The

D0030355

WITHDRAWN

DATE DUE

The Seattle School

10033486

CHRISTIAN COUNSELING ETHICS

A Handbook for Therapists, Pastors & Counselors

Edited by
Randolph K. Sanders

InterVarsity Press
Downers Grove, Illinois

©1997 by Randolph K. Sanders

All rights reserved. No part of this book may be reproduced in any form without written permission from InterVarsity Press, P.O. Box 1400, Downers Grove, IL 60515.

InterVarsity Press® is the book-publishing division of InterVarsity Christian Fellowship®, a student movement active on campus at hundreds of universities, colleges and schools of nursing in the United States of America, and a member movement of the International Fellowship of Evangelical Students. For information about local and regional activities, write Public Relations Dept., InterVarsity Christian Fellowship, 6400 Schroeder Rd., P.O. Box 7895, Madison, WI 53707-7895.

All Scripture quotations, unless otherwise indicated, are taken from the HOLY BIBLE, NEW INTERNATIONAL VERSION®. NIV®. Copyright ©1973, 1978, 1984 by International Bible Society. Used by permission of Zondervan Publishing House. All rights reserved.

Case studies in this book are representative of the kinds of cases faced by clinicians in practice. The cases are totally fictitious, are composites of a number of cases, or have been thoroughly altered to ensure anonymity and confidentiality. All names used for characters are fictitious, and any resemblance to persons living or dead is purely coincidental.

Appendix B, "Ethical Principles of Psychologists and Code of Conduct" (American Psychological Association, 1992). Copyright (c) 1992 by the American Psychological Association. Reprinted with permission.

Appendix B, Ethical Guidelines for the Christian Association for Psychological Studies. Copyright 1992, Christian Association for Psychological Studies. Reprinted with permission.

Appendix B, AAPC Code of Ethics. Amended April 28, 1994. Reprinted with permission.

Appendix B, Code of Ethics and Standards of Practice. April 1995. © ACA. Reprinted with permission. No further reproduction authorized without written permission of the American Counseling Association.

Appendix B, AAMFT Code of Ethics, copyright August 1991, American Association for Marriage and Family Therapy. Reprinted with permission.

ISBN 0-8308-1892-8

Printed in the United States of America ♾

Library of Congress Cataloging-in-Publication Data

Christian counseling ethics: a handbook for therapists, pastors, and
  counselors/Randolph K. Sanders, ed.
      p.   cm.
  Includes bibliographical references and index.
  ISBN 0-8308-1892-8 (alk. paper)
  1. Pastoral counseling—Moral and ethical aspects.   2. Counselors—
Professional ethics.   I. Sanders, Randolph K.
BV4012.2.C516   1997
241'.641—dc21   97-2866
                                                                                 CIP

22   21   20   19   18   17   16   15   14   13   12   11   10   9   8   7   6   5   4   3   2   1

15   14   13   12   11   10   09   08   07   06   05   04   03   02   01   00   99   98   97

*To Bette, my wife, whose intuitive
understanding of the relationship between love
and justice is a source of encouragement
to all those whose lives she touches.*

Patients Are Harmed
Patients Most Likely to Be Abused
Sexual Misconduct and the Abuse of Power
Other Types of Abuse of Power
The Abusing Therapist
Rehabilitation of Abusing Therapists
Prevention

Part 2: *Issues in Counseling Ethics*

Christian Ethics as a Guide to Forensic Practice
Using "Christian" Psychology as a Source of Authority
The Difficulties of Integration in a Forensic Setting

Part 4: *Current Trends in Ethics Education*

Chapter 1

EMBRACING OUR ETHICAL MANDATE

Randolph K. Sanders

---

*A*s a newly graduated Ph.D. I was, like most new psychologists, concerned with finding my first full-time position in the field. I discussed job possibilities with supervisors, made phone calls and sent résumés.

One day I received a call from the executive director of one of the Christian counseling centers to which I had sent my résumé. This agency was an established center, well known and well respected by many in the lay community.

After some preliminary discussion of my qualifications, I asked the director for more details about the programs at his center. "Just a minute," he replied. I could hear him rustling through some papers. "Take down these names and numbers," he said rather brusquely once he returned to the phone. I complied, but after taking down several listings, I felt myself becoming vaguely uncomfortable. "Dr. Doe [not his real name], exactly who are these people?" I asked.

"They're my clients," he replied. "I want you to call them and hear from their perspective what we do here and how they like what we do. If you like what you hear, you can call me back."

After pausing for a moment, certainly not wanting to question an older, seemingly wiser colleague, I ventured rather carefully, "Uh, Dr. Doe, have these clients given you permission to release their names and numbers?"

"Sure," he replied flippantly. With a hint of sarcasm he asked, "Why is that so important to you?"

"Well," I began hesitantly, "I was trained to follow the APA (American Psychological Association) Code of Ethics, which says—"

He cut me off abruptly. "APA Code of Ethics? Well, Dr. Sanders, that tells me something about you. We hold to a higher standard of ethics here—*Christian* ethics, *not* APA ethics!

"You know, Dr. Sanders," he continued, "I don't think we need your services at our center after all. Goodby!" And with that he abruptly hung up the phone. Several years later, this man's counseling center closed after serious allegations of misconduct and improprieties arose.

This example illustrates the danger of deciding, for whatever reason, to practice counseling without benefit of the basic rules agreed on by most others in the profession. By placing his counselees' rights to confidentiality below his desire to promote his counseling center, this man had put his clients in a potentially embarrassing and possibly harmful position.

This case also demonstrates rather dramatically why Christians should never presume that their faith inoculates them against the ethical dilemmas and moral temptations that face the rest of the world. This book attempts to understand better what constitutes ethical counseling practice, to explain why some Christian mental health professionals act unethically, to build a better understanding of the kinds of ethical dilemmas practitioners face and to help counselors become more ethical in their work.

Ethical Issues in Mental Health

Ethical dilemmas do occur in mental health work. Unfortunately they are a given. Some are more common than others:

☐ A therapist is counseling an adolescent boy. After several sessions the boy reveals that he is taking drugs. Should the therapist tell the boy's parents?

☐ A therapist teaches part time at a college in addition to her private practice. A student at the college begins seeing her for therapy but is not a student in any of her classes. A year later the student enrolls in one of her classes. What should she do?

☐ A therapist lives in a small town where there are few mental health professionals. A woman enters treatment for depression, but after several sessions it becomes evident that she is suffering from an eating disorder as well. The therapist has had no experience in treating eating disorders, but neither have any of the other therapists in town, and the closest referral is miles away. What should the therapist do?

☐ A therapist holds a Ph.D. in psychology but is licensed as a mental health counselor rather than a psychologist. The therapist tells clients at the Christian counseling center where he works that he is a Ph.D.-level psychologist. Has he acted unethically?

These are just a few of the many examples of ethical issues and dilemmas that mental health professionals face. In response to these dilemmas various groups and associations have devised rules and codes to help practitioners handle these problems. In addition to state and federal laws (Ohlschlager and Mosgofian, 1992), professional groups such as the American Psychological Association (1992), the American Association of Marriage and Family Therapists (1991), the American Counselors Association (1995), the American Psychiatric Association (1995), the National Association of Social Workers (1980), the American Association of Pastoral Counselors (1991) and several other organizations maintain codes of ethical conduct that their members are sworn to live by. In addition, the Christian Association for Psychological Studies (CAPS), a nonprofit organization made up of Christian mental health professionals, academics and paraprofessionals, has developed a statement of ethical guidelines for its members (1993) (see appendix B for examples of codes of conduct of various professional groups). Many state boards also have rules of practice for all individuals licensed or certified by that board.

As we will see later in this book, the codes of ethics vary in content and degree of specificity, but most deal with some essential elements of ethical practice. These elements include

☐ competence: Are you qualified professionally and personally to provide the services you are offering? (APA, 1992, Sects. 1.04, 1.05, 2.02-2.06)

☐ confidentiality: Do you understand the importance of holding information you receive in confidence? Do you recognize circumstances that could endanger your ability to be confidential? Do you know when it is appropriate to break a confidence? (APA, 1992, Sect. 5.00)

☐ dual or multiple relationships: Do you understand the dangers of working with people in professional relationships at the same time you are relating to them in other contexts, such as church, work or school? Do you understand why sexual intimacies with clients, students, etc., are always wrong and are clear examples of unethical multiple relationships? (APA, 1992, Sects. 1.17, 1.18, 4.05-4.07)

☐ public statements: Do you avoid making deceptive, false or manipulative statements about the services, products or activities you provide? Do you avoid making public statements that cannot be supported by evidence? Do you discourage public-relations people, book publishers and others who represent you from making inappropriate statements on your behalf? (APA, 1992, Sects. 3.01-3.06)

☐ third-party requests for services: When a third party (a court, parent, business, school) requests that you provide services for them (assess an alleged criminal or victim, see a child, evaluate an employee or student, etc.), do you clarify with all parties the nature of the relationship with each of them? For example, if you assess an accused individual for a court, do you make sure the person understands that the information they give you will not be confidential and will be given to the court? (APA, 1992, Sect. 1.21)

These are some of the issues that codes and laws attempt to cover. We will see in the chapters that follow how various rules apply specifically to different issues and areas of mental health work.

Responses to Codes of Ethics

When confronted with a professional code of ethics, counselors respond in different ways. In some respects their reactions mirror those of people confronted by an authority figure.

Some people oppose a code of ethics. Faced with the constraints that ethical systems impose, they ignore them and forge their own paths. In some cases they carry on a passive-aggressive relationship with ethical codes, verbally assenting to the codes while quietly disobeying them.

Sometimes, but less often, people openly defy the rules. For these individuals the rules represent restraints that stand in the way of their own self-serving motivations and impulses. These therapists often, consciously or unconsciously, use the client-therapist relationship as a means to meet their own personal needs and desires rather than to serve the best interests of the client. Disturbances in the therapist's character such as narcissism, impulsiveness or sociopathy may all be underlying factors affecting the therapist's ethical thinking and resulting in his or her forging a path outside the parameters of the ethical code. In the example that began this chapter, one can only speculate about the personal reasons a therapist who knew better would be willing to share so freely the names and addresses of "satisfied clients," showing little concern for the potential problems his hasty action might cause them.

Others faced with the authority of ethical codes react with anxiety. They believe that ethical codes are to be feared. People are always in danger of making a mistake, and those who fear the codes often ruminate excessively about the gray areas in practicing psychology and about whether they have met all the standards required by the code. As a result, anxious practitioners are sometimes less effective as therapists because they resist making any decision that might have the slightest chance of being questioned ethically or legally. At times, in their failure to be decisive, they behave unethically anyway. For example, the anxious practitioner might delay acting to protect someone who had seriously discussed suicide, fearing that he might make a mistake that would be seen later as having violated the patient's rights.

Some therapists tend to avoid their ethical codes. When the codes are revised, they don't read them, and they seldom consult them for help when questions arise. Unlike therapists who feel themselves above the rules, avoiders are more phobic than rebellious and avoid rules in order to escape dealing with difficult issues. These individuals hope they will do the right thing, and may feel guilty about not keeping abreast of their field's ethical code, but when all is said and done they do not consult the code because the gain in understanding hardly seems worth the discomfort of studying.

Thankfully there are mental health professionals who neither fear their ethical code nor rebel against it, but who instead have a healthy respect for it. These practitioners allow the code to guide and challenge them as they do their daily work, yet they don't deify the code. Such people recognize that there are gray areas that do not always fit the rules well and that part of behaving ethically is learning how to be ethical even when the rules do not apply or are contradictory. Later in this chapter we will discuss how the Christian practitioner can achieve this goal.

Yet even when there is basic respect for the ethics code, there are still a number of reasons why a therapist might behave unethically (Keith-Spiegel and Koocher, 1985). Inexperience and ignorance of the law are common causes of unethical behavior in otherwise sincere professionals. Some counselors may be naive, believing that being a dedicated Christian professional automatically ensures against ethical problems. Still others act unethically because they have not anticipated a potential problem in advance. For example, a therapist may promise confidentiality to a couple in marriage counseling but later finds herself in a dilemma when the couple eventually divorces and one spouse wants to use the records from counseling in a child custody dispute. Or, as sometimes occurs when controversial treatment techniques are used, a therapist may not have been able to adequately anticipate the problems that might arise from using a controversial intervention. One must proceed with great care when considering unusual treatment techniques.

Therapists may encounter situations in which the possiblity of behaving unethically was foreseen but unavoidable. Or therapists can end up in situations in which they must choose between various less-than-fully-ethical responses. For example, the therapist who receives a subpoena to release confidential information but does not have his client's permission may find himself in contempt of court if he does not release the information and guilty of a breach of confidentiality if he does. And finally, some therapists may act unethically because there are no ethical guidelines or laws that apply to the issue in question, or because the guidelines or laws that do exist are ambiguous or conflict with each other.

Christian Mental Health Care Today

Fortunately, most Christian therapists today are trained, service-oriented professionals who honestly try to behave ethically in their daily work. Many Christian practitioners hold advanced degrees in the helping disciplines. Many are state licensed and are bound by professional codes of ethics and state laws that regulate their practice in the community. "Christian psychology" is now a major movement within the larger Christian community and has had a profound impact for good. Hurting people whose personal problems went largely unnoticed and uncared for in years past are now receiving hope and help, all in the context of caring Christian community. People who in the past would have been avoided, blamed or maligned, even by the church, are now receiving understanding and intervention.

Yet despite all that is good about the mental health movement in general and Christian counseling in particular, and despite the development of good ethical codes of conduct, there is a downside. In general, the number of ethical and legal complaints against psychotherapists appears to be increasing (APA, 1995). And some data suggest that despite the ethics codes, psychotherapists often can't agree on a course of ethical action in particular situations (Haas, Malouf and Mayerson, 1986). It's not fully known whether Christian therapists as a whole are more ethical than their secular counterparts. However, as the introductory example illustrated, Christian therapists are certainly not immune to ethical misconduct.

Why are there more ethical complaints today than in the past? Clearly one reason is that there are more mental health practitioners than ever before. In the last decade we have witnessed a proliferation of mental health services offered from a Christian perspective. Christian mental health professionals, clinics and psychiatric hospital units have sprung up across the country. Bookstores are filled with Christian self-help books. Religious broadcasting serves a steady diet of programs on personal, emotional and family issues. Graduate-school programs help integrate psychological principles with Christian theology in training new psychotherapists. Where there are more practitioners and more services rendered, there is an increased probability that ethical and legal infractions will occur. As noted earlier, most practitioners are conscientious, but there is a minority who use the profession to serve themselves, and others who make mistakes due to ignorance, inexperience or lack of judgment.

The number of complaints may also have increased because consumers of mental health services seem increasingly willing to complain. Through the media people are exposed to the idea that the mental health professions are not sacred. There is a greater awareness that people do suffer as a result of professional misconduct. Victims of all sorts of abuse are often more willing to report the abuse if they realize that they are not to blame for the inappropriate behavior of another and if they discover that there are others out there who have suffered in similar ways.

The reality that we live in an increasingly litigious society should not be forgotten. This is another reason for the increase in formal complaints against counselors. Right or wrong, people in our culture are strongly encouraged to choose the adversarial process of court, or the threat of court, as the way to deal with their health care complaints.

In response to complaints, most professional organizations have expanded their ethics codes as well as their methods for adjudicating allegations of misconduct. Internship training programs in psychotherapy have increased their attention to ethical issues. Graduate students often take formal coursework in ethics and are encouraged to consider ethical issues in their practicums and internships. Yet ethical complaints continue to be made and appear to be on the increase.

Cultural and Religious Trends

Although there is an increased interest in ethics in the Christian counseling profession, there are other societal trends that can negatively influence the ethical decision-making process. For example, moral and ethical *relativism* assumes that there are no absolute standards, that what is right and wrong varies according to many factors, including the particular circumstances and one's own point of view. We shouldn't be so naive, this approach says, as to think that any code of conduct would be able to help us much in our complex age.

The mental health professions have clearly been affected by this thinking. Indeed, perhaps due to the complex nature of people's problems and the gray areas that inevitably arise in counseling, we are tempted to say that there are no absolutes, that all standards are relative. Once we have done that, though, we run the risk of raising the exceptions to the rules to the same level as the rules themselves. For example, we decide that because some parents do abuse their children, the ancient admonition to respect and honor parents has little value today.

The increasing emphasis on *individualism and the self* may also affect our ethical decisions. Popular culture teaches us that the healthy person takes care of himself and his "needs" first, is independent, values personal happiness over obligation, is assertive, copes well with stress and enjoys leisure. The increased emphasis on individualism has brought with it a decreased emphasis on the importance of community, interpersonal connectedness, family and God. Martin Seligman, the eminent psychologist, has called this the "waning of the commons" (1990, p. 284). As he puts it,

> The life committed to nothing larger than itself is a meager life indeed. Human beings require a context of meaning and hope. We used to have ample context, and when we encountered failure, we could pause and take our rest in that setting—our spiritual furniture—and revive our sense of who we were. I call the larger setting the commons. It consists of a belief in the nation, in God, in one's family, or in a purpose that transcends our lives. In the past quarter-century, events occurred that so weakened our commitment to larger entities as to leave us almost naked before the ordinary assaults of life. (p. 284)

Seligman, an expert on depression, believes that "a society that exalts the individual to the extent ours does will be riddled with depression" (p. 287). Such a society is likely to be overwhelmed by people who in their emphasis on the self will ignore the importance of empathizing with others and thus be less liable to behave ethically toward their fellows. What purpose is there in following the rules if it's "every person for him/herself"?

For the therapist, the current cultural as well as mental health emphasis on individualism raises ethical questions about the proper goals of therapeutic intervention. Is treatment always and only about self-actualization and personal happiness? If so, does therapy then degenerate into a narcissistic exercise that idolizes the desires of the self (Vitz, 1994)?

Economic factors can also affect ethical decision-making. Prior to the 1980s, Christian therapy was a helping profession provided by a relatively small number of practitioners, most of whom made a reasonable living but often had to defend their work to a sometimes skeptical church community. But in the eighties, all that changed. Christian counseling was "in," and the market was soon flooded with practitioners, authors and speakers. Most were sincere, but some were attracted to the field by the promise of fame and fortune in the latest Christian fad. For this latter group the importance of truth in advertising, competency in counseling and interprofessional cooperation took a back seat to inflated claims, lower standards of care and unbridled competition.

Now new economic changes are occurring in the mental health community. Today the industry is marked by an increasing number of practitioners and a decreasing number of health care dollars. With the advent of health care reform, the nation is beginning to restrict access to health care in general and mental health care in particular. Faced with a shrinking economic base, clinicians and institutions are forced to find creative ways to survive as well as serve. In such an environment some practitioners and administrators will inevitably allow their own desire to survive in the marketplace take precedent over the welfare of their patients. Clinical decisions become unduly influenced by money, and some patients of means receive unnecessary care while others go begging.

Religious factors also play a role in ethical decision-making. During the latter part of the twentieth century, a period in which psychology has been gaining great popularity, much of the emphasis in secular culture has been on permissiveness, and in the Christian church the emphasis has tended toward grace. Much of this grace emphasis developed as a reaction to the legalism and prejudices that have been all too prevalent in the church's history. Consequently, the prevailing message of many within the church has been "God is love." Having seen the problems of rules without grace, many call for a return to a higher ethic based on love (Stott, 1994).

Yet some who preach this emphasis on grace convince themselves that they are following a higher ethic of love, when in fact they are ignoring basic rules of human conduct and interpreting Christian love to mean whatever fits their own sentiments and impulses, like the counselor in the vignette that opened this chapter. Indeed, by ignoring the APA code, the counselor in that story had not lived above an inferior, secular code but had instead denied some fundamental rules of professional conduct and practice (the APA code) that were not at all inconsistent with a Christian ethic.

The shift of the Christian culture toward grace was a needed corrective to the legalism of previous days. But as has been true from the beginning of Christianity, there have always been those who would shift the balance of grace and law too far in one direction or the other, resulting in detrimental consequences on moral and ethical decision-making.

The Christian Mental Health Professional

Christian mental health professionals are confronted with all the same ethical dilemmas as their secular counterparts. Confidentiality, multiple relationships, competence and other fundamental issues of ethical practice will arise. Christian practitioners also work in a larger cultural context and for better or worse are affected by cultural trends and values.

The ethics codes that have been created by various secular professional guilds are fundamental rules of practice hammered out through years of common experience. For the most part, these codes are straightforward and place most of their emphasis on the patient's welfare. Recognizing that professional intervention can have negative as well as positive outcomes, the codes encourage practitioners to take all reasonable steps to "do no harm" to their patients (Fernhoff, 1993). As documents devised in a pluralistic culture, the codes usually avoid issues that would undoubtedly offend a particular cultural or religious group. In a certain respect they represent the minimum that a therapist should do to behave ethically, and there is relatively little in them that would clearly contradict a Christian ethic.

Even for those who do not belong to a particular professional counseling guild, such as pastoral and lay counselors, knowledge of fundamentals common to the more respected codes of ethics in the professional counseling field is very important. For example, Cruse and Russell (1994) indicate that since the American Psychological Association code is one of the most extensive, nonpsychologists who go to court could well find themselves confronted by attorneys who expect them to be familiar with it, particularly if the counselors are providing service in an area covered by that code.

Though technically not held to the same standards as professional therapists, noncertified pastoral counselors and lay counselors have a responsibility to know as much as they can about the ethics of counseling. At a minimum they should be aware of some common ethical pitfalls in counseling. In this way they will be more likely to recognize potential problems and can discuss these with a supervisor, seek consultation from other professionals or refer to others with more training.

But is compliance with secular codes enough? Surely those who hold themselves out to peers and the public as Christian counselors are called to consider additional ethical issues. Here are just a few of the special issues that confront the Christian who serves in mental health work.

☐ A young couple with two children comes to a Christian marriage counselor, insisting at the outset that she help them negotiate an end to their marriage. What responsibility does the counselor have to the sanctity of the marriage and family as well as to the individuals involved?

☐ A pastor who counsels regularly questions whether or not to gain further formal training in counseling, knowing that in his state "religious counselors" are given an exemption from the strict training requirements facing other counselors.

☐ A Christian therapist works in a government agency. During the course of therapy with one client, material is revealed that suggests that the client has serious concerns of a spiritual nature. Should the therapist talk about faith issues in therapy despite the fact that she works for a nonpartisan, government agency?

Beyond specific ethical dilemmas, Christians must also consider whether or not they are called to more than a mere practice of the "rules ethics" established by professional guilds. Surely those who live under grace are called to a higher ethic.

As Christians, we want to practice not only doing right but also being moral people. Morality is a state of *being* as much as it is *doing*. Ideally, if we are to follow a higher ethic, we must be growing in virtue as well as in principle (see Jordan and Meara, 1990, for a discussion of virtue ethics and principle ethics). Character traits such as trustworthiness, wisdom, humility and integrity must have been developed and be developing alongside a knowledge of the rules of conduct; otherwise we become legalistic, applying rules arbitrarily to situations where the spirit of the law—the internal law—might tell us to intervene more carefully. Growing in virtue broadens the ability to see through to the essence of all good law: promoting justice and love (Smedes, 1983).

Ethics and Scripture

During his earthly ministry Jesus frequently confronted prominent Jewish leaders who had become excessively legalistic in their attempts to make the "letter" of religious law determinative in every situation. Jesus argued that these leaders had become so obsessed with the ceremonial law and with tradition that they had missed the essence of the law (Maston, 1964, p. 146). He summed up all law in a positive frame by asserting that the two greatest commandments were to love God with all one's being and to love one's neighbor as oneself (Mt 22:36-39).

Yet Jesus was not a libertarian. He clearly stated that his mission on earth was not to abolish the Old Testament law but rather to fulfill it (Mt 5:17) "by bringing its essential teaching to its full development" (Maston, 1964, p. 147). To Jesus, the commandments were not rigid moralisms, passed down from an outmoded civilization. They were basic truths for living and conduct that would be given new life and humanized in a pervasive ethic of love.

Jesus' ethic of love, far from being relativistic and anemic, sometimes went beyond the ethical legalisms of the day. For example, he argued that there was little advantage in following the letter of the law if one harbored such things as bitterness or lust or greed in one's heart (Mt 5:28). Unlike those who would use an "ethic of love" as an excuse to act out, Jesus' followers are called by his ethic to a higher level.

Jesus' message proclaims a balance between grace and law. Nowhere is this balance better explained than in the book of Romans. Here Paul says that God's law functions to define what sin is and to condemn the sinner (Rom 3:27-28). No one, no matter how good or how moral or how much he or she follows the rules, can or will measure up to the level of the divine. But God in his mercy provides a means for forgiveness and a way to peace and eternal relationship with him. It is through faith in God's Son, Jesus Christ, that people access this gift of God (Rom 5:2). Followers of Christ do not live under law but under grace (Rom 6:14), which can be defined as the unmerited favor that God has bestowed on sinful humankind.

Paul does not stop here. He argues that through the sacrifice of Jesus Christ on the cross and the assistance of the Holy Spirit, believers are empowered to fulfill the law and live lives that are righteous and loving (Rom 8:4; 13:8). They are free from the condemnation of the law yet free to keep the law in response to the loving grace of God and the ongoing care of his Spirit. The new covenant ushered in by Christ is one in which "the Holy Spirit writes God's law in our hearts" (Stott, 1994, p. 196).

Ideally, then, being a person of virtue follows naturally from a close, intimate relationship with God. Such a relationship, like all excellent relationships, must be marked by warmth, love, accountability and responsibility. The Bible is the unfolding drama of God's desire for this kind of relationship with his people. In the beginning he created man and woman in his image and desired fellowship with them. In the Old Testament he sought a covenantal relationship with his people that was much more than a mere contract; it was a deeply personal commitment one to the other. In the New Testament is God's ultimate endeavor toward intimacy with humankind: God became man in the person of Jesus Christ and walked the earth as a human being, with all the blood, sweat and tears that accompany that. While here he became intimately familiar with people from all walks of life, not just the "good" people, but the outcasts and the sinners as well. He was persecuted by those who did not understand him, and he experienced the hurts, anguish and negative emotions common to those who live in this world. He suffered a cruel and hideous death that he did not deserve.

The God of the Bible is not a distant figure, completely removed from his people. He is not a foreign figure who shouts impossible edicts from afar and then leaves his subjects alone to grapple with the pronouncements. In the Christian faith, the rule of law takes place within the context of personal relationship, of covenant, of love. It is in this relationship of covenantal love that we are empowered to follow a Christian ethic.

To be sure, this is not an easy task. There can be no doubt that as leaders in the Christian community, Christian mental health professionals are called to a higher ethic. It is not out of context to argue that the qualities of the overseer and the elder in the early church are some of the same qualities that Christian therapists should aspire to. These qualities, enumerated by Paul in 1 Timothy 3:1-7 and Titus 1:5-9, include self-control, gentleness, temperance, respectability and avoiding greed.

Ethics and God's Call

The calling to be a Christian counselor is a high calling with exceptional expectations and responsiblities. Certainly it reflects a standard to which all will aspire but which not all will fully attain (Rom 7:21-25). But the good news is that for the Christian the process of being ethical and becoming ethical takes place in the context of relationship—with God, the Holy Spirit and our fellow Christians.

Earlier in the chapter we looked at the different responses that people have to ethics codes. Those who are fearful of the codes are often afraid of the code's power to "condemn" them, so they follow the codes legalistically in an effort to avoid judgment. In contrast, those who reject ethics codes sometimes take an antinomian position that the codes are of no value and rebel against them. Following Paul and assuming that the codes are in the main consistent with a Christian ethic, a Christian might face the codes secure in the grace of Christ yet determined to fulfill them with God's help.

The message of Scripture is that God is with us at all times, but most especially in life's hard places, much in the same way a close personal friend is—when we seek to help our clients in psychotherapy, when we struggle to teach others, when faced with tough ethical decisions. As a truly intimate friend God is there to both support and encourage us, and to hold us accountable and correct us. He walks with us and encourages us to embrace our ethical mandate.

Likewise the call to be ethical takes place best within the context of a Christian community in which we participate with other Christian people who are seeking as we are to fulfill God's will and ministry. Christianity takes place in *koinonia,* in close fellowship with one another. In fellowship with one another we benefit from the shared love, support, wisdom, accountability and obligation to each other.

The chapters that follow cover pertinent issues related to ethics and the Christian mental health professional. Chapter two reviews the fundamental relationship between Christian ethics and psychotherapy. Part one stresses some essential rules common to most ethical codes and how they apply practically to the daily work of therapy, as well as gives an overview of Christian professionals themselves and some problems that can occur in a client-counselor relationship. What qualifications appropriately define those who would call themselves Christian practitioners? What about pastors who counsel? What does it mean when we say that a therapist has abused his or her power? What are the most common ways in which therapists abuse their power, and what can be done to help therapists avoid doing it? What do we know about impaired professionals and how to respond in a way that is redemptive and maintains accountability?

The next section deals with some challenging issues in therapy, including chapters on marital therapy and deprogramming as well as chapters relating to specific client populations such as the homosexual client, the child client and clients with chronic conditions.

Part three looks at problems related to the business of counseling, the ethical issues that surface not in the counseling room but in the boardroom, where fees are set, billing is done and corporate decisions are made. Additional chapters deal with specific counseling settings and the ethical issues peculiar to them. Among the settings covered are lay counseling, college counseling centers, governmental agencies and forensic settings.

A final section looks at current trends in teaching ethics to Christian mental health professionals, offers a model for practicing ethically, and reviews some of the existing secular and Christian codes of practice. Appendix A is an important research article about the actual ethical behavior of Christian mental health professionals. Appendix B includes some examples of ethics codes that are presently available, and appendix C contains examples of the types of consent and other forms that are used in counseling today.

Case studies in this book are representative of the kinds of cases faced by clinicians in practice. The cases are totally fictitious, are composites of a number of cases, or have been thoroughly altered to ensure anonymity and confidentiality. All names used for characters are fictitious, and any resemblance to persons living or dead is purely coincidental.

To act ethically is difficult, to be ethical even more so. Our hope of approaching these ideals is found in God, who first loved us, who in his love encourages us to love others, and in the Holy Spirit and the community of friends who encourage us as we seek to live righteously in the world. God does not wish for us to run from his law in fear, but to embrace and fulfill his law with confidence—confidence in our inestimable worth before him, in his power to be with us in the midst of Christian community, and in his ultimate control of our destiny.

References

American Association of Marriage and Family Therapists. 1991. *Code of Ethics.* (Available from AAMFT, 1133 15th St. NW, Suite 300, Washington, DC 20005.)

American Association of Pastoral Counselors. 1991. *Code of Ethics.* (Available from AAPC, 9504A Lee Highway, Fairfax, VA 22031-2303.)

American Counseling Association. 1995. *ACA Code of Ethics and Standards of Practice.* (Available from ACA, P.O. Box 531, Alexandria, VA 20701.)

American Psychiatric Association. 1995. *Principles of Medical Ethics with Annotations Especially Applicable to Psychiatry.* (Available from APA, 1400 K St. NW, Washington, DC 20005.)

American Psychological Association. 1992. "Ethical Principles of Psychologists and Code of Conduct." *American Psychologist* 47: 1597-1611.

―――. 1995. "Report of the Ethics Committee, 1994." *American Psychologist* 50: 706-13.

Christian Association for Psychological Studies. 1993. *Ethical Guidelines for the Christian Association for Psychological Studies.* (Available from CAPS, P.O. Box 310400, New Braunfels, TX 78131-0400.)

Cruse, R., and R. Russell. 1994. *Ethical Thinking: New Standards.* Paper presented at the Christian Association for Psychological Studies Southwest Regional Conference, Abilene, Tex. (October).

Fernhoff, D. 1993. "The Valued Therapist," in *Against the Grain,* ed. M. Goldberg. Valley Forge, Penn.: Trinity Press International.

Gottlieb, M. C. 1993. "Avoiding Exploitive Dual Relationships: A Decision-making Model." *Psychotherapy* 30: 41-48.

Haas, L. J, J. L. Malouf and N. H. Mayerson. 1986. "Ethical Dilemmas in Psychological Practice: Results of a National Survey." *Professional Psychology: Research and Practice* 17: 316-21.

Jordan, A. E., and N. M. Meara. 1990. "Ethics and the Professional Practice of Psychologists: The Role of Virtues and Principles." *Professional Psychology: Research and Practice* 21: 107-14.

Keith-Spiegel, P., and G. P. Koocher. 1985. *Ethics in Psychology: Professional Standards and Cases.* New York: Random House.

Maston, T. B. 1964. *Biblical Ethics.* Cleveland: World Publishing.

National Association of Social Workers. 1980. *NASW Code of Ethics and Standards for the Private Practice of Clinical Social Work.* (Available from NASW, P.O. Box 431, Annapolis Junction, MD 20701.)

Ohlschlager, G., and P. Mosgofian. 1992. *Law for the Christian Counselor.* Dallas: Word.

Seligman, M. E. P. 1990. *Learned Optimism.* New York: Simon and Schuster.

Smedes, L. 1983. *Mere Morality.* Grand Rapids, Mich.: Eerdmans.

Stott, J. 1994. *Romans.* Downers Grove, Ill.: InterVarsity Press.

Vitz, P. C. 1994. *Psychology as Religion: The Cult of Self-Worship.* Grand Rapids, Mich.: Eerdmans.

Chapter 2

PSYCHOTHERAPY & CHRISTIAN ETHICS

Alan C. Tjeltveit

---

*S*ome schooled solely in secular psychotherapy might find the title of this chapter (and book) curious. Therapy, for them, is based solely on science. And Christian ethics is a neurosis-producing burden from which guilt- and anxiety-laden clients need liberation. That task being commonplace and well covered in most training programs, those therapists would expect a chapter (and book) that is brief, boring, or both.

While recognizing the problem of legalistic abuses of Christian ethics, Christians committed to helping people overcome problems tend to view Christian ethics in a more positive light. But even Christian therapists occasionally see therapy and ethics as entirely separate domains—between which dialogue is neither required nor desired.

In contrast, I contend that psychotherapy is a profoundly and pervasively ethical endeavor, and that Christian ethics both vigorously supports and sharply challenges the ethical positions represented (usually implicitly) in the different forms of therapy. I also believe that Christian ethicists have much to learn from psychotherapists, and that Christian clients and therapists therefore need to engage—regularly and rigorously—in substantive reflection on the ethical dimensions of therapy. Only when Christians take Christian ethical perspectives very seriously can we understand—and act on—the vitally important implications of Christian faith for psychotherapy that is conducted in full accord with the gospel.

Lurking in the background of this chapter and book is the question of the distinctiveness of psychotherapy as understood and practiced by Christians. Is therapy with a Christian therapist really different from therapy with a person who is not a Christian? Christian therapists of good will and undisputed competence diverge—at times sharply—regarding how to answer this question. Some emphasize the uniqueness of Christian therapy; others stress the essential equivalence of therapy provided by Christian and non-Christian practitioners. Some of this disagreement stems, perhaps, from focusing on different presenting problems and different client populations (see Worthington, 1988, 1993b). Christian ethics is more obviously relevant, and Christian therapy more likely distinctive, when Christian clients are involved and ethical issues in therapy are overt and controverted. However, Christian ethics may also be relevant, albeit nondistinctively, in cases involving subtle and noncontroversial ethical issues. For example, when a Christian provides behavior therapy for a snake phobia to a non-Christian in a secular setting, that intervention may be behaviorally indistinguishable from the intervention of a non-Christian therapist.

By way of contrast, consider this vivid case:

Brad, a middle-aged midlevel manager who attends a local Baptist church on a semiregular basis, sees a therapist at the insistence of his son, a psychology major at a nearby college. The son has discovered that Brad is sexually involved with Jennifer, the 20-year-old daughter of one of Brad's coworkers. Both families attend the same church. Brad is ambivalent about whether there is really a problem, explaining that his wife, Carol, has been an invalid for several years and has been unable to maintain an active sexual relationship. Brad says he thinks Carol may even know "on some level" about his relationship with Jennifer and be secretly relieved that she no longer has to engage in an activity she's never seemed to enjoy.

Although he says he sometimes feels a twinge of guilt about his behavior, he brightens when talking about Jennifer: "This relationship makes me very happy. And Jenny tells me she's very happy too. That's what it's all about, isn't it—being happy? Surely God wants that for us." Brad adds that he thinks therapy "wouldn't hurt," because he wants to figure out a way to get his son to be more accepting of his relationship with Jennifer and doesn't know how to do that. "It's not like I'm planning to do anything drastic like get a divorce," Brad adds. "I stand by my word; a promise is a promise. And Jenny knows about the situation. I've never made any false promises to her. She likes my wife very much."

About this case Christian ethics has much to say.

"Ethics" Versus "Christian Ethics"

If a group were asked to provide an ethical analysis of this case or to analyze it from the perspective of Christian ethics, a lively discussion would likely ensue. The discourse might involve several distinguishable dimensions of the case, each of which may legitimately be called "ethical," possibly resulting in confusion. To minimize such confusion, and to make clear the full spectrum of "ethical" aspects of therapy, these dimensions, or "facets," of ethics will be distinguished and discussed in turn: professional ethics; ethics in context and as content; ethical theory; social ethics, public policy and consensus. Following is a general overview of some of the implications of Christian ethics for psychotherapy.

Professional Ethics

Mention the word *ethics* to many psychotherapists and their thoughts turn immediately to codes of professional ethics (e.g., American Psychiatric Association, 1995; American Psychological Association, 1992; National Association of Social Workers, 1979; see appendix B); that is, to ethical principles set down by various professional groups and "based on the goals, objectives, and fundamental values of the profession" (Bennett, 1994, p. 124). A violation of these principles may result in expulsion from a professional association.

Suppose, for instance, that Brad's therapist is a Christian psychologist who works at a public counseling center and did not state at the outset of therapy that she is an explicitly Christian therapist. She asks in the first session, "Have you thought about the moral issues here?" And when Brad arrives at his next session, he finds—to his surprise—that his pastor is waiting there for him, fully briefed about his affair with Jennifer and insisting that Brad repent and immediately end the affair or be expelled from the church. The psychologist would, of course, be in grave trouble with a psychological association ethics committee, which would point to her violation of Brad's confidentiality and failure to obtain informed consent about the type of distinctively Christian therapy being provided.

Christians who publicly declare themselves to be mental health professionals should, for reasons of honesty and integrity, and for other substantive reasons, abide by the appropriate professional code of ethics. But such codes do sometimes limit the actions of professionals, including behaviors Christians may otherwise appropriately exhibit. Recruiting a pastor to confront a friend about his immoral behavior wouldn't be considered unethical, but recruiting a pastor about a client's behavior without the client's consent would be. Overt evangelism in the therapeutic relationship is likewise proscribed by codes of professional ethics but is encouraged or obligatory for the Christian in other relationships.

The relationship between Christian ethics and professional ethics is complex (see Reeck, 1982). Some assert that the two perspectives are rivals, so Christians need to decide whether their allegiance lies with "the world" or with Christ. If allegiance to Christ means trouble with a professional ethics committee, so be it. Christians should not be conformed to the world.

Christian therapists holding this perspective are unlikely to join a professional association or seek licensure.

Others see professional and Christian ethics as partially or fully compatible, because (a) Christian ethics provides a rationale for the professional standards, (b) logical equivalence (the eighth commandment, for instance, forbids bearing false witness, as do codes of professional ethics) or (c) codes of professional ethics exhaust what Christian ethics has to say about ethics in therapy. Some advocates of the last position hold that Christian ethics and professional ethics are functionally identical because the only obligation Christian ethics places on the therapist as therapist is conformity with professional ideals. The good Christian therapist is the therapist whose behavior is consistent with professional codes of ethics and standards, so any claim that there is a distinctively Christian ethic for therapists would be seen as suspect. Consequently, all Christians assuming compatibility between Christian ethics and professional ethics would likely join the ethics committee in viewing the behavior of Brad's therapist as unethical.

Still others argue that given careful thinking, creativity and a deep respect for both professional ethics and Christian ethics, codes of professional ethics give ample room for the expression of Christian positions in therapy. Constraints are placed on the therapist, but not absolute constraints. A therapist can communicate values in therapy, for instance, by upholding client freedom (by not eliminating or reducing the freedom of clients to choose their own values, not imposing values on clients, not being judgmental or moralistic, and not propagandizing), providing clients with adequate information about the particular therapeutic approach employed (including its Christian distinctiveness, if any), honoring the therapeutic contract, and limiting the practice to areas in which he or she is competent (Tjeltveit, 1986, 1992).

In addition, the American Association of Pastoral Counselors (1991) and the Christian Association for Psychological Studies (1993) have promulgated codes of ethics that *combine* the content of professional codes with Christian ethics.

One's understanding of the relationship of Christian ethics and professional ethics depends, of course, on one's approach to Christian ethics. I contend that Christian ethics is usually, but not always, consistent with standards of professional ethics. A Christian ethic that is exhausted by professional ethics is, at best, profoundly impoverished. However, Christian ethics undergirds professional ethics, so a therapist engaged in professionally ethical behavior (e.g., upholding client confidentiality) is engaged in fully Christian behavior. Although Christian ethics does sometimes limit the Christian's behavior, careful thinking and responsible professional behavior (especially centered around informed consent) will usually, though not always, result in a satisfactory resolution of dilemmas arising from conflicts between professional and Christian ethics.

Ethics in Context and as Content

In a general sense, ethics can also be understood as specific ideals or behavioral prescriptions that are either applicable to people in general or obligatory for Christians in particular. Ethics pertains to decisions and behavior having to do with what is good, right, obligatory and/or virtuous. For example, people with different ethical perspectives might make the following assertions: "Thou shalt not commit adultery"; "Brad should be more aware of his own feelings and desires and the reality that his marriage is failing"; "Brad ought to keep his marital promise to remain faithful to his wife"; "Brad would be healthier if he dropped his guilt-inducing Christian standards, got out of his failed marriage and into a more fulfilling partnership." Rules for living, morality, behavioral prescriptions and ideal or authentic ways of being human are all aspects of "ethics," broadly construed. Ethics can be understood as *content*.

Depending on one's perspective, the content of Christian ethics (e.g., "Thou shalt not commit adultery" for Brad, and "Thou shalt not bear false witness" for the therapist, who, by self-declaration as a psychologist, promised to uphold client confidentiality) will be more or less distinctive. Some hold that Christian ethics is based solely on reason and so is no different from other ethical perspectives. But others stress the authority of the Bible or Christian tradition and assert that Christian ethics often provides distinctive answers to ethical questions.

But Christian ethics has to do with far more than just the content of particular principles. To content must be added context. Every session of psychotherapy, every moment of human life must be seen in the context of creation, fall, redemption and eschaton. We are all created by God, have sinned, were redeemed though the death and resurrection of Christ, and are heirs of the promise of his coming again in glory. As forgiven children of God, we are free in Christ, saved by grace through faith. As such, we strive to "lead lives worthy of the Lord, fully pleasing to him" (Col 1:10 NRSV). God works in us, transforming us into his image and likeness. To sever ethics from this context, to proclaim law without gospel (however their relation is understood; cf. Forde, 1969; Fuller, 1980) is to irrevocably alter Christian faith and abandon truly Christian ethics. The contextual uniqueness is vital. An intellectual analysis of the abstract ethical principle "Thou shalt not commit adultery" would be very different if one were to add a little contextual background: "The Lord your God says to you, his child, you for whom Jesus died, 'Thou shalt not commit adultery.' "

Christians striving to make ethical decisions must take context into consideration when making judgments, but should not be relativistic. It is usually necessary to balance flexibility and firmness in addressing ethical issues. Christians should be pastoral at times and prophetic at others, with "pastoral" almost always characterizing therapeutic relationships, all the while trying to be neither legalistic nor antinomian.

This emphasis on the context of Christian ethics means practically that psychotherapy can never be seen simply as a relationship between therapist and client. Rather, it is a relationship taking place within the greater relationship of client, therapist, the families of each, the church (in local and global manifestations, as both visible and invisible body of Christ) and God. Christian ethics is thus inextricably systemic; to understand therapy requires an understanding not just of the client's family, but also of the system embracing the client, the client's family, the therapist, the church and God.

But if Christian ethics needs to be understood within the context of holy history, it also has specific content. Both are important. Christians disagree, however, about what constitutes the domain of ethics. Following are several distinctions regarding the meaning of ethics that are sometimes made, including some implications of Christian ethics for psychotherapy in each instance.

Ethics and morality. Ethics and *morality* are sometimes contrasted and sometimes "used interchangeably" (Annas, 1992, p. 329). *Ethics* is used in both a narrower and a broader sense. When used in a narrower sense, it is solely concerned with morality and can be used interchangeably with *morality.* When used in a broader sense, as in this chapter, *ethics* connotes a focus both on the traditionally moral questions of "how we should live and what we should do" (Annas, 1992, p. 329) and on nonmoral questions of goodness and value. For example, happiness and mental health can be considered nonmoral goods, because we are under no obligation to be happy or mentally healthy (and so we don't usually label as immoral the person who is unhappy or mentally ill simply because the person is unhappy or mentally ill). Ethics, broadly defined, includes both moral issues (e.g., "You should be faithful to your wife") and nonmoral issues (e.g., "It would be good for you to be happy").

Although rarely employing the term *moral,* codes of professional ethics, in their focus on professional obligations, tend to use *ethics* in the narrower sense. For instance, a therapist who sleeps with a client or violates confidentiality would be considered unethical, but the therapist who is unhappy or not fully self-actualized would not (unless, of course, those problems hurt clients, in which case harm to clients would be the problem rather than unhappiness or incomplete self-actualization per se). In other words, however much it may be good to be happy or self-actualized, a therapist is under no professional obligation to be so.

A similar distinction is sometimes made between Christian ethics, which focuses on obligation and morality, and the Christian life, which is a lifestyle motivated and lived by faith in Christ. The latter includes worship and prayer, for instance, which are considered good but are not generally considered "moral" issues. Most would tend not to label "immoral" or "unethical" a Christian who fails to pray or worship or "love the Lord your God with all your heart, and with all your soul, and with all your mind, and with all your strength" (Mk

12:30 NRSV). But if prayer and worship aren't moral issues, they do pertain to the Christian life, to the "good life" as understood in the Christian faith, and thus warrant careful reflection.

I use the word *ethics* in this chapter's title to refer both to nonmoral goods, like mental health, happiness, prayer and worship, and to moral issues, like adultery and the professional obligation to maintain client confidentiality. I prefer this broader usage of *ethics* because moral and nonmoral issues are not always easily separable and are often deeply intertwined in both therapy and Christian faith. Back to the earlier example: if a therapist thinks Brad's personal happiness (meaning the nonmoral good of experiencing happiness in the here and now) is the ultimate good for him, and no moral considerations are applicable, the outcome of therapy is likely to be different than if a therapist thinks that the happiness that comes from a right relationship with God is the ultimate human good and that Brad has a moral obligation to remain faithful to his wife. In general I think it preferable to use an intellectual perspective that embraces all of life and permits a consideration of both goodness and obligation. Moral and nonmoral should be distinguished, of course, while still recognizing their inseparability. Similarly, Christian ethics and the Christian life may need to be distinguished, but both require the careful attention of Christian therapists and clients.

Ethical principles regulating behavior, virtue or both. Another distinction regarding the meaning of ethics has to do with whether ethics is primarily concerned with (a) ethical principles, for instance, justice or autonomy (e.g., "Human beings should be just in their dealings with others" or "No one should infringe on the autonomy of another human being"), or (b) virtue, the optimal character of persons (e.g., "The ideal person is self-actualized, godly, prayerful, loving and self-aware"). Of course, both may also be emphasized. Although ethicists have long emphasized principles, attention has recently turned to virtue or character as a critical aspect of ethics (DuBose, Hamel and O'Connell, 1993; Kruschwitz and Roberts, 1987; MacIntyre, 1984; Roberts, 1991, 1993). Christian ethicists have, of course, focused on both ethical principles and virtue, the latter often under the heading of sanctification.

To varying degrees, therapists have convictions about both optimal principles for living and ideal human functioning. And whatever a therapist's intent, therapy may result in a client's adopting, abandoning or reprioritizing ethical principles, or in changes in the quality of a client's character. So to limit ethics to a discussion of principles would clearly pass over some of the other key ethical dimensions of psychotherapy (cf. Jordan and Meara, 1990; Weiner, 1993). The Christian concerned about the ethical dimensions of therapy should consider carefully both principles and virtue.

Whether principles or virtue is the more important may depend in part on a therapist's theoretical orientation. Cognitively oriented therapy may produce greater change in a client's ethical principles, while virtue ethics may be more pertinent in understanding psychodynamic therapy (seeking "character trans-formation") and humanistic therapy (stressing the emergence of a "self-actual-ized" person).

The influence of the therapist's ethical convictions can be subtle. For example, Taylor (1989) has argued convincingly that any notion of identity (arguably related to notions of character and virtue) includes some standard of goodness, to which an individual compares himself. For example, if Brad's identity were that of a "man's man" (as exemplified in *Playboy* magazine), the standards of "goodness" by which he would evaluate himself (e.g., sexual prowess) would be very different than if his identity were that of "good father" or "faithful, loving husband" (as exemplified by God's relationship with his children and the church). To the extent that therapy produces an altered identity, it may also produce an altered sense of what is good and best in life. Therapeutic change can be both psychological and ethical.

If different therapists were asked, "What kind of person would Brad ideally become in therapy?" they might propose a variety of answers: self-aware, able to communicate well, a faithful marital partner, guilt-free, spontaneous, one who loves God above all, a person who makes meeting his personal needs his first priority in life. From the perspective of Christian ethics, it is vitally important which of those "virtues" Brad chooses, especially if one virtue becomes the guiding vision he uses to shape his behavior, identity and life.

Minimal obligation versus ideals. Some prefer to limit ethics to indisputable moral obligations, to minimal ethical principles about which there is widespread societal or rational agreement, and to the conflicts between such obligations and principles. For others, ethics also encompasses ideals, that is, optimal states, behaviors or personal qualities to which persons may aspire. The APA's new ethics code, for instance, distinguishes between obligatory ethical standards, which are *"enforceable rules for conduct,"* and desirable ideals set forth in the Preamble and General Principles, which articulate *"aspirational* goals to guide psychologists toward the highest ideals of psychology" (APA, 1992, p. 1598). For instance, the code states that psychologists "have a primary *obligation* . . . to respect the confidentiality rights of those with whom they work or consult" (Standard 5.02, p. 1206, emphasis mine) but also should *aspire* "to advance human welfare" (Principle F: Social Responsibility, p. 1200).

The same distinction applies to clients. Many psychologists, if pushed, would hold that certain obligations are universally applicable. Even Carl Rogers, who argued that being unconditionally positive with clients was fundamental to good therapy, would likely have become somewhat conditional had his client Brad announced his intent to rapidly hasten the demise of his invalid wife. And Bergin (1985) reported that when eminent psychotherapy researcher Sol Garfield was asked "whether he believed there are [moral] absolutes," he stated that "he believed in 'moderation in all things,' with the exception of fidelity, which he said he considered absolute" (Bergin, 1985, p. 110). Setting forth such ideals, whether moral or nonmoral, is controversial, though I think most therapists commonly hold some sort of (often implicit) aspirational psychological ideals.

Ethics, even when focused on minimal ethical obligations, has often tended to focus on ethical dilemmas, on conflicts between indisputable moral obligations. Much attention is devoted to clarifying and resolving such conflicts.

Ethical dilemmas do arise in therapy (Lakin, 1991). Therapists wrestle with situations in which honoring one ethical principle (like confidentiality) may result in violating another (for instance, someone may be physically harmed unless the therapist breaches confidentiality). In our earlier example, Brad's therapist could argue that she invited Brad's pastor to the second therapy session because when faced with a conflict between (a) upholding confidentiality and (b) ensuring the integrity of Brad's family and furthering his moral and spiritual well-being, she chose the latter.

An exclusive focus on minimal obligations, or on conflicts between minimal obligations, falls far short of addressing all of the ethical issues in therapy, however. Indeed, the ideals therapists and clients bring to a therapeutic relationship represent one of the most important ethical aspects of psychology. Questions of ideals arise most pointedly when treatment goals are formulated. What is the ideal life (the optimal behavior, character and lifestyle to which a Christian should aspire) for a particular Christian client? for all clients? What is the ideal life for Brad and his therapist?

The aspirational goals of psychotherapy are often discussed under the rubric "mental health," a term that, ironically, rarely receives careful scrutiny by mental health professionals. Providing a simple, universally accepted definition of "mental health" has proven difficult in spite of the great efforts put forth to do so (Jahoda, 1958; Smith, 1961), and measuring the values associated with it is very difficult (Bergin et al., 1994; Kelly, 1990; Kubacki and Gluck, 1993; Tyler et al., 1983; Suan and Tyler, 1990). Any consensus besides the superficial remains elusive. This is partly because "mental health" is a value-laden term, one whose meaning is inextricably tied to the philosophical assumptions underlying it (Engelhardt and Spicker, 1976).

At its simplest, mental health means freedom from mental illness. The desirability of that ideal is indisputable, and there is nothing distinctive about a Christian seeking it. However, when mental health is viewed as a positive, ideal state, a goal toward which therapists strive to move people, divergences emerge. Here therapy's value-ladenness (cf. Bergin, 1991; Beutler and Bergan, 1991; Kelly and Strupp, 1992) is relevant. To the extent that therapy affects client values, the ethics-laden nature of concepts of mental health means that therapeutic approaches differ substantially. Christian ethics supports some understandings of mental health and challenges others. Thus the aspirational ideal of mental health may be different for the Christian therapist. Indeed, it may be the case that of all the ways in which therapy is tied to ethics, Christian ethics may provide the most distinctive perspective when addressing therapy ideals.

Mental health, however defined, is one good end toward which clients may aspire. Brad's mental health and happiness are indisputably good; other things being equal, we would presumably want him more, rather than less, happy and healthy. But other good ends exist as well, such as his personal integrity, his promise-keeping, and the quality of his relationship with God, with his family and with the Christian community. One vital task is to evaluate the relative merits of all those goods, to determine what is ideal or optimal for him, to clarify his highest good. Is his mental health more important than his relationship with God? Although many therapists—Christian and non-Christian—consider such a question to be beyond the scope of their expertise or calling, the therapy they provide often reflects their de facto balancing of good and obligations. And so in working with Brad, his therapist would likely weigh the goodness of mental health against other goods, and against moral obligations like marital fidelity.

Christian therapists cannot be indifferent to the direction in which Brad and others move in therapy, cannot be neutral about the ideals that shape and direct psychotherapy. Removal of distress, however good and valuable, cannot be equated with optimal human functioning. Some argue that a Christian counselor should strive to help clients reach not merely the minimal goal of decreased suffering, but deeper, more ultimate goals that reflect the highest ideals of the Christian life. Such goals would clearly be distinctively Christian.

One way in which therapists and counselors articulate their aspirations for their clients is in the treatment goals they establish. For example, a Christian counselor, articulating an aspirational ethic, might set as a treatment goal for all clients what the Shorter Catechism of the Westminster Confession says is the optimal goal for human beings: our "chief end is to glorify God and to enjoy Him forever" (Westminster Divines, 1648, 1745, p. 369).

More often, therapists emphasize limited behavioral treatment goals, like reduced depression. Indeed, some assert it is precisely the focus on mental health alone (and not the pursuit of more ambitious moral and spiritual goals in addition to better psychological functioning) that distinguishes psychotherapy from counseling. Clearly, therapists set goals at different levels. Herron et al. (1994) distinguish between "three levels of mental health—necessity, improvement, and potentiality" (p. 106), noting that current trends in health care funding limit financial assistance to the first level.

Even therapists who argue for therapy's role in helping clients achieve their potential, however, often exclude moral and spiritual dimensions of human potential. These limitations set by therapists themselves stem in part from genuine modesty about therapeutic efficacy, in part from an unwarranted assumption that "everyone knows" the goal of psychotherapy, in part from a focus on therapy process rather than on the ultimate goals of therapy, in part from a recognition of the limited function a therapist serves, and in part from a radical skepticism about the possibility of having any but subjective or conative grounds for selecting more ultimate treatment goals. Regarding the latter, MacIntyre (1984) argues that many believe "questions of ends are questions of values, and on values reason is silent; conflict between rival values cannot be rationally settled. Instead one must simply choose" (p. 26).

Nevertheless, therapists often have more fundamental underlying treatment goals (cf. Browning, 1987; Jones and Butman, 1991) that shape their relationships with clients. Different therapists may well reduce Brad's distress (mental health at the level of necessity), but each would do so by moving Brad away from his symptoms and toward a variety of "ideal" directions. These underlying visions of optimal humanity can and should be analyzed from an ethical perspective.

The extent to which Christian therapists and clients can and should include the full range of Christian ideals in the goals they establish is a thorny and divisive issue. The Christian mental health professional cannot maintain either extreme position. Strict neutrality regarding Christian moral obligations and ideals is neither possible nor desirable. However, mental health professionals must limit their actions to the realm of their expertise—mental health—and are thus not free to focus on the Christian life of clients in the way pastors and friends can. So the issue is not whether Christian ethics enters therapy, but how it enters. Specifically, how intentional should Christian therapists and clients be in formulating therapy goals in relationship to Christian ideals? For the Christian therapist, this issue is made more complex by the fact that many clients enter therapy deeply disturbed and confused. They know they want to suffer less but are unclear about what they want in terms of ideals and personal qualities they would like to develop. This can provide an opportunity for Christian therapists, but also potential peril. To avoid the peril, Christian mental health professionals need to act in concord with professional ethics and provide therapy fully informed by Christian ethics only when clients give their free, full and informed consent.

Ethical Theory
In the academic realm, ethicists often use the term *ethics* to refer to ethical theory. Philosophers and others concerned with ethical theory strive to clarify the meanings of the concepts employed in moral discourse in order to determine whether it is meaningful to talk about goodness, virtue and moral obligation (or whether all moral judgments are relative), to establish the basis of goodness and moral obligation, to set forth ethical principles by which we can decide what is right or good, to obtain ethical knowledge, and so forth.

Christians often give distinctive answers to questions of ethical theory (e.g., Birch and Rasmussen, 1989; Holmes, 1984; Mouw, 1990; Roberts, 1991, 1993; Smedes, 1982). When seeking to set ethical standards, some Christians focus on

God's commands (as found in Scripture and church tradition), some on reason, some on the relationship of persons to God, and some on a combination of these approaches (Long, 1967, 1982). Ethical theories held by Christians and non-Christians can diverge even when there is agreement on a particular ethical standard or virtue. But most Christians would agree that ethical questions are best addressed in the context of a Christian worldview. "What should I do?" is a very different question for the one called by grace through Christ to be a just, loving child of God than it is for the one who believes that the world consists entirely of physical matter and that ethical questions are meaningless.

Ethical theory applies to psychotherapy in different ways. It may serve as the source of therapeutic goals. Christian and non-Christian psychotherapists might agree that it would be good for Brad to end his present arrangement with Jennifer, and perhaps even that his infidelity is immoral, but might do so for different reasons. One therapist may object to the relationship solely because it is inconsistent with his or her vision of mental health for Brad. Another may agree that Brad's relationship with Jennifer is not mentally healthy but may also consider the affair to be immoral—promises are obligatory because of the damage to society if they are not kept. Still another therapist might add that the affair is immoral because it violates the clear command of God in the Ten Command-ments, or because the clear thrust of Scripture is in support of marriage. Of course, many psychologists never state their underlying ethical theories clearly, and some deny that they even hold such theories. Fortunately, Christian mental health professionals wishing to evaluate the ethical theories of psychotherapeutic approaches, including those that are implicit, can benefit from the substantial critical attention those theories have received in recent years (e.g., Browning, 1987; Jones and Butman, 1991; Roberts, 1991, 1993; Tjeltveit, 1992, 1993).

Another way in which ethical theory applies to psychotherapy is regarding clients' own ethical theories, which may (and perhaps sometimes should) be altered over the course of a therapeutic relationship. Brad, for instance, appears to hold a rather unreflective hedonistic ethical theory—"Living the good life means doing what makes me happy"—in contrast to the richer hedonism of the Westminster Confession—"enjoy [God] forever" (cf. Piper, 1986, 1991). But some therapists may convert clients from a Christian ethical theory to Brad's brand of hedonism and label the result "mental health."

Social Ethics, Public Policy and Consensus

Given the deep, unresolved tensions in society over ethical theory, the content of specific ethical principles and the deeply ethical nature of therapy, the task of determining how society should regard therapy, and especially its ethical dimensions, is daunting. At present, society clearly sanctions therapy in its role of reducing the suffering associated with mental illness. But other ethical questions remain, having to do with "ethics" in the sense of social ethics: Which ethical position (or positions) is consistent with the societally sanctioned activity of psychotherapy? What is the proper role of therapy in society?

Adequately addressing these questions requires Christians to participate in the general societal debate regarding a public philosophy for psychotherapy (cf. Browning and Evison, 1991; Drane, 1991; Michels, 1991). Assuming that full societal agreement about the ethical dimensions of psychotherapy is very unlikely in the foreseeable future, all who have a stake in the outcome of therapy, including Christians, need to participate (Stiles, Shapiro and Barkham, 1993). Christians can contribute to this discussion by affirming on theological grounds the positive contributions of mental health professionals in general, while also arguing that the rights of religious persons seeking to provide and receive therapy consistent with their faith traditions should be upheld.

Some propose that we solve the problem of religious pluralism by erecting a "wall of separation" between religion (and, for many, ethics and morality) and the rest of life, including therapy. As a solution to the problem of the value-laden nature of therapy, this supposedly solves the problem of pluralism by ensuring that religious ethical perspectives don't inappropriately insinuate themselves (or insinuate themselves at all) into a publicly funded therapeutic relationship. The problem with this solution, despite its merits when applied in the arena of government, is that faith, ethics and therapy all have to do with deeply personal matters, matters that don't neatly fall into the categories created by psychotherapists and social planners. Expecting clients and therapists to be neutral about religious matters in therapy seems neither realistic nor desirable.

A much better solution to the question of the proper role of therapy in society includes a recognition that therapy can be understood on several different levels. Neimeyer (1993), for instance, distinguishes between four levels of therapy, in order of increasing abstractness: strategies and techniques (e.g., interpretations in psychoanalysis); clinical theory (e.g., the role of transference in psychoanalysis); formal theory (e.g., Freud's theory of the ego, id and superego); and metatheory ("assumptions about the nature of human existence, plasticity, and the locus of change," p. 143, that are not generally empirically testable). He suggests that consensus may be most easily attained in the middle levels (cf. Saltzman and Norcross, 1990). Societal consensus about the role of ethics in therapy is also probably most achievable at an intermediate level of abstraction. Achieving ethical consensus about the goodness of freedom from disabling and deeply distressing psychological disorders, for instance, does not seem difficult. Such an ethical assertion falls somewhere between specific ethical assertions (e.g., "Thou shalt not commit adultery") and very general ethical assertions (e.g., "Reason and reason alone is the appropriate basis for ethical principles"). But there is no social consensus yet, nor is it likely to develop soon.

A public philosophy that assumes certain intermediate-level goals (e.g., reduced psychological symptoms) and permits a wide range of general and specific ethical assertions in support of those goals may be optimal. Distinctively Christian forms of therapy, and forms of therapy distinctive to other religious and philosophical traditions, would be supported so long as the consensual goals are met, permitting a genuine pluralism in society as a whole (Tjeltveit, 1996). Societal sanction would thus be given to therapy that uses a vision of humanity that is fully informed by Christian ethics (or Buddhist ethics, or Jewish ethics, or Wiccan ethics), so long as the therapist is clear about the philosophy and goals, clients are fully informed about them, and the intermediate-level goals about which society agrees are pursued and reached. Adopting this sort of public philosophy would, of course, require that Christians support different religious therapists and clients, ensuring they have the same level of autonomy and distinctiveness we want for ourselves.

Unfortunately, as Johnson (1993) and Worthington (1993a) point out, Christians have made too little progress in documenting the efficacy of Christian approaches to psychotherapy. Research needs to focus both on the effectiveness of Christian approaches to psychotherapy, as judged by traditional standards of therapy outcome, and on distinctively Christian standards. Until that research is conducted, justifying distinctively Christian psychotherapy to society will be far more difficult than it need be.

References

American Association of Pastoral Counselors. 1991. *American Association of Pastoral Counselors Code of Ethics*. Fairfax, Va.: Author.

American Psychiatric Association. 1995. "The Principles of Medical Ethics, with Annotations Especially Applicable to Psychiatry." (Available from APA, 1400 K St. NW, Washington, DC 20005.)

American Psychological Association. 1992. "Ethical Principles of Psychologists and Code of Conduct." *American Psychologist* 47: 1597-1611.

Annas, J. 1991. "Ethics and Morality," in *Encyclopedia of Ethics,* ed. L. C. Becker and C. B. Becker. Vol. 1. New York: Garland.

Bennett, T. S. 1994. "Professional Ethics," in *Encyclopedia of Psychology,* ed. R. J. Corsini. 2nd ed., vol. 3. New York: John Wiley.

Bergin, A. E. 1985. "Proposed Values for Guiding and Evaluating Counseling and Psychotherapy." *Counseling and Values* 29: 99-116.

———. 1991. "Values and Religious Issues in Psychotherapy and Mental Health." *American Psychologist* 46: 394-403.

Bergin, A. E., L. E. Beutler, A. J. Consoli, T. A. Kelly, S. R. Kubacki and A. C. Tjeltveit. 1994. "New Approaches to Measuring Values in Psychotherapy." Panel presentation at the meeting of the Society for Psychotherapy Research, York, England (July).

Beutler, L. E., and J. Bergan. 1991. "Value Change in Counseling and Psychotherapy: A Search for Scientific Credibility." *Journal of Counseling Psychology* 38: 16-24.

Birch, B. C., and L. L. Rasmussen. 1989. *Bible and Ethics in the Christian Life.* Rev. ed. Minneapolis: Augsburg.

Browning, D. S. 1987. *Religious Thought and the Modern Psychologies: A Critical Conversation in the Theology of Culture.* Philadelphia: Fortress.

Browning, D. S., and I. S. Evison, eds. 1991. *Does Psychiatry Need a Public Philosophy?*

Chicago: Nelson-Hall.

Christian Association for Psychological Studies. 1993. *Ethical Guidelines for the Christian Association for Psychological Studies.* New Braunfels, Tex.: Author.

Drane, J. 1991. "Doctors as Priests: Providing a Social Ethics for a Secular Culture," in *Does Psychiatry Need a Public Philosophy?* ed. D. S. Browning and I. S. Evison. Chicago: Nelson-Hall.

DuBose, E. R., R. P. Hamel and L. J. O'Connell. 1993. *A Matter of Principle? Currents in U.S. Bioethics.* Philadelphia: Trinity.

Engelhardt, H. T., Jr., and S. F. Spicker, eds. 1978. *Mental Health: Philosophical Perspectives.* Dordrecht, Netherlands: D. Reidel.

Forde, G. O. 1969. *The Law-Gospel Debate: An Interpretation of Its Historical Development.* Minneapolis: Augsburg.

Fuller, D. P. 1980. *Gospel and Law: Contrast or Continuum? The Hermeneutics of Dispensationalism and Covenant Theology.* Grand Rapids, Mich.: Eerdmans.

Herron, W. G., R. A. Javier, L. H. Primavera and C. L. Schultz. 1994. "The Cost of Psychotherapy." *Professional Psychology: Research and Practice* 25: 106-10.

Holmes, A. F. 1984. *Ethics.* Downers Grove, Ill.: InterVarsity Press.

Jahoda, M. 1958. *Current Concepts of Positive Mental Health.* New York: Basic.

Johnson, W. B. 1993. "Outcome Research and Religious Psychotherapies: Where Are We and Where Are We Going?" *Journal of Psychology and Theology* 21: 297-308.

Jones, S. L., and R. E. Butman. 1991. *Modern Psychotherapies: A Comprehensive Christian Appraisal.* Downers Grove, Ill.: InterVarsity Press.

Jordan, A. E., and N. M. Meara. 1990. "Ethics and the Professional Practice of Psychologists: The Role of Virtues and Principles." *Professional Psychology: Research and Practice* 21: 107-14.

Kelly, T. A. 1990. "The Role of Values in Psychotherapy: A Critical Review of Process and Outcome Effects." *Clinical Psychology Review* 10: 171-86.

Kelly, T. A., and H. H. Strupp. 1992. "Patient and Therapist Values in Psychotherapy: Perceived Changes, Assimilation, Similarity and Outcome." *Journal of Consulting and Clinical Psychology* 60: 34-40.

Kruschwitz, R. B., and R. C. Roberts, eds. 1987. *The Virtues: Contemporary Essays on Moral Character.* Belmont, Calif.: Wadsworth.

Kubacki, S. R., and J. P. Gluck. 1993. *Relating Values and Methods in Psychodynamic and Cognitive-Behavioral Therapy.* Paper presented at the 101st annual meeting of the American Psychological Association, Toronto (August).

Lakin, M. 1991. *Coping with Ethical Dilemmas in Psychotherapy.* New York: Pergamon.

Long, E. L., Jr. 1967. *A Survey of Christian Ethics.* New York: Oxford University Press.

———. 1982. *A Recent Survey of Christian Ethics.* New York: Oxford University Press.

MacIntyre, A. 1984. *After Virtue: A Study in Moral Theory.* Rev. ed. Notre Dame, Ind.: University of Notre Dame Press.

Michels, R. 1991. "Psychiatry: Where Medicine, Psychology and Ethics Meet," in *Does Psychiatry Need a Public Philosophy?* ed. D. S. Browning and I. S. Evison. Chicago: Nelson-Hall.

Mouw, R. J. 1990. *The God Who Commands.* Notre Dame, Ind.: University of Notre Dame Press.

National Association of Social Workers. 1980. *Code of Ethics of the National Association of Social Workers.* Silver Spring, Md.: Author.

Neimeyer, R. A. 1993. "Constructivism and the Problem of Psychotherapy Integration." *Journal of Psychotherapy Integration* 3 (2): 133-157.

Piper, J. 1986. *Desiring God: Meditations of a Christian Hedonist.* Portland, Ore.: Multnomah Press.

———. 1991. *The Pleasures of God.* Portland, Ore.: Multnomah Press.

Reeck, D. 1982. *Ethics for the Professions: A Christian Perspective.* Minneapolis: Augsburg.

Roberts, R. C. 1991. "Psychotherapeutic Virtues and the Grammar of Faith." *Journal of Psychology and Theology* 15: 191-203.

———. 1993. *Taking the Word to Heart: Self and Other in an Age of Therapies.* Grand Rapids, Mich.: Eerdmans.

Saltzman, N., and J. C. Norcross, eds. 1990. *Therapy Wars: Contention and Convergence in Differing Clinical Approaches.* San Francisco: Jossey-Bass.

Smedes, L. B. 1983. *Mere Morality.* Grand Rapids, Mich.: Eerdmans.

Smith, M. B. 1961. " 'Mental Health' Reconsidered: A Special Case of the Problem of Values in Psychology." *American Psychologist* 16: 299-306.

Stiles, W. B., D. A. Shapiro and M. Barkham. 1993. "Research Directions for Psychotherapy Integration," in *Research Directions for Psychotherapy Integration: A Roundtable,* ed. J. C. Norcross. *Journal of Psychotherapy Integration* 3: 91-131.

Suan, L. V., and J. D. Tyler. 1990. "Mental Health Values and Preference for Mental Health Resources of Japanese-American and Caucasian-American Students." *Professional Psychology: Research and Practice* 21: 291-96.

Taylor, C. 1989. *Sources of the Self: The Making of the Modern Identity.* Cambridge: Harvard University Press.

Tjeltveit, A. C. 1986. "The Ethics of Value Conversion in Psychotherapy: Appropriate and Inappropriate Therapist Influence on Client Values." *Clinical Psychology Review* 6: 515-37.

———. 1992. "The Psychotherapist as Christian Ethicist: Theology Applied to Practice." *Journal of Psychology and Theology* 20: 89-98.

———. 1993. "Christian Ethics and Psychological Explanations of 'Religious Values' in Therapy: Critical Connections," in *Religious Values in Psychotherapy,* ed. E. L. Worthington Jr. Grand Rapids, Mich.: Baker.

———. 1996. "Aptly Addressing Values in Societal Contracts About Psychotherapy Professionals: Professional, Christian and Societal Responsibilities," in *Psyche and Faith: Beyond Professionalism,* ed. P. J. Verhagen and G. Glas. Zoetermeer, Netherlands: Boekencentrum. Pp. 119-37.

Tyler, J. D., J. A. Clark, D. Olson, D. A. Klapp and R. S. Cheloha. 1983. "Measuring Mental Health Values." *Counseling and Values* 27: 20-30.

Weiner, N. O. 1993. *The Harmony of the Soul: Mental Health and Moral Virtue Reconsidered.* Albany: State University of New York Press.

Westminster Divines. 1648, 1745. The shorter catechism agreed upon by the Assembly of Divines of Westminster with the assistance of the Commissions from the Church of Scotland. In *A Compendium of the Westminster Confession of Faith and the Shorter and Longer Catechism.* Philadelphia: Benjamin Franklin. Pp. 367-410.

Worthington, E. L., Jr. 1988. "Understanding the Values of Religious Clients: A Model and Its Application to Counseling." *Journal of Counseling Psychology* 35: 166-74.

———. 1993a. "Critical Issues in the Study of Psychotherapy and Religious Values," introduction to *Psychotherapy and Religious Values,* ed. E. L. Worthington Jr. Grand Rapids, Mich.: Baker.

———. 1993b. "Psychotherapy and Religious Values: An Update," in *Psychotherapy and Religious Values,* ed. E. L. Worthington Jr. Grand Rapids, Mich.: Baker.

Part 1

THE CHRISTIAN
PRACTITIONER

Chapter 3

ESSENTIAL ELEMENTS FOR ETHICAL COUNSEL

Horace C. Lukens Jr.

---

*N*ever before have counseling and psychotherapy services been so familiar to and so widely used by the American public with such sophistication, understanding and candor. In years past such services were often sought quietly and with a sense of embarrassment, shame and failure.

In order for the Christian therapist to excel professionally and spiritually, it is essential to identify, understand and apply appropriate guidelines and limits to the services being provided. Only through such a thorough examination and understanding of the relevant issues and a deliberate and careful application of these principles in clinical practice will we be confident of delivering services in a highly ethical manner, bringing healing to our clients and glory to God. This chapter attempts to identify and discuss some elements and issues that every Christian mental health professional and paraprofessional (lay counselor) needs to be aware of and to deal with in order to deliver competent and ethical counseling services.

There are many increasingly complex issues that confront the counselor and that require a clear understanding and careful handling with clients, who are often in difficult or emergent circumstances. For example, informed-consent laws have expanded far beyond their more simple origins and require thoughtful scrutiny and application. Dual-relationship issues can be relatively benign or can lead to misunderstanding and harm, and they may arise often for therapists that work in church settings.

These and other issues discussed in this chapter apply to credentialed mental health professionals, pastors who conduct counseling as part of their ministries, and church counseling centers that may have both professionals and lay counselors providing service. Other issues that are equally relevant to the topic of this chapter are addressed elsewhere in the book: the nature and extent of formal training; internship experiences; confidentiality in marriage and family therapy; and business ethics in counseling, to name several. While paraprofessionals may not have to comply with some of the regulations and policies required of the professionals—and, in fact, there will be differences among professional disciplines regarding regulations—awareness of and compliance with regulations is not only prudent, but also assists in lowering liability exposure (Becker, 1987).

Confidentiality

Confidentiality is crucial to an effective and trusting counseling relationship. Without it, most counseling relationships would never begin, and those that did would be unlikely to survive. Few ethical constraints within the field of counseling are as universally accepted as confidentiality. There are, however, important limits to confidentiality that must be recognized by the counselor and must also be reviewed with and understood by the client at the outset of counseling in order to adhere to proper legal and ethical requirements. Clients need to understand that counselors are obligated to comply with laws regarding disclosure. It is often helpful to advise clients when a request for information has been made even though the therapist may have some leeway regarding exactly what information is provided. Should a client discover such disclosure after the fact, the sense of betrayal and the erosion of trust is likely to be increased.

According to C. D. Stromberg and his colleagues (1988), who authored a handbook for psychologists covering the full range of legal issues encountered in practice, there are three concepts—privacy, confidentiality and privilege—that must be understood and distinguished. *Privacy,* the broadest of these concepts, refers to an "individual's right to be left alone and to decide the time, place, manner and extent of sharing oneself (one's thoughts, behavior or body) with others" (p. 371). The right of privacy grows out of the Fourth Amendment to the constitution and is the foundation on which confidentiality and privilege are built.

Confidentiality is a professional and ethical term. It refers to the "quality of private information that is divulged with the implicit or explicit promise and the reasonable expectation that it will not be further disclosed except for the purpose for which it was provided" (p. 372).

Privilege, the narrowest of the concepts, is "a legal protection against being forced to break a promise or expectation of confidentiality in legal proceedings"

(p. 372). While the concept of confidentiality is most familiar to counselors, it is important that counselors also have a working knowledge of privacy and privilege.

The "Ethical Principles of Psychologists and Code of Conduct" (APA, 1992) states that "psychologists have a primary obligation and take reasonable precautions to respect the confidentiality rights of those with whom they work or consult" (p. 1606). This principle, which has become a standard among other professional associations, fundamentally holds that all information about a client that is obtained in the course of a professional psychological relationship, including an initial contact such as a telephone call, should be viewed as confidential. It is not proper for psychologists or counselors to assume that clients understand the concepts and their implications. Rather, it is imperative that expectations about confidentiality and the possible exceptions be clarified with each client at the outset of the counseling relationship. Similar clarification of the scope and limits of confidentiality needs to occur with others with whom the psychologist will be working, such as the pastor, physician or attorney.

Therapists need to have a clear understanding of the exceptions to the general rule of confidentiality. These may include (1) when the client consents in writing to disclosure, (2) when a law requires reporting of an event such as child abuse, (3) when there is a duty to warn or protect, (4) when reimbursement or other legal rules require disclosure, (5) when the client is deemed to waive confidentiality by bringing a lawsuit, or (6) in the case of an emergency. Therapists should be aware of the code of confidentiality mandated by their own professional organization. Equally important, every therapist must be familiar with state laws that govern confidentiality and privilege, and understand that laws can vary from state to state. In addition, professional rules and state laws occasionally disagree in what they require of therapists. In such a case it is incumbent on the professional to seek consultation and perhaps legal advice to determine the best course of action.

Written consent. When a client consents for information to be disclosed, it is essential that the client understand the information that will be provided, the individuals or entities to which it will be provided, and the reasons for divulging such information. The best way to accomplish this is in a detailed yet clearly understood written release-of-information form. Adherence to federal and state law is essential when creating such a form. For instance, federal law requires that such releases include information about communicable diseases (including HIV) yet prohibits the use of the same information to criminally investigate or prosecute an alcohol- or drug-abuse patient. For more information about sample forms see appendix C, as well as forms provided by most professional associations, state licensing agencies and those found in Tan's volume (1991).

Duty to report. When state law requires that certain information about a client's circumstances or behavior be reported, the counselor is obligated to do so. In many states there are laws requiring the reporting of child abuse, which typically includes sexual abuse, physical and even psychological abuse. Some states require the reporting of *suspected* child abuse and even gross neglect of a child. These laws have complexities that vary from state to state.

Medicare and Medicaid laws. Federal and state laws that regulate health and welfare programs require access to client records in order to assure "program integrity." Typically, providers whose services are reimbursed by Medicare and Medicaid are required to furnish, upon request, the names and addresses of clients, the dates of service, and a description of the services rendered (Stromberg et al., 1988). It should be recognized that there are occasions when such agencies also request treatment records as part of their investigation.

Patient as litigant. When a client initiates litigation against a therapist, the client places his or her own mental status at issue and thereby is considered to have waived confidentiality rights as far as they relate to the issues of the case. At times clients may place their own mental status at issue without even realizing it. For instance, when a parent seeks custody of his child, his own mental competency may be at issue, and thus he may be regarded as having waived his confidentiality rights.

Duty to warn and protect. Some of the most troublesome and complex issues counselors face have to do with managing the potentially or actually dangerous client. Even well-trained mental health professionals are not able to make reliable predictions of future danger. Nevertheless, certain obligations have been imposed on counselors who are working with potentially dangerous clients. The "duty to warn," which has grown out of the *Tarasoff* decision, has triggered more litigation and discussion than perhaps any other legal issue in the mental health field. The landmark Tarasoff case litigated in California (*Tarasoff* v. *Board of Regents of the University of California,* 1976) ruled that when a therapist determines or should determine that a patient presents a serious, violent threat to another person, that therapist has an obligation to protect and warn the intended victim and to notify others, including the police, against such danger.

Tarasoff is, however, not the only case focusing on the professional obligations of therapists. Therapists have also been held liable for issues such as a failure to diagnose accurately or to treat effectively in order to bring the client's violent tendencies under control.

While the *Tarasoff* decision has had tremendous impact on the evaluation and handling of the potentially dangerous client, Stromberg et al. (1988) note that there appears to be a judicial trend toward narrowing the ruling to apply it only to specifically articulated, credible threats to identifiable victims. Subsequent rulings have limited the duty to warn to revealing only information which is necessary to accomplish the intended purpose only to those who absolutely need to know (Stromberg et al., 1993).

Details of *Tarasoff*'s impact will not be reviewed here. Its central impact is that the counselor's duties are not limited to a duty to warn but may include the much broader stance of taking all steps of "reasonable care" to protect the intended victim. These steps, according to Stromberg et al. (1988), should include selecting clients carefully, taking a detailed history, advising the client of the limits of confidentiality, clarifying and exploring a client's propensity for violence, maintaining careful and thorough records, and taking action to protect victims. What appears to be simply a duty to warn is in fact a duty to protect potential victims. Steps of protection might include thorough and effective therapeutic management of the patient's propensity for violence, discussing the issue with the patient, warning potential victims, contacting the police, and taking any other steps which might fall under the rubric "reasonable steps." These might include seeking involuntary commitment, referring the patient for a medication evaluation, calling for an ambulance, obtaining assistance from friends or a pastor who may be able to intervene, and attempting to involve the patient's family to assist in resolving the threatening circumstance.

Not only does the duty to warn and protect apply to potential victims of dangerous patients, but it also applies to circumstances where there is *imminent danger* that a patient will commit suicide. It is essential that every counselor know the fundamentals of assessing suicide risk and be prepared to disclose confidential information to protect suicidal patients from harming themselves (APA, 1992; CAPS, 1993). Depending on the circumstances of each case, the therapist may have to contact law enforcement, emergency medical services, a responsible family member or some other party who is in a position to assist. Understand, however, that the information released in such circumstances is limited to that which is necessary to remove the patient from harm's way.

Future criminal behavior. With the exception of reporting child abuse, psychologists do not have an obligation to report to authorities when a client has committed a crime unless such activity suggests, by virtue of the duty-to-warn standards noted above, that future criminal behavior is likely to occur and future harm to a third party might be averted by the reporting of such information.

Emergencies. The courts have increasingly defined *emergency* narrowly with respect to reporting. That is, incidents in which the client's health is seriously or imminently at risk are viewed as appropriate for disclosure. For example, an emergency-room physician might contact a therapist in an effort to determine the source of a client's delirious behavior. In such circumstances it is probably appropriate for the therapist to disclose information pertinent to the client's care. The scope of the disclosure should, of course, be limited to that which is necessary.

Confidentiality with minors. When it comes to confidentiality and psychological care of minors, in most cases all information shared by a minor child in treatment is accessible by the parents, and the parents are responsible for giving permission for disclosure to others of information regarding their child. At times this requirement is in conflict with effective treatment strategies: rapport and trust may be compromised if a child or adolescent knows that anything he might say in treatment could be conveyed to his parents. Thus it is important to establish with both parents and minors early in treatment what guidelines will be followed. Legal and ethical considerations must be delicately balanced here.

Group therapy. The unique setting of group therapy raises some different and difficult issues regarding confidentiality. The usual rule—when personal information is shared with third parties, the right to confidentiality is waived— must be modified due to the unique nature of group therapy. In this setting, part of the therapeutic process involves the sharing of personal information with other clients. Many courts have recognized this unique situation and conse- quently have upheld the client-counselor privilege if other individuals have participated in or facilitated the treatment process. Care must be taken, however, to ensure an accurate understanding of confidentiality among group members so that inadvertent violations do not occur. By using first names only and by discouraging socialization outside the group, the risks of confidentiality viola- tions can be reduced. A written contract with each member may also further stress the importance of confidentiality and clarify its limits.

Confidentiality and a deceased client. The limits of confidentiality continue to apply following the death of a client. If this were not so, clients would be reluctant to share personal information, knowing that there would be no protection from disclosure following their death. A number of states permit a legal representative of the client to continue to protect the confidentiality of the client's records from posthumous disclosure.

Responding to requests and subpoenas. The counselor faces a wide array of requests for access to client records, many of which come from individuals with little understanding of the therapeutic process and who have nontherapeutic goals. It is not unusual to discover that professionals such as physicians, pastors, and even attorneys and other mental health professionals do not fully compre- hend or appreciate the delicate nature of the therapeutic relationship. Conse- quently, counselors need to be prudent and cautious in responding to such requests. All requests should be in writing with the purpose of the request and the requested information clearly stated. Except in true emergency circum- stances the client must be consulted for a signed consent to the request. If the request is denied, then the counselor should adhere to the client's decision. Even if records are subpoenaed, the subpoena can be refused based on the client's refusal to permit disclosure. In such instances, the client should be encouraged to consult his or her attorney about steps that can be taken to block such a release of records. If the court still orders that the records be made available, then the counselor must either produce the records or face contempt-of-court charges and possible imprisonment. In such an instance, the counselor has taken the most conservative stance in protecting the confidentiality of the client-counselor relationship and the confidentiality of client records.

Informed Consent to Treatment

The concept of informed consent as it applies to mental health circumstances is a relatively recent development. For years patients who assumed that their health care professional knew best deferred to that provider's judgment. Gradually the courts have recognized the importance of patients' rights and the need for greater equality in the doctor-patient relationship. Informed consent acknowledges the necessity of respect for individuals, their autonomy and their privacy rights. Today courts require that informed consent be obtained from the client prior to disclosure, and not having it may be considered malpractice. It should be noted that a client can sue for being treated without consent, even if the treatment was competent in all other aspects.

There are at least four basic aspects of informed consent (APA, 1992, Sect. 4.02). First, the patient must be legally competent in order to consent to treatment. Second, all information regarding treatment that a reasonable person would want to consider should be presented to the client, including the nature of treatment, the potential benefits and risks, alternative treatments with their benefits and risks, and the benefits and risks of no treatment at all. Next, the client must understand this information. And fourth, voluntary consent to the recommended treatment must be obtained and documented. In addition, counselors should discuss with clients as early as possible other relevant issues such as the anticipated length of treatment, fees and related financial policies, and the presence of a supervisor or student/intern (APA, 1992, Sect. 4.01). Therapists should also study their state board rules and professional codes of conduct carefully to ensure that they are providing all necessary information to clients.

Increasingly, attorneys and others recommend that therapists use signed consent forms or contracts to provide essential information to clients and obtain their written consent for treatment. These forms should be provided at the outset of treatment or as near to the outset of treatment as possible. While signed consent forms are very important from the standpoint of risk management, there are admittedly times when their use may be somewhat awkward. If presented with poor timing and taste, they could make the establishment of rapport difficult. For instance, for a client in crisis to spend most of his first session going over the therapeutic contract rather than receiving immediate assessment and intervention would be inappropriate. Unusual circumstances require special care. But overall, obtaining informed consent, preferably using a signed consent form, has become the standard in the field.

In addition to the general information suggested above, a number of specific items listed below should be provided to clients as a part of informed consent (Texas State Board of Examiners of Psychologists [TSBEP], 1995). Appendix C also provides examples of how a written consent form might be organized.

1. *Information about the services provided.* In understandable language, explain something about your services and your philosophy of treatment. This may include information about the types of counseling you provide, your theoretical orientation, and something about what clients can expect assessment and treatment to be like. Some information about alternative choices for treatment should also be given: clients' rights to withdraw from treatment, and side effects, stresses or strains that could occur as a byproduct of treatment. If you offer Christian therapeutic services, you should provide some information about the nature of these services so that your clients will know how you apply Christian concepts in treatment. The primary purpose of these explanations is to give clients the opportunity to decide whether or not they want these concepts to be a part of their treatment. Providing this information may be especially important if you offer Christian services and work in a center where this is not otherwise clearly indicated.

2. *Goals of therapy and procedures to be used.* What problems will you be treating in therapy, and what techniques will you use? Since each case is different, this information is not usually included in a basic information form. However, it can be discussed early on in the therapeutic relationship, and the treatment plan and the client's consent to it can be documented in the chart. Since goals and procedures may change as therapy progresses, this topic will likely be revisited over the course of treatment, and the client should be encouraged to ask questions about goals and procedures as a part of therapy. Also included in this discussion could be some estimate of the frequency of sessions and length of treatment, albeit with some understanding that specific pronouncements may not always be possible early on in therapy.

3. *Financial issues.* Clients should clearly understand the cost of services, when they will be expected to pay and the method of payment. How are insurance matters handled? Who is ultimately responsible for the bill? What is the policy for overdue accounts, and does the counselor reserve the right to use collection agencies?

4. *Confidentiality.* Clients must be told that therapy is confidential to the extent provided by law. They should understand that while confidentiality may be assumed in the majority of circumstances, there are exceptions. Admittedly, a focus on all the exceptions to confidentiality could raise worries for some clients. Notable exceptions to confidentiality have been presented earlier in this chapter. Other situation-specific issues might center around confidentiality in marriage and family cases (see chapter eight) or on child cases (see chapter ten). When insurance or managed care is involved, clients will need to sign and understand releases to permit information to be sent to third-party payors.

5. *Qualifications.* What are your qualifications, licensing, degrees and certification? It may be helpful to share where you received your academic as well as clinical training. If you are a trainee under supervision, the client needs to know that and who your supervisor is.

6. *Other pertinent information.* Other important information to be discussed may include how phone calls or emergencies are handled, what clients should do if they have a concern or complaint, and information about office hours. In any case, the information needed for informed consent depends somewhat on the nature of the counseling setting and the type of services provided.

One of the primary goals of informed consent is to prevent misunderstanding between client and therapist. Many of the complaints that come to a state licensing board have to do with miscommunication between therapist and client (TSBEP, 1995). While formal consent procedures should help keep serious miscommunication at a minimum, misunderstandings can and do occur in counseling relationships, as they do in all relationships. Therapists who respond to misunderstandings with a spirit of concern and consideration, and who work closely with their client to deal with the issues and correct the misunderstanding, do much to restore, maintain and develop the trust factor so important to all successful therapy.

There are some exceptions to informed consent. The courts have recognized that there are circumstances in which "disclosure poses such a threat of detriment to the patient as to become infeasible or contraindicated from a medical point of view" (Stromberg et al., 1988, p. 452; APA, 1992, Sect. 4.02). However, in most situations, the burden of proof is likely to be on the therapist to show why their client was not informed.

Documentation

Many, if not most, state boards now require that licensed professionals keep accurate records of evaluation and counseling services. In addition, professional guilds, counseling agencies and institutions have their own rules about documentation. Specific requirements regarding the content of records may vary from place to place, but records usually must include as a minimum information about (1) the date of service, (2) type of service rendered and by whom, (3) assessment and progress information, and (4) billing information. Of course, copies of release and other consent forms should be kept as well.

Accurate records can help the therapist in the process of assessment, in devising and maintaining consistent treatment plans, and in recalling important therapeutic information. They can also serve a risk-management function, allowing the therapist to document important information of an ethical or legal nature. As is sometimes said in the legal community, "If it isn't in writing, it didn't happen." Even negative findings should be documented as evidence that they were in fact evaluated. For example, if an evaluation showed there was no suicidal ideation, that should be noted. Good records are also helpful if the case is transferred to a new therapist at some point.

Documentation is not without its dilemmas, however. Therapists must realize that records could at some point be seen by someone other than themselves. The trend in law over recent years has been to allow clients more and more access to records of their treatment. As noted earlier, exceptions to the rules of confidentiality may lead to the release of records. Managed care is requesting greater and greater documentation. Questions also abound regarding what is appropriate for release. Some state boards consider materials like raw data and test protocols appropriate to release only to other professionals who have training in how to interpret them. The overriding concern in these situations is that misinterpretation, misunderstanding and misuse of records could occur the more available they become to others. Bennett et al. (1990, pp. 76-78) provide an excellent checklist for determining how to keep accurate and careful records.

Ending Treatment

When the therapeutic relationship must be interrupted or terminated, it is important to do so properly. Arrangements should be made for provision of services in the event of the therapist's absence due to illness, relocation or death, or as a result of the client's financial limitation. When the client no longer needs service, is not benefiting from service or is at risk of being harmed by continued service, termination of treatment and possible referral to another resource is appropriate.

Every counselor has experienced the dilemma of whether or not to refer a client to another professional. Sometimes the therapist-client mix is simply a mismatch. On other occasions issues such as age, sex of the therapist or personality style hamper the development of an effective therapeutic alliance. Limits in training and experience can also dictate the need for referral. A greater difficulty is encountered when there has been a positive treatment relationship but a poor response to treatment. Under such circumstances, appropriate referral is often clouded by issues such as the therapist's sense of failure, the therapist's positive or negative countertransference with the client, the therapist's reputation among her colleagues, or the therapist's not wanting to acknowledge to the client that she has reached the limits of her expertise. At times even financial and caseload pressures can cloud a therapist's objective evaluation of when to refer.

Ethical constraints and concern for the welfare of counselees require that clients not be abandoned. Abandonment can be avoided by carefully discussing the treatment plan with the client, providing thorough pretermination interventions, suggesting alternative service providers and taking any other reasonable steps to facilitate transfer of care to another provider if it is indicated (APA, 1992, Sects. 4.08-4.09). The sensitive therapist will realize that transfer or termination, though it may ultimately be in the client's best interest, can raise ambivalent or confusing feelings for some clients. A therapist's handling of such situations should be measured and compassionate (CAPS, 1993, Sect. 5.3).

Dual Relationships

Dual relationships (also called multiple relationships) are those in which "therapists assume two roles simultaneously or sequentially with a person or persons engaging their professional assistance" (Huber, 1994, p. 67). Huber notes that the dual relationships could both be professional, as when a practitioner serves as both a therapist and a supervisor to a person, or could involve the combination of professional and nonprofessional roles such as therapist and friend, therapist and relative, or therapist and lover.

The issue of sexual and romantic relationships with clients will be covered at length in chapter six. However, it is important to realize that sexual misconduct is by no means the only kind of dual-relationship problem that can occur. A nearly endless variety of situations can, in some circumstances, raise questions about whether or not an inappropriate dual relationship is occurring. Should a therapist ever provide therapy for a student, relative, neighbor or fellow church member? Should a therapist ever loan a client money, allow a client to stay in his home, or see a client socially?

Dual-relationship issues are a particular concern for the Christian therapist, especially for counselors who work in a church counseling center where, for example, the potential client could be an emotionally troubled person as well as a fellow Sunday-school class member or a member of the church board. Pastors often struggle with these issues and often do so without the clear professional boundaries that assist traditional psychotherapists in avoiding dual relationships.

Several writers have formulated guidelines for dealing with dual relationships, and these guidelines are worthy of careful consideration (Gottlieb, 1993; Kitchener, 1988). Some dual relationships are clearly a problem and are always inappropriate: intimate relations with clients; counseling with close relatives, students or employees; loaning clients money. However, it must be realized that it is impossible to avoid every kind of dual relationship and that, in fact, not all dual relationships are necessarily harmful (Huber, 1994; Keith-Spiegel and Koocher, 1985; Kitchener, 1988). Indeed, there may be some circumstances in which knowing the client in another setting is beneficial to the client therapeutically. Nevertheless, the APA code is clear that professionals should avoid dual relationships that "might impair the psychologist's objectivity or otherwise interfere with the psychologist's effectively performing his or her functions as a psychologist, or might harm or exploit the other party" (APA, 1992, Sect. 1.17).

Clinical situations must be examined on a case-by-case basis to determine the best course of action. Based on his own experience and that of others,

Sanders (1996) highlights a number of points a prudent therapist should consider and weigh if the possibility of a dual relationship arises.

1. *The divergence of obligations* (Kitchener, 1988). "As the divergence between the obligations imposed by different roles increases, the potential for divided loyalties and loss of objectivity increases" (Huber, 1994). Other things being equal, there is a difference between providing services for the daughter of your best friend at church and counseling a member of your church of 5,000 whom you know only by name. You have obligations to your best friend that may well be incompatible with your obligation to be a good therapist to her daughter. The more the divergence in obligations, the greater the chance that misinterpretations, misunderstandings and mixed allegiances will occur.

2. *Locale and availability of other practitioners.* It is more difficult for rural therapists to avoid dual relationships, and some allowances must be made in these circumstances. Counselors who practice more specialized types of treatment are sometimes less available in some areas. If Christian counseling is the treatment of choice for an individual, but the only Christian counselor in the area participates in a church outreach program with that individual, it is possible that the individual would do better to see the local Christian counselor anyway. One should weigh the different factors involved to discover which ones are the most important. One must be very careful and analyze each situation separately, however. Christian counselors sometimes enter dual relationships out of a need to please or a sincere desire to help and are surprised later when a problematic dual relationship they did not anticipate emerges.

3. *The nature of the presenting problem and the treatment needed to resolve it.* The severity of the presenting problem(s) and the necessary treatment should be considered. Three sessions of relaxation training for stress management is much different from long-term therapy for a family with an anorectic daughter. Dual relationships can become more problematic either when the issues in therapy are more convoluted or when the therapy itself is complicated.

4. *The ability of each party to define and maintain appropriate boundaries.* Some clients have difficulty understanding and respecting appropriate boundaries. Since dual relationships by definition blur boundaries between different interpersonal roles, these problems are likely to become more severe when the client has difficulty maintaining boundaries in the first place. When boundaries are unclear, the likelihood increases that the client will develop false expectations about the therapy and/or the therapeutic relationship (Kitchener, 1988). Though therapists should be able to define and respect boundaries, it is nevertheless true that they may also have difficulty maintaining boundaries either because of personal problems or because of transference issues with the client. It is the therapist's responsibility to remain aware of additional factors in the client or in himself that might blur the boundaries of a dual relationship even more than would normally be expected.

5. *The power-prestige differential.* Dual relationships are more problematic when there is a definite power-prestige differential (Kitchener, 1988). That is, the more power or prestige the therapist has relative to the client, the more possible that exploitation of or harm to the client could occur. This is one reason why counseling between a therapist and his employee or student is undesirable.

6. *Potential confidentiality problems.* Dual relationships are an increased concern when the social context in which they take place makes it difficult for confidentiality to be maintained. Encountering a client and her friends at the grocery store may be unavoidable but can usually be handled constructively by the sensitive therapist. Some clients are not troubled by such occurrences, but others are. Many situations are far more complicated, however. Parishioners in counseling with their pastors sometimes become upset when they assume, albeit incorrectly, that the generic illustration used in the pastor's Sunday sermon was related to the material they brought up in counseling. Other pastors have had the opposite problem: pastoral counselees become disturbed when the pastor doesn't automatically acknowledge their personal problems during a prayer service.

It is easy to see how different issues can overlap with one another. For example, suppose a counselor serves on the personnel committee at the church and is asked to evaluate someone for a job with whom they have had a counseling relationship. At the least this example includes power-prestige differential issues, confidentiality problems and divergence in obligations.

It can be helpful for the therapist to talk openly with the client about a potential for a dual relationship and seek their input in how to deal with it. For example, if the counselor and the client both live in a very small town and have frequent interaction outside of counseling, they might discuss in detail the pros and cons of working together in therapy, taking into consideration the different issues involved. Frequently counselees are not aware of and have not really considered the possibility that a dual relationship either exists or might emerge. Often they are appreciative when the counselor brings it up, invites them to consider possible options and to take part in the decision about what will be done. Such discussions can prove invaluable to the therapist too, because they may provide the therapist with much-needed information about the client's ability to maintain boundaries and other factors that may be helpful in forming a decision about whether to proceed with treatment.

Counselors who work in churches or Christian institutions should work with other leaders in the institution to develop policies and guidelines for handling dual-relationship issues before problems ensue (Deal and Parish, 1996). If nothing else, doing this will sensitize other church leaders and members to the potential problems, help them avoid asking counselors to overstep appropriate roles and decrease the probability of misunderstandings when actual situations arise. Becker (1987) recommends that lay counselors in the church be allowed to make the helping relationship with their counselees their primary obligation and not be placed in dual roles or functions that will conflict with this primary obligation.

Counseling, and even more so Christian counseling, is accompanied by a host of complex and multifaceted issues and responsibilities. Unless each of us as Christian counselors has a thorough understanding of these issues and is able to effectively apply them for ourselves and hold one another lovingly accountable to the legal, ethical and professional issues and to God's fundamental truths, we will fall short of an authentic response to God's call on our lives. Let us each be thoroughly competent, professional and Christlike in all that we do. By this will God be glorified.

References

American Psychological Association. 1992. "Ethical Principles of Psychologists and Code of Conduct." *American Psychologist* 47: 1597-1611.

Becker, W. W. 1987. "The Paraprofessional Counselor in the Church: Legal and Ethical Considerations." *Journal of Psychology and Christianity* 6: 78-82.

Bennett, B. E., B. K. Bryant, G. R. VandenBos and A. Greenwood. 1990. *Professional Liability and Risk Management.* Washington, D.C.: American Psychological Association.

Christian Association for Psychological Studies. 1993. *Ethical Guidelines for the Christian Association for Psychological Studies.* New Braunfels, Tex.: Author.

Deal, R. L., and W. E. Parish. 1996. "Family Therapy in a Congregational Setting: Assessing and Utilizing the Impact of the Larger Church System." *Journal of Psychology and Christianity* 15: 232-45.

Gottlieb, M. C. 1993. "Avoiding Exploitive Dual Relationships: A Decision-Making Model." *Psychotherapy* 30: 41-48.

Huber, C. H. 1994. *Ethical, Legal and Professional Issues in the Practice of Marriage and Family Therapy.* 2nd ed. New York: Macmillan.

Keith-Spiegel, P., and G. P. Koocher. 1985. *Ethics in Psychology: Professional Standards and Cases.* New York: Random House.

Kitchener, K. S. 1988. "Dual Role Relationships: What Makes Them So Problematic?" *Journal of Counseling and Development* 67: 217-21.

Sanders, R. K. 1996. "Issues to Consider When a Dual Relationship Emerges." Unpublished manuscript.

Stromberg, C. D., D. J. Haggarty, R. F. Leibenluft, M. H. McMillian, B. Mishkin, B. L. Rubin and H. R. Trilling. 1988. *The Psychologist's Legal Handbook.* Washington, D.C.: Council for the National Register of Health Service Providers in Psychology.

Stromberg, C. D., D. Lindberg, B. Mishkin and M. Baker. 1993. *The Psychologist's Legal Update: Privacy, Confidentiality and Privilege.* Washington, D.C.: Council for the National Register of Health Service Providers in Psychology.

Tan, S. Y. 1991. *Lay Counseling: Equipping Christians for a Helping Ministry.* Grand Rapids, Mich.: Zondervan.

Tarasoff v. *Board of Regents of the University of California.* 1976. In vol. 551 of *Pacific Reporter.* 2nd ed., p. 334 (California Supreme Court).

Texas State Board of Examiners of Psychologists (TSBEP). 1995. "Informed Consent." *Newsletter,* Winter, pp. 11-12.

Chapter 4

QUALIFICATIONS
OF THE CHRISTIAN MENTAL
HEALTH PROFESSIONAL
Richard E. Butman

---

*O*ne of the most interesting discussions in any standard text on ethical and legal issues in the helping professions is the section that develops the concept of professional competence (e.g., Corey, Corey and Callanan, 1993; Keith-Spiegel and Koocher, 1985). The assumption is usually made that a client's welfare is directly affected by whether or not the mental health professional knows his or her limitations and weaknesses, as well as his or her strengths and skills. In other words, *competence* is usually defined as some combination of clinical expertise, high levels of self-awareness and interpersonal effectiveness (cf. Corey and Corey, 1989). Obviously the ability to explore one's motives and relationships insightfully is a skill that is hard to teach, difficult to assess and impossible to perfect, yet few skills are more central to effective ethical and legal functioning as a mental health professional (Keith-Spiegel and Koocher, 1985, p. 223). Perhaps in no other profession does the behavior and personality of the professional make such a significant and potentially lasting impact on the client, or such a direct contribution to the eventual success and satisfaction of the change agent (Meier, 1989, p. 55).

"Knowing thyself" is certainly a challenge for any Christian mental health professional, but it must be coupled with genuine wisdom and humanness (cf. Evans, 1989). Further, the Christian mental health professional is called to serve God and his church and to imagine the Father in all professional work (cf. Jones and Butman, 1991, pp. 401-14). These "lofty concerns" vie with more mundane and often preoccupying matters like intense competition for the mental health dollar, widespread interdisciplinary conflict over "turf," or financial security for business, self, or family. Consequently it can become terribly tempting to "shrink from self-knowledge" and largely avoid the difficult challenge of thinking clearly about a truly Christian understanding of persons and their suffering (Anderson, 1990; Benner, 1983; Oden, 1984; Tidball, 1986).

This chapter will explore the challenge of defining *competence* for the Christian mental health professional. The implications are enormous not only for training, licensing and credentialing issues, but also for the challenge of maintaining excellence through continuing education, supervision and spiritual growth (cf. Collins, 1991). This should also include some form of group accountability for true Christian distinctiveness and integrity beyond the maintenance of professional welfare only. Perhaps this would prompt the entire Christian counseling movement to stretch beyond its scientific infancy and current credibility problems toward more responsible statements in the marketplace and mass media (cf. Butman, 1993).

Our discussion will be limited to professional applications for certified or licensed counselors, marriage and family therapists, psychiatrists, psychiatric nurses, psychologists, and social workers. This in no way should be interpreted as diminishing the importance of lay and paraprofessional counselors (see chapter fourteen) or the tremendous example of the great tradition of pastoral care throughout the centuries (see Clesch and Jaekle, 1975; Holifield, 1983; chapter five in this volume). Recent work by Scannish and McMinn (1994) and McMinn and Meek (1996) would be especially helpful for applications in these areas.

Defining Competence

Competence in the helping professions is difficult to define and even harder to assess. Standards and credentials in the mental health disciplines vary, and much controversy surrounds any attempt to discuss boundaries of competence and limitations of technique. Fortunately, each of the major professional associations has made an attempt to do so in their respective professional codes of ethics (see appendix B). To date, only one major Christian organization, the Christian Association for Psychological Studies (CAPS), has a published statement. Another document is in the process of development for the American Association of Christian Counselors (AACC). Consider the relevant section from the CAPS *Ethical Guidelines:*

4.1. I pledge to be well-trained and competent in providing services.

4.2. I will refrain from implying that I have qualifications, experiences, and capabilities which are in fact lacking.

4.3. I will comply with applicable state and local laws and regulations regarding competency in the psychological and pastoral professions.

4.4. I will avoid using any legal exemptions from professional competency afforded in certain states to churches and other nonprofit organizations as a means of providing services that are beyond my training and expertise.

4.5. I will diligently pursue additional education, experience, professional consultation and spiritual growth in order to improve my effectiveness in serving persons in need. (CAPS, 1993, pp. 4-5)

On the matter of self-representations in the public sector:

6.1. I will advertise or promote my services by Christian and professional standards, rather than only commercial standards.

6.2. Personal aggrandizement will be omitted from advertising and promotional activities. (CAPS, 1993, p. 5)

In examining these documents and exploring recent trends in the field, a number of conclusions are inescapable. First, it is not clear how the professional should determine the boundaries of his or her competence. Advanced degrees alone don't confer, nor does the process of credentialing or licensing necessarily guarantee, specific clinical skills and sensitivities. Second, individuals who work in existing structures charged with detecting and then adjudicating incompetent professional behavior (e.g., state licensing or certification boards, third-party payer quality-assurance programs, review committees, professional associations, etc.) often have great difficulty applying existing criteria to specific complaints against mental health professionals. Next, expulsion from professional associations—or even the loss of certification and/or licensure—hasn't always served as a deterrent against unethical behavior. It is not surprising, then, that there has been a proliferation of litigation in situations (including the church setting) where alleged harm has been done (cf. Ohlschlager, 1991). Fourth, the codes can't force the practitioner to accept existing practice criteria, review and carefully study the results of treatment outcome data, consult with more experienced practitioners, learn new skills or pursue appropriate levels of training. The sad reality is that professional licensure and credentialing are less than adequate indicators of an ongoing and continuing commitment to excellence. Professional codes of ethics don't necessarily prompt a practitioner to utilize peer review or consultation groups, participate in continuing education or take advantage of supervision (Corey and Corey, 1989).

At a minimum, then, *competence* implies a recognition of a therapist's strengths and weaknesses, and the humility to pursue further consultation, training and supervision throughout one's professional career. It includes not allowing others to assume that one has training or experience one does not have. Honest and sobering self-appraisal likewise requires wisdom and discernment, capacities that are probably best developed in the context of some type of accountability group. A therapist should not expect academic and practical preparation only to guarantee competence, or leave it to the judgments of professional licensing or credentialing bodies only. Since ethical codes tend to be "too general in nature and give too few specifics to permit an easy identification of incompetent practice" (Keith-Spiegel and Koocher, 1985, p.

226), the challenge remains of developing a consensus about those qualities that embodies a commitment to excellence beyond formal education and credentials only.

Peterson and Bry (1980), in one of the few high-quality studies on the subject of competence, discovered that four factors emerged in their analysis that consistently differentiated "incompetent" and "outstanding" student-clinicians toward the end of a doctoral training program. These were professional responsibility, interpersonal warmth, intelligence and experience. These factors are strikingly similar to those reported by McLemore (1982) in a more anecdotal account of an unusually gifted Christian mental health professional. According to McLemore (pp. 171-72), this psychologist was "genuinely loving," "not afraid to care" and "communicated integrity." He goes on to say that "her core beliefs were manifestly Christian . . . in accord with the infrastructure of life." Further, "there was nothing that smacked of 'religion in the service of defenses,' of trying to avoid distressing thoughts and feelings by clinging to empty religious language. . . . My awareness of her faith on many occasions nourished my own."

Yet it was a fifth quality, which he described as her "clear professional competence," that was most impressive:

On the surface, there seems to be nothing particularly Christian about this. Many unbelieving practitioners are competent; in fact, I know a good number of avowed agnostic therapists to whom I would rather refer clients than to some of the Christian professionals I know. However, if God is the Source of all good, regardless of who does it, there is something Christian about competence after all. Moreover, I strongly believe that her Christian love for people is largely what has motivated her to develop her clinical expertise. (p. 172)

So competence in professional practice might best be understood as a cluster of virtues (cf. Roberts, 1993), or even as a process of character formation (cf. Holmes, 1992). At the most basic level, interpersonal skills and sensitivities must be coupled with clinical expertise. It is probably beyond the scope of any licensing or credentialing body, or even professional association, to define these qualities. It is not surprising, then, that admission committees can have difficulty recognizing a candidate's potential, or that training programs struggle in defining these criteria, or that professional associations are unclear about how best to encourage members to maintain and develop a commitment to excellence in their work.

Additional challenges face the Christian mental health professional who is willing to engage in much-needed honest and sobering self-appraisal in the context of a discerning and wise accountability group. As the CAPS code implies, he or she should "diligently pursue additional education, experience, professional consultation and spiritual growth in order to improve [his or her] effectiveness in serving persons in need" (1993, Sect. 4.5, p. 5). Toward those desirable end goals there are a number of guidelines for the express purpose of fostering a dialogue between committed Christian clinicians and the communities of which they are a part. As Scannish and McMinn (1994) have observed, the Bible nowhere directly addresses the issue of competence as it applies to Christian mental health professionals, yet certain themes beyond clinical expertise and interpersonal warmth alone seem highly relevant to the discussion.

Ten Guidelines for Improving the Competence of Christian Clinicians

1. *Rigorous training in one of the major mental health disciplines.* Specifically this should include formal education through at least the master's level at a regionally accredited college or university. In certain disciplines specialized degrees and extensive clinical training are required (e.g., MSW [master's in social work] plus practicum for social work, Ph.D. or Psy.D. plus internship for clinical or counseling psychology, M.D. plus residency for psychiatry). I agree with Levicoff's concern (1993) about the "chaff" that all too often accompanies the "wheat" in the burgeoning Christian counseling movement. Since at least thirty-five of the fifty states have some kind of credentialing legislation in place "that range[s] from voluntary title acts to mandatory practice acts" (p. 58), it behooves us to take seriously the prerequisite education and training necessary to be even considered as a candidate for the appropriate credentials and licensure required for professional practice in any given state.

I share Noll's anguish (1994) about the "anti-intellectual" attitudes evident far too often in some conservative Christian circles. I would be greatly encouraged by a more engaging mindset, one that would be open and receptive to God's truth in all of the academic disciplines (e.g., Browning, 1987; Collins, 1989; Holmes, 1977). I am deeply convinced that in my particular discipline (clinical psychology) there is much in the theoretical and applied scholarly literature that bears directly on the many activities of the Christian mental health professional (cf. Jones and Butman, 1991).

All systems of psychological thought have their points of compatibility and incompatibility with Christian thought. I think it is a mistake to assume that the Bible declares itself to be sufficient to meet all human needs (cf. Bobgan and Bobgan, 1987, p. 11) or that it is necessary to study only the Holy Scriptures in order to equip oneself to become the servant of God (cf. Adams, 1979, p. 46). At the most basic level, such a position runs the risk of denying "general revelation" or "common grace" (i.e, all truth is God's truth). Consequently, the widespread distrust of the mental health disciplines and the tendency for some Christians to "shoot their wounded" (cf. Carlson, 1994) is deeply troubling.

Granted, the ultimate task of the Christian mental health professional is the "interrelating of Christian belief and practice with the best of contemporary scholarship and professional standards" in his or her particular discipline (*Inform,* 1994). We can't establish or maintain true Christian distinctiveness as mental health professionals unless we are conversant in the major theories, paradigms, values and culture of our chosen mental health discipline. How this could be done apart from extended study and residence in a high-quality academic setting is beyond my comprehension. *Only* in a residential setting is there opportunity for regular dialogue and discussion that is so essential for integrative learning. *Only* in a residential setting can close community, modeling and mentorship occur. *Only* in a residential setting can the student be regularly held accountable by peers and professors. I believe the sacrifice is "worth it" and can be an expression of good Christian stewardship of our time, talents and resources.

No doubt certain programs and institutions are better than others, and choices about which discipline to pursue are seldom easy. We need to help the next generation make wise and informed decisions about whether or not to pursue the helping professions, and give them the kind of practical information that can help them get the most out of their education and training (see chapters one and two in Corey and Corey, 1989). For those of us who have already made our choices and commitments, we must realize that the responsibility for educating ourselves must transcend the confines of prior educational and training settings. Learning is a never-ending process.

For those who serve in academic and clinical training settings, it is imperative to give careful attention to selecting students, how best to train and supervise students, the curriculum offered, and the criteria for certification and graduation (cf. Corey, Corey and Callanan, 1993, especially chapter seven). The qualifications of mental health professionals reflect in no small measure the academic milieu in which they were shaped, the training and supervisory experiences they were exposed to, and the modeling they directly observed (see Guy, 1986). This process of "imprinting" can place certain limits on an individual's capacity for personal and professional growth, one vital expression of a commitment to excellence.

2. *Exposure to diversity in initial training and beyond*. This includes but is not limited to contemporary models of multicultural psychotherapy. Traditional approaches to people-helping are not always applicable in the crosscultural context. Ours is a pluralistic culture that demands the ability to be "uncommonly decent"—being civil without being entirely relativistic, being "convicted" without being overly dogmatic and rigid (Mouw, 1992). We need to develop a kind of humility and openness that allows us to see the essential humanity of all persons. Arrogance and inflexibility regarding our theories, paradigms and values will certainly impair our ability to relate with others whose experiences can be vastly different from our own. We live in a society in which there is far too much intolerance and unnecessary conflict surrounding issues of racial or ethnic identification, age, socioeconomic status, religious affiliation, or gender.

Ideally, professional preparation would include coursework and training experiences that would stress issues of diversity, and licensed and credentialed professionals would actively pursue the kind of continuing education and supervision that would challenge and stretch them in these areas. This would hopefully bring a heightened awareness of those who have been marginalized and wounded by living in a nonpluralistic society (see chapters ten and eleven in Corey, Corey and Callanan, 1993) or silenced by ethnocentric and culture-bound attitudes and behaviors (Van Leeuwen et al., 1993).

A respect for diversity should also be reflected in one's primary theoretical allegiances. A strong argument can be made for responsible eclecticism in clinical practice (see chapter fifteen in Jones and Butman, 1991). There is no warrant for theoretical exclusivism in training, supervision or practice. The demands of most contemporary mental health settings necessitate flexibility and "epistemic humility," a willingness to learn much about (and from) those being served. "Knowing thyself" must be coupled with an equally strong desire to get to know others, including those whose experiences are very different from our own (Palmer, 1993).

3. *A commitment to careful supervision and regular consultation for all Christian mental health professionals and students.* This is a requirement in nearly every practicum and training setting, although the quality and quantity of that supervision and consultation vary widely. When it is good, the recipient can learn much about ethical issues associated with carrying out professional roles and responsibilities, the need to maintain clear boundaries between those roles, and the potential dangers of dual relationships (Corey, Corey and Callanan, pp. 209-10). In that context, awareness of strengths and weaknesses and insights about the helper in the healing process can develop. Ideally, supervision can be a catalyst for self-exploration and growth and a context for both modeling and mentoring.

Careful supervision and regular consultation should last far beyond the formal requirements of a practicum or training setting. Becoming certified or licensed should not somehow signal the end for the need of this kind of intimate, one-on-one accountability. Exposure to a variety of styles or orientations is potentially useful, and a combination of individual and group involvement is ideal. This kind of regular feedback, and the opportunity to hone clinical skills, is necessary and very relevant to the complex and often confusing tasks of the Christian mental health professional.

Of course, high-quality supervision beyond credentialing and licensure can be expensive and time-consuming. But when coupled with a commitment to continuing education and training, it has the potential to be a most worthwhile investment and a very tangible expression of a commitment to excellence. Indeed, it may speak deeply to whether or not we as therapists aim toward achieving greater measures of wholeness and holiness, and being the best that we can be (cf. Malony, 1994).

4. *The pursuit of legitimate credentials and professional licensure.* Mental health professionals usually recognize that most credentials and licenses are generic; that is, they don't specify the problems or populations the practitioner is qualified to work with, nor do they indicate the nature of the practitioner's clinical expertise. In most states legislation has been passed that presumably protects the public against untrained or potentially unqualified practitioners. The assumption is that those who are credentialed or licensed will engage only in those psychotherapeutic tasks for which they have received specialized education and training. Fretz and Mills (1980) define licensure as "the statutory process by which an agency of the government, usually a state, grants permission to a person meeting predetermined qualifications to engage in a given occupation and/or use a particular title and perform specified functions" (p. 7). Certification, in contrast, pertains more directly to judgments made by members of a professional association about a particular individual's credentials (e.g., graduate education, supervised practica, internship or highly specialized postdoctoral training). The relationship between certification and/or licensure and clinical competence has not, unfortunately, been clearly documented (Keith-Spiegel and Koocher, 1985).

There are strong arguments for and against professional licensing and credentialing. According to Corey, Corey and Callanan (1993), "The essence of the argument for licensure is the contention that the consumer's welfare is better safeguarded with legal regulation than without it. Challenges to this assumption often maintain that licensing is designed to create and preserve a 'union shop' and that it works more as a self-serving measure that creates monopolistic helping professions than as a protection for the public from misrepresentation and incompetence" (p. 183).

No doubt there are competent counselors who are shut out because they are not certified or licensed, and this has the potential to produce adversarial rather than collaborative relationships (cf. Collins, 1991). In some Christian circles a strong argument is made that any biblically grounded Christian is competent to counsel, a position that is critiqued and evaluated at length elsewhere (see chapter one in Jones and Butman, 1991). A major concern regarding this is the limited availability of any empirical data beyond anecdotes and "case studies" to support this view. Advocates of this position are sometimes unwilling to strive toward the development of a more inclusive and responsible eclecticism in theory or practice. Nor does there seem to be a willingness to engage in discussions that could be characterized as evidencing a "convicted civility" (respectful and attentive dialogue with others with whom one differs; cf. Butman, 1993). This position might be best viewed as a "creedal assertion," a virtue statement that is difficult to confirm or refute and that needs to be put into the terms of a researchable hypothesis.

I am personally encouraged by the inclusion of Statement 4.4 in *Ethical*

Guidelines for the Christian Association for Psychological Studies (CAPS, 1993): "I will avoid using any legal exemptions from professional competency afforded in certain states to churches and other nonprofit organization as a means of providing services that are beyond my training and expertise" (p. 5). I share Ohlschlager's (1991) concern that by too loosely appealing to "church-state separation issues," one can avoid the more rigorous and demanding approach being advocated in this chapter for the Christian mental health professional. There are certainly delicate tensions for credentialing or licensing pastoral counselors, tensions fully appreciated by groups like the American Association of Pastoral Counselors or movements like Clinical Pastoral Education. I certainly have sympathy for positions that stress church-state separation. My fear, however, is the temptation on the part of the counselor not to pursue additional education, experience or professional supervision, or the blatant disregard for any kind of peer review or system of accountability. I suspect that Ohlschlager (1991) is right when he argues that in the "grave new world" of Christian counseling, the threat of litigation may be the greater incentive for pursuing excellence, rather than a strong sense of personal or professional integrity that should undergird the desire for competency.

I seriously doubt whether the licensing or credentialing debate will be resolved in the near future. A bigger concern, however, is the attitude and belief on the part of a practitioner that he or she is somehow beyond the need to take these issues seriously or is satisfied to settle for less than fully legitimate credentials. I share Levicoff's (1993) conviction that it is "better not to be certified at all than to be certified by a bogus organization that will reflect poorly on the counselor's professional reputation" (p. 58). No doubt regulation can be a "hassle"—but I remain convinced that market forces alone should not drive the activities of Christian mental health professionals, since the risk of personal aggrandizement or the temptation to promote oneself in a self-serving manner is tremendous. Regulation, I firmly believe, is a much-needed potential corrective for these tendencies.

An even more effective way to capture the spirit and letter of the law is to engage in professional disclosure. I would like to see Christian mental health professionals take the initiative by preparing an annual "professional disclosure statement" that would be submitted to regulatory boards—and perhaps even to a representative group of discerning peers, including members of their local churches (cf. Bernstein and Lecomte, 1981). Unlicensed or noncredentialed clinicians would be asked to demonstrate clinical skills that are clearly related to positive client outcomes (via audio, video or written transcripts). Licensed and credentialed clinicians might consider submitting evidence of their continuing commitment to academic and professional excellence, and providing an updated and mature statement of their philosophy of psychotherapeutic change and records of their attempts to measure client outcomes.

This idea is not particularly new. It follows logically from the practice of preparing informed-consent documents for new and potential clients (see chapter three in this volume and Collins, 1991, pp. 185-87). These documents provide clients with the information necessary for making intelligent decisions about whether or not to utilize the provider's services and what to expect from treatment.

The pursuit of legitimate credentials and professional licensure is to be commended, although it is not without its limitations. Beyond these regulatory considerations, it would be exemplary for Christian mental health professionals to develop the habit of offering annual professional-disclosure statements and utilizing informed-consent documents with all their clients. Such accountability would most likely have a humbling and humanizing effect on the current practice of psychology and would make the Christian mental health professional far more sensitive to the legal as well as ethical considerations that are involved in a variety of psychotherapeutic endeavors. Recent research by McMinn and Meek (1996) indicates that far too many Christian counselors fail to see that all their actions are subject to the mechanisms of ethical restraint and regulation, whether they are credentialed, licensed or not. The freedom from these "restraints" is illusory if it leads to the disintegration of competence within the lay counseling and pastoral care movements. Indeed, clergy malpractice suits have become a painful reality in the past two decades (Malony, Needham and Southard, 1986).

5. *Develop good treatment plans and use them as a basis for peer review.* One very tangible expression of a commitment to excellence is the development of adequate treatment plans. It can seem at times that Christian mental health professionals are too casual about their work and rather poorly focused (Collins, 1993). Careful assessment prior to intervention and a willingness to evaluate the effectiveness of these efforts afterward should be marks of professionalism (McMinn, 1994). The inherent risks of "going with the flow" include the potential for becoming unreflective about problem identification, intervening in an unsystematic hodgepodge manner and being cavalier about engaging in the kind of outcome evaluation that has the potential to sharpen and refine clinical skills. This lack of focus can only lead to personal and professional isolation, which contributes little to the legitimization of our collective efforts.

Networking on the basis of a shared commitment to develop effective treatment plans is one of the most important means of building accountability and improving professional communication. It also provides impetus for continuing crucial discussions of the ethical and legal questions facing Christian mental health professionals (What am I trying to accomplish? What are the identified problems? What are options for intervention? What does the available research evidence suggest about the differential effects of those strategies? How do I know that I was able to reach the stated goals and objectives of treatment?).

Our approach to helping others should be flexible and responsive to the particulars of individuals in any given situation, as well as deeply informed by our understanding of how to intervene and so best enhance human welfare (Butman, 1993).

Christian mental health professionals should meet often with colleagues to exchange information as well as to ensure the quality of their work. Peer review in itself has the potential to encourage healthy self-regulation. I suspect that these groups do more to foster ethical practice than the major professional associations, certification and licensure boards, or any particular ethical code of conduct. Further, they may provide much-needed interpersonal and intellectual stimulation, absolutely essential for helping the clinician to stay alive as a person and as a professional. I doubt that there are more effective ways to ensure quality or to provide an opportunity for consultation about matters that most directly concern professionals.

Recent research (Lewis, Greenburg and Hatch, 1988) indicates that about half of the psychologists in the sample studied belonged (23 percent) or had belonged (24 percent) to a peer-consultation group. Of the remainder, the majority (61 percent) would join a peer review group if it were available. There is obviously a "felt need" for the kind of challenge and support that can be found in such settings.

6. *Regular participation in continuing education.* More than two decades ago Dublin (1972) suggested that the half-life of a doctoral degree in psychology was somewhere between ten and twelve years. Keith-Spiegel and Koocher (1985) observed that obsolete information might be an even greater risk in the field of psychology than in fields like medicine or law. If they are right, it is essential for professional associations as well as regulation boards to require continuing education. It seems almost unethical to be unaware of innovative methods, recent advances in theory and research, multicultural concerns, or the host of professional resources available to Christian mental health professionals today.

Of course, mandated continuing education is no guarantee that the clinician has actually incorporated the information. As Corey, Corey and Callanan (1993) have observed, "One of the weak points of mandatory continuing education is that it cannot require intellectual and emotional involvement. A practitioner's résumé may look impressive in terms of knowledge acquired, but the amount of this knowledge that is absorbed and is integrated into practice may be less than a piece of paper indicates" (p. 186).

A deeper value of continuing education—mandatory or voluntary—may be that it teaches the practitioner that he or she is not immune to mistakes. Experience alone does not guarantee clinical expertise. Christian mental health professionals need to strive for constant awareness of their limitations, recognize that these limitations may increase with the passage of time, and seek to develop constructive helps to maintain their professional capabilities. Further education may also help the practitioner recognize the potential for burnout or exhaustion and take action accordingly.

7. *Understand and use Scripture wisely.* Any of the previous guidelines can be just as relevant to the "generic," non-Christian mental health professional as to the Christian professional. The challenge to Christian clinicians is more complex since we are called to be competent in two worlds—the world of faith and the world of professional practice (Scannish and McMinn, 1994). All our activities as practitioners should be grounded in, informed and shaped by the practices of the Christian faith (*Inform,* 1994). Not only do we need to be "practitioner-scholars," but we must be adept in our understanding of the significant interface between mental health disciplines and Christian beliefs and practice. The ability to articulate that understanding is at the core of what it means to be truly distinctive as a Christian mental health professional (see chapters fifteen and sixteen in Jones and Butman, 1991).

The ethical behavior of Christian mental health professionals is ultimately grounded in obedience to the Word of God. Christian practitioners, whether they acknowledge it or not, are representatives of the church (Anderson, 1990). It is imperative, then, that Christian clinicians have the ability to articulate the basis for their faith and lifestyle, and a certain amount of philosophical and theological sophistication is essential (cf. Evans, 1989; Holmes, 1977; Roberts, 1993). I would argue that Christian mental health professionals who are informed about the points of compatibility and incompatibility between their mental health discipline and the world of Christian thought are more likely to be analytic and sophisticated in how they think about the many dimensions of the human condition, able to clarify the core constructs of major psychotherapeutic approaches, and more willing to strive toward the goal of developing a responsible eclecticism in their clinical work.

The essential discipline of the Protestant tradition is personal study of the Bible (Smith, 1993). Through spending time reading and studying the Scriptures, we learn to listen to Christ's teaching on the importance of hearing and doing his word. A good understanding of the Bible and theology can make our interventions complete and at the same time respectful of the fundamental commitments in life that are so central to society. We are more likely to see the implications of our faith beyond merely the clinical context. We will come to see our work as a means of grace, thoroughly built on a theological as well as a psychological foundation (cf. Anderson, 1990). A solid knowledge of Scripture is one aspect of what it means to be held accountable for Christian distinctiveness, and one expression of being more "responsive to and centered on the will of God and the welfare of the church over and against our individual professional welfare" (Jones and Butman, 1991, p. 416). We will be less likely to equate psychological wholeness (health) with spiritual maturity (holiness)—or vice versa (Malony, 1994). Biblical literacy and a certain theological sophistication are essential competencies for the Christian mental health professions to cultivate (see Foster and Smith, 1993).

8. *Develop a strong link with a local church.* The culture of professionalism can be both a blessing and a burden for the Christian mental health professional, as well as a source of profound "ethical ambivalence." As Anderson (1990) has noted, "Professionals self-consciously embody and attempt to model the higher ideals of the general society. . . . [They] want to be known for their altruistic service, concern for all persons regardless of economic and social status, and sacrifices made for the general good of society." Yet it is that same culture which all too often provides the cues for values that are "basically pragmatic, opportunistic, and entrepreneurial" (p. 202). The potential risk for the Christian mental health professional is that survival in the marketplace can replace an idealistic and deeply Christian value system as the modus operandi. In other words, kingdom ethics and professional priorities clash.

Thus it is imperative for the Christian mental health professional to establish a strong link with a local church. This is essential for several reasons. First, the church can serve as a place where Christian mental health professionals are ministered to; a source of support, accountability and empowerment (Anderson, 1990, p. 209). Second, the church is a place where Christian professionals can minister to others. Christian clinicians must fully grasp the idea that the issues they face daily in their offices are not just psychological concerns, but matters that have significant implications for furthering the kingdom of God. Such a realization can help promote a greater concern for the welfare and status of those individuals who are marginalized in society, in contrast to the world of professionalism, which tends to focus almost exclusively on the elite and powerful. Third, the church is a source of community, whereas the culture of professionalism tends to be highly individualistic and rather isolated. And finally, the local church can provide a context in which practitioners can reflect deeply on their implicit or explicit goals and objectives for their clients, and measure those against kingdom criteria for wholeness and holiness (cf. Malony, 1994). Consider the keen insights of Anderson (1990):

> Clinical problems . . . are related to a client's domestic, marital, family, and social structures. These networks of relationships contain moral, often religious, and occasionally legal issues that impinge on the therapist's role. The therapist's own values, convictions, religious beliefs, and commitments also influence this role. Probably no people in our society other than pastors and priests provide access to the core of life in all these areas as much as professional counselors. (p. 209)

Without that vital link between practitioner and parishioner, there is a potential loss of genuine wisdom and humanness (cf. Evans, 1989), much-needed social support and empowerment, and an ethical context for wholistic healing beyond the confines of a very private office. The very *outward* discipline of service needs to be undergirded by the more *corporate* disciplines of confession, worship and celebration, and the more *inward* disciplines like prayer and meditation (cf. Foster, 1992; Foster and Smith, 1993). Confessing Jesus Christ as Lord was never intended to be a solitary pursuit only. Linking arms with a local church is perhaps the most tangible and visible way to bring one's work under the lordship of Jesus Christ (Col 3:23).

9. *Become actively involved in a support group of Christians who are* not *therapists*. Qualities like compassion, servanthood, agape love, transparency, holiness, wisdom, humanness and integrity (see chapter sixteen in Jones and Butman, 1991) require an interpersonal context *outside* the consulting room to develop in. The Christian mental health professional is not called to be merely compliant with ethical and professional codes, but is instead challenged to develop a life of integrity, deeply transformed by the Spirit and empowered by the gospel.

To accomplish these ideals it is strongly recommended that the Christian mental health professional engage in regular and intentional dialogue with other believers who are *not* therapists. This is important not only for intellectual stimulation, but also for interpersonal support. Involvement in a support group of nontherapists is an expression of courage and openness toward being held accountable for Christian distinctiveness and integrity in everyday work (Jones and Butman, 1991, p. 416). Not only should these members ask the tough questions about our professional commitments and priorities, but they should also challenge us to take our own spiritual formation seriously (cf. Smith, 1993). This type of substantive and formative feedback can get to the heart of what it means to be engaged in distinctively Christian counseling.

Ideally, this support group can provide a context for integrative growth for both the professional and the nontherapist participants. The focus is *not* on the direct discussion and supervision of the professional's clinical cases. Indeed, this would be a clear violation of confidentiality. Rather, a group such as this provides "perspective, spiritual support, and a representation of the culture of the kingdom of God" (Anderson, 1990, p. 210). It is also perhaps one of the best "antidotes" for the burnout, exhaustion and loneliness often felt by those who care deeply about the pain and agony of others and who feel called to bear those burdens and help transform that pain (see chapters seven and eight in Corey and Corey, 1989).

10. *Take up the challenge of personal and spiritual growth*. Christian therapists, whether they acknowledge it or not, are representatives of the church and should image God in their work. If this is indeed true, then certain qualifications for Christian leaders ought to apply to therapists as well. Consider the challenging words of Titus 1:5-9 (NRSV):

I left you behind in Crete for this reason, so that you should put in order what remained to be done, and should appoint elders in every town, as I directed you: someone who is blameless, married only once, whose children are believers, not accused of debauchery and not rebellious. For a bishop, as God's steward, must be blameless; he must not be arrogant or quick-tempered or addicted to wine or violent or greedy for gain; but he must be hospitable, a lover of goodness, prudent, upright, devout, and self-controlled. He must have a firm grasp of the word that is trustworthy in accordance with the teaching, so that he may be able to preach with sound doctrine and to refute those who contradict it.

Scannish and McMinn (1994) respond to these challenging words in several ways. First of all, it is clear that the Christian mental health professional should not be living in blatant sin. We are all broken and fallen persons—and none of us is blameless (cf. McLemore, 1982)—but a consistent pattern of clear disregard for God's command on a personal level raises fundamental questions about the nature of our Christian commitment. Second, it seems evident from the passage that our families and marriages should be spiritually and emotionally healthy (and when problems occur, are we willing to acknowledge them and seek appropriate help?). Finally, we need to be able to articulate the basis for our faith and lifestyle. Our holiness, then, is not merely a private matter; it should be an integrated expression of word *and* deed, cultivated in the context of peer review, a support group or the local church.

The end goals of spiritual and psychological growth—holiness and wholeness—are absolute ideals, hopes to be aspired to (Malony, 1994). Quite frankly, life does not demand perfection in either of these areas: "You can exist without achieving either one. You can be well without being healthy. You can be healthy without being whole. You can be moral without being religious. You can be religious without being holy" (Malony, 1994, p. 6). Indeed, these are ideals, hopes, dreams—perhaps even utopias. Still, they are certainly not irrelevant to a ministry of caring and service (Groeschel, 1992).

In the seventeen years since I have left graduate school I have increasingly seen the benefit of "help for the helper" (cf. chapter six in Corey and Corey, 1989). The issue is not just the clinician's personal development. As McMinn and Meek (1996) have observed, personal distress commonly precedes unethical relationships. This is especially troubling since nonprofessional Christian counselors are generally less cautious about multiple-role relationships in counseling than Christian professionals (reported in Scannish and McMinn, 1994). It is imperative, then, that we Christian counselors seek help—be it formal therapy and/or spiritual direction—when personal problems arise that could affect our work. Wholeness and holiness are goals we should take to heart—and be the best that we can be. As Foster (1992) has noted, we desperately need *deep* people in the world today. Who we are—and who we intend to become—

speaks volumes about our qualifications to be Christian mental health professionals. It is hard to imagine how we could help others if we haven't been willing to seek help ourselves.

Conclusion

I am encouraged that many of these issues are being raised in publications, professional associations and peer accountability groups. These guidelines are given in the hope that they might prompt more discussion among the second and third generation of Christian mental health professionals. Yet it is doubtful that consensus will emerge on many of the themes raised in this chapter. Since the Christian counseling movement is hardly a monolithic enterprise, we should expect a plurality of voices in this much-needed dialogue. Currently there are no legal restraints on the title *"Christian* mental health professional." I would like to see us establish some kind of clarity or standardization of that title, if only to better educate ourselves and the public at large. Many of the abuses we see in the marketplace can be directly traced to the current ambiguity surrounding the title. It would also be useful to be as concrete and specific as possible about the meaning of the phrase "clear professional competence." I would like to believe that Christlike love is what motivates the Christian mental health professional to develop his or her clinical expertise.

If we are serious about becoming effective imagers of God as therapists, we will resist the temptation to go with the flow. The times demand that Christian clinicians evidence greater measures of congruence, courage and commitment. Our desire to be excellent in all that we do should motivate us to take seriously the challenge implicit in these guidelines, which, I humbly admit, are far easier to describe than to embody. As Christian mental health professionals, we are called to take our disciplines seriously. This can be a very tangible expression of our compassion and service (cf. Noll, 1994).

I suspect that we are a long way from developing standardized definitions for many of our key terms. This is unfortunate, since it will directly affect the welfare of clients and deeply influence the training, supervisory and credentialing processes. The issues can be complex and often confusing. Yet if we continue to ask the right kind of questions and resist the temptation to "shrink from knowledge," perhaps we will someday hear, "Well done, thou good and faithful servant."

References

Adams, J. 1979. *More Than Redemption: A Theology of Christian Counseling.* Phillipsburg, N.J.: Presbyterian and Reformed.

Anderson, R. S. 1990. *Christians Who Counsel.* Grand Rapids, Mich.: Zondervan.

Benner, D. G. 1983. "The Incarnation as a Metaphor for Psychotherapy." *Journal of Psychology and Theology* 11: 287-94.

Bernstein, B. L., and C. Lecomte. 1981. "Licensure in Psychology: Alternative Directions."

Professional Psychology 12: 200-208.

Bobgan, M., and D. Bobgan. 1979. *Psychoheresy: The Psychological Seduction of Christianity*. Santa Barbara, Calif.: Eastgate.

Browning, D. 1987. *Religious Thought and the Modern Psychologies*. Philadelphia: Fortress.

Butman, R. E. 1993. "Where's the Beef? Evaluating Counseling Trends." *Christian Counseling Today* 1: 20-24.

Carlson, D. L. 1994. *Why Do Christians Shoot Their Wounded?* Downers Grove, Ill.: InterVarsity Press.

Christian Association for Psychological Studies. 1993. *Ethical Guidelines for the Christian Association for Psychological Studies*. (Available from CAPS, P.O. Box 310400, New Braunfels, TX 78131-0400.)

Clebsch, W., and C. Jaekle. 1975. *Pastoral Care in Historical Perspective*. New York: Jason Aronson.

Collins, G. R. 1989. *Can You Trust Psychology?* Downers Grove, Ill.: InterVarsity Press.

―――. 1991. *Excellence and Ethics in Counseling*. Waco, Tex.: Word.

―――. 1993. "Hot Topics in Christian Counseling." *Christian Counseling Today* 1: 12-14.

Corey, G., M. S. Corey and P. Callanan. 1993. *Issues and Ethics in the Helping Professions*. 4th ed. Pacific Grove, Calif.: Brooks/Cole.

Corey, M. S., and G. Corey. 1989. *Becoming a Helper*. Pacific Grove, Calif.: Brooks/Cole.

Dublin, S. S. 1972. "Obsolescence of Lifelong Education: A Choice for the Professional." *American Psychologist* 27: 486-98.

Evans, C. S. 1989. *Wisdom and Humanness in Psychology*. Grand Rapids, Mich.: Zondervan.

Foster, R. J. 1992. *Prayer: Finding the Heart's True Home*. San Francisco: HarperCollins.

Foster, R. J., and J. B. Smith. 1993. *Devotional Classics*. San Francisco: HarperCollins.

Fretz, B. R., and D. H. Mills. 1980. *Licensing and Certification of Psychologists and Counselors*. San Francisco: Jossey-Bass.

Groeschel, B. J. 1992. *Spiritual Passages: The Psychology of Spiritual Development*. New York: Crossroad.

Guy, J. 1986. *The Personal Life of the Psychotherapist*. New York: Wiley-Interscience.

Holifield, B. 1983. *A History of Pastoral Care in America*. Nashville: Abingdon.

Holmes, A. 1977. *All Truth Is God's Truth*. Grand Rapids, Mich.: Eerdmans.

―――. 1992. *Shaping Character*. Grand Rapids, Mich.: Eerdmans.

Inform. 1994. (The occasional bulletin of Wheaton College.) Wheaton, Ill.: Wheaton College.

Jones, S. L., and R. E. Butman. 1991. *Modern Psychotherapies: A Comprehensive Christian Appraisal*. Downers Grove, Ill.: InterVarsity Press.

Keith-Spiegel, P., and G. P. Koocher. 1985. *Ethics in Psychology: Professional Standards and Cases*. New York: Random House.

Levicoff, S. 1993. "In Search of Legitimate Credentials." *Christian Counseling Today* 1(4): 58.

Lewis, G. J., S. L. Greenburg and D. B. Hatch. 1988. "Peer Consultation Groups for Psychologists in Private Practice: A National Survey." *Professional Psychology Research and Practice* 19(1): 81-86.

Malony, H. N. 1994. "Wholeness and Holiness Revisited." Keynote address, Christian Association for Psychological Studies Annual Meeting, San Antonio, Texas.

Malony, H. N., T. L. Needham and S. Southard. 1986. *Clergy Malpractice*. Philadephia: Fortress.

McLemore, C. W. 1982. *The Scandal of Psychotherapy*. Wheaton, Ill.: Tyndale.

McMinn, M. 1994. "RET, Constructivism and Christianity: A Hermeneutic for Christian Cognitive Therapy." Unpublished manuscript.

McMinn, M., and K. Meek. 1996. "Ethics Among Christian Counselors: A Survey of Beliefs and Behaviors." *Journal of Psychology and Theology* 24: 26-37.

Meier, S. 1989. *The Elements of Counseling*. Pacific Grove, Calif.: Brooks/Cole.

Mouw, R. 1992. *Uncommon Decency*. Downers Grove, Ill.: InterVarsity Press.

Noll, M. 1994. *The Scandal of the Evangelical Mind*. Grand Rapids, Mich.: Eerdmans.

Oden, T. 1984. *Care of Souls in the Classic Tradition*. Philadelphia: Fortress.

Ohlschlager, G. 1991. "Liability in Christian Counseling: Welcome to the Grave New World," in *Excellence and Ethics in Counseling*, ed. G. R. Collins. Dallas: Word.

Palmer, P. J. 1993. *To Know As We Are Known: Education as a Spiritual Journey*. San Francisco: HarperCollins.

Peterson, D. R., and B. H. Bry. 1980. "Dimensions of Perceived Competence in Professional Psychology." *Professional Psychology* 11: 965-71.

Roberts, R. 1993. *Taking the Word to Heart: Self and Other in an Age of Therapies*. Grand Rapids, Mich.: Eerdmans.

Scannish, J., and M. McMinn. 1994. "The Competent Lay Christian Counselor." Unpublished manuscript.

Smith, J. B. 1993. *A Spiritual Formation Workbook*. San Francisco: HarperCollins.

Tan, S. 1991. *Lay Counseling: Equipping Christians for a Helping Ministry*. Grand Rapids, Mich.: Zondervan.

Tidball, D. 1986. *Skillful Shepherds: An Introduction to Pastoral Theology*. Grand Rapids, Mich.: Zondervan.

Van Leeuwen, M. S. 1993. *After Eden: Facing the Challenge of Gender Reconciliation*. Grand Rapids, Mich.: Eerdmans.

Chapter 5

PASTORS WHO COUNSEL

Bill Blackburn

---

*P*astor, can I talk with you sometime this week? I need some help." "I am
so torn up about what I need to do with my mother. Can you see me this week?"
"I lost my job, and I need to talk." "Pastor, my wife told me that she wants a
divorce and that she hasn't loved me for a long time. I don't know what to do.
Can we get together?" "I think the Lord may be calling me into the ministry, but
I'm not sure. I just need to talk with you." "I've never felt anything like this
before. Somebody told me I might be depressed. Can you help me?"

As a pastor I receive numerous requests such as these, many of which result
in pastoral counseling sessions. Each story is different, and new dimensions of
the original request are discovered once the story unfolds. But what is similar
in each instance? Here are people who are hurting and reaching out for help,
and they are reaching out to a pastor of a church, implying a recognition that
there are spiritual dimensions to their dilemmas.

This chapter will address the major ethical issues involved in pastoral
counseling. These issues center around how a pastor sees his or her role as
pastor and the particular dimensions of that role when he or she is doing pastoral
counseling. The kinds of questions this article will address include: How is
pastoral counseling understood in light of the total work of the pastor?
Considering the biblical image of the pastor as shepherd, how does that affect
the understanding and practice of pastoral counseling? What about the common
tendency in pastoral counseling that "uses" God as a means to the end of

personal peace? What are some of the limits of what a pastor can or should do in the area of pastoral counseling? What are the ethical dimensions of referral? What are some basic guidelines for pastors who counsel? Searching for answers to these and other questions will, I hope, aid pastors and others who counsel to explore some of the ethical dimensions of counseling.

Pastoral Counseling in Context

Many pastors divide their work as pastor into three main areas: (1) preaching/teaching, (2) pastoral care and (3) leadership/administration. Obviously, the three areas overlap and are intertwined.

I include pastoral counseling in the area of pastoral care (2). Whereas pastoral care would include such things as hospital visitation, telephone calls expressing concern or reassurance, and informal, brief conversations about needs in people's lives, pastoral counseling, as used in this chapter, refers to those times when an appointment is made and a parishioner comes asking for help, guidance or perspective on a problem she or he is facing.

It is important for a pastor to set guidelines and limits as to the amount of time he or she will spend on various duties. In my own case, I explained to my church when I became their pastor that I would do only three to four hours a week of pastoral counseling and that I would see persons for no more than three sessions.

Why did I set these guidelines, and why do I still hold to them? I do not believe that a pastor can do more than three to four hours a week of counseling and get the rest of his job done. My major thrust as a pastor is preacher/teacher. My mornings are spent in my study and are given to prayer, study and preparation of sermons and Bible studies. My main focus as a pastor is not on counseling, although I do much pastoral-care work. But I do not believe a pastor can lead and build a church with the emphasis on pastoral counseling. And as a fellow pastor noted, "When the body of Christ functions as it should, a lot of problems will be resolved at a 'grass roots' level, the first level where counseling ought to take place" (Getz, 1980, p. 132).

Second, I keep these guidelines to protect myself and my parishioners. Ministers can get into trouble in sexual relationships with persons they were first counseling. It is striking how dangerously intimate and even seductive a counseling session can become when a woman is pouring out her heart to a male minister, especially if she is in a bad marriage or is unmarried. He can be providing with his listening and acceptance something no other male is giving her, and the issues of transference and countertransference loom large (Seats, Trent and Kim, 1993). Additionally, if there is not a general guideline regarding the number of sessions, it can be easy to start selecting who will have more sessions and who will have fewer. Often those decisions are made even unconsciously by such needs as affirmation, dependence or sexual desire.

Third, research has concluded that many parishioners who do in-depth, long-term counseling with their minister will end up leaving the church. The parishioners can end up feeling exposed and feeling that the accepted veneer of social contact has been removed. They can also believe that the pastor is singling them out from the pulpit in his sermon examples when in fact he is speaking more generally.

Finally, by following these guidelines I limit my counseling to brief, supportive counseling and referral counseling. I believe that these are the forms of counseling most appropriate for pastors (Stone, 1994). Although I have the educational requirements and experience necessary to do counseling, I do not feel that long-term counseling is what I should be doing as pastor. That is not what God has called me to do as a pastor of this local congregation. By adhering to these guidelines, other pastors are able to decide this for themselves as well.

The Pastor as Shepherd

The most basic image of the pastor in the New Testament is a shepherd. That is, of course, what the word *pastor* literally means. And what is the role of the shepherd? Looking at the key passages of Ezekiel 34 and John 10 as well as Matthew 18:10-14 and Luke 15:3-6, we see that the shepherd (1) *provides* for the sheep, (2) *protects* the sheep and (3) *guides* the sheep.

What does this tell us about the pastor as counselor? Counseling is an extension or different dimension of the pastor's total work. In the context of counseling the pastor *provides* scriptural and spiritual insight as well as perspective on what is happening in the counselee's life, given the pastor's training and experience and the exercise of the gifts of wisdom, discernment and teaching.

The pastor offers *protection* in several ways. In the trusting and confidential counseling relationship, the individual, couple or family can pour out what is being felt or report what has happened, knowing that what is heard is listened to with openness, concern, confidentiality and prayer. Protection is provided when a couple or family has come for counseling and the pastor serves as interpreter/mediator. The pastor acts in this role as one who helps the counselees deal with conflict but also keeps the conflict in bounds.

There is another way the pastor provides protection. He or she can warn the counselee(s) about the destructive ways other persons have dealt with the same kinds of problems. And he or she can caution the client from seeking help in either destructive or inappropriate ways, such as abusing alcohol or drugs, "looking for love in all the wrong places," or wrongful sexual encounters. It is important to discuss the danger of major decisions made during a crisis, which can sometimes include suicide.

A pastor also provides *guidance,* which can include various ways of listening, responding, and offering observations and possible suggestions. For example,

I was initially trained in the somewhat stereotypical Rogerian nondirective approach to counseling, and although I continue to benefit greatly from that training, which taught me to listen carefully and to let the person know by some form of reflection that they were being heard, I moved some time ago to a more directive stance in counseling, which I believe is thoroughly biblical.

In the more directive approach to guidance, a pastor listens carefully and explores through questions and clarification what the client's issues are, how they are viewed by him or her, how they have been responded to and what the person sees as the options. Then the counselor shares what he or she has heard from the counselee, some perspective on what is happening, and initial guidelines or suggestions about how to deal with the issues. Here the pastor can deal with biblical principles that seem pertinent and can point to particular Scripture passages, and can even assign some specific tasks to do, such as reading certain Bible verses or other books. Here the pastor may also discuss with the counselee the importance of taking care of him- or herself in regard to diet, exercise, sleep, hobbies, social contact and spiritual disciplines.

Integrity of the Pastor

In any discussion of ethics, integrity is central. Integrity implies soundness, adherence to principle, completeness in the sense of being undivided. What shape does integrity take for pastors who counsel?

First, integrity is seen as faithfulness to the Lord. It must be understood that whatever problems are presented in a pastoral counseling session, the ultimate issue is the person's relationship to the Lord. Oates, a pioneer in the fields of pastoral counseling and psychology of religion, deeply desires to help pastoral counselors see "the difference it can make if you and I make the presence of the Eternal God the central dynamic in our dialogue with counselees." He adds, "In essence, I want to move *from dialogue to trialogue* in pastoral counseling" (1986, p. 23).

This does not mean that every counseling session should become a mini-sermon. But when pastoral counseling is understood this way, it can dramatically change the counseling event. How the counselee presents himself, what issues he raises, what he does not want to talk about, what history he reports—all become facets of the deepest issue of his life, his relationship to the Lord.

In a classic work in the field of pastoral care, *The Minister and the Care of Souls*, Williams writes, "To bring salvation to the human spirit is the goal of all Christian ministry and pastoral care" (1961, p. 23). He goes on to observe, "The key to pastoral care lies in the Christological center of our faith, for we understand Christ as bringing the disclosure of our full humanity in its destiny under God" (p. 13).

God is not just a utility player called in as one among others to help the client. In a prophetic message to pastors and other Christian leaders at Leadership Network's 1993 annual conference, "The Church in the 21st Century," Crabb detailed how easy it is to so focus on the needs of people that God is then used to meet a need. God becomes part of the recipe given to people to help them feel better. Crabb suggests that a crucial question to ask when a counselee presents symptoms is "What are the obstacles in the soul of this person that are blocking them from God?" (1993).

Consider a distinction made by Oates between the teachings of Jesus and the teachings of psychoanalysis concerning the issue of leaving one's father and mother. Oates observes that psychoanalysis

> dwells on the fixation and looks to the individual to use the insight to manage his or her life better by a courageous act of will. The New Testament, to the contrary, says that "in the beginning it was not so," i.e., the Creator intended that a person leave father and mother. He or she is empowered to do so by reason of the larger love of God and neighbor. (1986, p. 47)

This is another illustration of the importance of faithfulness to God in pastoral counseling. When God is at the center of the counseling session, he is never just one of those "things" trotted out to help someone.

A second facet of integrity is integrity of role. A continuity exists between who you are as pastor of the church and who you are in the counseling session. Who you are, your perspective and how you present yourself have unity, completeness. In the pastoral counseling session you are still the pastor; you are not now junior psychologist or psychiatrist. You are not now a counselor applying the latest technique learned in the last workshop you attended. You are a pastor seeking to be faithful to the Lord and to your calling as you listen and address a person who is seeking help.

Third, there is integrity in regard to Scripture. The person seeking out the pastor may not be directly asking, as did King Zedekiah, "Is there any word from the Lord?" (Jer 37:17), but that question is certainly in the background of the session. Therefore what is shared and advised must have integrity with Scripture and not be in violation of scriptural principles.

Fourth, there is an integrity with the congregation. In the pastoral counseling setting the pastor represents the congregation. Pastoral counseling occurs within the body of Christ. The pastor acts as agent for the congregation in the sense that he or she symbolizes the care of the congregation, speaks as the leader of the congregation and represents the congregation's further resources to help deal with what is raised in counseling. What happens in the counseling session should not be in conflict with the pastor's role as representative of the congregation.

Integrity must be kept in regard to what has been promised. The pastor must take opportunities directly and indirectly to interpret and reinterpret his or her role in the counseling setting. Care must be taken not to promise too much or to hold out unrealistic hope. My mentor and professor of pastoral counseling,

Wayne Oates, used to tell students of pastoral counseling, "It's the promises I make that keep me awake. It's the promises I keep that let me sleep."

Sixth, integrity can concern the limits of the pastor's training, experience or responsibility. Many laypeople do not understand what pastors have been trained to do and what their training did not include. I have found, however, that when this is discussed, most persons appreciate the pastor's being honest in confessing a lack of training, background or time to deal with the particular issue being faced. In regard to such things as substance abuse, unrelenting depression, sexual abuse, bulimia or the serious threat of suicide, for instance, I am careful to explain why I cannot provide all of the help that is needed and why another professional needs to be called on.

Sullender and Malony state in an article in *The Journal of Pastoral Care*, "Clergy must be mature enough and professional enough to know their limits when it comes to counseling troubled persons. These limits may involve training, available time, conflict of interest, or just available energy" (1990, p. 206).

All pastors and other Christian ministers would do well to meditate on this verse describing King David and his leadership of the people of Israel: "And David shepherded them with integrity of heart; with skillful hands he led them" (Ps 78:72).

The Ethics of Referral

It is important for pastors who counsel to be willing to refer their counselees to other professionals and to be knowledgeable about when and to whom a counselee should be referred. Following are some general guidelines that can be used in this regard.

First, a minister has a responsibility to know the variety of professionals to whom she or he might refer. In my situation, I minister in a semirural area but have the good fortune to have competent professionals in two nearby towns and a metropolitan area about an hour away. If I am going to refer a parishioner to another professional, I will want to know his or her (1) reputation, (2) training, (3) experience, (4) professional supervision, (5) network of other professionals or hospitals to call on, and (6) faith commitment or appreciation of such a commitment in the client. The first three points are self-explanatory, but the last three may require some explanation.

It is very important that the professional, whether a pastoral counselor, clinical social worker, psychologist or psychiatrist, is receiving some form of supervision or consultation on their work. This indicates their professional ethics and their desire to keep perspective in the midst of helping people in need. What is the extent of the professional's network of consultation and referral? And if hospitalization is a possibility, what arrangements can they make for the client?

Should a pastor refer parishioners only to Christian counselors? No. I do so whenever I can, and I am fortunate that I have many to whom I can refer.

However, I will refer to a non-Christian if I know she has the best skills and background in dealing with this particular need and that she would neither demean religious faith nor suggest that the person do something in violation of their faith commitment.

Second, a pastor has the responsibility to appropriately present the referral to the client. The pastor must interpret carefully why she is making this referral and why it is being made to the particular professional. She should explain her own limitations of time and/or training, and the qualifications of the other professional, while being careful not to promise what the professional will do. It is a good idea for the pastor to reassure the counselee at this point that he isn't crazy (and I do use that word sometimes) or about to lose his mind. This is what many clients have been afraid of, and that fear can be reinforced with a referral to a mental health professional.

Next, the pastor should explain how to get in touch with the person referred to and something of what the client can expect from the sessions. If the cost is raised, provide what information is available and let the person know that the church has a fund to help with these sorts of costs (if it does). In some situations the pastor can make the call to the professional and help set up the first appointment.

Fourth, the pastor should reassure the client about their relationship together. I do this so that the counselee knows I am not rejecting him or her. I explain that I will be in touch and that along the way we can get back together to talk things over and to pray. I am, of course, careful here not to serve as another therapist, but as pastor.

Fifth, after reassuring the client I as pastor have a responsibility to maintain that relationship. I do this myself by having the client on my prayer list so that I am reminded regularly to pray for him or her and to maintain contact through phone calls, notes and visits.

Finally, it is appropriate for the pastor to keep proper contact with the professional to whom the client has been referred. Some professionals want information prior to the first visit, and others do not. Personally, I do not seek to get a report on the sessions, but with appropriate consent from the counselee I do want to know how things are going and what I can do to be of further help. And because of the continuing relationship with the client through the church, I will sometimes consult with the professional on any relationship issues that may come up due to this.

Boundary Issues

How should pastors decide how much to counsel, whom to see, appropriate boundaries in counseling, and how available to be to persons in need? These boundary issues are crucial, because if they are not decided in some reasonable manner, the pastor can risk his or her effectiveness, mental health, family life and leadership of the congregation.

In the guidelines outlined earlier I noted that I do only three to four hours a week of counseling. That obviously varies week by week, but that is still almost half a day per week of pastoral counseling, and depending on the size of the church, even that can be too much time for this facet of pastoral ministry. In order to hold to a limited amount of counseling it is important that the pastor not communicate an unlimited availability to the congregation. One of my professors of preaching, George A. Buttrick, used to tell us, "Many pastors are a quivering mass of availability." I cannot be the husband, father and pastor I need to be and also be constantly available for counseling.

Most pastors could end up counseling twelve hours a day if it were allowed. But a failure to draw boundaries and deal with the limits of what one can do often implies other issues. Is there such a need to please that the pastor cannot say "No" or "Later"? Is there a feeling of impotence in other areas of ministry that leads the minister to do an inordinate amount of counseling and thereby feel the power and helpfulness and adulation that often comes from counseling? Is there a problem in the pastor's marriage or family that encourages getting emotional needs inappropriately met in counseling? Does the pastor have a messiah complex, seen in rescuing persons in trouble? Is there withdrawal from other duties and relationships and into counseling? In looking at those who are seen for counseling and those who are not, is there a clue to the underlying issues related to too much counseling?

On this last question of who is or is not seen for counseling, a troubling issue for many pastors is whether or not to do counseling with persons who are not members of the congregation. I generally do not see persons for counseling who are from outside my congregation. I will see someone who is attending and not a member, and I will on occasion see persons in crisis whom I know in the community and who request to see me. In this latter instance, it is almost always for one session in which a referral is made if that is needed. One of the issues for pastors today is that there is a greater possibility of legal liability when counseling persons who are not members of your congregation (ABA, 1989).

Concerning boundaries, in looking at the Gospels, did Jesus see every troubled soul in each village he visited? Did he stay in one place until every sick person was healed? Was Bartimaeus the only blind person in Jericho? Didn't Jesus in fact retreat either with the disciples or by himself when he needed to? And when he retreated, were there not still persons who could have been helped who were left behind? And didn't Jesus in his ministry move more toward preaching and the training of the disciples and less toward healing and other miracles?

From the time of Satan's testing in the wilderness at the beginning of Jesus' public ministry, to how Jesus presented himself to the crowds and the authorities in his last days in Jerusalem, to his resurrection appearances and final discourses prior to the ascension, Jesus was setting boundaries and defining limits according to who he was and what his mission was. Look again at the repeated "I am" statements of Jesus, and you will see boundaries, limits and possibilities.

As a contemporary pastor, how does one deal with these boundary issues? I myself find it necessary to continue interpreting to the congregation what my role is as pastor, how I spend my time, and what my guidelines are for counseling. It is important to set aside time for the various parts of pastoring, such as preparation for preaching and teaching, administration, and pastoral care. My secretary has my schedule and sets appointments for me within the time that is already allotted to certain things. Time is protected for sermon preparation, worship planning, administrative matters, meetings with staff and other key leaders, and pastoral visitation. I also protect time for my family and for my own personal renewal and rest.

General Guidelines for Pastoral Counseling

Following are some general guidelines for pastors who counsel to keep in mind. Some of these have been discussed earlier in the chapter but bear repeating here.

1. *Maintain confidentiality.* The exception to this rule would be if there are ethical or legal reasons dictating the breaking of a confidence. It is imperative that pastors familiarize themselves with the laws in their state pertaining to privileged communications with the clergy and to the exceptions to confidentiality. Usually these exceptions will include such things as suspicion of child abuse. These kinds of situations point to the necessity of not making a blanket promise that nothing will be shared out of the counseling session.

2. *Avoid manipulating the counselee.* This almost goes without saying, but because there is such a risk due to the vulnerability of many persons in crisis who seek pastors out, it needs to be stated.

3. *Avoid making decisions for the person seeking help.* Because the pastor is an authority figure who is knowledgeable about the Bible and is assumed to have a strong prayer life, many persons come to him or her expecting a divinely revealed answer to the problem at hand. As I've indicated earlier, I believe the pastor should be directive in his or her approach in counseling but should be careful about simply making decisions for the counselee.

4. *Do not inappropriately carry messages.* There are times in the ministry of reconciliation when interpreting the behavior or words of one person to another can be appropriate and healing. However, because the pastor often has contact with the family or group the client may be in conflict with or alienated from, sometimes there is the desire or expectation on the part of the client that the pastor act as a Western Union messenger. This is inappropriate.

5. *Do not be a voyeur.* Particularly in the area of sexuality, the pastor must be careful not to seek, directly or indirectly, information that is not germane to

the issue at hand. Seeking information for sexual titillation is inappropriate, unfair and counterproductive.

6. *Never become romantically or sexually involved with a counselee.* This is assumed, of course, but needs to be stated because it is such an important and pervasive issue. A one-on-one counseling relationship with a person of the opposite sex can be powerfully seductive. This is why I make sure someone else is in the office area if I am counseling a woman counselee, and why I have maintained a guideline for myself of seeing a person for only three sessions. In a study done of Southern Baptist ministers through the Baptist Sunday School Board, it was found that among ministers who became involved in adulterous affairs, 71 percent of those affairs started through counseling sessions (Booth, 1994).

Wayne Oates used to tell his students that he knew he was beginning to cross over a dangerous line when he woke up in the morning and began thinking about a female counselee he would see that day. If, in anticipation of seeing her, he was careful to think about which tie to wear, he knew danger was lurking.

Conclusion

The opportunity, responsibility and calling to be a shepherd is awesome and ought to be so intimidating that we go to our knees before the Lord, knowing that we cannot do what must be done and be who we need to be without God's help. I firmly believe that in the years ahead, the task of the pastor will grow more difficult because of the needs of the people, the expectations that grow into demands, and the confusion and deterioration of our society. Only by prayer, wisdom and much discipline will pastors be able to carry out their God-given assignment and maintain their spiritual, mental, physical, familial and social health.

My deep conviction, borne of experience as a pastor, is that time management that grows out of faith and a clear understanding of the mission of the church and the work of the pastor is crucial to maintaining health. In that regard, I highly recommend two books that have proved invaluable to me in this area: *First Things First* by Stephen R. Covey, A. Roger Merrill and Rebecca R. Merrill (New York: Simon and Schuster, 1994), and *The Management of Ministry* by James D. Anderson and Ezra Earl Jones (San Francisco: Harper & Row, 1978).

Finally, my prayer for those reading this book is that God will use it to help you be a shepherd with integrity of heart and skillful hands (Ps 78:72).

References

American Bar Association. 1990. "Tort and Religion." Symposium held in San Francisco, May 3-4, 1990. Cited in R. S. Sullender and H. N. Malony, "Should Clergy Counsel Suicidal Persons?" *Journal of Pastoral Care* 44: 206.

Booth, G. 1994. *The Baylor Messenger,* Spring, p. 4.

Crabb, L. 1993. "Vision Versus Community." Presentation made at "The Church in the 21st Century," Orlando, Florida (June), a conference sponsored by Leadership Network.

Getz, G. 1980. "Leadership Forum: The Demands, Dilemmas and Dangers of Pastoral Counseling." *Leadership* 1: 132.

Oates, W. E. 1986. *The Presence of God in Pastoral Counseling.* Dallas: Word.

Seats, J. T., J. T. Trent and J. K. Kim. 1993. "The Prevalence and Contributing Factors of Sexual Misconduct Among Southern Baptist Pastors in Six Southern States." *Journal of Pastoral Care* 47: 363-70.

Stone, H. W. 1994. "Brief Pastoral Counseling." *Journal of Pastoral Care* 48: 33-43.

Sullender, R. S., and H. N. Malony. 1990. "Should Clergy Counsel Suicidal Persons?" *Journal of Pastoral Care* 44: 206.

Williams, D. D. 1961. *The Minister and the Care of Souls.* New York: Harper & Brothers.

Chapter 6

SEXUAL MISCONDUCT & THE ABUSE OF POWER

John F. Shackelford & Randolph K. Sanders

*A*s he approached Dr. Malpractice's door, Dr. Fairfax felt a gnawing discomfort in the pit of his stomach. Fairfax had arranged this meeting, but now a part of him wished to avoid what was to come. Taking a deep breath, he entered Dr. Malpractice's front door.

As he walked through the lobby and up to the desk, he was surprised at how nice Malpractice's office looked. Perhaps he had thought a man accused of sexual misconduct by his colleagues would have a shabby office. But this office was neat and nicely appointed.

The secretary at the front desk acknowledged him and asked him to take a seat for just a moment. As he waited, he thought about the reason he was here. Throughout the town in which they both worked, a persistent rumor had circulated that Dr. Malpractice had been romantically involved with one of his patients for a number of months. The rumor was so prevalent that several physicians had approached Fairfax in the last month, wondering what it would take for the state board of examiners to get involved.

Just now, Fairfax wondered why he had been the one to come. What if Malpractice became indignant and threw him out of his office? Still, Fairfax felt it was his responsibility to at least talk to Malpractice about the rumors. And besides, both he and Malpractice represented themselves as Christian therapists. *Surely,* Fairfax thought, *that makes me the person to talk to him.*

The door to the lobby suddenly swung open, and there was Malpractice standing in the doorway. "Frank Fairfax, it's good to see you!" Malpractice exclaimed as he ushered him into his office. "I haven't seen you since the state convention a couple of years ago. What brings you over here to see me?"

"Well, I'm afraid what I have to talk about is rather unpleasant," Fairfax began. "You see, there is a rumor around town that you are having a relationship with one of your patients. I would have discounted it, but I hear the rumor again and again, mostly from people who would have no reason to lie. I know how these rumors are, but I thought I should—"

Malpractice cut him off. "Well, the rumors are true," he said rather matter-of-factly. "A wonderful thing has happened to me in the last few months. God has brought a very special person into my life. I never planned to get involved with her, but this is different. We both feel the same way about each other. It just seems like we were led to be together. She had been a patient in a psychiatric hospital in the state where her parents live. She is from a very enmeshed family. It's fortunate for her that she moved back here and got in to see me when she got out of the hospital. The psychiatrist at the hospital diagnosed her as having major depression with borderline personality, but I'm sure he was wrong about the diagnosis of personality disorder. She may have a few problematic traits, but I guess anybody would who came from a family like that. But you know, I've always thought that diagnostic categories label people and prevent us from seeing the richness of the unique individuals we counsel."

"But what about your wife? Aren't the two of you still together?" Fairfax asked.

"Oh, Frank, we have a marriage in name only. The relationship has been over for years. Don't get me wrong; I care for my wife, but it was hardly ever a marriage to begin with. I know that by the letter of the law we are still married, but I've come to learn that if you're ever going to live abundantly, you have to live out the spirit of the law."

Malpractice talked on while Fairfax sat quietly on the couch. *How could a therapist be this far off center?* he thought to himself. *How could he miss so many obvious red flags? And what could have been done to prevent something like this from happening?*

Incidence of Sexual Misconduct

How prevalent is sexual misconduct in the counseling profession? Kardener, Fuller and Mensh (1973) were among the first to research this problem when they surveyed 114 male psychiatrists in Los Angeles and found that 10 percent admitted sexual contact with patients. Holroyd and Brodsky (1977) conducted a national survey of licensed doctoral-level psychologists, with 70 percent of surveys completed. They found that 5.5 percent of 347 male respondents and 0.6 percent of 310 female respondents had engaged in sexual intercourse with their patients. Eighty percent of the abusers admitted sexual contact with more than one patient. Bouhoutsos et al. (1983), with 704 respondents, found a similar incidence, with 4.8 percent of male therapists and 0.8 percent of female therapists acknowledging sexual involvement.

The largest research project on therapist-patient sexual intimacy was done by Gartrell et al. (1986), in which psychiatrists were surveyed nationwide. Questionnaires were sent to 5,574 psychiatrists, with a return by 1,423 respondents (26 percent return). Similar to earlier studies, 6.4 percent acknowledged sexual intimacies with a patient. Eighty-seven percent of the victims were female, with a mean age of 33. Genital contact was involved with 74 percent of these patients, and other sexual contact consisted of kissing, fondling and/or undressing.

Pope and Vetter (1991) surveyed 1,320 psychologists, with a 50 percent return rate, asking if they had treated a patient who reported sexual involvement with a prior therapist. Almost 50 percent of the psychologists had seen at least one patient reporting previous sexual involvement, and some psychologists had treated several patients who were previously sexually involved with a therapist.

These studies show that a serious problem exists in the mental health profession, with a percentage of therapists abusing their position of power and becoming sexually involved with their clients. Borys and Pope (1989) surveyed the three major mental health professional groups—psychiatrists, psychologists and social workers—and found no significant difference among the rates at which the various professionals acknowledged engaging in sex with their patients. What is of most concern is the problem of underreporting. Vinson (1987) has illustrated the potential magnitude of the problem with the following scenario: In 1982 there were 31,300 licensed psychotherapists in California, and if one projects that approximately 7 percent of the total, or 2,200 therapists, have sexually abused a patient, and some of these have abused several patients, then one could expect there to be roughly 6,000 patients who have been abused and psychologically damaged. In the same year in California, records show that at least twelve but no more than sixteen therapists were disciplined by their licensing boards.

Interestingly, some later surveys reveal only 1 to 2 percent of therapists reporting that they have been sexually involved with a patient, which represents a marked decline (Borys and Pope, 1989; Gechtman, 1989; Pope, Tabachnick and Keith-Spiegel, 1987). Borys and Pope observe that this may either represent a true decline in sexual involvement or indicate a greater reluctance to report since such involvement is now recognized as a felony in many states.

A recent study of Christian counselors indicates that 2 percent admitted to having had sex with a client they were seeing in therapy. About 6 percent said they had been involved with a former client (see McMinn and Meek, 1996).

Ethical Standards

The APA's code of ethics (1992) states:

Psychologists do not engage in sexual intimacies with current patients or clients. . . .

Psychologists do not accept as therapy patients or clients persons with whom they have engaged in sexual intimacies. . . .

(a) Psychologists do not engage in sexual intimacies with a former therapy patient or client for at least two years after cessation or termination of professional services.

(b) Because sexual intimacies with a former therapy patient or client are so frequently harmful to the patient or client, and because such intimacies undermine public confidence in the psychology profession and thereby deter the public's use of needed services, psychologists do not engage in sexual intimacies with former therapy patients and clients even after a two-year interval except in the most unusual circumstances. The psychologist who engages in such activity after the two years following cessation or termination of treatment bears the burden of demonstrating that there has been no exploitation. (Sects. 4.05-4.07)

The idea behind the prohibition against sex with former patients was expressed by Brodsky in a 1983 paper given at the APA's annual meeting: "Father-daughter incest does not become acceptable one year after the daughter has left home. No matter how the therapy contract ends, the *imbalance of power* of the initial interactions can never be erased" (italics added).

Patients Are Harmed

Bouhoutsos et al. (1983) surveyed therapists who were treating patients who had sexual intimacy with a previous therapist. The therapists rated that all told, some 90 percent of the patients had experienced some kind of negative effects, which included personal factors such as "increased depression, loss of motivation, impaired social adjustment, significant emotional disturbance . . . increased drug or alcohol abuse" (p. 190), or negative effects on their therapy. Eleven percent were hospitalized and 1 percent committed suicide. It is interesting to note that a later paper by Holroyd and Bouhoutsos (1985) revealed that the psychologists in the survey who had claimed that their patients had *not* been harmed by previous intimacies were 2.5 times more likely to have sexual intimacies with patients themselves.

Feldman-Summers and Jones (1984) took a different approach and collected their data by directly interviewing and testing patients. They found that women who had been sexually active with their therapists had significantly more mistrust and anger toward men and their own therapists than women who had not been sexually intimate with their therapists. These abused women also had signifcantly more symptoms one month posttherapy than the nonabused women. This study also discovered that the women with a prior history of childhood sexual abuse or sexual victimization who were also involved with a married therapist suffered the greatest negative effects. Instead of finding healing, their previous wounds were reopened.

Pope and Sonne (1991), who have extensively researched the harm done by sexual intimacy with therapists, coined the diagnostic phrase "therapist-patient sex syndrome" to refer to the symptom-picture of those who are victims of sexual misconduct. The symptoms include ambivalence, guilt, emptiness and isolation, sexual confusion, impaired ability to trust, identity and boundary confusion, emotional lability, suppressed rage, increased suicidal risk, and cognitive dysfunction (p. 175). They note similar symptoms in those suffering from rape, incest and other forms of child sexual abuse. Solursh, Solursh and Williams (1993) summarize that the harmful effects of therapist-patient sexual intimacy for women patients include chronic distrust of therapy, increased sexual problems, anger at being exploited and lower self-esteem.

In a thought-provoking article Baylis (1993) makes the point that it is impossible for a therapy patient, who comes to treatment feeling vulnerable, to give "consent" for sexual involvement with her doctor, who is in a position of power. Baylis argues that the components of consent are intentionality, substantial understanding, substantial voluntariness and autonomous authorization. Baylis concludes that "therapist-patient sexual relations are always non-consensual and inherently harmful . . . irrespective of who initiates the sexual contact" (p. 503).

Patients Most Likely to Be Abused

In their book *Sexual Intimacy Between Therapists and Patients* Pope and Bouhoutsos (1986) describe from their clinical experience three categories of patients who have become sexually involved with their therapists: low-risk, middle-risk and high-risk.

1. *The low-risk group*. These patients have no history of prior hospitalizations and usually function on a high level with a history of stable, long-term relationships. What is distinctive about this group is that they had recently been highly stressed by a loss, such as a divorce or the sudden death of a parent. The therapist took advantage of their temporary vulnerability.

2. *The middle-risk group*. This group of patients is seen as more dependent and needy, and they often receive a diagnosis of personality disorder. They have a history of relationship problems. Chesler (1972) interviewed eleven such women and described them as feminine, intellectually insecure, economically limited and "frantically" attractive. They were sexually fearful as well as sexually compulsive, with marked self-contempt. They were likely to blame themselves when they were mistreated by men.

Gorkin (1985) describes the masochistic female patient whose sexual fantasies and feelings toward her therapist take the tone of being injured or hurt by him. This particular patient frequently has a background of sexual excitement with a father or brother that is also tinted with punishment or abuse. Despite this negative family relationship, it was often the only consistent relationship that provided attention. Belote (1974) found in a study of twenty-five women who had been sexually intimate with their therapists that most reported a negative relationship with their mothers and a close relationship with their fathers. Most of these women reported being attracted to relationships with older authority figures. Stone's (1980) research seemed to support her hypothesis that women who suffer from "severe anxious attachment" caused by separation-individuation failures are more vulnerable to becoming sexually involved with their therapist. The reason advanced is that they are trying to repair early ego damage and preserve the symbiotic relationship that helps them feel loved and complete.

3. *The high-risk group.* This third group consists of two subgroups: incest survivors and borderline personality disorder.

To date there has not been a large-scale empirical study of the premorbid personalities of patients who are sexually abused by their therapists. Pope and Bouhoutsos (1986) observe from their clinical experience that many of the high-risk patients have been incest victims. Therapist-patient sexual involvement has frequently been compared to incest, and the phenomenon of repetition compulsion is no doubt at work here. These authors write:

The usual incest victim has been involved . . . with a person in authority, either father or someone else, over a period of years and has had to keep the secret. She has learned to take the blame for what happened and has learned to exonerate the adult offender. The paternal role is fulfilled by the therapist with whom she is sexually involved. The therapist is assured of a pliable, often pathetically naive, needy patient who will not tell and who will not blame the therapist but who will frequently remain in the therapeutic relationship for years, paying for the damage and feeling guilty for causing the inevitable abuse and neglect by the therapist. Even with support . . . such women may find it almost impossible to admit to themselves that victimization has occurred. (p. 53)

Thus the therapist, consciously or unconsciously, abuses his powerful parent role to inflict more damage on this most vulnerable type of patient, a patient who has been scripted for victimization.

Guntheil (1989) has written about the borderline personality and sexual intimacy in therapy. He makes the observation that the borderline may be a likely victim because the neurotic patient may have better perception and judgment than to succumb to sexual involvement and the psychotic patient may not be seen as very attractive by the therapist.

He further explains that the dynamics of the borderline, especially their neediness, their demandingness, and their desire to be rescued and taken care of, can make it very difficult for the neophyte therapist to maintain boundaries. The therapist may fear that if he confronts and sets boundaries, then he will be accused of rejecting the patient "as everyone else has."

Sexual Misconduct and the Abuse of Power

Sexual misconduct is an abuse of a therapist's power. When people consult therapists, they most often do so in times of great personal vulnerablity. They step into an office where they have never been, confused about painful issues they may not clearly understand, tell their innermost secrets to a person they hardly know, and, largely by faith, trust that the therapist will be able to help them. The therapist has a tremendous obligation to honor and respond appropriately to the patient's trust and to avoid doing anything that might harm the patient.

But some therapists relish the power they hold in the therapeutic relationship, using it to direct and even manipulate the patient's life. These therapists are the most dangerous. However, experience suggests that many therapists are naive about the degree of power they hold in some patients' lives, and that this naiveté may also be problematic.

There may be several reasons therapists are naive about the power they hold. Some therapists are trained to see themselves as "facilitators of change" rather than aggressive change agents. Therapists trained in this more passive approach perhaps fail to see the tremendous power that some patients project onto them, however client-centered these therapists believe themselves to be.

Alternatively, some therapists may be blind to the power they hold because they have seen that a number of patients in therapy do not change markedly despite all the "powerful" therapeutic techniques therapists have at their disposal. Typically these practitioners are more experienced therapists who have realized that the therapeutic interventions they learned in graduate school do not always produce happy endings. Such therapists may conclude quite incorrectly that their power in the therapeutic relationship is much less than it really is.

Some therapists may be naive to their power because of the ambivalence that various groups within society have had toward the mental health profession in the past. For example, Christian mental health professionals have sometimes had to defend the effectiveness of their work to portions of the Christian community that have viewed Christian counselors with skepticism. Perhaps therapists who have experienced this skepticism doubt the extent to which patients ascribe power to them. One has only to listen to Christian radio therapists, however, to realize that there is also a huge Christian public that is quite willing to follow without question the advice of radio counselors whom they do not know and perhaps have never seen.

Some may argue that viewing therapists as the ones who hold the power in the relationship is unfair and does not take into account the power and impact the patient has to affect the course of the therapeutic relationship. To be sure, therapy is not a one-way street, and the patient is never truly a passive participant. One of the things that makes therapy complicated, particularly for the young practitioner, is that therapy is not unilateral. A complicated interaction occurs between therapist and client in which the terms and process of therapy are negotiated and refined at each new turn.

For example, if during the third therapy session a woman client who is in despair about her life becomes tearful and slides off the couch and onto the floor near her male therapist's chair, the therapist is left with a decision about how to respond. Among the extreme range of responses he could make are the following: (1) he could sternly tell her that sitting on the floor is inappropriate and direct her to sit back on the couch; (2) he could wonder out loud about her despair and the possible reasons, both good and bad, for her behavior; (3) he could verbally express his care and empathy for her deep despair, but say little about her sitting on the floor next to him; (4) he could reach out and touch her hand while expressing empathy for her; (5) he could get down on the floor with her and embrace her while speaking warmly to her; or (6) he could act with some combination or variation of any of these responses. Though a therapist might rationalize a response like (5), arguing that it represents the most genuine, caring response, responses of this kind clearly enter a danger zone and could set a collision course for blatant misconduct later.

The point is that however active patients may be in the direction of therapy, the burden falls on therapists by virtue of their training and expertise to recognize and deal with patient behaviors that could become countertherapeutic. Indeed, the therapist is also responsible to recognize the thoughts and feelings within him- or herself that could become countertherapeutic.

In the field of law, the term *fiduciary* is used to refer to those people in a society who are, because of special expertise or knowledge, typically accorded special authority by others. It is assumed that such people have special obligations to act in good faith toward those who put their trust in them (Feldman-Summers, 1987). Feldman-Summers has suggested that the mental health profession would do well to see itself as fitting the definition of a fiduciary and to understand that "even with the strongest feelings on the part of the client, sexual contact is unlikely to occur in the absence of a willing fiduciary" (p. 203).

Other Types of Abuse of Power

Sexual misconduct is not the only means by which therapists abuse their power. Any circumstance in which the therapist takes undue advantage of the patient or another person may be seen as an abuse of power.

In addition to sexual misconduct, the APA code describes a number of other circumstances that represent abuse of power. Like others, therapists can be guilty of sexual or other forms of harassment of patients, employees or other people. Therapists sometimes exploit persons over whom they have authority (APA, 1992, Sects. 1.08-1.12, 1.15-1.16, 1.19). They can be guilty of discrimination toward people who are different from themselves, or can sometimes misuse their influence, as when a therapist allows her name and professional standing to be used in an effort to endorse a commercial product whose clinical effectiveness is unknown.

In his book *Against Therapy* Masson (1994) argues that all therapy is inherently abusive no matter how altruistic it may appear. He believes that the very fact that therapists make their income from the emotional pain and suffering of others sets up an unavoidably unequal relationship that is certain to lead to problems. While some would agree that there are always dangers of abuse in therapeutic relationships, most would disagree that all therapy necessarily results in abuses of power.

Increasingly, however, writers are raising questions about the probability of abuse of power that may be inherent in certain forms of psychotherapy. For example, writers have expressed concern about the propensity for abuse in strategic therapy (Doherty, 1989; Solovey and Duncan, 1992) and hypnotherapy (Masson, 1994).

Doherty (1989) points out that strategic family therapists sometimes use deception in an effort to move families toward a desired end in therapy. A therapist using a paradoxical intervention, for example, might prescribe that a "resistant" client do the opposite of what she really wanted the client to do, hoping that the client would then do the desired behavior. Or a therapist attempting to move a family to carry out a behavior might say that several other professionals recommended such an intervention when in fact she really had not consulted any other professionals at all. Proponents argue that such deception is appropriate when attempting to overcome blocks to progress, so long as the therapist is not purposefully trying to take advantage of the client and the intervention is intended to lead the client toward a therapeutic end (in other words, the ends justify the means).

Critics counter that deceiving clients, even if the client never becomes aware of the deception, "undermines one of the cornerstones of the therapist-client relationship—trustworthiness" (Doherty, 1989). Further, deception allows the therapist to exert power over someone who has voluntarily surrendered much of his or her power by revealing to the therapist his or her innermost feelings, thoughts and secrets.

Most critics would admit that not all clients come to therapy in such a passive, revealing way and that many clients do resist open, transparent therapeutic intervention even when ostensibly they claim they want change. Many critics would agree that some "passive concealment" (Doherty, 1989) of therapist impressions and directions may be necessary if, in the therapist's best judgment, the client is not ready to deal with these impressions. Still, they would argue that frequent use of deception "in the patient's best interest" can set up a kind of paternalistic relationship between therapists and clients in which therapists think they have the power to unilaterally decide what is best for clients. In such an atmosphere, abuses of power are sure to occur.

Questions about hypnosis as a manipulative technique have been raised for years. The more obvious questions have to do with whether clients under hypnotherapy can be led to do things against their will. Traditionally hypnotherapists have argued that clients cannot be led to do things that they truly do not wish to do or that go against their values (King, 1990). More complicated are the indirect approaches to hypnosis, such as Ericksonian hypnosis. In these approaches trance and suggestions are accomplished in much less obvious ways. For example, the therapist may paradoxically induce a trance by suggesting verbally that the patient might wish to fight the trance, but then making indirect suggestions and providing a therapeutic environment that subtly encourages the patient to go into a trance.

The power of hypnosis to manipulate will likely be debated for years to come. Surely some therapeutic approaches are more likely to be misused than others. But such arguments may miss the most important issue. Perhaps the greatest danger for abuse in hypnosis, strategic therapy or any other therapeutic technique, for that matter, lies not primarily in the therapeutic technique itself but in the therapist's personality, and to some extent the client's. We have already seen how some types of patients are more susceptible to sexual abuse than others. Surely there are some patients who are more open to abuse in hypnotherapy; in all probability many of them are the same patients who are most open to sexual abuse. In the same way, there are certain types of therapists who are more likely to abuse their patients sexually, and at least some of these may be the same types who would abuse their patients in hypnotherapy, strategic therapy or some other therapeutic technique.

The Abusing Therapist

Who are the therapists most likely to sexually abuse patients? In 1986 Pope, Keith-Spiegel and Tabachnick surveyed 575 psychologists and found that 95 percent of the men and 76 percent of the women acknowledged having been sexually attracted to their patients on occasion. While most therapists would consider feelings of sexual attraction to patients normal, acting on those feelings is recognized as harmful and an abuse of the therapist's power. Pope (1987) warns that the therapist who doesn't acknowledge and examine his or her sexual feelings toward patients "blocks its therapeutic potential and unleashes its destructive effects" (p. 150).

In an attempt to learn more about therapists who become sexually involved with clients, Butler and Zelen (1977) performed a study that found abusing therapists had a mean age of 43.5 years and were needy or lonely at the time the sexual contact occurred. A number of these therapists had recently become separated or divorced. As a group, they were generally well-trained, private-practice clinicians.

Zelen (1985) concludes, "It might possibly be assumed that the therapists shifted the sources of gratification to their patients during these vulnerable or needy periods of time" (p. 182). He also observed that the therapists experienced few unrewarding or punishing consequences. Butler (1975) reported that 95 percent of therapists surveyed felt conflict and guilt about what they had done, yet most continued their sexual acting-out. Rationalization was frequently used, such as their desire to help the patient feel she was an attractive and desirable woman. Some 40 percent of therapists sought professional consultation regarding their unethical behavior, but it was most often with a therapist friend, so the value of this help is possibly questionable.

Gabbard (1994) offers insights from his years of clinical practice at the Menninger Clinic, where he has treated a number of sexually abusing therapists. He offers the following broad categories describing abusing therapists and their reasons for abuse: (1) psychotic disorders, (2) predatory psychopathy and paraphilias, (3) lovesickness and (4) masochistic surrender.

1. *Psychotic disorders.* This is the smallest group and includes bipolar disorder, paranoid psychosis, schizophrenia and organic brain syndromes. These therapists usually require pharmacotherapy and often vocational counseling to steer them away from their careers as therapists.

2. *Predatory psychopathy and paraphilias.* Here Gabbard (1994) includes antisocial personalities and severe narcissistic personalities with antisocial features. Most of these offenders are male and have been involved with many female patients during their practice. They are refractory to rehabilitation and are highly skilled at manipulating the legal system to avoid consequences for their behavior. When caught, they often appear remorseful and claim they were in love with the patient. In reality, the patient is only an object for their gratification, and their poor superego development keeps them from feeling true guilt or remorse.

3. *Lovesickness.* Gabbard (1994) sees most therapists who become sexually involved with their patients as being predatory or lovesick. Sixty-five percent of therapists who sexually abuse claim to be in love with their patient (Gartrell et al., 1986). These therapists have a strong need to be loved and idealized by the patient. They use the patient to boost their own self-esteem. Gabbard writes that the most frequent scenario is the middle-aged male therapist who, while in the midst of his marital or family crisis or loss, falls in love with his younger female patient. Such therapists often begin to share their own problems and needs, activating a role reversal which may lead to sexual involvement. Gabbard elaborates:

> Both therapist and patient are refinding forbidden objects from the past, and the therapist colludes in an enactment rather than interpreting the unconscious wish to repeat past trauma, all under the guise of "true love." (p. 128)

Some of Gabbard's (1994) additional observations about therapist dynamics include:

☐ The therapist sees the patient's wish for maternal nurturance as a sexual overture.

☐ The therapist believes that love is curative for the patient.

☐ Both patient and therapist have interlocking rescue fantasies.

☐ Sexual involvement can be a manic defense against grieving at the end of therapy.

☐ The therapist feels this relationship is so special that it is an exception to ethics.

☐ Sexual involvement is thought to be a validation of masculine identity.

☐ The female therapist believes her love will settle down the "rowdy" man.

☐ Anger with a patient's lack of progess leads the therapist to cover over their anger with "love."

4. *Masochistic surrender.* Gabbard (1994) describes the therapist with masochistic tendencies who allows him- or herself to be intimidated and controlled by the patient. The patient's increasing demands on the therapist have power because the therapist fears the patient will commit suicide if the various demands are not met. Often setting limits on the patient feels sadistic to the therapist. The therapist feels tormented, becomes angry, then feels guilty about being angry or showing anger toward the patient. Out of this guilt the therapist may succumb to sexual demands.

These therapists, unlike the lovesick, "are not in love with their patient and often feel they are being 'dragged down' by the patient" (Gabbard, 1994, p. 133). These therapists often feel tremendous guilt after the sexual experience, and some have turned themselves in to their licensing board. If litigation becomes a part of the picture, they often are very straightforward and honest, admitting their guilt. They often suffer more serious legal or professional consequences than the predatory type, who is so skilled at manipulating the system.

Gorkin (1985) is another analyst who has written about the therapist's vulnerability to a demanding patient. He believes that the patient is really attempting to merge and form the symbiotic relationship with the therapist that the client lacked with his or her mother. Such a sexualized relationship would bring instant utopia and dispense with the tough work of dealing with hostility and grief. When the patient realizes that the relationship is not permanent, he or she may be engulfed with rage and feelings of abandonment so familiar from childhood.

Claman (1987) writes from the perspective of self-psychology about the therapist who did not have adequate mirroring during his early development. He has missed the experience of having the supportive and proud mother watch him and empathize with his excitement as he individuates. Kohut and Wolf (1977) write: "With mirror hunger as the underlying psychodynamic, the therapist falls in love with his mirroring self-object, rather than with the patient as a separate and individual person" (p. 414). In other words, the therapist has such a deep unmet need to be admired and enjoyed that he can't see the patient's idealization of him as a childlike or infantile need.

Rehabilitation of Abusing Therapists

Pioneering work in the rehabilitation of abusing therapists at the Walk-In Counseling Center in Minneapolis has been cataloged by Gartrell et al. (1988). Here therapists are assessed at the request of licensing boards or agencies. Therapists must fully acknowledge their sexual involvement and cooperate with the evaluation and treatment. They are usually quite motivated to do so in order to preserve their licenses and maintain their careers. Part of the assessment process is to interview the key people involved if need be, such as the victim, supervisors, colleagues, employers or family members. After interviews and psychological testing, treatment recommendations are made. Therapists with sociopathic features may receive a recommendation to change careers. Others may receive practice restrictions, such as no individual therapy with the opposite sex. It is usually up to the employer or agency to monitor the treatment plan and restrictions. If the therapist does not comply with the treatment plan, or if the agency suspects the therapist may be in danger of abusing patients again, they must report him or her to their state licensing board or ethics committee.

Pope (1987) reviewed current literature, searching for principles of therapy to treat abusing therapists, and found nothing. He presents a hypothetical case of a therapist who comes for psychotherapy because of his strong attraction to a female patient. Pope encouraged the therapist to sign a "no sexual acting-out contract." He also assigned readings about the normalcy of sexual attraction and about the issue of sexual intimacy with patients.

Pope puts great emphasis on having abusing therapists read first-person accounts by victims of their abuse in therapy (Freeman and Roy, 1976; Plasil, 1985; Walker and Young, 1986). These accounts are sobering and helpful in preventing acting-out. Pope also uses some conditioning "thought-stopping" techniques to deal with obsessive fantasies. Another part of treatment is positive imagery or rehearsal on how to work effectively with the particular patient.

Pope (1989) believes rehabilitation should offer four procedures:

1. *Establish a coordinator.* An accountability person separate from the therapist and who has access to all the information.

2. *Distinguish between rehabilitative and therapeutic tasks.* There should be a rehabilitative specialist who focuses on issues of practice limits, professional attitudes and work setting. There should also be an individual therapist who works with the personal issues of the offending therapist.

3. *Identify the appropriate professional to implement rehabilitation.* The coordinator or licensing board, which may be the same, should identify competent people for the two roles under (2) above. These two individuals

should not have any prior professional, business or personal relationship with the offending therapist, and they must be knowledgeable about therapist-patient sexual involvement.

4. *Evaluate the success of rehabilitation.* There should be another professional who can objectively evaluate the results of the rehabilitation. The rehabilitation specialist and the treating therapist should both submit reports to the coordinator for evaluation by an objective professional.

Celenza (1991) has made a further contribution by presenting a case study of the therapy of an abusing therapist. She notes frequently that abusing therapists make the mistake of seeing the patient's transference as real. On a human, and humorous, note, she quotes veteran therapist Elvin Semrad, who once said to an adoring female patient: "You feel this way for neurotic reasons, and when you get better, I will be sad" (pp. 501-2). Celenza makes the point that erotic countertransference feelings are often a defense against disappointment or rage in the transference. As has been noted by other authors, this erotic relationship sustains positive, idealizing feelings in the patient, which meets the narcissistic needs of the therapist.

Prevention

Strasburger, Jorgenson and Sutherland (1992) have written on prevention, stressing the point that nonsexual boundary violations almost always precede sexual contact. For example, they list the following as part of "the slippery slope" of boundary violations: (1) scheduling a favorite patient as the last of the day so more time can be spent, (2) excessive telephone conversations with the patient, (3) extended sessions, (4) laxity with fees, (5) excessive self-disclosure, (6) meetings arranged outside the office, (7) asking the patient to perform work at the therapist's home or office, and (8) exchanging gifts. Any of these behaviors may cause detrimental effects on the therapy and are warning signs of escalating boundary violations.

A number of other authors have offered suggestions for preventing therapist-patient sexual involvement:

☐ Graduate schools could do a better job of screening therapist candidates if they are familiar with personalities prone to be offenders (Pope and Bouhoutsos, 1986).

☐ There should be more educational efforts in graduate training on the "risk areas" in practicing psychotherapy (Zelen, 1985).

☐ Graduate schools should have strict regulations about faculty and supervisors not being romantically involved with students. Research has indicated that these students are more at risk of becoming sexually involved with a client later (Glaser and Thorpe, 1986).

☐ Agencies and employers should strictly prohibit sexual intimacies between therapists and patients. They should evaluate "the risk factor" when hiring new therapists (Pope and Bouhoutsos, 1986).

☐ Professional organizations should take an active role in educating members about the problem of abuse and informing them how to have their patients report past therapists who were sexually abusive. Such an organization might also develop a rehabilitation program for therapists (Pope and Bouhoutsos, 1986).

☐ State consumer affairs departments could require therapists to display a sign which states that sexual contact is unethical and never a part of therapy (Bouhoutsos, 1985).

☐ State licensing boards, which have the responsibility for governing entry into the counseling profession, might begin requiring an oral ethics interview that covers the area of sexual intimacies between therapist and patient (Pope and Bouhoutsos, 1986).

Conclusion

This chapter has examined how counselors might abuse their power in the counseling relationship, and in particular has presented sexual misconduct as one very damaging abuse of power. Perhaps most alarming is that many of those involved in sexual misconduct have been fully trained and licensed mental health professionals who knew better. Yet somehow the intellectual knowledge of simply "knowing better" has not prevented the abuse of power when it is competing with strong emotional needs that have not been adequately addressed by personal psychotherapy and spiritual growth. Both professional ethical standards and our Christian ethics direct the responsibility back to us as counselors to know ourselves, resolve our own issues, and become more aware of and responsible with the power we have.

References

American Psychological Association. 1992. "Ethical Principles of Psychologists and Code of Conduct." *American Psychologist* 47: 1597-1611.

Baylis, F. 1993. "Therapist-Patient Sexual Contact: A Non Consensual, Inherently Harmful Activity." *Canadian Journal of Psychiatry* 38: 502-7.

Belote, B. 1974. "Sexual Intimacy Between Female Clients and Male Therapists: Masochistic Sabotage." Unpublished doctoral dissertation, California School of Professional Psychology, Berkeley.

Borys, D. S., and K. S. Pope. 1989. "Dual Relationships Between Therapists and Clients: A National Survey of Psychologists, Psychiatrists and Social Workers." *Professional Psychology: Research and Practice* 20: 283-93.

Bouhoutsos, J. C. 1985. "Therapist-Client Sexual Involvement: A Challenge for Mental Health Professionals and Educators." *American Journal of Orthopsychiatry* 55(2): 177-82.

Bouhoutsos, J. C., J. Holroyd, H. Lerman, B. R. Forer and M. Greenberg. 1983. "Sexual Intimacy Between Psychotherapists and Patients." *Professional Psychology: Research and Practice* 14(2): 185-96.

Butler, S. 1975. "Sexual Contact Between Therapists and Patients." Unpublished doctoral dissertation, California School of Professional Psychology, Los Angeles.

Butler, S., and S. Zelen. 1977. "Sexual Intimacies Between Psychotherapists and Their Patients." *Psychotherapy: Theory, Research and Practice* 139: 143-44.

Celenza, A. 1991. "The Misuse of Countertransference Love in Sexual Intimacies Between Therapists and Patients." *Psychoanalytic Psychology* 8(4): 501-9.

Chesler, P. 1972. *Women and Madness.* New York: Avon Books.

Claman, J. M. 1987. "Mirror Hunger in the Psychodynamics of Sexually Abusing Therapists." *The American Journal of Psychoanalysis* 47(1): 35-40.

Doherty, W. J. 1989. "Unmasking Family Therapy." *Networker,* March/April, pp. 35-39.

Feldman-Summers, S. 1987. "Sexual Contact in Fiduciary Relationships," in *Psychology, Ethics and Change,* ed. S. Fairbairn and G. Fairbairn. London: Routledge and Kegan Paul.

Feldman-Summers, S., and G. Jones. 1984. "Psychological Impacts of Sexual Contact Between Therapists, Other Health Care Professionals and Their Clients." *Journal of Consulting and Clinical Psychology* 52(6): 1054-61.

Freeman, L., and J. Roy. 1976. *Betrayal.* New York: Stein and Day.

Gabbard, G. O. 1994. "Psychotherapists Who Transgress Sexual Boundaries with Patients." *Bulletin of the Menninger Clinic* 58(1): 124-35.

Gartrell, N., J. Herman, S. Olarte, M. Feldstein and R. Localio. 1986. "Psychiatrist-Patient Sexual Contact: Results of a National Survey, I: Prevalence." *American Journal of Psychiatry* 143: 1126-31.

Gechtman, L. 1989. "Sexual Contact Between Social Workers and Their Clients," in *Sexual Exploitation in Professional Relationships,* ed. B. O. Gabbard. Washington, D.C.: American Psychiatric Press.

Glaser, R. D., and J. S. Thorpe. 1986. "Unethical Intimacy: A Survey of Sexual Contact and Advances Between Psychology Educators and Female Graduate Students." *American Psychologist* 41: 43-51.

Gorkin, M. 1985. "Varieties of Sexualized Countertransference." *Psychoanalytic Review* 72(3): 424-40.

Gutheil, T. G. 1989. "Borderline Personality Disorder, Boundary Violations and Patient-Therapist Sex: Medicolegal Pitfall." *American Journal of Psychiatry* 146(5): 597-602.

Holroyd, J. C., and J. C. Bouhoutsos. 1985. "Sources of Bias in Reporting Sexual Contact with Patients." *Psychotherapy: Research and Practice* 16: 701-9.

Holroyd, J. C., and A. M. Brodsky. 1977. "Psychologists' Attitudes and Practices Regarding Erotic and Non-erotic Physical Contact with Patients." *American Psychologist* 32: 843-49.

Kardener, S. H., M. Fuller and I. N. Mensh. 1973. "A Survey of Physicians' Attitudes and Practices Regarding Erotic and Nonerotic Contact with Patients." *American Journal of Psychiatry* 130: 1077-81.

King, R. R. 1990. "Hypnosis," in *Dictionary of Pastoral Care and Counseling,* ed. R. J. Hunter, H. N. Malony, L. O. Mills and J. Patton. Nashville: Abingdon.

Kohut, H., and E. S. Wolf. 1977. "The Disorders of the Self and Their Treatment." *International Journal of Psychoanalysis* 59: 413-25.

Masson, J. M. 1994. *Against Therapy.* Monroe, Maine: Common Courage Press.

McMinn, M. R., and K. R. Meek. 1996. "Ethics Among Christian Counselors: A Survey of Beliefs and Behaviors." *Journal of Psychology and Theology* 24: 26-37.

Plasil, E. 1985. *Therapist.* New York: St. Martin's/Marek.

Pope, K. S. 1987. "Preventing Therapist-Patient Sexual Intimacy: Therapy for a Therapist at Risk." *Professional Psychology: Research and Practice* 18(6): 624-28.

———. 1989. "Therapists Who Become Sexually Intimate with a Patient: Classifications, Dynamics, Recidivism and Rehabilitation." *The Independent Practitioner* 9(3): 28-34.

Pope, K. S., P. Keith-Spiegel and B. G. Tabachnick. 1986. "Sexual Attraction to Clients." *American Psychologist* 41(2): 147-58.

Pope, K. S., and J. C. Bouhoutsos. 1986. *Sexual Intimacy Between Therapists and Patients*. New York: Praeger.

Pope, K. S., B. G. Tabachnick and P. Keith-Spiegel. 1987. "Ethics of Practice: The Beliefs and Behaviors of Psychologists as Therapists." *American Psychologist* 42: 993-1006.

Pope, K. S., and V. A. Vetter. 1991. "Prior Therapist-Patient Sexual Involvement Among Patients Seen by Psychologists." *Psychotherapy* 28(3): 429-38.

Pope, K. S., and J. L. Sonne. 1991. "Treating Victims of Therapist-Patient Sexual Involvement." *Psychotherapy* 28: 1174-87.

Solovey, A. D., and B. L. Duncan. 1992. "Ethics and Strategic Therapy: A Proposed Ethical Direction." *Journal of Marital and Family Therapy* 18: 53-61.

Solursh, D. S., L. P. Solursh and N. R. Williams. 1993. "Patient-Therapist Sex: 'Just Say No' Isn't Enough." *Medicine and Law* 12(3-5): 431-38.

Stone, L. G. 1980. "A Study of the Relationships Among Anxious Attachments, Ego Functioning and Female Patients' Vulnerability to Sexual Involvement with Their Male Psychotherapists." Unpublished doctoral dissertation, California School of Professional Psychology, Los Angeles.

Vinson, J. S. 1987. "Use of Complaint Procedures in Cases of Therapist-Patient Sexual Contact." *Professional Psychology: Research and Practice* 18(2): 159-64.

Walker, E., and T. D. Young. 1986. *A Killing Cure*. New York: Henry Holt.

Zelen, S. L. 1985. "Sexualization of Therapeutic Relationships: The Dual Vulnerability of Patient and Therapist." *Psychotherapy* 22: 178-85.

Chapter 7

CHRISTIAN RESPONSES TO THE UNETHICAL HEALER

Ioma L. Hawkins &
Colleen K. Benson

---

*A*s Christians, we are a people set apart. Yet our salvation does not come with an iron-clad mantle of protection from sin. Neither does being a Christian confer on mental health professionals immunity from the temptations that assault our secular counterparts. Although research up to this point has been scant, a clear picture emerges of *Christian* healers struggling with issues of ethical and professional accountability, and where there are struggles, there will also be defeats (Hawkins and Bullocks, 1995).

While professional Christian counseling has had a brief history, pastoral or lay counseling in the church has had a long and rich history (Lau and Stelle, 1990; Tan, 1991). But longevity alone has not given pastors or lay counselors in the church immunity from complaints and ethical dilemmas (Fortune, 1990). In fact, as recent media publicity reflects, abuses are occurring at an alarming rate. Ohlschlager (1991) states: "Like the explosive trends in the secular mental health professions, the church has begun to face an epidemic of spiritual, moral, ecclesiastical, and legal trouble due to sexual misconduct in the counseling ministry" (p. 64).

While there is growing attention in the secular community to the needs of impaired therapists (Guy, 1989; APA, 1988), the Christian professional community has not adequately begun to investigate this phenomenon (Oordt, 1990). CAPS has published a statement of ethical guidelines containing protocol for dealing with impaired members, but more still remains to be done in the field at large. Many questions remain: What are the areas of ethical vulnerability for the Christian practitioner? Do we know what the focus of preventive measures should be? What is the restorative process? What are some examples of redemptive responses toward one who has made ethical mistakes?

This chapter represents a preliminary effort to address these concerns by (1) surveying what Christian practitioners perceive as primary problems and (2) demonstrating possible responses to unethical behavior that would be redemptive.

A Survey of Christian Counselors and Ethical Behavior
The survey explored the following four questions: (1) In what areas are Christian mental health workers vulnerable to unethical behavior in counseling and psychotherapy? (2) What is the relationship between law (as it pertains to professional practice), grace and discipline? (3) What are some psychological and interpersonal factors behind unethical behavior? (4) Once a Christian counselor or psychotherapist has been identified as having committed an unethical act, should there be anything "unique" in the response from the Christian professional community? A series of vignettes follow the survey results to illustrate redemptive responses on the part of caring professionals in helping to restore the unethical healer.

Survey data were collected from a sample of twenty psychologist-acade- micians who (1) teach in accredited doctoral-level training programs of psychology that include a Christian focus, (2) hold doctorate degrees and licensure, and (3) practice the integration of Christian principles in psycho- therapy. Five of the respondents were female, and fifteen were male. Although the survey subjects were professionally trained, licensed Christian therapists, much of what is concluded is applicable to lay and pastoral counselors as well.

The data were collected in the form of either in-person or telephone interviews. A portion of the responses to the first question were grouped into frequency categories. Two raters determined the category fit by agreement. If agreement could not be reached, a third rater determined the category.

Results of the Survey
Question 1: *In what areas are Christian mental health workers vulnerable to unethical behavior in counseling and psychotherapy?*

The twenty respondents cited fifty-four violations in response to this inquiry. Forty-one (76 percent) of the most frequently reported instances of unethical behavior fell into seven categories: (1) sex, (2) money, (3) boundary violations, (4) dual roles, (5) confidentiality, (6) unfinished business (referring to therapist's personal issues) and (7) retention of clients in therapy longer than needed. Of these seven categories, sexual misconduct, money issues and professional boundary violations were most frequently cited (see table 7.1). The seven categories are fairly consistent with those cited in the secular psychology field (APA, 1988; Borys and Pope, 1989; Bouhoutsos, 1983; Holroyd and Brodsky, 1977; Pope, Tabachnick and Keith-Spiegel, 1986, 1987).

Response	Number of Respondents Citing
1. Sexual misconduct	15
2. Money and business issues	10
3. Professional boundary violations	6
4. Dual role relations	4
5. Confidentiality not maintained	3
6. Unfinished business of therapist	5
7. Holding client unduly in therapy	3

(Frequencies are not actual occurrences but are perceptions of Christian therapist's vulnerability.)

Table 7.1. Christian professionals' vulnerability

Interestingly, there were five violations that, though mentioned only once, were "uniquely religious" in nature: (1) over spiritualizing both psychological and spiritual issues; (2) lay counselors in the church working without ethical limits; (3) the indiscriminate use of questionable exercises such as demonic deliverance and exorcism in counseling; (4) using Scripture to abuse or pressure counselees; and (5) authoritarianism—imposing therapist values on the client.

The category of unethical behavior mentioned the most for Christian therapists was sexual misconduct. This is the greatest problem for secular therapists as well. However, it should be reiterated that this does not necessarily suggest that sexual misconduct *is* the most frequent ethical violation in the Christian professional community (Oordt, 1990).

Question two: *What is the relationship between law, grace and discipline in response to the unethical healer?*

The responses reflect the general thought that law defines unethical behavior or provides the parameters (n=8), while grace is restorative and related to repentance by the offender (n=10). Following are several specific responses to question two.

☐ "Law defines unethical behavior. Grace is meant to restore a person back to proper relationship, with the goal of restoration."

☐ "Unethical Christian professionals should follow the laws and discipline of our profession. Grace should be shown in accordance with Scripture to those who have fallen."

☐ "The law needs to be obeyed. Grace has more to do with how a person is treated. I don't believe in excusing Christians. Discipline needs to be there— grace is more the manner in which it's done."

☐ "The state law is to keep order. Grace is the freedom to take responsibility to keep the law."

☐ "Grace provides motivation for rehabilitation, but competency cannot be sacrificed."

The respondents agreed that the law must be upheld, recognized and obeyed by Christian counselors. The law sets the parameters that define unethical behavior. Discipline is seen as a consequence of committing the unethical act. The Christian professionals surveyed here support laws and the need for discipline but believe strongly in the restoration of the fallen person back into the community when proper repentance is displayed and discipline exacted. They described the idea of grace with words such as *restoration, repentance* and *forgiveness*. The term *restoration* was used most frequently.

Question three: *What are some psychological and interpersonal factors behind unethical behavior?*

The majority of the responses dealt with psychological factors in the therapist: unresolved personal issues such as an inability to recognize boundaries and roles, issues related to a dysfunctional background, and other factors such as depression, burnout, narcissism, power issues and character flaws. Only two related to interpersonal issues specifically. Here is a sample of the responses:

☐ "Confusing good Christian intentions with lack of professional boundaries; the blurring of roles. People come into Christianity with unresolved issues. Others may be using the Christian environment as a cloak to better hide their unethical desires and actions. The Christian community is not using the powers of discernment."

☐ "Unresolved personal issues that are not ever addressed. Therapists may feel this isn't applicable to them. They are not growing as persons themselves."

☐ "Psychological factors—emotional needs or conflicts which the healer hasn't acknowledged or resolved. Interpersonal factors—subtle violations of professional and emotional boundaries and the healer's working in isolation."

☐ "Motives of psychologists that enter the profession—they need to be needed. Curiosity is out of proportion. Unresolved dealings with very disturbed clients who are depressed or borderline. We need to be open with supervisors in relation to sexuality issues."

☐ "Role fuzziness. Our roles need to be clear: I am the doctor, you are the patient. Therapists with an impoverished life outside the office and therapists who have not experienced their own didactic therapy are particularly vulnerable."

Question four: *Should there be anything "unique" in a Christian response to unethical behavior?*

Eighteen of the twenty respondents (90 percent) clearly supported the idea that there should be a uniqueness in a Christian's response to unethical behavior. This uniquely Christian response should have elements of humility, redemption, grace, restoration, understanding and forgiveness.

While those surveyed identified a uniquely Christian response to the unethical healer, they also believed that the unethical behavior itself should not be excused or go unaddressed. Respondents clearly indicated that when proper repentance is shown by the offender, restoration with forgiveness should follow from the Christian community. Some responses include:

☐ "We should restore one another in humility, not being condemning or judgmental. We should not waver in our standards but help to restore the fallen one who submits to the prescribed discipline."

☐ "The only unique aspect is that a Christian should be more ethical and definitely address anything in a way that will lead to redemption."

☐ "Christian ethics ought to emerge out of Christian faith. Morality emerges out of a Christian base. My morality determines my response to someone who has committed an unethical act."

☐ "What is unique is our God, who doesn't just restore us to appropriate ethical behavior professionally, but restores us spiritually so we can become whole people."

☐ "If the law defines unethical behavior and punishment is prescribed for it, then the person must undergo it. There is still a spiritual nature; that's where grace and redemption come in. If God forgives, we should too, yet restoration is needed—spiritually and socially—internal, for the person, and external, for the community."

☐ "Christians must see unethical behavior as not just a professional issue but also a moral issue. This should strengthen our commitment to being ethical. We should also respond to the person needing restoration and growth as well as to the behavior and consequences."

Conclusions Reached

Although this was a sample survey, the information obtained gives an interesting picture of the perceptions of a group of well-trained Christian professionals about their approach to understanding and approaching the unethical healer. The findings first suggest that these professionals believe that Christian practitioners are most vulnerable in the same areas as secular practitioners (APA, 1988). It therefore seems appropriate to recommend that graduate training programs bolster their focus on the fundamentals of ethical practice and professional behavior. Additionally, Christian professionals who practice fringe Christian therapies or use extreme methods should seek consultation and supervision from their colleagues, since practice in these areas could lead to ethical abuses. Currently malpractice suits are actually quite low in the area of unethical or unlawful abuses by therapists who do "Christian oriented psychotherapy" (Bogie, 1994), but one must keep in mind that Christian therapy may refer to quite a broad range of techniques.

The survey also reveals some important insights into the psychological and interpersonal factors leading to unethical behavior. Psychologically, the unethical healer is seen as a person who may have unresolved personal issues. Some respondents suggest that a type of narcissism may be evident. Interpersonally, factors centering around power issues and boundary violations are particularly salient. In light of this, it is important to closely examine the admission process in Christian graduate training programs. Incorporating personal didactic therapy for students also can be a good preventative dimension of training. Last, supervision and consultation should be an ongoing process that does not end with graduate training. Being a Christian provides no automatic immunization against psychological and interpersonal problems for the practitioner.

None of the survey responses suggests that one's Christianity alone negatively influences the counseling/therapy process. However, a few respondents urged caution regarding extreme forms of religious practices in the therapeutic context. One respondent cautioned that even the sharing of the same faith by both therapist and client may be a cause of enmeshment and could act as a therapeutic blind spot. This, however, is true of many areas of similarity that arise within the therapeutic process and should be addressed objectively by the therapist.

Christian professionals seem unique in their emphasis on showing grace toward the unethical offender. While they respect the need for law and discipline, there is general agreement that grace should be extended to the offender who has adequately responded to disciplinary measures and who can be restored back into the community. (See the CAPS [1993] ethical guidelines for more detail regarding this position.)

What does being redemptive and restorative mean in actual practice? Are there specific suggestions on how to mix accountability and grace, or restoration? What practical recommendations or illustrations are there for how a practitioner might confront a colleague yet also remain available for care and support?

The Response to the Impaired Healer

The question that continues to beg for an answer is, What are we as Christians to do when we know that a colleague is impaired or in trouble ethically? It seems evident to us how to give a "Christian" response to someone in a personal crisis, for example, the death of a family member or even a divorce. But in terms of the unethical healer, if our goal is a redemptive one, how do we uphold a standard and still be an agent of reconciliation? Following are some case studies that will help us think through the issues. The case studies have been thoroughly disguised by combining elements of several cases into one and by significantly altering information. Names are purely fictitious.

A Case of Boundary Violations

Dr. Smith and Dr. Jones are both members of the same church denomination and see each other at regular citywide denominational functions. John, a former client of Dr. Smith's, began seeing Dr. Jones. During the course of therapy, John revealed to Dr. Jones that Dr. Smith had often spent time during or at the end of their sessions discussing the difficulty he was having with his marriage and how he was becoming romantically involved with someone else. At times Dr. Smith would mention sexual matters concerning both his wife and his girlfriend, which to John felt inconsistent with the biblical concepts and values that were talked about in many sessions. John had been victimized in the past, and now again was unable to set limits with his therapist, even though he was very uncomfortable. The only thing he knew to do was to leave the relationship.

As he entered therapy with Dr. Jones, John began to deal with this most recent violation experienced at the hands of a supposedly "helping" person. John wanted to confront Dr. Smith about what had happened, and Dr. Jones felt this would likely be therapeutic for him. Dr. Jones consulted with two colleagues and came to realize that he had some responsibility to talk to Dr. Smith also. Further, he felt some responsibility because they were both members of the same denomination as well as the same profession. John also wanted Dr. Jones to go with him to meet with Dr. Smith.

Dr. Jones helped to arrange a meeting between the three of them. During the meeting, John was able to talk to Dr. Smith about what had happened and to state the impact it had on him. He shared how he felt victimized again, this time by someone he was paying to help him. Dr. Smith did not deny John's description and to some degree expressed the hope that John would forgive him. Later, Dr. Jones ascertained that this had happened during a stressful period of Dr. Smith's life and that he had taken steps to resolve some of the issues that had been bothering him at the time.

While the outcome of the case was not satisfactory in every way, Dr. Smith had acknowledged his problem and had taken some responsibility for what happened. In other situations, the ethical violations can be much more serious and the outcome much less restorative.

The Elusive Professional

Dr. East was on the faculty of a large Christian university when she became enchanted with a graduate student seeing practicum clients at the student counseling center. Her colleagues would frequently see the two of them together on campus, although no one talked to her about what she was doing. It was only when her husband called the dean of the graduate school to tell her that his wife had moved out, had filed for divorce and was planning to marry the graduate student that the university administrators realized there was a problem.

The dean, Dr. West, set up an appointment to talk with Dr. East. When the dean confronted Dr. East with her actions and the implications, she indicated that she realized what she was doing violated both professional ethics and Christian standards. But she went on to explain with a great deal of rationalization that this situation was different in that the grad student was such a special man, and she couldn't imagine God would want to keep her in a marriage that had been miserable for some time. She did ask the dean if she wanted her to resign. At this point the dean spelled out a process that would allow Dr. East to maintain her employment with the school and be rehabilitated professionally. This would involve both regular individual therapy and regular appointments with the dean to discuss her progress. In addition the dean asked Dr. East to confess her lack of good judgment and resulting harmful relationship with the graduate student to the entire faculty, since by now they were all aware of much that had gone on.

Dr. East refused to confess anything to the faculty, again reiterating that she really didn't think she was doing anything particularly wrong. And if she was, God would forgive her, and that was all that mattered. On hearing this, the dean indicated that she would need to ask Dr. East for her resignation. Dr. East said she would be glad to leave an institution that was so rigid and apparently had no idea of what grace is.

Dr. East got a divorce, married the student, got a job in another city doing therapy and is involved with a church only as an occasional attender. She left her faculty group divided on how to handle the ethical violations. They were split down the middle, with one half thinking they should file charges with both the professional association and the licensing board, and the other half feeling that the Christian response was to do nothing. Because they could not reach a consensus, no official action was taken.

If this case follows the pattern revealed in research (Pope and Bouhoutsos, 1986), charges could be filed by the therapist's second husband if they divorce and he gets into therapy and becomes healthy enough to realize the power differential in a marriage which started as supervisor-supervisee relationship (even more of an issue if the relationship begins as a therapist-client relationship) is something he can no longer tolerate. One may ask why this woman's first husband didn't file charges. There are no clear-cut answers to that question, but it is something that seldom happens. Perhaps even ex-spouses struggle to arrive at a "Christian" response to a mate who seems to have become quite deranged and is acting out of character. Also, the spouse may be caught up in the personal devastation of losing the relationship, leaving little energy to be concerned with filing a professional complaint.

This case illustrates several other features that are often part of the picture when someone violates professional ethics in a major way. The professional is usually not in a relationship with colleagues or a group of church laypeople in which there is mutual accountability for living within acceptable guidelines of the profession and/or Christian community. As the CAPS *Ethical Guidelines* states:

Difficulties, power struggles, trials and tribulations are normal and to be expected. . . . We are to grow and mature through the conflicts, problems, trials, tribulations and discipline that we experience. . . . We are to support and encourage each other. . . . We are to admonish and confront each other, especially those Christians in positions of leadership and trust. However, such confrontation is to be constructive rather than judgmental, done in love and with caution about our own shortcomings. . . . We are to demonstrate the lordship of Christ in our lives by servantlike leadership, a sense of community and a lifestyle that reflects the will of God. . . . We are to reach out to others in love and concern. . . . These guidelines are meant in part as an encouragement for all CAPS members to reach out to other members who are in distress. (1993)

Later in this same document:

I will do my best to be aware of my human limitations and biases. I admit that I do not have complete objectivity or spiritual maturity. Thus, I also will endeavor to establish and maintain a relationship of mutual accountability with another Christian colleague or mentor.

Thus we see that at least one reason professionals get into this kind of difficulty is they have chosen *not* to be in relationships of mutual accountability. This leads directly to another question, however: What might explain the lack of interpersonal relationships in a person's life? What are the emotional and spiritual factors (and perhaps physical factors as well) that are often present?

Burnout can sometimes be a precursor to the kind of idiosyncratic thinking seen in Dr. East's actions. The professional who is working twelve to fourteen hours a day with limited time for friends or colleagues has little opportunity for her thinking to be challenged when it begins to move outside social or professional norms. Professionals who become sexually involved with clients tend to be well established in practice, oftentimes leaders in the field (Pope and Bouhoutsos, 1986). Perhaps psychologists are particularly at risk for believing the myth of their own invincibility (Sleek, 1994), a risk which increases the longer one is in practice.

Emotionally, the individual may actually be suffering from a depressive disorder. If this is undiagnosed and untreated, the person is often just looking for something, *anything,* that will help her feel better. The feelings of worth-lessness, loss of meaning, lack of pleasure and low self-esteem may actually send her looking for something or someone outside herself that initially promises to "fix" all of these problems. This may take the form of various kinds of addictive behaviors. Underlying all of this may be some level of narcissism or narcissistic thinking, which defends against the symptoms of depression with an exaggerated sense of importance, a sense of being unique and "special," and a sense of entitlement. Longer-term relationships no longer provide the level of admiration and attention desired, so a new relationship is sought to supply what is perceived as missing. The therapist's empathic ability is limited to the extent that the impact these actions will have in the lives of clients, family, friends and colleagues is distorted and grossly underestimated.

This suggests a level of arrogance, which is described spiritually as pride or a lack of humility (Prov 16:18). In 2 Chronicles 7:14 God clearly outlines elements of the healing process: humility; prayer, or listening to God; being teachable; and repentance, or turning from the sinful way. This results in being heard, being forgiven and being healed. The implication is that this process should take place in the context of community, in the midst of loving people who are able to be agents of God's grace and at the same time not overlook the required steps of repentance and turning from sin. The case of Dr. East illustrates what happens when a person decides he or she is willing to live outside of being accountable to either God or a community of loving persons. And typically it means that the person physically moves to another professional and personal environment. He or she finds a new practice which is more accepting (if members of the new practice even know) and settles into a new life. The person's new church might place him or her in leadership, either unaware of the past behavior or convinced by the person that all of that has been dealt with and is no longer an issue. This is not to be confused with those individuals who truly have gone through a process of confession, reconciliation and restoration, however. Usually the person who changes environments does so to resist the confrontation of colleagues and to avoid the restorative cycle that begins with repenting and ending the abusive or unethical behavior.

A Means to Healing

Dr. Run was practicing in a counseling center sponsored by several churches in the community when someone he supervised accused him of sexual harassment. The woman said she felt that Dr. Run was seductive. Because Dr. Run was an ordained minister as well as a psychologist, the supervisee filed a complaint with the church governing body that oversees the churches in his area. Even though this group responded in a punitive way in dealing with Dr. Run, they did insist he receive some therapy to deal with his inappropriate behavior.

Dr. Run welcomed the opportunity to work on several issues, not just the area related to his sexual harassing. He was actually quite surprised by the allegations and decided that there must be some unconscious process that would explain his actions. Leaving the situation was not an option, and denial and rationalization were not a part of his response. He felt there must be something he needed to look at in himself if someone had misread his motives and actions. He used the situation as an opportunity to grow personally, in his family relationships and professionally.

This case stands in stark contrast to another:

There was a man who was a pastor of a church in which several women accused him of having sexual relations with them. He had little choice about leaving the church and the ministry. His response was a combination of contrition and rationalization: he was sorry for creating such a big problem but would never acknowledge the extent of injury he caused in the lives of these women. He continued to justify his actions by saying he'd only done what they wanted and that he always had their best interests as his priority. He left the church and began working independently as a counselor, a role even more susceptible to boundary violations.

This points out the difficulty licensing boards have in getting an adequate background check of applicants in order to avoid credentialing high-risk individuals. While there are usually checks for criminal background, there are usually no judicial records if problems have been dealt with outside the civil arena (e.g., by an ecclesiastical governing body).

When to Take Action

With the variety of interpersonal, emotional, personality and spiritual factors involved in nonethical behavior, it becomes problematic to predict the outcome of becoming involved with someone who appears to be impaired. Our responsibility is to uphold the standards of our profession and of Christianity. The process for doing this is delineated in Matthew 18:13-17. There are a variety of professional resources to guide our intervention as well (APA, 1992; Keith-Spiegel and Koocher, 1985; Pope and Bouhoutsos, 1986; Sleek, 1994). The *Ethical Guidelines* for CAPS (1993; see appendix B) includes suggestions for CAPS members to follow in responding to troubled members. One of the differences between Christian and secular models of intervention centers around the first step: whether intervention should be done on a one-to-one basis or as a team. The severity of the problem and the nature of one's relationship with the professional in question can provide some guidance in this matter.

Prior to taking any overt action, it is important that we are in touch with our own motivation to engage in or avoid confrontation. This implies a strong need for consultation with a trusted and experienced colleague. When initiating the process of confrontation, whether alone or as a team, it is important to be educative and constructive in our approach. Our role is not to be that of judge, jury or punisher. In fact, we should attempt to help our fallen colleagues before they harm patients or are disciplined by regulatory boards. Official action should be necessary only for those professionals who refuse referral for treatment.

Clearly, the most problematic situations are when the therapists themselves fail to recognize the severity of their disturbance or behavior. This possibility argues for a team approach to confrontation, including colleagues, family members and friends. All those involved should be committed to ongoing support for the professional through the period of treatment and full rehabilitation and restoration (APA, 1994; see also the video *Colleague Assistance: Routes to Recovery*). No matter how pessimistic we are about the outcome, or how much we might dislike the colleague, we need to avoid gossip about the situation as well as the temptation to anonymously threaten the therapist with reporting the behavior to the licensing board. Neither of these actions has the possibility of a constructive outcome.

We should be cautious in relation to ourselves as we realize the circumstances that can lead to impaired or unethical behavior. We need to be continuously evaluating our own lives so we can proactively prevent burnout, the resulting social isolation, and the emotional and spiritual difficulties that can ensue. Pope and Bouhoutsos (1986) have a therapist checklist (p. 166) that provides some warning signs for self-evaluation. In addition to these we need to be alert to major changes in the usual pattern of professional conduct, including excess absenteeism, incomplete work assignments, complaints from clients or students, questionable judgment and denial of problems in the midst of high levels of stress.

As professionals we have the responsibility to be always aware of our own humanness and that of our colleagues. Even though this may be a sensitive and uncomfortable area, there is no room for denial in relation to either ourselves or others. Being constantly open to the vulnerability of the human condition is inherent in the task of being a responsible professional.

References

American Psychological Association. 1992. *Ethical Principles of Psychologists*. Rev. ed. Washington, D.C.: Author.

————. 1988. *Trends in Ethics Cases: Common Pitfalls and Published Resources*. Ethics Committee of the APA: Author.

Bogie, M. March 1994. Interview at California Psychological Convention, San Francisco, California.

Borys, D. S., and K. S. Pope. 1989. "Dual Relationships Between Therapist and Client: A National Study of Psychologists, Psychiatrist and Social Workers." *Professional Psychology* 14: 185-96.

Christian Association for Psychological Studies. 1993. *Ethical Guidelines for the Christian Association for Psychological Studies*. New Braunfels, Tex.: Author.

Collins, G. R. 1992. *Excellence and Ethics in Counseling*. Dallas: Word.

Fortune, M. M. 1990. "Betrayal of the Pastoral Relationship: Sexual Contact by Pastors and Pastoral Counselors," in *Psychotherapists' Sexual Involvement with Clients: Intervention & Prevention,* ed. G. R. Schoener et al. Minneapolis: Walk-In Counseling Center. Pp. 81-89.

Guy, J. 1987. *The Personal Life of the Psychotherapist*. New York: John Wiley.

Hawkins, I. L., and S. L. Bullocks. 1995. "Informed Consent and Religious Values: A Neglected Area of Diversity." *Journal of Psychotherapy* 32: 293-98.

Holroyd, J. C., and A. M. Brodsky. 1977. "Psychologists' Attitudes and Practices Regarding Erotic and Nonerotic Physical Contact with Patients." *American Psychologist* 32: 843-49.

Keith-Spiegel, P., and G. P. Koocher. 1985. *Ethics in Psychology*. New York: Random House.

Lau, G. K., and R. Steele. 1990. "An Empirical Study of the Pastoral Mental Health

Involvement Model." *Journal of Psychology and Theology* 18: 261-69.

Margiolis, R. *Colleague Assistance: Routes to Recovery.* Videotape. Available at 404-431-7050.

Ohlschlager, G., and P. Mosgofian. 1992. "Law for the Christian Counselor: A Guidebook for the Clinicians and Pastors," in *Excellence and Ethics in Counseling,* ed. G. R. Collins. Waco, Tex.: Word.

Oordt, M. S. 1990. "Ethics of Practice Among Christian Psychologists: A Pilot Study." *Journal of Psychology and Theology* 18: 225-60.

Pope, K. S., and J. C. Bouhoutsos. 1986. *Sexual Intimacy Between Therapists and Patients.* New York: Praeger.

Pope, K. S., P. Keith-Spiegel and B. G. Tabachnick. 1986. "Sexual Attraction to Clients: The Human Therapist and the Sometimes Inhuman Training System." *American Psychologist* 41: 147-58.

Pope, K. S., B. G. Tabachnick and P. Keith-Spiegel. 1987a. "Good and Poor Practices in Psychotherapy: National Survey of Beliefs of Psychologists." *Psychology: Research and Practice* 9: 547-52.

―――. 1987b. "Ethics of Practice: The Beliefs and Behaviors of Psychologists as Therapists." *American Psychologist* 42: 993-1006.

Sleek, S. 1994. "Impairment Issue Is Gaining Visibility." *Monitor,* November, pp. 28-29.

Tan, S. 1991. *Lay Counseling: Equipping Christians for a Helping Ministry.* Grand Rapids, Mich.: Zondervan.

Part 2

ISSUES IN COUNSELING ETHICS

Chapter 8

ETHICS IN MARITAL THERAPY & PREMARITAL COUNSELING

Steven J. Sandage &
Everett L. Worthington Jr.

*C*hristian therapists today are confronted with the challenge of discerning ethical convictions in a pluralistic postmodern culture. Ambiguity, chaos and alternative perspectives are prominent cultural themes, which can make ethical discernment seem almost impossible. The field of family therapy has made ethics a prime topic of articles, textbooks and conferences in recent years (Huber and Baruth, 1987; Patten, Barnett and Houlihan, 1991; Vesper and Brock, 1991). Yet the commitment of most family therapists to relativism as one pillar of their worldview makes ethical standards slippery.

Many Christians pursue truth and believe that moral absolutes exist. Even so, this does not make ethical reflection simple. Humility about the limits of our knowledge should lead therapists into professional dialogue with the goal of value-informed decisions. This chapter examines ethical principles and how they can be derived, then considers ethical issues in marital therapy and premarital counseling.

Ethical Principles

Counselors inevitably find themselves in situations involving ethical dilemmas. Marital therapy may be even more ethically complex than individual counseling because the client is the marriage—its quality and stability—with additional considerations of two spouses (each with a different agenda) and of children (and sometimes elders) who are in the care of the spouses. The competing agendas can make the therapist feel like he or she is lost in an unfamiliar city.

To navigate unfamiliar territory, one needs a map. The same is true of therapists, and our maps are made up of the ethical principles we embrace. But from where do we derive our ethical principles?

Ethics is a philosophical and, for the Christian, theological endeavor. Bloesch (1987) suggested a differentiation between philosophical and theological types of ethics. Philosophical ethics seeks to understand the good in light of the human plane, whereas theological ethics looks to the divine revelation of God in human history.

Christian Ethics

Christian ethics are inspired by God's Word, God's community and God's character (Collins, 1991).

1. *God's Word.* Christians consider the Bible to be the inspired and authoritative Word of God. As such, the Bible provides general guidelines for morality as well as for doctrine. It charts our course through commandments, promises, specific principles and an overall worldview. Ethical issues are fleshed out in the Bible through narrative examples. As Joshua prepared to lead the rebellious and fickle Hebrews out of the desert, through hostile enemy territory and into the Promised Land (a job description often similar to that of a marital therapist), God spoke to him:

> Do not let this Book of the Law depart from your mouth; meditate on it day and night, so that you may be careful to do everything written in it. Then you will be prosperous and successful. (Josh 1:8)

2. *God's community.* God is relational. He intends for his truth to be understood by his people in the context of a community—the church. Christian counselors are a part of the body of Christ whether they work in private practice, schools, hospitals, prisons, churches or other settings. Some counselors may feel distant from the church, especially since a few church leaders have criticized counseling. But the church can provide a community of fellow believers to enhance theological integrity. Interpreting the Bible and formulating ethical principles in isolation is dangerous. Our own biases can easily influence our interpretations. A Christian community subjects interpretations and biases to public scrutiny. This is the same reason science is done in a community of scholars where interpretations of data are published and evaluated.

A church community can provide support, encouragement and ethical accountability for Christian counselors (Anderson, 1990; Dueck, 1987). Anderson (1990) recommends that Christian therapists consider forming a spiritual support group of Christians who are not professional therapists. This group would not be used as a substitute for supervision or an excuse to violate confidentiality, but could still offer therapists the opportunity to discuss the broader issues of personal growth and counseling practice within the culture of Christian community. Christian counselors may be wise to consider the role of the body of Christ in defining their sense of "calling" as agents of healing (Anderson, 1990; Jones and Butman, 1991).

3. *God's character.* God has not only revealed specific principles in the Bible; he has revealed the Word in his Son. Jesus is called "the radiance of God's glory and the exact representation of his being" (Heb 1:3). Christians have much more than just a set of rules to follow. Christ offers us a person to pattern ourselves after.

Some modern ethicists have emphasized that virtues are a missing foundation in our popular focus on ethical dilemmas and in the question "What should I do?" (Hauerwas, 1981; MacIntyre, 1981). Virtues involve the question "Who shall I be?" Ethical decision-making then arises from a person's character or virtue. God not only models righteous character but also promises through Christ to transform our character to become more like his (2 Cor 3:18). Bloesch (1987) prefers to speak of "graces" instead of virtues because it is God's grace that produces anything virtuous in people's characters. In addition to reflecting on ethical dilemmas, counselors should strive to develop virtues such as humility, honesty, integrity, prudence, fidelity, benevolence and discretion (Jordan and Meara, 1990). Another virtue is fidelity to one's profession, which raises another dimension of ethics for mental health professionals who deal with marriage relationships.

Professional Ethics

Christian counselors fulfill various professional roles and are members of different professional organizations. Psychologists, marriage and family therapists, and social workers all have the opportunity to join professional organizations that have specific ethical codes of conduct. These secular ethical codes contain little that, in principle, is objectionable to Christians. Some of the general principles that shape these codes, such as concern for others' welfare in the APA code, are highly consistent with Christian virtues. One study of the ethical practices of Christian psychologists found that most reported being very consistent with the APA's ethical code (Oordt, 1990). The major differences between secular ethical codes and the CAPS code, for instance, are the explicit statements about members' commitments to the Bible, the church, the family and godly living. The CAPS code also emphasizes love as the motive for service.

This leads us to a practical question: How does one integrate biblical principles and virtues with professional principles and virtues?

Integrative Ethics

No ethical code will cover all ethical situations or dilemmas a family counselor will face. Moreover, it is not always clear how to apply either Christian or secular ethical codes to tough situations. A schema for understanding how ethical principles can be arranged for the Christian counselor is provided in figure 8.1.

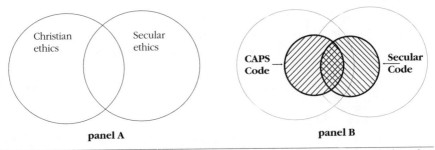

Figure 8.1. The relationship between secular and Christian ethics and codes of ethics that reflect each

In panel A, one circle represents the principles covered in secular ethics, and the other circle represents the principles of Christian ethics derived from the Bible and the Christian community. While there is substantial overlap, the circles are not identical. They may cover different areas or may conflict over some issues. In panel B, superimposed over the two full sets of ethics are secular and Christian codes of ethics. The codes necessarily cannot address all issues, but they usually address the issues frequently encountered at the core of professional practice. Christian ethical codes will be explicit about some issues, such as adultery, that will not be a part of the secular professional codes. The professional codes may be explicit about things not clearly addressed in the Bible, such as the use of current clients for testimonials in advertising. There will obviously be some overlap, some conflict and some issues not clearly addressed by either code. The CAPS code is one attempt to bring secular and Christian domains of ethical reflection together. But ethical principles arise out of an underlying ethical theory that provides the moral context of the entire therapy enterprise. Thus codes may differ at their philosophical bases in some crucial ways.

Ethical Theories

Christian psychologist Dueck (1991) has pointed out that most literature on ethics in family therapy focuses on specific issues and principles. Yet every theory of therapy involves a commitment to metaphors, models, paradigms and narratives of the marriage and the family that guide ethical decisions. For example, constructivist approaches, such as those of Bowen, emphasize the core metaphor of the idea. The ethical injunction will be to think differently. Strategic models, represented by Haley, emphasize the core metaphor of the machine and prescribe acting differently. Theoretical commitments involve notions about the purpose of a marriage, the roles of partners within a marriage, the boundaries of outside influences on a marriage, the appropriateness of certain behaviors within a marriage and a host of other ethical issues. Integrative ethics would require that Christian marital therapists reflect on the ethical implications of their theoretical commitments in light of their Christian values.

Ethical Themes

A point of departure for developing an integrative Christian ethical approach is to recognize that every ethical theory suggests an underlying *theme*. The secular professional codes are generally built on the pragmatic theme of the greatest good for the greatest number of people (utilitarianism) or the theme of self-realization (hedonism).

The Christian story suggests a quite different theme. Dueck (1991) suggests the theme of the Christian story is the reign of God. We are to draw our ethical convictions from God's character as the Sovereign of all creation. Ethics, as a prescription of what is just and right, finds correspondence in who God is and what he has done in history.

A basic New Testament paradigm for ethical living is "faith working through love" (Gal 5:6; 1 Thess 1:3 RSV; see Worthington and McMurry, 1994, for an elaboration). Faith is allegiance or trust in Jesus as the representative of God's reign in history. Work is the obedience that does not merit justification but fulfills our responsibilities as members of God's kingdom (Jas 2:14-24). Love is the motive of our service to God and to our neighbor, which encourages us to do good (beneficence) and prevents us from seeking to do harm (nonmaleficence). Faith working through love as an ethical theme reminds us that ethical principles are not simply abstract ideals. Christian ethics grow from the narrative context of the cross, where law and gospel meet and we gain the freedom for obedience (Bloesch, 1987). Seen within this context, marriage is a special relationship of mutual discipleship. That is, marriage is one very special God-ordained way of helping each other become better citizens living under the reign of Christ (Worthington and McMurry, 1994).

Let's examine a case briefly. A woman comes to counseling puzzling about a decision to return to work after childbearing. She doesn't feel fulfilled picking up toys all day, and she believes that she'll be more fulfilled in the work force. Her husband argues that they don't need the money, and he believes that her work responsibilities will result in a substantial increase in his homemaking and child-care responsibilities. Both husband and wife worry about the effects of daycare on their young child and the effects of increased workloads for both of them on the quality time they have with each other and their child. How does the therapist counsel these individuals, this marriage and this family?

From the standpoint of utilitarianism, the counselor will help the participants explore what decision maximizes benefits for the greatest number of participants and what decision minimizes costs. From the standpoint of hedonism, the central question will revolve around what makes each of the people the happiest or creates the least disruption in their happiness. A reign-of-God perspective, though, will ask an altogether different question: Which decision is in line with what God desires for each person, for the marriage and for the family? Note that people in different circumstances may answer each of these questions differently and thus arrive at different decisions. The therapist must know his or her own ethical stance prior to guiding the individual, couple or family in their decision-making.

Issues Arising in Professional Practice

Several issues related to marital therapy merit special consideration. We will look at how four ethical principles influence some challenging issues faced by marital therapists. These principles are *competence, responsibility to clients, confidentiality* and *integrity*. These principles are drawn from the American Association of Marriage and Family Therapists (AAMFT) code of ethics but are also covered in the APA code of conduct.

1. *Competence.* Both the APA and the AAMFT codes emphasize that therapists should recognize the boundaries of their competence based on their education, training and supervision. A competent therapist is thought to best be able to promote the client's self-betterment or self-fulfillment. For the Christian a commitment to competence is an expression of the Christian virtues of honesty and humility. Further, professional competence is motivated by love and sacrifice for others.

How does one determine competence as a marital therapist? Most psychologists are trained in psychology programs where they may have taken one course in family therapy. Yet two-thirds of all psychologists do marital or family therapy (VandenBos and Stapp, 1983). This raises a question as to the adequacy of training of psychologists in marriage and marital therapy. One might respond that once a therapist has experience with couples, this serves as the necessary training. However, Wiley and Ray (1986) found that *supervised* counseling experience, not counseling experience itself, leads to competence. Therapists without formal training in marital therapy should seek supervision from someone with adequate credentials and training in marital therapy.

Professional organizations have tried to establish minimum standards for both initial and continuing training. But what happens if there is a conflict in the competency requirements of different fields? This happened in the case of one psychologist (from an APA-approved program) who accepted a faculty position with a marriage and family therapy training program accredited by the AAMFT. Once he began work he was surprised to learn that he would be expected (after receiving additional training) to supervise many times the number of therapists that he had been trained to supervise at any one time throughout his doctoral program. This raised an ethical dilemma for him. Could he in good conscience supervise such a large number of therapists? After prayerful reflection this psychologist agreed with others on his faculty not to provide supervision that he felt would stretch him beyond his ability to provide competent training. Instead he fulfilled his teaching obligations through teaching additional lecture courses. At issue were different ethical standards, which the Christian faculty resolved in faith working through love.

Consider another example. Nancy and Jim have been married for five years. They saw a pastoral counselor to whom they had been referred. Their basic complaint was that they had argued intensely about sex as a result of Jim's difficulties with impotence. The counselor met with the couple for ten sessions using a program of conflict resolution. She prayed with the couple at the end of each session. After counseling, Nancy and Jim argued less hurtfully but were frustrated that their sexual difficulties had not improved.

A competent assessment of Jim and Nancy's problem would have indicated that the conflict difficulties were a result of the sexual dysfunction. In this case the counselor chose an intervention familiar to her rather than one appropriate to the problem. A marital therapist could be expected to be familiar enough with sexual dysfunctions to make it part of assessment. A therapist should also know that some sexual problems, such as impotence, are frequently treated successfully through medical or behavioral interventions. The counselor should have referred the couple to a therapist competent to work with couples who had sexual dysfunctions.

2. *Responsibility to clients.* Marital therapists have the responsibility of seeking to advance the welfare of their clients. This raises the pivotal question: Who *is* the client? When a couple comes to marital therapy, they can be viewed as separate individuals, or the relationship can be seen as the client. Unless the therapist thinks clearly about who the client is, treatment goals are likely to become muddled amidst conflicting interests.

Some marital therapists believe that individual married partners are the clients and that the therapist should maximize each client's happiness (see Harper, 1985). Others believe that the marriage must be seen within the context of the broader family (Haley, 1984). Our clinical judgment is that usually, in marital counseling, the client is the marriage relationship (see Worthington and DeVries, 1990, for an extended discussion of this topic). If individual psychopathology were the primary diagnosis, then marital therapy would rarely be the primary treatment. (Note that major depression *as a result of marital distress* has been successfully treated by marital therapy; Beach, Sandeen and O'Leary, 1990.) If a family problem is the main concern—even if marital disruption is present— then family therapy is recommended, not marital therapy (unless the couple recontracts for marital therapy).

Some argue that many people who attend marital counseling are seeking an excuse for divorce or are genuinely conflicted about whether to divorce. Should the focus of marital counseling, then, be neutral? Or should the focus be on improving the marriage? The client-is-the-marriage perspective, of course, does not resolve all ambiguity. At times an individual focus is called for. Issues of divorce (once one partner has decided to pursue divorce) or the presence of physical abuse may require individual focus.

The therapist should communicate his or her understanding of who the client is early in counseling. The therapist might say, "It seems that the focus of your problems is with your marriage. I would like to work with you primarily to improve your relationship. Does a focus on your marriage sound good to you, or are you interested in counseling for something else?" Without this clarification one or both partners may not agree with the focus of therapy being on improving the marriage, resulting in misunderstanding.

Some argue that marital therapists should remain more neutral, not presupposing that successful therapy should restore a more positive marriage. They say, "Through therapy we will determine whether the marriage should continue or whether divorce is the most beneficial course of action." But we liken that reasoning to the individual therapist who counsels a suicidal client by arguing that the therapist must remain neutral on suicide merely because the client is ambivalent about it. God prefers life to suicide, and he also prefers marriage to divorce. Marital therapists should align with a promarriage ethic unless clients demonstrate irrefutably that they intend to divorce—at which time marital therapists should recontract with both partners for divorce therapy.

3. *Integrity.* Integrity generally implies a commitment to honesty and fairness toward clients and other professionals. There are three key issues in marital therapy that relate to the principle of integrity.

a. Integrity is required in diagnosis. Insurance generally does not pay for marital therapy unless it is clearly the treatment of choice for a medical problem. Therapists can be tempted to make some other diagnosis, such as depression in one spouse, that is covered under insurance reimbursement. Billing marital therapy sessions as individual sessions not only violates integrity but runs the risk of insurance fraud (Ohlschlager and Mosgofian, 1992). In recent years more managed-care companies are allowing marital therapy as an approved treatment when it can be demonstrated that marital disruption is affecting work or psychological functioning.

b. Integrity is required for informed consent. Integrity requires an effort to inform clients about process, boundaries and goals of therapy. A more comprehensive discussion of informed consent can be found in Vesper and Brock, 1991, and chapter three in this volume, but a few issues are particularly relevant to marital therapy.

The description of integrity in the APA code requires psychologists to reflect on their own values and biases to determine how they may influence therapy. A Christian worldview will inform therapists' values about marriage in numerous ways, just as a secular worldview will. A marital therapist may have views about the permanence of marriage or roles within marriage that are different from those of the client. Ethical principles suggest that the therapist examine his or her values and decide whether to work with the client or to refer.

If the therapist decides to work with the client, how and when should the therapist inform the client of the values that might influence therapy? Analogue studies have suggested that potential clients may need more information about a therapist's values than merely the label "Christian" or "feminist" to decide whether or not to work with that therapist (Lewis and Epperson, 1991; Lewis and Lewis, 1985). Opinions differ on how or when to inform clients of one's values.

The myth of value-neutral therapy has largely been exposed. A values-informed approach (Dienhart, 1982) seeks to inform clients what the therapist's own relevant values are, while at the same time advocating clients' freedom to hold different views. It is the clients' responsibility to develop their own value positions. Informing clients is not the same as imposing one's values.

Further, not every client decision requires that clients know the therapist's values. A good practice could be to inform clients at the outset that the therapist holds a Christian worldview and that Christian beliefs could be an explicit part of therapy if the clients desire. If clients are not interested in including Christian beliefs in therapy, the counselor should either respect this and proceed accordingly or refer the couple to another therapist. Therapists should remain cognizant of the potential influence of their own beliefs and culture and should be knowledgeable about the beliefs and cultures of their clients.

c. Integrity is required in use of paradoxical interventions. Many marital therapists use paradoxical interventions (Weeks and L'Abate, 1982). How can a therapist maintain honesty while deliberately concealing the purpose of certain techniques or even misleading the client about the purpose? Paradoxical interventions pit two Christian values against each other: truth and love (i.e., helpfulness to the client).

The use of paradoxical interventions has been debated for years. On one side are those who feel honesty and trust are violated by deception in therapy and that effectiveness does not justify deceit (Whan, 1983). On the other side are those who argue that paradoxical interventions can be used ethically (for the client's benefit and with little deceit) or unethically (for the benefit of the therapist and with direct deceit) and that failure to disclose everything to a client occurs with *all* interventions (Deschenes and Shepperson, 1983). Basically, then, the use of an effective technique is a compassionate act that is seen as more important than full disclosure.

Regardless of one's view, two ethical issues are relevant. First, therapists should examine their own motives to ensure that self-aggrandizement is not the goal. Point 2.3 of the CAPS code of ethics says, "I will avoid exploiting or manipulating any client to satisfy my own needs." Second, paradoxical interventions should be used cautiously by the novice therapist unless appropriate supervision is available, because incompetent use of such interventions might result in premature termination of treatment or direct harm to the partners or their relationship.

4. *Confidentiality.* An essential part of being a therapist is protecting appropriate client confidentiality. The APA code describes maintaining confidentiality as a "primary obligation" of psychologists (1992). It is widely understood that there are certain limitations to confidentiality (see chapter three). The specific boundaries of confidentiality should be discussed with clients as part of the informed-consent process.

But what about individual confidentiality in marital therapy? Marital therapists often have sessions or parts of sessions with one partner. How should a marital therapist handle secrets divulged by one partner that he or she doesn't want his or her spouse to know?

Anne and Mike were in marital therapy for four sessions. Anne revealed in private to the therapist that she had just terminated an affair of two years. She asked the therapist not to tell Mike because she was sure he would not forgive her. Ethically, what should the therapist do?

Marital therapists generally take one of three approaches to secrets:

1. All information, whether received in an individual or conjoint session, is public information. This would mean telling the spouse everything.

2. All individually divulged information is private. This would mean keeping secrets confidential.

3. Certain information divulged by one spouse to the therapist may be withheld from the partner by the therapist (based on the therapist's clinical judgment), but confidentiality is not promised. This would make the therapist the arbitrator of what to share as public knowledge.

Whichever approach a therapist chooses should be agreed on with the couple up front. The therapist should try to meet with the couple conjointly as much as possible, because this seems to be the most effective therapeutically and removes one ethical dilemma of dealing with secrets (Gurman and Kniskern, 1981), since the therapist has no knowledge of any. This is also consistent with the idea of the marriage as client in marital therapy. If meeting or communicating with an individual, then, the therapist can tell the person to communicate as if the partner were present. Also, the therapist should let the person know that anything he or she says might come up in future sessions with the partner (position 1), explaining that this seems the best way to ensure fairness, since the husband and wife are being treated as a couple.

This approach, however, can result in the client's not telling the therapist some piece of information that is important to the case. Another risk is that the partner with the secret will drop out of therapy, feeling that the secret is important but being unwilling to reveal it in front of the spouse. If individual therapy is not available to the spouse, then the spouse might be frustrated at not being able to receive counsel on a troublesome issue. That may not be in the client's best interest—whether the client is seen as the married individual or the relationship.

Secret affairs present a common dilemma to marital therapists. Virkler (1992) recommends confession of the infidelity in almost all cases. He suggests that in some rare cases a spouse may have had a one-night affair that did not continue or represent a significant pattern in the marriage. In that case Virkler recommends the repentant client confess the sin to God and work on the marriage in other ways. This approach involves the risk that the partner may one day find out about the affair and come looking for the therapist.

Ohlschlager and Mosgofian (1992) suggest that secrets be considered a process issue, as well as a legal or ethical issue. Many couples have difficulties because they keep numerous secrets. That pattern is relevant to address in marital therapy.

Confession in the case of infidelity involves balancing many complex considerations. For example, what is the motive for confession by the offending spouse? Is there a genuine concern for the partner, or is confession simply a means to relieve the person's own pain? An even more difficult scenario is raised by a passive-aggressive spouse whose "confession" feels like a manipulative attempt to injure. Therapists may also have to make decisions about confession of infidelity in cases where there is some indication that the offended spouse may become violent or seek divorce immediately. The duty to protect one's client from physical harm is a deciding factor in such cases. In other cases, a victim may employ significant defenses against knowledge of an affair and appear to lack the psychological strength to handle the full impact of a revelation. Certainly decisions about whether to encourage an unfaithful spouse to confess his or her transgressions should be done with the welfare of the client (whether marriage or individual partner) in mind and not merely because confession might make things easier for the therapist. Finally, practical limitations must figure into decisions about whether to encourage confession. The number of therapy sessions is often limited by insurance or managed care companies. The therapist must judge whether the affair can be adequately dealt with within the confines of allowable therapy. All of these considerations make an ethical policy about secrets in marital therapy extremely challenging.

Related to confidentiality is the legal issue of privileged communication (which doesn't exist in all states). The legal right of privilege belongs to the client and protects confidential information shared with the therapist from being used in legal proceedings. Clients can waive privilege, which leaves the therapist with no grounds for withholding information (Huber and Baruth, 1987). Privilege is most often an issue for marital therapists regarding divorce proceedings. One partner may want the therapist to testify, while the other does not.

States differ on how they handle client privilege. For example, in both Tennessee and New Jersey judges have ruled that therapists do not have to testify if one spouse objects. In Virginia, however, a judge ruled that a three-way conversation is public information. In this view privilege does not exist and the therapist must testify. This highlights the importance of knowing state laws and how those laws have been interpreted in actual cases.

Issues Arising from Theological Views

Marriage is an important theological construct for Christians. Christians see marriage as a visible symbol of God's faithful commitment to his people and of our need for faithful commitment to him (Worthington, 1989). Marriage was designed by God to be a permanent, intimate and giving relationship between a man and a woman (Eph 5:22-33). This spiritual union of two people into one flesh points to the nature of God's covenant (Gen 2:24).

Marital therapists, however, usually see relationships not characterized by intimacy or giving, and partners are often ambivalent (at best) about its permanence. This often leads to the question of whether these relationships *should* be permanent. Is it ethical and moral, within a Christian framework that values marriage, for the therapist to focus on the partners' ambivalence, pain and distress? Is it ethical and moral *not* to bring up the positive? At what point does the therapist give up trying to help the couple salvage the marriage? What then?

Divorce. Divorce is something every marital therapist faces and realistically cannot prohibit regardless of personal beliefs and values. Three issues confront the Christian therapist: What is a biblical ethic on the permissibility of divorce? How should a therapist handle his or her own values about divorce in the therapeutic process? And how should a Christian therapist respond to a couple's decision to divorce?

Theological interpretations of divorce are varied. Barber (1984) suggests that Christian positions tend to fall into four main categories (see also House, 1990; Worthington, 1990a):

1. Marriage is permanent—period. This view sees no exceptions to marriage being permanent (Laney, 1981).

2. Marriage is permanent—except for adultery and abandonment. This position sees adultery as violating the marital covenant and leaving open the possibility of divorce (Mt 5:32; 19:9). In the early church non-Christian spouses of Christian converts sometimes wanted to abandon or divorce their Christian spouse. Paul handled this by saying the Christian should stay with the partner, but divorce is permissible if the non-Christian initiates it (1 Cor 7:19). These two exceptions form the only legitimate grounds for divorce in the view of many evangelical Christians (Bromily, 1980; Thompson, 1989).

3. Marriage is permanent—except for exceptional circumstances. This view broadens the scope of legitimate grounds for divorce from only adultery and desertion in the previous view. Some interpret the "hardness of heart" mentioned by Jesus (Mk 10:4-5) as including adultery, physical abuse, unrepentant substance abuse or possibly severe verbal abuse.

4. Marriage is permanent—except when annulled by a church tribunal. In the Roman Catholic tradition church tribunals can annul a marriage.

Divorce can become a complicated issue even within these various positions. One might be tempted to be comforted by the idea that delineating ethical positions is not the main role of a therapist. The AAMFT code of ethics even says, "In all circumstances, the therapist will clearly advise a client that the decision to separate or divorce is the responsibility solely of the client" (1979). Margolin (1982) points out, however, that client responsibility for decisions does not preclude influence from the therapist. It would be naive to suggest that clients were not influenced by therapist values, and the desirability of this reflects a strong individualistic bias. The main issue seems to be whether the therapist seeks to impose a view on the client in a manner that violates client autonomy. Principle D of the "Ethical Principles of Psychologists and Code of Conduct" (APA, 1992) states the importance of respect for people's rights and dignity. Autonomy and self-determination are two essential rights psychologists are to respect.

Principle B of the code of conduct says that integrity involves psychologists' being "aware of their own belief systems, values, needs, and limitations" (APA, 1992). Margolin (1982) likewise indicates that family therapists should become aware of their own values. If therapist values inevitably influence clients, then it would seem wise for the marital therapist to reflect on what his or her position is regarding divorce.

How does the Christian therapist deal with divorce once he or she has sorted out a theological interpretation? First, therapists should ask themselves how their own values may influence clinical practice (Margolin, 1982). Does the therapist become anxious or angry when clients mention divorce, or avoid the topic altogether, even when clients mention it repeatedly? What are the therapist's personal experiences with divorce? Did the therapist's parents or a sibling divorce? Has the therapist divorced? People often deceive themselves to justify their own experiences, so a therapist has an ethical and moral responsibility to examine his or her personal experiences and reflect on how those influence his or her attitudes and behaviors concerning divorce. Discussing the issue of divorce with other Christian marital therapists may also be helpful.

Second, marital therapists can clarify their role to the client. While a therapist can assist clients in considering ethical positions, particularly if the therapist is familiar with the client's religious tradition, the therapist is not a professional theologian. Therapists should show the humility to work within their competence and refer clients to religious professionals for more extensive theological reflection. Unfortunately, according to research, such referrals rarely are made (Meylink and Gorsuch, 1988). Care should be taken to understand the client's expectations about the therapist's role, preferably at the outset of therapy.

Therapists can facilitate clients' understanding of their own values in light of the potential spiritual and psychological consequences regarding divorce. Some clients who are serious about divorce may believe that divorce will solve all of their problems. Therapists who treat the research on divorce fairly can challenge such idealism supportively without interfering with client autonomy. For example, divorce does not end conflict with the spouse in at least half of all cases; divorce usually results in economic burdens on both the man and the woman, but especially the woman; the man generally experiences decrements of happiness and health after divorce; children of divorce experience short- and long-term negative results of divorce (see Emery, 1988; Wallerstein and Blakeslee, 1990, for two reviews).

Fourth, Christian therapists can inform their clients of their own theological positions on divorce in a spirit of grace and humility (Margolin, 1982). Many clients may wonder about the therapist's values without ever asking directly. At the same time, informing a couple of one's theological position on divorce may not always be necessary even if divorce is mentioned by the clients. Some partners will threaten divorce during marital therapy in a manipulative manner that does not represent their true feelings. Therapists can overreact to such coercion rather than recognizing the purpose behind it.

What if the clients decide to divorce? How does a therapist who may be ideologically opposed to divorce behave if the partners decide to divorce? Christian marital therapists should remember that the Christian faith deals with grace and forgiveness. Many Christians will see divorce as unfortunate in any situation. Christian marital therapists can offer troubled couples the opportunity to work out their problems rather than simply giving in to the permissive attitudes toward divorce advocated by our culture. But even when divorce involves sin, it is not unforgivable. Christian therapists who live by faith working through love can model God's redemptive love to those who choose divorce.

Christian therapists can work with pastors to educate congregations about divorce, to foster a climate of acceptance and forgiveness, and to encourage couples to seek counseling before problems get out of control.

Spouse abuse. Spouse abuse is ugly. Christian therapists often don't want to believe that other Christians can actually act violently against a spouse. Therapists thus may avoid such painful revelations by failing to acquaint themselves with the signs of abuse, not asking spouses if they act violently toward one another, and even making excuses when violence is uncovered. But spouse abuse happens—more frequently than we might think (Alsdurf and Alsdurf, 1989; Whipple, 1987).

Probably the most quoted verse in the case of spouse abuse is Malachi 2:16: " 'I hate divorce,' says the LORD." Pastors, counselors and friends sense the threat to a marriage's stability when physical abuse becomes evident, and they may react by trying to preserve the marriage through quoting this verse. Ironically, the second part of the verse is almost continually ignored: "and I hate a man's covering himself with violence." Given that the two statements occur within the same sentence, therapists and clients should engage in careful theological analysis prior to deciding which principle is the more important.

Physical abuse in a marriage presents a difficult moral decision. Glib admonitions to the wife to submit to her husband's authority and glib assurances by the husband, wife or both that the violence won't happen again are belied by research, which shows that an abusing spouse will usually continue to abuse unless actively stopped (Gelles, 1982).

The therapist has the dual ethical duty first to ensure that the client comes to no harm and second to attempt to promote beneficence. This would suggest that the first approach to a marriage in which the wife has been (or might reasonably be expected to be) harmed is to protect her through separation or even legal recourse. Rather than assume that the abusive behavior can be eliminated through promoting better communication, conflict resolution or intimacy, the therapist must deal directly with the physical threat. Then and only then should marriage therapy seek to improve the relationship.

Definitions of marriage. The job of the Christian marital therapist is further complicated by the plethora of definitions of marriage that exist in our society. Postmodern culture celebrates diversity, and marriage has been largely stripped of its symbolic religious significance. Christians are likely to face important issues with regard to defining marriage when confronted by couples who cohabit or by homosexual couples.

For Christians who see cohabitation and homosexuality as clear violations of God's Word, these clients will present obvious difficulties. Should a Christian counsel such couples at all? Christian therapists are likely to differ in their ethical decisions about these situations. One approach would be for therapists to make their own values clear to the cohabiting couple by telling them the potential spiritual and psychological risks if they continue in their sin (Worthington, 1989). Spiritual risks might involve consequences of a rebellious spirit or of deliberately sinning, if the couple believed their cohabitation to be sin. Psychological risks might include the clearly demonstrated likelihood of increased divorce after marriage and all the negative psychological outcomes of divorce.

The therapist might then help the cohabiting couple improve their relationship with the goal of terminating the cohabitation through marriage, breaking up or separating, and ending sexual relations. Sexual counseling for the cohabiting couple and couples therapy with homosexuals are not recommended for the Christian therapist.

Of course, problems can occur if the therapist's goals and the clients' goals do not coincide. For example, the clients might not want to end sexual relations, marry or end their cohabitation. What should the therapist do then? Goals in psychotherapy are not always shared between client, therapist and community representatives. Strupp, Hadley and Gomez-Schwartz (1977) have described therapy as a negotiation among the involved parties. For instance, a client might have a paranoid delusion that the therapist wants to eliminate but the client does not. One obligation of the therapist is to show the client why the behavior is perceived as bad or harmful by the therapist, even though the client perceives the behavior as good. The therapist does not discontinue therapy merely because disagreement exists concerning goals. Further, community representatives might have different goals for the client than do the counselor or client. For instance, a mother might want her adolescent son to obey her, while the son might want independence and the counselor might want the son to mature. Goals are negotiated throughout therapy—sometimes more overtly than at other times.

Issues Arising from Research and Practice

Counseling approaches must be evaluated to see whether the intended goals are accomplished. Some approaches to marital therapy may prove more effective with clients of a certain age, ethnicity, religious orientation or level of marital adjustment. Research can and must be done on Christian marital counseling, premarital counseling and marriage enrichment programs.

Marriage counseling. Christian counseling might be considered still in the early stages of development. But the paucity of research on Christian marriage counseling (Worthington, Shortz and McCullough, 1993) should be a major concern to Christian therapists. How do we know the counseling we are doing is effective? How long do we continue to practice without demonstrating treatment effectiveness? The APA code of conduct (1.06) says psychologists will "rely on scientifically and professionally derived knowledge when making scientific or professional judgments or when engaging in scholarly or professional endeavors" (1992). A commitment to excellence requires consistently evaluating one's work.

Many Christians are less committed to an epistemology of empiricism than are secular psychologists. Many would look first to Scripture for its revelation about counseling. However, Scripture is silent about the technology of marital counseling. True, it offers guidelines about love, marriage and helping others, but *justifying* a particular counseling approach by using Scripture is inappropriate. Supporting one's stance as more or less consistent with Scripture is clearly desirable for Christians, but one should not claim scriptural approval of a particular counseling method. Without unambiguous scriptural guidance, marital therapists should look to general revelation (evidence in the natural realm) for support. This should be an ethical mandate, but it has seldom been considered to date.

Premarital counseling. Many churches require or strongly recommend premarital counseling for couples pursuing marriage, yet almost no empirical research has been done on Christian premarital counseling. Stanley and Trathen (1994) have developed Christian PREP (Prevention and Relationship Enhancement Program) based on Markman's well-researched PREP, which uses cognitive-behavioral skills for conflict resolution (Markman et al., 1993). Research on Christian PREP's effectiveness has not yet been published. The research on many secular premarital counseling programs generally demonstrates that programs are not very effective unless couples receive training in communication and conflict-resolution skills, and feedback about their performance (Stanley and Trathen, 1994).

There is also some debate as to whether it is better to intervene prior to marriage, in the first six months following marriage, or both (Worthington, 1990). This depends in part on whether one adopts a philosophy that stresses rehabilitation of troubled marriages, prevention of marital problems or promotion of positive marriages. Still, evidence suggests that couples might be more realistic about and invested in interventions six months or so after the marriage ceremony than they are before marriage. These are fundamentally questions for empirical evaluation. Since pastors still do most of the premarital counseling (Williams, 1992), the role of Christian therapists might be to assist pastors in evaluating their programs or at least consulting about the research literature on premarital counseling.

Marriage enrichment. Programs for marriage enrichment are aimed at improving the marriages of well-functioning couples. Churches often enthusiastically recommend these programs to all their members, and research has shown several marriage enrichment programs can be effective (Markman et al., 1993; Worthington, Buston and Hammonds, 1989). But churches rarely help couples to assess their marriage to see if the level of conflict indicates that an enrichment program is not appropriate. Extremely troubled couples may become more frustrated by an enrichment program that only glosses over issues that are producing tremendous strain on their marriage. In an even worse scenario, highly troubled couples may begin to approach enrichment programs as though they were counseling sessions and escalate their conflict without trained professionals to assist them in managing it. If this becomes obvious to other couples it might even interfere with the effectiveness of the entire program. Again, Christian therapists could help churches develop and evaluate marriage enrichment programs that are based on competent assessment and informed by research on effective programs.

Conclusion

We have attempted to provide an approach to ethics that integrates Christian and professional principles. We have also tried to remain true to Christian virtues and the theme of "faith working through love." It is always tempting to suggest an invariant ordering of ethical principles or to imply that reliance on a single principle or small set of principles would clarify most ethical issues, but that is not the case. Ethics is an enterprise that must be engaged in light of Scripture, theology, the Christian community (including the community of Christian professionals) and even the secular community. In many ways ethics will always be based on value-informed discussions of dilemmas. However, Christians need not rely only on situation ethics or secular codes of ethics. Christians are informed by the greatest story ever told—that of Jesus laying down his divinity to take human form and then laying down his human life to purchase people. Primary Christian virtues are faith working through love and humility, and this should lead those who follow Christ to remember the limitations of human knowledge. Given such humility, we must recognize our weaknesses. Grace, confession and forgiveness should always have a prominent place in Christian ethical reflection.

References

Alsdurf, J., and P. Alsdurf. 1989. *Battered into Submission: The Tragedy of Wife Abuse in the Christian Home*. Downers Grove, Ill.: InterVarsity Press.

American Psychological Association. 1992. "Ethical Principles of Psychologists and Code of Conduct." *American Psychologist* 47: 1597-1611.

Anderson, R. S. 1990. *Christians Who Counsel: The Vocation of Wholistic Therapy*. Grand Rapids, Mich.: Zondervan.

Barber, C. J. 1984. "Marriage, Divorce and Remarriage." *Journal of Psychology and Theology* 12: 170-77.

Beach, S. R. H., E. E. Sandeen and K. D. O'Leary. 1990. *Depression in Marriage: A Model for Etiology and Treatment*. New York: Guilford.

Bloesch, D. G. 1987. *Freedom for Obedience: Evangelical Ethics in Contemporary Times*. San Francisco: Harper & Row.

Bromily, G. W. 1980. *God and Marriage*. Grand Rapids, Mich.: Eerdmans.

Christian Association for Psychological Studies. 1992. *Ethical Guidelines for the Christian Association for Psychological Studies*. New Braunfels, Tex.: Author.

Collins, G. R. 1991. *Excellence and Ethics in Counseling*. Dallas: Word.

Deschenes, P., and V. L. Shepperson. 1983. "The Ethics of Paradox." *Journal of Psychology and Theology* 11: 92-98.

Dienhart, J. W. 1982. *A Cognitive Approach to the Ethics of Counseling Psychology*. Washington, D.C.: University Press of America.

Dueck, A. C. 1987. "Ethical Contexts of Healing: Ecclesia and Praxis." *Pastoral Psychology* 36: 49-62.

Dueck, A. C. 1991. "Metaphors, Models, Paradigms and Stories in Family Therapy," in *Family Therapy: Christian Perspectives*, ed. H. Vande Kemp. Grand Rapids, Mich.: Baker.

Emery, R. E. 1988. *Marriage, Divorce and Children's Adjustment*. Newbury Park, Calif.: Sage.

Gelles, R. 1982. "Applying Research on Family Violence to Clinical Practice." *Journal of Marriage and the Family* 44: 9-20.

Gurman, A. S., and D. P. Kniskern. 1981. "Family Therapy Outcome Research: Knowns and Unknowns," in *Handbook of Family Therapy*, ed. A. S. Gurman and D. P.

Kniskern. New York: Brunner/Mazel.

Haley, J. 1984. "Marriage or Family Therapy?" *American Journal of Family Therapy* 12(2): 3-14.

Harper, R. A. 1985. "Limitations of Marriage and Family Therapy." *Voices* 21(2): 26-31.

Hauerwas, S. 1981. *A Community of Character: Toward a Constructive Christian Social Ethic.* Notre Dame, Ind.: University of Notre Dame Press.

House, H. W., ed. 1990. *Divorce and Remarriage: Four Christian Views.* Downers Grove, Ill.: InterVarsity Press.

Huber, C. H., and L. G. Baruth. 1987. *Ethical, Legal and Professional Issues in the Practice of Marriage and Family Therapy.* Columbus, Ohio: Merrill.

Jones, S. L., and R. E. Butman. 1991. *Modern Psychotherapies: A Comprehensive Christian Appraisal.* Downers Grove, Ill.: InterVarsity Press.

Jordan, A. E., and N. M. Meara. 1990. "Ethics and the Professional Practice of Psychologists: The Role of Virtues and Principles." *Professional Psychology: Research and Practice* 21: 107-14.

Laney, J. C. 1981. *The Divorce Myth.* Minneapolis: Bethany.

Lewis, K. N., and D. L. Epperson. 1991. "Values, Pretherapy Information and Informed Consent in Christian Counseling." *Journal of Psychology and Christianity* 10: 113-31.

Lewis, K. N., and D. A. Lewis. 1985. "Pretherapy Information, Counselor Influence and Value Similarity: Impact on Female Clients' Reactions." *Counseling and Values* 29: 151-63.

MacIntyre, A. 1981. *After Virtue.* Notre Dame, Ind.: University of Notre Dame Press.

Margolin, G. 1982. "Ethical and Legal Considerations in Marital and Family Therapy." *American Psychologist* 7: 788-801.

Markman, H. J., M. J. Resnick, F. J. Floyd, S. M. Stanley and M. Clements. 1993. "Preventing Marital Distress Through Communication and Conflict Management Training: A Four- and Five-Year Follow-up." *Journal of Consulting and Clinical Psychology* 61: 70-77.

Meylink, W. D., and R. L. Gorsuch. 1988. "Relationship Between Clergy and Psychologists: The Empirical Data." *Journal of Psychology and Christianity* 7(1): 56-72.

Oordt, M. S. 1990. "Ethics of Practice Among Christian Psychologists: A Pilot Study." *Journal of Psychology and Theology* 18: 255-60.

Ohlschlager, G., and P. Mosgofian. 1992. *Law for the Christian Counselor: A Guidebook for Clinicians and Pastors.* Dallas: Word.

Patten, C., T. Barnett and D. Houlihan. 1991. "Ethics in Marriage and Family Therapy: A Review of the Literature." *Professional Psychology: Research and Practice* 22: 171-75.

Pope, K. S., B. G. Tabachnick and P. Keith-Spiegel. 1987. "Ethics of Practice: The Beliefs and Behaviors of Psychologists as Therapists." *American Psychologist* 42: 993-1006.

Stanley, S. M., and D. W. Trathen. 1994. "Christian PREP: An Empirically Based Model for Marital and Premarital Intervention." *Journal of Psychology and Christianity* 13: 158-65.

Strupp, H. H., S. W. Hadley and B. Gomez-Schwartz. 1977. *Psychotherapy for Better or Worse.* New York: Jason Aronson.

Thompson, D. A. 1989. *Counseling and Divorce.* Dallas: Word.

VandenBos, G. R., and J. Stapp. 1983. "Service Providers in Psychology: Results of the 1982 APA Human Resources Survey." *American Psychologist* 38: 1330-52.

Vesper, J. H., and G. W. Brock. 1991. *Ethics, Legalities and Professional Practice Issues in Marriage and Family Therapy.* Boston: Allyn and Bacon.

Virkler, H. A. 1992. *Broken Promises: Understanding, Healing and Preventing Affairs in Christian Marriages.* Dallas: Word.

Wallerstein, J. S., and S. Blakeslee. 1990. *Second Chances: Men, Women and Children a Decade After Divorce.* New York: Ticknor & Fields.

Weeks, G. R., and L. L'Abate. 1982. *Paradoxical Psychotherapy: Theory and Practice with Individuals, Couples and Families.* New York: Brunner/Mazel.

Whan, M. 1983. "Tricks of the Trade: Questionable Theory and Practice in Family Therapy." *British Journal of Social Work* 13: 321-37.

Whipple, V. 1987. "Counseling Battered Women from Fundamentalist Churches." *Journal of Marital and Family Therapy* 13: 251-58.

Wiley, M. O., and P. B. Ray. 1986. "Counseling Supervision by Developmental Level." *Journal of Counseling Psychology* 33: 439-45.

Worthington, E. L., Jr. 1989. *Marriage Counseling: A Christian Approach to Counseling Couples.* Downers Grove, Ill.: InterVarsity Press.

———. 1990. *Counseling Before Marriage.* Dallas: Word.

Worthington, E. L., Jr., B. G. Buston and T. M. Hammonds. 1989. "A Component Analysis of Marriage Enrichment: Information and Treatment Modality." *Journal for Counseling and Development* 67: 555-60.

Worthington, E. L., Jr., and H. DeVries. 1990. "Individual, Marital and Family Therapy: Empirical, Pragmatic and Value Considerations." *Journal of Couples Therapy* 1(1): 77-90.

Worthington, E. L., Jr., and D. McMurry. 1994. *Marriage Conflicts.* Grand Rapids, Mich.: Baker.

Worthington, E. L., Jr., J. L. Shortz and M. E. McCullough. 1993. "A Call for Emphasis on Scholarship on Christian Marriage and Marriage Counseling." *Journal of Psychology and Christianity* 12: 13-23.

Chapter 9

THE
HOMOSEXUAL
CLIENT

Mark A. Yarhouse &
Stanton L. Jones

---

*H*ow to be a Christian clinician, in particular how to bring one's Christianity
to bear on one's professional or clinical work, is extraordinarily difficult, and
there is not much by way of guidance or precedent with respect to it. Part of
what makes our professional work so complicated is that clinicians, like all
Christian professionals, are members of several communities, as Plantinga (1993)
observed as he reflected on the responsibilities of Christians in philosophy. For
Christian mental health practitioners these include the Christian community, a
local church community, the community of Christian clinicians, the professional
community of practitioners and many others. Although Christian clinicians may
identify self-consciously with the Christian community, we are still members of
the mental health community. Plantinga notes that although our first responsibility is to Christ and to the Christian community, and not to the psychological
community at large, we still have a responsibility to the psychological community, made serious in part because of its connection with our first responsibility.

This concern for the ordering of our responsibilities should be most directly
evident to Christian practitioners in the care and treatment of homosexual
persons. As we consider therapy with homosexuals we must ponder regularly
and often the question of what form a distinctively Christian response to
homosexuality should take. At the same time we carry responsibilities to the
professional mental health community: ethical standards set in place to ensure
the ethical treatment of all clients and to hold practitioners accountable within

and to their profession. Clinical practice is malleable; the Christian who engages in clinical work will seek to learn from the practice and from the ethical standards as well as contribute to the shaping of both. However, there are appropriate forums for shaping practice and standards, and the clinical setting (as opposed to professional journals, conventions and so on) is *not* an appropriate place to challenge, shape or take liberties with ethical standards, even if we believe Christians have an "inside track" on the ethical care of persons and perspectives on sexual behavior.

This chapter focuses on the treatment of persons who are struggling with a homosexual orientation or inclinations toward homosexual behavior. We recognize, however, that many homosexuals who enter therapy do not seek treatment for change of orientation or behavior; rather, they enter therapy for concerns related to mood disorders, anxiety disorders, sexual dysfunctions, interpersonal conflicts and so on. The question of the Christian's responsibility to assist homosexual persons in these and other areas (and how that responsibility relates to the existing ethical principles) is beyond the scope of this chapter. However, we urge Christian clinicians to consider and apply each of the ethical principles, especially those pertaining to competency and concern for others' welfare, and to critically evaluate their capacity to work effectively with homosexual persons who come for help for a variety of reasons.

The ethical considerations inherent in the treatment of homosexuals who are looking for a change in their orientation or behavior are concerns Christian practitioners may not have thought through explicitly and in a focused way. Although there is much diversity in the training and education of Christian clinicians (spanning such fields as social work, pastoral care, clinical and counseling psychology, and marriage and family therapy), each mental health profession is guided by ethical principles that are generally equivalent, in that each addresses issues of competency, integrity, concern for others' welfare and so on.

For clarity of presentation we will consider the APA's code of conduct, making application to the treatment care of homosexual clients by Christian clinicians. The APA's "Ethical Principles of Psychologists and Code of Conduct" (or "Ethics Code"; APA, 1992) consists of a preamble, six general principles and a number of specific ethical standards. The preamble and general principles are "aspirational goals"; although they are not enforceable rules, they are intended for consideration by mental health providers in arriving at an ethical course of action in a particular circumstance. They are also used to interpret the ethical standards, which are specific, enforceable rules pertaining to the ethical conduct of clinicians.

Principle A: Competence
Psychologists strive to maintain high standards of competence in their work.

They recognize the boundaries of their particular competencies and the limitations of their expertise. They provide only those services and use only those techniques for which they are qualified by education, training, or experience. Psychologists are cognizant of the fact that the competencies required in serving, teaching, and/or studying groups of people vary with the distinctive characteristics of those groups. In those areas in which recognized professional standards do not yet exist, psychologists exercise careful judgment and take appropriate precautions to protect the welfare of those with whom they work. They maintain knowledge of relevant scientific and professional information related to the services they render, and they recognize the need for ongoing education. Psychologists make appropriate use of scientific, professional, technical, and administrative resources. (APA, 1992, p. 1599)

The emphasis of this first principle is that practitioners "recognize the boundaries of their particular competencies and the limitations of their expertise." Competence is determined by such things as education and training, and competencies required for ethical treatment of groups of people vary according to the "distinctive characteristics of those groups." This principle also notes that if professional standards do not yet exist in a given area, clinicians are to be cautious to protect the welfare of their clients, exercising "careful judgment" on their behalf.

What are the implications of this principle for Christian practitioners and the ethical treatment of homosexuals? To begin, not every Christian clinician is competent to treat homosexuals on the basis of being either a Christian or a clinician. Christians sometimes confuse Christian morality and religious belief with professional ability, substituting orthodoxy for competency. We might be inclined to believe that because of the power of the Holy Spirit, Christians are able to do "all things" (Phil 4:13), including offering successful treatment for change to all homosexual clients. However, we must distinguish between the power of the Holy Spirit to do good works through us and our own competence as indicated by the APA ethics code. As Christians working under the ethical standards of our profession, if we are not competent—if we do not have the education, training, supervised experience or appropriate professional experience to offer treatment—we should not attempt to provide such services to our clients.

There is also no guarantee we can always provide effective treatment as clinicians. However the orientation toward homosexual preference develops, there is substantial agreement that it is not a preference that is easily amenable to change by a simple act of the will. Various methods have been used for the treatment of homosexual persons, including psychoanalysis (Bieber et al., 1962; Bieber, 1976; Socarides, 1978) and directive behavioral sex therapy (Adams and Sturgis, 1977; Masters and Johnson, 1979). Reported "success" rates have never been outstanding or suggestive of an easy path to change for the homosexual person, ranging between 33 percent (Bieber, 1976) and 50-60 percent (Masters and Johnson, 1979) at best. In addition, there is no one treatment program for homosexuals recognized by most practitioners, and there is debate as to the appropriateness of providing reorientation treatment under any circumstances (e.g., Nicolosi, 1991; cf. Haldeman, 1994; Ritter and O'Neill, 1989; Shannon and Woods, 1991; Youngstrom, 1991).

As one might suspect, homosexuality is an area in which recognized standards for preparatory training do not yet exist, either in secular or in Christian professional training programs. The general consensus in the mental health community is that no one theory of homosexuality can explain such a diverse phenomenon. It certainly seems that there is no completely determinative genetic, hormonal or psychological cause of homosexual orientation. Instead there appear to be a number of facilitating influences that provide a push in the direction of homosexuality for some persons (see Byne and Parsons, 1993). What steps ought we to take, then, to ensure the competence of our work and to protect our homosexual clients from harm? First, those offering treatment to homosexual clients are obligated to maintain a high level of awareness of current scientific and professional information. The most frequently cited scientific topics are those in the areas of prevalence, etiology, status as a mental disorder and efficacy of change methods (see Burr, 1993; Byne and Parsons, 1993; Jones and Workman, 1989; Jones and Yarhouse, 1997). Christian clinicians should be aware of the current state of thinking in these areas.

Second, we should rely on "scientifically and professionally derived knowledge when making . . . professional judgments" (APA, 1992, 1.06). Theory, practice and research are interrelated. Therapists have an ethical responsibility to ground their practice in both theory and research. Practitioners operating without a theoretical and empirical foundation are left without a compelling rationale for formulating therapeutic goals and for developing techniques or interventions for accomplishing these goals. As professional mental health care providers we should not perform extraordinary interventions that have no ground in scientific and professional findings (e.g., Ross and Stalstrom, 1979). Finally, in addition to acquiring specialized knowledge about homosexual people in general, we should be increasingly aware of and sensitive to the meaning of a homosexual orientation, identity (including stigma or feelings of self-contempt) and behavior to the particular individuals to whom we offer therapy.

Principle B: Integrity

Psychologists seek to promote integrity in the science, teaching, and practice of psychology. . . . In describing or reporting their qualifications, services, products, fees, research, or teaching, they do not make statements that are false, misleading, or deceptive. Psychologists strive to be aware of their own belief systems, values, needs, and limitations and the effect of these on their work. To the extent feasible, they attempt to clarify for relevant parties the roles they are performing and to function appropriately in accordance with those roles. Psychologists avoid improper and potentially harmful dual relationships. (APA, 1992, p. 1599)

As professionals we are to promote integrity in the science and practice of our work. We are to be honest, fair and respectful of others, particularly as we describe our qualifications and services and as we become aware of our own belief systems and values and the effect of these beliefs and values on our work. As we offer treatment to homosexual clients we are to inform them of our services, using grammar and language that is "reasonably understandable to the recipient of those services," and offer "appropriate information beforehand about the nature of such services" (APA, 1992, 1.07).

In addition, we are to be honest about the current research findings on homosexuality or homosexual behavior as we discuss treatment with homosexuals. For example, we have an obligation to be honest that current research on what homosexuality *is* has been tremendously problematic. We can concur with Haldeman (1994) that the construct of sexual orientation is nebulous. Not only do definitions of sexual orientation vary, but individuals experience their own subjective sense of sexual orientation differently. Those who describe themselves as homosexual range from the male who cannot remember a time when he did not feel "different" to the female who embraces homosexuality after years of abuse at the hands of a male or as a self-consciously chosen political statement.

The complex nature of what constitutes sexual orientation and its development in individuals has left many questions unanswered. As Byne and Parsons (1993) observe, some scientists, dissatisfied with psychosocial explanations of homosexuality, are turning to biology "by default," even though "the biologic alternatives seem to have no greater explanatory value" for uncovering the causes of homosexuality (p. 236). Even neurobiology, which accounts for much of the current research, offers few clear answers. The remarkable publicity that certain findings have received may merely confuse the matter. "It is imperative that clinicians and behavioral scientists begin to appreciate the complexities of sexual orientation and resist the urge to search for simplistic explanations, either psychosocial or biologic" (Byne and Parsons, 1993, p. 236; for a discussion of the factors that may contribute to a homosexual orientation and the difficulties faced by scientists researching in this area, see Byne and Parsons, 1993; Jones and Workman, 1989).

Part of what it means for practitioners to work with integrity is admitting that we do not know why homosexual proclivities exist in each and every person who experiences such inclinations. For the non-Christian as for the Christian, this can be a deeply perplexing, deeply disturbing realization. But given the ethical standard of integrity, and despite the consideration that the subject matter is politically charged and that much research is motivated by personal as well as scientific concerns, we are called to honesty regarding the current knowledge and *lack of available knowledge* in the study of homosexuality.

Finally, as was mentioned earlier, Christians must avoid the assumption that because they have a moral evaluative framework they therefore have the professional qualifications to do good work with homosexual clients. As Principle B states, we are to "strive to be aware of [our] own belief systems, values, needs, and limitations and the effect of these on [our] work." Although we do not believe that our moral evaluative framework limits our professional capacity to work with homosexual clients, we are concerned that Christians may assume that their moral evaluation of homosexual behavior sufficiently qualifies them to work with homosexuals in a professional capacity. Professional integrity and competency overlap to some extent conceptually and practically, and Christian mental health care providers must examine whether or not their belief systems and values substitute for the qualifications necessary to work with integrity with homosexual clients.

Principle C: Professional and Scientific Responsibility

Psychologists uphold professional standards of conduct, clarify their professional roles and obligations, accept appropriate responsibility for their behavior, and adapt their methods to the needs of different populations. Psychologists consult with, refer to, or cooperate with other professionals and institutions to the extent needed to serve the best interests of their patients, clients, or other recipients of their services. . . . When appropriate, they consult with colleagues in order to prevent or avoid unethical conduct. (APA, 1992, p. 1599)

The emphasis of this third principle is that clinicians accept responsibility for the work we do with our clients and that we consult with or refer to other professionals if doing so is in the best interest of our clients. In addition, we are to adapt our services to the best interests of our clients.

Some practitioners assume that being a professional means having the ability to assist anyone with any problem. A more accurate understanding of being a professional involves recognizing that at times therapists' values and those of their clients will conflict to such an extent that therapists will be ethically obligated to assess their ability to function professionally. Tjeltveit (1986) suggests that therapists should consider referring clients when moral, religious or political values are central to the client's presenting problem and (a) the limits of their professional competence have been reached, (b) they experience significant discomfort with their client's values, (c) they are unable to work objectively or (d) they have reason to believe that if therapy continues they will impose their value commitments on their client. If these circumstances arise, Tjeltveit suggests therapists refer such clients to a therapist who shares or is closer to sharing the client's moral, religious or political values or is not struggling in the areas identified above.

It is important for clinicians to sort out what we believe and how we feel about homosexuality and homosexual behavior. Christian clinicians must be honest about our own limitations, and we must be honest with potential clients when we think value conflicts will interfere with the therapeutic relationship. The beliefs (including moral evaluations) and feelings we have about homosexuality and homosexual behavior contribute to the way the presenting problem is conceptualized. Different background assumptions will lead to different formulations, which will, in turn, lead directly to decisions to refer, to affirm the homosexual inclinations, behavior and lifestyle, or to pursue a theoretically based change process or strategy. Clinicians who do not refer these clients for whatever reason choose between affirming homosexual orientation and behavior, attempting to facilitate change of sexual orientation or behavior if the client indicates interest, or accepting a client's homosexual orientation as a given but attempting to modify behavior to fall within the parameters of a moral evaluative framework held by the client. Keeping in mind the ethical obligation to adapt our services to the best interests of our clients, Christian clinicians must carefully assess the client's desire to change orientation or behavior.

Principle D: Respect for People's Rights and Dignity

Psychologists accord appropriate respect to the fundamental rights, dignity, and worth of all people. They respect the rights of individuals to privacy, confidentiality, self-determination, and autonomy. . . . Psychologists are aware of cultural, individual, and role differences, including those due to age, gender, race, ethnicity, national origin, religion, sexual orientation, disability, language, and socioeconomic status. Psychologists try to eliminate the effect on their work of biases based on those factors, and they do not knowingly participate in or condone unfair discriminatory practice. (APA, 1992, pp. 1599-1600)

Perhaps what is most relevant to our discussion of homosexuality is that this principle calls clinicians to respect clients' rights to "privacy, confidentiality, self-determination, and autonomy," and that we are to be aware of differences, including those of sexual orientation.

One way to help ensure a sense of autonomy and self-determination in our clients is through informed consent. Clients should be able to decide whether or not to attempt to modify their sexual orientation or to learn new behaviors and coping mechanisms that do not have as their goal the modification of sexual orientation. If we are proficient with treatment approaches that might prove efficacious, and if clients, after exploring the consequences of various treatment modalities and other alternatives to treatment, choose to be involved in the change process, we are in the position to assist them by attempting to modify their sexual orientation or behaviors. Debate exists as to what constitutes "efficacious treatment," what appropriate alternatives are, and what the goals of the change process might entail (see Haldeman, 1991, 1994). The critical point under this principle for ethical conduct, however, is that informed consent is required at these levels of intervention to ensure proper respect for individual autonomy and self-determination.

The amount and kind of information relevant to our client's decision-making suggests that a truly comprehensive presentation is warranted regarding the dictates of research findings. Informed consent to any intervention is directly related to the amount of information clients have as to what is causing their difficulties, the potential benefits and risks of treatment, the various treatments available, and the possible course of their behavior with or without treatment (Corey, Corey and Callahan, 1993; Keith-Spiegel and Koocher, 1985). To the extent that we seek true informed consent from our clients, our obligation is to provide them with a maximum amount of information pertaining to the various options available and under consideration.

It is increasingly common in the literature advocating homosexual behavior and lifestyle to assert that no homosexual freely chooses to modify his or her sexual orientation (Davison, 1976, 1982; Haldeman, 1991; Halleck, 1976; Murphy, 1992). It is argued that voluntary treatment is a myth and that any "volunteer" is merely succumbing to cultural and societal pressures and internalized homophobia:

> Some will say that an individual has the "right to choose" conversion treatments. Such a choice, however, is almost always based on the internalized effects of a hostile family and an intolerant society. . . . To view self-negating homosexuals seeking change otherwise is to deny the significant impact of negative social stigma that confronts the gay person at every step. (Haldeman, 1991, p. 160)

Despite the generalization that homosexuals who choose treatment "almost always" do so because of internalized familial hostility and societal intolerance—a generalization lacking empirical support—we can agree with proponents of homosexual behavior that our culture is undoubtedly heterosexual in majority, and that it is probably the case that some homosexuals are drawn to treatment out of powerful feelings of lack of acceptance. This of course has no logical bearing on whether many of those same homosexuals or other homosexuals evaluate their behavior and inclinations and choose to enter therapy for a variety of other reasons or a combination of reasons (e.g., the homosexual who has come to the conclusion that homosexual behavior is immoral). The unsubstantiated claim that the majority of homosexuals who enter treatment programs do so only (or even primarily) because they are succumbing to societal pressures explicitly denies the "autonomy" and "self-determination" of the homosexual seeking change.

A Christian account of homosexuality takes seriously the question of whether or not people are free or capable of "agency," which is defined as "the capacity for an organism to behave in compliance with, in addition to, in opposition to, or without regard for biological or sociological stimulations" (Rychlak, 1988, p. 84). Rather than ask whether it is moral or immoral to act on one's orientation or predisposition toward a given behavior, proponents claim that the behavioral sciences have rendered that question irrelevant (e.g., Sedgwick, 1988). However, Christian clinicians assume that persons are by and large capable of sorting out and identifying principles regarding what they ought to do and not do. We also assume that persons can exert their will in a desired direction and have some success in doing so independent of antecedent physiological, neurological, psychological and environmental conditions. Moreover, even in cases where individuals may be predisposed to a given act, the behavioral sciences have increasingly shown that causation cannot be understood in simplistic "caused" versus "free choice" terms. Rather, human behavior is seen to be the result of a *network* of factors that work together, and human choice cannot be eliminated as one of these factors.

In what sense is the concept of agency relevant to the ethical treatment of homosexual clients? If therapist and client take the concept of agency seriously and agree that homosexual behavior is a moral concern with various related or overlapping psychological aspects, then the human capacity to choose becomes enormously relevant to therapeutic conceptualizations and interventions. Clients can choose to make moral concerns a priority in therapy, and a homosexual client can legitimately choose to seek change.

Further, although we are to respect our client's rights to "privacy, confidentiality, self-determination and autonomy," all therapists have ideals to which they believe healthy, mature adults should aspire. A recent study by Bergin and Jensen (1990) indicated that over 50 percent of therapists value heterosexuality as preferable for clients. This admission implies that certain value assumptions undergird one's account of healthy adult behavior. Although it is not always clear what serves as the basis for secular ideals of health and maturity, Christian clinicians should not be surprised to find that their ideals for persons are generated from or find confirmation in their Christian belief system, just as alternative ideals for health and maturity are generated from alternative philosophical presuppositions, metaphysical and ethical sources (Jones, 1994; O'Donahue, 1989). As Halleck (1976) admits, accepting homosexuality and affirming the gay lifestyle is as much a value judgment as condemning it. Furthermore, it is conceivable that the therapist's acceptance of homosexual behavior as the necessary expression of self-actualization, and the concomitant effort to promote it as morally justified, may serve to exacerbate the potential guilt reaction of clients who, with equally compelling justification, see their homosexual behavior as morally unacceptable.

A final concern is that those who would deny homosexuals access to treatment for reorientation or behavior change may be advocating an unethical position. What happens to the individual homosexual who does not wish to affirm his or her homosexual identity through homoerotic behavior? Denying the right of the individual homosexual to seek treatment aimed at curbing homosexual inclinations or modifying homosexual behaviors is ethically questionable, as this "therapeutic" stand denies the client's right to dignity and autonomy as a person presumed capable of freely choosing treatment modalities and behavior.

Principle E: Concern for Others' Welfare

Psychologists seek to contribute to the welfare of those with whom they interact professionally. In their professional actions, psychologists weigh the welfare and rights of patients or clients. . . . When conflicts occur among psychologists' obligations or concerns, they attempt to resolve these conflicts and to perform their roles in a responsible fashion that avoids or minimizes harm. Psychologists are aware of real or ascribed differences in power between themselves and others, and they do not exploit or mislead other people during or after professional relationships. (APA, 1992, p. 1600)

The upshot of Principle E is that clinicians are ethically obligated to promote their clients' welfare. To sort out various ways in which client "welfare" can dovetail with a Christian understanding of homosexuality, it will be helpful to first review the status of homosexuality and the assumed implications of that status in the *Diagnostic and Statistical Manual of the American Psychiatric Association.*

In *DSM-I* homosexuality was categorized as "psychopathic personality with pathological sexuality" (1952). More than a decade later, in *DSM-II* (1968), it was listed under the category of "sociopathic personality disturbance," until it was removed from this category by the American Psychiatric Association's 1973 decision. The *DSM-III* did not list homosexuality as a mental disease, although a category existed called "egodystonic homosexuality," which referred to homosexuals who are dissatisfied with their homosexuality and seek help to change it (1980). There was no reference to homosexuality in the *DSM-IIIR,* and all that remained was mention of "sexual orientation distress," the suffering associated with an unwanted sexual orientation (1987). The *DSM-IV* also makes no reference to homosexuality and only briefly recognizes "persistent and marked distress about sexual orientation," which is cited as an example of a "Sexual Disorder Not Otherwise Specified" (1994, p. 538).

Proponents of homosexual behavior take the removal of homosexuality from the *DSM* and various published research on homosexuality to suggest or prescribe something about the wholesomeness and hence morality of homosexual acts: "The scientific evidence is sufficient to support the contention that homosexuality is not pathological or otherwise an inversion, developmental failure, or deviant form of life as such, but is rather a human variant, one that can be healthy and whole" (Majority Committee of the United Methodist Church, 1991, pp. 27-28). Interestingly, the removal of a behavioral pattern from a list of psychopathologies bears no necessary logical relation to endorsement of that pattern as healthy or whole.

The question of whether homosexuality is a pathology or whether individuals who manifest homosexual behavior should be regarded as mentally ill continues to be debated in psychological circles and also throughout the church. Many people in the mental health field continue to believe homosexuality is a pathology (Rudulph, 1988). Interestingly, the majority of psychiatrists around the globe continue to view sex between people of the same gender as a mental illness (APA, 1993). The debate tends to center around whether homosexuality is normal or pathological. If homosexuality is normal, it is argued, then clients who seek to change their sexual orientation should be discouraged or not allowed to seek such change (Haldeman, 1991). If, at the other extreme, homosexuality is a pathology, the failure to develop programs or provide therapeutic services for people who wish to change their behavior or become heterosexual would be unethical (Bieber, 1976). Of course, some conditions, behaviors or practices can be abnormal yet not fall into the category of psychopathology (e.g., "phase of life problem"; V62.89; APA, 1987). Along these same lines, practitioners might consider John Harvey's (1987) alternative designation of homosexuality as a "developmental abnormality." He notes that the debate over designating homosexuality as a pathology is a battle Christians do not have to fight.

In either case, psychologists work from conservative criteria for defining psychopathology. Homosexuality is therefore not regarded as a psychopathology in the same sense as schizophrenia or bipolar depression, and Christians should be the first to agree that the mental health system should have reservations about attaching a label to variant behavior patterns simply because they differ from those in the majority. We can also agree that the practice of diagnosing homosexuals ipso facto as suffering from psychopathology may be inappropriate depending on one's theoretical orientation; that is, the fact of being homosexual *in and of itself* may not warrant labeling a person as suffering from a mental illness. However, Christians have traditionally held that genital homosexual acts are immoral and that immorality is an abnormal (i.e., unintended by God) condition for persons. Consequently, homosexuality can and perhaps must be regarded by Christians as a problematic erotic orientation and homosexual acts as behavior from which to refrain.

Nevertheless, many advocates of homosexuality continue to argue that a homosexual lifestyle is an alternative lifestyle and that any questioning of this status as healthy and whole on the part of homosexuals themselves is simply (necessarily) a manifestation of internalized homophobia (e.g., Davison, 1982; Haldeman, 1991; Murphy, 1992). What is overlooked in such a conclusion is the alternative explanation that even in the case where guilt, anxiety or concern about an inclination for homoerotic behavior is experienced, it does not necessarily follow that this is an indication of internalized homophobia. One could with equal justification argue that guilt, anxiety or concern over one's involvement in homosexual behavior (or one's concern over inclinations toward such behavior) is due to questions of morality. Yet Haldeman (1994), a proponent for the morality of homosexual behavior, is representative of mental health professionals who allow the "sociocultural landscape" (p. 222) alone to determine personal morality: "For many individuals, sexual orientation is a variable construct subject to changes in erotic and affectual preference, as well as changes in social values and political philosophy that may ebb and flow throughout life" (p. 222). Surely one's personal moral philosophy must also be considered a variable in assessment and treatment planning. There is no compelling reason for clinicians to allow the sociocultural landscape alone to determine the morality of homosexual behavior or the extent to which we advocate the morality of homosexual behavior over and against personal moral convictions.

Despite the resistance of many therapists to acknowledge the moral dimension of the work they do with their clients, religious beliefs and moral questions affect many facets of human experience that are brought up in therapy. How people respond to guilt feelings, anxiety and moral questions are just a few of these areas. It is important for clients to understand what their beliefs mean to them, and Christian practitioners are in a unique position to provide a place where clients can explore their religious or moral concerns.

Ironically, some advocates of homosexual relations rely on similar assumptions concerning the place and magnitude of morality in therapy. Consider the following argument by an advocate for the morality of homosexual behavior:

Issues of morality are part of the fabric of the technology of psychotherapeutic change. . . . We risk much by not confronting the overwhelmingly lopsided power relationships in any therapeutic alliance and the fact that psychological interventions inevitably entail a judgment by the therapist of how, in a moral sense, a given client should shape his or her existence. Even therapies that view themselves as hands-off . . . set parameters for interventions. And if one refrains from suggesting a change, lest he impose his values on the client, is one not willy-nilly sanctioning the status quo, and is that not in itself a therapist decision about the goals of therapy? (Davison, 1991, p. 147)

Christian clinicians can concur that a "heavy moral responsibility is inherent to the conduct of psychotherapy" (p. 147). Christian practitioners must not maintain the illusion of so many of our peers that it is possible to offer therapy dispassionately, from a totally uncommitted standpoint. Many fail to see that supposed objectivity may be a hindrance (or worse) to good psychotherapy and that it may be far better to ground one's assumptions in an established, historic belief system, such as that found in the Christian tradition (see Jones, 1994).

If we agree that it is impossible to adopt a neutral value system with respect to any behavior, and that religious beliefs alter our valuative frame of reference, it becomes obvious that therapists who advocate an alternative lifestyle of homoerotic expression also exert an influence on their clients because of a new belief that homosexual acts are not necessarily undermining their client's (moral) welfare. Advocates of the morality of homoerotic behavior simply disagree with the traditional Christian account that such behavior is immoral. But where do we turn to resolve such a fundamental debate? Significantly, the behavioral sciences do not offer an answer to the moral debate: "To sustain a value claim requires the introduction of some form of reasoning beyond the statement of the facts. Thus, the empirical sciences, including psychology, cannot in themselves be used to settle questions of moral values" (Waterman, 1988, p. 291; cf. Haan, 1982; Jones and Yarhouse, 1993). Moral questions are philosophical and speculative by their very nature, and because no empirical observation will make certain which moral answers are correct, the debate over the morality of homosexual behavior may be at an ideological impasse.

In light of the above, are therapists ethically obligated, as some have argued, to address homosexual behavior in an affirmative manner (e.g., Buhrke and Douce, 1991)? No. The absence of pathology or even developmental abnormality (if such is the case) in homosexuality does not mean that psychologists are obligated to view all forms of behavior with moral indifference. Despite there being a significant number of people who engage in homosexual acts and whose behavior is supported by a subculture and its sexual ideology, some clients question the appropriateness of identifying with a class of people defined solely by sexual preference or orientation, especially as many are questioning the morality of homosexual acts. Homosexuality appears to be a case where moral latitude in problem formulation is especially applicable. Clinicians should also keep in mind that Principle E is concerned with the ethical obligation practitioners have for the welfare of clients. The term *welfare* suggests an appreciation for broader considerations than concepts such as psychopathology or even developmental abnormality can, by definition, include. For instance, consider the V Codes in the *DSM-IV,* which designate conditions that are not pathological yet are taken to be the focus of treatment (American Psychiatric Association, 1994). An example might be "partner relational problem" (1994, V61.1), a condition that does not indicate a mental disorder but that may nonetheless lead people to seek help from a psychologist. Another example, which is a recent addition in the *DSM-IV*, is that of "religious or spiritual problem" (1994, V62.61). The kinds of religious or spiritual problems that may lead people to seek help include "distressing experiences that involve loss or questioning of faith, problems associated with conversion to a new faith, or *questioning of other spiritual values*" (p. 685; our emphasis). For many clients religiously motivated moral concerns over homosexual behavior and the inclination to engage in such behavior fall under the category of religious or spiritual problem. Further, in light of evidence suggesting a modest but significant correlation between the similarity of therapist and client values and positive outcome in therapy (Kelly and Strupp, 1992), clients who consider homosexual acts immoral and seek help in curbing such desires and inclinations may increase the likelihood of positive outcome in therapy if they are seen by therapists with a similar understanding.

How should Christian clinicians proceed? It is probably best to assess the client's desire for change, including motivations, as well as the psychosexual history of the client's homoerotic inclinations. An investigation of an individual's total situation might suggest whether or not treatment should be indicated. We can assist clients as they weigh past experiences of homosexual identity and behavior against future repercussions if that role is abandoned, as they consider what they will give up as well as gain if they attempt to change their sexual behavior or identity, and as they consider the emotional as well as the economic price of such change. Christian practitioners should have as their aim to thoroughly discuss (a) possible gains and losses for the client if therapeutic intervention is successful, (b) possible consequences for the client if therapeutic intervention is unsuccessful, (c) current biological and psychological theories of homosexuality and how they relate to the client, (d) success rates of various treatment modalities, (e) alternatives to therapy, such as support groups and the like (e.g., Homosexuals Anonymous or the Exodus-affiliated ministries), and (f) possible consequences of not pursuing treatment. Christian therapists should be concerned to support their client's ability to make informed, responsible decisions in the area of sexual behavior.

Therapists and clients may spend some time in the stage of considering arguments for and against a direction for therapy, but at some point clients, in collaboration with their therapists, make a commitment to the beliefs they want to see govern their lives, as well as the goals for therapy. For those clients who are interested in pursuing treatment, it makes a great deal of difference how Christian clinicians proceed with a particular client, whether homosexual proclivities are to a large extent dependent on the client's actions, choices or efforts, or whether they emerge in an individual largely by seemingly immutable factors. In instances where clients can identify circumstances at home or among peers that shape their inclinations in one way or another, therapy will involve examining how participation in one environment over another might alter the nature and strength of tendencies, attitudes, habits, desires, emotional proclivities and so forth. Other cases may involve clients who find their homosexual inclinations to be largely immutable. So far as initial inclinations or tendencies are concerned, these clients experience their homosexuality as a "given," as a matter of predisposition to behavior. Previous attempts to change orientation have only led to frustration. In these cases, although we cannot answer all of the questions regarding the etiology—biological, environmental or both—of homosexual orientation, we can still raise the question whether such a predisposition should be acted on or whether it should be resisted. To the extent our clients feel that acting on such inclinations is immoral, we can work with them to develop strategies for resisting the habits and inclinations that may have been strengthened by past experiences.

Discussing treatment for those clients struggling with homosexual inclinations and behavior, McConaghy (1990), a highly regarded specialist in the field, notes that there "are treatments to enable [homosexuals] to control homosexual feelings or behaviors they experience as compulsive and to reduce anxiety concerning heterosexual activity" (p. 576). A number of treatment interventions can be considered, including behavior therapy, emphasizing imaginal desensitization, modeling and behavioral rehearsal of effective behavior for dealing with both heterosexual and homosexual persons, and cognitive and group therapy, providing support for developing more rational perspectives on common problems as well as increasing levels of self-esteem, cultivating habits and relationships conducive to achieving realistic goals for personal growth, strengthening the capacity to manage not only adverse external situations but internal inclinations, habits and emotions, and eliminating self-defeating, unrealistic standards of self-appraisal and self-reinforcement.

Furthermore, it is appropriate to challenge the presupposition among advocates of homosexual behavior that human health and well-being requires that sexual desire be acted upon and satisfied. Self-discipline or restraint has been popularly depicted (versus empirically supported) as unhealthy, unjust and dehumanizing. Our clients can be reminded that it is certainly possible for some people to lead a gratifying life without genital sexual expression, and that there is no evidence that persons need to express their erotic inclinations to find self-fulfillment. No major theory in academic psychology asserts that the expression of erotic urge is essential to human well-being. It is important not to maintain the illusion that sexual expression is either necessary or sufficient for health and happiness.

Principle F: Social Responsibility

Psychologists are aware of their professional and scientific responsibilities to the community and the society in which they work and live. They apply and make public their knowledge of psychology in order to contribute to human welfare. Psychologists are concerned about and work to mitigate the causes of human suffering. . . . Psychologists comply with the law and encourage the development of law and social policy that serve the interests of their patients and clients and the public. They are encouraged to contribute a portion of their professional time for little or no personal advantage. (APA, 1992, p. 1600)

In addition to all of the ethical considerations related to work with clients, clinicians also have an ethical responsibility to society. We are not necessarily spokespersons for traditional cultural attitudes, nor are we mandated to speak for support of social action groups. Our responsibility as professional mental health care providers is related to the presentation of theoretically and empirically based data.

What is our social responsibility as it relates to homosexuality? First, in the area of research, keeping in mind that we are limited in our understanding of the factors that may shape a homosexual identity, we must present current findings with modesty. As Burr (1993) observes, many researchers are concerned that "certain well-publicized findings . . . could turn out to be milestones on the road to an intellectual dead end" (p. 48). For example, consider the appropriateness of modesty when discussing the etiology of homosexuality. As was mentioned earlier, no one theory of homosexuality can explain such a diverse phenomenon. The movement toward biologic theories seems to have been fueled by dissatisfaction with the psychosocial theories, but in fact the biologic theories at this point "seem to have no greater explanatory value" than the psychosocial models they seek to displace (Byne and Parsons, 1993, p. 236). There appear to be a variety of factors that can provide a push in the direction of homosexuality for some persons, but there is no evidence that this "push" renders human choice utterly irrelevant. Some of these influencing factors may be genetic in origin, but genetic influence may not mean a "sexual orientation gene"; rather, other higher-order traits may dispose some children to atypical social relationships, patterns of psychological identification and so forth. A more accurate reading of the literature suggests an interactional hypothesis for the formation of sexual orientation, one which suggests varying ratios of influence from different sources for different persons. "This is not meant to imply that one consciously decides one's sexual orientation. Instead, sexual orientation is assumed to be shaped and reshaped by a cascade of choices made in the context of changing circumstances in one's life and enormous social and cultural pressures," and, we would add, in the context of predispositions toward certain types of preferences (Byne and Parsons, 1993, p. 237; see also Yarhouse and Jones, 1997).

Second, we must strive for clarity and honesty as we present research. Consider the opening sentence of a recent journal article by Morgan and Nerison (1993): "Given that lesbians and gay men comprise 10-15 percent of the general population, today's psychotherapist cannot afford to be ignorant of the mental health needs specific to these groups" (p. 133). The statement that 10 to 15 percent of the general population is gay is simply wrong. The 10 percent figure has been attributed to the Kinsey studies (e.g., Kinsey, Pomeroy and Martin, 1948), but today's psychotherapist needs to be aware that the Kinsey data has been convincingly discredited (see Reisman and Eichel, 1990). Recent and more credible studies reveal a much lower prevalence estimate, suggesting 1 to 3 percent of males are homosexually active in a given year and that the rate of males who engage in sustained homosexual practice over a significant period of adult life is probably less than 5 percent. Female homosexuality continues to be estimated at roughly half the rate attributed to males (cf. Fay et al., 1989; Stoll et al., 1991).

Christians must also be honest about the efficacy of change methods. At an anecdotal level there are a number of "former" homosexuals who report changing the object of their sexual desire, in addition to their habits and behaviors, after living the homosexual lifestyle for a number of years. Research indicates that sometimes this alteration occurs as a result of therapy (Bieber et al., 1962), while for others it is related to religious or spiritual factors (Pattison and Pattison, 1980).

Be that as it may, the existing data on efficacy of change methods suggest that most homosexuals do not find a "cure" in reorientation programs. Many struggle all their lives with homosexual inclinations, self-hatred and guilt. Even in cases of reorientation or behavior modification, many individuals are still tempted by lustful thoughts and homoerotic urges. To present treatment less realistically or to assume too much of current treatment procedures is to engage in ethically questionable practice.[1]

In addition, many homosexuals turn to Christian support groups for treatment. Directors of such programs should be careful to promote their programs accurately. Haldeman (1994) is correct in saying that Christian conversion programs have enormous power over many individuals. With power comes responsibility. What we know currently is that the effectiveness of Christian ministries is not clear, as little empirical data has been collected. With not much empirical validation for successful conversion, can such providers ethically advertise their services as reorientation programs? Or should these programs more conservatively publicize themselves as supportive environments for homosexuals struggling to curb homoerotic desires and behaviors? In other words, if celibacy rather than reorientation is the realistic goal for most individuals who enter such programs, service providers should advertise accordingly.

Also, we should question the role psychology plays in supporting social and political policies in general, and the role it should play specifically in the promotion of social change and politics concerning homosexuality. "Psychology, conceived as either the human science of consciousness or the natural science of behavior, cannot validate moral imperatives and therefore cannot support social policies because of their presumed ethical underpinnings" (Kendler, 1993, p. 1050). In the case of homosexuality, the debate over the morality of homosexual behavior comes to an impasse at its ethical foundations. Psychology, in particular the APA as a professional organization, cannot resolve the moral debate and therefore has no empirical or scientific justification for supporting social policies grounded in moral philosophy. A professional organization such as the APA could justify arguing for social policies based on a particular moral philosophy, but this kind of forthright pronouncement of a *philosophical* moral position, grounded not in science but in ideology or philosophy, has not been made to date.

There are additional ethical concerns for Christian clinicians offering treatment to homosexual clients. For instance, Christians should consider how they arrange charges for their services. From an ethical standpoint, the actual fee charged for services is not as important as the manner in which it is set, communicated, managed and collected. "From the outset of a relationship with a new client, the psychologist should carefully explain the nature of services to be offered, the fees to be charged, the mode of payment to be used, and other financial arrangements that might reasonably be expected to influence the potential client's decision" (Keith-Spiegel and Koocher, 1985, p. 155). Clinicians generally operate on a "fee for service" model where the client is charged for each service delivered. If treatment is desired and indicated, we must be clear with the client about the duration of treatment. In addition to offering a sliding-fee scale for clients who cannot afford to pay a customary charge, we should give clients the opportunity to consider alternative mental health treatment modalities, such as group therapy or self-help treatment programs such as Homosexuals Anonymous or the Exodus-affiliated ministries. As a matter of stewardship Christian practitioners must consider whether or not to work toward reorientation or behavior modification with clients when there are not-for-profit agencies that offer similar treatment programs. Of course, this consideration must be weighed against the fact that professional therapy currently has far more empirical research backing than ministry or support groups. This ethical principle also specifies that clinicians render at least some pro bono services; in light of the controversy and debate surrounding the efficacy of change methods, perhaps work with homosexual clients should be the portion of our professional time contributed for "little or no personal advantage."

In addition, Christian practitioners should consider the ethical obligations we have to third-party reimbursers. Most coverage by third-party reimbursers is limited to treatment for illness or health-related problems. Considering the current status of homosexuality, behavior modification programs and reorientation programs are not, strictly speaking, health or mental health services, and insurance companies will not cover treatment. Attempts to conceal the actual nature of the treatment or otherwise attempt to obtain payment in light of third-party payment restrictions may constitute fraud. In cases where clients suffer from depression related to their homosexual proclivities we must be honest with third parties that when the depression is alleviated—when there is no justification for further professional intervention for depression—further work on modifying homosexual behavior cannot be covered.

As this principle on social responsibility suggests, clinicians have ethical responsibilities beyond the work we do with people who come for counseling. We have an opportunity and an ethical obligation to use our skills to educate communities and to promote mental and emotional health in the community at large. In light of the many unanswered questions concerning homosexuality, therapists have a responsibility to dispel myths generated by advocates of homosexual behavior and to challenge unsubstantiated claims by treatment program spokespersons. We must also avoid the unethical billing practice of submitting fraudulent claim forms to insurance carriers.

Conclusion

What can we conclude from this review of the General Principles of the APA and the relevance of these principles to our work as Christian practitioners? First, ethical concerns surrounding homosexuality are not simply answered once and for all; to become ethical Christian clinicians we must be willing to continually raise questions about the nature of the work we are doing and the assumptions and values that undergird our problem formulation and treatment planning. In addressing the ethical problems encountered by Christian therapists who treat homosexual clients wanting to change orientation or behavior, it is incumbent upon practitioners to critically evaluate various concepts such as our own competence, client autonomy and informed consent.

Christian clinicians must walk a fine line. Christians are called to a set of values that are meant to set us apart from the numerous forces shaping our society; we face a constructive task that involves identifying ideals for healthy adult behavior that are grounded in a Christian evaluative framework (Tjeltveit, 1991). We must also be prepared to clarify existential and contextual concerns of ultimate meaning (cf. Jones, 1994; O'Donahue, 1989). At the same time, with regard to our responsibilities to the mental health community, we are challenged to articulate our value commitments in ways that respect the autonomy and rights of our clients and further their welfare, and to offer therapy within the framework of existing ethical principles and standards for accountability and professionalism.

References

Adams, H., and E. Sturgis. 1977. "Status of Behavioral Reorientation Techniques in the

Modification of Homosexuality: A Review." *Psychological Bulletin* 84: 1171-88.
American Psychiatric Association. 1952. *Diagnostic and Statistical Manual: Mental Disorders.* Washington, D.C.: American Psychiatric Association.
———. 1968. *Diagnostic and Statistical Manual: Mental disorders.* 2nd ed. Washington, D.C.: American Psychiatric Association.
———. 1980. *Diagnostic and Statistical Manual: Mental Disorders DSM-III.* Washington, D.C.: American Psychiatric Association.
———. 1987. *Diagnostic and Statistical Manual: Mental Disorders DSM-IIIR.* Washington, D.C.: American Psychiatric Association.
———. 1993. "Psychiatrists' Views on Homosexuality." *Psychiatric News,* September. A survey conducted by the APA's Office of International Affairs.
———. 1994. *Diagnostic and Statistical Manual: Mental Disorders DSM-IV.* Washington, D.C.: American Psychiatric Association.
American Psychological Association. 1992. "Ethical Principles of Psychologists and Code of Conduct." *American Psychologist* 47(12): 1597-1611.
Bergin, A. E., and J. P. Jensen. 1990. "Religiosity of Psychotherapists: A National Survey." *Psychotherapy* 27: 3-7.
Bieber, I. 1976. "A Discussion of 'Homosexuality: The Ethical Challenge.' " *Journal of Consulting and Clinical Psychology* 44(2): 163-66.
Bieber, I., H. Dain, P. Dince, M. Drellich, H. Grand, R. Gundlach, M. Kremer, A. Rifkin, C. Wilber and T. Bieber. 1962. *Homosexuality: A Psychoanalytic Study.* New York: Basic Books.
Buhrke, R. A. 1989. "Incorporating Lesbian and Gay Issues into Counselor Training: A Resource Guide." *Journal of Counseling and Development* 68(1): 77-80.
Buhrke, R. A., and L. A. Douce. 1991. "Training Issues for Counseling Psychologists in Working with Lesbian Women and Gay Men." *The Counseling Psychologist* 19(2): 216-34.
Burr, C. 1993. "Homosexuality and Biology." *The Atlantic Monthly,* March, pp. 47-65.
Byne, W., and B. Parsons. 1993. "Human Sexual Orientation: The Biologic Theories Reappraised." *Archives of General Psychiatry* 50: 228-39.
Carrier, J. M. 1980. "Homosexual Behavior in Cross-cultural Perspective," in *Homosexual Behavior: A Modern Reappraisal,* ed. J. Marmor. New York: Basic. Pp. 100-122.
Coleman, E. 1982. "Changing Approaches to the Treatment of Homosexuality: A Review," in *Homosexuality: Social, Psychological and Biological Issues,* ed. W. Paul, J. D. Weinrich, J. C. Gonsiorek and M. E. Hotvedt. Beverly Hills, Calif.: Sage. Pp. 81-88.
Corey, G., M. S. Corey and P. Callanan. 1993. *Issues and Ethics in the Helping Professions.* 4th ed. Pacific Grove, Calif.: Brooks/Cole.
Davison, G. C. 1976. "Homosexuality: The Ethical Challenge." *Journal of Consulting and Clinical Psychology* 44: 157-62.
———. 1982. "Politics, Ethics and Therapy for Homosexuality," in *Homosexuality: Social, Psychological and Biological Issues,* ed. W. Paul, J. D. Weinrich, J. C. Gonsiorek and M. E. Hotvedt. Beverly Hills, Calif.: Sage. Pp. 89-98.
———. 1991. "Constructionism and Morality in Therapy for Homosexuality," in *Homosexuality: Research Implications for Public Policy,* ed. J. C. Gonsiorek and J. D. Weinrich. Newbury Park, Calif.: Sage. Pp. 115-36.
Fay, R., C. Turner, A. Klassen and J. Gagnon. 1989. "Prevalence and Patterns of Same-Gender Sexual Contact Among Men." *Science* 243: 338-48.
Haan, N. 1982. "Can Research on Morality Be 'Scientific'?" *American Psychologist* 37: 1096-1104.

Haldeman, D. C. 1991. "Sexual Orientation Conversion Therapy: A Scientific Examination," in *Homosexuality: Research Implications for Public Policy*, ed. J. Gonsiorek and J. Weinrich. Newbury Park, Calif.: Sage. Pp. 149-60.

———. 1994. "The Practice and Ethics of Sexual Orientation Conversion Therapy." *Journal of Consulting and Clinical Psychology* 62(2): 221-27.

Halleck, S. L. 1976. "Another Response to 'Homosexuality: The Ethical Challenge.'" *Journal of Consulting and Clinical Psychology* 44(2): 167-70.

Harvey, J. F. 1987. *The Homosexual Person: New Thinking in Pastoral Care*. San Francisco: Ignatius Press.

Jones, S. L. 1994. "A Constructive Relationship for Religion with the Science and Profession of Psychology: Perhaps the Boldest Model Yet." *American Psychologist* 49(3): 184-99.

Jones, S. L., and D. Workman. 1989. "Homosexuality: The Behavioral Sciences and the Church." *Journal of Psychology and Theology* 17(4): 213-25.

Jones, S. L., and M. A. Yarhouse. 1992. "Contemporary Scientific Research on Homosexuality: A Critique of Its Relevance to the Contemporary Moral Debate." Paper presented at the Second International Congress for Christian Counseling, Atlanta, Georgia.

———. 1997. "The Status of Recent Scientific Research of Relevance to the Contemporary Ecclesiastical Debate About Homosexuality." *Christian Scholar's Review* (in press).

Keith-Spiegel, P., and G. P. Koocher. 1985. *Ethics in Psychology: Professional Standards and Cases*. New York: Random House.

Kelly, T. A., and H. H. Strupp. 1992. "Patient and Therapist Values in Psychotherapy: Perceived Changes, Assimilation, Similarity and Outcome." *Journal of Consulting and Clinical Psychology* 60(1): 34-40.

Kendler, H. H. 1993. "Psychology and the Ethics of Social Policy." *American Psychologist* 48(10): 1046-53.

Masters, W., and V. Johnson. 1979. *Homosexuality in Perspective*. Boston: Little, Brown.

McConaghy, N. 1990. "Sexual Deviation," in *International Handbook of Behavior Modification and Therapy*, ed. A. S. Bellack, M. Hersen and A. E. Kazdin. 2nd ed. New York: Plenum Press. Pp. 565-80.

Money, J. 1980. "Genetic and Chromosomal Aspects of Homosexual Etiology," in *Homosexual Behavior: A Modern Reappraisal*, ed. J. Marmor. New York: Basic. Pp. 59-74.

Morgan, K. S., and R. M. Nerison. 1993. "Homosexuality and Psychopolitics: An Historical Overview." *Psychotherapy* 30(1): 133-40.

Murphy, T. F. 1992. "Redirecting Sexual Orientation: Techniques and Justifications." *The Journal of Sex Research* 29(4): 501-23.

Pattison, E. M., and M. L. Pattison. 1980. " 'Ex-gays': Religiously Mediated Change in Homosexuals." *American Journal of Psychiatry* 137: 1553-62.

Pillard, R. C. 1982. "Psychotherapeutic Treatment for the Invisible Minority," in *Homosexuality: Social, Psychological and Biological Issues*, ed. W. Paul, J. D. Weinrich, J. C. Gonsiorek and M. E. Hotvedt. Beverly Hills, Calif.: Sage. Pp. 99-114.

Plantinga, A. 1993. "A Christian Life Partly Lived," in *Philosophers Who Believe: The Spiritual Journeys of Eleven Leading Thinkers*, ed. K. J. Clark. Downers Grove, Ill.: InterVarsity Press. Pp. 45-82.

Reisman, J., and E. Eichel. 1990. *Kinsey, Sex and Fraud: The Indoctrination of a People*. Lafayette, La.: Huntington House.

Ritter, K. Y., and C. W. O'Neill. 1989. "Moving Through Loss: The Spiritual Journey of

Gay Men and Lesbian Women." *Journal of Counseling and Development* 68(1): 7-15.

Ross, M. W., and O. W. Stalstrom. 1979. "Exorcism as Psychiatric Treatment: A Homosexual Case Study." *Archives of Sexual Behavior* 8(4): 379-83.

Rudulph, J. 1988. "Counselors' Attitudes Toward Homosexuality: A Selective Review of the Literature." *Journal of Counseling and Development* 67: 165-68.

Rychlak, J. F. 1988. "Explaining Helping Relationships Through Learning Theories and the Question of Human Agency." *Counseling and Values* 32: 83-92.

Sedgwick, T. 1988. "Christian Ethics and Human Sexuality: Mapping the Conversation," in *Continuing the Dialogues: Sexuality: A Divine Gift.* New York: Episcopal Church, Task Force on Human Sexuality, Education for Mission and Ministry Unit. Pp. 1-14.

Shannon, J. W., and W. J. Woods. 1991. "Affirmative Psychotherapy for Gay Men." *The Counseling Psychologist* 19(2): 197-215.

Sobocinski, M. R. 1990. "Ethical Principles in the Counseling of Gay and Lesbian Adolescents: Issues of Autonomy, Competence and Confidentiality." *Professional Psychology: Research and Practice* 21(4): 240-47.

Socarides, C. 1978. *Homosexuality.* New York: Jason Aronson.

Stoll, R., J. Gagnon, T. Coates, J. Catania and J. Wiley. 1990. "Prevalence of Men Who Have Sex with Men in the United States." In "Results from the First National AIDS Behavioral Survey." Symposium presented at the convention of the American Psychological Association, San Francisco, California (August).

Tjeltveit, A. C. 1986. "The Ethics of Value Conversion in Psychotherapy: Appropriate and Inappropriate Therapist Influence on Client Values." *Clinical Psychology Review* 6: 515-37.

————. 1991. "Christian Ethics and Psychological Explanations of 'Religious Values' in Therapy: Critical Connections." *Journal of Psychology and Christianity* 10(2): 101-12.

Weinrich, J. D. 1982. "Is Homosexuality Biologically Natural?" in *Homosexuality: Social, Psychological and Biological Issues,* ed. W. Paul, J. D. Weinrich, J. C. Gonsiorek and M. E. Hotvedt. Beverly Hills, Calif.: Sage. Pp. 165-68.

Yarhouse, M. A., and S. L. Jones. 1997. "A Critique of Materialist Assumptions in Interpretations of Research on Homosexuality." *Christian Scholar's Review* (in press).

Youngstrom, N. 1991. "Lesbian and Gay Men Still Find Bias in Therapy." *APA Monitor,* July, pp. 24-25.

---

[1]Interestingly, skeptics of reorientation programs argue that any lustful thoughts or homoerotic urges experienced by clients directly refute the claim of a "cure." At issue here is the question of how to view continuing experiences of homosexual attraction and arousal after treatment. This *may* indicate an ineffectiveness of treatment as alleged. An alternative hypothesis is to view continued struggles with homoerotic urges not as signaling failure in and of themselves, but rather as expected residual effects from years of homosexual fantasy, behavior and general lifestyle. Certainly the criterion for successful treatment of alcohol dependency is not whether the person in question ever experiences cravings. In either case this is certainly an area where definitions and expectations for change must be made clear.

Chapter 10

THE CHILD CLIENT
Jeffrey S. Berryhill &
Angela M. Sabates

*T*he ethics regarding the evaluation and treatment of children is a broad subject about which numerous articles and books have been written. Anyone who chooses to treat a child, either as the primary focus of treatment or as a member of a family in treatment, should be familiar with the issues addressed in this literature. These include research participation, assessment, diagnosis and labeling, informed consent, willing versus unwilling participation in treatment, environmental manipulation, treatment with medications, and many more. In addition, the therapist should be familiar with the APA's ethical principles and guidelines for psychologists, or with the ethical guidelines observed by the therapist's particular discipline. Of particular value to Christians is the CAPS *Statement of Ethical Guidelines* (1993). Specific references to the APA's ethical codes will be made throughout the chapter and cited as "Ethical Principles."

Many members of the evangelical community espouse particular concepts and practices regarding family structure and functioning, including child development and child rearing, frequently with reference to Scripture. These practices are increasingly divergent from those promoted within our society, due to changes in the way our society views and treats children and families, such as protecting children's rights more than their responsibilities. While Christian communities and parents are adapting their behavior somewhat to the demands of society, many of them are resistant to changes that they perceive to be contrary to the teachings of Scripture and to the needs of their children. Therapists who work with such families should be sensitized to these areas of tension and should be able to articulate their own views regarding them.

This chapter discusses several topics that have particular relevance to the therapist who treats children from Christian families or within the Christian community, with the idea of outlining the ethical responsibilities and struggles that face Christian therapists and helping therapists make more informed and reasoned decisions regarding ethical treatment of children. "Who is the client?" is the crucial question to keep in mind throughout the chapter (cf. APA, 1992, Principle E, Stand. 4.03). If an individual is the client, then that individual is the primary, if not sole, object of ethical concern. If the family is considered to be the client, then the therapist becomes responsible for protecting the interests of the family as an entity, and individual interests may at times be considered subordinate to the interests of the family. Treating a child without regard for that child's familial and community context can easily lead to interventions that are *not* in the child's best interests.

Protection of Children

As followers of Jesus, Christians are clearly expected to value and protect children. Jesus welcomed contact with children (Lk 18:15-17) just as he did with women, lepers and "sinners," even though they were devalued by his society. He told adults that they must become like children if they want to enter God's kingdom. He also urged adults to demonstrate kindness to children, and warned that "whoever causes one of these little ones who believe in Me to stumble, it is better for him that a heavy millstone be hung around his neck, and that he be drowned in the depth of the sea" (Mt 18:6 NASB).

Jesus' attitude toward children flows naturally from Old Testament writings. God values human life from conception forward (Ps 139:13), and children are considered a direct reward or blessing from the Lord (Ps 127:3). God is exemplified as the model parent. The "right" of children to be valued and protected, then, should be a high priority to Christian people.

But who is responsible for this protective action, and what degree of freedom should be allotted to the person or persons who carry that responsibility? While all writings on mental health ethics and children affirm that children must be protected, most are less clear about who really carries this responsibility. In reviewing a number of these writings we encountered only one (a psychiatric textbook) that directly and without apology stated that parents are responsible for the welfare of their children (Graham, 1991, p. 341). Stein (1990) notes that parents are held responsible for their children but then refers to a possible connection between this practice and the Anglo-Saxon view that children were the property of their fathers. The majority of mental health writers seem to hold parents responsible for failure to protect their children while indicating that protection is to be defined and enforced from outside the family. Society in general and social agencies or agents (including therapists) in particular appear to carry final responsibility for the protection of children. This collective responsibility implies that children "belong" more to their society than to their families, as Wagner of the Family Research Council has suggested (1993).

Our own view is that at the human level the child "belongs" first to the family, then to the subcommunity or social subgroup, and finally to the larger community or society as a whole. This hierarchy is appropriate from a human relationship perspective and from a biblical perspective. In this context belonging means to be taken care of by and be accountable to another person or group. The more direct the relationship, the higher the degree of belonging. This is a critical point because it implies that the family should exercise the greatest responsibility for (and action toward) the protection of children. The immediate community should take secondary responsibility, and the society should carry the least responsibility. For Christians the local church should function as the entity that most directly empowers parents and holds them accountable for the protection of their children. The church should thus function as the primary "social service agency" for Christian families, with public agencies serving as an additional safety net. We are not arguing here against mandatory reporting laws or the authority of social service agencies, but rather pointing out that local churches should be better positioned than public agencies to assist Christian families with protecting and nurturing children.

Christian therapists are often uniquely able to work with both the church and child protective agencies. For example, a therapist learns during an initial interview that an adolescent (the identified client) and his father have had physical altercations that have left bruises on both. The mother also states that her husband has "a temper problem" that has led to physical marital fights. Both parents have discussed these problems with the pastor of their church and have agreed to a plan to provide accountability through a parenting class. In this situation the church has already been engaged in addressing the problem. The family is likely to consent for the therapist to consult with their pastor about the problem and appropriate interventions. With proper consultation the intervention process may be pursued jointly by the therapist, the church staff and the appropriate social service agency (since a report is likely to be required). The family thus receives assistance without becoming alienated from the church, and the church is able to provide its available services to the family in coordination with public services.

While Christian therapists may be best equipped to interface between the Christian and secular communities in protecting children, they also may be most likely to encounter conflicting opinions about what constitutes abuse and protection from abuse. Society gets its definitions from prevailing norms and from persons or organizations considered to be authoritative. Christians, by contrast, often seek to define protection primarily through Scripture and the teaching within the Christian community, even though they are usually cognizant of society's concepts. Although public and governmental standards for child protection often seem to override family standards, the family deserves much consideration because it carries the greatest direct accountability and has (potentially, at least) the greatest understanding of and concern for the child. If we are to advocate effectively for the child, we must support those structures that are most able to recognize and affirm the individual child.

Consider this example: A conservative Christian family desires to keep their children "unstained by the world" by preventing access to television or movies, despite the children's very vocal opposition. While this practice is consistent with the family's concept of protection, it might be viewed by society at large (and perhaps by therapists) as repressive and contrary to successful social development, and therefore harmful to the children. Which therapeutic objective should be pursued?

1. The parents adjust their standards to reflect their children's preferences or society's norms.

2. The children internalize their parents' standards.

3. The children accept their parents' right to regulate access to the media without agreeing with their parents' choices.

4. The parents and children negotiate a compromise that reflects everyone's wishes.

The approach taken by the therapist should be based on concern for the welfare of the children and of the family (Ethical Principles D and E) but will reflect his or her beliefs about appropriate family authority structure. Therapists should explain their own assumptions and biases to the parents, and usually to the children, when addressing this type of situation.

A possible implication of the above example is that parents, and indeed families, may need protection for the same reasons that children need protection. Just as children are vulnerable to abusive control by their families, families are vulnerable to abusive control by persons or agencies that regulate them. While parents and families do receive certain protections under the present legal code, and while parents' rights are discussed sparingly in the mental health literature (e.g., Garinger, Tankenoff and Brant, 1976; Schnaiberg and Goldenberg, 1989), the societal emphasis seems to have been slanted noticeably toward protecting only the children. It might be argued that society has been concerned more with protecting children from "conservative" influences (e.g., required parental notification for abortions or forced church attendance) than from more "liberal" ones (e.g., exposure to overly sexualized material on television or required education on "alternate lifestyles"). Christian parents are beginning to articulate their own rights, however, and legislative proposals to protect the rights of parents seem likely to follow.

Christian therapists must look beyond the perspectives of society, parents and children to assess what types of protection and what types of freedom are needed to help the individual child progress in a developmentally appropriate way. Having made that assessment, they often must mediate between those perspectives in order to truly support the welfare of the client.

Child Abuse

A quick review of the literature or even of popular talk shows is sufficient to point out that child abuse is a pervasive and high-profile problem in our society. The incidence of reported physical, emotional and sexual abuse of children continues to increase, and it is clear that many more abuses go unreported. Child protection agencies stagger under the volume of abuse complaints and ongoing cases. Countless adults are coming to terms with abuse that they suffered as children when it was not called abuse. It is evident that many children in our society are not adequately protected, including children from Christian homes. Children are vulnerable in numerous ways and should be carefully protected. Developmental research makes it clear that experiences during the first years of life have a profound impact on later development. At the time when a child is most deeply affected by his or her environment, he or she is least able to exert control over it and therefore is in greatest need of protection.

Any therapist who treats children must know the legal definitions of child abuse and neglect and must follow prescribed rules for reporting it. In instances of abuse or possible abuse, the therapist's greatest responsibility is to the victim of the abuse, even if the victim is not the identified client. In fact, abuse laws usually state that *suspicion* of abuse is grounds for reporting, even if the suspicion has not yet been or cannot be substantiated.

In clear cases of abuse or neglect (e.g., a parent who literally beats or starves a child) the therapist obviously must follow the prescribed reporting procedures. When the situation is less clear, as is often the case, the therapist needs to systematically gather information from available sources in order to determine as clearly as possible if abuse has occurred or might be occurring, and what actions or conditions are in the child's best interests. Once again, states often require reporting even if the therapist is not certain about what has happened or is happening. Although professional liability is not the primary concern, therapists should know that if a child experiences physical harm from an offender whom a therapist previously suspected but did not report, that therapist may be successfully sued for professional neglect. In addition, the therapist may receive such consequences as reprimands from state professional or licensing boards, suspension of license to practice, or fines.

Abuse must be reported and dealt with even if the alleged abuser is a "good Christian" or leader in the church, if the report will be disruptive to the family or to the church, or if the therapist will risk severe criticism from members of the Christian community for doing so. It is imperative that therapists not assume that abuse does not happen to Christian children or that Christians will respond appropriately to abuse situations.

In one case a family brought their two young children to a therapist because they had claimed that an older child had molested them. The alleged abuse occurred at church during various meetings, and the abuser was an adopted child of the pastor. Child protective services had already been contacted, and it seemed clear that the abuse had happened. The children responded well to therapy, and treatment was concluded within a relatively short period of time.

Within the church, however, the response was less than satisfactory. The pastor and his family minimized the abuse and continued allowing their son to roam unsupervised throughout the church during services. This was very distressing to the abused children and their parents, who protested to the church elders. The therapist consulted with the church counselor about monitoring the pastor's son and determining if other children had been abused. The counselor agreed but felt somewhat constrained by her relationship with the pastoral staff. The therapist urged the parents to maintain pressure on the elders, which they eagerly did. Ultimately the pastor left the church without telling the congregation why and sought to keep the matter quiet while transferring to another, unsuspecting, church. The younger children in the church were later interviewed discreetly to detect other abuses, and church staff were provided with training to prevent further abuse within the church.

This example points out the implications of abuse within the church context and illustrates the variety of responses that can occur within a single case. The therapist's greatest responsibility was to the abused children and their family, but responsibility to the church and its members was also taken into account.

The case also illustrates the need for churches to establish and maintain policies that seek to ensure that child abuse does not occur, and that if it does there are standards in place for dealing with it. Increasingly, with the help of mental health professionals and attorneys, churches are developing policies for screening employees for church daycare centers, nurseries, youth ministries and other sensitive positions, and for intervening when violations are suspected or reported. Korb and Bourland (1995) have prepared a notebook to help churches with these issues, and informed therapists can do much to direct church leaders toward resources that will help them deal with these kinds of problems. For example, a therapist may be enlisted by a church to evaluate a parent's claim that his child had been abused by a Sunday-school teacher, to provide support to the family as needed (at the family's discretion), to consult with child protective services if necessary and to advise the church's education director on how to address the alleged abuser. In such cases confidentiality issues must be handled very delicately, and the rights of both the family and the church must be protected so that church receives the consultation it needs to respond appropriately to the situation.

Determining if abuse has occurred, or if what is occurring is in fact abuse, can be rather difficult. Official definitions of and policies for handling child abuse vary from state to state, and sometimes the guidelines are written in vague or unclear terms. The legal parameters of abuse are not fixed but rather evolve along with the societal or popular definitions of abuse. For a number of years these parameters have been expanding, and they now include many actions that formerly were considered acceptable, particularly in the area of discipline. Thus the therapist must know how the courts and the child protection agencies are defining abuse at that particular time. In addition, however, the therapist must take into account the views of the parents or other responsible parties. This includes the responsibility of the therapist to handle such reporting in as sensitive a manner as possible.

Finally, Christian therapists should bear in mind that child protection workers are usually inundated with cases to manage, with the result that they are often unable to provide the supervision or rehabilitative services that are needed to truly assist the family. The therapist should seek cooperatively to fill in the gaps and, where possible, involve other persons or agencies to help the family take needed steps to prevent further abuse. The church, once again, can be a resource of inestimable value, particularly when the therapist can help coordinate the church's efforts.

Children's Rights

Although child abuse has been relatively visible in the mass media for decades, the subject of children's rights has only recently gained prominence in both popular and professional literature. Therapists are being called on more and more to address what rights children should have and how those rights should be protected within the family and the community. Within the Christian community, where rights are sometimes emphasized less than responsibilities, the Christian therapist may encounter widely divergent responses to the notion of children's rights.

It should be noted from the outset that adults probably cannot truly avoid exercising authority over children until the children become adults themselves. Even a decision to limit adults' influence or control over children would be made by adults, and hence adults would still be exercising control over children. The debate over children's rights may actually be about which adults or adult organizations will decide what freedoms children will have. Social activists and political leaders who advocate "children's rights" do not advocate unlimited freedoms, but rather those freedoms which fit within their own set of standards. The issue of children's rights, therefore, may primarily have to do with who gets to set the limits for children. Since therapists are considered experts in this area, Christian therapists may be able to help Christian families secure appropriate rights for their children through direct contact and by becoming involved in public policymaking at various levels.

Some authors seem to believe that children have been not only underprotected but also overcontrolled or dominated. One respected writer on mental health ethics refers to socialization of children as a "benign oppression" and states that socialization generally means that "older, bigger, stronger and more experienced (although not necessarily wiser) people are constantly trying to guide, educate, bully, or otherwise direct smaller, less sophisticated, dependent, and more vulnerable people" (Koocher, 1976b). He goes on to argue that children should be regarded as a minority group and afforded the same considerations that are given to other minorities. In discussing the ethics of assessment with children, Hoghughi (1992) states that "the assessor is usually an adult in a position of power and the assessed child is relatively powerless, and in a minority position." It follows, according to his argument, that the clinician must safeguard the interests of the child against inappropriate use of power through the process of assessment.

Many people seem to reject the concept of older persons' having authority over younger persons, because younger persons may then be more vulnerable to being misguided, mistreated or misused. If older people are prevented from directing or controlling children, then children should be safer and more free to direct their own lives, and their quality of life should be enhanced. We should bear in mind that the children's-rights movement has occurred during a cultural preoccupation with individual rights and freedom, at least in the United States. Palmeri (1980) examined this view in her fascinating article on children's liberation. She agreed that "interfering with a child's liberty should be as serious a matter as interfering with an adult's liberty" (p. 113). However, she later divides liberty into two parts: (1) freedom from external constraints and (2) being responsible and "acting with intentions and purposes" (p. 119). She goes on to say that "what has been missed, or confused, in 'liberation' talk is that giving people complete liberty, in the sense of letting them do whatever they want, may undermine liberty in the second sense," and she concludes that true liberation may require "more interference with the first sense of liberty rather than less."

An approach to children's rights that seems consistent with Palmeri's comments, and one that is more commonly advocated among people in the Christian community, is that children need guidance from responsible adults in order to develop properly. According to this view children are not yet competent to exercise full autonomy and therefore need to be under the authority of adults until they are ready to take responsibility for themselves. Children are viewed as having rights, but within the context of parental and community responsibility and authority. Authority over another person is not seen as inherently bad, and even being denied some of one's wishes is considered an appropriate part of preparing for adult life.

This approach fits rather well with the apparent inverse relationship between freedom and protection: the more freedom you give a child, the less protection you can offer him or her. It is simply not possible to give a child maximum freedom and also maximum protection. In fact, if you give a young child too much freedom you will be considered guilty of inadequate protection or neglect. Children crave freedom, to be sure. But if increased freedom is a mixed blessing for adults, it is even more so for children. Further, we have observed that children seem to be more secure and confident when given limits to their freedom that allow them to experience their world with reasonable safety.

Some leaders in our society are trying to give children levels of freedom that are not healthy for them, because children are not developmentally equipped to bear the responsibility of such freedom. Laws allowing minors to have abortions without parental consent were developed to eliminate harmful or unwanted interference by parents, but they also place sole responsibility for the consequences of the choice on the shoulders of minors. While minors may be quite willing to make this decision, they may not be developmentally capable of fully understanding the issues involved. As is always the case, freedom is accompanied by responsibility.

The therapist, then, needs to determine what freedoms are appropriate at different ages in order to advocate effectively for children and their families. This requires comprehensive knowledge and understanding of developmental psychology, as well as the ability to integrate this understanding with biblical principles regarding children's and parents' rights and responsibilities. Therapists who acquire such knowledge will possess a more balanced perspective when counseling parents and children, and will be able to address issues of children's rights during the therapeutic process in a more ethical and responsible way. Therapists must also seek to understand the child's and family's perspectives on children's rights, as well as those of the local church community. Since these various views may often conflict, the therapist will at times need to mediate between them and help the different persons or groups reach agreement on how to handle a particular situation.

Consider the example of a Christian therapist who is told by a fifteen-year-old female client that she is pregnant and has planned an abortion. This adolescent has a long history of depression and suicidal thinking. The therapist is concerned that her emotional state may impair her ability to make important decisions, and also that the abortion would worsen her depression. In this case the Christian therapist is concerned not only with the client's welfare but also with the moral dilemma of an abortion, which the therapist cannot personally endorse.

The therapist encourages the client to confide in her mother about the pregnancy in order to receive emotional support (which most likely would be provided) and to have an opportunity to consider alternate solutions for the problem. The client declines and emphatically directs the therapist *not* to divulge information about the pregnancy to her mother. The client is well aware, as is typical, of state laws regarding adolescents' rights to choose abortion without parental consent. The client ultimately decides to follow through with the abortion.

Cases of this sort, which unfortunately are common in Christian circles, present therapists with at least two ethical dilemmas with respect to APA standards. First, the therapist is required by both APA and state laws to maintain clients' confidentiality despite moral concerns. Second, the Christian therapist who does not consider abortion a viable option for moral reasons may not ethically "harass" or "coerce" clients into changing their minds, even with strong appeals to scriptural principles. In cases where the client proceeds with the abortion (or other morally unacceptable action) therapists must determine whether their convictions regarding that action would hinder their continued work with the client. If so, the therapist would be ethically bound to refer the client to another competent professional in a tactful manner.

Discipline

Since a large percentage of children who are brought to therapy have various behavior problems, discipline is frequently a central topic for child therapy. Parents often report that they have "tried everything" to no avail, and they look to the therapist to provide an intervention that will eliminate or produce certain behaviors or attitudes. Once again the therapist must bear in mind who the "client" is and provide extra protection for the child who is in a dependent position. Even if the parent is the client, the therapist cannot help the parent intervene with a child without considering the needs and interests of the child. The ethical therapist should be prepared to point out where parental expectations are inappropriate or unreasonable and to help the parent understand the child's needs or views. On the other hand, a therapist should not automatically become the child's ally against the parent.

Disciplinary practices vary widely, and many different approaches can be ethically implemented when guided by the needs of the child (including the need for structure and limits). Christian author Campbell (1992) defines discipline as *"training* a child in mind and character to enable him to become a self-controlled, constructive member of society" (p. 88). He also states that *"making a child feel loved is the first and most important part of good discipline."* He lists a number of methods and includes punishment, but calls it "the most negative and primitive factor." Yet it is punishment, and in particular physical or corporal punishment, that has sparked a major controversy, with secular authorities on childhood taking the negative side and many Christian authors (and apparently most Americans in general) taking the positive side. According to one writer, "Fundamentalists today are among the most outspoken defenders of physical punishments, but they write and say what others believe" (Greven,

1990, p. 6). Strauss (1994) similarly notes that conservative Christian authors and 80 percent of the population "believe that hitting a 'willfully disobedient' child is an act of love and concern, not abuse" (p. 15). Christian therapists should be aware of the arguments against physical punishment but also aware that most of their clients will believe in using it. We will briefly cite some of these arguments as well as a more positive view, since Christian therapists will have to deal with the subject repeatedly.

In 1976 Feshbach and Feshbach outlined the history of methods of punishing children, arguing that many punishments that previously had been used and approved were later considered abusive and were prohibited. They then posited the question of "whether there are extant parental punishment practices that we consider legitimate methods of child training and discipline that in a few decades will be perceived as examples of child abuse" (p. 152). Their own answer to this rather prophetic question was that "it seems reasonable to infer that the path of future change will be in the direction of more compassionate caring for children and will be in part reflected in a decline of corporal punishment and its psychological equivalents." Although Strauss's study of trends from 1975 to 1985 did not find an overall decline in hitting, it did indicate a major decrease in more severe forms of physical punishment (1994, p. 33) and thus partly supported Feshbach and Feshbach's prediction.

"Modeling of aggression" has commonly been used to depict corporal punishment in both scholarly and popular writings. Spanking is frequently described by detractors as a big person hitting a little person. Such arguments would seem to insult the intelligence of children, since even young children can usually tell the difference between a spanking and an unmatched fistfight. A more defensible contention is that punishment often fails as a method of behavior change. Feshbach and Feshbach (1976) conclude in their review of available research that "the use of physical punishment tends to be counterproductive. It often fails to suppress the response it is intended to inhibit, and in the case of aggression, may even exacerbate the behavior." Strauss (1994) cites data linking physical punishment in early teen years and higher levels of adult depression and suicidal ideation. He discusses possible connections between physical punishment and a variety of later problems such as crime and sexual violence but stops short of definitive conclusions. Greven (1990) similarly discusses several possible effects of physical punishment, ranging from anxiety to dissociation and paranoia, but makes no firm conclusions.

Perhaps the best known Christian advocate of physical punishment as a legitimate tool is James Dobson. In the 1992 revision of his *Dare to Discipline* he offers a rationale for the use of physical punishment as one available intervention, and in fielding specific questions provides guidelines for appropriate use of physical punishment. In another book Dobson (1985) draws a distinction between two types of noncompliance in children and indicates how these can be handled by parents. The first type of noncompliance is what Dobson associates with "usual" childhood behavior (e.g., a five-year-old needs to have commands repeated occasionally because he may become distracted by other activities). The second type of noncompliance is the result of active, willful defiance, which Dobson proposes has to be dealt with more sternly (including, if necessary, corporal punishment). Along with understanding this distinction it is imperative that the therapist be aware of possible underlying reasons for apparently willful noncompliance (e.g., depression, anxiety, attention deficit disorder) and not assume that all noncompliance is deliberately chosen or energized by a desire to thwart the parent. We suggest that Christian therapists be familiar with Dobson's approach, especially since many of their clients will be.

Despite the writings of Dobson and others like him, the legitimacy of corporal punishment is being challenged within Christian circles as well, as can be seen from several articles in the *Journal of Psychology and Theology* (Summer 1993). Oosterhuis calls on Christians to "abolish the rod," while respondents argue for appropriate applications of spanking (Gangel and Rooker, Larzelere) or for a focus on more effective alternatives (Pike). Campbell, in *How to Really Love Your Child* (1992), refers to Christian advocates of harsh physical punishment without naming them and indicates that their claims of biblical justification for such punishment is not valid (pp. 92-93). He goes on to note that the Old Testament shepherd's rod was more an instrument of compassionate guidance than of punishment. Two well-balanced discussions of spanking can be found in books by Narramore (1995, chapter eight) and Sanders (1992, chapter fourteen).

This discussion suggests that the use of physical punishment cannot automatically be either endorsed or condemned on the basis of data or philosophical argument. What the Christian therapist must bear in mind is that a person's willingness to accept particular disciplinary measures depends considerably on his or her assumptions about discipline and child rearing. At the conclusion of their article Feshbach and Feshbach (1976) assert that "what is needed to serve the interests and the rights of both the child and the parents is *an invasion of parent privacy* in the area of child rearing. . . . In our hierarchy of values, protecting the child is a more important principle than protecting parental privacy" (p. 164). This is a statement of opinion, not of fact. It makes an untested assumption that intervening (or interfering) with parents' methods of discipline will always enhance the child's overall well-being.

A responsible therapist cannot afford to make such sweeping assumptions in working with families. Rather, the therapist should serve as an expert consultant, providing guidelines for appropriate and effective use of all disciplinary measures, including punishments, with a constant eye toward the welfare of the child and of the family. It is not uncommon for a therapist who works with Christian families to be told that the parents use spanking as a form of discipline and then asked if the therapist intends to report them for child abuse. Although some Christian parents use corporal punishment to vent frustration, frighten their children into compliance or demonstrate their "God-given authority," as do some non-Christian parents, others seem to use it carefully and effectively as one of many tools for guiding their children toward mature adulthood.

Consider the example of a single mother of two boys who no longer was able to regulate their abusive behavior toward her. During the course of treatment she used discipline methods that were commonplace a decade ago but that might be unacceptable by current standards (most notably, spanking). She did not appear to use these methods abusively (i.e., her behavior did not appear to meet the state criteria for child abuse or neglect or to cause any type of harm to the children), and they helped her regain control over her home and avoid unnecessary outplacement for the boys. In this instance the Christian therapist did not involve outside agencies but continued helping the woman to build her authority with the boys, reduce the incidence of rebellious behavior, and develop nonphysical interventions to manage her sons' behavior.

Consider another example in which a father uses punishment harshly in a manner that reflects his internal anger and inability to tolerate misbehavior in his children and that provokes the children to rebellion and hopelessness. When challenged about his discipline practices, he comments that his father did the same things, with obviously satisfactory results, and also quotes biblical passages such as "He who spares the rod hates his son" (Prov 13:24). Depending on the father's openness the therapist may best intervene by referring the father to other scriptures that address parenting strategy, such as "Fathers, do not exasperate your children; instead, bring them up in the training and instruction of the Lord" (Eph 6:4). In some instances church leaders may be brought into the process (with appropriate releases, of course), especially for fathers who are more inclined to listen to clergy than to therapists. If the father resists the therapist's input but is not actually committing abuse, the therapist may alternatively work with the children or other family members to minimize the likelihood of harsh punishment by the father. If the father's discipline constitutes abuse, then the appropriate agency will have to be notified as mandated by the particular laws of the state.

Another arena where discipline comes into question is the school. Christian therapists may be asked by concerned parents to evaluate the methods of discipline being employed at their child's school. At times this has resulted in the therapist's reporting abusive school personnel to the appropriate agency. Whereas public schools are rarely criticized for disciplining too severely, Christian schools may sometimes employ measures that are abusive. Physical punishment is generally regulated fairly well, but allegations of physical abuse may certainly arise.

Perhaps more common, social or emotional consequences for misbehavior may seem abusive to the therapist. Humiliation in front of peers is sometimes used to encourage better compliance, but for some children it may be emotionally quite damaging. Scriptures may also be invoked or applied in ways that are developmentally or otherwise inappropriate. For example, a very anxious child may be told that his behavior is placing him at risk for going to hell. The primary result of such an intervention may be increased anxiety and a decreased ability to function. Therapists, then, may need to help schools understand the child's characteristics and devise more appropriate and effective ways to intervene with the child. In any case, it is imperative for the therapist to gather sufficient information from both the family and the school before intervening directly in the situation.

Informed Consent

On many occasions initial sessions are held with families in which the child in question was told little or nothing about treatment prior to arriving at the therapist's office. Parents frequently wonder how to tell their child about going to psychotherapy, especially when they fear an adverse reaction. One therapist commonly asks older children and teenagers during the initial session, "Are you here voluntarily or with your arms tied behind your back?"

Corey, Corey and Callahan (1988) assert that informed consent is a critical consideration for therapists who treat children, since children often are not included in their parents' decision to seek psychological treatment for them. In its "Ethical Principles" the APA warns psychologists to take special care in protecting the rights of children, since they generally are often "unable to give voluntary, informed consent" (1992). Koocher (1976a) comments that "generally the parents have had prior contact or conversation with the therapist about a child's problems, and in some way [this] represents a kind of benevolent conspiracy." He calls for direct conversation with child clients regarding their feelings about participating in treatment and their opinions of the goals being pursued.

How should the Christian therapist handle situations where the parents or other adults want treatment for the family or the child, but the child does not? We believe that treatment is more likely to succeed when all those involved are willing to participate. If a child initially is resistant to treatment, the therapist should show respect by acknowledging the child's wishes and perhaps by communicating an understanding that the child is being forced to participate. The therapist then may seek to enlist the child in the treatment process without resorting to coercion, such as by pointing out potential benefits of treatment for the child. A therapist may tell the child, for example, that he or she has the freedom to tell parents where they are making unreasonable demands on the child, or that the child may stand a better chance of being heard by the parents in the context of therapy. Therapists obviously must only say what they believe to be true and must be careful not to cross the line between encouragement and manipulation. The therapist may also work with the parents to provide appropriate incentives or concessions for participating in treatment. Although parents certainly have the right to seek treatment for their children, both in society and within God's established order, they may gain more therapeutic ground by respecting and negotiating with their children than by simply asserting their authority.

Thompson (1990) states that recent research indicates that adolescents aged fifteen or older are developmentally capable of giving informed consent and thus should be afforded the same rights as adults. State laws vary, however, in whether or not and under what circumstances they allow minors to consent to treatment without authorization from parents (cf. Stein, 1990). Usually these situations involve a crisis for the minor, and strict limitations are placed on the number of sessions that can be received without parental authorization. We believe that children's and adolescents' interests are generally best served when the parents are informed about the treatment, although there may be instances where treatment of a minor without parental knowledge may be appropriate. Therapists should be aware of state regulations regarding consent for treatment.

Confidentiality

Confidentiality can become a complex issue even when treating adults, since the "welfare of the client" varies considerably depending on the circumstances. This complexity is frequently compounded when the client is a minor or the family includes a minor, because privacy within the family can be a very difficult matter. Most Christian parents will support a certain level of privacy for their children, at least for encouraging openness with the therapist, and many will trust the therapist to know when to disclose information about their children. On the other hand, most Christian parents also have strong convictions about what behaviors are acceptable from their children, and they understandably do not want those convictions to be undermined by the therapist. At the extreme, some parents see therapy as a way to access information about their children, and thus they expect a direct report of what their child said and did during each session.

A child's right to privacy depends on a number of factors: the child's age and maturity, the reason for referral, the source of the referral (e.g., with court-ordered therapy confidentiality is essentially waived), state and local regulations, the content of the therapy, and parents' preferences. Parents generally have control over confidentiality for children under the age of sixteen, although there are often notable legal exceptions, such as pregnancy or drug abuse. Minor children should generally be made aware of the limits to their privacy.

The therapist must be aware that adolescents, especially older or more mature ones, may be legally entitled to privacy in areas where their parents might quite reasonably want to be informed. Furthermore, in general confidentiality can be *legally* violated only in cases of suspected abuse or threat of imminent harm to the client or another person (i.e., suicidal or homicidal risk), or in cases where the court requires access to the records.

Many problems with confidentiality can be avoided by addressing confidentiality directly during the initial contact with the family. Thompson (1990) recommends that confidentiality within the family be explicitly spelled out and agreed upon in writing (p. 78), but a verbal understanding may be sufficient for some families. All family members should be encouraged to state their understanding and expectations about confidentiality, and an agreement should be sought that is acceptable to all parties. All relevant legal parameters should be explained to the family members. When parents request a level of access that seems inappropriate to the therapist, he or she should discuss the matter with them and reach a mutual agreement. The parents may have concerns that the therapist will consider compelling, such as when certain behaviors have preceded actions of self-harm in the past. On the other hand, the parents may tend to violate the child's boundaries, and that tendency will need to be addressed. In any case, parental concern for the child's spiritual well-being does not automatically eliminate the child's right to some privacy. Therapy should not continue unless an understanding between parent and therapist can be reached; otherwise difficulties are almost certain to arise.

The therapist who works with children will undoubtedly encounter situations where information provided in private by the child must be reported to a parent in order to protect the welfare of the child. As with adults, the therapist must be convinced that a more crucial issue than confidentiality is at stake (such as personal safety) before breaking confidence with a child. All of the reasons for breaking confidence with an adult apply to a child, but other valid reasons unique to children may arise. For example, while an admission that a teenager is smoking marijuana may not automatically warrant a report to a parent or other appropriate adult, an admission of potentially self-injurious behavior while smoking marijuana may well warrant such a report. Since children are not held fully responsible for their behaviors they are not afforded the same level of privacy that adults are. As is the case in all therapy situations, the fundamental question is: What will best serve the overall welfare of this person? Therapists must be prepared to violate confidentiality when necessary and to deal with the aftermath as effectively as possible.

One problem that can arise within Christian communities is the regulation of information about the child or family to people within the church. Ideally, the client's church and church leaders are the extended spiritual family, and as such they can provide a wealth of healing resources. In many cases the church family provides more appropriate assistance to the child than the family does; indeed, it is often within the church community that family malfunction is brought to light and treatment is recommended.

Nonetheless, if the therapist must be cautious about dispensing information to the parent or other family members without the child's permission, he or she must be much more cautious about giving such information to a pastor, youth group leader or fellow parishioner. These persons have no legal right to information, even if they made the referral for treatment. Pastors will sometimes assume that they have a right to know what is being worked on in therapy, what the therapist is trying to accomplish or what methods are being employed. While it is often appropriate for church leaders to learn about a therapist's style or theology, it is a violation of confidence for the therapist to indicate without permission how a particular case is being handled. In extreme cases therapists have been threatened with being "blacklisted" among local church pastors for not divulging information about persons in question. When a parent asks for a report to a church leader when the child has not given permission, the therapist should discuss the matter with the parent.

Participation in Direction of Treatment

Stein (1990) points out that "studies have shown that substantial benefits accrue to minor clients when they are allowed a degree of self-determination in the counseling process" (p. 97). He goes on to note that this communicates the counselor's respect for the client and fosters a better working relationship.

The Bible certainly endorses a higher level of adult authority over and responsibility toward minors than does our society (e.g., Ps 1), but we have found nothing in Scripture to indicate that children are not to participate in the direction of their lives. Child or adolescent clients should be permitted and even encouraged to understand the purpose of treatment and to participate in deciding how to proceed, at a level that is appropriate for their level of development and type of problem. This will both protect their personal integrity (i.e., respect their boundaries) and improve the probability of a successful outcome, since clients will most likely have a higher investment in projects where they have input.

The degree to which a child should participate in the direction of treatment will depend on the nature of the problem and the developmental level of the child. In a case of sexual abuse, for example, a six-year-old will usually be given a concrete explanation of the purpose and objectives for therapy, whereas a thirteen-year-old (who probably has a greater understanding of the issues involved) will be more able to help decide how the therapy will proceed and what goals will be pursued. If the issue is bed-wetting, however, the six-year-old may participate as fully as a thirteen-year-old in deciding what approach to use in treating the problem.

Christian parents may sometimes balk at allowing their children to participate in the therapeutic decision-making process (or in any other decisions, for that matter). Some may view this as a threat to their biblical authority within the home, particularly when the child is demonstrating rebelliousness. In such cases therapists will need to reassure parents that they have legitimate authority, but also challenge them to use that authority to empower their children toward maturity, rather than to simply hold on to as much control as possible. It can be useful to remind parents that their children will eventually have full decision-making power for themselves, and that it is better to make some mistakes while still under their parents' care. It may also help to work with the parents to determine which treatment decisions are appropriate for the child or adolescent to participate in and which should be determined by the adults alone.

Spiritual Issues

How can a Christian therapist espouse a value system that is Christian without inappropriately influencing a child or adolescent client? Although as Christians our highest calling is to "make disciples of all nations" (Mt 28:19), as therapists we are professionally bound not to coerce our clients into thinking or feeling the way we want them to. This can be particularly complicated when the parent is a Christian but the child is not and a major reason for coming to therapy is a clash over moral values or behaviors. Bear in mind, also, that Christians vary tremendously on their moral codes (e.g., whether rock music is acceptable, at what age dating is acceptable, etc.).

The notion that therapy is, should be or can be "value free" has received considerable criticism since Carl Rogers popularized it decades ago. But all therapists have a value system, and that value system influences the way they do therapy. We believe it is more honest and ethical to be open with clients about our value systems so that the clients can interact with those systems and make personal choices. This is not to say that therapists should outline everything they believe during an initial session, but rather should give clients information as needed so they can understand their therapist's perspective and make informed choices. We obviously need to consider the child's age in deciding how to express our own views as well as other factors that determine our level of influence over the child.

Since many adolescents and children are brought to therapy because of inappropriate behaviors, the therapist must be able to confront such behaviors while supporting the worth of the person. In one case a Christian therapist had been working for approximately two years with a nineteen-year-old woman who had been molested as a child by several different older male relatives. This client had, until early adolescence, subscribed to conservative sexual standards. By age sixteen, however, she had become very promiscuous. The therapist was aware that such behavior is quite common among sexually abused girls and worked with the client to perceive the connections between her abusive past and her current sexual behavior. Over the course of two years the young woman became increasingly aware of her unhealthy behavior pattern, but she used her abusive past as justification for that pattern. She also developed considerable trust in her therapist.

During this time period the therapist gradually challenged the client regarding her use of the past as an excuse for willfully engaging in promiscuity. The client initially became quite angry with the therapist, who remained nonjudgmental and loving while continuing to challenge the client. Ultimately the young woman was able to recognize her power to alter her dangerous behavior, acknowledge the sinfulness of the behavior and make a decision not to remain a victim of her past. The likelihood of this successful outcome was enhanced by the tactful manner in which the therapist confronted the client, the absence of coercive tactics and the context of a trusting relationship.

A related idea is the use of prayer and Scripture in therapy. Since prayer and Scripture are the means by which we communicate with God and also communicate and fellowship with each other, they obviously have tremendous value in therapy. As with any other action or "intervention" in therapy, therapists must consider the needs, wishes and developmental level of the child or adolescent with whom they wish to pray or share Scriptures.

The blending of ethical standards and Christian faith can be a significant struggle. Often the attitudes of the therapist have a profound impact on how successfully they can integrate the two. In general it is essential for the therapist to maintain as balanced a perspective as possible and be well informed.

Some Christian therapists unfortunately err on the side of being "too spiritual." That is, they neglect the study of non-Christian professional literature or focus too much on the spiritual aspects of a case, thereby overlooking other important factors, such as emotional or physical factors. Although much non-Christian literature may contain information that is not consistent with the Christian faith, it is nevertheless a valuable resource that often turns out to be consistent with biblical teachings. Furthermore, Christian therapists who do not provide their clients with as comprehensive assessments as possible may later be sued for neglect by clients or their parents when an oversight results in harm to the client.

The "Ethical Standards" (e.g., 1.09) also explicitly warn against the use of techniques that the client may consider harassment. Specifically for the Christian therapist this may include attempts at coercing clients to think, feel or believe as they do, "forcing" a client to embrace the Christian faith, forcing the use of prayer or Scripture when the client does not want it, or challenging a client in a harsh manner regarding "sinful behavior."

It is true that the use of prayer and Scripture in therapy can have a very healing effect on the client. It is also true that it is appropriate at times to directly confront particular clients' unacceptable behaviors as sin. However, a coercive attitude by a therapist often comes across as judgmental to the client and may alienate him or her. Usually these techniques (e.g., prayer, biblical confrontation) are most successful within the context of a trusting therapeutic relationship.

Essentially, the Christian therapist's attitude should be like Christ's: loving, uncompromised, nonjudgmental (usually) and at times confrontive.

The "Ethical Standards" (1.13) also stipulate that therapists be careful not to allow personal conflicts or problems to interfere in the treatment process. For Christian therapists this can apply, for example, to a bias toward certain denominations or theological systems. In addition, therapists who feel that their "bias" against particular behaviors (e.g., homosexuality) may result in a judgmental attitude that would impair their ability to work empathically with certain clients are responsible for safeguarding those clients by referring them or by otherwise neutralizing the effects of those attitudes.

Conclusion

Christian therapists are playing a growing role in the lives of Christian families and Christian churches, as well as in the professional and social community. We are convinced that well-trained Christians are better able than non-Christians to provide the mental health services that Christian families need. In order to do this Christian therapists need to function competently in the secular professional community as well as in the church community. As representatives of Christ, Christian therapists should seek to bring excellence to their work and to follow a higher level of ethics than is required by secular agencies. Christian therapists are called to value persons and to treat them with respect not because an ethics code says so but because each person has infinite worth to God.

Many Christian parents and church leaders are justifiably concerned about the negative effects that secular psychology may have on their children or families. It is impossible to adequately understand or intervene in the functioning of children or families without an understanding of how they are regarded in the Bible. Christians who work as therapists must be alert to and able to resolve a variety of issues that are generally not a concern for non-Christian therapists. We must work harder to do what we do well. But the results, both in the lives of clients and in the Christian community, can be more than worth the effort.

References

American Psychological Association. 1992. "Ethical Principles of Psychologists and Code of Conduct." *American Psychologist* 47(12). (Reprints available from APA Order Department, 750 1st Street NE, Washington, DC 20002-4242.)

Campbell, R. 1992. *How to Really Love Your Child*. Wheaton, Ill.: Scripture Press.

Christian Association for Psychological Studies. 1993. *Ethical Guidelines for the Christian Association for Psychological Studies*. (Available from CAPS, P.O. Box 310400, New Braunfels, TX 78131-0400.)

Corey, G., M. S. Corey and P. Callahan. 1988. *Issues and Ethics in the Helping Professions*. 3rd ed. Pacific Grove, Calif.: Brooks/Cole.

Dobson, J. 1985. *The Strong-Willed Child*. Wheaton, Ill.: Tyndale.

————. 1992. *The New Dare to Discipline*. Wheaton, Ill.: Tyndale.

Feshbach, N. D., and S. Feshbach. 1976. "Punishment: Parent Rites Versus Children's Rights," in *Children's Rights and the Mental Health Professions,* ed. G. P. Koocher. New York: Wiley. Pp. 149-70.

Gangel, K. O., and M. F. Rooker. 1993. "Response to Oosterhuis: Discipline Versus Punishment." *Journal of Psychology and Theology* 21: 134-37.

Graham, P. "Ethics and Child Psychiatry," in *Psychiatric Ethics,* ed. S. Bloch and P. Chodoff. Oxford: Oxford University Press. Pp. 341-64.

Greven, P. 1990. *Spare the Child: The Religious Roots of Punishment and the Psychological Impact of Physical Abuse*. New York: Knopf.

Hoghughi, M. 1992. *Assessing Child and Adolescent Disorders: A Practice Manual*. London: Sage.

Koocher, G. P. 1976a. "A Bill of Rights for Children in Psychotherapy," in *Children's Rights and the Mental Health Professions,* ed. G. P. Koocher. New York: Wiley. Pp. 23-32.

————. 1976b. "An Introduction: Why Children's Rights?" in *Children's Rights and the Mental Health Professions,* ed. G. P. Koocher. New York: Wiley. Pp. 1-4.

Korb, W. R., and M. V. Bourland. 1995. *Keeping Your Church out of Court*. (Available from Christian Life Commission, Baptist General Convention of Texas, 333 N. Washington, Dallas, TX 78246-1798.)

Larson, D., and S. Larson. 1992. *The Forgotten Factor in Physical and Mental Health: What Does the Research Show?* (Seminar study guide.) Arlington, Va.: National Institute for Healthcare Research.

Larzelere, R. E. 1993. "Response to Oosterhuis: Empirically Justified Uses of Spanking— Toward a Discriminating View of Corporal Punishment." *Journal of Psychology and Theology* 21: 142-47.

Melton, G. B. 1981. "Children's Participation in Treatment Planning: Psychological and Legal Issues." *Professional Psychology* 12: 246-52.

Narramore, B. 1995. *Help! I'm a Parent*. Grand Rapids, Mich.: Zondervan.

Oosterhuis, A. 1993. "Abolishing the Rod." *Journal of Psychology and Theology* 21 (Summer): 127-33.

Palmeri, A. 1980. "Childhood's End: Toward the Liberation of Children," in *Whose Child? Children's Rights, Parental Authority and State Power,* ed. W. Aiken and H. La Follette. Totown, N.J.: Rowman and Littlefield.

Pike, P. L. 1993. "Response to Oosterhuis: To Abolish or Fulfill?" *Journal of Psychology and Theology* 21: 138-41.

Sanders, R. K. 1992. *A Parent's Bedside Companion*. St. Davids, Penn.: Herald Press.

Schnaiberg, A., and S. Goldenberg. 1989. "From Empty Nest to Crowded Nest: The Dynamics of Incompletely Launched Young Adults." *Social Problems* 36(3): 251-69.

Stein, R. H. 1990. *Ethical Issues in Counseling*. Buffalo: Prometheus.

Strauss, M., with D. Donnelly. 1994. *Beating the Devil out of Them: Corporal Punishment in American Families*. New York: Lexington.

Thompson, A. 1990. *Guide to Ethical Practice in Psychotherapy*. New York: Wiley.

Wagner, D. M. 1993. "The Family and American Constitutional Law." *Insight*, January. (Published by the Family Research Council, 700 13th Street NW, Suite 500, Washington, DC 20005.)

Chapter 11

CLIENTS WITH CHRONIC CONDITIONS

James H. Jennison

Many Christian counselors and mental health professionals approach patients who have chronic conditions with the same presuppositions that they might hold regarding patients with more transient life problems. Models that work well for simple emotional problems may not be as useful for dealing with chronic problems based on organic conditions or psychological disorders that are, by definition, chronic and intractable. This chapter will examine the professional ethical principles that are most pertinent to the evaluation and treatment of chronic conditions and will discuss in particular the conditions of schizophrenia, major depression, character disorders, Alzheimer's disease, traumatic brain injury and chronic pain.

Christian mental health workers may be trained in a variety of academic disciplines and may hold different professional licenses and certifications. In this chapter the terms "mental health professional" and "counselor" will refer primarily to the professions of psychiatry, psychology, clinical social work, licensed or certified mental health counseling, and licensed marriage and family therapy. Parts of the discussion may be helpful to pastoral counselors and paraprofessionals who will undoubtedly encounter individuals suffering from chronic conditions in the course of their work and may need to know how to recognize and refer them to other mental health professionals. Some of the information should also be helpful to chaplains who work in hospital settings.

Presuppositions regarding illness and health influence the thinking of the Christian mental health worker. Scriptural accounts of miraculous healings of what appeared to be chronic, intractable conditions (blindness, paralysis, etc.)

may contribute to a presupposition that all conditions are subject to the patient's choice of emotional and spiritual health. We run the risk of spiritualizing the physiological or psychological condition of the patient and in so doing may frustrate and harm rather than help. We must avoid the example of Job's friends, who interpreted his malady as symptomatic of some spiritual lapse and thus contributed to his suffering rather than comforting or helping. Job's response to their exhortations was "Now you too have proved to be of no help" (Job 6:21).

The apostle Paul in 2 Corinthians 12:7-10 refers to his "thorn in the flesh," which appears to be some type of physical or emotional malady. The Scriptures do not give any further clue as to the nature of his condition, and to specify it is merely speculative. Rather than discuss his condition, or its physical ramifications, Paul proceeds with a discussion of the spiritual impact and meaning of the "thorn" in his life. He describes how it fostered humility and a dependence on God. But the text also indicates that he truly suffered, he wished to be delivered from it, and he asked God for deliverance from it but apparently did not receive the deliverance he hoped for. Therefore he resigned himself to having the condition chronically. Scripture does not indicate that his condition was resolved or that he ceased to suffer—even though he was able to recognize a spiritual value in the experience.

The role of the Christian mental health worker is to address not just the spiritual significance of the patient's condition but the ongoing human experience as well. In the case of chronic conditions this not only may pose difficult and unanswered questions (why do the righteous suffer?) but may challenge the theoretical presuppositions on which the counselor bases his or her work.

Professional Codes of Ethics

The ethical principles referred to in this chapter—most notably the APA's code of ethical conduct—are applicable to mental health professions other than just psychology. The principles chosen for discussion here are those that address particular issues that arise with regard to chronic patients. This is not to imply that the many other principles and ethical codes do not apply or are less important. It is assumed that mental health professionals will follow the full ethical standards of their profession as applicable to all types of practice.

The most basic principle of the APA's code is contained in the preamble: "Psychologists work to develop a valid and reliable body of scientific knowledge based on research. They may apply that knowledge to human behavior in a variety of contexts" and will "rely on scientifically and professionally derived knowledge when making scientific or professional judgments" (1992, p. 1599). A psychologist identifies with a profession that is based on scientific method or on information that is "professionally derived." Professionally derived information is that which is held by consensus based on the collective experience of others in the profession, on generally accepted theory within the profession and on information that may be extrapolated from known scientific data. While mental health professionals other than psychologists or psychiatrists may place different emphasis on the scientific inquiry, all of them rely on a body of knowledge held by consensus within the profession. That body of knowledge is central to the professional identity of that group. While there may be considerable diversity of viewpoints within a professional group, there is the expectation that those who identify themselves as professionals (psychologist, social worker, psychiatrist, etc.) work responsibly within the scope of the knowledge of that profession. Thus it is inappropriate, for example, for a Christian to present herself as a psychologist but summarily reject the principles and concepts held by consensus within the profession of psychology.

There is a growing body of knowledge about various chronic conditions and unique aspects of these conditions, as well as the aspects shared in common. Within the mental health professions there is a proliferation of subspecialties. As knowledge grows it becomes impossible for the "general practitioner" model to serve the mental health professions as it has in the past. The Christian mental health professional has an opportunity and a responsibility to those with chronic conditions to contribute to the knowledge base. Careful research and writing that adds to knowledge and dispels misconceptions not only helps the chronically afflicted individual but helps to shape the profession as well. There may be no better way for the Christian to be sure that Christian principles are accepted and integrated by both Christian and non-Christian mental health professionals.

A second general principle has to do with competence. Psychologists are expected to recognize the boundaries and the limitations of their competence and expertise as established by their education, training and experience. The psychologist should also keep up to date with new information as it becomes available. As we consider various chronic conditions, it will become clear that dealing with particular diagnostic groups may require specialized knowledge and experience. An experienced, competent mental health professional, when beginning to practice with an unfamiliar type of patient, must learn new information and will need consultation and perhaps supervision by other professionals who are experienced with that diagnostic group or type of treatment. Continuing education, whether formal or informal, is also a necessity. New information becomes available constantly, at an ever-increasing rate. Keeping current is hard work but is necessary in order to practice ethically.

A third general principle has to do with integrity. "Psychologists strive to be aware of their own belief systems, values, needs, and limitations and the effect of these on their work" (APA, 1992, p. 1599). The Christian mental health worker must not only consider the beliefs, values, needs and limitations of his or her own personality and experience, but must specifically be aware of the implication of Christian beliefs and worldview and the effect those have on his or her work. (This is also discussed in chapter ten.) This includes respecting the rights of others who hold different beliefs, whether Christian or non-Christian. The issue at stake is the well-being of the patient and the administration of professional services consistent with the profession. The professional may want to think of the spiritual condition of the patient as a variable, much as one might consider ethnicity or level of education as a variable. Providing the best mental health services to a Christian patient may include using Christian terms, concepts and Scripture, while to do so for the non-Christian patient would be inappropriate. While it is not appropriate for Christian psychologists to evangelize patients, their role with the chronic patient may extend over many years, providing ample opportunity for the demonstration of Christian principles.

A fourth principle has to do with dual or multiple relationships with patients (see chapter three for a detailed discussion). The "Ethical Principles" recognizes that in some cases it is not possible to prevent some contact with patients in other, nonprofessional settings. This is particularly true in small towns, and may also be true in the Christian community within a larger city. For those with chronic conditions the relationship with the mental health professional may extend, at least intermittently, over decades. The patient and the significant others may begin to perceive the therapist as "a friend of the family." Involvement in organizations that promote the welfare of specific chronic groups may bring the therapist into contact with the patient outside of the treatment setting, for instance. Subtle issues arise in such cases and may require considerable thought and consultation with other professionals to avoid unethical conduct. The power differential between patient and therapist and the need for objectivity on the part of the professional make these multiple contacts problematic. The length of the ongoing professional involvement compounds the difficulty, whereas in cases of more brief professional service multiple roles may be much easier to avoid.

Confidentiality is another pertinent principle. With patients who have chronic conditions, the circle of confidentiality may include a multidisciplinary treatment team, family or personal caregivers, social service or legal systems, depending on the issues or situations involved. The circle of confidentiality may also need to change as the severity of the chronic condition may wax and wane or as degenerative conditions progress. Any change in the limits of confidentiality should be specifically discussed with the patient or the patient's guardian or conservator in cases where the patient cannot give informed consent.

Chronic Clinical Conditions

There are many chronic conditions that may be presented to the professional mental health worker. As the provision of health care has broadened from a traditional medical model, mental health workers are increasingly involved in nonpsychiatric treatment settings. The chronic clinical conditions discussed here are only a sampling of the wide variety that may be encountered and were chosen simply to provide a context for the understanding of the ethical issues involved. As each chronic condition is presented a brief discussion will relate particular ethical concerns that may arise with regard to that patient group. Again, this discussion is not exhaustive but is designed to highlight the ethical concerns discussed earlier in this chapter.

Schizophrenia. Scientific knowledge about schizophrenia is advancing rapidly. A recent edition of a well-respected psychiatric text (Kaplan, Sadock and Grebb, 1994) reviews the current state of knowledge. Recent studies indicate that as many as two to three million Americans may be afflicted directly, with many others suffering as family members and loved ones. While there have been significant advances in pharmacological management of the disease, there is still no cure. While about one-third of those afflicted will have some social adjustment, the majority will live unproductive lives, dependent on others for support. Aimlessness, alienation, frequent hospitalizations, homelessness and poverty are more often than not characteristic of the life of the chronic schizophrenic. The prognosis is not positive. Five to ten years after the first hospitalization only 10 to 20 percent can be said to have a good outcome. The probability of readmission within two years of the first hospital discharge is 40 to 60 percent. Lack of knowledge about this disease and the limitations of effective management have multiplied the suffering not only for the identified schizophrenic individual but for the parents, siblings and loved ones as well.

In the past five years major advances in brain imaging, introduction of new medications and an increased interest in psychosocial factors relevant to the onset, relapse and treatment outcome have increased understanding of this disorder and improved clinical management. Brain imaging studies, together with postmortem studies, have provided increasing evidence of a biological basis for schizophrenia. A wide range of studies support a genetic component in the etiology of the disorder.

It is equally important to consider what has *not* been demonstrated by research studies. There is no well-controlled evidence of any specific pattern of family interpersonal relationships that plays a causative role in schizophrenia. This misconception, which for many years was strongly held by many professional mental health workers, has caused great suffering for many parents of schizophrenics and has resulted in a lingering anger toward the mental health community.

There have been significant advances in pharmacological management of schizophrenia, particularly the introduction of Clozapine (Clozaril), and promising research on other atypical antipsychotic medications that do not have the devastating neurological side effects of previous antipsychotics. It is important for nonmedical mental health professionals to be informed and assist their patients in getting whatever help may be available via medication. At the same time it is usually the case that optimal clinical improvement is based on a combination of pharmacological, psychological and social interventions.

As the biological basis of schizophrenia has become better established there has been an increased interest in psychosocial factors that may affect the onset of symptoms, relapse or treatment outcomes. The unexplained fact that nearly half of monozygotic twins do not become schizophrenic, even when the other twin has the disorder, suggests that the interaction between biological and environmental factors is not well understood. While part of the answer may lie in the complexities of the genetic predisposition or physiological development of the individual, it is also reasonable to assume that the course of the disease may be affected by psychosocial stress, much like diabetes or heart disease. While it is important not to "blame" such psychosocial factors for the etiology of schizophrenia, careful management of psychosocial stresses may be important in delaying onset, preventing relapses or obtaining best treatment outcomes.

The mental health worker who works with schizophrenic patients must be careful to keep informed of advances in knowledge regarding this disorder. Theoretical approaches that emphasize family or psychosocial factors as the cause of the disorder are inconsistent with recent evidence. There are very specific criteria for diagnosis outlined in the *DSM-IV* (American Psychiatric Association, 1994) as well as in reputable psychiatric textbooks. Knowing these criteria will help the worker in understanding the disorder and will help to prevent misdiagnosis or mislabeling of symptoms. A knowledge of resources available to the patient and family is also important in making appropriate referrals and assisting the family or caregivers in obtaining the support they may need.

The importance of addressing both biological and psychosocial factors increases the need for involving multiple disciplines in effective treatment. It is highly unlikely that optimal treatment will be rendered by a single professional dealing only with the identified patient, as was often the case in the past. This raises issues of confidentiality, as effective treatment will be likely to require information sharing between several treating professionals, caregivers and others. The limits of this "circle of confidentiality" need to be defined and made explicit to all involved. There may also be occasion to modify the limits based on the current mental status of the patient. The patient who is actively psychotic may be unable to give consent to information sharing, in which case the issue falls to the responsible guardian or caregiver.

Ethical issues pertaining to professional integrity may arise in the case of schizophrenia. There continues to be significant stigma with regard to schizophrenia, in both the Christian and the non-Christian communities. Bizarre behavior raises levels of discomfort, and attempts to explain the disorder in terms of spiritual concepts, such as demon possession, may increase stigma by adding a moral quality to it. Christian mental health professionals must carefully consider the current knowledge of schizophrenia in relation to their own beliefs and worldview. Such a devastating illness inevitably leaves unanswered questions in the mind of the careful Christian thinker.

Major depression. Major depression is a mood disorder prevalent in 15 percent of the population—maybe as high as 25 percent in the female population. This gender discrepancy is found in all cultures. Since major depression is relatively common, it is the subject of countless popular books and articles as well as volumes of scientific literature. As with all subjects in the popular literature there is a maze of differing opinions and "cures" being promoted. The popular literature often treats all depressed moods as if they were a single disorder.

There is increasing evidence of a biological etiology for this disorder, as with schizophrenia. The strongest evidence is biochemical, with a number of studies showing abnormalities of biogenic amine metabolites or neuroendocrine regulation in patients with a diagnosis of major depressive disorder. Brain imaging studies are less conclusive. Genetic factors are strongly implicated in the etiology as family studies show that first-degree relatives of those with major depressive disorder are two to three times more likely to develop the disorder than are those in the general population. Adoption studies show a 50 percent concordance rate among monozygotic twins (Kaplan, Sadock and Grebb, 1994).

Many nonpsychiatric medical conditions and treatments can produce symptoms of a major depression. Medications that the patient is taking for other reasons, for instance, should always be considered possible causes of depressive complaints.

Psychosocial factors are also important in the onset of a major depression. Clinical observations indicate that the first episode is more often preceded by stressful life events than are subsequent episodes. Some clinicians believe strongly that life events play the primary role in the etiology of depression, while others lean toward a more limited role. Personality studies have failed to identify any single personality trait or type that predisposes one to depression.

The role of psychosocial stressors in the etiology of major depression is an example of a situation where scientific knowledge is not definitive and professionally derived knowledge has not reached strong consensus. Such differences of professional opinion provide the motivation to continue to investigate, gather data and seek understanding.

Issues of differential diagnosis in the patient with depressive complaints draw attention to the fact that not all depressions fit the criteria for major depressive disorder. Other diagnoses are provided by the *DSM-IV* (American Psychiatric Association, 1994), including dysthymic disorder, depressive disorder not otherwise specified, mood disorder due to a general medical condition, and substance-induced mood disorder. Other disorders with primarily depressive symptoms include adjustment disorder with depressed mood, and bereavement (which is not considered a disorder but rather a condition that may be a focus of clinical attention).

This wide array of diagnoses may indicate that there are many different conditions or processes that might be popularly labeled "depression." In fact the range of depressive states ranges from normal to serious psychopathology. Concepts or presuppositions that may serve one diagnosis well may be limited or ineffective for another. The Christian mental health professional may struggle with the relative salience of biological factors as he or she considers the issue of patient responsibility or the contribution of spiritual, religious or philosophical issues to the patient's condition. While spiritual struggles may result in symptoms of depressed mood, it is also true that clinical depression of other etiology may keep an individual from a full appreciation of spiritual truth or a full participation in the church.

Major depressive disorder becomes chronic and/or recurrent in a portion of cases. For this group the general conclusion of most studies indicates a long course with many relapses. Most studies show that a combination of medications and psychotherapy is most effective in treating this disorder. The duration and recurrence of the disorder can be problematic for the clinician who emphasizes the patient's responsibility for his or her own condition. Whether or not patients are seen as responsible for their condition affects the clinician's behavior toward the patient, as will be discussed later.

Personality disorders. Personality disorders have a broad range of presentation, including a variety of behavioral patterns and encompassing a range of pathology from mild to serious. Behaviors associated with some manifestations of personality disorder are particularly distasteful or may violate Christian moral standards. These types of personality disorder are likely to create the most tension for the Christian mental health professional. The ethical principle of integrity must be applied here. The counselor's need to preserve and advance Christian moral principles must not stand in the way of an objective appraisal of the patient. Negative feelings and biases with regard to the patient's behavior may at times result in early termination of the therapist-patient relationship or a lower level of service due to the therapist's discomfort.

On the positive side, the Christian counselor has the advantage of a well-ordered set of moral and behavioral values that may be communicated both directly and indirectly to the character-disordered client. Lacking internal controls, these individuals can profit from external structuring and limit-setting. In the Christian's perspective there is an external moral reality that transcends the operation of conscience or human will. Philosophies that rely on looking within oneself for guidance are not likely to be helpful to these patients. The application of Christian moral principles must be made openly, with consent of the patient, taking care not to confuse the role of therapist with that of evangelist.

All personality disorders are chronic by definition: "The essential feature of a Personality Disorder is an enduring pattern of inner experience and behavior that deviates markedly from the expectations of the individual's culture" (*DSM-IV,* 1994, p. 634). The pattern is most often lifelong, though some types of disorder ease with maturity and aging. Some disorders are somewhat available to therapeutic modification, while others are extremely resistant. People with personality disorders often do not feel anxiety about their behavior, and in the absence of discomfort lack motivation to change. Their maladaptive pattern of perceiving themselves and the world makes it unlikely that they will understand or recognize the problem as others do. While some modification may result from therapeutic intervention, the change may be small and slow. Concepts of spiritual regeneration and rebirth that are central to Christian belief may predispose the therapist to expect more change and more rapid change than is often seen in personality-disorder patients.

The ethical consideration of multiple relationships is also pertinent to the character-disordered patient. Some personality-disordered patients fail to distinguish clear boundaries between themselves and others. Setting and clarifying such boundaries is central to the therapeutic task. The therapist must be especially careful regarding dual relationships with these patients. Relationships that might be inconsequential with another type of patient may disrupt the therapeutic process with the character-disordered patient.

Traumatic brain injury. Improved neurosurgical management techniques and the availability of emergency medical services have resulted in a significant increase in the survival rate for individuals who sustain traumatic brain injury. Penetrating injuries, such as gunshot wounds, often result in focal brain lesions—areas of brain tissue that are destroyed by the penetrating object. Closed-head injuries, as often occur in automobile accidents, usually result in more diffuse brain damage. Loss of function based on damage to brain tissue is addressed in rehabilitation services from acute hospitalization to outpatient services to long-term chronic care facilities. Damage from penetrating injuries may be dramatic and specific, with areas of functioning left quite intact. Closed-head injuries, on the other hand, may result in a tremendous variety of neurobehavioral deficits.

While traumatic brain injury may be seen as a single diagnostic category, treatment must address a wide range of medical, surgical, perceptual, cognitive, emotional, behavioral and social problems. Rehabilitation efforts typically include physicians of multiple specialties, nurses, physical and occupational therapists, speech and language therapists, neuropsychologists, clinical psychologists, social workers, vocational counselors, chaplains and others. Despite the best efforts of all these professionals and the huge expenditure of resources in rehabilitation, long-term studies of the brain injured suggest that neurobehavioral deficits often become permanent barriers to the total restoration of function (Tellier et al., 1990).

The mental health professional is most likely to be asked to address some of the specific behavioral deficits that are often seen in the brain-injured patient. These include altered expression of emotion, decreased initiative and behavioral directedness, impulsivity and disinhibition, denial, depression, and social and family consequences. While the condition and functioning of the injured person's brain is a major causal factor, the effects of learning and conditioning, interpersonal interactions, intrapsychic factors, and environmental contexts must be considered as well.

Patients with injuries to the prefrontal cortex often display flattened or dull affect, and those with right-hemisphere lesions may be unable to accurately perceive emotional cues from other persons or situations. Emotional lability may also be based on brain damage. Decreased initiative and lack of goal-directed behavior are classic symptoms of frontal-lobe damage. Diffuse cortical damage often results in decreased inhibition and increased impulsivity. Denial may be organic, as seen in the condition of anosagnosia (the failure to see or appreciate one's deficits), or psychological. Depression is common and appropriate in those who have suffered disability due to traumatic brain injury. It is usually a transient phase of adjustment but can become more chronic and problematic. Though seen as a "normal" response, it must receive proper attention as a focus of treatment to minimize the negative impact it may have on the patient's recovery and rehabilitation.

Denial is a normal phase in the adjustment to disability after physical trauma. Both the patient and the family may fail to appreciate the reality of the situation and the prognosis. In similar fashion, patients or family members may have a religious conversion experience, a sudden flight into religious faith, or may appeal to miraculous healing. The needs of the Christian mental health professional to see others expressing faith in God may prompt reinforcement of these behaviors in the patient. This can be counterproductive therapeutically and may later be disruptive of the relationship between patient and therapist, as most patients reject their early statements of faith as they become more aware of the permanence of their disability. Understanding the typical course of recovery and adjustment is essential to avoiding these pitfalls. For example, understanding the "bargaining" phase of adjustment to the patient's losses will allow the counselor to lay the groundwork for a more mature and broadly based faith and help the patient to see the importance of the resource of faith, regardless of his or her physical condition.

The issue of confidentiality must also be considered for these patients. Since there are typically multiple professionals involved, particularly in rehabilitation settings, effective treatment requires sharing of information and coordination of efforts among all professionals involved, as well as family members or significant others. The extent to which information will be shared must be discussed with the patient, though some patients at some times may be unable cognitively to understand the issue. There may be certain information, shared with the mental health counselor, that is very personal and may not be essential information for the treatment team. This can be held in confidence. At times the high-functioning patient may want to have the option of selectively sharing some information that will be kept confidential.

Issues of confidentiality are important in the forensic arena as well. Patients with traumatic brain injury are sometimes involved in civil or criminal litigation, and the mental health professional may be required to testify. As early as possible in the treatment this possibility should be discussed with the patient and/or guardians.

Alzheimer's disease. Alzheimer's-type dementia (AD) is the most common type of dementia, affecting about 5 percent of persons at age 65 and increasing in percentage with increasing age. The prevalence is higher in women than in men. Patients with Alzheimer's-type dementia have been estimated to occupy half of all nursing-home beds in the United States.

The onset of the disease is insidious, and the cause is unknown. The hallmarks of AD include impaired intellectual functioning, memory loss, impaired ability to name objects (dysnomia) and visuospatial deficits, though patients may not show all of these in early stages. A useful guideline for the early presentation is memory impairment plus one other area of impaired cognitive functioning. The disease is degenerative, with a mean survival time of eight years. It can progress rapidly (death in one year) or slowly (death in twenty years). There is no known cure.

The psychosocial difficulties presented by the AD patient are substantial. Often family members become the major caretakers. The burden of the caretaking role may precipitate breakdown in the physical and emotional health of the caretaker. As the patient becomes more impaired, the resources of the family caretaker may become exhausted, and institutionalization is required.

In addition to cognitive deterioration, there are behavioral and affective disturbances associated with AD. Considering these is equally important for the mental health professional, since they are common presenting complaints and may affect decisions regarding institutionalization. Unlike the cognitive aspects of the disease, which do not respond to treatment, the behavioral disturbances and agitation can sometimes be managed pharmacologically.

Depression in an elderly patient may masquerade as dementia but is potentially reversible, yet symptoms of depression are also common in those clinically diagnosed with AD. The mental health professional must be aware of the potential for misdiagnosis, which may result in effective treatments being denied to the elderly depressed person.

Psychotic symptoms such as hallucinations and delusions may also be seen in the AD patient. Frequently persecutory delusions may cause the patient to become suspicious of loved ones and caregivers, and this may precipitate early institutionalization. Pharmacological intervention is often effective in managing these symptoms.

Other behavioral disturbances, including apathy, agitation, irritability and inappropriate patterns of activity, may complicate the management of the AD patient. These are areas in which the mental health counselor can be of assistance. A combination of behavior modification, environmental modifications and community support services may allow the AD patient to remain in the home setting much longer than would otherwise be possible.

As the disease progresses the mental health professional may need to give more direct attention to supporting the caregivers. Support groups are often available, as well as temporary respite care for the patient, allowing the caregivers a break. The physical and emotional demands of taking care of the AD patient are substantial and can become overwhelming even in the strongest caregiver. The caregiver may feel that he or she has failed the loved one, and the sense of guilt may require psychotherapeutic intervention. The spouse or child may need grief counseling as they see their loved one slipping away.

One of the difficult ethical issues the counselor may face is to provide accurate, timely information to the AD patient early in the course of the illness. At that time there may be symptoms of depression, and the patient may be aware that their mental faculties are deteriorating. Diagnosis is an important issue, as other treatable conditions may be present with the same symptoms as early Alzheimer's disease. If diagnostic examination indicates probable Alzheimer's, the patient and family may need to make preparations for what lies ahead by estate planning and modification of living arrangements. It is important to include family members or significant others in the circle of confidentiality, even at early stages, since the disease will have a profound effect on them as well. In some cases the patient may want to "protect" his or her loved one from the pain of knowing, or the family member who brought the patient to the doctor may want to protect the patient. Both patient and family have a right to know the diagnosis, and it is in the best interest of all to be informed.

Chronic pain. Chronic pain is defined as pain that persists beyond normal healing time for a disease or injury (usually longer than six months) and is often associated with functional disability. Distinctions between acute and chronic pain are not always clear, and some diseases (such as malignant cancers) pose special cases of chronic pain that do not necessarily fit the pattern discussed here. Chronic pain patients typically exhibit pain symptoms and disability in excess of that which can be explained by physical pathology, so the mental health professional is often involved in their treatment. Multidisciplinary pain centers, often in hospital settings, have proliferated in recent years due to the large numbers of such patients and the substantial problem they present to health care systems. Effective treatment often depends on the communication and cooperation of multiple professionals of various specialties in a carefully designed treatment regimen.

Fordyce and his colleagues at the University of Washington were pioneers in what is now commonly recognized as an operant conditioning model of chronic pain (Fordyce, Fowler and Delateur, 1968; Fordyce, 1976). Understanding that the clinician is dependent on patient behaviors (including verbal behavior) to determine the frequency, intensity, duration and locus of pain, they proceeded to analyze "pain behaviors" in terms of conditioning. Pain behaviors are subject to both classical and operant conditioning. The interaction of learning factors, emotional state and situational circumstances was found to produce a wide variety of pain behaviors. Pain behaviors could often be modified by manipulation of external contingencies. As pain behaviors were modified, subjective distress and functional disability often diminished as well.

In the operant-conditioning model of chronic pain "secondary gain" was seen as reinforcement of pain behaviors. There was no need to attribute blame or intention to the patient or the caregivers, but there was rather a simple recognition that all persons are subject to the effects of reinforcement. The frustration of health care personnel with the chronic pain patient had often led to a derogatory labeling and to an effort to simply quiet their complaints by offering some intervention, even if it was known to be ineffective. Iatrogenic problems often resulted, including dysfunction from multiple surgeries and addiction to narcotic analgesics.

In the treatment of the chronic pain patient the counselor must be extremely aware of the reinforcing quality of his or her interaction with the patient. Professional attention can be among the most powerful reinforcers. Physicians must be aware of the conditioning factors at work in medication regimens. Family members and significant others must be part of the treatment team for effective outcome and generalization of therapeutic gains to the natural environment.

While chronic pain may occur in conjunction with a variety of physiological conditions, it also often coexists with psychopathology, particularly anxiety, depression and personality disorders. Typical approaches to these disorders must be integrated with a broader consideration of the pain problem for successful treatment.

Ethical issues concerning confidentiality are important in these cases, since multidisciplinary treatment with the cooperation of many professionals is often necessary. The issues here are similar to those discussed for the traumatic brain injury patient.

The problem of pain has been discussed by many Christian writers and theologians. A familiarity with works such as C. S. Lewis's *The Problem of Pain* may benefit the Christian mental health professional in dealing with patients' philosophical and spiritual questions regarding their condition. Anger is a frequent companion to many of these patients and their families. The counselor must be prepared to discuss issues of meaning without losing focus on concrete and behavioral therapeutic goals.

Sources of Bias

There are hundreds of types of psychotherapy, each with its own set of beliefs regarding psychopathology, causes of particular diagnoses and the efficacy of various approaches to treatment. Such beliefs may be a function of academic training and support of one's professional peers, published information about a particular form of therapy, or personal clinical experience. Snyder and Thomsen (1988) discuss how bias can develop and operate in the clinical context from an information-processing perspective by using hypothesis testing and confirmation as a model to understand therapist-client interactions. Therapist beliefs and theoretical orientations affect not only the hypotheses they generate, but also the outcome of the hypothesis testing. Behavioral confirmation is often the outcome of hypothesis testing in the clinical context. The process is similar to that demonstrated by Rosenthal and Jacobsen (1968) in their now-famous experiments in classroom settings. There is extensive research demonstrating that people treat others in ways that serve to cause behavioral responses consistent with their beliefs and expectations (self-fulfilling prophecy).

Consider the clinical functions of diagnosis, causation and treatment. The therapist forms a working hypothesis regarding diagnosis, often within the first few minutes of contact. This initial diagnosis may be influenced by the client's own presenting statements, previous diagnoses or information from the referring party. Chronic patients of all types accumulate a legacy of diagnostic opinions and labels from professionals they have seen. The counselor must guard against simply going along with previous diagnoses without thinking through the patient's symptoms and presentation. All sources of data, including previous records, need to be considered. The therapist's habits and experience are reflected in a tendency to make diagnoses that are frequently utilized or have been recently utilized by that therapist. This initial diagnosis influences the questions that the therapist may then pose to the client, and by selective questioning, influences the data provided by the client. This process may account in part for the wide differences in symptoms reported by a client, depending on the therapist conducting the interview.

In similar fashion the hypothesis testing and confirmation process may introduce bias into the determination of the cause of a disorder and the selection, utilization and evaluation of treatment procedures and outcomes.

The issue of bias can also be conceptualized within the framework of attribution theory (Jordan, Harvey and Weary, 1988). Attributions are inferences about people, events, behaviors and causal relationships. The inferences regarding the patient or client made by the mental health worker may be biased by differences of perspective (actor versus observer), theoretical perspective or aspects of the patient's behavior. Bias may also be based on the needs or wishes of the clinician. For example, treatment failures may be attributed to resistance, secondary gain or character defects, while successes are attributed to the positive influence of the therapist or the efficacy of a favored intervention.

Of particular importance for chronic conditions is the issue of the patient's responsibility for his or her own predicament. Jordan et al. (1988) cite research indicating that the clinician's willingness to offer help is influenced by the perception of the "controllability" of the life events of the patient. Other research suggests that clinicians who perceive the patient as similar to themselves are more apt to attribute the negative life events of the patient to external rather than internal factors. Weiner (1993) discusses the relationship of controllability and responsibility. Persons who are suffering conditions thought to be brought on by their own actions are more likely to be treated with anger and withholding of help, while those perceived as "innocent victims" are treated with empathy and helping behaviors. These attributions are not unique to the health care arena but are common to all aspects of the human experience. Many patients encountered by the mental health professional are stigmatized by association with the diagnosis of their condition. Weiner describes research of attributions made with regard to a number of diagnoses (such as Alzheimer's disease, heart disease, AIDS, drug addiction, etc.). He concludes that "stigmatized persons were generally not held responsible for uncontrollable physical problems, whereas stigmas for which individuals were held responsible were primarily behavioral and mental problems, which are typically regarded as controllable" (1993, p. 960). In the absence of mitigating information regarding causation, certain conditions may evoke attributions regarding personal responsibility.

Certain chronic conditions are most likely to be seen as uncontrollable and their sufferers as not responsible for their plight. Dementia of the Alzheimer's type is one of these. The AD patient is not likely to be seen as responsible even though the cause of the disease is unknown. In other conditions, attributions of personal responsibility may be made. In the absence of specific causal information the chronically depressed person may be seen as responsible for his or her condition. If information is available to link the condition to a neuroendocrine imbalance, the patient is more likely to be seen as a victim. In regard to the traumatic brain injury patient, there is a natural tendency to inquire about the circumstances of the injury. Was the gunshot wound a hunting accident, a war wound, a gang-related shooting, or a wound from a police officer as the patient was attempting a holdup? Do we see the patient as responsible for, and perhaps even deserving of, the pain he now suffers? As we observe the chronic pain patient, do we observe increases of pain behaviors in the presence of family members, while the patient appears quite comfortable when no one is watching? Do we attribute personal responsibility to that patient?

The Christian counselor must be aware of all sources of bias and attempt to maintain objectivity. If there are conditions that the counselor finds him- or herself unable to consider in an objective manner, the most ethical course of action may be to refer that patient to some other professional.

Ethical Issues and the Chronic Patient

Scientific and professional basis for treatment. This pertains specifically to the professional mental health worker. All recognized mental health professions have similar codes of ethics, and each has a body of knowledge, part of which is scientifically derived and part of which has been derived by consensus within that profession.

Earlier we referred to the "Ethical Principles of Psychologists," where it is stated that psychologists "rely on scientifically and professionally derived knowledge when making scientific or professional judgments" (APA, 1992). In his thought-provoking book *The Scandal of Psychotherapy* McLemore states, "While it is patently clear that Christian beliefs are not scientific (using the word in its modern sense), it is less obvious that much of what psychotherapists believe, and do, is equally nonscientific." He further argues that "a psychiatrist, psychologist, psychiatric social worker, or marriage counselor has no special qualification for dispensing opinions about the meaning of life, the nature of the universe, or what is ethically good" (p. 48). The Christian mental health professional is faced with a task of carefully delineating his or her role and making clear to both patients and the professional community the limits of that role. While an integration of one's beliefs as a Christian with one's psychological thought is desirable, neither Christian belief nor professional knowledge should be obliterated by the other.

In the varieties of chronic conditions discussed throughout this chapter we have attempted to draw attention to the need of the mental health professional for knowledge and information. Typical psychotherapeutic models may or may not be applicable to specific chronic conditions, and in some cases recent evidence has shown previous assumptions to be false. For example, previous theories regarding the role of parenting in the etiology of schizophrenia have proved untrue as research has demonstrated a biological basis of the disorder. To continue to base one's professional work on theories now disproved only causes unwarranted pain for the "accused" parents and fails to meet ethical standards for a professional.

Competence. It is incumbent upon all professionals to recognize the limits of their own expertise and limit their practice to areas of competence. Some global approaches to Christian counseling have minimized the need for competence with regard to areas of mental health practice, emphasizing spiritual principles that transcend diagnostic categories. Lacking knowledge, the counselor may act in ways that are harmful to the patient. An approach that is appropriate for the borderline personality disorder may not be appropriate for the Alzheimer's patient. A misunderstanding of the emotional lability or disinhibition of the patient with traumatic brain injury may lead to expectations for change that are sure to lead to failure.

Integrity. To maintain integrity Christian mental health professionals must be aware of the effect of their own beliefs, values, needs and limitations on their work. In the discussion of sources of bias, the importance of attributions regarding the causation of a condition was noted. Based on causal attributions, further attributions are made regarding the controllability of the condition. Whether or not the patient is seen as personally responsible for his or her condition often depends on whether it is seen as controllable. Studies have shown differences in responses of health care professionals to patients perceived as responsible for their condition versus those seen as innocent victims.

Theological beliefs may influence the Christian mental health worker's view of personal responsibility. But Christian mental health professionals are subject to all the same human failings as non-Christians. As McLemore (1982) observes, "The doctrinal assertion that we are all imperfect sinners has not deterred Christians from hiding their psychological hurts and struggles, out of the fear that these imperfections would reveal moral failings and thus lead to social censure" (pp. 36-37).

Confidentiality. All mental health professionals, regardless of faith, encounter the same issues with regard to confidentiality and the chronic patient. All must make the boundaries of confidence explicit and be careful to indicate when those boundaries must change in order to effectively treat the patient. Multidisciplinary settings such as rehabilitation services or pain clinics require communication between professionals and cooperation on implementing the treatment plan. The sharing of information must always be done carefully and purposefully, and only information pertinent to the treatment should be shared. On occasion the mental health professional may have information from the patient that is very personal and that has little bearing on the treatment program or the rest of the treatment team. Such information should be held in confidence.

A Christian Perspective on the Chronic Patient

The chronic patient often requires professional intervention over a period of many years. An appropriate professional relationship can provide significant service both to the patient and to family members and loved ones, yielding a lifelong impact. While it may require an enduring commitment and the exercise of patience on the part of the professional, working with chronic patients provides a unique opportunity to communicate God's love in a very tangible way.

Counseling the chronic patient addresses three broad goals: restoration of function, environmental modification and maintenance. The first goal is to increase the patient's functional abilities by either retraining and strengthening preexisting ability or by teaching coping and compensatory mechanisms to circumvent areas of deficit. The second goal is to assist in the modification of the patient's natural environment to maximize the "fit" between the patient's preserved or retrained abilities and compensatory strategies and the demands of the environment. The third goal is to provide support, comfort and encouragement, to prevent isolation and to assist in the adjustment to disability.

Direct intervention to increase the patient's functional ability may include such diverse activities as insight-oriented psychotherapy, behavior modification, medication management, social skills training, cognitive rehabilitation and education.

The counselor's role in the modification of the patient's environment also encompasses diverse functions. Family members or significant others are perhaps the most important environmental context to be addressed. Education of these caregivers is essential. They must have a clear understanding of the strengths and limitations of the patient and how they can best assist the patient. They often must learn new roles and expectations. Vocational counseling may also be involved and may even extend to the counselor's involvement on behalf of the patient in the workplace. An interface with community agencies may also be part of the counselor's role. The counselor can be an important source of information regarding social programs, and reports from the counselor often are essential for establishing the patient's eligibility for certain social resources.

The chronic patient and counselor may establish a long-term, even lifelong professional relationship, unlike most traditional mental health counseling relationships. This is similar to the relationship of a patient and a family physician that may extend over decades. The support of the counselor can be key to successful maintenance.

In many cases the counselor will need to be actively involved with family members or significant others in order to achieve these goals. The efforts of even the most well-meaning and highly motivated significant others can be counterproductive and can increase disability. Particularly in the early stages of a chronic disabling condition, the counselor may need to provide instruction and modeling for family members in providing the proper level of care while encouraging the patient to function as independently as possible. It is difficult to watch a loved one struggle to perform a task that could be accomplished so easily by the caregiver. But it is the struggle and the achievement that serves to enhance self-esteem and a proper sense of independence in the patient.

Conclusion

The suffering of chronic disabling conditions is not exclusively that of the identified patient but extends to family members and significant others as well. The greatest indignity of all may be the apparent meaninglessness of the suffering. The counselor's role in helping to identify meaning for both patient and family members could help make the suffering more "bearable" and prevent the additional suffering of deepened depression.

Contemporary models of grief and loss typically describe stages or levels of adjustment that may be encountered by the patient. For the chronic patient, adjustment to the loss of function and its meaning at the present may resemble stages of death and dying, as described by Kübler-Ross (1969). The phases of adjustment include denial, anger, bargaining, depression and acceptance. Faced with a lifetime of permanent loss, the chronic patient has an adjustment task similar to that of the dying patient. With a model to assist in understanding, both patient and family members will be more able to move toward an experience of meaningful suffering rather than despair. The movement toward acceptance requires a clear view of reality, an understanding of one's finite limitations, a sense of compassion for others and relationships that include a balance of necessary dependency and separateness. If the experience of suffering engenders compassion, true humility, and a deeper appreciation for life and relationships, the suffering has not been useless or meaningless.

References

American Psychological Association. 1992. "Ethical Principles of Psychologists and Code of Conduct." *American Psychologist* 47: 1597-1611.

American Psychiatric Association. 1994. *Diagnostic and Statistical Manual of Mental Disorders.* 4th ed. Washington, D.C.: American Psychiatric Association.

Fordyce, W. E. 1976. *Behavioral Methods for Chronic Pain and Illness.* St. Louis, Mo.: Mosby.

Fordyce, W. E., R. S. Fowler and B. J. Delateur. 1968. "An Application of Behavior Modification Technique to a Problem of Chronic Pain." *Behavior Research and Therapy* 6: 105-7.

Jordan, J. S., J. H. Harvey and G. Weary. 1988. "Attributional Biases in Clinical Decision-Making," in *Reasoning, Inference and Judgment in Clinical Psychology,* ed. D. C. Turk and P. Salovey. New York: Macmillan. Pp. 90-106.

Kaplan, H. I., B. J. Sadock and J. A. Grebb. 1994. *Synopsis of Modern Psychiatry.* 7th ed. Baltimore: Williams & Wilkins.

Kübler-Ross, E. 1969. *On Death and Dying.* New York: Macmillan.

Lewis, C. S. 1961. *The Problem of Pain.* London: Collins.

McLemore, C. W. 1982. *The Scandal of Psychotherapy.* Wheaton, Ill.: Tyndale.

Rosenthal, R., and L. Jacobsen. 1968. *Pygmalion in the Classroom.* New York: Holt, Rinehart & Winston.

Snider, M., and C. Thomsen. 1988. "Interactions Between Therapists and Clients: Hypothesis Testing and Behavioral Confirmation," in *Reasoning, Inference and Judgment in Clinical Psychology,* ed. D. C. Turk and P. Salovey. New York: Macmillan. Pp. 124-52.

Tellier, A., K. M. Adams, E. A. Walker and B. P. Rourke. "Long-Term Effects of Severe Penetration Head Injury on Psychosocial Adjustment." *Journal of Consulting and Clinical Psychology* 58: 531-37.

Weiner, B. "On Sin Versus Sickness." *American Psychologist* 48: 957-65.

Chapter 12

DEPROGRAMMING
H. Newton Malony

*D*eprogramming is the intentional and forceful attempt to change another person's beliefs. The term itself implies that there has been a stringently designed "program" or plan to adopt convictions that are new or strange. For example, after the Korean War it was thought necessary to "deprogram" the attempts by Chinese communists to change the political persuasions of U.S. servicemen by coercion, seduction and threat. More recently (Richardson, 1983) the term has come to stand for high-pressure efforts of friends and families to change the minds of those who have become members of new religious movements (NRMs).

Thus deprogramming could be conceived of as the forceful and aggressive extreme on the influence continuum, where more mild and unoffensive persuasive attempts to convince persons of the error of their actions have failed (Malony, 1988). Descriptively, deprogramming has come to include the abduction of individuals against their will followed by imprisonment for a period of days during which they are exposed to deprivation and required to listen to forceful rationales as to why they should dissociate themselves from their NRM affiliations. The Cult Awareness Network, which has been very active in deprogramming, has attempted to soften the implied violence of this definition and has renamed the process "exit counseling." The procedures used are nevertheless very similar.

These seemingly coercive efforts to change people are rationalized on the basis that their beliefs are so outlandish and their behavior so irrational that the only way to understand them is to contend that they have been "programmed" against their will in the same manner as were American soldiers under communist imprisonment. Thus deprogramming is excusable under the "necessity defense" whereby such actions are bad but excusable; it would be worse to allow persons to remain in their "false" state of mind. In various court cases both those who kidnapped members of NRMs and those who did the deprogramming have been declared not guilty on the basis of this defense. Although it did not occur in the Patty Hearst-Symbionese Liberation Army case, many people would agree this was a case in which deprogramming would have been excused under the "necessity defense."

In exploring what professional and/or ethical role Christian counselors should play in these endeavors, this chapter includes several case studies. As you read the case studies, imagine that you have been asked to take part in these situations. Think about possible alternatives that are available. Although these descriptions are based on real events, the situations have been thoroughly disguised to protect individuals' identities. While most of the details are part of court records and, thus, are public knowledge and available under freedom of information laws, the details have been changed as a matter of courtesy and professional ethics.

Families Can Overreact

1. As a student at the University of Rhode Island, a young woman was befriended by some members of a large NRM. She joined the group and became one who collected donations on the streets of a large city. She had a goal of $100 each day and often met her quota. She was very happy, although she worked hard and the hours were long. Her family was very distressed about what she was doing. They were an active Catholic family and were deeply embarrassed to tell others where she was and what she was involved in.

When she came home to attend a family gathering, they secreted her off to a remote spot and talked her out of staying with the NRM. She returned to the small town where she had grown up, but she no longer felt comfortable worshiping in the Catholic church. She began to attend a Baptist church. After about six weeks at home her parents said, "It is simply too upsetting and embarrassing for us to have you not go to our church. This is a small town, and all our friends are asking where you are on Sunday. Either come back to the Catholic church or leave home." She left and moved back to the university, where she became part of an evangelical Christian group.

Had you been a counselor for this young woman or her family, what would you have advised? Did they do the right thing? The young woman was glad to be away from the NRM, but she was a misfit at home. Would she have left without the forced deprogramming? Did the end justify the means?

2. For over thirteen years a mother of five children had been a member of a church commonly thought to be a cult. Her husband disapproved of her

participation in the group but tolerated it. Her mother and brothers thought she was too involved and that it was not good for the children. However, her four sons seemed well adjusted and often went with their mother to church.

The matter came to a head when the couple decided to divorce. The husband and the mother arranged for the wife to be kidnapped and kept against her will for a week. Friends in her church became concerned and called the police. Some days later she was released by her deprogrammers, who had ultimately failed to convince her to leave. At her insistence the district attorney filed kidnapping charges against the assailants as well as the deprogrammers who attempted to force her to change her mind.

During the trial the attorney for the kidnappers and deprogrammer used the "necessary evil" defense. He did not deny that his clients had kidnapped and attempted to force this woman to change her mind. He contended, however, that it was reasonable and permissible to commit such crimes where not to do so would expose a person to a greater evil. The church was this "greater evil" because its members considered their leader to speak with the voice of a prophet and because the group reportedly was stockpiling guns. The lawyer insisted this woman was in such a state of deterioration that deprogramming was a necessity.

At this point the woman's mental status became a consideration, and an evaluation was requested. Was she mentally deteriorated? Had she been unduly influenced and coercively persuaded against her will to be a part of this group? Was she emotionally disturbed to the point where she could not make rational decisions?

What would you have done if you were asked to do the evaluation in this case? Would you have agreed to take part in a court trial involving a non-Christian religion? Would you have felt it was important to protect religious freedom whether you agreed with their beliefs or not, or would you have felt that society would be better off without groups such as this church?

Abusing Authority

3. A family had a son who had become involved in a break-off group from a large Episcopal church. Several couples in the church had begun to feel that the church was not being true to New Testament Christianity and decided to invite those who agreed with them to become part of a residential community who would all live together and share their resources. This family's son had joined the group. The group met daily for Bible study, worship and housekeeping chores.

As time went on the discipline recommended by the leaders increased. The leaders insisted they were to be obeyed because they were closer to God's will than the younger followers were. They instructed the members to cut off regular contact with their families. The family's son no longer came home to visit, and when the parents went to see him, the leaders would not let him be alone with them.

The parents requested the help of a therapist with experience dealing with different religious movements. They were sad and wanted contact with their son and felt that his church was separating them as a family. The therapist agreed to try to make contact with their son. He never succeeded, though he left a number of phone messages and at one point even attempted a home visit. After all efforts to bring the family together failed, he reluctantly advised the parents that he would not recommend forcible deprogramming since the young man was an adult. He encouraged them to pray for the son and be patient.

What would you have done? Would you have tried harder to make contact with the son? Would you have contacted a deprogrammer and helped make arrangements for the son to be kidnapped? You probably would not agree with his cutting off contact with his family and would feel that a religious group that separated people from their loved ones was wrong, but would you affirm the son's right to make his own religious choices?

Satanic Ritual Abuse and Brainwashing

4. An older couple had been told by one of their adult children that a counselor had concluded that they, the parents, had subjected the child to satanic ritual abuse. Shortly after spending a happy holiday together, the child cut off all contact with the parents. The adult child was being counseled by a therapist known to have strong convictions that many problems could be traced back to satanic ritual abuse, memories of which had been repressed. In treatment the adult child client had been encouraged to recall early memories of satanic abuse. The client was diagnosed to be suffering from multiple personality disturbance and, in order to protect a fragile alter ego, was advised by the counselor to cut off contact with the parents. When the parents contacted this counselor, he would offer the parents no chance to counter the accusations. They were told by the child to stay away, without any promise of a time when they could be a family again or see their grandchildren.

The parents consulted with another counselor, who told them that from one point of view the other therapist's rationale was legitimate. Protecting the several alter egos that were revealing themselves in dissociative treatment was a very respectable way of trying to achieve personality integration.

But the parents strongly denied any satanic involvement. They said they had never abused their children in any manner. They thought that they were being falsely accused without any chance to defend themselves. While they did not deny the diagnosis of multiple personalities or that their child could benefit from counseling, they felt that their being judged as the cause of their child's problems was unfair. These people seemed to be good Christian persons. They were long-time church members who said they had no connection with satanism. They reported that the other three children denied any such abuse and in fact thought the fourth sibling was lying.

The parents' counselor agreed to contact the child's therapist. He told the therapist what the parents had said and asked if the family members could get together for consultation and dialogue. The child's therapist suggested that most ritual abuse perpetrators denied any involvement, and he insisted that it was best to keep the child away from the parents. The therapist refused to talk with the parents, and the parents eventually instituted legal action against him.

Was the counselor in this case guilty of "brainwashing"? Should deprogramming have been recommended to the parents? Since the alleged satanic abuse was a crime, should the counselor have reported the parents to the proper authorities? The grandchildren might have been exposed to the grandparents' abuses as well, so should the counselor have notified protective services? Could the parents really have been satanic abusers? Could there have been better ways to assess the situation and determine what had occurred?

When *Cult* Is an Unfair Label

5. A psychologist had evaluated former members of an NRM. Some of these people had been deprogrammed, while others had gotten angry and left. In every person she evaluated she found evidence of emotional disturbance. This psychologist routinely attributed psychopathology to the recruitment and membership practices of this particular new religion. In her reports the group was labeled a "cult" that used coercive persuasion or brainwashing. The group protested that they were being unjustly labeled and sued to recover losses of members and money because of the stigma of being called a cult.

I was asked by this NRM to critique the testimony of this psychologist. I became concerned that the same type of pathology seemed to appear in every case, and I felt that this psychologist made judgments on the basis of quick impressions and problematic clinical procedures. I wondered whether the psychologist would find the same psychopathology in those who were still members of the NRM. I concluded that what we were hearing in these reports was a subjective opinion based on prejudgments and an antireligious bias. Although I did not necessarily agree with the beliefs of this particular group, I wondered to what extent they were being unfairly condemned on the basis of what they believed and because of their strange practices. My perception was that this particular psychologist had a negative attitude toward all religion and was taking out her general disapproval on this small and vulnerable group.

I agreed to critique her testimony even though the group had been called a cult. At that time I did not know how the term *cult* was being defined, so I was a bit afraid that I was getting involved in some dangerous group. However, I agreed to look into the situation. I interviewed members of the group who were still involved and attended several of their worship services. I noted that although the group was definitely different from the mainline Christianity of which I was a part, clearly it considered itself to be a Christian organization. In fact I learned that several of its ministers had attended the seminary where I teach.

Subsequently I participated in testifying for this NRM in a court trial where they were awarded $11 million in damages for being falsely accused of being a dangerous and destructive cult. I judged them to be a Christian sect out of the Plymouth Brethren tradition which had a high-demand type of church life that required members to attend many meetings and submit many life decisions to the elders of the group. (See Melton et al., 1995, for the complete story.)

What would you have done? Would you have been as willing as I was to associate yourself publicly with such a different kind of group? What would you say to Christian friends about defending a group whose beliefs and practices they felt were heretical? Was I right to become involved on the basis of what I felt to be an antireligious bias in another psychologist? Was this really an issue of defending the freedom of religion against antireligious persons?

6. The campus ministry office of a major university engaged a well-known deprogrammer to address them on dealing with cults on campus. I called one of the campus denominational chaplains to inquire about the concerns that had prompted them to extend an invitation to such a controversial person. I told her I was concerned that through such an invitation they would align themselves with a person who had a reputation for kidnapping persons against their will and trying to force them to change their opinions.

The chaplain said that a conservative Christian group had been holding Bible study groups in the dormitories. I paused, waiting to hear more. Finally I replied, "So?" She immediately answered, "We don't do that."

As we talked further it became clear that those denominations that had offices in the campus ministry building had agreed among themselves that they would not attempt to evangelize outside the building, much less in the dormitories. Other religious groups that were not members of the Office of Campus Ministry or did not have full-time chaplains on campus had not agreed to these regulations, so when this conservative Christian group held Bible studies in the dormitories, they were considered deviant. In my conversation with the denominational chaplain she called the group "one of those cults."

I asked the chaplain if the members of the Office of Campus Ministry would be willing to use force to keep such "cults" under control—even to following the advice of a deprogrammer. I told her that I felt this might be a violation of First Amendment rights and I thought they should invite someone on campus to offer a different point of view about new or different religious groups. Since I had grown uneasy with forcible deprogramming of persons against their will, I offered to be that person.

That was the last contact I had with the chaplain—even though we were both ordained in the same mainline denomination and had known each other in the past. No invitation to speak to the Office of Campus Ministry ever came.

I felt that arbitrary power was being used to curtail the behavior of Christian groups who were not playing the mainline "game." Was there an ethical or professional issue here? What would you have done?

7. A Mormon psychology professor received a call from a Mormon family in another state who expressed their concern that their daughter had been persuaded to become part of an evangelical Christian group on the professor's campus. The daughter had become very active in trying to persuade other students to leave the Mormon church as she had done. The girl's mother wanted the professor's help in getting her daughter out of this dangerous "cult."

The professor called the girl in for a conference and found her to be well oriented and in good mental health. She had not been brainwashed or coerced as her mother had contended; she had become persuaded of the errors of Mormonism and had decided to leave the church. Although personally he felt that this was not wise, he honored this student's decision as right for her. He advised the mother to be patient and not to take any drastic action. He took no further action other than to invite the daughter to come see him again if she wanted to talk.

Had you been this psychology professor, what would you have done? What is interesting in this case is that the situation is reversed for Christian psychologists. What many Christians consider a cult was being perceived as normal, and the evangelical Christian group was being accused of being the cult. It appears as if attempts to deprogram someone may depend on who is the dominant group and who is the outsider. Does this make a difference in terms of what is ethical? Or professional? Are there larger issues than just which religion a counselor thinks is the *true* religion?

The Hazards of Extreme Beliefs

8. The final case studies involve NRMs considered to be truly abusive and coercive: the Jim Jones and David Koresh affairs. Almost one thousand people followed Jim Jones's suicidal commands in Guyana, and over seventy adults and children burned to death in the Branch Davidian compound in Waco. Most people joined in condemning these atrocities and wondered what could have been done to save these people from dying. Many felt that Jim Jones and David Koresh were hyperauthoritarian leaders who exercised an almost irresistible control over their followers. Even though the government's actions backfired, there was little public protest over the force used in Waco, and there was a strong wish that something equally strong had been done to stop the suicides in Guyana.

Yet there are other facets to both stories. In both cases people died for believing that the world was coming to an end. We applaud the Jewish Zealots at Masada, who at the end of the first century ritualistically murdered each other and committed suicide rather than be conquered by the Romans. Many visitors to Israel take a trip to this mountaintop site on the coast of the Dead Sea. Although Jones and Koresh took their beliefs to the extreme, they were not unlike Christian groups through the centuries that have thought the world was coming to an end. It is clear that David Koresh, for example, was intensely studying the "signs" in the book of Revelation. He sincerely thought that the government forces were the antichrist and that surrendering to them was an act of apostasy.

These viewpoints do not excuse these debacles in the least, and I do not want to be seen as condoning groups that are violent or encourage drastic behavior. However, my illustrations do suggest that often little attention is paid to the sincerity with which certain nonheretical Christian beliefs were held by these groups. There were some elements of both groups that were outlandish, but child abuse was never proved in either group, and adultery, though reprehensible, is not illegal. Further, as the movie *Deceived* clearly demonstrated, Jim Jones's People's Temple served a vital function in the religious life of the disinherited in San Francisco for a number of years. As the pastor of the First United Methodist Church of Reno said on the Sunday after the suicides, "My two children perished at Guyana, but they received more warmth and acceptance from the People's Temple in a few short years than they received their whole lives from the Methodist Church."

There were other ways to deal with these tragically different groups than to storm them with force. The Branch Davidians were a sect of the Seventh-day Adventist faith. They were not new to Waco. They had been there for over twenty years. One scholar at Baylor University had spent his academic life studying them. A report commissioned by the FBI after the fire concluded that the government paid very little attention to the advice of such scholars. Instead they followed the warnings of some ex-members and anticultists who rely on the necessity defense. In Waco there was little evidence that people were being held against their will. As one father said on national television, "I visited my son at Waco and determined that he had made a rational and serious decision to be there. I was not going to force him to leave. Someone tried to force me in this way when I was a young man, and I was not going to do that to my son."

These two situations have implications for counselors involved in deprogramming. Should counselors join with those who think that whatever force is necessary should be used? Or should we conclude that some of these groups are sincere even though they take their beliefs to the extreme? Human life is precious, and there may come a time where we make a distinction between freedom of religious belief and religious practice. Maybe we do need to protect people from their own foolishness, particularly if their convictions involve life and death.

Available Alternatives
There are a variety of ways in which Christian counselors have been and can

become involved in issues such as those discussed in the first half of this chapter.

☐ Parents can come seeking advice on how to handle their children who have become alienated from their families by joining new or strange religious groups.

☐ Parents can come insisting that you intervene in the lives of their offspring and/or take action against the group in which their children are involved.

☐ Counselees can share with you their involvement in religious groups you think are harmful, coercive and manipulative.

☐ Counselees can share with you their involvement in religious groups you think are heretical.

☐ You can be asked to do the actual deprogramming—either coercive or persuasive.

☐ You can become involved in groups, such as the former Cult Awareness Network (CAN), that propagate knowledge about or governmental control of NRMs.

☐ You can become involved in groups that propagate religious freedom—for new religions, old religions or no religion.

☐ You can be asked to make public statements in support of or against NRMs.

☐ You can be asked to evaluate the mental health of members or former members of NRMs.

☐ You can be asked to testify in court trials involving NRMs.

What are the standards of professional ethics that you should keep in mind as you contemplate involvement in any one or more of these alternatives?

First, it is important for professional Christian counselors to keep their role clear. In spite of their own convictions about what is and what is not *true* religion, their unique skills are in the areas of human behavior. They are not in the business of identifying theological heresy or defending the Christian faith. Some may insist that where counselors are theologically trained they have the right as well as the duty to point out heresy when they see it. On the one hand I agree. However, this is where academic freedom enters in. One has the right to speak out in the area in which one is an expert, not in the area where one has just "some" training.

This does not mean that Christian counselors should have no opinions about the beliefs of new or different religious groups. As Christians they have a right, and even an obligation, to make these judgments. However, they should express these opinions in their role as Christian persons, not as professional counselors. The two roles should not be mixed. It is not ethical to use the weight of one's prestige as a counselor to influence others to accept one's faith convictions. This would be an illegitimate conflict of interest.

I recognize that encouraging persons to keep their faith and their work separate may come as a surprise, since many readers will recall that I have given much of my professional career to the issues of integration (cf. Malony, 1986). I acknowledge that the issue is not a simple one (Enroth, 1986). However, I am convinced that it is very tempting to cloak our disagreement with the beliefs and practices of certain groups under the disguise of our professional expertise in an unacknowledged, and often unconscious, manner.

I remember a mental status evaluation in which an anticult psychologist said twenty minutes into the examination, "My goodness, what have they done to you? Let me get you some material that will help you better understand this group [an NRM]." This psychologist's conviction that the NRM was wrong and dangerous was perfectly appropriate. However, she had been hired by an attorney to unbiasedly evaluate the mental status of an ex-member. The evaluation eventually took a number of sessions of testing, interviewing and observing. What was inappropriate, and in my opinion unethical, was to reach a conclusion twenty minutes into the first session and shift the professional role from evaluator to educator. She was hired to be a neutral evaluator and not an opinionated educator—but those who would later read her report did not know this.

Next, not confusing one's role or becoming involved in a conflict of interest does not mean that one should never evaluate the internal processes of new, or old, religious movements. There is such a thing as "toxic faith" (Arterburn and Felton, 1991). Certain practices of religious groups can evoke pathology (Sloat, 1986). As counselors, Christians have an obligation to evaluate these practices in terms of their possible harmful effects on people. Great care should be taken, however, that the critique is based on sound psychological principles and broad views of normality and human development and not on some subjective judgment of what is true or false (cf. Malony, 1987). Nevertheless, while influence is always present, force is not acceptable where religion is concerned. Healthy religion is that which is always growing and where reflection and questioning is encouraged.

However, Christian counselors should remember the saying "There are many ways to live a life" and that just being different does not always mean that one is destructive. The accusations about child abuse among the Branch Davidians in Waco and The Family in Argentina have both been proved false. Although Singer et al. (1987) proposed a very logical four-step model of influence strategies, their contention that certain NRMs utilize "controlling/destructive" methods different from those used throughout society in both business and evangelism has yet to be demonstrated. In fact, the Singer et al. (1987) report in which this influence model appeared was rejected by the Board of Social and Ethical Responsibility of the APA as not representative of the field because it singled out NRMs and failed to recognize that it was presenting a biased, subjective judgment.

Third, counselors should take care when dealing with families that they not forget what they know about adolescent development. Rather than quickly engaging in suspicious, paranoid projection that youth have been coerced or seduced by some evil manipulators, counselors should first consider the possibility that what looks like coercive persuasion may be an indication of a striving for independence and/or counterdependent behavior. As Stewart wrote in *Adolescent Religion* (1967), youth react to the religion of their parents in three different ways: (1) they affirm it and remain loyal and active in the faith of their childhoods, (2) they reject it entirely and either become irreligious or join strange groups, or (3) they alter it by joining groups that are similar but different. Developmentally, all three reactions should be considered normal. Children who do not follow their parental religious training are just as common as those who do (cf. Brown and Hunsberger, 1984).

However, the reaction of parents should also be understood and appreciated (cf. Singer, 1986). They are hurt over their loss of influence and may feel that they have failed. They are going through deep pain and desperation at the rejection they are feeling and as they see their hopes and dreams disappear when their children make radical decisions. Parents may attempt to reexert influence and power. The relationships they have nurtured and planned are dissipating, and they feel a need to take drastic action. Counselors should be cautious at first about blaming something other than family dynamics and the need for youth to take charge of their own lives in these situations (cf. Kilbourne and Richardson, 1984a).

When Christian counselors give advice to either parents or adolescents, they should first of all encourage them to be calm and listen to each other before panicking (cf. Melton and Moore, 1982, for more good advice). "Tell me about it" should be the first thing parents say. After all, in almost all of these situations the young person has decided to act on the basis of a goal higher than simply achieving success or making money. Most often they have decided to be idealistic and altruistic—not criminal. Of course, at some point adolescents should also be willing to listen to what their parents are feeling.

It is also important for counselors to be aware of two other issues: the history of religion and the psychology of religion. In regard to religious history, there have been many different interpretations of "religion" both across cultures and within cultures. A clear example is the first half of the nineteenth century in America (Marty, 1984). There was much public criticism and prejudice about various new religious groups, such as the Millerites and other millenarians. Many parents were disturbed by the choices their offspring made and felt that the government should take action. So concern over youths' deviant decisions is not a new phenomenon.

Counselors should also be aware of church-sect theory in church history, which conclusively demonstrates how many mainline denominations were originally sects that evoked great disapproval (Handy, 1977). "Throughout American history the prevailing tendency among sectarian movements has been toward reconciliation with the environing culture, resulting in the transformation of sect into denomination" (Persons, 1961, p. 399). There is the strong possibility that some NRMs, which today are considered cults or sects, may become the respected denominations of tomorrow. Certainly this is true of the Methodism of which I am a part. Our church was considered a troublesome sect of the Church of England in the eighteenth century.

Furthermore, counselors need to know about the psychology of religion—particularly Beit-Hallahmi's (1986) contention that religion serves primarily as social identity. In both parents' and youths' lives religion is worn as a badge for all the world to see. While beliefs are central to our identity, what we tell others about who we are is also important. Being a Baptist or a Jew or a Muslim or a Moonie means, among other things, belonging to a group that is different from other groups. It is the badge of our social, or interpersonal, identity. Everyone has this kind of label, whether it is religious or not.

Fourth, Christian counselors need to reflect on modern social constructionism in epistemology (Kuhn, 1970). Grounded in Kant's contention that we never know reality as it really is but are confined by our own human limitations, it is now understood that all knowledge—including religious knowledge—is socially conditioned and culturally constructed. As theologian Tillich asserted, there is a "God above God"—God over and beyond even our best understandings of him (Tillich, 1951).

Many Christians never had the chance to be anything but Christian. Their religious decisions were socially conditioned. For instance, I have to accept the truth that I never had the chance to seriously consider being a Muslim or a Buddhist. While I firmly agree that the Christian faith is the true faith, I have to acknowledge it is not the only faith. We live in a pluralistic world, as the title of Marty and Greenspahn's (1988) book suggests.

How to be open to others' ideas and still committed to Christianity—this is the big issue for Christian counselors. We need to remain humble about our faiths and allow others freedom to take different paths. Allport suggested that being humble and open were characteristics of mature religion (Allport, 1951). And we should remember that psychiatry and psychology have always been handmaidens of the society in which they existed (Szasz, 1961). During the Cold War we bemoaned the fact that Russian psychiatrists sent people who rebelled against the state to mental hospitals. But we fail to see how being different in our own society can be condemned as well. It is very easy to discount the mental stability of those who choose to be different or to claim that participation in a culturally different group causes emotional disturbance. Robbins and Anthony (1982) call this the "medicalization of deviance."

Sociologists Kilbourne and Richardson (1986) have demonstrated the tendency to characterize unpopular religious decisions as based on hypersuggestibility or mental disturbance. They suggest that society has adopted a very passive view of human nature and falsely assumes that those who join NRMs are unfairly influenced or coercively persuaded. Such people had to be under mind control or they never would have joined these groups, this reasoning explains. So because they are "out of their minds" some feel they should be treated, hospitalized or deprogrammed against their wills.

I once heard a speech by a Polish psychologist at an international convention. He spoke on nontraditional religion within Poland. He described Methodists in Poland and said that studies revealed they were hysteric or hypersuggestible, emotionally weak and disturbed. I turned to a friend sitting next to me and said, "I think he is talking about us!" The same sort of accusations have been made about those who choose to become a part of NRMs in the United States. Culture has a great impact on what we consider deviant or normal.

It is interesting that some counselors have concluded that NRMs target disturbed people and influence them coercively, while they do not make the same accusations about the far greater number of people who choose not to be religious in any manner. Nor have they applied the same line of reasoning to used-car sales, advertising, military training and a host of other high-demand sectors of society.

Last, Christian counselors should attempt to follow the ethics of the APA (1992) in "Principle D: Respect for People's Rights and Dignity." As noted earlier, in some cases religious professionals use psychological jargon to cover up their own prejudgments that NRMs are heretical and that society should take any measures necessary to protect people from joining them. They do not realize that they are using political and sociological data to buttress what is basically a religious judgment. Most counselors are trained to exude empathy and warmth by entering into the perceptual world of the counselee. They should do no less when attempting to understand religious and philosophical positions that may differ radically from their own. This is what respect is.

In such biases there is a further danger that counselors will inadvertently espouse "civil religion" (Marty, 1976). Civil religion has become a major part of American history. It follows the common presumption that the United States is chosen and blessed by God to be the representative of God's will on earth. Mormons exemplify this in their belief that Jesus visited America and that the United States is a chosen nation. But Christian and Jewish faiths are grounded in the eighth-century B.C. prophets whose legacy calls us to judge all civil arrangements and to be sensitive to how the state might be unjust in its treatment of marginal minorities.

Yet sometimes these same religious groups have accommodated themselves to their cultures in a conformist manner. They falsely identify Christianity with culture, as Niebuhr poignantly noted in his book *Christ and Culture* (1951). In contemporary America the values of individualism, privatism, civility and anonymity reign supreme and color mainline attitudes toward new or different religious movements that do not share the same social status and power.

One of my closest friends is the president of a prominent theological seminary that prides itself on its inclusiveness and social concern. However, when I mentioned the Moonies' habit of greeting and befriending forlorn youth who got off out-of-town buses as they arrived in San Francisco, he immediately called this brainwashing and coercive behavior. This practice was not coercive persuasion; it was simply the intentional application of good social science theory. Perhaps the United Methodist Church, of which both I and my friend are a part, would not be losing members if it met youth who got off buses in the major cities of our nation!

To bolster our concerns about NRMs with false accusations of brainwashing—which, if it ever even occurred, happened under conditions of extreme deprivation and life threats—is to take comfort from ideas that may be fashionable but have no ultimate value beyond the culture in which they appear.

A personal example of this occurred in the conversion of one of my sons to a very conservative religious group while he was in college. He called me late one Sunday night and said, "Dad, I thought you'd like to know I just accepted Jesus as my Savior and Lord." Fortunately for both of us, I replied, "Tell me about it," even though I was thinking, *You didn't just do that; you were raised as a Christian and have been a member of the United Methodist Church for many years.* He shared with me that he had begun to feel guilty about some things he had been doing and shared his feelings with a Bible study group that was led by a minister from a very conservative church who came every Sunday night to work with the university swimming team, of which my son was a part. As a result of "praying it through," as my son said, he felt converted. He never returned to my church and remains a serious Christian whose priorities are different from mine.

The university has a full-time chaplain from my denomination, and I have often asked myself, *Where was this chaplain the night my son needed somebody to talk to about the guilt he was experiencing?* He was not there when my son needed him, as was the minister from the conservative church. He didn't follow the norms or the rules about who could or could not go into the dorms. I have no right to complain. It was certainly not coercive persuasion. I would even have no right to complain if the volunteer had been from the Moonies or the Church of Scientology. I might have argued long and hard with my son had he decided to join one of these NRMs, but I would be out of order to claim that the group had brainwashed him. Although I, like any father, might prefer my son to affirm the particular denomination in which I raised him, after reflecting on the matter I realized that it was his serious commitment to Christ that really mattered. The church he joined is a strong evangelical congregation in which I have many friends.

Conclusion

This chapter has considered the ethical implications for participating in deprogramming. Although *deprogramming* was narrowly defined as "forceful attempts to change beliefs and practices of persons against their will," the discussion was broadened to include any and all counselor efforts in relation to decisions that are different from the dominant culture.

The recommendations suggested here are biased toward respecting the rights of individuals to make "strange" decisions. This bias is grounded in the ethics of the APA (1992) and the constitution of the United States, which guarantees freedom of religious belief and assembly.

Recommendations about honoring others' religious beliefs should not be taken as a blanket approval of all groups—particularly those that espouse or condone violence. Yet I do not believe that becoming involved in coercive attempts at change (deprogramming) is morally or professionally ethical. In fact, my opinion is that deprogramming usually involves the criminal act of kidnapping and is a clear example of coercive persuasion. Deprogramming, or "exit counseling," meets all the criteria for "brainwashing" as it supposedly occurred in Chinese prisons around the time of the Korean War. Falsely attributing such processes to NRMs, as Langone (1980) has done, is erroneous.

Although there is great pain involved for families in which such religious deviations occur, I believe Christian counselors can provide services that are professionally ethical, compassionate and effective if they follow the guidelines suggested in this chapter. In most cases, I believe, counselors should avoid participating in any degree of deprogramming.

References

Allport, G. W. 1961. *The Individual and His Religion.* New York: Macmillan.

American Psychological Association. 1992. "Ethical Principles of Psychologists and Code of Conduct." *American Psychologist* 47: 1597-1611.

Arterburn, S., and J. Felton. 1991. *Toxic Faith: Understanding and Overcoming Religious Addiction.* Nashville: Oliver Nelson.

Beit-Hallahmi, B. 1986. "Religion as Art and Identity." *Religion* 16: 1-17.

Brown, L. B., and B. Hunsberger. 1984. "Religious Socialization, Apostasy and the Impact of Family Background." *Journal for the Scientific Study of Religion* 23: 239-51. Reprinted in *Psychology of Religion: Personalities, Problems, Possibilities,* ed. H. N. Malony. 1995. Pasadena, Calif.: Integration Press.

Handy, R. T. 1977. *A History of the Churches in the United States and Canada.* New York: Oxford University Press.

Kilbourne, B. K., and J. T. Richardson. 1984a. "Cults Versus Families: A Case of Misattribution of Cause." *Marriage and Family Review* 3-4: 81-100.

———. 1984b. "Psychotherapy and New Religions in a Pluralistic Society." *American Psychologist* 39: 237-51.

———. 1986. "Cultphobia." *Thought* 61: 258-65.

Kuhn, T. 1970. *The Structure of Scientific Revolutions.* 2nd ed. Chicago: University of Chicago Press.

Langone, M. D. 1986. "Cultism and American Culture." *Cultic Studies Journal* 3: 157-71.

Malony, H. N. 1986. *Integration Musings: Thoughts on Being a Christian Professional.*

Pasadena, Calif.: Integration Press.
————. 1987. "Anticultism: The Ethics of Psychologists' Reactions to New Religions."
Paper presented at the meeting of the Christian Association for Psychological Studies,
Memphis, Tennessee.
————. 1988. "The Psychology of Proselytism," in *Pushing the Faith: Proselytism and Civility in a Pluralistic World,* ed. M. E. Marty and F. E. Greenspahn. New York: Crossroad. Pp. 125-42.
————. 1989. "Confessions of a 'Cult' Watcher: An Alternative Point of View." *Cultic Studies Journal* 6: 117-18.
Marty, M. E. 1976. *A Nation of Behavers.* Chicago: University of Chicago Press.
————. 1984. *Pilgrims in Their Own Land.* Boston: Little, Brown.
Marty, M. E., and F. E. Greenspahn. 1988. *Pushing the Faith: Proselytism and Civility in a Pluralistic World.* New York: Crossroad.
Melton, J. G., and R. L. Moore. 1982. *The Cult Experience: Responding to the New Religious Pluralism.* New York: Pilgrim Press.
Melton, J. G., J. A. Saliba, E. V. N. Goetchius, R. Stark, H. N. Malony and E. S. Gaustad. 1995. *The Experts Speak Concerning Witness Lee and the Local Churches.* Anaheim, Calif.: Living Stream Ministry.
Niebuhr, H. R. 1951. *Christ and Culture.* New York: Harper.
Persons, S. 1961. "Religion and Modernity: 1865-1914," in *The Shaping of American Religion,* ed. J. W. Smith and A. L. Jamison. Princeton, N.J.: Princeton University Press. Pp. 369-401.
Richardson, J. T. 1983. "The Brainwashing/Deprogramming Controversy: An Introduction," in *The Brainwashing/Deprogramming Controversy: Sociological, Psychological, Legal and Historical Perspectives,* ed. D. G. Bromley and J. T. Richardson. New York: Edwin Mellen. Pp. 1-11.
Robbins, T., and R. Anthony. 1982. "Deprogramming, Brainwashing and the Medicalization of Deviance." *Social Problems* 29: 283-97.
Singer, M. T. 1986. "Consultation with Families of Cultists," in *Systems Consultation: A New Perspective for Family Therapy,* ed. L. C. Wayne, S. H. McDaniel and T. T. Weber. New York: Guilford. Pp. 270-82.
Sloat, D. E. 1986. *The Dangers of Growing Up in a Christian Home.* Nashville: Thomas Nelson.
Stewart, C. 1967. *Adolescent Religion: A Developmental Study of Religion and Youth.* Nashville: Abingdon.
Szasz, T. 1961. *The Myth of Mental Illness.* New York: Harper & Row.
Tillich, P. 1951. *Systematic Theology.* Vol. 1. Chicago: University of Chicago Press.

Part 3

COUNSELING CONTEXTS

Chapter 13

BUSINESS ETHICS IN MENTAL HEALTH SERVICES
Randolph K. Sanders

*I*magine you are a young psychotherapist fresh out of graduate school. After several years of the graduate-school grind you naively assume that Christian counseling clinics will be standing in line to hire you, anxious to make use of the outstanding skills in talk therapy you have developed in school. Instead you struggle to find a position, eventually landing a decent job as a beginning case manager at a new psychiatric hospital with a Christian therapy unit. One month after you arrive the hospital decides to hold a depression screening day. Advertisements will be listed encouraging people from the community to come to the hospital and be evaluated for depression. As one of the new case managers, you draw the responsibility of being one of the screeners. At the orientation meeting for the screeners, the hospital administrator announces that it is his goal that 35 percent of the people who are assessed to be depressed should be admitted to the hospital, and he promises bonuses to all screeners who are able to get at least 35 percent of their interviewees to enter the hospital. In addition, the administrator promises a vacation to the screener who obtains the highest number of admissions.

The Business of Mental Health
Idealistic young psychotherapists seldom think, at least at first, about their work as business. We go to graduate school with the primary purpose of "helping

people," but time and the realities of our world cause even the most idealistic to consider the "business" of what they are doing before long.

It's not just young psychotherapists who fail to think about the business ethics of psychotherapy. Seasoned professionals also neglect these issues. Much of our professional thinking about ethics is focused on issues in the therapy room such as confidentiality and multiple relationships. Comparatively little thought is given to the ethical issues of the business office and the boardroom. Unfortunately, when business matters are considered, ethical decisions may be driven by expediency (e.g., "What must I do to survive financially?") rather than with consideration for what is moral or ethical.

What would you do if you were the therapist in the example? Would you raise questions about the legitimacy of a screening day whose primary purpose is to find patients to fill empty beds in a new hospital? Or will you look the other way, concerned that to say anything would be to endanger your fledgling career? Perhaps you would tell yourself that many facilities probably do screenings like this and that it surely will help the lay public in some ways, even if the motivations are not entirely noble.

At their lowest common denominator many of the ethical issues surrounding the business of counseling involve issues of money or power or both. There is a natural tension inherent in providing psychotherapy and other forms of professional mental health services. The tension is in the fact that psychotherapy is at once a service to a hurting individual and at the same time a way of producing income for the professional person. On the one hand, the professional is sworn to attend to the welfare of the client or patient. On the other, professionals are also engaged in an occupation, seeking to provide an income for themselves and their families. Some radical critics who oppose psychotherapy altogether see this conflict as an indictment of psychotherapy, clear proof that psychotherapy is inherently unethical because it allows so-called professionals to profit from the pain and suffering of others (Masson, 1994). Most people would not go that far. Many professions make their income by providing special services to people with needs, whether physical, emotional, legal or financial.

We must not miss the critics' warning, however. Whenever one is providing special services to someone in some type of pain or distress, whether it be providing clean water to victims of a hurricane, providing emergency surgery, giving legal counsel or helping someone through a depression, there is the danger that providers of the service will take advantage of their position, manipulating or unfairly profiting from their clients or patients. It should concern us all that the place where Scripture most clearly highlights Jesus' righteous rage is when he threw the traders out of the temple, a definitive indictment of those who would "merchandise" the faith or, in the context of our present discussion, those who would "use" Christian counseling for selfish personal gain (Mt

21:12-14; Mk 11:15-18; Lk 19:45-47; Jn 2:13-16).

This chapter focuses on the ethical issues attached to the business of service provision. We will discuss the more obvious issues: advertising, fee-setting and third-party payments. But we will also review other less discussed but no less important issues such as the ethics of managed care and the unique issues that face clinicians in for-profit and nonprofit settings.

Truth in Advertising

The fundamental rule when advertising mental health services is *tell the truth*. Many of the problems in advertising could be avoided if this rule were considered before public statements were made.

Advertising covers a broad range of activities. It can include brochures and newspaper ads, broadcast media announcements, directory listings, résumés, testimonials or information presented by others, book and tape announcements, and so forth. Taken broadly, advertising could even be construed to mean any statement you make that gives information about your services to the public. When therapists and mental health clinics advertise, they should be particularly careful about certain areas.

Training and experience. Prospective clients have a right to know about therapists' background, degrees and experience. Therapists must be truthful about their training, providing the facts and not giving misinformation either by stating things about their training that aren't true or by omitting certain facts that mislead the client into thinking they have training they don't have.

Case A: A counselor with an M.A. in counseling and a Th.D. in biblical studies advertises himself as Dr. Z, professional counselor, but nowhere in his brochure does it explain that his doctorate is in biblical studies. In fact throughout the brochure he is always referred to as Dr. Z. This counselor was not being entirely clear, leaving potential counselees with the distinct possibility of assuming he had a doctorate in counseling.

Case B: Dr. Y had obtained a doctorate and certificate in counseling from a mail-order school of Christian counseling that was not accredited by any recognized credentialing body. Her training consisted of several brief correspondence courses in "Counseling from the Bible" and the payment of a tuition and processing fee. She told counselees she had her doctorate in counseling.

Case C: Dr. X advertised in the phone book that he had been trained by a well-known Christian therapist, and he named the therapist in his ad. In fact Dr. X had only attended a weekend seminar given by the famous therapist. Therapists should be clear and avoid misunderstanding when stating their degrees, their licensing or certification, and their training experiences. They should not imply that membership in certain organizations such as the APA or CAPS implies special competency or training unless the organization specifically makes it clear that it is appropriate to advertise in this way (APA, 1992, Sect. 3; CAPS, 1993, Sect. 6.3).

Services. Therapists and clinics have an obligation to be clear and truthful about the services they offer. They should not suggest that they provide a certain service when they are, for whatever reason, not equipped to provide the services in a manner which matches the prevailing standard of care.

Case D: Mrs. A, a psychotherapist, announced that she was opening a pain management clinic. A solo practitioner, Mrs. A had no medical consultant for her clinic and had no ready referral network in the medical community. Her pain management treatment program consisted solely of trying to help patients restructure their cognitions about their pain. While Mrs. A's treatment approach might be considered part of an appropriate treatment program, she was implying that she had a comprehensive pain management program when in fact she did not.

Mental health professionals should also avoid making exaggerated claims about the services they provide.

Case E: Dr. Q's telephone advertisement contained the slogan "You've tried the rest, now counsel with the best." Her colleague reported her to the state board, complaining that Dr. Q could not possibly substantiate her claim that she was "the best." Dr. Q countered that several of her clients had told her she was the best therapist they had ever seen. The state board ruled against Dr. Q, stating that "a small unscientific sample of happy clients was hardly proof of superior skill." They required her to receive additional education and supervision (APA, 1992, Sect. 3.03a; CAPS, 1993, Sect. 6.2).

When advertising in the phone book, newspaper or other media, it is best to first study carefully the ethical code of one's professional group to clarify what is considered appropriate and what is not. Rules vary from one professional group to another and from one jurisdiction to another.

Defining appropriate advertising has been complicated in recent years with the entry of government regulations into the process. Until the mid-1970s one could assume that "moderation" and "conservatism" in advertising were basic givens. Therapists were usually encouraged by their professional guilds to use very simple ads that gave basic information with no "bells or whistles."

Then the Federal Trade Commission and the U.S. Department of Justice issued rulings indicating that guild rules on advertising that were too stringent might in some cases inappropriately limit competition (Keith-Spiegel and Koocher, 1985; Koocher, 1977, 1994). The government rulings were supposedly intended to encourage healthy competition and were not intended to endorse flamboyant, sideshow advertising. However, it could be argued that at the least such rulings make deciding what constitutes appropriate advertising more difficult, and thus increase the probability that inappropriate advertising will go unregulated.

Surely Christian therapists should err in the direction of conservatism in advertising. They should not hesitate to state their credentials and training in a clear, forthright manner that helps the consumer understand their skills and be able to make an informed choice about their services. But they should avoid statements that could mislead a layperson and should eschew statements that smack of self-aggrandizement (CAPS, 1993, Sect. 6.2). Most of all they should realize that some things that are fairly acceptable by commercial standards and by the culture at large may not necessarily be acceptable by Christian standards, which encourage care and concern for the welfare of others (CAPS, 1993, Sect. 6.1). They should check state or professional guild standards for advertising and do their best to remain in compliance. They should ask for consultation from fellow professionals when they are in doubt.

Advertising Christian counseling. "Christian" counseling has become very popular. Indeed, laypeople request Christian counseling frequently enough that some managed care and other referral networks now specifically ask therapists to indicate in their applications for provider privileges whether they provide Christian counseling services. In this environment it is not surprising that a few professionals use these terms as much for financial gain as for anything else.

Case F: A private, for-profit Christian psychiatric therapy unit operating out of several hospitals advertised itself as "a ministry to the emotional needs of God's people." However, the program routinely turned away individuals with severe or chronic mental disorders as well as those lacking the financial means to pay for services. Upon being told that his schizophrenic son was "not appropriate" for the unit and referred to a state hospital, a father questioned the program director regarding whether this program was indeed a ministry to God's people if his son, a Christian and a schizophrenic, was not acceptable.

This case should not be taken to suggest that Christian mental health institutions must be capable of dealing with every type of mental disorder presented to them. But they must be sensitive to the way in which Christian language used too broadly, too carelessly or too simply in an effort to sell services may be misunderstood by their public.

Care must also be taken in the use of Christian language because such terms mean different things to different people. Though there is a huge evangelical population in this country, great individual differences exist between Christians of different denominations in such matters as religious practice, religious knowledge, beliefs and opinions. Also, "Christian counselor" may mean different things to different people and could imply everything from a Ph.D.-level Christian psychologist to an inquirer's counselor at an evangelistic crusade. The mental health professional should be clear enough to allow the average person to understand who he or she is and the nature of the Christian services provided.

Advertising by third parties. Not only do therapists have a responsibility to manage their own advertising, they also bear ultimate responsibility for statements made for them by others. Today many therapists and agencies hire public-relations professionals to advertise their clinical services, their continuing education programs and so forth. Other therapists write popular books that are advertised by publishers. Ad agencies, book publishers and the like may not know what is appropriate and may use advertising practices that are unacceptable by the therapist's ethical standards. Therapists must assist these persons in knowing what is acceptable. Most will be responsive; a few, however, may view the therapist as impeding their ability to "sell" the therapist's work, and in such cases the therapist will have to be appropriately assertive about what constitutes ethical advertising or will have to find another public-relations service. Therapists must also gently correct well-meaning but mistaken individuals in the community who advertise incorrectly or give misinformation.

Case G: Mrs. D was doing a weekly marriage seminar at a local church. Each week the associate pastor, who served as emcee, introduced her as Dr. D, psychiatrist, even though Mrs. D was a marriage and family therapist and not an M.D.

The incorrect announcement likely represented simple misunderstanding on the part of the pastor. Nevertheless, the therapist should gently correct the pastor and explain or model an appropriate response.

Celebrity endorsements of professional services are a questionable practice. Actors or sports stars, particularly those who have little or no knowledge about professional counseling, are likely to attract potential clients with their name rather than with their understanding of counseling.

Using counselees' testimonials in advertising is also debatable. Potential counselees under stress may have special difficulty evaluating one testimony and generalizing to their own circumstances. What's more, single-case successes do not necessarily suggest a pattern of success across a number of cases.

Case H: A client with a history of bipolar disorder received help from Dr. R. The client then spoke at several of Dr. R's seminars and in the ebullient, expansive style of someone in a hypomanic state explained in glowing terms how Dr. R had changed his life and told the groups that if Dr. R could help him, he could help anybody.

Potential clients could not know the extent to which the person's bipolar disorder could affect his style of testimony, nor could they gauge how the treatment of bipolar might involve skills different from those needed to treat other disorders. To be sure, one of the best ways that seasoned therapists receive new clients is through word of mouth from former clients. However, these recommendations typically occur in the context of more personal one-on-one relationships in which the prospective client may be better able to judge the veracity of the testimonial and its applicability to his or her own needs.

In addition, one must be concerned about the welfare of the clients who give testimonials. In most cases there may be few long-term negative consequences, but what if clients reveal something in the testimonial that causes significant problems for them in the days ahead? For example, what if they share something that causes them to be ostracized by friends, family or community?

Testimonials are considered appropriate for such things as books, workshops and seminars, and tests or other products. But even here testimonies should not take the place of objective data, nor should they be used in a misleading manner.

Endorsements. Occasionally mental health professionals are asked to endorse a product. These requests may be based on the assumption that the therapist's professional credentials will enhance the perception of the product and increase the purchaser's willingness to buy. Therapists must take care about allowing their status to be used in this way. If the product has nothing to do with mental health, the therapist's professional credentials may create a "halo effect" for the product where none rationally exists. If the product is of a mental health nature, the therapist must take care that the endorsement not substitute for objective data about the efficacy of the product.

Therapists and clinics must avoid misleading the public about their services. They shouldn't make statements that sound positive but can easily be misinterpreted or leave false impressions in the mind of the listener.

Payment for Services

Fees. Fees are a part of the therapy business. Sometimes both therapists and clients ignore this, but it is a fact (Knapp and Vandecreek, 1993). The therapist who avoids discussing money matters is likely to be unclear with clients about the procedures of payment or billing, and perhaps even about the amount to be charged, and may confuse the client or create the mistaken impression in the client's mind that the fee is not particularly important.

For other therapists the business of therapy seems to clearly take precedence over the service of therapy. Every billable hour is accounted for down to the second, and no exceptions are made. Occasionally therapists inflate their fees over those of comparably trained professionals and implicitly or explicitly assert that their high fees are proof of the high quality of their services. Fees should not be misrepresented and should not be exploitive. They should be consistent with the law (APA, 1992, Sect. 1.25; CAPS, 1993, Sect. 2.7).

The APA ethics code states that psychologists should clarify fee and billing arrangements as early as is feasible in the therapeutic relationship. Basic information about fees and billing arrangements may be discussed in the first phone contact between the client and the therapist's office. Therapists should do their best to ensure that their office staff has a clear understanding of the office financial policies so that both staff and therapist will be able to communicate these clearly and consistently to the client. More extensive written information about fees can be provided at the first visit as part of the written informed consent procedures (see chapter three). The therapist or staff can then respond to any questions the client has during early sessions.

Some patients use health insurance to help pay the cost of certain types of mental health treatment. It is up to the practitioner to set forth the policy by which third-party payments are handled. Will the patient be required to pay at the time service is rendered, or will the practice bill the insurance company on the patient's behalf? Some third-party payors define the way and the amount the practitioner will be paid. In any case, if the counselor is to contact the insurance company directly for any reason having to do with the billing, he or she should have a signed release from the patient.

Some therapists and agencies have been known to tell clients that they will accept "insurance only." Under this arrangement the therapist bills the insurance company for the full amount of the session, for example, $80. If the insurance company normally pays 80 percent of such claims, the therapist accepts $64 from the insurance company as the full payment and asks the client to pay nothing.

While therapists who do this might see it as a positive gesture toward the client, it constitutes fraud toward the insurance company. The insurance company assumes that the fee stated on the bill is the customary fee and pays the claim, believing that the client will pay the other 20 percent. If the therapist actually charged only $64, then the insurance company should have paid 80 percent of that amount.

Another fraudulent practice occurs when a practitioner who is eligible to receive third-party payments bills for sessions actually conducted by a practitioner who is ineligible. For example, a board-certified psychiatrist might "sign off" for therapy sessions conducted by a professional counselor in his office who was not on the insurance company's provider list. Or a licensed psychologist might bill the insurance for sessions that were actually conducted by her unlicensed trainee without informing the insurance company that this was what she was doing. Such practices are not only wrong, but could expose the therapist to legal prosecution as well.

When fees and billing arrangements have been established and the client does not pay the bill, the therapist should first attempt to come to terms with this issue directly with the client. Therapists should learn to anticipate those clients who, for psychological or other reasons, display a high potential for not paying their obligations, and where appropriate the therapist should respond to these issues in session.

Case I: During his first session Mr. P told his therapist that he had bill collectors at his door "all the time" and that he had had problems throughout his life with "procrastination." Near the end of the session Mr. P mentioned that he needed to work out a "time payment plan" with the therapist for his sessions. In some cases it may be necessary to use a collection agency or legal measures to obtain compensation for services rendered (APA, 1992, Sect. 1.25). However, the therapist or the agency should inform the client ahead of time that such measures may be taken if no response to a bill is forthcoming. When obtaining informed consent at the onset of therapy, the therapist should tell clients that he or she reserves the right to utilize a collection agent for unpaid accounts. Even so, therapists should realize that using collection agencies or legal measures to obtain uncollected fees is a factor that seems to trigger some clients to file malpractice suits against their therapists (Knapp and VandeCreek, 1993).

Fees and persons of limited means. There is an undeniable biblical mandate for helping the poor. The poor may be with us always, but we have a responsibility to open ourselves to them (Deut 15:11). Jesus and the early church expressed a solidarity with the poor that is clear and unmistakable. Christ announced that he came to set free the poor and downcast (Lk 4:16-21). He gave strong warnings about not being sensitive to the needs of the poor (Lk 16:19-21). We who have are encouraged to share with those who have not (Heb 13:16; 1 Tim 6:17-18) and to avoid favoring the rich over the poor (Jas 2:1-5).

Mental health ethics usually encourage therapists to donate some measure of their services pro bono or on a sliding scale (APA, 1992, Principle F; CAPS, 1993, Sects. 2.1, 2.7). This is easier to do in some work settings than in others. The clinician who works in a community mental health setting may have the fees of poor clients subsidized by the state, foundations or charitable gifts. The private practitioner usually has no such subsidies and must carefully balance services to those with limited means against the financial survival of the practice. Fee scales should be set up carefully, balancing the needs of the community against the real costs of providing quality service (Hinkle, 1981).

In truth, Christian mental health professionals possess a responsibility at two levels when providing services to those of limited means. The first is at the *micro* level: being concerned about the way they respond to the needs of individual clients who come before them. Christian therapists, whether they work in nonprofit or for-profit settings, need to contemplate carefully any conscious or unconscious prejudices they make between people of various socioeconomic groups who come for counseling. They should develop policies that are realistic and compassionate. If a therapist sincerely feels that he or she cannot by virtue of personal skill or financial stability provide services to a person of limited means, he or she should develop a network of resources to which such persons can be referred.

Professionals must also be concerned about the larger issues involved in providing services to the poor: service provision at a *macro* level. Developing a network of referral sources for poor clients is good, unless these sources are, as they so often are, overburdened, understaffed and underfinanced. What responsibility does the Christian mental health professional have to be an advocate for a more humane mental health system for all people, not just the affluent?

To cut costs some states have severely restricted the services they provide to the chronically and acutely mentally ill, who, coincidentally, are often poor and without means. These people, who at one time would have been provided for through the state hospital or community mental health systems, are often relegated to skid-row tenements, bus stations and other places where they try to survive with minimal assistance.

On the other side of the proverbial "tracks," some of the "haves" in the health industry have structured systems that threaten to drive the wedge between services to rich and poor even deeper. Eisenberg (1986) has described the process of "cream skimming" in the medical world in which some hospitals provide only those services that are the most profitable and leave more costly services and the care of the indigent to public hospitals. This practice increased rapidly during the eighties, severely taxing the country's already burdened public hospitals. According to Eisenberg some for-profit institutions structure their entire program, from choosing hospital sites in economically advantaged areas to avoiding certain disorders that are more costly to treat, in such a way as to exclude certain patients. In these settings losing money on a patient is only "profitable" if it leads to some type of public-relations gain for the hospital.

"Cream skimming" takes place in mental health settings as well. Some institutions actively avoid patients with conditions that may be more intractable or patients who for various reasons have little in the way of financial resources.

From a Christian perspective, profits should not take precedent over patients. People, whatever their means, need care, and a system that rewards great profits partly by rejecting certain people is not humane. There is the issue of balance, however. On the one side is the need to provide effective, caring service to as many as possible whatever their means. On the other side is the need to have financially sound agencies, institutions and practices to provide the services. Each individual Christian practitioner needs to be willing to look at the bigger picture of how his or her treatment patterns do or don't integrate with other service delivery systems in the community in order to provide for the needs of the total population.

Fee splitting and kickbacks. No one would argue that therapists should refer clients to those whose skills and integrity they know and trust. Likewise teachers, physicians, pastors, attorneys and other referral persons should feel comfortable with the persons they refer to. However, when money changes hands between referral sources and professionals, there is always the danger that money is more the issue in the referral than is treatment excellence and the needs of the client (APA, 1992, Sect. 1.27).

Case J: A counselor in a Christian high school referred adolescents with serious problems to a Christian ranch for adolescents four hundred miles away, even though there was another well-respected Christian program within fifty miles. The counselor received $150 for each patient she referred.

Ostensibly, the payment was for a brief "background report" on the patient. In this case one must question whether the counselor is referring to the far-removed facility because she really believes its program is far superior or because she is receiving cash payments for sending them there.

Third-party payors and managed care. Insurance companies and other third-party payors have detailed regulations in their policies specifying what conditions are covered and the financial amount of coverage. It is unethical for a practitioner to misstate or mislead a third-party payor with the intention of extracting additional insurance benefits. In general, misleading the insurance carrier can occur in at least two different ways.

First, the practitioner might bill one amount and actually accept a lesser amount so as to maximize the amount received from the insurance.

Case K: A therapist uses a sliding scale for clients with financial hardship. The usual fee is $80, but the therapist offers a $30 fee to a client whose income has dropped. However, when billing the client's insurance company, the therapist states that the bill was $80.

In such a case the therapist should note on the billing to the insurance company that the patient was charged a rate based on financial hardship and that the total amount of charges was $30, not $80.

The practitioner might also mislead the insurance carrier by misstating the diagnosis. Third-party payors reimburse for certain conditions and not for others, and by giving the wrong diagnosis the practitioner might improperly receive payment for a condition he or she was not treating. Both of these behaviors represent fraud, and a person convicted of this can face serious penalties.

The rise of managed care has ushered in a whole new set of ethical dilemmas for the mental health profession. Managed care can be defined as an organized effort "to regulate the utilization of health care" by the "prospective or concurrent review of care provided to individual patients, with the power to deny payment for care thought to be unnecessary or not cost effective" (Appelbaum, 1993). According to its proponents, the purpose of managed care is "to control price and service use, while maintaining quality and assuring that care is rendered in the most appropriate setting" (from *NASW News,* cited in Dworkin and Hirsch, 1994, p. 2).

In fact, many questions are being raised about the quality of care under managed care and the responsibility of individual therapists whose clinical decision-making is sometimes dictated by managed care reviewers whose primary goal may be cost savings for the insurance provider more than service to the patient (Landerman et al., 1994).

Case L: Mr. H suffered from severe and chronic depression that was marginally responsive to any and all medical treatments. The goal of outpatient psychotherapy treatment had been to stabilize Mr. H as much as possible and then to provide maintenance therapeutic sessions on a monthly basis to maintain gains and ensure no relapse. After six months the managed care company refused to provide any more benefits for Mr. H, despite the fact that his doctors filed extensive paperwork documenting the dangers of destabilization that would likely occur if Mr. H was not maintained in treatment.

This case raises many of the salient ethical issues about providing mental health treatment in the age of managed care. With managed care new responsibilities arise both for therapists and for managed care reviewers. Some of these have been reviewed elsewhere (Applebaum, 1993; Sanders, 1996). First, clinicians have a responsibility to appeal the decisions of a managed care company when they feel the decisions adversely affect their patients. As never before therapists are being called on to be advocates on behalf of their patients, asserting their need for care when it is appropriate. Some therapists may feel rightly frustrated that they should be called on to carefully assess and treat clients and then repeatedly have to justify their treatment plan, not once but perhaps numerous times, to persons often far away who may claim to have personal commitment to the patient but in truth have little such commitment.

Yet Christian therapists do bear an ethical imperative to serve in an advocacy role where appropriate. Indeed, we not only should be advocates for the patient, we must, in love and without being heavy-handed, call managed care representatives to their own ideals, encouraging them to ensure that the people who have entrusted their companies with their premiums will be properly cared for (Sanders, 1996). Likewise, Christian therapists have a responsibility to self-regulate and assure that the level of care their patients are receiving is truly needed and that it is being provided at an appropriate price.

Though it is arguably managed care companies' responsibility to do this, therapists may also need to educate patients at the beginning of therapy about the potential limitations managed care may place on therapy. Many patients are totally unaware of managed care's new role in overseeing how much and what kind of care the patient will receive as well as who they will see for the care. For patients with problems of character or other circumstances that may not remit quickly, there may be hard choices to face about how much treatment is enough. This is an issue that therapist and patient should discuss candidly in therapy, deciding together what is best and taking all circumstances into account.

Therapists also have to struggle with issues of confidentiality in dealing with managed care companies. How much detail does the company need to have about a client's case in order to authorize treatment? What if the managed care reviewer is closely allied to the client's workplace, and the information revealed in therapy could have negative consequences for the client if it were known in the work setting?

Clinicians must try to project contingency plans into the future, should their patient's managed care plan deny further coverage but the patient still needs therapy and has no financial resources. The therapist's goal in such circumstances is to ensure that the patient gets the needed help and to avoid any suspicion of abandonment. The therapist may also need to consider what effect if any the patient's current episode of treatment might have on his or her ability to receive covered treatment services in the future.

As therapists sign numerous agreements to provide managed care services, they must also read the fine print and be careful to ensure that the terms of the contract are in keeping with the therapist's code of ethical practice (Dworkin and Hirsch, 1994). Not every managed care contract provides therapists the freedom to consider the patient's needs first.

Mental health practitioners who work as reviewers for managed care companies bear responsibility to review cases with care and to contemplate carefully the often contradictory values of saving money for the insurance company and allowing appropriate care for policyholders. Reviewers also must ensure that they have the appropriate training necessary to judge a treatment plan. For example, is it appropriate for a nurse practitioner reviewer with no training in cognitive behavior therapy to judge a treatment plan consisting of cognitive therapy for depression? Or consider the psychologist who contacts a managed care reviewer to precertify psychological testing for a client. Suppose that the therapist reviewer refuses to certify the testing, but he himself has no training in testing. Clearly the reviewer is working outside his area of competence.

Interactions Inside and Outside the Workplace

Mental health professionals have the obligation to treat colleagues, employees, employers and students with the same level of respect they afford to clients. The business of mental health is seriously impeded by professionals who do not conduct themselves with integrity in these relationships (APA, 1992, Principles B, C, E, F, Sects. 1.09-1.13, 1.19, 1.22).

Relationships with colleagues, staff and students. Every workplace needs clear policies and procedures governing the conduct of the workplace, the terms of employment, the manner for handling conflicts and difficulties, and the manner for handling hiring, firing and promotions. Mental health professionals must respect colleagues and avoid discriminating against, exploiting or harassing (sexually or otherwise) employees, students and colleagues. Written policy and procedure manuals do much to clarify the rules of the workplace.

Interprofessional relationships. Therapists should seek as much as possible to work collegially with fellow professionals outside the immediate workplace. This not only benefits the therapist, but may indirectly benefit clients as well. Mental health professionals should avoid "guild wars" and as much as possible recognize the contribution of each of the therapeutic professions. Therapists need to be able to work closely with other allied professionals in mental health, medicine or ministry who may be able to add their unique talents to help the patient. In this age of intense competition over health care dollars there is an increasing tendency to engage in unethical turf wars with other practitioners. Therapists should avoid such practices as "patient stealing" and should clarify the circumstances carefully with clients who see them during or after they have seen another mental health professional (APA, 1992, Sect. 4.04).

Case M: Dr. C was seeing a female patient in therapy. It soon became clear that the patient's husband required treatment also, but for various reasons Dr. C felt that the patient's husband might have a better outcome if he referred him to another therapist. He sent the patient's husband to another clinic, explaining his concerns to the therapist there. After one visit the therapist there told the patient's husband that he should see both husband and wife individually and that for each of them to go to a different clinic was unethical. The new therapist did not communicate at all with Dr. C about this recommendation, and it was several weeks before Dr. C learned what the other therapist had done.

The keys to good interprofessional relationships are integrity and communication. Professionals, like other groups, build relationships and trust, which can only be solidified when the people involved talk to one another.

Relationships with employers and boards. Seemingly forgotten in the modern workplace is the virtue of loyalty, whether loyalty of employee to employer or vice versa. Without loyalty, workplace relationships take on a transient quality. But loyalty, particularly the loyalty of employee to employer, does not grow in a vacuum. Loyalty springs up where there is legitimate authority.

Where there is legitimate authority employees have the responsibility to work toward the advancement of the organization and to keep its standards. When there is conflict between the organization and the needs of clients or the requirements of one's ethical standards, the employee works to try to resolve these conflicts.

Nonprofit counseling agencies have active boards to which the mental health professionals in the agencies answer. Interaction with boards raises some unique ethical questions. First is the issue of honesty with the board. Boards frequently consist of bright, caring individuals who nevertheless know a limited amount about the daily work of a counseling center. Counselors have a responsibility to educate board members honestly about their work, giving the board the knowledge it needs to intelligently direct the center. This doesn't mean that board members become amateur mental health professionals; it means they have enough information to use the special talents they each bring to the board effectively in the development of the agency's work.

Second, the integrity of relationships between mental health professionals and the board must be sufficiently strong to withstand the fact that it is inappropriate for boards to know everything about what transpires in the agency each day. Sometimes board members may unknowingly ask therapists to breach confidentiality. It is, of course, inappropriate to breach confidentiality, even with board members, but if the relationship between agency leadership and the board is strong, it is likely to withstand such conflicts.

Mental health administrators must also be careful about potential dual relationships with board members. These may include but are not limited to accepting board members as clients and entering into outside financial liaisons with board members.

Case N: Mr. F, an accountant, was asked to join the board of a counseling center and become its treasurer. Soon after joining the board Mr. F approached the director, telling him that he was glad he was on the board because it reminded him of something he had known for years: he really needed to get some marriage counseling. Mr. F asked the director to provide marriage counseling for him in exchange for Mr. F's serving on the board and doing the agency's bookkeeping.

Finally, since boards and their committees often serve in a fundraising capacity for agencies, mental health administrators should promote appropriate fundraising. To do this boards must be appropriately educated about what the agency does as well as what funds are used for. Boards must be honestly apprised of the financial status of the organization through regular financial reports, which should be verified through regular audits or official financial review.

Conclusion

Ethical problems in conducting the business of counseling frequently arise because therapists and administrators often fail to consider consciously the potential problems that might arise. Many of the worst problems stem from a failure to deal well with the inherent tension that exists between mental health as a service to people in pain and mental health as a vocation providing professionals a means for making a living. To avoid problems and build goodwill therapists need to develop honest relationships with others about the business of running the counseling center. They must set clear standards that allow them to serve clients' best interests first and still maintain and run their businesses efficiently and effectively.

References

American Psychological Association. 1992. "Ethical Principles of Psychologists and Code of Conduct." *American Psychologist* 47: 1597-1611.

Appelbaum, P. S. 1993. "Legal Liability and Managed Care." *American Psychologist* 48: 251-57.

Christian Association for Psychological Studies. 1993. *Ethical Guidelines for the Christian Association for Psychological Studies.* (Available from CAPS, P.O. Box 310400, New Braunfels, TX 78131-0400.)

Dworkin, M., and G. Hirsch. 1994. "Responding to Managed Care: A Roadmap for the

Therapist." *Psychotherapy in Private Practice* 13: 1-21.

Eisenberg, L. 1986. "Health Care: For Patients or for Profits." *American Journal of Psychiatry* 143: 1015-19.

Hinkle, J. E., Jr. 1981. "Central Issues Related to the Use of Fee Scales," in *The Organization and Administration of Pastoral Counseling Centers,* ed. J. C. Carr, J. E. Hinkle and D. M. Moss III. Nashville: Abingdon. Pp. 123-30.

Keith-Spiegel, P., and G. Koocher. 1985. *Ethics in Psychology.* New York: Random House.

Knapp, S., and L. VandeCreek. 1993. "Legal and Ethical Issues in Billing Patients and Collecting Fees." *Psychotherapy* 30: 25-31.

Koocher, G. P. 1977. "Advertising for Psychologists: Pride and Prejudice or Sense and Sensibility?" *Professional Psychology* 8: 149-60.

———. 1994. "APA and FTC: New Adventures in Consumer Protection." *American Psychologist* 49: 322-28.

Landerman, L. R., B. J. Burns, M. S. Swartz, H. R. Wagner and L. K. George. 1994. "The Relationship Between Insurance Coverage and Psychiatric Disorder in Predicting Use of Mental Health Services." *American Journal of Psychiatry* 151: 1785-90.

Masson, J. M. 1994. *Against Therapy.* Monroe, Maine.: Common Courage Press.

Sanders, R. K. 1996. "Integrity in the Age of Managed Care." Manuscript in preparation.

Chapter 14

LAY COUNSELOR TRAINING
Siang-Yang Tan

*T*he field of lay counseling, or the provision of people-helping services by nonprofessionals or paraprofessionals with little or no training in mental health counseling, has mushroomed in recent years, both in secular and in Christian contexts (e.g., see Tan, 1990, 1991a, 1991b, 1992, 1993a, 1994b). Increasingly churches are training laypeople to minister as caregivers to facilitate support and recovery groups, do grief counseling, and provide a number of other helping services to hurting people in need. Often Christian mental health professionals are called on to develop and oversee or supervise lay counselor training programs and lay counseling services. Ethical issues pertinent to lay counselor training include the appropriate selection of persons to be lay counselors, the adequacy of the training provided for them, the types of counseling they should be trained for, and the responsibility of professionals to properly supervise such lay counselors. Many of these issues have been covered elsewhere (see Tan, 1991a, pp. 212-26) but will be briefly summarized and updated here.

Lay counseling is a biblically based ministry that has received much support from the research literature for its effectiveness (see Tan, 1991a). Lay counselors in general have often been found to be as effective therapeutically as professional therapists (Berman and Norton, 1985; Christensen and Jacobson, 1994; Durlak, 1979, 1981; Hattie, Sharpley and Rogers, 1984; Nietzel and Fisher, 1981). More research is needed to evaluate the specific effectiveness of lay *Christian* counselors, especially in the local church context (see Toh et al., 1994; Toh and Tan, 1997).

Ethical and Legal Issues

A number of important and helpful books have recently been published on legal issues and Christian counseling (Levicoff, 1991; Ohlschlager and Mosgofian, 1992), but the literature on ethical issues and Christian counseling is more limited (Collins, 1991; Tan, 1994a). The literature on ethical and legal issues related to lay counselor training and ministry is sparse, but it does exist, and I will briefly review it here.

Becker (1987) has written a helpful article covering the main legal and ethical considerations pertinent to the paraprofessional or lay counselor in the church context. He emphasizes the need to develop trust in the counseling relationship in three major areas: the *confidentiality* of the relationship, the *competence* of the counselor and the client's freedom of *choice*.

Confidentiality

In the area of confidentiality Becker notes that lay counselors should follow the legal and ethical standards of professional counselors, which usually require professional counselors to report incidents of child or elder abuse, or situations involving potential danger to self or to others. There are therefore limits to confidentiality that lay counselors should explain to their clients or counselees at the beginning of counseling as they obtain informed consent from them, preferably in writing (or at least verbally, in more informal contexts of lay helping). Even if lay counselors are not mandated by law in some states to report such situations, I agree with Becker (1987) that it is wiser that they do. They definitely should abide by such reporting laws if they are being supervised by a licensed mental health professional. Apart from such limits to confidentiality, lay counselors need to ethically preserve confidentiality with the greatest of care.

A related issue in this regard has to do with whether lay counselors should also be directly involved in church discipline of clients who have broken the moral codes subscribed to by church members, and therefore whether confidentiality can be broken for the sake of church discipline. Becker (1987) has specifically recommended that lay counselors *not* act as agents of church discipline, although they can encourage clients to confess their transgressions to appropriate church leaders. They should *not* break confidentiality for the purpose of church discipline. Some churches may not agree with such a recommendation, especially those using a nouthetic counseling approach that emphasizes providing scriptural direction, including appropriate church discipline. In such churches lay counselors should inform their clients of this further limit to confidentiality for the sake of necessary church discipline as part of obtaining informed consent before starting counseling. The implementation of church discipline, however, still requires much sensitivity, love and wisdom (see Southard, 1986; White and Blue, 1985).

There are also some limits to confidentiality when counseling with minors (see chapter ten). Becker (1987) especially stresses the need to maintain confidentiality in the context of group counseling and the necessity of keeping records on clients safe and secure, preferably by putting them in the care of a licensed professional supervisor.

Competency

Becker (1987; see also Scanish and McMinn, 1996) notes the need to adequately and carefully select, train and supervise lay counselors so that they can function effectively within the limits of their helping abilities and training, and so they can learn to refer more difficult clients to appropriate mental health professionals. I have written a text on lay Christian counseling that describes in detail how to do this (see Tan, 1991a). Briefly, lay counselors should be carefully selected, using criteria such as (a) spiritual maturity; (b) psychological or emotional stability; (c) love for and interest in people, including having empathy, genuineness, and warmth or respect for people; (d) appropriate spiritual gifts for helping ministries (e.g., encouragement or exhortation, healing, knowledge, wisdom, discerning of spirits and mercy); (e) some life experience; (f) previous training or experience in people-helping (if possible, but not essential); (g) age, sex and ethnic/cultural background appropriate to the needs of the clients served; (h) teachability and availability; and (i) ability to maintain confidentiality. Potential lay counselors should be interviewed either individually or in a group context as an essential part of the screening process, which can also include other requirements such as letters of recommendation and psychological/personality testing if a mental health professional is available to conduct it (see Collins, 1980). The use of measures of spiritual gifts, spiritual well-being and spiritual maturity may also be helpful (see Tan, 1991a).

When it comes to training lay counselors, I have noted elsewhere (Tan, 1992; also see Tan, 1991a) that while a systematic training program is essential, there is great variety in the *length* of training and the *counseling approaches* (e.g., Rogerian, psychodynamic, cognitive-behavioral or systems) or *modalities* (e.g., individual, couple, family or group) covered. Usually a minimum of twenty-four to fifty or more hours of basic training in listening and helping skills over a period of several weeks to several months are provided for the lay counselors. However, it should not be assumed that longer and more complicated training programs are necessarily better or more effective than shorter and simpler ones, as Collins (1987) has pointed out.

Collins has raised a further question as to whether professionals are always the best people to provide training for lay counselors. The following are some components of a good training program: (a) practical and clear lectures; (b) homework reading; (c) watching good counseling skills modeled by the trainer or other more experienced counselors (live or through videotapes); and (d) experimental practice through role-playing, or the use of an "experimental client" or friend, or even real-life cases (with consent obtained). Collins (1980) has suggested that the content of a training curriculum for lay counselors should include (a) basic Bible knowledge, particularly that which is pertinent to people-helping ministries (see Collins, 1993); (b) knowledge of counseling skills (including experiential practice or role-plays); (c) understanding of common problems like depression, anxiety, stress and spiritual dryness; (d) awareness of ethics and dangers in counseling; and (e) awareness of the importance of referral and knowledge of referral techniques. While lay counselors can help people who are experiencing a broad range of problems, they should be taught their limits and the need to refer clients to appropriate professionals in difficult situations, such as when the clients or counselees are severely depressed and suicidal, show extremely aggressive behavior, make excessive use of alcohol or drugs, seem to be severely disturbed, have great financial needs, are in legal difficulties, require medical attention, want to switch to another counselor, will need more time than the lay counselor can provide, or arouse strong feelings of dislike, sexual stimulation, or threat in the lay counselor (Collins, 1976, p. 113). The lay counselor should make referrals sensitively and supportively, for example by pointing out that the client deserves help from better trained or more qualified professionals than the lay counselor, not by disparaging or putting down the client.

With regard to the supervision of lay counselors, it is usually recommended that they be supervised by a licensed mental health professional (see Adair, 1992; Lukens, 1987). However, I have noted that although this is ideal or preferable, it is *not* essential. In some churches in rural areas of the country, for example, it may not even be possible because such a professional may not be available. Nevertheless, the supervisor of lay counselors should at least have some basic training and experience in pastoral care or counseling, and also have a licensed mental health professional nearby as a consultant (Tan, 1991a). Lay counselors should receive ongoing, regular supervision of the counseling services they are providing. Usually such supervision is conducted weekly for an hour, whether individually, in pairs or in small groups. The supervision can also occur in small groups on a biweekly basis (meeting for about two hours once every two weeks) or monthly basis (meeting for two to four hours once a month), with individual supervision provided as needed. As Worthington (1987) has pointed out, there should be some observation of the lay counselor's actual counseling work as far as possible. This can be done through audiotapes or videotapes of actual counseling sessions, direct observation through a one-way mirror, or cocounseling, in which the lay counselor and supervisor conduct the counseling session together.

Lay counseling can be provided through a formal, organized model, like a lay counseling center in the church or community, or through an informal, organized model, in which the counseling is provided in more informal settings like homes, hospitals, nursing homes, restaurants and so forth (Tan, 1991a). In such informal contexts cocounseling appears to be the most practical and ethical way of observing lay counselors in action.

Worthington (1987) has also emphasized the need for supervisors to stress what friends and laypeople do well in helping one another, including providing excellent emotional support and empathy for people in crisis, giving good advice after careful empathic listening and understanding, and making available daily, multisituational support. Supervisors should also provide the best supervision they can, making use of the latest developments in the supervision literature (e.g., Bernard and Goodyear, 1992; Estadt, Compton and Blanchette, 1987; Haber, 1996; Hart, 1982; Hess, 1980; Hoffman, 1990; Kaslow, 1977; Mead, 1990; Stoltenberg and Delworth, 1987; Williams, 1995; also see Tan, 1991a, pp. 135-58; and Worthington, 1987).

There are ethical and legal issues pertaining specifically to the supervision of counselors (see Harrar, VandeCreek and Knapp, 1990; Stoltenberg and Delworth, 1987), including lay counselors. These issues include the need for lay counselors to obtain clients' permission to share information from their counseling sessions with supervisors and other lay counselors if group supervision is used. Such information, of course, is to be kept confidential by those present at supervision sessions. Clients or counselees should be informed regarding who will be providing the supervision, how often it will take place and who else will be present.

Adair (1992) has also stressed the need for lay counselors to take and keep good records as part of the supervision process, and she agrees with Becker (1987) that such records should be kept safe and confidential, preferably with a licensed professional supervisor, or at least separate from other church member records. Clients should also be informed before counseling is started that records on them will be kept. Most churches with formal, organized lay counseling centers do require their counselors to keep brief notes or records on their clients. However, there are other churches, especially those involved in more informal but organized models of lay counseling and caregiving, that do not require their counselors or caregivers to keep records on clients. Each lay counseling service or center must decide clearly about record keeping. It is probably wisest to keep some brief records on clients, especially if a formal, organized model of lay counseling is used.

Adair (1992) also noted that the Christian Counselors of Texas recently added the requirement that lay counselors obtain malpractice insurance as part of their guidelines for supervision. However, not all churches have obtained malpractice insurance for their lay counselors, because in some states it is very expensive to do so (see Tan, 1991a), and some churches may not be able to afford it. Also, in some states such malpractice insurance may be very difficult, if not impossible, to obtain.

Choice

In the area of choice Becker (1987) emphasizes that freedom of client choice or informed consent requires the lay counselor to provide accurate and sufficient information on his or her qualifications, training and values, as well as the process, goals and possible consequences of counseling so that the client can make educated choices, including whether to stay with a particular lay counselor or switch to another one. Lay counselors must be particularly careful not to misrepresent themselves as being professionally trained, and they should not use terms like *psychologist* or *psychotherapy* to refer to who they are and what they do. In some states even the term *counselor* cannot be used by lay counselors because of licensing laws, and therefore other alternative titles like *lay helper, lay minister, lay caregiver* or *lay shepherd* may need to be used instead.

Becker (1987) also recommends that lay counselors follow the ethical standards and guidelines of professional counseling or psychological organizations like the American Association of Counseling and Development (now called the American Counseling Association), the American Association of Marriage and Family Therapists (AAMFT) and the APA. As I have noted elsewhere (Tan, 1991a), it is not as easy or clear-cut a task as Becker suggests for lay counselors to follow all of the professional ethical guidelines. Most of them do apply, but one particular guideline having to do with avoiding dual relationships cannot be applied as clearly to lay counselors, since many of them are involved in peer or friendship counseling. I believe that it is appropriate for lay counselors to help peers or friends, especially in church contexts, but they still need to be careful to refer clients to other lay or professional counselors when their objective judgment is in danger of being impaired. Good supervision is crucial to help lay counselors keep appropriate limits or boundaries, even if these are somewhat different from those that professional counselors need to maintain.

Lay counselors should follow other ethical guidelines for professionals that may clearly apply to them as well—for example, avoiding sexual or romantic relationships with clients, and helping within the limits of their competency. There are at least two codes of ethics written from a Christian perspective that can be helpful for Christian mental health professionals as well as lay Christian counselors to follow: a code of ethics for Christian counselors (Beck and Mathews, 1986) and the ethical guidelines for CAPS (1993; see appendix B; see also King, 1986).

Possible Hazards Faced by the Lay Counselor

Becker (1987) warns lay counselors to avoid the following high-risk situations, partly to reduce the possibility of being sued for malpractice: charging fees or asking for "donations"; using psychological tests without adequate training or supervision; having simplistic beliefs that can lead to superficial intervention, misdiagnosis or harm (e.g., believing that all problems are spiritual); counseling clients with severe problems that require professional help; giving advice against psychological or medical treatment; ignoring client statements regarding intent to harm or signs of violent behavior; counseling with an employee or relative; and developing a romantic or sexual relationship with the client.

Needham (1986) has also written a helpful chapter in a book on clergy malpractice (Malony, Needham and Southard, 1986). He stresses the need to care carefully, and in so doing lists twenty high-risk situations that pastors and lay counselors would do well to avoid, many of which are unethical or illegal and which overlap with those mentioned by Becker (1987). Needham also suggests the following steps in caring for others while reducing the risks of litigation: (a) develop a formal counseling policy, covering a number of important areas (e.g., determining target needs, assessing resources, determining organizational channels and accountability, establishing selection procedures, setting up training and supervision standards, formulating guidelines on issues like fees or contributions, checking malpractice insurance coverage, and developing a feedback loop); (b) develop adequate selection, training and supervision; (c) avoid misleading claims; (d) conduct a thorough evaluation of the problem(s) presented by a client; (e) learn to benefit from testing (where appropriate and using properly trained and qualified persons); (f) determine the level of intervention (appropriate to the competence of the lay counselor); (g) make use of consultation and referrals; (h) take advantage of continuing education; (i) keep records and information confidential and secure; and (j) provide follow-up care.

Collins (1988), in his well-known text on Christian counseling, has a good chapter on the counselor and counseling in which he describes the potential problems or hazards a Christian counselor, including a lay Christian counselor, may experience. The areas covered include the counselor's motivation, effectiveness, role, vulnerability, sexuality, ethics and burnout. I have summarized elsewhere these potential problem areas and stressed the need to minimize or avoid them (see Tan, 1991a, pp. 213-15).

Adair (1992), in a paper on ethical considerations of a professional supervising lay counselors, also pointed out that lay counselors do a significant amount of religious counseling, usually without any remuneration. It is my recommendation that fees should not be charged or donations requested by lay counselors in a lay counseling ministry (Tan, 1991a). In providing explicitly religious or Christian counseling, lay counselors often use spiritual resources like prayer,

Scripture and referrals to church or parachurch groups where appropriate (see Tan, 1991b). Sensitivity and competence in dealing with religion as a crucial dimension of human diversity are now mandated by the latest revision of the APA's "Ethical Principles of Psychologists and Code of Conduct" (1992). However, explicitly religious counseling should still be conducted in an ethical and competent way (Tan, 1993b, 1994a, 1996), because there are potential ethical pitfalls in religious counseling that should be avoided (see Younggren, 1993). For example, Nelson and Wilson (1984) have suggested that it is ethical for counselors to share or use their religious faith in counseling contexts if they are dealing with problems that would be helped by spiritual interventions, if they are working within the client's belief system (and therefore avoid forcing their own religious beliefs on the client), and if they have clearly defined the counseling contract to include the use of religious or spiritual resources or interventions, thereby obtaining the informed consent of the client. Lay Christian counselors need to follow these guidelines in order to do lay counseling that is explicitly Christian or religious in an ethical and helpful way. They can share openly or expose their Christian values without imposing them on their clients and can give the clients the freedom to ultimately choose their own values and courses of action.

Richard (1987) briefly described a number of potential perils that the professional counselor may face in being involved with local paraprofessional mental health organizations, lay counselor training or lay counseling ministries. They include the following scenarios: (a) other professionals may feel threatened by the work of lay counselors and may therefore need to be educated about the effectiveness of lay counselors as well as the cooperative way in which lay counselors usually work together with professionals, making referrals to them where necessary and serving constituencies not currently being served adequately by the existing mental health system; (b) some churches or Christian organizations may still be antipsychology and anticounseling, and this attitude may be difficult, but not impossible, to change; (c) there is the danger of burnout and exhaustion for the professional counselor who overcommits to a lay organization, and therefore the work should be shared with others; (d) there could be a conflict of interest for a professional counselor in private practice, so he or she should avoid using a lay counseling organization to further private endeavors.

Proper Evaluation of Lay Counselors
One final ethical guideline that has not been sufficiently emphasized is the need for evaluating lay counselors. Both the effectiveness of lay counselor training programs and the efficacy of the counseling provided by lay counselors should be comprehensively evaluated in better controlled studies, particularly for lay Christian counselors (see Toh et al., 1994; Toh and Tan, 1997). I have elsewhere

made detailed suggestions as to how such careful evaluation research can be conducted (see Tan, 1991a, pp. 159-87). There is also a need for further research that more closely examines the skills, deficiencies and limitations of lay counselors (Durlak, 1979). A particularly important area in need of more research and data has to do with the question of how ethical is the actual practice of lay counselors. More specifically, we do not yet know how many lay counselors actually obtain informed consent from their clients prior to counseling with them, keep confidentiality appropriately and follow the other ethical guidelines discussed in this chapter. Although lay counselors have been found generally to be as effective therapeutically as professional therapists, some may question whether lay counselors are as ethical as professional therapists. Only further research and data obtained from lay counselors and professional therapists can answer this crucial question more adequately. Evaluation is important in adding to and furthering the knowledge we already possess.

Conclusion

Lay counselor training and lay counseling ministries are significant areas of service for Christian mental health professionals to be involved in. The ethical and related legal issues discussed in this chapter, as well as recommendations or suggestions provided, will hopefully help such professionals to develop and supervise lay counselors effectively and ethically, so that the lay counselors can learn themselves how to function effectively and ethically in people-helping ministries.

References

Adair, J. 1992. "Ethical Considerations of a Professional Supervising Lay Counselors." Paper presented at the Second International Congress on Christian Counseling, Atlanta, Georgia (November).

American Psychological Association. 1992. "Ethical Principles of Psychologists and Code of Conduct." *American Psychologist* 47: 1597-1611.

Beck, J. R., and R. K. Mathews. 1986. "A Code of Ethics for Christian Counselors." *Journal of Psychology and Christianity* 5(3): 78-84.

Becker, W. W. 1987. "The Paraprofessional Counselor in the Church: Legal and Ethical Considerations." *Journal of Psychology and Christianity* 6(2): 78-82.

Berman, J. S., and N. C. Norton. 1985. "Does Professional Training Make a Therapist More Effective?" *Psychological Bulletin* 98: 401-7.

Bernard, J. M., and R. K. Goodyear. 1992. *Fundamentals of Clinical Supervision.* Needham Heights, Mass.: Allyn and Bacon.

Christensen, A., and N. S. Jacobson. 1994. "Who (or What) Can Do Psychotherapy: The Status and Challenge of Nonprofessional Therapies." *Psychological Science* 5: 8-14.

Christian Association for Psychological Studies. 1993. *Ethical Guidelines for the Christian Association for Psychological Studies.* New Braunfels, Tex.: Author.

Collins, G. R. 1976. *How to Be a People Helper.* Santa Ana, Calif.: Vision House.

———. 1980. "Lay Counseling Within the Local Church." *Leadership* 7(4): 78-86.

————. 1987. "Lay Counseling: Some Lingering Questions for Professionals." *Journal of Psychology and Christianity* 6(2): 7-9.

————. 1988. *Christian Counseling: A Comprehensive Guide.* Rev. ed. Waco, Tex.: Word.

————. 1991. *Excellence and Ethics in Counseling.* Dallas: Word.

————. 1993. *The Biblical Basis of Christian Counseling for People Helpers.* Colorado Springs: NavPress.

Durlak, J. A. 1979. "Comparative Effectiveness of Paraprofessional and Professional Helpers." *Psychological Bulletin* 86: 80-92.

————. 1981. "Evaluating Comparative Studies of Paraprofessional and Professional Helpers: A Reply to Nietzel and Fisher." *Psychological Bulletin* 89: 566-69.

Estadt, B. K., J. R. Compton and M. C. Blanchette. 1987. *The Art of Clinical Supervision: A Pastoral Counseling Perspective.* New York: Paulist Press.

Haber, R. 1996. *Dimensions of Psychotherapy Supervision: Maps and Means.* New York: W. W. Norton.

Harrar, W. R., L. VandeCreek and S. Knapp. 1990. "Ethical and Legal Aspects of Clinical Supervision." *Professional Psychology: Research and Practice* 21: 37-41.

Hart, G. M. 1982. *The Process of Clinical Supervision.* Baltimore: University Park Press.

Hattie, A., C. F. Sharpley and H. J. Rogers. 1984. "Comparative Effectiveness of Professional and Paraprofessional Helpers." *Psychological Bulletin* 95: 534-41.

Hess, A. K., ed. 1980. *Psychotherapy Supervision: Theory, Research and Practice.* New York: John Wiley and Sons.

Hoffman, L. W. 1990. *Old Scapes, New Maps: A Training Program for Psychotherapy Supervisors.* Cambridge, Mass.: Milusik Press.

Kaslow, F. W., ed. 1977. *Supervision, Consultation and Staff Training in the Helping Professions.* San Francisco: Jossey-Bass.

King, R. R., Jr. 1986. "Developing a Proposed Code of Ethics for the Christian Association for Psychological Studies." *Journal of Psychology and Christianity* 5(3): 85-90.

Levicoff, S. 1991. *Christian Counseling and the Law.* Chicago: Moody Press.

Lukens, H. C., Jr. 1987. "Lay Counselor Training Revisited: Reflections of a Trainer." *Journal of Psychology and Christianity* 6(2): 10-13.

Malony, H. N., T. L. Needham and S. Southard. 1986. *Clergy Malpractice.* Philadelphia: Westminster Press.

Mead, D. E. 1990. *Effective Supervision: A Task-Oriented Model for the Mental Health Professions.* New York: Brunner/Mazel.

Needham, T. L. 1986. "Helping When the Risks Are Great," in *Clergy Malpractice,* ed. H. N. Malony, T. L. Needham and S. Southard. Philadelphia: Westminster Press. Pp. 88-109.

Nelson, A. A., and W. P. Wilson. 1984. "The Ethics of Sharing Religious Faith in Psychotherapy." *Journal of Psychology and Theology* 12: 15-23.

Nietzel, N. T., and S. G. Fisher. 1981. "Effectiveness of Professional and Paraprofessional Helpers: A Comment on Durlak." *Psychological Bulletin* 89: 555-65.

Ohlschlager, G., and P. Mosgofian. 1992. *Law for the Christian Counselor.* Dallas: Word.

Richard, R. C. 1987. "The Professional Counselor and Local Paraprofessional Mental Health Organizations." *Journal of Psychology and Christianity* 6(2): 35-38.

Scanish, J. D., and M. R. McMinn. 1996. "The Competent Lay Christian Counselor." *Journal of Psychology and Christianity* 15(1): 29-37.

Southard, S. 1986. "Church Discipline: Handle with Care," in *Clergy Malpractice,* ed. H. N. Malony, T. L. Needham and S. Southard. Philadelphia: Westminster Press. Pp. 74-87.

Stoltenberg, C. D., and U. Delworth. 1987. *Supervising Counselors and Therapists: A Developmental Approach*. San Francisco: Jossey-Bass.

Tan, S. Y. 1990. "Lay Counseling: The Next Decade." *Journal of Psychology and Christianity* 9(3): 59-65.

———. 1991a. *Lay Counseling: Equipping Christians for a Helping Ministry*. Grand Rapids, Mich.: Zondervan.

———. 1991b. "Religious Values and Interventions in Lay Christian Counseling." *Journal of Psychology and Christianity* 10(2): 173-82.

———. 1992. "Development and Supervision of Paraprofessional Counselors," in *Innovations in Clinical Practice: A Sourcebook*, ed. L. VandeCreek, S. Knapp and T. L. Jackson. Sarasota, Fla.: Professional Resource Press. 11:431-40.

———. 1993a. "Lay Christian Counseling," in *Clinical Handbook of Pastoral Counseling*, ed. R. J. Wicks and R. D. Parsons. Mahwah, N.J.: Paulist Press. 2:27-50.

———. 1993b. "Training in Professional Psychology: Diversity Includes Religion." Paper presented at the National Council of Schools and Programs of Professional Psychology (NCSPP) Midwinter Conference on "Clinical Training in Professional Psychology," La Jolla, California (January).

———. 1994a. "Ethical Considerations in Religious Psychotherapy: Potential Pitfalls and Unique Resources." *Journal of Psychology and Theology* 22: 389-94.

———. 1994b. "Lay Counseling: A Christian Approach." *Journal of Psychology and Christianity* 13(3): 264-69.

———. 1996. "Religion in Clinical Practice: Implicit and Explicit Integration," in *Religion and the Clinical Practice of Psychology*, ed. E. Shafranske. Washington, D.C.: American Psychological Association.

Toh, Y. M., S. Y. Tan, C. D. Osburn and D. E. Faber. 1994. "The Evaluation of a Church-Based Lay Counseling Program: Some Preliminary Data." *Journal of Psychology and Christianity* 13(3): 270-75.

Toh, Y. M., and S. Y. Tan. 1997. "The Effectiveness of Church-Based Lay Counselors: A Controlled Outcome Study." *Journal of Psychology and Christianity* 16.

White, J., and K. Blue. 1985. *Healing the Wounded: The Costly Love of Church Discipline*. Downers Grove, Ill.: InterVarsity Press.

Williams, A. 1995. *Visual and Active Supervision: Roles, Focus, Technique*. New York: W. W. Norton.

Worthington, E. L., Jr. 1987. "Issues in Supervision of Lay Christian Counseling." *Journal of Psychology and Christianity* 6(2): 70-77.

Younggren, J. N. 1993. "Ethical Issues in Religious Psychotherapy." *Register Report* 19(4): 1, 7-8.

Chapter 15

ETHICAL ISSUES IN
SPECIAL SETTINGS:
AN INTERVIEW WITH
STEPHEN H. ALLISON &
RICHARD L. PRICE

Randolph K. Sanders

*S*ome Christian mental health professionals work in institutional settings where ethical conflicts occur as a function of discrepancies between the individual practitioner's professional or Christian ethics and the mission and standards of the institution in which they work. Therapists and mental health administrators who work in federal, state or military institutions are good examples of professionals who may experience these conflicts. Psychologists in Christian college counseling centers or other Christian agencies may also experience conflicts with college or agency administrators. While the two sides share a common faith, they may have different perspectives on the purposes and appropriate conduct of counseling.

The interview that follows focuses on the ethical conflicts that may arise when the mental health professional works in one of these special settings. Being interviewed are Stephen Allison, the director of a Christian university counseling center, and Richard Price, a military psychologist. Practitioners in other types of state or Christian agencies and institutions are likely to find much in the experiences of Dr. Price and Dr. Allison that would apply in their own settings, at least in a general way. It should be noted that the opinions expressed by Dr. Price are his own and not to be construed as the official policy or position of the U.S. government, the Department of Defense or any branch of the service.

Ethical Issues in Military and University Counseling

Many of the ethical issues present in your work settings are similar to those that most mental health professionals face. However, there are some issues that are particularly pertinent to your settings. Using the APA's "Ethical Principles of Psychologists and Code of Conduct" (1992) as a reference, please mention several issues particularly prevalent in your workplace.

Price: In a military mental health setting one of the most frequently encountered ethical issues is that of client welfare. Seldom does a day go by that I don't feel some degree of tension between the interests of the military and those of the military client. I am constantly challenged to clarify my roles and responsibilities depending on the nature of the client contact. As a general rule I try to abide by the principle that to do a good job for the client will serve the best interests of the military as well in the long run. In addition, by training and by personal disposition I am inclined to try to make each client encounter a therapeutic one, or at least to leave open the possibility of a therapeutic encounter in the future. However, in practical application it is sometimes difficult to abide by these general guidelines.

One area where the issue of client welfare arises in a military setting is that of performing commander-directed mental health evaluations. Sometimes these evaluations are fairly straightforward and free of conflict, particularly when the evaluation discloses no significant diagnosis or other information that would require any action deemed undesirable by the client. On the other hand, however, the evaluation may reveal significant psychopathology requiring hospitalization or a medical evaluation board to review the client's fitness for military duty. This course of action may be met with a great deal of resentment on the part of the client, depending on his or her agenda and perspective. The evaluation might also reveal a personality disorder or other diagnosis that interferes with military service to a degree that the client must be recommended for administrative separation from the service. If the client wants to separate from the service, this may be a welcome recommendation. However, if the client wants to remain in the military or believes he or she should be compensated for a disability rather than administratively separated, the client may believe the mental health provider is not acting in his or her best interest.

Still another outcome of an evaluation might be a diagnosis of alcohol abuse or dependence, which requires certain mandatory rehabilitative actions as well as administrative restrictions—some of which may significantly affect the client's current job and even his or her career, in some cases. The client's psychological denial may make it difficult to accept the existence of an alcohol problem. However, to an even greater degree, the client often finds it hard to agree that the mandatory rehabilitation and administrative restrictions will be beneficial. The military mental health professional is often in the position of either making an unwelcome recommendation or compromising his or her clinical judgment in order to avoid conflict with the client or a negative impact on the client's career.

Another factor contributing to the military provider's dilemma is command influence. Command influence refers to the circumstance in which the evaluator and evaluee serve under the same commander. Although the clinician may be able to refer clients to mental health professionals at other installations to avoid direct command influence, indirect command influence can still be present. The clinician's performance appraisals are written in part on the basis of the quality of service provided to the local unit commanders. In other words, our customers are the commanders as well as the clients. Naturally, a clinician who has decided to stay in the military will ordinarily try to maintain good rapport with commanders, legal officers, supervisors and helping agencies throughout the installation. It sometimes challenges our integrity to be true to our clinical judgment while recognizing our professional limitations, particularly when making recommendations that are unpopular with commanders, clients or both.

One of my primary responsibilities in dealing with the conflicts of interest I've described is to continually clarify expectations with my superiors, my clients and the clients' commanders. At the onset of my contact with the military client who is referred for a commander-directed evaluation, I explain that I will be sending the commander a written report of my evaluation and recommendations. I also confirm that the client has been advised in writing by the commander of the reason for the referral and the client's rights. After the evaluation I discuss my findings and recommendations with the client and provide the client a copy of the evaluation report if requested.

Another technique for coping with conflicts of interest is to stay current in my understanding of diagnostic and administrative decision criteria through reading, seminars and discussions with colleagues. Being able to adequately explain these decision criteria to clients or commanders is very important in helping all parties understand the ground rules. In addition to reviewing decision criteria, I like to discuss specific difficult cases with other providers, sometimes asking for second evaluations. This helps me avoid developing "tunnel vision" or accepting forced choices when better options may be available. Finally, I try to mix enough "therapy cases" into my workload to maintain a sense of fulfillment and job satisfaction. Otherwise a steady diet of commander-directed evaluations would be a sure recipe for burnout due to the constant tension I've mentioned.

From a Christian perspective I find it helpful in dealing with conflict of interest to remember that I am called to serve God by loving others. I strive to keep this call a higher priority in my life than pleasing others, particularly those in positions of power and influence. I also believe it is important to pray for God's help in doing mental health work—for the client to receive healing in time of crisis and personal growth and for me to have wisdom and a loving spirit, especially when bearing unwelcome news.

Allison: University counseling centers have a number of organizations and publications, in addition to the ethical principles published by the APA, that serve as ethical guidelines for our practices.[1] Undoubtedly the most critical ethical concern in our counseling center is confidentiality. Since we are a fairly small university, there is a lot of concern expressed among our clients about other people knowing that they are coming in for services. We have statements guaranteeing confidentiality on a "guidelines for services" page that students read and sign upon intake [see appendix C]. Part of what is ensured in this document is confidentiality. Any exceptions that would allow us to legally breach confidentiality are outlined very specifically. These include the client's becoming suicidal, homicidal, emotionally or mentally decompensated to the point where they cannot take care of themselves, or involved in or reporting knowledge of sexual or physical abuse of a minor. The other issue that we have to address regarding confidentiality, since we are a training site for master's-level therapy, is taping. State supervision guidelines require us to audio- and/or videotape therapy sessions conducted by subdoctoral trainees. There is a separate release form that is discussed and signed with the counselee in the first session to ensure confidentiality of the audio- or videotapes. These are viewed solely for supervisory purposes. Students that do not agree to taping are reviewed and typically assigned to a doctoral-level staff member.

On occasion we are called on to consult with legal counsel about the mandatory withdrawal of a student. This is a very touchy issue and has many legal and ethical considerations. The primary guideline that we have used is to avoid mental health reasons for withdrawal and to focus on behaviors that are in violation of school policy, such as academic failure or suspension for breaches of student rules. We try to stay away from using psychological language in any kind of withdrawal decision. Coll (1991) has a good review of the critical issues germane to this, and Burch has developed a very helpful document outlining guidelines for dismissal of impaired students.[2] Each state also has legal guidelines that should be consulted.[3]

One final ethical consideration that arises in our staff meetings quite often is multiple relationships. On college campuses that are both small and Christian there is a push to blur the lines of distinctions in relationships, because a lot of what we do on this campus is termed "ministry." One has to be very careful about honoring the ethical guidelines about multiple relationships in settings such as these. For example, I never counsel anybody who is a current student of mine. We also refer any student with whom we have an outside social relationship who asks to see us. For instance, one of our therapists serves as a minister on a local church staff, so he does not do psychotherapy with any students involved in his campus ministry program. Our student trainees do not do psychotherapy with people who are fellow students in classes with them.

Issues Beyond the Ethics Code

I am sure there are potential issues that arise for you as a Christian mental health professional that are beyond the professional ethics code. Please mention a few of these.

Price: I think the biggest issue for the Christian mental health professional serving in the military is the issue of wartime service. A Christian friend once asked me if it would be good for our nation to have a military force with no Christians in it. Of course, it would be best if there were no need for any country to have a military force. Unfortunately, however, as most would agree, military strength appears to be necessary for the security of our nation. Accepting that premise, I have to answer my friend by saying that I am glad Christians are a part of our nation's military. However, this means that Christians can be engulfed by something that is basically evil—war itself. This is true for the health care professional as well as the combat soldier, fighter pilot or bomber crew.

Even though the health care provider is not expected to be a combatant, the fact remains that our efforts are geared to support the war-fighting capability of our country. The private citizen may believe a particular military action is warranted, but to actually be deployed to the combat theater in support of combat troops entails a different level of involvement. It links the military mental health professional very closely to the war effort and may also expose him or her to a certain degree of danger.

As a Christian military psychologist deployed to Saudi Arabia during Operations Desert Shield and Desert Storm, I was faced with the possibility that I might not return to my home and family, as well as the grim knowledge of the devastation caused by our successful bombing campaign against the Iraqi forces. It was important for me to remember that my wife and I had prayed together over the years at many decision points, which eventually led to my being deployed to Saudi Arabia. I had to trust that I was where God had placed me and accept that I was part of something far beyond my ability to fully comprehend—especially in light of all the talk about Armageddon prior to the war. I also relied heavily on the promise in Romans 8 that not even death could separate me from God's love in Jesus.

Although I had prayed that the conflict with Saddam Hussein would not lead to war, this was not to be the case. Obviously, once the air war started, I wanted our efforts to be successful in destroying the war-fighting capability of the Iraqi forces in Kuwait. However, I found it extremely painful to hear the reports of all the Iraqi soldiers killed in the process. Perhaps my pain is no different from the pain any other Christian might have felt at that time. But I think being a part of the military made it hard to ignore the tragedy of it all, since I directly supported the forces that brought it about. Perhaps one reason it is good that the military is not devoid of Christians is that the desire for victory needs to be tempered with an acknowledgment of the evil inherent in war and a sensitivity to the suffering it causes.

Another problem, perhaps of less dramatic proportions but more frequently faced by the military mental health professional, is that of failing to value the client. In an atmosphere in which there is a steady and sometimes overwhelming flow of clients, there is no economic necessity to seek out new clientele. This is especially true when the demands for services far exceed our ability to satisfy them. In addition, except for internally generated quality improvement efforts there is no systemic pressure to see each client as a valuable entity. This is especially true in the case of those clients who have run afoul of the system and are awaiting disciplinary action. In fact, I have found it a significant challenge to avoid burnout and to maintain a sense of reverence and gratitude for the healing ministry with which I have been entrusted. I am glad that other Christian mental health professionals in the military have helped remind me of the spiritual nature of my calling. One colleague told me that he continually experiences a sense of awe and humility when he considers how blessed he is to have been given the opportunity to serve others in such a personal and intimate way through his practice of psychology. In addition, the fundamentals of our Christian faith provide a basic framework that affirms the worth of every client by reminding me that each person is precious to God and therefore to me.

Allison: The most pervasive issue in my work that deals with spirituality and Christian issues is the developmental problem of students questioning, challenging and internalizing their own belief system. A number of students have grown up in homes where their religion was "spoon fed" to them. Leaving home and going away to school is seen by them as the first opportunity they have had to really question things. Some of this questioning is done in a very healthy, straightforward way. At other times there is a lot of negative acting out that accompanies it. Learning to sensitively question students about their own value system in the context of psychotherapy, without appearing to be proselytizing, is tough. Although most of our students expect some spiritual component to their counseling, one has to be careful to pace and word these things appropriately in order to establish and maintain adequate rapport with the counselee.

The other real dilemma for us is when students in the course of the counseling session present to us clear violations of Christian principles and values in terms of behavioral acting out. We have discussed this at length in our staff meetings and feel like we have to follow APA ethical guidelines. Students are assured that we will not break confidentiality and "rat on them" to the administration for breaches such as alcohol and drug use, sexual acting out and the like, unless these behaviors spill over into potentially life-threatening situations as defined by APA code.

Conflict Between Ethics and Organizations

One area I think most institutional therapists deal with is conflict between your professional ethics and the demands of your organization. The APA code (1992) speaks to this in Section 8.03. For example, many Christian colleges subscribe to some form of in loco parentis, *maintaining that they bear some responsibility to serve as surrogate parents or guardians to students, while at the same time providing a quality education. Dr. Allison, in what ways could this philosophy conflict with the work of the college psychology clinic?*

Allison: We feel very strongly that we are not surrogate parents to these students. We want to be an extended support system for them. It is very important that we be perceived as professional therapists and not mom and dad. Part of doing this requires that we not assume responsibility for students' behaviors or decisions. Most parents are understanding about the dilemma we are in regarding releasing information, although we have to very diplomatically explain our ethical guidelines to many parents each semester when they call asking for information. Some students are willing to sign releases that will allow us to consult with parents. Here again, we discourage students from signing blanket releases allowing us to confer with their parents about any aspect of their treatment, preferring that they put some limits on the content that can be revealed. Given that most of our students are over eighteen years old, we are bound by the same confidentiality laws that govern others. We get a lot of calls from concerned parents wanting to know the status of their students in counseling. Learning how to respond to concerned parents poses a real dilemma for both our counseling and our office staff.[4]

Another issue that poses a considerable dilemma for us is referrals from the dean's office, making counseling a mandatory alternative to dismissal. This has been widely debated in the profession, and you will find quite a variety of stances that college counseling directors take in regard to these kinds of referrals. At a recent meeting of Texas University counseling-center directors we took an informal survey. Some counseling centers refuse to accept any of these kinds of referrals. Most of us are willing to work with the dean's office but put clear limits on our availability for ongoing consultation with the referral source. We want the students to feel they have the same access to confidentiality as any other student seeking our services would have. There is also a problem with compliance, given that these students are not voluntarily seeking counseling. There is considerable discussion of all these issues in the counseling-center literature.

With regard to the confidentiality of student counseling records, are there times when the college should have a right to know what is in a student's record?

Allison: The incidents where the university or outside agencies have had to know material contained in the student records have involved cases where students became psychotic, suicidal or homicidal. There have also been instances where child abuse has been involved and records have been subpoenaed.

Here again, following APA guidelines and state law is the rule. No administrator has ever asked for access to student records because of concerns about breaking university policy alone (for example, violations of drinking guidelines, sexual misconduct, etc.).

What are some ways that a Christian college counseling-center director can help college administrators be sensitive to ethical dilemmas?

Allison: The best way for counseling-center directors to help administrators be more aware of our own ethical dilemmas is to develop a good consulting relationship with them. As my college vice president, who is an attorney, has indicated, he is in an entirely different profession from me that is guided by a different set of ethical guidelines, and unless I am willing to communicate with and educate him, there is no way that he can know our position. There are, however, parallel organizations within higher-education circles that administrators should be encouraged to join and whose journals they should subscribe to, which periodically address university counseling-center issues. My own vice president just returned from a convention of university counseling-center attorneys. An entire day of the program was devoted to better understanding the stresses and dilemmas inherent in the university counseling centers on their campus. On his return from the conference he and I had a lengthy conversation that was quite eye-opening for both of us. Providing copies of any guidelines or laws governing the ethics of your profession to your administrators would be an essential first step. I will refer you to the AUCCD [American Association of University and College Counseling Center Directors] document bank for samples of policy statements and papers that could be supplements to APA materials and that university administrators could find helpful and educational.

Of course, the famous Tarasoff case is one which grew out of services provided at a university clinic. Dr. Allison, please discuss this case and tell us, are there things that college administrators and counseling-center professionals can learn from it?

Allison: The Tarasoff case did establish the precedent for duty to warn. It is a rare semester that we don't encounter a similar dilemma. On our own campus we use *Tarasoff* as a basis for having to breach confidentiality when students are at risk of hurting themselves or others in the dorm. We have an understanding with the deans that dorm directors and/or resident assistants will always be notified if a student is in this critical condition.

Dr. Price, the right of the institution to know versus the confidentiality of the client's record is also an issue in military facilities. What are the special issues in this setting, and how can the therapist deal with them?

Price: The lack of confidentiality of the client's record poses a serious concern for the military mental health professional. Under certain circumstances military regulations allow government agencies to have access to client records without the client's consent. This inhibits the client in sharing information and reinforces the common fear that seeking military mental health care might at some point be damaging to one's career or legal standing. Although clients in a private setting may sometimes face the possibility of a court-ordered subpoena of their records (and in some cases of their therapist as well), this seems to be a frequent issue in a military setting. Clients are often investigated, either for security clearances or for criminal charges.

In my years of military practice the only solution I've found for dealing with this dilemma is to be certain that the client is fully advised at the onset of counseling or assessment about the limitations on the confidentiality of his or her record. If it appears that legal issues may be at stake, I advise the client of his or her rights against self-incrimination and inform the client that I can be required to testify in court or other military proceedings about information they may share with me.

Spiritual Resources in Counseling

Another concern that arises for the Christian professional in any state or federal institution is the question of the use of spiritual resources or concepts in therapy. Dr. Price, are there times when you may utilize spiritual or Christian resources in therapy? If so, when would this be, and how would it be done ethically? What are some examples?

Price: Just as I would not condone a therapist of another faith using his or her government-paid position to solicit converts, I feel it is unethical for me to evangelize non-Christians, particularly in my official capacity as both a therapist and an officer. However, I do believe the client's religious practice and social support system are legitimate areas of psychosocial functioning that warrant assessment. As long as I don't try to pressure the client to accept my beliefs, I consider it to be acceptable to ask the client about his or her religious background and current practice—partly to understand the client's value system and partly to appreciate how the client's personal faith and religious affiliations may be helping or hindering his or her attempts to achieve emotional, physical or spiritual healing.

On the other hand, Christian clients sometimes invite me to share my personal faith or to comment on specific spiritual issues. When asked to do so, I do feel more freedom to share my faith with my clients. However, I still believe it is important not to take advantage of my position as a therapist and an officer and unduly pressure a person to accept my religious perspective. In addition, I want to avoid allowing spiritual issues to become a diversion from cognitive, emotional or behavioral issues that may be painful but extremely important for the client to face. I basically try to be sensitive to spiritual issues in therapy. However, as a general rule I don't try to do pastoral counseling in the military mental health setting. If the client seems to need in-depth spiritual counseling, I usually suggest they see a chaplain or a pastor instead of (or in addition to) me. I believe this approach helps me focus my energies in those areas of ministry for which I am best equipped and helps the client better address both spiritual and cognitive-emotional concerns.

Dr. Allison, it might seem that on the Christian campus there would be no limits to using spiritual resources, including evangelizing. But are there issues in this setting as well?

Allison: Our student trainees—practicum students and student workers—are put through an orientation before they are allowed to work at the university counseling center. Part of this involves considerable dialogue about the difference between incorporating spiritual discussion in the healing process and evangelizing in the counseling center. We are strong proponents of an integrative approach to therapy and view our role as holistic healers very seriously. We would, however, have to be sensitive to the developmental needs of each individual client. Student trainees are encouraged to use the client's language and to address issues at the level each client can tolerate. This would include any discussion about spiritual issues like grace and forgiveness. Some clients come in eager to address these issues. Others are in a state of spiritual rebellion and would not return if this language was "crammed down their throats." We have seen some students come to faith and many others deepen their Christian walk through counseling in the university counseling center.

Ethical Dilemmas in Secular Settings

Dr. Price, Christian professionals who have administrative or policymaking roles in secular institutions must also face ethical dilemmas. What are some examples, and how might these be dealt with?

Price: In a military setting a Christian mental health officer often exercises supervisory authority over other professionals, technicians and administrative personnel. The emphasis in recent years on a "total quality management approach" has challenged those in positions of authority to value the ideas of everyone involved in a given process. Previously, a Christian mental health officer may have felt it was fine to run a tight ship in a benevolent, though somewhat dictatorial, fashion. However, under total quality management we are challenged to maintain a dynamic balance between directive and participatory management styles that can be tailored to address a wide variety of situations. This forces the Christian to look beyond rank, position, power and recognition for deeper and more abiding sources of emotional security. I find that power assertion is rarely an effective strategy for conflict resolution in the long run. If I am able to participate in a win-win solution to conflicts, then all parties seem to be happier. To do this I find I frequently need to remind myself that as Christians we are called to serve one another in love.

In addition to my relationship with subordinates, my relationship with superiors also challenges my Christian principles at times. The most common temptation for me is to overvalue the approval of senior officers. When I do this, I lose sight of my primary allegiance to God. I think it is important for us as Christians in the military to show respect for our superiors—tempered with an inner awareness that our ultimate commander is Jesus.

Suggestions for the Young Professional

With regard to ethical issues, what suggestions would the two of you have for young professionals who are planning or beginning careers in Christian or secular institutional settings?

Price: My most significant source of help in dealing with ethical issues has been my wife. Her commitment to her faith and to the church have strengthened me on many occasions when my own strength was exhausted. Another source of strength has been the support of Christian friends who uphold me in prayer and provide an example for living out the faith in practical circumstances. In addition, teaching Bible study classes has helped me stay in touch with biblical truths that enrich my life, establish my ethical parameters and help me focus my prayer life. Finally, networking with caring Christian colleagues has often proven to be a source of encouragement, instruction and constructive admonition. I encourage young professionals to maintain an open dialogue with their spouses, cultivate Christian friendships, study the Bible and develop networks of Christian colleagues. I believe this strategy will provide an excellent foundation for dealing with ethical dilemmas, both personal and professional.

Allison: Young Christian professionals who wish to work in a university counseling center should familiarize themselves with the current literature, as this will give them some awareness of the breadth and depth of ethical dilemmas posed in this setting. However, I think that attendance at and participation in professional and Christian professional organizations and conferences would be an even better way of gaining an understanding of the concerns at hand. We hosted the southwestern regional convention of CAPS recently. This was an invaluable experience for our students. One of the presentations was entitled "Ethical Thinking: New Standards," and material was presented by Drs. Ron Cruse and Roger Russell, professionals who have expertise as well as a sensitivity to spiritual issues.

Young professionals certainly need to be familiar with the ethics codes and other ethics information published by their professional organizations [see appendix B]. These documents contain the fundamental principles for good practice.

There is no substitute for mentoring. Getting your feet wet with volunteer work or employment will give you the best feel for ethical dilemmas. When you are faced with dilemmas in real life, in real counseling situations, you have to deal with the issues. They are no longer distant and academic. Seeing ethical problems arise in my own practice has been the primary impetus for my students and me to explore ethics in depth.

References

American Psychological Association. 1992. "Ethical Principles of Psychologists and Code of Conduct." *American Psychologist* 47: 1597-1611.

Coll, K. 1991. "Mandatory Psychiatric Withdrawal from Public Colleges and Universities: A Review of Potential Legal Violations and Appropriate Use." *Journal of College Students Psychotherapy* 5.

---

[1]In addition to the AUCCD, we also have state affiliates such as the Texas chapter (TUCCD). These groups have annual meetings in which we discuss ethical issues that affect university counseling centers. There is information published through Division 17 (counseling psychology) of the APA in the *Journal of Counseling Psychology* and the *Counseling Psychologist*. There is a *Journal of College Student Psychotherapy,* published by Hayward Press, that includes information about ethics. For example, there is an article in a 1991 issue (vol. 6, no. 1) entitled "Ethical Dilemmas in College Counseling: The Doctor Is In," by D. Kaplan and D. Rothrock. The other excellent resource pertaining to specific ethical guidelines for university counseling centers is the AUCCD document bank. There are a number of white papers and policy statements that have been issued through this national body, including papers on confidentiality, job performance ratings, interventions for crises such as rape and sexual offenses, suicide management, and other critical ethical concerns. This document bank can be accessed by writing the University of North Carolina at Wilmington, 601 South College Road, Wilmington, NC 28403-3297, attention: Division of Student Affairs. There is also an accrediting body for university counseling centers called the International Association of Counseling Services, 101 S. Whiting St., Suite 121, Alexandria, VA 22304, (703) 823-9840.

[2]A copy of these guidelines can be obtained by writing Dr. Wade Burch, director, Student Counseling Service, Texas A&M University, Henderson Hall, College Station, TX 77843-13263, (409) 845-4427.

[3]In the state of Texas, sourcebooks include *Texas Law and the Practice of Psychology* (Texas Psychological Association) and *Forensic Psychology for the Journeyman Clinician* (Texas Psychological Foundation).

[4]There is a double issue of the *Journal of College Student Psychotherapy* devoted to parental concerns and college student mental health published in 1987 (vol. 2, nos. 1 and 2) that addresses a number of these issues.

Chapter 16

FORENSIC PSYCHOLOGY

James M. Alsdurf

*F*orensic psychology is one of the most complicated areas a psychologist can be involved in. He or she must weigh complex psychological matters within the context of legal factors and reach determinations that can have profound implications for individuals being evaluated. Consider the following scenarios, typical of what a forensic psychologist might address:

☐ A fifteen-year-old enters the home of a woman in the late afternoon and stabs her twice, resulting in her death. He has no criminal record and claims that he simply was startled and overreacted when the victim entered the bedroom where he was hiding. Further evidence shows that the victim was sexually assaulted before her death. When interviewed by police he denies any past problems. His parents, however, tell police that he has a psychiatric history. A box of his writings, which involve sexually violent images and references to Satan, is found in his bedroom.

☐ A young man in his twenties is charged with criminal sexual conduct for coercing an adolescent female to repeatedly engage in sexual acts of bondage and domination. He is a leader of his church's youth group and a graduate of a Christian college. The pastor and members of his church and community come forward in outrage over these charges and are tenacious in their advocacy of his innocence. The pastor announces in a Sunday-morning service that it is not his or the church's role to take sides. The young man's wife lies during the trial, claiming she was with her husband the night of the offense, despite later proof that this was impossible. The defendant is found guilty. The judge considers a range of sentencing options in light of the man's complete denial of guilt, finally ordering a psychological evaluation.

☐ A man is charged with stalking after a four-year history of harassing a woman. He has pursued her in public, surreptitiously entered her home, sent her love letters, flowers and candy, and makes contact despite several restraining orders. Convinced that he has been enlisted by a secretive group of psychiatrists who telepathically communicate with him and want him wedded to this woman, the man is being evaluated to determine if he is competent to stand trial. His attorney is urging the examiner to view her client as meeting the standard for a McNaughton ruling (not guilty by reason of insanity).

When the activities of forensic psychology are carried out within the framework of a Christian faith, ethical and moral dilemmas are brought to the fore, which makes the task of integration especially challenging. This chapter will examine the basic tasks of forensic psychology and the role of Christian ethics within that context, in the hope that the reader will not only gain an understanding of the basic components of forensic psychology but also be helped in deciding whether to pursue this area of professional activity.

The Nature of Forensic Psychology

Forensic psychology is that area of mental health evaluation which relies on behavioral science to address issues of law. Given that human behavior is the main concern of both fields, the use of psychology in the context of law seems to be a natural fit. However, a closer look at the attempt to apply the behavioral sciences to the legal arena reveals that psychological insights are often compromised by the frequent interest of the court to predict human behavior. The prediction of human behavior is very complicated and has been described as a "perilous, narrow path," particularly as it relates to predicting violent behavior (Growth et al., 1978, p. 39).

Forensic psychology, as defined by those in the field, refers to all forms of "professional psychological conduct when acting, with definable foreknowledge, as a psychological expert on explicitly psycho-legal issues, in direct assistance to courts, parties to legal proceedings, correctional and forensic mental health facilities, and administrative, judicial and legislative agencies acting in a[n] adjudicative capacity" (APA, 1991b, p. 657). A forensic psychologist, then, is one who regularly engages in the practice of forensic psychology as defined above. A distinction should be made, however, between psychologists who may be asked to provide professional psychological services without knowing that they will be employed for a forensic task and those who understand their task to be forensic in nature.

One foundational question raised by the very nature of forensic psychology is whether mental health professionals should even be considered experts.

According to the Federal Rules of Evidence, Article 7, "If scientific, technical, or other specialized knowledge will assist the trier of fact to understand the evidence or to determine a fact in issue, a witness qualified as an expert by knowledge, skill, experience, training or education may testify thereto in the form of an opinion or otherwise" (Melton et al., 1987, p. 14).

Expert testimony must therefore be able to disclose the data base or underlying facts that serve as the foundation for expert opinion. For instance, testimony should not recommend a certain type of treatment on the basis of "intuition" unless supported by other reliable data, such as treatment outcome studies. Or, as is more often the case, the forensic psychologist should not use psychological testing that lacks solid validity or reliability measures just because it fits the clinician's theoretical framework. These standards are intended to prohibit careless or uninformed testimony and clarify the fact that mental health professionals are to refrain from giving opinions as to the ultimate legal issues involved. The task of the mental health professional, then, is to inform the court and not to serve as a fact finder.

Professional Guidelines and Codes of Conduct
Within the APA's code of conduct (1992) is a section that addresses the issue of forensic activities. This section deals with professionalism related to forensic psychology and specifically challenges psychologists who are involved in forensic activity to have an awareness of the impact of their reports and testimony on the legal process. When one explores this section, what is most apparent is that forensic activity requires constant attention to the limits of one's role and the effect this has on both the court and the parties involved.

In addition to the APA's ethics code there are state guidelines and rules of conduct that govern the behavior of psychologists. While generally there are no specific sections dealing with forensic practice, many states require the practitioner to declare his or her areas of competence in which proficiency has been gained through experience in clinical training. Most people involved in the area of forensic assessment generally have declared this as an area of specialty.

A recent guideline for providers of psychological service to ethnic, linguistic and culturally diverse populations has also been published by the APA (1991a) with the hopes of improving the quality of psychological services to ethnic and culturally diverse populations. This requires attention to different "values, interactional styles, and cultural expectations." Given the increased attention in mental health activity to ethnic, racial and multicultural factors, and given that forensic activity often includes persons of color, familiarity with these guidelines is essential.

Furthermore, guidelines for "child custody evaluations in divorce proceedings" are also now available from the APA, having been drafted recently by the Committee on Professional Practice and Standards (COPPS). These guidelines are constructed on the APA's "Ethical Principles of Psychologists and Code of Conduct" (1992) and are intended to promote "proficiency in using psychological expertise in conducting child custody evaluations" (APA, 1994, p. 677). Noting the important role psychologists often play in such custody studies, the guidelines call for particular competencies and understanding in order for such evaluations to "provide adequate and appropriate psychological services to the court" (p. 677). Emphasizing that the primary purpose of such evaluations is the "best psychological interests of the child," the APA outlines sixteen concerns under three categories: the purpose of evaluation, how to prepare for such an evaluation and the actual conducting of the evaluation. A helpful list of references and pertinent literature is contained in this article, essential for all psychologists engaged in this task.

What is quickly apparent to the reader from a cursory overview of these various standards is the range of responsibilities that rest on the psychologist or evaluator who undertakes this work and the expectations of just what makes up competent, objective and impartial evaluation. For instance, the primary emphasis within child custody evaluations is essentially which of the two parents is most capable to meet their child's needs. These APA child custody guidelines address issues of competency to perform evaluations, confidentiality, expert witnesses, the role of psychologists as evaluators, how to advise the court, the risk of bias in evaluating families and more. One admonition from these guidelines is that therapy and evaluation do not blend and that psychologists should not be involved in both tasks for the same client. Ethical considerations also exist for psychologists involved in divorce mediation (Ewing, 1985, pp. 243-79) and stress that psychologists, as mediators, should always remain neutral. And, while not available at this time, specialty guidelines for the practice of forensic psychology with juveniles will be forthcoming soon from the APA, Division 37, Child, Youth and Family Services.

Specialty Guidelines for Forensic Psychologists
Specific guidelines for forensic psychologists have also been created by the Forensic Psychology/American Law Division of the APA to help improve the quality of forensic psychological services.

For those who are clearly functioning in a forensic capacity, the code outlined by Division 41 emphasizes a model of "desirable professional practice" associated with forensic practice. Psychologists should first be aware of the areas in which they have specialized knowledge, skill, experience and education and be able to communicate the factual basis legitimating their qualification as an expert. Along with this awareness of "competence" is the ability both to understand the civil rights of parties in legal proceedings and to manage their professional conduct in a manner that does not diminish or threaten those rights (APA, 1991b, p. 658). Such responsibilities require that the psychologist recognize the impact of what the specialty guidelines label "personal values, moral beliefs" on his or her professional practice. This is particularly an issue for the Christian psychologist and will be discussed at length later in this chapter.

Under the heading "relationships" the specialty guidelines outline obligations that forensic psychologists have to inform their clients about factors that might affect a decision to enter into a contract with a forensic psychologist. Following these recommendations can help to limit conflict between the psychologist and client, to establish a clear contract between professional and client, and to guide this relationship according to professional standards. Unless an assessment is court-ordered, psychologists must obtain the informed consent of the client or party (or the client's legal representative) before proceeding with such an evaluation. One should never procced if a client appears unwilling to cooperate and until a thorough notification has been given to the particular client in tandem with his or her attorney.

In cases where the forensic evaluation has been court-ordered, if the client's attorney objects to the evaluation, the psychologist should notify the court and request further direction before proceeding. Within this context all clients should be given a Tennessen Warning, a statement given to a client which specifies the limitations of confidentiality (e.g., a report may be sent to the court based on the therapy conversation).

The section on "confidentiality and privilege" within the specialty guidelines affirms the obligation of forensic psychologists to be aware of legal standards that affect a client's confidentiality. In situations "where the right of the client or party to confidentiality is limited," the psychologist is obligated to protect data which do not specifically pertain to the purpose of the evaluation. This section essentially challenges professionals to conduct their activities "in a manner that respects those known rights and privileges" (APA, 1991b, p. 660).

When discussing "methods and procedures," issues of documentation, preparation of reports to the court or use of psychological methodology for forensic assessment are reviewed. The guiding principle within this section is that forensic psychologists should avoid giving "written or oral evidence about the psychological characteristics of particular individuals when they have not had an opportunity to conduct an examination of the individual adequate to the scope of the statement, opinions, or conclusions to be issued" (APA, 1991b, p. 663). The emphasis here is on clinical rigor as the legitimate, essential basis for forensic opinion. This requires the clinician to be careful in forming opinions and attentive to the special responsibility to gather data "in a manner standard for the profession" and maintain professional integrity by examining "the issue at hand from all reasonable perspectives" (p. 662).

The final section, "public and professional communications," may seem very clear, but in light of recent high-profile cases (e.g., the O. J. Simpson case) and the release of confidential information by mental health professionals it is apparent that this is sometimes disregarded. The ethical burden for forensic psychologists is that they make every reasonable effort to ensure that the product of their services is not exploited or miscommunicated in ways that promote deception. In court this means clearly disclosing sources of information used to reach a particular opinion. Outside of court this means releasing only the information required and legally authorized.

Ethical Issues in Forensic Psychology

One of the first ethical issues that faces the forensic psychologist is deciding who the client is. Monahan's (1980) notable publication provides a very informative discussion and review of the complications surrounding this matter. As Melton et al. (1987) note in their seminal work, *Psychological Evaluation for the Courts,* the APA's task force in the criminal justice system found this question "to be of overriding significance" because the primary goal of assessment is not "to assure the individual's psychological adjustment or well-being, but to assist the courts in making fully informed dispositional decisions" (p. 51).

Given the competing concerns of the judicial system and the individual parties in question, some professionals may decide not to be involved in forensic evaluation. For those who do it is essential that from the beginning expectations of attorneys, the court or individuals be clearly delineated regarding issues of confidentiality. Since forensic evaluations are done to provide information to the court, sensitive material must be reviewed and sometimes revealed for the first time. It is not unusual for an examiner to learn information that even the client's attorney did not know and that the examiner may decide is essential to disclose. As no assurances can be given to client or counsel about the outcome of an evaluation, particularly when a professional is obligated to report his or her findings to the court, assurances of confidentiality cannot ethically be made. It is best in these situations to be clear with all parties that confidentiality cannot be assured and to have the person being examined (assuming a client is competent) sign a statement that he or she has been so informed. When an attorney wants to obtain a private evaluation without the court's knowledge in order to determine if an initial evaluation is credible, confidentiality must be maintained by the private examiner. It is not infrequent that an "adverse" evaluation ends up in the wastepaper basket.

An ethical issue that rarely arises but that can cause great anxiety for the professional when it does is what to do when, in the process of an evaluation, information is revealed that if ignored may compromise a clinician's ethical standards. For instance, threats of violence would call for warning potential victims if they are specifically named or notifying the court or the police if a client is incarcerated. One should also always make a record of this warning.

Often, however, the type of information revealed is complicated because it involves competing courses of action that could affect the client in a variety of ways. For example:

□ A client reveals information about his spouse that suggests that previous bruises and injuries to his daughter were caused by his wife, who is now the sole guardian due to his pending prison term. He provides you with a letter in which the wife threatens to beat the daughter once he goes to prison unless he himself takes the blame for her actions and discourages the involvement of child protection.

□ A woman charged with felony theft reveals in the process of a court-ordered assessment that her psychologist has been having sex with her regularly for two years (a felony in some states). She also claims that she will deny this if you reveal it to anyone because she is in love with him. Rules of conduct within your state dictate that you report such information to the Board of Psychology or face disciplinary measures. This same psychologist is in the private-practice setting where you work, and you could be listed as a defendant if civil litigation were brought against him.

These and other circumstances reveal the broader ethical considerations forensic examiners may face that point to the importance of not only being alert to ethical issues, but having access to legal counsel specializing in professional behavior. As Melton et al. (1987) recommend, where situations of "ethical-legal conflict exist, clinicians must ultimately establish some priorities in order to select a course of action" (p. 59). The principles they recommend include considering first the physical welfare of the client and then the "personal health and safety concerns" (p. 59) of others. Again, consulting with either the referral source or outside agencies may be necessary, and in cases that are court-ordered, the primary obligation is to the court. All information to the court should be well documented and as objective and specific as possible.

Central to the literature on ethics and forensic psychology is the standard that one not overstep his or her areas of expertise by attempting to act as an expert in areas in which one is not trained or has little experience. The APA states that "psychologists only provide services for which they are qualified by training and experience" (APA, 1992, p. 1597). Psychologists are to be exceedingly careful that the data they present are not given in a distorted fashion. For reasons that are often evident (given the consequences that criminal defendants in particular may face), attorneys may attempt to employ psychological data or expert opinion in a misguided or clearly dishonest fashion. It is the responsibility of the psychologist in these situations to be alert to potential misuses of his or her data and clarify, as best as possible, any distortions. Psychologists must remember that it is their professional responsibility to "remain scrupulously close to the data" (Shapiro, 1991, p. 234) and not just to satisfy the attorney who hired them (sometimes more difficult than is initially apparent).

Predicting Behavior
Courts' frequent admission or use of forensic testimony is due to the desire to

obtain predictions of behavior. Diagnosis is one dimension of psychological evaluation/testimony that guides the court in its decision-making. For example, did a defendant charged with shooting at a passing airplane do so because he has posttraumatic stress disorder from his years as an infantry soldier in Vietnam, and will he under similar circumstances repeat this behavior? Or was this a random act of violence caused by drinking and a recent fight with his girlfriend? Some would argue that the influence of psychological theory on diagnostic labels (improved by the publication of *DSM-III, III-R* and *IV*) and the variation among professionals despite attempts to standardize diagnosis should exclude diagnostic information from the court.

The ability to predict dangerous or violent behavior is often a concern for the court. However, clinical and actuarial methods both are very limited in their accuracy (see Monahan, 1981, pp. 71-75; Wenk, Robison and Smith, 1972, who found an 86 percent false positive prediction of violence). Generally a much higher percentage of violent behavior is predicted than actually occurs. Given the possibility that an expert's prediction of future violence may influence the court to impose restrictions on an individual, even to the point that repeat sexual offenders can in some states now be permanently institutionalized as sexual predators (Farnsworth et al., 1994, outline the history of this process and the treatment design for such offenders in the state of Minnesota), mental health involvement in violence prediction has been criticized by many as unethical. Melton et al. (1987) express concern because of the many factors that can influence a clinician's judgment, including political factors, cultural difference, a belief that correlations exist between two variables when they do not (i.e., the more psychotic the person, the more likely he or she is to be violent), the low base rate for violence, and a failure to appreciate contextual factors rather than personal pathology as an explanation of violence.

Predictions of dangerousness by clinicians have been seen as poor at best by all who have investigated this area. Some would suggest that any attempt to predict dangerousness is unethical (Monahan, 1981), while others suggest that "mental health professionals should not offer unqualified and categorical predictions in individual cases" (Melton et al., 1987, p. 205). Melton et al. further admonish clinicians who function as experts for the court and make statements only about an individual's violence potential "by describing the risk factors associated with a particular class of individuals whose violence potential is known and to which the subject belongs" or by conducting "a careful inquiry into the personal and situational factors that have contributed to the individual's behavior in the past, in an effort to identify those conditions under which the likelihood of a future aggressive act is increased" (p. 205). As another qualification they warn that when reporting the results of their assessment of violence potential, clinicians minimize reference to diagnostic labels in reports addressing dangerousness and offer no long-term "clinical predictions of dangerous behavior couched in absolute terms. . . . [They should] volunteer prefatory comments, both in written reports and in oral testimony regarding the poor validity (i.e., no better than one in three) of clinicians' positive predictions of dangerousness" (p. 207).

These strong cautions should not ignore, however, a growing area of literature that indicates that some factors do increase predictive validity regarding dangerousness. Grisso and Appelbaum (1992), well-regarded forensic experts, propose that such predictive testimony is not necessarily unethical and that past opposition to such predictions was based on the "lack of scientific support for the validity of predictions . . . derived primarily from publications in the 1970's" (p. 624). They propose a variety of forms prediction can take (dichotomous, dichotomous with qualified confidence, risk but individual-based, risk but class-based) and cite recent studies that contradict "the generalized assertion that all predictive testimony regarding future violence is unethical for lack of a scientific basis" (p. 626). Overall the burden is still on the professional to be familiar with the literature on prediction and to provide comprehensive information to the court on this issue.

New assessment measures for the prediction of violence using theoretical constructs have also been proposed by Hare and Hart (1994) using Hare's "psychopathic checklist" (PCL-R). They claim that violence levels for psychopaths can be measured, are fairly constant and therefore relatively predictable. Other researchers have presented similar findings, focusing on psychopathic offenders (Harris, Rice and Cormier, 1991), with some proposing a statistical prediction model (Harris, Rice and Quinsey, 1993). And a recent publication on assessing the dangerousness of sexual offenders, batterers and child abusers summarizes the "research in this area, as well as the instruments that may be helpful and the criteria by which to judge them" (Campbell, 1995).

Christian Ethics and Forensic Psychology

In his book *A Passion for Justice* philosopher Solomon (1990) states that "true human justice involves real human passions." Justice is wisdom applied in the midst of the tensions and dilemmas of life. It is "the Will of God conscientiously applied to the ways of humanity" (p. 5). Perhaps no area of professional activity is more closely related to the difficult task of applying the will of God to the evil ways of humanity than forensic psychology.

Just as Monahan challenged forensic psychologists to begin by focusing on who the client is, the Christian forensic psychologist must, in turn, be concerned with not just the rights of the client but also the client's dignity. The Christian begins with the understanding that Christian faith establishes a value system based on moral and ethical considerations. These considerations are informed by Scripture, guided by faith and founded on the belief that certain principles from Scripture are to be applied to human relationships with wisdom. The application of clinical skills and knowledge from psychology is part of that process of wisdom. These skills are to be respected, not mistrusted or disregarded over and against a theological system that may use biblical language to explain and describe human behavior and be uninformed about the role of science and the insights gained from psychology. In fact, for the Christian psychologist not to rely primarily on the knowledge of psychology is to act unethically, because by so doing he or she is ignoring the ethics of the profession and thereby placing his or her client at risk.

What is being advocated here is a model of integration that prioritizes the place of Christian ethics so that very careful attention is given to each situation. For instance, a psychologist doing a child custody evaluation will attend to issues of faith and religious identity very differently from the person doing a sex-offender evaluation for the court. The former would require a careful assessment of both parents and their strengths and weaknesses along with the primary focus of the child's needs, while the latter would necessitate consideration of dispositional possibilities (permanent or temporary incarceration, type of treatment, probationary stipulations, etc.). Because treatment outcome research with sex offenders indicates a rather low level of success, particularly when diagnostic factors are carefully examined (e.g., pedophiles are particularly resistant to treatment; cf. Barbaree and Marshall, 1988), one might hope for change but in reality place little confidence in this outcome, even if the offender claims newfound religious faith.

Christian Ethics as a Guide to Forensic Practice

The Christian forensic psychologist must function within the context of a redemptive love in order to cope with the outrage he or she may feel when evaluating those charged with or convicted of various crimes. Such love is redemptive because it allows contact with those who suffer or, as is more often the case in forensic psychology, with those who create suffering, and it provides a conduit for both accountability and healing.

The presence of Christian ethics also requires theological grappling on the part of the forensic psychologist, with a willingness to ask, "What does Scripture say about this?" It requires one to integrate good theology with good psychology and not to set aside one's faith but to constantly struggle with faith and practice in the context of warring forces. It requires keeping in mind that while psychology informs and theology guides, in the forensic setting the court decides.

The Christian mental health professional should realize that things are not always as they seem and that using prescription biblical passages as a cure-all for psychological problems seldom proves efficacious. Such is even more true for the Christian forensic psychologist. The following ethical guidelines for those engaged in forensic psychology are offered as a guide for determining professional behavior.

1. *The ethic of redemptive love.* Ethicist Smedes (1983) calls this the power to move "in the direction of kindness" (p. 19). The source of this power is divine love, the love of God, which exhibits an "uncommon power to cope with common suffering" and gives us the ability to endure what we don't want to endure (p. 1). Only redemptive love can empower forensic psychologists to confront and overcome their fears and liberate them to move toward clients who, by the very nature of their often despicable deeds, are treacherous and disgusting. While grounded in servanthood, the ethic of love is not a synonym for weakness, however. Rather, such love must be integrated with the wisdom of clinical rigor and with justice so that it doesn't become a sort of naive pity that could easily be exploited. The forensic psychologist must understand that doing good is not the goal—truth telling is. For example:

☐ Dr. John Doe, a Christian forensic psychologist, was called on to examine a man charged with a serious criminal offense. The man's pastor attempted to advocate for the accused with Dr. Doe, appealing to the common identity they all shared in Christ. Having heard only the defendant's story, the pastor minimized the offense and the man's pathology. He insisted that Dr. Doe act with Christian charity by suggesting to the court that special circumstances accounted for the man's actions. By securing records and performing many interviews, Dr. Doe learned that this man's "indiscretion" was illustrative of a long history of reckless, provocative and angry behavior. He recommended, and the court agreed, that the man should be on probation, receive counseling and make restitution for his crime—a decision that was very unpopular but was nevertheless ultimately helpful to the man.

Christian love in the context of forensic psychology must be capable of looking at a bigger picture than that presented by the immediate circumstances. It must remain clear about the court's goal in the matter at hand and not allow reality to be distorted by fear or the need for approval. Such a redemptive love also requires discernment, what Smedes calls the "ability to see the difference between things" and to "know what is really going on when others are camouflaging the issues" (1978, pp. 43, 44). The forensic psychologist must keep in clear perspective the substance of his or her recommendation to the court and the information upon which that recommendation is based. Because few people will have access to this information, the ethics of love for the Christian forensic psychologist requires an acceptance of the standards of the task and a commitment to truth telling when it seems to others that justice has not been served.

2. *The ethic of respect for the dignity of personhood.* This ethic requires that one respect human life even when to do so necessitates looking beyond the person being evaluated. It is predicated on a belief that the stamp of the divine is imprinted on every human being, however distorted by sin. Not uncommonly do forensic cases involve despicable acts of violation that result in torment and

suffering to innocent parties. But in God's eyes even the reprobate—one who has so disregarded the dignity of another's personhood—must be given the respect that is accorded to all of God's fallen creatures. Christians in particular are called to affirm life and the dignity of personhood, knowing that it is only God's grace that separates us from death and judgment.

This ethic of respect for the dignity of personhood must be balanced by an understanding of personal accountability that prevents the clinician from ignoring as well as overidentifying with the client. Because it allows for personal accountability, punishment for breaking the law both affirms the rights of a human being and authenticates his or her humanness (Lewis, 1970). The concept of getting one's "just deserts," Lewis said, holds people to be responsible for their actions. The responsibility for personal choice, then, is the mark of their having been made in the image of God. The view of crime as pathology—a sickness from which one needs healing—has led to the court's being overly influenced by "technical experts whose special sciences do not even employ such categories as rights or justice" (p. 289), thereby viewing lawbreakers as simply in need of healing rather than responsible for restitution. For psychological professionals who do forensic work, the issue of personal accountability must inform their decision-making.

3. *The ethic of justice.* Justice from a Christian viewpoint concerns human rights. It is the recognition that the Bible gives us a powerful motive for doing what is right because God through Christ established justice and righteousness as the "primary character component in the biblical model of the new creature in Christ (Eph. 4:24; 1 Tim. 6:11; 1 Pet. 2:24)" (Smedes, 1983, p. 23). Justice seen from the kingdom of God disposes one to treat others fairly even when it may not be popular or result in self-gain. Such justice does not depend on personal attitudes toward others but the undeniable standard revealed in the gospel of grace to which God calls all Christians in Christ.

The biblical ethic of justice is manifested in clinical standards of *fairness and objectivity* in recognizing the legal rights of the client. For instance, familiarity with the research on decision-making and the flaws therein helps balance out the clinician's confidence. Influenced by success and the desire not to fail, we often predict falsely rather than balance our decisions by objective data. All information that could bear on our decisions should be considered. The controversy surrounding suggestions of sexual abuse and the attempts by clinicians to delineate true from false memories of childhood sexual trauma is an area of intense disagreement between mental health professionals currently. Yet the difficulty of confirming such abuse is extreme, short of physical evidence or eyewitness documentation. Still, on more than one occasion I have heard psychologists quote from one recovery book that states, "If you think you were abused and your life shows the symptoms, then you were" (Bass and Davis, 1988). Such assertions are sometimes based on symptoms like "poor self-esteem, phobias, depression and fearing abandonment," symptoms which "may relate to abuse in some cases" but may have "nothing at all to do with abuse in others" (Yapko, 1994, p. 114).

4. *The ethic of hope.* This is the beginning of promise for the future, the belief that the future can hold profound, even miraculous change. It is what German theologian Jürgen Moltmann described as "forward looking and forward moving, and therefore also revolutionizing and transforming the present" (1967, p. 16). Hope is a statement of promise. Like Christ's words to the thief on the cross, "Today you will be with me in paradise" (Lk 23:43), Christian hope provides opportunity for change in the future. It allows for the miracle of resurrection and offers a guarantee for "righteousness as opposed to sin, life as opposed to death, glory as opposed to suffering, peace as opposed to dissension" (Moltmann, 1967, p. 18). This ethic of hope is balanced by an understanding and acceptance of the limits of clinical prediction and the limits of treatment.

5. *The ethic of reconciliation.* This ethic is based on Christ's redemptive act in history. The cross provides the model for reconciliation on a relational level. The source of reconciliation is God, "who reconciled us to himself through Christ and gave us the ministry of reconciliation" (2 Cor 5:18). The substance of reconciliation "is a hope grounded in the fact that Christ overcame death and provided the avenue for us to be reconciled to God and one another" (Alsdurf and Alsdurf, 1989, p. 99). When Paul speaks of reconciliation over and against enmity, alienation and other conditions of estrangement from God, God's purpose in reconciling the world to himself was to make peace and cease violence. When reconciliation is applied interpersonally, it is a call to radically transform damaged relationships.

However, reconciliation is not just *inter*personal but *intra*personal as well. The inner torment and violence that accompanies the exploitation of one person by another is no small matter, and the clinician must recognize the magnitude of the psychological roadblocks to change. The ethic of reconciliation is therefore balanced by commitment to one's task as an expert, using clinical skills within a contentious system in which consequences, not reconciliation, are often the court's primary goal.

The Christian forensic psychologist must recognize that his or her primary task is not reconciliation either but well-founded assessment. Such assessment may raise troubling questions about the role of religious faith in the context of a client's behavior and personal responsibility. It requires professionals to accept the tension of their task—to evaluate rather than to be agents of reconciliation.

Using "Christian" Psychology as a Source of Authority

When using psychological references that are specifically Christian in perspective, we need to examine whether they are based on solid psychological findings and clear theological thinking. Quasi-scientific statements or theories presented by Christian writers should not be presented as a factual basis for recommendations to the court unless they can be clinically justified. For instance, suppose an attorney for a sexual offender obtains a private evaluation for his client from a psychologist who assesses the man's problems as a "sexual addiction" and recommends a Christian recovery program that includes many unproven assumptions and untested treatment techniques, including assumptions that sexual addiction is an accepted diagnosis, that sexual addicts have chemical changes in the brain that make them just like drug addicts, and that pedophiles are sexual addicts. When these problems are exposed in court, it places the psychologist in a negative light and ultimately proves detrimental to the client's case.

Indeed, the use of addiction as an explanation for so many different types of pathological behaviors today is based largely on unproven assumptions. When used in a court of law, the argument presumes that the accused was not responsible for his or her behavior because he or she was "addicted" to the behavior. Christian psychologists have an obligation to present in a courtroom only that information which they can validate and provide substantiation for.

If one understands that the consequences to an individual resulting from a court's decision may be extreme and permanent, it is imperative to avoid misusing Christian psychology as an authority source. Material on religious factors should be presented with sensitivity and caution. For instance, claims that a Christian treatment approach is uniquely successful, without having any supporting data, can be very detrimental.

The Difficulties of Integration in a Forensic Setting
Pseudoscientific statements that are based on theological grounds and are untested or unable to be integrated into a scientific system will be quickly confronted and usually rejected by the court. Particularly suspect are systems that place women in subordinate positions to men, especially given the increased role of victim advocates within the judiciary. Perspectives that make assertions about the inequality of husbands and wives but offer no data should be avoided. For instance, one Christian psychology textbook (Meier, Minirth and Wichern, 1982) states that a major characteristic of a healthy family is that "the husband has the final authority in the home" (p. 377). Unless claims like these can be clearly substantiated, such attempts at integration of faith and psychology only confuse the court.

It is also essential that the Christian professional not underestimate a Christian client's capacity for mischief. While this might be true in all evaluation/treatment settings, it is even more true in the forensic setting. A certain functional paranoia is necessary when doing forensic psychology, as one should not underestimate the strategies people will employ to persuade you or the court in their favor.

This requires that one be alert to the assumptions and requests of religious clients and to any indication that, because you are a Christian, you will have a unique understanding of their dilemma. Suppose, for example, a woman involved in a custody dispute contacts you on the advice of a minister. She wants someone to do an evaluation that would offset the recommendations of the court-appointed evaluator. She claims that the court-appointed evaluator is very antireligious and doesn't understand her. She says she called you because she knows that as a Christian you will understand and support her need to have her child and because she knows God wants him in a Christian home. What she fails to reveal is that child protection had identified her as abusive. With such a person you would need to clarify that while being a Christian might help you better understand some of her struggles, it would not necessarily lead to the recommendation that she have custody. As a professional you must be prepared to set clear boundaries so that you are not taken advantage of and so that the person who seeks your services will be clearly informed about what you can and cannot do.

The discrepancies between an individual's proclaimed faith and his or her actual behavior can be painful and perplexing for the Christian professional. A forensic setting probably reveals more of these contradictions than any other. Such discrepancies may involve the pastor who has a vibrant ministry until he's arrested and charged with sexually abusing a child, the abusive husband who claims biblical authority for his actions, the Christian family whose adopted adolescent becomes violent and incorrigible. Contradictions such as these are common within forensic evaluation and require an ability to provide thorough assessment without losing hope and becoming cynical. Such a task is both challenging and rewarding and necessitates constant review of oneself and one's understanding of faith and practice.

References

Alsdurf, J., and P. E. Alsdurf. 1989. *Battered into Submission*. Downers Grove, Ill.: InterVarsity Press.

American Psychological Association. 1991a. *Guidelines for Providers of Psychological Services to Ethnic, Linguistic and Culturally Diverse Populations*. Washington, D.C.: American Psychological Association.

———. 1991b *Specialty Guidelines for Forensic Psychologists*. Washington, D.C.: American Psychological Association.

———. 1992. "Ethical Principles of Psychologists and Code of Conduct." *American Psychologist* 47: 1957-1611.

———. 1994. "Guidelines for Child Custody Evaluations in Divorce Proceedings." *American Psychologist* 49: 677-80.

Barbaree, H. E., and W. L. Marshall. 1988. "Deviant Sexual Arousal, Offense History and Demographic Variables as Predictors of Reoffense Among Child Molesters." *Behavior Science and the Law* 6:267-80.

Bass, E., and L. Davis. 1988. *The Courage to Heal*. New York: Harper & Row.

Campbell, J. C., ed. 1985. *Assessing Dangerousness.* Thousand Oaks, Calif.: Sage.

Ewing, C. P., ed. 1985. *Psychology, Psychiatry and the Law: A Clinical and Forensic Handbook.* Sarasota, Fla.: Professional Resource Exchange.

Farnsworth, M. 1994. "Psychopathic Personality Commitment." Paper presented at Association for the Treatment of Sexual Abusers conference, San Francisco, California (November).

Grisso, R., and P. S. Appelbaum. 1992. "Is It Unethical to Offer Predictions of Future Violence?" *Law and Human Behavior* 16: 621-33.

Growth, N. 1978. "A Clinical Prediction of Dangerousness." *Crime and Human Delinquency* 24: 28-39.

Hare, R. D. 1991. *Manual for the Revised Psychopathy Checklist.* Toronto: Multi-Health Systems.

Hare, R. D., and S. D. Hart. 1994. "Psychopathy and the PCL-R: Clinical and Forensic Applications." ATSA [Association for the Treatment of Sexual Abusers] Preconvention Workshop, San Francisco, California.

Harris, G. T., M. E. Rice and C. A. Cormier. 1991. "Psychopathy and Violent Recidivism." *Law and Human Behavior* 15: 625-37.

Harris, G. T., M. E. Rice and V. L. Quinsey. 1993. "Violent Recidivism of Mentally Disordered Offenders: The Development of a Statistical Prediction Instrument." *Criminal Justice and Behavior* 20: 315-35.

Lewis, C. S. 1970. *God in the Dock.* Grand Rapids, Mich.: Eerdmans.

Meier, P. D., F. B. Minirth and F. B. Wichern. 1982. *Introduction to Psychology and Counseling.* Grand Rapids, Mich.: Baker.

Melton, G. B., J. Petrila, N. G. Poythress and C. Slobogin. 1987. *Psychological Evaluation for the Courts.* New York: Guilford.

Moltmann, J. 1967. *Theology of Hope.* New York: Harper & Row.

Monahan, J., ed. 1980. *The Ethics of Psychological Intervention in the Criminal Justice System.* Washington, D.C.: American Psychological Association.

———. 1981. *The Clinical Prediction of Violent Behaviors.* Washington, D.C.: U.S. Government Printing Office.

———. 1985. "Evaluating Potentially Violent Persons," in *Psychology, Psychiatry and the Law,* ed. C. Ewing. Sarasota, Fla.: Professional Resource Exchange. Pp. 5-39.

Shapiro, D. L. 1991. *Forensic Psychological Assessment.* Needham Heights, Mass.: Allyn & Bacon.

Smedes, L. B. 1978. *Love Within Limits.* Grand Rapids, Mich.: Eerdmans.

———. 1983. *Mere Morality.* Grand Rapids, Mich.: Eerdmans.

Solomon, R. C. 1990. *A Passion for Justice.* New York: Thomas Nelson.

Wenk, E. A., J. O. Robison and G. W. Smith. 1972. "Can Violence Be Predicted?" *Crime and Delinquency* 18: 393-402.

Yapko, M. 1994. *Suggestions of Abuse.* New York: Simon & Schuster.

Part 4

CURRENT TRENDS IN ETHICS EDUCATION

_____

Chapter 17

TRAINING PROGRAMS
Mark R. McMinn &
Katheryn Rhoads Meek

*R*eading the many ethical guidelines and dilemmas described in this book may leave many mental health practitioners feeling overwhelmed, as if they were caught in a hailstorm and trying to avoid being hit by any of the hailstones. Although this is a normal reaction to the changing field of mental health ethics, the anxiety that results is useful only if it leads to professional development. One purpose of training programs is to teach practical ways of converting anxiety about ethical problems into specific actions and attitudes that ultimately prevent ethical violations.

The challenge for Christian counselors is to continue ministering with confidence to those in need while maintaining current awareness of relevant ethical and legal standards. This is not an easy task, because one can err in either direction. Some work with confidence but fill their schedules too full and fail to keep current with reading, courses, continuing education, supervision or peer consultation. They sometimes commit unethical acts out of ignorance. Others remain current but become overwhelmed with the possibilities of lawsuits and ethical violations. As a result they often become tentative and hesitant in their clinical judgments and interventions, and sometimes fail to provide the confident leadership necessary for good mental health care. The following example demonstrates the dilemma:

> After meeting with you weekly for twenty sessions to discuss his depression, your client decides he can trust you with his painful memories of being

sexually abused as a child. Because you have very little experience with males who have been sexually abused, you consider making a referral to a colleague across town who works extensively with survivors of sexual abuse. This raises troubling questions for the therapist: *If I refer, I am being cautious not to work outside my specialty area, but what will I communicate to my client, who has taken a risk to tell me about the abuse? If I don't refer, I will affirm the trust the client has placed in me, but will I be practicing outside of my area of competence?* At first glance this appears to be an irresolvable dilemma. However, the confident therapist with ethical awareness will look for *training programs* to resolve the dilemma. For instance, the therapist might arrange for supervision with a professional more experienced in treating sexual abuse, obtain informed consent from the client and continue with therapy. Alternatively, the therapist might consult with a more experienced colleague and eventually conclude that referral is the most responsible action. Either way, the therapist should seek training.

This chapter considers four types of training experiences: graduate training, continuing education, consultation or supervision, and personal therapy. Though the major portion of the chapter pertains to graduate training, each of these training opportunities can play an important role in the ongoing professional development of Christian mental health practitioners.

Throughout the chapter we make reference to the results of a recent survey of Christian counselors. In 1994 we surveyed 900 members of the American Association of Christian Counseling (AACC) to assess their beliefs about the ethical implications of 88 specific behaviors. The same survey instrument has been used in several earlier surveys of mental health practitioners (Gibson and Pope, 1993; Oordt, 1990; Pope, Tabachnick and Keith-Spiegel, 1987). Respondents also rated the adequacy of various training programs in preparing them for the ethical decisions they face as practitioners. Of the 900 AACC members surveyed, 5 surveys were undeliverable because of address changes, 27 were returned incomplete with letters of explanation, and 496 were completed and returned, resulting in an overall response rate of 57 percent. Basic demographic information about the respondents is given in table 17.1, found on page 291. The specific nature of the survey and a more detailed analysis of our findings are reported elsewhere (McMinn and Meek, 1996).

At times we will compare our work with a survey of psychologists conducted by Pope, Tabachnick and Keith-Spiegel (1987). This survey was conducted without regard to the psychologists' religious background, and this should be understood when evaluating the results.

Graduate Training

Except for those trained as paraprofessionals, graduate training provides a foundation on which mental health practitioners build their professional identity. An essential part of this foundation is an awareness of relevant ethical principles and standards of conduct.

In our sample, 60 percent of Christian counselors described their graduate training program as having done a good or excellent job in preparing them for effective, appropriate and ethical practice. Nineteen percent felt their graduate training provided them adequate preparation, and only 6 percent reported dissatisfaction with their training program. Another 12 percent rated the question as not applicable, presumably because some respondents were paraprofessional counselors without graduate training in counseling.

Thus it seems that most Christian mental health professionals believe they receive important ethics training during graduate school. To understand the nature of effective graduate training, two important questions are considered here. First, what is the essential content of graduate education for Christian mental health professionals? And second, what methods are most helpful in teaching ethics?

What Is the Essential Content of an Ethics Curriculum?

Although the nature of the training curriculum will depend on the specific profession being studied, there are common elements that are essential to cover in all mental health training programs. Students need to learn a philosophical or theological context for professional ethics, general principles that apply to the caring professions, specific ethics codes that apply to their profession, pertinent professional issues and sensitivity to cultural diversity.

Setting a philosophical or theological context. Most mental health professions have a specific ethics code to regulate those within the profession. Although the specific ethics code is an essential part of the ethics curriculum, a more general foundation is also important. Students leaving graduate school thinking that the essence of ethics is defined in their profession's code of conduct will not be prepared to deal with the rapid changes in the mental health professions or to fully understand the relationship of their professional behavior with Christian ethics. Thus it is important to provide students with a philosophical and/or theological understanding of ethics.

Those teaching and studying in Christian colleges and universities often have opportunities to consider theological and Christian ethics during graduate school. Psychology doctoral students at Wheaton College, for example, are required to take a theological ethics course. Similarly, doctoral students at George Fox College take a course in Christian ethics, those at Biola University take integration courses related to Christian ethics, and those at Fuller Seminary choose between a variety of theological ethics courses as part of their church history and theology requirement.

Even when teaching an ethics course designed specifically for a mental health profession, it is important to discuss the diverse philosophical systems that inform professional ethics. This broader philosophical discussion provides a basis for more specialized discussions of professional ethics.

Valuing general ethical principles. Although the ethics codes of the American Counseling Association, the APA, the AAMFT and the National Association of Social Workers (NASW) all appear quite different from one another at first glance, they share some common principles that are important for students to understand and appreciate. Kitchener describes the relationship between these general ethical principles and the prescribed rules found in professional ethics codes:

> Principles are more general and fundamental than moral rules or codes and serve as their foundation. Because ethical codes may be too broad in some cases and too narrow in others, ethical principles both provide a more consistent framework within which cases may be considered and constitute a rationale for the choice of items in the code itself. (1984, p. 46)

Redlich and Pope (1980) have described seven such principles. The first five are found in ancient texts, including the Hippocratic Oath. First, those in the helping professions are to *do no harm.* Although unethical behavior and legal definitions of malpractice may not coincide entirely, the issue of harm is at the center of the definition of malpractice. Malpractice occurs when a mental health professional has a professional duty to a client and violates that duty, resulting in harm to the client (Stromberg et al., 1988). Without harm there can be no malpractice.

Second, it is important that mental health professionals *practice only with competence.* Results of survey research suggest that practicing beyond competence is a prevalent problem. In our survey of Christian counselors approximately 65 percent said they had, at least on rare occasions, worked when they were too distressed to be effective. In their survey of psychologists, Pope, Tabachnick and Keith-Spiegel (1987) found similar results, with 60 percent giving the same answer. Moreover, 25 percent of psychologists and 38 percent of Christian counselors reported having provided services outside their area of competence at least on rare occasions. Finally, 6 percent of the psychologists reported having done therapy under the influence of alcohol. This appears to be less problematic for Christians—only 1 percent of our sample endorsed this item.

Next, the client-practitioner relationship is unique in that there is a clear power differential. Christian mental health professionals need to be aware of the inherent dangers associated with such a relationship and ways to *avoid exploiting* those they are trying to help. Christian counselors and pastors may face unique vulnerabilities in this area, especially because dual relationships are often difficult or impossible to avoid (see Craig, 1991).

Our survey results reveal the difficulties Christian counselors face in multiple-role relationships. Many more Christian counselors (58 percent) than psychologists (29 percent) reported having provided therapy to one of their friends. It should be noted that almost one-third of our respondents identified a church as their primary place of counseling. These counselors may frequently be called on to give mental health services to those in their congregation. Fortunately we did not see evidence that Christian counselors are more inclined toward exploitative dual relationships. For example, 98 percent of the Christian counselors and 98 percent of the psychologists reported they have never engaged in sexual contact with a current client, and 94 percent of Christian counselors said that they had never become sexually involved with a former client, compared with 88 percent of the psychologists in the Pope survey (Pope et al., 1987). So despite being in professions that are more likely to require multiple-role relationships, Christian counselors may not be at higher risk for exploitative dual relationships, at least sexual ones.

One way Christian counselors may cope is by not allowing personal fantasy or feelings of attraction to enter into their awareness as often as their non-Christian counterparts do. Interestingly, 41 percent of the Christian counselors surveyed reported never experiencing sexual attraction to a client. In contrast, Rodolfa and his colleagues (1994) assessed 908 APA-member psychologists and found that only 12 percent reported never having been attracted to a client. Other surveys of psychologists have reported similar rates of 13 percent (Pope and Tabachnick, 1993) and 9 percent (Pope, Tabachnick and Keith-Spiegel, 1987). There are several possibilities for this discrepancy. One is that Christian counselors are somehow different from those in the other studies. If this is true, future research may help delineate what characteristics account for this discrepancy. Another possibility is that Christian counselors are less comfortable with sexual feelings toward clients and therefore tend to suppress them. Or perhaps both are true. Christian counselors may be more inclined to deliberately limit thoughts and feelings as a way of controlling their behavior because they are more often in multiple-role relationships. However, they may also be inclined to deny feelings of sexual attraction when they occur. A number of the Christian counselors surveyed wrote comments next to this question, suggesting that it is not immoral to be sexually attracted to a client, but it is immoral to act on these feelings. We concur with this assertion and believe that the best preventative measure one can take is to openly discuss sexual feelings with a clinical supervisor or trusted colleague. It is vitally important for Christian mental health training programs to prepare students for feelings of sexual attraction and to provide an atmosphere where students feel that they can safely disclose struggles in this area. Students should also be made aware of the different avenues through which they can seek help in the years following graduate school.

Fourth, mental health professionals *treat people with respect for their dignity as human beings.* The key component of this principle is an attitude of humility.

It is sometimes tempting for counselors to categorize people based on psychiatric diagnoses or perceived similarities and "prescribe" a cure. This medical model can create a relationship that is patronizing and hierarchical. Therapy is best seen as a collaborative endeavor in which the client must assume equal responsibility for his or her treatment (McMinn and Lebold, 1989).

In our survey of Christian counselors we found that the majority attempt to establish a collaborative therapeutic environment. Ninety-eight percent address clients by their first names, approximately 99 percent will offer or accept a handshake from their clients, and 94 percent have used self-disclosure as a therapy technique. It should be noted, however, that collaboration can be overemphasized in some therapy situations, resulting in the client becoming excessively dependent on the therapist.

Fifth, mental health professionals are bound to *protect client confidentiality.* This is an essential principle of all mental health professions, and it deserves a prominent place in ethics training. Nonetheless, practitioners are sometimes called on to reveal certain relevant information when there is a clear and imminent danger to an individual or society. This duty to protect encompasses situations where there is suspected child abuse (Brosig and Kalichman, 1992a, 1992b; Nicolai and Scott, 1994), risk of suicide (Jobes and Berman, 1993) or risk of harm to another identified person (Monahan, 1993). In our survey of Christian counselors we found that most are aware of their responsibility to break confidentiality in order to prevent harm. Even so, just under 5 percent view breaking confidentiality in cases of child abuse, suicide or homicide as unquestionably unethical. In terms of actual practice, 80 percent reported having broken confidentiality in cases of child abuse, 83 percent in cases where the client was suicidal, and 62 percent in cases with homicidal clients.

Sixth, mental health professionals should *act only with informed consent.* The client has the right to make an informed decision about whether or not to engage in therapy (Somberg, Stone and Claiborn, 1993). Having a detailed, written informed-consent form that describes the nature, expected outcomes and possible side effects of the treatment both fulfills a therapist's ethical obligation and enhances the consumer's perceptions of the therapist's credibility (Sullivan, Martin and Handelsman, 1993).

Finally, mental health professionals are committed to *promoting equity and justice.* Ideally, professors and students in Christian mental health training programs are passionately concerned with becoming advocates of those who have been marginalized. Although Christian therapists need to make a living, they are also motivated by ministry and often concerned for those who cannot afford mental health services. In our survey of Christian counselors, over three-fourths said that they have provided therapy at no cost to the client, as compared to two-thirds of the psychologists surveyed by Pope et al. (1987). Furthermore, over half reported that they have never terminated therapy in situations where the client was no longer able to pay, as compared to 36 percent of psychologists in the Pope survey.

These principles represent only one possible scheme for organizing ethics. Other schemes have been proposed and are equally useful. For example, Kitchener (1984) proposes five general principles: autonomy, beneficence, nonmaleficence, justice and fidelity.

Knowledge of specific ethics codes. In addition to understanding general ethical systems and principles, students in mental health training programs learn the ethics code of their specific profession. In our survey of Christian counselors, 63 percent reported that a professional ethics code is a good or an excellent way to maintain awareness of effective, appropriate and ethical practice. Only 5 percent reported it to be ineffective.

Some examples of current ethics codes and guidelines are found in appendix B. Most organizations revise and update ethics codes every few years, and it is important to teach the most current form of the ethics code in graduate training programs. The most recent revision of the APA's ethics code (1992), for example, involved an extensive reorganization and updating of the previous code (1990). Also, professional organizations often publish casebooks that demonstrate the various ethical guidelines with actual cases considered by the organization's ethics committee (e.g., APA, 1987a).

Beyond ethics codes, other professional guidelines and standards are important to include in ethics training. In most professional psychology training programs students are expected to read and be familiar with a number of documents published by the APA. These include the *Specialty Guidelines for the Delivery of Services by Clinical Psychologists* (1981), the "General Guidelines for Providers of Psychological Services" (1987b), the "Guidelines for Providers of Psychological Services to Ethnic, Linguistic and Culturally Diverse Populations" (1993a) and "Record Keeping Guidelines" (1993b).

In order to relate specific ethics codes to prevailing legal standards and case laws, students need a basic knowledge of the state and federal laws governing mental health professions. A number of useful textbooks and professional books are available on ethics (Corey, Corey and Callanan, 1993; Huber and Baruth, 1987; Hummel, Talbut and Alexander, 1985; Keith-Spiegel and Koocher, 1985; Pope and Vasquez, 1991) and on relevant legal standards (Bennett et al., 1990; Myers, 1992; Shah and Sales, 1991; Stromberg et al., 1988; VandeCreek and Knapp, 1993). Many state organizations have publications that summarize pertinent state laws for mental health professionals (e.g., Foster et al., 1993). Finally, Collins (1991) has written a helpful book for Christian counselors that includes a discussion of relevant ethical principles and legal/liability issues.

Awareness of relevant professional issues. The mental health professions share some common issues, and yet each mental health profession faces unique challenges. These shared and unique professional issues are introduced in graduate school. Examples of common mental health issues are the rapid changes in health care reimbursement (Austad et al., 1992; Newman and Bricklin, 1991), billing and collecting fees (Knapp and VandeCreek, 1993), care of those with AIDS and those who are HIV-positive (Kelly et al., 1993; Mapou and Law, 1994; Robiner et al., 1993; Trezza, 1994), ways to address physical safety needs when dealing with dangerous consumers (Guy, Brown and Poelstra, 1992), and the use of touch in counseling (Kertay and Reviere, 1993). Examples of unique professional issues include psychologists' consideration of prescription privileges (Brentar and McNamara, 1991a, 1991b; Chafetz and Buelow, 1994; DeLeon, Fox and Graham, 1991; DeNelsky, 1991), licensing criteria and examinations (McGaha and Minder, 1993), and career satisfaction (Hershey, Kopplin and Cornell, 1991; Walfish, Moritz and Stenmark, 1991).

Sensitivity to diversity. As American society becomes more ethnically and culturally diverse, training students to be sensitive to issues of diversity becomes more important. Whereas courses in diversity may have been perceived as a training option in the past, they have now become an essential component of graduate training. Competent practice in today's mental health fields requires an ability to work with those of different religious, economic and ethnic backgrounds.

Kanitz, Mendoza and Ridley (1992) reported a survey of multicultural training in religiously oriented counselor education programs. Of the forty-two programs responding, 88 percent offered specific training in multicultural issues. This is heartening, but it must also be noted that most of the programs offering multicultural training relegated the diversity curriculum to separate courses. Kanitz et al. wisely suggest that true multicultural training occurs throughout the curriculum and is considered in every graduate course. Thus issues of diversity should be an integral part of professional ethics courses.

The first-year ethics and diversity course in the Psy.D. program at Wheaton College has been designed to provide students with a rigorous introduction to both topics, though discussions of ethics and diversity are found in most other courses as well. During the four-semester-hour course, students read a number of articles and one book on diversity (Allison et al., 1994; Atkinson, Morten and Sue, 1993; Bergin, 1991; Bernal and Castro, 1994; Betancourt and Lopez, 1993; Darou, Hum and Kurtness, 1993; Kelly and Strupp, 1992; Lopez et al., 1989; Mintz, Rideout and Bartels, 1994; Morgan and Nerison, 1993; Ridley et al., 1994; Rothblum, 1994; Sue, 1988; Sue and Zane, 1987; Szapocznik and Kurtines, 1993; Vachon and Agresti, 1992), participate in group presentations on religious, gender, ethnic, age and socioeconomic diversity, and listen to special speakers with expertise in multiculturalism. In this way they are exposed to the relevant ethical guidelines pertaining to multicultural sensitivity before beginning their first practicum at the beginning of their second year.

Of course not all professional literature on ethics or diversity (for example, gay and lesbian issues) is compatible with orthodox Christian doctrine. Rather than avoiding this literature, we advocate assigning it as reading material and using class sessions to evaluate the authors' perspectives from a Christian worldview (e.g., seek students' reactions to Haldeman, 1994). This helps students better define their own values and beliefs and understand how the values of future clients may conflict with their own.

What Are the Effective Methods of Teaching Ethics?

Graduate training is the primary way students learn about the ethics of their profession. In fact, the APA requires doctoral programs to provide an ethics course in order to receive accreditation. In many states completion of an ethics course is also required for professional licensure. Unfortunately, there is little empirical data evaluating the effectiveness of these courses. Welfel (1992) reviewed the available literature in an attempt to determine if there is any evidence that graduate training courses in ethics effectively produce professionals who think and behave ethically. She concluded that "the association between ethics courses and ethical sensitivity and ethical reasoning is weak and inconsistent" (p. 186). Although this suggests a need for more systematic evaluation of graduate courses in ethics (McGovern, 1988), we will speculate here about the factors that contribute to the successful teaching of ethics.

One goal of good graduate training in ethical issues is prevention of future violations, but most mental health professionals involved in ethics training have an even more ambitious goal: to instill a sensitivity, even a passion, for the place of ethics in a profession. In this sense ethics training is shaping the professional and, to some extent, personal identity of students. How does this shaping occur? As with understanding diversity and multiculturalism, a good working knowledge of ethics cannot be gleaned from one course. Ethics must be considered in a variety of courses, emphasized in clinical placements, and demonstrated in interactions with faculty members, clinical supervisors and program administrators.

Formal coursework. Most of the discussion so far has focused on the role of formal coursework in ethics. This appears to be an important component of graduate training, though it has not been researched adequately (Welfel, 1992). McGovern (1988) tested students before and after his ethics course and found significant improvement. For example, students knew an average of 1.2 of the 10 "Ethical Principles for Psychologists" (APA, 1992; these principles have since been revised) before the course, and an average of 9.2 after. They showed similar gains in understanding philosophical assumptions, federal laws and regulations, and the distinction between licensing laws and ethical principles.

Welfel (1992) cites a 1990 dissertation in which Vanek reports that most psychology ethics instructors use lecture, discussion and case studies as their primary methods of instruction. The topics most frequently covered include the profession's ethics code, confidentiality, informed consent, sexual exploitation and professional responsibility. We suggest two additions to these lists.

First, with regard to teaching methods, McMinn (1988) described a computerized modification of the traditional case study method. In the *Ethics Case Study Simulation* students are presented with a small amount of information and then asked what action they would take. In a case called "The Secret" a client comes for therapy and asks the therapist to guarantee confidentiality. The students must decide whether or not to agree to this request. Based on their choice, they are given additional information and asked to make additional choices. The "secret" in this case is that the client is abusing his child and fears being reported to the authorities. At each step in the decision process students must make difficult ethical choices and then cope with the outcome of their decisions. Eventually students are given a case outcome and evaluated based on the "Ethical Principles of Psychologists and Code of Conduct" (APA, 1992).

Whereas the traditional case-study method provides all the relevant information and then appropriate choices are discussed, actual clinical situations are rarely this easy. Typically, the decisions a clinician makes will affect the course of events and change the information he or she receives. The computer simulation software provides students with case-study opportunities that resemble actual clinical situations. "The Secret" can be obtained by sending a blank Macintosh diskette and a stamped, self-addressed envelope to Mark R. McMinn, Ph.D., Department of Psychology, Wheaton College, Wheaton, IL 60187.

Second, with regard to topics covered, Christian mental health training programs may also consider the relationship of Scripture, Christian tradition and spiritual wisdom to professional ethics. This is not to suggest that a superficial application of Bible verses is necessary or helpful. Rather, students in Christian training programs have opportunities to contemplate the meanings of Christian principles, virtues and character and to relate those meanings to professional practice. For example, it is important for Christians to wrestle with Christ's example of servanthood and find ways to incorporate sacrificial acts of service into their future careers. In our Psy.D. program all students in their second- or third-year practicum placements meet individually with a faculty preceptor on a regular basis and participate in a weekly group discussion led by the preceptor. One purpose of these meetings is specifically integrative—each preceptor has the goal of helping students grasp the practical implications of their Christian faith as they develop professionally.

Clinical supervision. If the introductory ethics course is the formal academic component of training, then the clinical practicum is the laboratory component. The ideas taught in the classroom are practically evaluated and applied as students learn to function professionally. An important part of clinical training is in the supervision students receive.

Vasquez (1992) describes supervision as an opportunity to guide students through James Rest's four components of moral and ethical behavior. The first component is the development of moral sensitivity, when students see that their actions will affect the client's life. Second is moral reasoning, when students differentiate between an ethical and an unethical choice. Third, students choose an action, though such a choice is not always easy in the presence of competing values. The final stage is to implement the ethical choice. As supervisors help students navigate these components of ethical behavior, they also carefully evaluate students' knowledge of ethics, competency and personal functioning (Vasquez, 1992). In training programs that emphasize research, students are guided through a similar process of sensitization to ethics as they design studies, consider the potential effects on participants, analyze results and publish their findings (see Goodyear, Crego and Johnston, 1992).

Faculty in most training programs find it important to regularly evaluate students' clinical functioning and suitability. Not every student has the capacity to function competently and ethically in a clinical environment. Even students who excel in the classroom may face difficulties in the laboratory of clinical practice. Thus semiannual or annual evaluations of students' clinical perform-ance are an important component of mental health training programs.

Modeling and mentoring. It is tempting to think of clinical ability as a set of skills that we learn in training and then "put on" as we enter the therapy office. If this were true, then it would seem reasonable that some sets of skills or theoretical perspectives would produce better results than other sets of skills. Although this may be true for some specific disorders, the general trend of psychotherapy-outcome research suggests that no one set of skills is better than any other (Smith, Glass and Miller, 1980). Rather, it appears that the therapeutic relationship is the most important ingredient in therapy outcome (Whiston and Sexton, 1993). Although the relational variables have sometimes been called "nonspecific" factors, they may actually be undefined rather than nonspecific. That is, future research may help us understand the healing relationship in more specific terms. Until such research is reported, we are left to speculate on the nature of the therapist-client relationship.

Given this self-determined license to speculate, we suspect that the character of the therapist may be of crucial importance and that matters of character cannot be "put on" as a professional persona or a set of clinical techniques. In moments of crisis, for example, the therapist's character, and not the specific theoretical orientation, will largely determine the response he or she will have to a client (McMinn and Wilhoit, 1994). However, character traits cannot always be transfused via textbook or class assignment.

Thus faculty members and clinical supervisors in Christian mental health training programs have a responsibility to develop and model virtuous character in their dealings with students, colleagues and clients. This is not to say that mentors must be or think themselves to be flawless—such a delusion points to a significant character problem and questionable clinical insight. Rather, those involved in Christian training programs ought to experience and demonstrate passion for the spiritual life and spiritual disciplines, intellectual curiosity, love for ministry, concern for justice, and sincere care for students.

Although not writing about Christian training programs, Kitchener (1992) affirms the importance of mentors treating students ethically. Despite psychologists' awareness of the importance of modeling, faculty members have often prescribed ethical actions for others and not behaved ethically themselves. Perhaps this is what James had in mind when he instructed, "Not many of you should become teachers, my brothers and sisters, for you know that we who teach will be judged with greater strictness. For all of us make many mistakes" (Jas 3:1-2 NRSV).

Continuing Education

Because of the complexities and rapid changes in mental health care and theory, receiving an advanced graduate degree is not sufficient preparation for the ongoing challenges therapists face. In recognition of this, most mental health professions provide continuing-education (CE) opportunities, and most states mandate CE for licensure. For example, thirty-five states now require psychologists to participate in CE (ranging from five to fifty hours per year), and the APA is considering mandatory CE for all members (deGroot, 1994). In our survey of Christian counselors, 62 percent reported that CE has been a good or an excellent way to maintain awareness of effective, appropriate and ethical practice. Only 12 percent reported it to be ineffective.

In 1972 Dubin suggested that the half-life of a psychology doctorate is ten to twelve years. That is, ten to twelve years after receiving a doctorate, half of the information learned will be obsolete, irrelevant or incorrect. Since 1972 information has become more easily accessed, journals have proliferated, and the rate of knowledge has generally accelerated. Thus the ten-to-twelve-year half-life is probably now an overestimate of the stability of information in the mental health professions. This rapid rate of change requires mental health professionals to look to CE for ongoing training in ethics and other professional issues (VandeCreek, Knapp and Brace, 1990).

There are numerous ways to obtain CE, and states and professions vary in what they accept as legitimate forms. All state boards give credit for seminars and workshops that are approved by the board's professional organization. In psychology, for example, approximately four hundred organizations, including CAPS, have been approved by the APA to sponsor continuing-education programs. These sponsors are listed bimonthly in the *APA Monitor* and annually in *American Psychologist*. Other activities that sometimes qualify for continuing-education credit include attending conventions, presenting papers at conventions, taking a college or university course, publishing a paper, teaching a new course, receiving clinical supervision or personal therapy, studying at home, and participating in leadership of a state or national professional organization.

Obtaining CE in professional ethics has several benefits. First, it allows professionals to keep informed of recent occurrences in case laws and revisions in ethical standards. Given the busy schedule of most mental health practitioners, it is necessary to rely on ethics experts to stay informed about laws and standards regarding child abuse reporting, third-party reimbursement, sexually transmitted diseases, informed consent and other topics. Second, workshops and seminars on ethics give opportunities to meet other professionals and discuss ways they handle difficult ethical issues. Helpful ideas are often generated in informal conversations during the lunch hour or coffee breaks. Third, CE experiences often motivate professionals to think more carefully about the ethical implications of their work and the choices they make.

However helpful CE may be, it is best seen as necessary but not sufficient for establishing new clinical skills and specialty areas. Other forms of training are necessary in many situations, including supervision, consultation and personal therapy.

Consultation and Supervision
While sitting in the waiting area prior to an oral licensing exam, a candidate for mental health licensure may imagine a question such as this:

> You are working with a male who is HIV-positive. He has not yet told his spouse but continues to have sex with her on a regular basis. Although he claims to use a condom most of the time, you are concerned about the possible risk of disease transmission. What would you do as a therapist?

If the candidate is well coached, the rehearsed response might be something like

> This is a difficult situation. I would be concerned about both confidentiality and my duty to protect my client's spouse. My first response would be to consult with a respected colleague.

This response, quite natural for the licensure candidate who has just finished training, may not always be as natural for those facing busy private-practice schedules. However, 66 percent of the respondents in our survey reported that colleagues are a good or excellent resource to help them practice in ethical and appropriate ways. Although this survey does not provide us with information about how many Christian counselors actually are consulting with colleagues on a regular basis, it is encouraging to see positive opinions about the usefulness of consultation.

Two types of interactions with colleagues are often helpful in ongoing professional development. First, peer consultation occurs when two or more professionals regularly discuss the difficult clinical issues and decisions they are facing. Sometimes these consultations are formalized into peer consultation groups that meet weekly or biweekly (Greenburg, Lew and Johnson, 1985). In some states these groups qualify for continuing-education credit. Of course, consultation can also occur on a less formal basis.

Second, clinical supervision with a more experienced colleague is a widely used form of professional development. In a survey of masters- and doctoral-level psychologists, McCarthy, Kulakowski and Kenfield (1994) reported that 80 percent had a designated clinical supervisor and 88 percent received some type of designated or peer supervision. Those obtaining supervision received an average of 7.4 hours per month. A higher portion of master's-level than doctoral-level therapists reported having a clinical supervisor. Although the expense of supervision is often unwelcome, the benefits in professional development and ethical wisdom can be enormous.

Personal Therapy

When Guy, Poelstra and Stark (1989) surveyed 312 practicing psychologists, they found both good news and bad news. The bad news was that 74 percent reported significant personal distress in the previous three years, and 37 percent admitted that their distress decreased the quality of their clinical work. The good news is that most psychologists facing personal distress did something about it—most commonly they arranged to get individual or family therapy.

Although these findings may not seem relevant to a discussion of ethics training, we believe they are relevant, because distressed professionals appear to be at high risk for blurred relationships with clients. One of the most common ethical violations among mental health professionals is having an inappropriate relationship with a client (Pope and Vetter, 1992), and 90 percent of therapists who become sexually involved with clients describe feeling vulnerable and needy when the sexual contact began (Pope and Bouhoutsos, 1986). Thus it seems likely that personal therapy can serve as a preventive measure for some forms of ethical violation.

Another reason for personal therapy is that many people entering the mental health professions have experienced past trauma that may impede their work as therapists. For example, Pope and Feldman-Summers (1992) reported that 70 percent of the female and 33 percent of the male psychologists they surveyed had been physically or sexually abused in the past. Because therapy is a personal interaction, the past pain of the therapist will often affect the way a client is perceived and treated. Personal therapy, then, may lead to greater competence in the practice of one's profession because it helps counselors become more self-aware (MacDevitt, 1987).

Though some therapists find it difficult to admit to personal needs and seek therapy, it is encouraging to note that 71 percent of a sample of psychologists reported having personal therapy at least once during their career (Norcross,

Strausser-Kirtland and Missar, 1988). An overwhelming number (over 90 percent) reported personal therapy to be helpful (see also Pope and Tabachnick, 1994).

Characteristic	Category	N	Percentage
Sex	Male	300	60.5
	Female	180	36.3
	Not reported	16	3.2
Age	Under 30	8	1.6
	30-45	181	36.5
	46-60	215	43.3
	Over 60	85	17.1
	Not reported	7	1.4
Degree	No graduate degree	71	14.3
	Master's	228	46.0
	Doctorate	170	34.3
	Not reported	10	5.4
Work Setting	Private office	162	32.7
	Clinic	40	8.1
	Hospital	14	2.8
	University	13	2.6
	Church	148	29.8
	Other	68	13.7
	Not reported	51	10.3
Licensure	Nonprofessional	344	69.4
	Professional	152	30.6

Table 17.1. Demographic information about survey respondents

Conclusion

One of the privileges educators enjoy is watching the remarkable transformation students make during their graduate-school years. This is certainly true in ethics education. Those completing graduate school can often see ethical implications in situations and decisions that they would not have noticed as beginning students. Through coursework, interactions with faculty and clinical fieldwork they develop new insights regarding the ethical implications of their work.

But the journey is only beginning for students completing their graduate degree. All of us in mental health professions—students, faculty, therapists and supervisors—must continue learning in order to keep current with the rapid changes our professions face (Dubin, 1972). These changes sometimes cause anxiety, but fortunately we work in professions where we teach people to convert anxiety into proactive solutions. Perhaps the best solution is the golden rule found in Matthew 7:12: "In everything do to others as you would have them do to you; for this is the law and the prophets" (NRSV). When counselors are passionately concerned about their clients' welfare, they have little need for anxiety. We concur with Kendler (1993) that the golden rule "gains validity because it is experientially compelling, a self-evident truth" (p. 1048).

References

Allison, K. W., I. Crawford, R. Echemendia, L. V. Robinson and D. Knepp. 1994. "Human Diversity and Professional Competence." *American Psychologist* 49: 792-96.

American Association of Marriage and Family Therapy. 1991. *AAMFT Code of Ethics.* Washington, D.C.: Author.

American Counseling Association. 1988. *Ethical Standards.* Alexandria, Va.: Author.

American Psychological Association. 1981. *Specialty Guidelines for the Delivery of Services by Clinical Psychologists.* Washington, D.C.: Author.

———. 1987a. *Casebook on Ethical Principles of Psychologists.* Washington, D.C.: Author.

———. 1987b. "General Guidelines for Providers of Psychological Services." *American Psychologist* 42: 712-23.

———. 1990. "Ethical Principles of Psychologists." *American Psychologist* 45: 390-95.

———. 1992. "Ethical Principles of Psychologists and Code of Conduct." *American Psychologist* 47: 1597-1611.

———. 1993a. "Guidelines for Providers of Psychological Services to Ethnic, Linguistic and Culturally Diverse Populations." *American Psychologist* 48: 45-48.

———. 1993b. "Record Keeping Guidelines." *American Psychologist* 48: 984-86.

Atkinson, D. R., G. Morten and D. W. Sue. 1993. *Counseling American Minorities: A Cross-cultural Perspective.* 4th ed. Madison, Wis.: Brown and Benchmark.

Austad, C. S., W. O. Sherman, T. Morgan and L. Holstein. 1992. "The Psychotherapist and the Managed Care Setting." *Professional Psychology: Research and Practice* 23: 329-32.

Bennett, B. E., B. K. Bryant, G. R. VandenBos and A. Greenwood. 1990. *Professional Liability and Risk Management.* Washington, D.C.: American Psychological Association.

Bergin, A. E. 1991. "Values and Religious Issues in Psychotherapy and Mental Health." *American Psychologist* 46: 394-403.

Bernal, M. E., and F. G. Castro. 1994. "Are Clinical Psychologists Prepared for Service and Research with Ethnic Minorities?" *American Psychologist* 49: 797-805.

Betancourt, H., and S. R. Lopez. 1993. "The Study of Culture, Ethnicity and Race in American Psychology." *American Psychologist* 48: 629-37.

Brentar, J., and J. R. McNamara. 1991a. "The Right to Prescribe Medication: Considerations for Professional Psychology." *Professional Psychology: Research and Practice* 22: 179-87.

———. 1991b. "Prescription Privileges for Psychology: The Next Step in Its Evolution as a Profession." *Professional Psychology: Research and Practice* 22: 194-95.

Brosig, C. L., and S. C. Kalichman. 1992a. "Child Abuse Reporting Decisions: Effects of Statutory Wording of Reporting Requirements." *Professional Psychology: Research and Practice* 23: 486-92.

———. 1992b. "Clinicians' Reporting of Suspected Child Abuse: A Review of the Empirical Literature." *Clinical Psychology Review* 12: 155-68.

Chafetz, M. D., and G. Buelow. 1994. "A Training Model for Psychologists with Prescription Privileges: Clinical Pharmacopsychologists." *Professional Psychology: Research and Practice* 25: 149-53.

Collins, G. R. 1991. *Excellence and Ethics in Christian Counseling.* Dallas: Word.

Corey, G., M. S. Corey and P. Callanan. 1993. *Issues and Ethics in the Helping Professions.* 4th ed. Pacific Grove, Calif.: Brooks/Cole.

Craig, J. D. 1991. "Preventing Dual Relationships in Pastoral Counseling." *Counseling and Values* 36: 49-54.

Darou, W. G., A. Hum and J. Kurtness. 1993. "An Investigation of the Impact of Psychosocial Research on a Native Population." *Professional Psychology: Research and Practice* 24: 325-29.

deGroot, G. J. 1994. "Should CE Be Mandated for Every Psychologist?" *APA Monitor* 25: 41.

DeLeon, P. H., R. E. Fox and S. R. Graham. 1991. "Prescription Privileges: Psychology's Next Frontier?" *American Psychologist* 46: 384-93.

DeNelsky, G. Y. 1991. "Prescription Privileges for Psychologists: The Case Against." *Professional Psychology: Research and Practice* 22: 188-93.

Dubin, S. S. 1972. "Obsolescence or Lifelong Education: A Choice for the Professional." *American Psychologist* 27: 486-98.

Foster, L. M., B. E. Bennett, W. K. Carroll, M. B. Epstein and M. C. Weber, eds. 1993. *Illinois Mental Health Professional's Law Handbook.* Chicago: Illinois Psychological Association.

Gibson, W. T., and K. S. Pope. 1993. "The Ethics of Counseling: A National Survey of Certified Counselors." *Journal of Counseling and Development* 71: 330-36.

Goodyear, R. K., C. A. Crego and M. W. Johnston. 1992. "Ethical Issues in the Supervision of Student Research: A Study of Critical Incidents." *Professional Psychology: Research and Practice* 23: 203-10.

Gottlieb, M. C. 1993. "Avoiding Exploitive Dual Relationships: A Decision-Making Model." *Psychotherapy* 30: 41-48.

Greenburg, S. L., G. J. Lewis and M. Johnson. 1985. "Peer Consultation Groups for Private Practitioners." *Professional Psychology: Research and Practice* 16: 437-47.

Guy, J. D., C. K. Brown and P. L. Poelstra. 1992. "Safety Concerns and Protective Measures Used by Psychotherapists." *Professional Psychology: Research and Practice* 23: 421-23.

Guy, J. D., P. L. Poelstra and M. J. Stark. 1989. "Personal Distress and Therapeutic Effectiveness: National Survey of Psychologists Practicing Psychotherapy." *Professional Psychology: Research and Practice* 20: 48-50.

Haldeman, D. C. 1994. "The Practice and Ethics of Sexual Orientation Conversion Therapy." *Journal of Consulting and Clinical Psychology* 62: 221-27.

Hershey, J. M., D. A. Kopplin and J. E. Cornell. 1991. "Doctors of Psychology: Their Career Experiences and Attitudes Toward Degree and Training." *Professional Psychology: Research and Practice* 22: 351-56.

Huber, C. H., and L. G. Baruth. 1987. *Ethical, Legal and Professional Issues in the Practice of Marriage and Family Therapy.* Columbus, Ohio: Merrill.

Hummel, D. L., L. C. Talbutt and M. D. Alexander. 1985. *Law and Ethics in Counseling.* New York: Van Nostrand Reinhold.

Jobes, D. A., and A. L. Berman. 1993. "Suicide and Malpractice Liability: Assessing and Revising Policies, Procedures and Practice in Outpatient Settings." *Professional Psychology: Research and Practice* 24: 91-99.

Kanitz, B. E., D. W. Mendoza and C. R. Ridley. 1992. "Multicultural Training in Religiously Oriented Counselor Education Programs: A Survey." *Journal of Psychology and Christianity* 11: 337-44.

Keith-Spiegel, P., and G. P. Koocher. 1985. *Ethics in Psychology: Professional Standards and Cases.* New York: Random House.

Kelly, J. A., D. A. Murphy, K. J. Sikkema and S. C. Kalichman. 1993. "Psychological Interventions to Prevent HIV Infection Are Urgently Needed: New Priorities for Behavioral Research in the Second Decade of AIDS." *American Psychologist* 48: 1023-34.

Kelly, T. A., and H. H. Strupp. 1992. "Patient and Therapist Values in Psychotherapy: Perceived Changes, Assimilation, Similarity and Outcome." *Journal of Consulting and Clinical Psychology* 60: 34-40.

Kendler, H. H. 1993. "Psychology and the Ethics of Social Policy." *American Psychologist* 48: 1046-53.

Kertay, L., and S. L. Reviere. 1993. "The Use of Touch in Psychotherapy: Theoretical and Ethical Considerations." *Psychotherapy* 30: 32-40.

Kitchener, K. S. 1984. "Intuition, Critical Evaluation and Ethical Principles: The Foundation for Ethical Decisions in Counseling Psychology." *The Counseling Psychologist* 12: 43-55.

———. 1992. "Psychologist as Teacher and Mentor: Affirming Ethical Values Throughout the Curriculum." *Professional Psychology: Research and Practice* 23: 190-95.

Knapp, S., and L. VandeCreek. 1993. "Legal and Ethical Issues in Billing Patients and Collecting Fees." *Psychotherapy* 30: 25-31.

Lopez, S. R., K. P. Grover, D. Holland, M. J. Johnson, C. D. Kain, K. Kanel, C. A. Mellins and M. C. Rhyne. 1989. "Development of Culturally Sensitive Psychotherapists." *Professional Psychology: Research and Practice* 20: 369-76.

MacDevitt, J. W. 1987. "Therapists' Personal Therapy and Professional Self-Awareness." *Psychotherapy* 24: 693-701.

Mapou, R. L., and W. A. Law. 1994. "Neurobehavioral Aspects of HIV Disease and AIDS: An Update." *Professional Psychology: Research and Practice* 25: 132-40.

McCarthy, P., D. Kulakowski and J. A. Kenfield. 1994. "Clinical Supervision Practices of Licensed Psychologists." *Professional Psychology: Research and Practice* 25: 177-81.

McGaha, S., and C. Minder. 1993. "Factors Influencing Performance on the Examination for Professional Practice in Psychology EPPP." *Professional Psychology: Research and Practice* 24: 107-9.

McGovern, T. V. 1988. "Teaching the Ethical Principles of Psychology." *Teaching of Psychology* 15: 22-25.

McMinn, M. R. 1988. "Ethics Case-Study Simulation: A Generic Tool for Psychology Teachers." *Teaching of Psychology* 15: 100-101.

McMinn, M. R., and C. J. Lebold. 1989. "Collaborative Efforts in Cognitive Therapy with Religious Clients." *Journal of Psychology and Theology* 17: 101-9.

McMinn, M. R., and K. R. Meek. 1996. "Ethics Among Christian Counselors: A Survey of Beliefs and Behaviors." *Journal of Psychology and Theology* 24: 26-37.

McMinn, M. R., and J. Wilhoit. 1996. "Becoming Spiritually Sensitive." *Christian Counseling Today,* Winter, pp. 21-25.

Mintz, L. B., C. A. Rideout and K. M. Bartels. 1994. "A National Survey of Interns' Perceptions of Their Preparation for Counseling Women and of the Atmosphere of Their Graduate Education." *Professional Psychology: Research and Practice* 25: 221-27.

Monahan, J. 1993. "Limiting Therapist Exposure to *Tarasoff* Liability: Guidelines for Risk Containment." *American Psychologist* 48: 242-50.

Morgan, K. S., and R. M. Nerison. 1993. "Homosexuality and Psychopolitics: An Historical Overview." *Psychotherapy* 30: 133-40.

Myers, J. E. B. 1992. *Legal Issues in Child Abuse and Neglect.* Newbury Park, Calif.: Sage.

National Association of Social Workers. 1993. *Code of Ethics of the National Association of Social Workers.* Washington, D.C.: Author.

Newman, R., and P. M. Bricklin. 1991. "Parameters of Managed Central Health Care: Legal, Ethical and Professional Guidelines." *Professional Psychology: Research and Practice* 22: 26-35.

Nicolai, K. M., and N. A. Scott. 1994. "Provision of Confidentiality Information and Its Relation to Child Abuse Reporting." *Professional Psychology: Research and Practice* 25: 154-60.

Norcross, J. C., D. Strausser-Kirtland and C. D. Missar. 1988. "The Processes and Outcomes of Psychotherapists' Personal Treatment Experiences." *Psychotherapy* 25: 36-43.

Oordt, M. S. 1990. "Ethics of Practice Among Christian Psychologists: A Pilot Study." *Journal of Psychology and Theology* 18: 255-60.

Pope, K. S., and J. C. Bouhoutsos. 1986. *Sexual Intimacy Between Therapists and Patients.* New York: Praeger.

Pope, K. S., and S. Feldman-Summers. 1992. "National Survey of Psychologists' Sexual and Physical Abuse History and Their Evaluation of Training and Competence in These Areas." *Professional Psychology: Research and Practice* 23: 353-61.

Pope, K. S., and B. G. Tabachnick. 1993. "Therapists' Anger, Hate, Fear and Sexual Feelings: National Survey of Therapist Responses, Client Characteristics, Critical Events, Formal Complaints and Training." *Professional Psychology: Research and Practice* 24: 142-52.

————. 1994. "Therapists as Patients: A National Survey of Psychologists' Experiences, Problems and Beliefs." *Professional Psychology: Research and Practice* 25: 247-58.

Pope, K. S., B. G. Tabachnick and P. Keith-Spiegel. 1987. "Ethics of Practice: The Beliefs and Behaviors of Psychologists as Therapists." *American Psychologist* 42: 993-1006.

Pope, K. S., and M. J. T. Vasquez. 1991. *Ethics in Psychotherapy and Counseling.* San Francisco: Jossey-Bass.

Pope, K. S., and V. A. Vetter. 1992. "Ethical Dilemmas Encountered by Members of the American Psychological Association." *American Psychologist* 47: 397-411.

Redlich, F. D., and K. S. Pope. 1980. "Ethics of Mental Health Training." *Journal of Nervous and Mental Disease* 168: 709-14.

Ridley, C. R., D. W. Mendoza, B. E. Kanitz, L. Angermeier and R. Zenk. 1994. "Cultural Sensitivity in Multicultural Counseling: A Perceptual Schema Model." *Journal of Counseling Psychology* 41: 125-36.

Robiner, W. N., S. A. Parker, T. J. Ohnsorg and B. Strike. 1993. "HIV/AIDS Training and Continuing Education for Psychologists." *Professional Psychology: Research and Practice* 24: 35-42.

Rodolfa, E., T. Hall, V. Holms, A. Davena, D. Komatz, M. Antunez and A. Hall. 1994. "The Management of Sexual Feelings in Therapy." *Professional Psychology: Research and Practice* 25: 168-72.

Rothblum, E. D. 1994. " 'I Only Read About Myself on Bathroom Walls': The Need for Research on the Mental Health of Lesbians and Gay Men." *Journal of Consulting and Clinical Psychology* 62: 213-20.

Shah, S. A., and B. D. Sales. 1991. *Law and Mental Health: Major Developments and Research Needs.* Rockville, Md.: National Institute of Mental Health.

Smith, M. L., G. V. Glass and T. I. Miller. 1980. *The Benefits of Psychotherapy.* Baltimore: Johns Hopkins University Press.

Somberg, D. R., G. L. Stone and C. D. Claiborn. 1993. "Informed Consent: Therapists'

Beliefs and Practices." *Professional Psychology: Research and Practice* 24: 153-59.

Stromberg, C. D., D. J. Haggarty, R. F. Leibenluft, M. H. McMillian, B. Mishkin, B. L. Rubin and H. R. Trilling. 1988. *The Psychologist's Legal Handbook*. Washington, D.C.: Council for the National Register of Health Service Providers in Psychology.

Sue, S. 1988. "Psychotherapeutic Services for Ethnic Minorities: Two Decades of Research Findings." *American Psychologist* 43: 301-8.

Sue, S., and N. Zane. 1987. "The Role of Culture and Cultural Techniques in Psychotherapy." *American Psychologist* 42: 37-45.

Sullivan, T., W. L. Martin Jr. and M. M. Handelsman. 1993. "Practical Benefits of an Informed-Consent Procedure: An Empirical Investigation." *Professional Psychology: Research and Practice* 24: 160-63.

Szapocznik, J., and W. M. Kurtines. 1993. "Family Psychology and Cultural Diversity." *American Psychologist* 48: 400-407.

Trezza, G. R. 1994. "HIV Knowledge and Stigmatization of Persons with AIDS: Implications for the Development of HIV Education for Young Adults." *Professional Psychology: Research and Practice* 25: 141-48.

Vachon, D. O., and A. A. Agresti. 1992. "A Training Proposal to Help Mental Health Professionals Clarify and Manage Implicit Values in the Counseling Process." *Professional Psychology: Research and Practice* 23: 509-14.

VandeCreek, L., and S. Knapp. 1993. *Tarasoff and Beyond: Legal and Clinical Considerations in the Treatment of Life-Endangering Patients*. Rev. ed. Sarasota, Fla.: Professional Resource Press.

VandeCreek, L., S. Knapp and K. Brace. 1990. "Mandatory Continuing Education for Licensed Psychologists: Its Rationale and Current Implementation." *Professional Psychology: Research and Practice* 21: 135-40.

Vasquez, M. J. T. 1992. "Psychologist as Clinical Supervisor: Promoting Ethical Practice." *Professional Psychology: Research and Practice* 23: 196-202.

Walfish, S., J. L. Moritz and D. E. Stenmark. 1991. "A Longitudinal Study of the Career Satisfaction of Clinical Psychologists." *Professional Psychology: Research and Practice* 22: 253-55.

Welfel, E. R. 1992. "Psychologist as Ethics Educator: Successes, Failures and Unanswered Questions." *Professional Psychology: Research and Practice* 23: 182-89.

Whiston, S. C., and T. L. Sexton. 1993. "An Overview of Psychotherapy Outcome Research: Implications for Practice." *Professional Psychology: Research and Practice* 24: 43-51.

Chapter 18

A MODEL
FOR ETHICAL
DECISION-MAKING

Randolph K. Sanders

W henever Christian counseling is critiqued, the most frequently posed criticisms have to do with theological purity. Is psychological counseling, the critics query, something that is in harmony with the truths of the faith, or is it an alternative philosophy of humankind that poses a threat to the Christian church? Christian leaders worry about whether psychological techniques taught and promoted are in keeping with a biblical view of human beings.

These are real concerns and will continue to be as long as the field of professional counseling exists. But this critical vigilance and singleness of focus may well have prevented us from dealing with an equally valid concern: the ethical integrity of the Christian counseling profession. For the clients who see us in counseling and the professionals who work with us daily, theological purity may make little difference if we do not practice with integrity. It is at the point of practice that our clients best see our faith at work.

In view of the rapid growth of Christian counseling, the relative lack of concern in the profession with ethical issues is frightening. At its worst this lack of concern could foretell a movement that while theologically correct is morally deficient. Indeed, it could be argued that the time is ripe for episodes of scandal and misconduct. It could suggest that lurking side by side with counseling programs of solid integrity are some programs that look good to the eye, but are morally bankrupt at their core.

It remains to be seen whether the same scandals that ripped through the nearly unregulated world of televangelism several years ago will occur in the Christian counseling arena. Certainly the counseling field has established some ethical guidelines. But the profession is big, it is faddishly popular, it contains a number of superstars and it has not yet given the same priority to ethics that it has given to marketing itself.

Learning to act with integrity in the everyday world of the therapy room, the classroom and the boardroom is imperative for the Christian therapist who would aspire to excellence. To do this, Christian models for ethical decision-making are needed. These models, while not perfect, can assist therapists in dealing with the difficult ethical issues that face them in the real world. They can allow therapists to maintain their objectivity in the face of stress and help them avoid the disillusionment that comes when they find themselves drawn into dilemmas they dislike but feel powerless to respond to.

Ethical Foundations

Any decision-making model must begin with a set of foundations. These overarching principles and standards must be internalized by the individual practitioner in order for ethical dilemmas to be recognized and dealt with. Basic internalization of rules and principles is a prerequisite for providing services. Internalization also develops as a result of continuing and increasing familiarization with the principles through ongoing educational and clinical experiences.

1. *Thoroughly familiarize yourself with the adopted rules of professional conduct.* This is absolutely essential. Without a thorough knowledge of one's code of ethics, the counselor will be largely unaware of ethical dilemmas when they present themselves. While one hopefully has some intuitive respect for fundamental concepts like confidentiality and dual relationships, the standards of conduct such as those adopted by the APA, CAPS and ACA provide specificity, translating ideas into practicalities. At their best they remove some of the guesswork, self-serving biases and rationalizations that can often arise when considering moral or ethical decisions (Miller, 1991).

In addition to knowing professional codes of conduct, competent professionals must also be aware of the laws governing the practice of counseling in their state. For instance, laws regarding confidentiality of mental health information and the way in which confidentiality is handled in various legal proceedings is essential for any counselor to know.

Finally, therapists who practice in agency, institutional or church settings must be aware of the institutional rules and policies that apply to their professional activities. In an ideal situation, state laws, institutional rules and professional standards agree and make decision-making clearer and easier. That is not always the case in real life; however, knowledge of adopted rules and laws is absolutely necessary as a foundation for processing ethical dilemmas.

2. *Internalize basic principles that undergird rules of conduct.* Underlying

the rules of professional conduct are ethical principles. These principles form the bedrock on which the rules of conduct are based. In situations where application of the rules is difficult or confusing, the principles can assist in interpreting the application of the rules and in coming to a decision. Kitchener (1984) identified five moral principles that are foundational to many mental health codes: (1) autonomy, (2) nonmaleficence, (3) beneficence, (4) justice and (5) fidelity. Many of these principles are rooted at least in part in a Christian tradition. In addition, there are other principles that are important for the Christian to consider when attempting to apply the professional rules of conduct.

a. The comprehensive nature of the reign of God. "For the Christian, the kingdom of God constitutes the primary ethical community" (Anderson, 1990, p. 204). The Christian faith makes the bold assertion that God's reign extends into all aspects of life (Christian Life Commission, 1981). This includes the professional life. God is as present with us when we are in the therapy room as he is when we are at church. He is in our presence when we make business decisions about our professional practice. He is concerned with the philosophies that inform our therapies and our ethical decisions.

This is a source of great comfort. It makes clear God's desire to be involved in the present realities in which we live, encouraging and supporting us, and affirms God's care for us in the midst of the difficult, stressful decisions that we face. It also confronts us with the fact that we cannot separate our faith from our vocation when it would be convenient for us to do so. God challenges us to make our decisions with more than ourselves in mind. We must avoid the temptation to live as if God's rules were fine for Sunday school but impractical for the world of complicated client issues or the competitive world of the counseling business. To do so is to live as if our faith were impotent in the world in which we live, and it leaves us open to hypocrisy in our thinking and behavior.

b. Stewardship of talents. From a Christian perspective one's talents, including professional talents, are a gift from God. As such, the gift is a sacred trust, and the recipient is expected to prove faithful to that trust (1 Cor 4:2). Thus in training and service the professional is called to the highest standards of competence and practice. In a real sense the work of counseling can be seen as an extension of Christ's healing ministry. In fact, historically in Western society many professions were at one time viewed as forms of ministry (Campbell, 1982).

c. Humility. Sin is a very real presence in our world (Rom 3:23). Generally forgotten in most professional codes, it is nevertheless an extremely important reality to which we are all prone (CAPS, 1993). Though traditional codes have done little to remind us of the presence of sin, psychology has certainly documented some of its characteristic patterns. Attribution theory, for example, recognizes that human beings tend to make excuses and find extenuating circumstances for their own mistakes while blaming other people for theirs. We readily take responsibility for success even when it isn't justified, but we tend to blame our failures on others (Myers, 1981). Rationalization, one of a number of psychodynamic defense mechanisms, illuminates our tendency to justify our unacceptable behaviors, attitudes and beliefs.

The reality of sin calls professionals to practice the art and science of therapy with humility. Ethical therapists remain vigilant to their own human limitations and avoid the notion that their professional standing and knowledge ever fully inoculate them from error.

d. The image of God in humanity. The Bible states that each person is created in the image of God (Gen 1:27). As such, human beings have a special quality, a uniqueness among creatures. The message of Scripture is that each person is of inestimable value to God and, by extension, to us also. Because of this we have a responsibility to practice beneficence as well as nonmaleficence toward the people we serve (Kitchener, 1984). In other words, we have a duty to contribute to our clients' welfare, to do good by them and above all else to avoid harming them.

As Christian mental health professionals we are concerned about the dignity and needs of each individual, whether they are clients we serve or colleagues we serve with. Clients are far more than diagnostic categories that need treatment. Employees are more than "hired hands" to be used. Employers are not adversaries who deserve to be cheated or taken advantage of simply because they represent the established institution. Professional colleagues are not competitors to be destroyed. All are people created in God's image. All are people of worth in God's eyes and in ours as well (Christian Life Commission, 1981).

e. Autonomy. Autonomy (Kitchener, 1984) refers to the therapist's responsibility to ensure clients' rights to make their own informed decisions and actions. Part of the task of the therapist is often to help clients learn how to view various options and make their own decisions. Obviously there are limits to this principle, as when the client is a child or is someone who is unable to make competent choices.

Though autonomy is a principle developed mostly out of the emergence of democratic societies, it is not without foundation in Christian thought, so long as by *autonomy* one means the ability to self-manage, self-control or self-discipline rather than to be self-willed (Tit 1:7-8). An important aspect of disciplined autonomy is recognizing how one's own actions affect others.

f. Concern for community. We are called to recognize the larger community in which we and those we counsel live (McCloughry, 1995). The New Testament emphasis on koinonia fellowship illustrates God's concern with healthy community. Our counselees live as part of larger communities: nuclear family, extended family, church, neighborhood, God's world. Decisions that are made affect others as well as oneself. When a client ends a marriage, for example, it has repercussions that reach far beyond just the individual and the spouse. Children are affected, of course, but so are extended family, friends and associates. The therapist should be sensitive to the needs of the larger body in which the person lives (Eberlein, 1987, pp. 356-57) and though encouraging autonomy should assist the client in understanding how his or her behavior may or may not affect others. A sensitivity to community also has implications for the therapist. It implies that therapists should not practice in isolation but in the context of the larger community. This community provides support and accountability. For the professional, the wider community is both a source of sustenance and a group to which one is responsible (Reeck, 1982).

g. *Covenant as trust.* The Old Testament concept of covenant establishes the trustworthy relationship between humankind and God. It forms the basis of the Old Testament ethic (Dumbrell, 1995). Likewise trust and fidelity are essential to the therapeutic relationship. Without them the relationship is unlikely to be beneficial. Trustworthiness encompasses keeping promises, being faithful and remaining loyal.

h. *Concern for honesty.* The ninth commandment says, "You shall not give false testimony," and with good reason. Lying destroys relationships, both individual and communal. Honesty and integrity are fundamental to good mental health practice. Clients have a right to expect it of us.

At times being honest may mean talking through an ethical dilemma forthrightly with a client. Sometimes clients will trigger an ethical concern without being fully aware of the ramifications of what they have done. For example, if the mother of a client asks you to record her name rather than the child's for insurance billing purposes, you could talk with her about the negative ramifications of doing this. Though clients may sometimes be unhappy that the therapist didn't accede to their request, most will understand and appreciate that the issue was discussed openly and rationally. Therapists who conduct themselves in this way set a tone of honesty and reasonableness for the therapeutic relationship, modeling these behaviors themselves and thus encouraging clients to do likewise.

i. *Christian love.* Love is the bedrock of the New Testament ethic (1 Cor 13). We are to love others with the love that God has bestowed on us (2 Cor 1:3-7) and that is rooted in Christ's sacrifice for us. Jesus is our model of love in action (Smedes, 1983). In the context of therapy, it means that we are called to express a Christlike love toward those with whom we work.

Obviously the principle of love can be rationalized into a self-seeking focus. Therapists having affairs with clients frequently insist that they are in love. But Christlike or agape love is love that exists for the other's sake, both now and in the future.

j. *Justice.* Justice has to do with treating others fairly. It doesn't necessarily mean treating everyone exactly alike: "equals must be treated as equals and unequals must be treated in a way most beneficial to their own circumstances" (Huber, 1994). Justice and love belong together, and in a sense justice gives "backbone" to the concept of love (Tillich, cited in Field, 1995). Justice can also include trying to remedy unfair situations where they exist without creating greater harm.

A Model for Ethical Decision-Making

Ethical decision-making is not always easy. Some dilemmas do not fit nicely within the guidelines of an ethical code. Others create such strong emotions within us that it is difficult for us to remain objective, or at least to give our emotions no more due than they deserve. Some decisions require us to consider the conflicting claims of different parties.

What follows is a model for making ethical decisions. It presumes an understanding of the rules and principles discussed in the previous section. Several models of ethical decision-making have informed the present model (Eberlein, 1987; Forester-Miller and Davis, 1995; Keith-Spiegel and Koocher, 1985; Kitchener, 1986; Sileo and Kopala, 1993; Tymchuk, 1982; Welfel and Kitchener, 1995). The current model is not intended to be all-inclusive. It does not provide a "canned program" by which one can solve every ethical dilemma. The sequence in which the steps are listed may fit many dilemmas. Certainly the first two steps should occur as early as possible in the decision process. However, the exact sequence in which the steps are taken is not as important as making sure each step is given its due. Not all steps are equally important in each individual case, but do not ignore steps that are truly necessary.

The model does not take the place of personal character and virtue, which are learned from significant others through a life of commitment to Christian discipleship. Christian maturity is a process gained through a combination of making oneself vulnerable to God's nurture and acting out the principles one learns, allowing them to become deeply imbedded in one's being so that they become a natural outflow of one's everyday behavior. This speaks to the importance of the kind of learning that begins long before one enters formal training to become a mental health professional or counselor.

Still, a model can assist in piercing through much of the confusion that often surrounds ethical decision-making. It can help in making the decision at hand and gaining skills for making future decisions. The model is outlined as follows:

1. Assess a situation for its ethical dimensions.

2. Seek to define the problem using codes and principles.

3. Understand and process your emotional reaction to the problem.

4. Seek consultation as needed. (This step may actually be enacted at any point during the decision-making process.)

5. Determine whom you should be considering in making an ethical decision and why you should consider them.

6. Determine if there is precedent in other cases that would help you in making your decision.

7. Consider the options you could take.

8. Consider the possible consequences of each option.

9. Make the decision and be prepared to take appropriate responsibility for the consequences of your action.

Each step in this decision process should offer one the option of seeking consultation with other professionals who may be able to offer perception and insight that may, in the midst of the ethical dilemma, be difficult to see oneself. Indeed, the ethical therapist should never work too long in relative isolation from peers. Each of us needs developing relationships with God and with other therapists that offer consultation, support and accountability. Ideally these relationships allow us to see the unconscious blind spots and frailties in our own thinking, which can make us susceptible to ethical lapses.

1. *Assess a situation for its ethical dimensions.* Potential ethical dilemmas are often first experienced as a vague uncomfortableness felt in response to something that has just occurred: the affable and persuasive client who asks you to code her bill some other way so she can obtain insurance payments, the friendly pastor who innocently asks you to tell him about his teen daughter's counseling session with you, the attorney in a divorce case who assures you that he has both parties' welfare at heart and just needs to see their marital therapy records in order to help them settle their divorce as amicably as possible. Prior to ever defining the problem specifically, you often experience the sensation that there might be a problem.

Such recognition is not automatic, especially in situations in which the emerging dilemma is less than clear. It requires ethical sensitivity, which is more likely when the practitioner is well acquainted with the ethical codes and the principles that underlie them.

At this stage the therapist gathers information in an effort to add definition to the situation and decide if there are indeed ethical dimensions to the problem. This requires a deliberateness on the part of the therapist, first to be conscious that some difficulty exists, and then to investigate its meaning. Sometimes making a list of the facts and problematic circumstances can help to organize one's thinking. Consultation (see step 4) may also be beneficial.

2. *Seek to define the problem using codes and principles.* Once information has been gathered, turn to the codes, laws and other guidelines. Are there standards that apply directly to the matter at hand? Keep in mind that codes, laws and institutional polices do not always agree. Ultimately it is the therapist's responsibility to review all applicable laws and guidelines. In many cases the guidelines speak directly to the issue at hand with clarity, and contradictory or complicating concerns do not arise. When the guidelines are clear, following the rules should lead to resolution (Forester-Miller and Davis, 1995). When

resolution doesn't occur, and even when it does, it may be important to review the principles listed earlier that undergird ethical rules of conduct. These principles are likely to add insight as one attempts to apply the rules. Even so, if a dilemma persists, then considering at least some of the additional steps listed below will be necessary.

3. *Understand and process your emotional reaction to the problem*. Traditional training in mental health ethics focused on studying cases in the classroom at an intellectual level, applying codes of conduct to cases in an analytical or logical manner. Real clinical dilemmas do not take place in that kind of environment. Most are emotionally charged, and a few take place under crisis conditions.

If the ethical problem triggers an emotional reaction, it's very important to be consciously aware of that reaction, because these emotions may affect one's judgment and the decisions one makes about the problem. Research indicates that when faced with an ethical conflict, therapists have a tendency to rely on the ethical codes when defining what they should do, but are more likely to rely on personal values and expediency when actually deciding what to do (Smith et al., 1991).

When faced with an ethical dilemma, the therapist may *fear* the possible legal consequences that could occur if the wrong decision is made. For instance, suppose a therapist believes that a client is not abusing his children, but he is. The therapist could be held accountable. Or the therapist may feel *angry* about an ethical dilemma—she may not want this dilemma to come up now at this time and place or may feel *frustrated* because the dilemma inconveniences her or slows the client's progress in therapy. And s*exual or affectionate feelings* can further complicate ethical dilemmas.

If the ethical dilemma involves business issues in your clinical practice, other types of feelings could emerge. You may feel *threatened* by new competitors who move into the "catchment area" of your clinical practice, or you may feel *greed* as you consider moving into someone else's territory.

The problem may raise issues from the therapist's own past. If you were abused as a child, your client's report of abuse may trigger feelings of *hatred, bitterness or anger* that make it difficult for you to look objectively at your responsibility. If you are under a great deal of stress in your personal life you may find the ethical dilemma deeply frustrating. You may have difficulty focusing objectively on the issues at hand or may allow your own difficulties to distract you from following a carefully thought out decision path in dealing with the issues.

Whatever the case, accepting your emotional state and then taking steps to deal with it is a prerequisite to being able to deal conscientiously with the ethical issue before you. Contemplative prayer combined with the help and support of a trusted colleague may do much to help you deal with the feelings and move on to responsibly dealing with the ethical dilemma. And sometimes the added stress of an ethical dilemma accents other problems in the personal life of the psychotherapist and triggers the realization of the need for professional help.

4. *Seek consultation as needed.* Consultation may actually be considered at any point in the decision-making process. It may be considered as soon as the therapist experiences the uncomfortable feeling signaling that a situation is emerging. Indeed, consultation with another professional may even help define exactly what the problem is. Seeking consultation with valued colleagues is one of the most important things a therapist can do at any time during the process of decision-making.

Ideally the consultant should be mature, experienced and have good ethical decision-making skills. The consultant may be a colleague or a supervisor, or a member of a professional ethics committee. If dealing with a particular type of clinical case (i.e., an issue of abuse, family confidentiality, drugs or alcohol) it is helpful if the person has expertise in that area. If the case includes legal ramifications, consultation with an attorney may be needed.

There are several reasons consultation is very important. The consultant will add a measure of *objectivity* that a clinician who is personally involved in the case will not have. The consultant can often help the therapist define the problem more accurately and, in the decision-making phase, can help the therapist evaluate competing courses of action and choose the course of greatest integrity.

The consultant also multiplies the amount of *experience* available to consider the ethical problem. At the very least the consultant will have a different history of clinical experiences than the clinician directly involved in the case. In many cases the consultant will have more experience, and in the best-case scenario will have had specialty training in the areas that pertain to the case at hand.

If a consultant is more experienced and has known or worked with the clinician for some time, then he or she may serve as an effective *mentor and model* for the clinician (see chapter seventeen). The clinician may already have benefited from observing the consultant's model in similar cases. In a more general way, the consultant's model of key virtues, sound thinking and measured actions may motivate the clinician to imitate such behaviors, thus providing a solid foundation from which good decision-making can develop.

An effective consultant will encourage *accountability* on the part of the clinician. The best consulting relationship is one in which the two parties feel comfortable enough with one another that the clinician will be completely truthful regarding the case and his or her thinking about it. Likewise, the consultant will be able to lovingly confront and hold accountable the clinician without this impairing the effectiveness of the relationship.

Documenting the consultation may help the clinician keep focus and may also be helpful from a risk-management standpoint. If the clinician is ever called to defend his or her behavior, it will be important to show that the clinician recognized that there was a dilemma and sought help. In one case a court recognized that while therapists admittedly do sometimes encounter conflicting ethical dilemmas, they have a responsibility to seek appropriate consultation (*Rost* v. *State Board,* 1995).

5. *Determine whom you should be considering in making an ethical decision and why you should consider them.* Obviously a clinician's first and foremost concern should be for the client or patient. The clients' welfare, their autonomy and their right of self-determination are extremely important.

However, as Eberlein (1987) has pointed out, respect for the client does not absolve the clinician from considering others as well. In fact it can be argued that what makes many ethical dilemmas difficult is that they place the therapist in the uncomfortable position of trying to consider the needs and rights of more than one person. Therapists should never assume that commitment to the patient releases them from considering competing ethical claims.

This can be most apparent in family therapy, group therapy or any other setting where there is more than one client involved. If a therapist promises a child client complete confidentiality, what will she do if the child's father decides that, as guardian, he wants to know the details of what the child has told her?

Considering the competing ethical claims of different people and groups is extremely important if the practitioner is to proceed beyond the tendency to simply apply ethical rules legalistically and impulsively to clinical situations. Suppose a client who has a history of bipolar disorder enters therapy. The client has recently married, and his wife knows nothing of his condition and what the ramifications of it are. The client refuses to have his new wife come with him to a session to understand more about his condition and discuss things they might both do to maintain his health. What are the responsibilities of the therapist to the different people involved?

At the simplest level the therapist has a duty to accept the client's autonomy and right to privacy. But does the therapist also have any duties to the client at other levels or to the client's wife, family or to herself as a therapist attempting to behave responsibly and appropriately? How should the therapist proceed in a case like this? What are the potential risks and benefits to each of the parties involved, both immediate and long-term, of any action she might take?

6. *Determine if there is precedent in other cases that would help you in making your decision.* Other case material may help in discovering possible courses of action for the present dilemma. Past cases may help clarify more clearly the potential outcomes of various decisions the therapist might make to solve the dilemma.

The APA periodically publishes articles that include case material presented by the APA Ethics Committee, and a number of books on ethics in psychology and counseling contain good case illustrations (APA, 1987; Bennet et al., 1990; Bersoff,

1995; Corey, Corey and Callanan, 1979; Keith-Spiegel and Koocher, 1985). Previous legal cases, such as *Tarasoff*, allow the clinician a chance to view how the courts have evaluated problem situations and may assist the therapist in building a defensible course of action. Research studies of ethical behavior and journal articles on ethical decision-making can also help.

A therapist's own past cases and the experiences of colleagues may also help. In addition to having a host of his or her own clinical experiences, a trusted colleague can help a therapist view the dilemma from a different perspective. This shows again why consultation with an experienced colleague can be so important.

7. *Consider the options you could take.* Here the therapist considers all the possible options to take to deal with the ethical dilemma. All options are considered before critically evaluating or discarding any. Sometimes more than one option may have merit, and no option may be perfect.

8. *Consider the possible consequences of each option.* What effect will each decision likely have on each of the people considered in step 5? The clinician should consider both costs and benefits, whether these are of a psychological, social or economic nature, as well as long-term and short-term consequences (Tymchuk, 1982).

9. *Make the decision and be prepared to take appropriate responsibility for the consequences.* Taking appropriate responsibility acts as an additional check, encouraging the therapist to look carefully at the potential consequences to all parties involved of any action he or she might take to solve the dilemma. It encourages those therapists who would decide impulsively to reconsider their actions. If seen rightly, it can also encourage the reticent therapist to move toward the response of greatest integrity. And though it might not immediately seem like it, considering one's responsibility for any action taken can actually empower the actor to move forward with courage, recognizing that in the most difficult decisions selecting a course of action is sometimes a matter of choosing the best from among several less-than-satisfactory possibilities and courageously hoping for a positive outcome while preparing for negative consequences. It is also important to recognize that the right choice may not necessarily be the choice that feels right (Huber, 1994); for instance, a therapist may feel bad about having to call law enforcement to protect a person who is openly suicidal, even though the action is necessary.

Case One: Temptation

After the second session with Martha Riley,[1] Dr. Anthony Case was completing his progress note. He paused and looked out the window. He was surprised that he and this new client had developed rapport so easily. When he first received the referral, he wondered if the pleasant first impression often needed for a positive therapeutic outcome to occur would be present.

Martha was a likable woman who opened up quickly and seemed motivated for therapy. By the second session she was talking about how much his counsel had helped already, and though Dr. Case was usually skeptical of success that arrived too quickly, he thought he sensed that Martha's improvements were genuine.

He hoped things continued to progress. He was looking forward to his third session with her, and he found himself spending extra time thinking about and preparing for the session.

Once again the session went well. It seemed as though every interpretation he made was on target and all his suggestions and recommendations were gladly received. Martha was sitting near the window today, and he couldn't help but notice how pretty she looked with the light cast across her face. He thought she reminded him of someone out of his past, but he couldn't quite remember who it was. He found it difficult to end their time together. One insight led to another, and both of them seemed to want to stretch the session longer. When they rose and walked toward the door, Martha paused to ask him something, and he realized that she was standing rather close, closer than most clients in similar situations. A moment later, the question answered, the session was over.

In the days ahead he thought about Martha a number of times. He knew their rapport seemed excellent. He knew he sensed she was a special client. He wasn't allowing himself to know what else was building in the relationship.

But by the end of session four the truth was difficult to ignore (step 1). As they walked to the door, Martha was too close again. She lingered and smiled as she spoke appreciatively about his help and lightly touched his arm as she moved out the door. He felt paralyzed by the mixture of opposing feelings all occurring at once. He knew what temptation felt like, but part of him didn't want to admit that he knew.

In a way he knew exactly what the problem was (step 2), and he knew he should get consultation (step 4), but he was also aware that to give the problem a name and to share it with a wiser colleague was to shed the light of day on it.

He resisted, even rationalized at first, but his extensive knowledge of the rules combined with spiritual and character values, as well as some fear and guilt, pushed him to call his old mentor. He and the mentor discussed the fact that this was indeed a budding dual relationship (step 2) and also talked about his emotional reactions to the problem (step 3). He began to realize more clearly the confusing array of emotions he had been feeling: relieved that rapport was easily established, empathetic toward Martha's problems, encouraged by her appreciation, exhilarated that she seemed to find him attractive, tempted by someone in "the forbidden zone," embarrassed about revealing his feelings to a colleague, and anxious about the entire situation.

His mentor asked him to consider each person in this situation and what their needs were (step 5). He also encouraged him to consider some Christian principles that applied to the problem. The two brainstormed some concerns, realizing that their list was not all-inclusive.

☐ Concern for Martha as one of God's people and the importance of trust in the therapeutic relationship: Martha had told Dr. Case that she had been seriously hurt in her relationship with her own father. Now she was beginning a therapeutic relationship with another male that if handled poorly could further harm her.

☐ Concern for honesty: The longer the present situation continued, the less likely that what was occurring in the office could properly be defined as therapy.

☐ Stewardship of talents: Dr. Case's career and personal integrity could be in jeopardy if he made poor decisions about his present circumstances.

☐ Christian responsibility: Since Dr. Case believed that God's kingdom does extend to the therapy room, he knew he had a responsibility to be honest with God about his feelings and deal responsibly and with agape love toward Martha.

Dr. Case also thought about other therapists who had "fallen from grace" and began to wonder what it would be like to be in their shoes (step 6). He agreed with his mentor that prior to his next session with Martha he would make a list of the options he could take. His list of options included the following:

1. Discuss the situation with Martha, terminate therapy and refer her to another therapist.

2. Discuss the situation with Martha but encourage a "talking through" of the issues in a therapeutic manner.

3. Commit to remaining ethical and therapeutic in the sessions, but unless necessary try not to deal directly with the sexual innuendo yet, choosing to wait until the therapeutic relationship was better solidified.

Dr. Case considered the possible consequences of each action (step 8). He knew, for example, that following option 2 would certainly open up the issue but might also surprise Martha and trigger a premature termination of therapy. Option 3 might allow more time, but also might leave him more vulnerable. Once he thought about the possible consequences of each action, and about his responsibility for whatever action he took, he was ready to make a final decision about what to do.

Which direction do you think he should have taken? Why? What would be the potential positive and negative consequences of that course of action?

Case Two: Confidentiality Versus the Client's Welfare

Dr. Sally Vernon, a therapist, begins counseling Jack Burns for depression and job stress. Jack is also taking antidepressant medication, which is prescribed by his internist. Several weeks into therapy Jack reveals that he has been drinking quite a bit, especially in the evenings. He started drinking prior to beginning the antidepressant as a way of trying to help himself sleep, but he has continued the practice in spite of the fact that his physician told him not to mix this particular medication with alcohol.

With some probing, Dr. Vernon learns from Jack that he has not informed his physician of his drinking. Dr. Vernon reminds Jack that the physician has warned him against drinking and taking medication and recommends that Jack contact his physician prior to the next session, inform him of what he is doing and request instruction. Dr. Vernon also suggests that Jack tell the physician that he is now in therapy.

When Jack returns for his next session, he admits that he has not contacted his physician and that he is still mixing medication and alcohol. Dr. Vernon asks Jack to sign a release so that she can talk to the physician herself, but Jack refuses. He says he doesn't want his physician to know because he and the physician attend the same church, and he thinks the internist will think much less of him if he knows. He tells Dr. Vernon that he'll just stop drinking and that will "take care of the problem." But Dr. Vernon believes that this is not likely to happen and feels an ethical as well as a therapeutic problem growing in the relationship (step 1). She is sworn to confidentiality and should not release information without her client's signed release. She believes that Jack's course of action is not healthy, and she has promised to be concerned about his welfare (step 2).

As she prepares to talk to her mentor about her dilemma (step 4), she becomes more aware of her conflicted feelings about the case—wanting to help, feeling trapped in her efforts to properly serve the client and somewhat anxious about the potential risks of continuing service to Jack (step 3).

She thinks carefully about the persons she should consider in this case. Of course there is Jack, who obviously needs treatment but seems tenuously committed at this point. There is some concern about Jack's physician, who apparently is trying to treat Jack without needed facts about the case. Finally, Dr. Vernon is concerned about herself in her efforts to serve Jack appropriately (step 5).

She is also concerned about the denial apparent in Jack's behavior, and she wants to foster a therapeutic relationship of honesty. She is concerned about Jack as one of God's people struggling, albeit haphazardly, to deal with many problems. She considers past cases where people had wanted her to participate in their denial and what she did about them (step 6).

She considers her options and their possible consequences (steps 7 and 8). She could refuse to continue to be Jack's therapist, indicating her inability to work with him based on his refusal to follow appropriate professional advice. She could discuss the matter further with him, reviewing carefully the therapeutic problems of continuing his current actions, discussing the bind she is in and considering the alternatives available to him. She could also confront him about his denial. She considers these and other options as well as the possible consequences of pursuing any one of them.

What would you do if you were Dr. Vernon? Is there one best solution?

Conclusion

The Christian counseling movement has become a powerful force within the modern church. It is imperative that professionals in this field know how to discern what is right and what is good, and learn to act with integrity in the everyday world of the therapy room, the classroom and the boardroom. An ever-maturing faith coupled with good models for decision-making can help the Christian professional structure the ethical decision-making process and make wise judgments. In addition, the professional who would act with integrity cannot do so in professional isolation. Relationships with others within the profession marked by frequent consultation, support and accountability will help the Christian counselor avoid the biases and blind spots that lead to ethical errors and lapses. These personal relationships, which can take place at a local level as well as through one's relationships in professional organizations, mirror the intimate relationship of love, support and accountability the Christian counselor or therapist should develop with God.

References

American Psychological Association. 1987. *Casebook on Ethical Principles of Psychologists*. Washington, D.C.: Author.

———. 1992. "Ethical Principles of Psychologists and Code of Conduct." *American Psychologist* 47: 1597-1611.

Anderson, R. S. 1990. *Christians Who Counsel*. Grand Rapids, Mich.: Zondervan.

Bennett, B. E., B. K. Bryant, G. R. VandenBos and A. Greenwood. 1990. *Professional Liability and Risk Management*. Washington, D.C.: American Psychological Association.

Bersoff, D. N., ed. 1995. *Ethical Conflicts in Psychology*. Washington, D.C.: American Psychological Association.

Campbell, D. M. 1982. *Doctors, Lawyers, Ministers: Christian Ethics in Professional Practice*. Nashville: Abingdon.

Christian Association for Psychological Studies. 1993. *Ethical Guidelines for the Christian Association for Psychological Studies*. (Available from CAPS, P.O. Box 310400, New Braunfels, TX 78131-0400.)

Christian Life Commission. 1981. *Business Ethics Issues and Answers Series*. Dallas: Christian Life Commission, Baptist General Convention of Texas.

Corey, G., M. S. Corey and P. Callanan. 1979. *Professional and Ethical Issues in Counseling and Psychotherapy*. Monterey, Calif.: Brooks/Cole.

Dumbrell, W. J. 1995. "Covenant," in *New Dictionary of Christian Ethics and Pastoral Theology*, ed. D. J. Atkinson, D. H. Field, A. Holmes and O. O'Donovan. Downers Grove, Ill.: InterVarsity Press. Pp. 266-67.

Eberlein, L. 1987. "Introducing Ethics to Beginning Psychologists: A Problem-Solving Approach." *Professional Psychology: Research and Practice* 18: 353-59.

Field, D. H. 1995. "Love," in *New Dictionary of Christian Ethics and Pastoral Theology*, ed. D. J. Atkinson, D. H. Field, A. Holmes and O. O'Donovan. Downers Grove, Ill.: InterVarsity Press. Pp. 9-15.

Forester-Miller, H., and T. E. Davis. 1995. *A Practitioner's Guide to Ethical Decision-Making*. (Available from American Counseling Association, P.O. Box 531, Annapolis Junction, MD 20701-0531.)

Huber, C. H. 1994. *Ethical, Legal and Professional Issues in the Practice of Marriage and Family Therapy*. 2nd ed. New York: Merrill.

Keith-Spiegel, P., and G. P. Koocher. 1985. *Ethics in Psychology: Professional Standards and Cases*. New York: Random House.

Kitchener, K. S. 1984. "Intuition, Critical Evaluation and Ethical Principles: The Foundation for Ethical Decisions in Counseling Psychology." *Counseling Psychologist* 12: 43-55.

———. 1986. "Teaching Applied Ethics in Counselor Education: An Integration of Psychological Processes and Philosophical Analysis." *Journal of Counseling and Development* 64: 306-10.

Ladd, G. E. 1974. *A Theology of the New Testament*. Grand Rapids, Mich.: Eerdmans.

McCloughry, R. K. 1995. "Community Ethics," in *New Dictionary of Christian Ethics and Pastoral Theology,* ed. D. J. Atkinson, D. H. Field, A. Holmes and O. O'Donovan. Downers Grove, Ill.: InterVarsity Press. Pp. 108-15.

Miller, D. J. 1991. "The Necessity of Principles in Virtue Ethics." *Professional Psychology: Research and Practice* 22: 107.

Myers, D. G. 1981. *The Inflated Self: Human Illusions and the Biblical Call to Hope*. New York: Seabury.

Reeck, D. 1982. *Ethics for the Professions: A Christian Perspective*. Minneapolis: Augsburg.

Rost v. *State Board*. 1995. Cited in "Legal Briefs." *Register Report* 22 (1996): 18-19.

Sileo, F. J., and M. Kopala. 1993. "An A-B-C-D-E Worksheet for Promoting Beneficence When Considering Ethical Issues." *Counseling and Values* 37: 89-95.

Smedes, L. B. 1983. *Mere Morality*. Grand Rapids, Mich.: Eerdmans.

Smith, T. S., J. M. McGuire, D. W. Abbott and B. I. Blau. 1991. "Clinical Ethical Decision-Making: An Investigation of the Rationales Used to Justify Doing Less Than One Believes One Should." *Professional Psychology: Research and Practice* 22: 235-39.

Tymchuk, A. J. 1982. "Strategies for Resolving Value Dilemmas." *American Behavioral Scientist* 26: 159-75.

Welfel, E. R., and K. S. Kitchener. 1995. "Introduction to the Special Section: Ethics Education—An Agenda for the 90s," in *Ethical Conflicts in Psychology,* ed. D. N. Bersoff. Washington, D.C.: American Psychological Association.

---

[1]The case studies and the names of all characters in this chapter are fictitious.

Chapter 19

CHRISTIAN CODES: ARE THEY BETTER?

James R. Beck

*I*n recent years professional organizations for Christian mental health service providers have developed their own codes of ethics. These codes have appeared as part of a larger movement to organize Christian psychotherapists into professional associations. As the mental health field itself expands, so does the number of Christian participants in that field. These Christian psychotherapists find themselves experiencing a curious combination of contradictory allegiances. On the one hand, they feel great kinship with their secular colleagues in the mental health field. But on the other hand, they sometimes feel more affinity with other Christian professionals, regardless of their respective professional identities, than they do with secular colleagues in the same professional group. Hence many psychotherapists find value in aligning with their own secular professional group as well as with a multidisciplinary Christian group.

As these Christian associations mature and develop they inevitably face the necessity of codifying standards of professional behavior that are expected of all members. This chapter will compare two such Christian codes with existing secular codes to evaluate how these newer codes compare and contrast with their secular equivalents. The chapter will conclude with a review of the distinctives and deficiencies of the Christian codes as well as a review of the problems inherent in the production of codes of ethics that these respective Christian organizations will have to face in the future.

Codes of ethics set forth for the members of an organization a general consensus concerning acceptable and unacceptable standards of behavior (Van Hoose, 1979). While these standards can never be so precise as to cover every imaginable contingency, they do serve the valued purpose of setting an ethical direction for the organization and provide a basis for the discipline of errant or wayward members. As such these codes of ethics fit well with many of the general themes of Christianity. The New Testament ethic for adherents to the Christian faith calls for standards of behavior and for the gentle discipline of those who do not conform. In some ways one could argue that major sections of the New Testament's epistolary literature are, in fact, codes of ethics for the followers of Jesus. So when Christian organizations produce professional codes of ethics for their members, they are acting in congruence with their Christian heritage. A minority of critics have charged that the only basis of professional operation for Christians ought to be the New Testament itself and that any additional codes of ethics for Christians are redundant and unnecessary. Most Christian professionals, however, concede that guidelines additional to those found in the pages of the New Testament are helpful if not necessary (Beck and Mathews, 1986).

The content of professional codes also brings to our discussion another point of contact between secular codes and Christian convictions. The ethical content of current codes has its roots in ancient standards, both Greek and Roman, as well as in the New Testament itself. Consider the following list of basic ethical principles that guide most all existing codes: autonomy, beneficence, fidelity, justice and nonmaleficence (Swenson, 1993). Pope and Vasquez (1991) summarize that ethical codes comprise three major themes: trust, power and caring. These themes have their roots in ancient sources, whether the Code of Hammurabi, the oath of Hippocrates or the Bible. "Thus our contemporary codes are products of a long, slow, sedimentary process and represent both a gradual accumulation of the experience of the ages and shaping by contemporary social values, economic pressures, and political developments" (Reeck, 1982, p. 61).

In addition to these slow, centuries-long processes, ethical codes are also greatly affected by quickly changing societal trends. Christian and secular codes both are significantly influenced by changing standards for what is acceptable in the mental health field. As ethical breaches occur, professional societies tend to incorporate new or expanded statements and standards into their codes. As offended clients file lawsuits and follow them through to victory, associations add new standards of conduct to their codes. As legislatures respond to recent consumer-rights philosophies and add new procedures to statutory law, writers of ethical codes have to catch up and continually upgrade their codes. All of these societal pressures affect religious counselors and professional societies. "Religious counseling can occur in almost every function of a religious organization—and so can lawsuits" (Bullis and Mazur, 1993, p. 1). Bullis and Mazur also write, "First, the United States has become a litigious society, and second, religious institutions no longer have the 'charitable immunity' once afforded to them" (p. 2). Christian codes stand in constant need of revision and conformity to these ever-changing trends (Ohlschlager and Mosgofian, 1992; Steere, 1984).

Christian Codes

The first code we will examine is that of the American Association of Pastoral Counselors (AAPC, 1994). This organization is unique for two reasons. First, it represents a single category of Christian mental health professionals— namely, pastoral counselors. The AAPC has developed an impressive system of credentialing psychotherapists who build their careers in mental health on a foundation of theological training and ministerial experience. All full members of the AAPC must possess the M.Div. degree or its equivalent and must be ordained or licensed by a denominational group. Members must be active participants in their faith group. Members are not just pastors who counsel; they are women and men who have carved out for themselves a distinct form of psychotherapy called pastoral counseling.

The second distinctive of the AAPC is that it is a religiously pluralistic group. Although primarily Christian in its ethos and membership, the association does welcome clergy from other faiths into its ranks. Jewish rabbis and Buddhist clerics are among the membership of the AAPC. For the purposes of this chapter, however, we are considering the code of ethics of the AAPC as a Christian code.

The AAPC code begins by listing seven foundational premises in the prologue that undergird the remaining themes of the document: church participation, nondiscrimination, continuing education, collegial relationships, personal problems, competence and professional boundaries. The remainder of the code consists of six principles, each of which consists of several subpoints. The six principles deal with professional practices, client relationships, confidentiality, supervisee/student/employee relationships, interprofessional relationships and advertising.

When this edition of the AAPC code first appeared in 1991, an extended section of the document entitled "Code of Ethics Procedures" was an integral part of the code. In 1993 the membership of the AAPC voted to separate the procedures section from the code itself. Now the organization's board of governors can alter the procedures, whereas the code itself can be modified only by the membership as a whole. The section dealing with procedures is as long as the body of the code itself.

The second code of ethics examined in this chapter is much more recent in origin. In 1993 the Christian Association for Psychological Studies adopted its first statement of "Ethical Guidelines" for its members. The process of developing this statement began on a regional level in 1982 (King, 1986). Association leaders revised the document several times before its final membership approval in 1993.

As an organization, CAPS has two features that make it unique in comparison to the features of the AAPC. First, CAPS is multidisciplinary in composition. CAPS members come from the psychiatric profession, from clinical psychology, from social work and from other varieties of master's-level mental health professions. This multidisciplinary quality of membership has necessitated a somewhat broader code than the AAPC's.

A second distinctive of CAPS is that its membership is totally Christian. Members must affirm a Christian doctrinal statement upon joining the organization. The membership is transdenominational in nature; most CAPS members would identify themselves as Protestant evangelicals, although people from other branches of Protestantism and some Roman Catholics belong to CAPS as well. This unique feature of CAPS allows its code of ethics to be more explicitly Christian than the AAPC's code, which is designed to serve a much broader constituency.

The CAPS code begins with a general statement describing its evolution and development. In the code itself is a preamble that reiterates the statement of faith found in the constitution of CAPS as well as a summary of biblical principles, actually theological convictions, that undergird the balance of the statement. The code itself consists of eleven articles, each of which consists of several subpoints. The eleven principles are (1) personal commitment as a Christian, (2) loving concern for clients, (3) confidentiality, (4) competency in services provided, (5) personal, human limitations, (6) advertising and promotional activities, (7) research, (8) professional liability, (9) pastoral care network, (10) membership revocation and restoration, and (11) a general prudential rule. The last section attempts to deal with issues not otherwise treated in the code.

> Recognizing that no ethical guidelines are complete, I make my day-to-day decisions based on the criteria and principles stated in the Preamble. I will do my best to serve and to live an a way that is congruent with the stated basic principles of these guidelines and with my faith as a Christian. (CAPS, 1993, p. 6)

The final two pages of the ethical guidelines consist of a protocol for giving service to troubled or noncompliant members of the organization. CAPS deals with ethical guidelines violations through its pastoral care network.

Secular Codes

We will now compare these two Christian codes with two existing secular codes. Both of the secular codes are much older and more expansive than both the CAPS and the AAPC codes.

APA code. The latest code of the APA appeared in 1992 under the title "Ethical Principles of Psychologists and Code of Conduct." The first APA code issued in 1953 was revised in 1959 and in 1981. The 1992 edition is both the longest and the most evolved of the four codes considered in this chapter. The APA code has always been accompanied by a casebook that describes the core of the code by giving illustrations of how the national APA ethics committee has adjudicated cases based on it.

The 1992 APA code follows the pattern of others as described by Keith-Spiegel and Koocher (1985).

Most professional ethics codes echo similar themes: to promote the welfare of consumers served, to maintain competence, to protect confidentiality and/or privacy, to act responsibly, to avoid exploitation and to uphold the integrity of the profession through exemplary conduct. (p. 3)

Even though the current APA code may be similar to other codes, it clearly wins the prize for length and comprehensiveness. The fifteen pages of double-column type include an entire page that indexes the preamble and the eight basic areas consisting of over one hundred subitems. At this rate of growth secular codes may soon graduate from pamphlet size to tomelike length.

The content of the APA code is divided into the preamble, a statement of general principles and the ethical standards themselves. The preamble is aspirational in tone and intent and includes statements of the knowledge base for psychology, the importance of the protection and welfare of individuals, and an appeal to follow the highest standards of conduct. The six general principles deal with competence, integrity, professional and scientific responsibility, respect, concern for the welfare of others, and social responsibility. The eight ethical standards are (1) general standards; (2) evaluation, assessment and intervention; (3) advertising and other public statements; (4) therapy; (5) privacy and confidentiality; (6) teaching, training, supervision, research and publishing; (7) forensic activity; and (8) resolving ethical issues.

The 1992 edition of the APA code deals with several issues that surfaced subsequent to the 1981 edition, such as information stored in databases and sexual intimacies with former patients. As new issues surface in the mental health disciplines, the tendency of associations is to add them to the current code but not to drop issues previously incorporated. As a result, these codes grow and grow.

ACA code. The American Counseling Association, formerly known as the American Association for Counseling and Development, represents a large number of master's-degree therapists in the United States. The first edition of their current code appeared in 1961; the association has revised that code several times since. The current format of the code includes a preamble that sets forth the basis for the association's interest in pursuing high levels of ethical conduct among its members: "The worth, dignity, potential, and uniqueness of each individual" (1995, p. 1).

A very brief preface is followed by a lengthy code of conduct section that covers some fifty items. Areas covered include the counseling relationship, confidentiality, professional responsibility, and research and publication. Following this is a section called Standards of Practice. The Standards of Practice are intended to represent the *minimum* requirements of the code of ethics. Apparently this was done to make the document more functional, as the size and scope of these newer codes are almost overwhelming to the beginning practitioner.

Again, the newer ACA code of ethics treats topics that have only recently emerged as issues of ethical importance: treatment planning, informed consent, family involvement in counseling and nondiscrimination.

Both of these secular codes stand in stark contrast to the smaller and more recent Christian codes we are considering here. These secular codes reflect the needs of organizations that are massive in size compared to either the AAPC or CAPS, but we can still profitably use these two secular codes for comparison purposes with the Christian codes, because both the APA and ACA codes reflect the best and most up-to-date approach to professional ethics in the mental health field. Both codes treat the seven most important areas of concern for psychotherapists: (1) do not harm; (2) practice only with competence; (3) do not exploit; (4) treat people with dignity; (5) protect confidentiality; (6) act with informed consent; and (7) practice in accord with social equity and justice (Pope, Tabachnick and Keith-Spiegel, 1987). One could only wish that the codes could still be as brief as this list of seven issues.

Williams's Ethical Descriptors

One means of comparing secular codes to Christian codes is to use Williams's Index of Ethical Code Terminology (Austin, Moline and Williams, 1990). Williams found seventy-nine descriptors of ethical issues addressed in six major secular codes (NASW, American Psychiatric Association, AAMFT, AACD, APA and ASGW [Association for Specialists in Group Work]). Twenty-three of the descriptors represent issues found in each of the six codes. Thus we can assume that the two secular codes we are using for comparison purposes, ACA and APA, both deal with these twenty-three items. We can examine the two Christian codes to determine how many of the twenty-three topics are found in them. Table 19.1 summarizes this investigation.

| | Christian Codes | |
	AAPC (1991)	CAPS (1992)
Duties to clients		
Competence	X	X
Confidentiality	X	X
Conflict of interest	X	
Danger	X	X
Discrimination	X	X
Exploitation	X	X
Fees	X	X
Protection		X
Records	X	

Refusal of treatment	X	
Sexual intimacies	X	X
Duties to the profession		
Colleague relationships	X	X
Continuing education	X	X
Measurement/testing		
Personal problems	X	
Referrals	X	X
Reporting colleagues		
Research		X
Teaching/training		
Techniques		
Relationship to society		
Community standards		
Fraud/deception	X	X
Governmental law/regulation	X	X

Table 19.1. Williams's code descriptors and Christian codes[1]

With regard to duties to clients and to society, both the CAPS code and the AAPC code compare quite favorably. The AAPC code does not appear to address directly the idea of protection of clients or the role of community standards in helping to set the tone for professional functioning. The CAPS code does not expressly deal with conflict of interest, records, community standards or refusal of treatment.

The biggest deficits found in the two Christian codes appear to be in the area of duties to the profession. For example, the AAPC code does not address the subjects of measurement/testing, reporting colleagues who are unethical, research, teaching or training, and the proper use of techniques. The CAPS code does not directly deal with measurement/testing, personal problems in the life of the therapist, reporting unethical colleagues, teaching or training, or the proper use of techniques. The issues of reporting unethical colleagues and personal problems of a therapist are addressed, however, in the Pastoral Care Network Protocol that is attached to the CAPS ethical code. Drafters of these two codes of ethics might well argue that the other omitted topics are covered by implication in other sections of the codes.

One could also argue that the more limited range of the Christian codes regarding duties to the profession may simply reflect the fact that the two Christian associations involved have a more narrowly defined professional scope than either the APA or the ACA. A second argument to explain the apparent deficiency of at least the CAPS code with regard to duties to the profession has to do with the relative recency of its experience with an ethical code. As more and more years pass by, the organization will undoubtedly uncover more examples of lapse of duty toward the respective professional groups among its members that will have to be addressed by new and additional ethical standards.

Malony's Comparison

Malony (1986) conducted a similar review of several codes of ethics. He compared four professional codes (APA, AAMFT, CAPS and AAPC). The four he selected vary slightly from the four we are using here in this study. Also, the four he reviewed represented, in some cases, earlier editions of the codes we are considering here. Nonetheless, his findings were that these four codes, while differing slightly in their composition, each dealt with ten major areas of ethical conduct: (1) a primary concern for human welfare; (2) a respect for all with a commitment to human rights; (3) a respect for the client's privacy and confidentiality; (4) a ban on all forms of exploitation, including sexual exploitation; (5) an encouragement to pursue continuing education; (6) a requirement to control advertisement; (7) an advocacy of competence; (8) a prohibition on kickback fees; (9) a requirement to refer in cases of lack of therapeutic response; and (10) a standard of respect for other professionals.

Thus we can conclude that the two secular codes and the two Christian codes we are comparing tend to cover the same general areas. No single code of ethical conduct will be free of problems. All codes have their limitations (Corey, Corey and Callanan, 1993). Secular codes have their limitations, and so do the Christian codes.

Distinctives of the Christian Codes

Having established that secular and Christian codes share a great deal of similarity and scope of coverage, we now move to an exploration of two major distinctives that the Christian codes have when compared to the two secular codes used in this study. These distinctives are the bases given for psychotherapeutic practice and enumerated procedures for dealing with ethical violations and violators.

Foundations. Grounding psychotherapeutic practice in philosophical assumptions seems to be the hardest task faced by creators of secular codes. Codes have used various philosophical underpinnings in the past. Utilitarianism has at times served as the compass for ethical decision-making (Carroll, Schneider and Wesley, 1985). Steininger, Newell and Garcia (1984) have argued that professional ethicists must adopt some moral theory with attendant secondary moral principles in order to anchor their prescriptions for ethical conduct on a reliable and supportive base. Adherents to an ethical code would thus be moral agents. But in our day the adoption of any moral theory is challenged by the immoralist, the relativist and the subjectivist. Secularists want to be morally neutral and to leave morality to religion, even though such efforts are futile. "We maintain that their attempt at moral neutrality is doomed to failure" (Steininger, Newell and Garcia, 1984, p. 37).

The APA code (1992) anchors its preamble statement in science: "Psychologists work to develop a valid and reliable body of scientific knowledge based on research," the goal being to "apply it pragmatically to improve the condition of both the individual and society" (p. 3). The APA code admits that "this Ethics Code provides a common set of values upon which psychologists build their professional and scientific work" (preamble, p. 3). Yet the code thus suffers from the lack of any grounding for these values. This scientific/pragmatic foundation for the APA code is fraught with internal inconsistencies. Does science yield a common set of values? Or do those values have another source that remains unidentified in this preamble? How do pragmatics and high ethical values fit together? How do pragmatics and pure scientific research fit together? What happened to the primary concern for the welfare of the individual that formerly held sway in the APA preamble? In the 1992 edition the rights, dignity and worth of all people have been relegated to a position of less prominence in Principle D, Respect for People's Rights and Dignity. The APA code thus rests rather tenuously on a curious blend of scientism, humanism and pragmatic values.

The 1988 revision of the ACA code put its foundational principles in the first paragraph of the preamble. The worth, dignity, potential and uniqueness of individuals is prominent. Some would argue that such a humanistic standard, while not very impressive in itself as the foundation for a social science, is at least the best that a secular and pluralistic profession can use as the basis of its work. The 1995 revision of the ACA code says almost nothing about foundational principles beyond the one statement. It merely calls on all ACA members to abide by the code and standards. It appears almost to give up on any attempt to anchor the counseling profession on a philosophical worldview. Reeck's 1982 commentary on this dilemma among secular professions is even more true today than when he first wrote the following:

> Professions seem to be riding on the shrinking religious capital of modern society, inherited from earlier generations, without contributing to its main-tenance. Like society at large, professions are becoming secularized, but this may be a greater danger than is generally recognized. (p. 68)

In sharp contrast to this dismal picture that the secular codes present to us, the Christian codes excel on this very point. The Christian foundation for the AAPC code is implicit since that organization has suppressed its explicit expression for the benefit of its non-Christian members. But the code assumes that all members will anchor the ethical preachments of the code in their own personal theology. The AAPC code also assumes a belief in the dignity and worth of each individual. "We are dedicated to advancing the welfare of those who seek our assistance and to the maintenance of high standards of professional conduct and competence" (1991, p. 1).

The theological grounding of the CAPS code is even clearer. Love is the implicit guiding principle for all professional conduct, according to the CAPS guidelines (Malony, 1986). Their guidelines are anchored in the CAPS statement of faith: "These guidelines are aimed at helping each member apply the message of the Gospel to his or her professional or pastoral service" (1992, p. 2). An extended paragraph of biblical principles (regarding human nature, the theology of conflict and struggle, the need for corporate support, and the lordship of Christ) also serves as a set of foundational guidelines to undergird the ethical guidelines.

Clearly the Christian codes, in spite of their other shortcomings, excel on the important issue of foundational principles. The Christian associations that have produced these codes have the obvious advantage of organizing themselves around common assumptions that the secular agencies struggle with due to their very diverse and pluralistic ethos.

Procedures. A second distinctive of the Christian codes centers on their description of procedures that must be used when a member violates the letter or the spirit of the code. The secular codes do address this issue, but only in the briefest manner. For example, the APA code devotes the final eight paragraphs to resolving ethical issues. This section requires members to be informed regarding the content of the code; to confront ethical issues; to resolve conflicts so as to permit fullest possible adherence to the code; to resolve issues informally where possible; to report all remaining, unsolved ethical violations; to cooperate with the ethics committee in its investigations; and to avoid frivolous and improper complaints. Yet this section is allotted a rather minor role when compared to the size of the document as a whole. To be fair, one can assume that the APA ethics committee does indeed have elaborate procedural guidelines. But the association has chosen not to elevate them to the same level of importance as the code itself.

The ACA (1995) code includes two small sections that deal with resolution of ethical conflicts. However, it also has added an attachment that deals with policies and procedures for processing complaints of ethical violations.

In great contrast, nearly half of both the CAPS and the AAPC codes is devoted to the procedures used in resolving ethical issues. In the case of the AAPC, these procedures were separated from the ethical standards so that the procedures could be changed more easily than the ethical principles. However, the ethical principles and the procedures continue to be printed in the same document. This presentation suggests that the association highly values its conduct toward members, just as the code has urged members to value highly all of their clients. The AAPC code and procedures document is commendably consistent at this point.

Likewise CAPS devotes a great deal of space to a description of its pastoral care network for troubled members.[2] The code expects CAPS members to be as ethical with one another as they are with their clients. The code represents balance and consistency here that is missing in the secular codes.

Future Issues

Several problems loom on the horizon for the Christian associations that have produced the Christian codes we have been examining. We will discuss three of those future issues.

Inherent problems. All codes, including Christian codes, face the problem of becoming too elaborate. Ethical codes grow and expand with the years. They can begin to carry around excess pounds that mitigate against good health. In some cases codes begin to codify common sense. Issues are added because some member violated the spirit of the code, and now the letter of the code must be devoted to that breach. An example is found in the AAPC code: "We do not harass or dismiss an employee who has acted in a reasonable, responsible and ethical manner to protect, or intervene on behalf of, a client or other member of the public or another employee" (1991, p. 4). Presumably some AAPC member unjustly fired an employee at some point, prompting the association to add this principle. But is this item really a principle? Is not the issue actually a commonsense extension of other existing principles? Wouldn't the code be leaner and more precise if such extensions or extrapolations of existing principles were left to the reader and to the ethics committee to decide or perhaps were included in a separate casebook? The Christian associations in question will have to struggle with the issue of how to keep their codes from becoming too elaborate, too similar to case law and too unwieldy in size.

Another inherent problem Christian associations must face in the future has to do with the triangulation of obligation. With secular codes, adherents face the occasional dilemma of a dual obligation that conflicts: duty to the code of ethics in question and duty to the law (Keith-Spiegel and Koocher, 1985). The conflict is difficult enough for the secular practitioner, but the Christian psychotherapist faces an even more difficult eventuality: at times conflicting obligations can be triangulated among duty to the code, duty to the law, and duty to scriptural conviction (Levicoff, 1991). The controversial issue of reparative therapy for homosexuals who are seeking to change is a good example. The law might obligate the therapist to comply with accepted standards of care that might preclude reparative therapy, ethical standards might insist that the therapist assist the client to adjust to his or her homosexuality, and scriptural convictions might compel a therapist to accede to the client's request for therapy. Somehow Christian associations must face this issue and offer help to their members on how to handle the problem.

Omissions. The Christian codes do not sufficiently address the issue of the personal problems of therapists. Kilbourg, Nathan and Thoreson (1986) have demonstrated that the professional in distress is an increasing problem in the mental health industry. Christian therapists will not be immune to this trend. Work in the psychotherapeutic arena is by definition stressful and difficult. Once a professional begins to function poorly because of this stress, others are affected, and the damage can be extensive. The codes must address this issue.

Also, the Christian codes, like most ethical codes, fail to deal adequately with the inner life of the practitioner. Of the four codes we are considering here, the CAPS code does the most comprehensive job of addressing this realm. Yet more needs to be done. "The codes in general pay scant attention to the issue of the inner life of the practitioner" (Reeck, 1982, p. 65). It is easy for us to assume that the practitioner will have good inner character and the desire to obey the rules, yet such assumptions are risky for associations to make.

Another omission concerns the victim of a member's ethical lapse. We do well to pay attention to the offender and to care for that person. But what about the victims? Should they not also receive some of our caring and healing attention?

A final omission is a treatment of the legitimate self-interest a practitioner may have in the field of mental health work. Is any self-interest legitimate? For example, how should therapists view marketing? Are marketing services a self-interest, or are they in the interest of and for the welfare of the client? If some legitimate self-interests do exist, in what areas and to what degree are they ethical?

Future Work. Christian associations must also decide on criteria for what to include in future revisions and what not to include. The tendency to codify a rule that would have prevented every possible breach of performance is a totally inadequate criterion for the construction of ethical guidelines. The production of casebooks to accompany the Christian codes may help solve this dilemma.

Conclusion
The Christian associations examined in this chapter have made great strides in producing usable, complete and philosophically grounded codes of ethics. While more work remains to be done, both CAPS and the AAPC have laid an impressive foundation for the future. It is important for Christian therapists and other mental health practitioners to have helpful, up-to-date and complete guidelines to follow in order to prevent or help ease the difficulties of ethical dilemmas.

References
American Association for Counseling and Development. 1988. *Ethical Standards.* Alexandria, Va.: Author.

American Association of Pastoral Counselors. 1994. *Code of Ethics.* Fairfax, Va.: Author.

American Counseling Association. 1995. *Code of Ethics and Standards of Practice.* Alexandria, Va.: Author.

American Psychological Association. 1992. *Ethical Principles of Psychologists and Code of Conduct.* Washington, D.C.: Author.

Austin, K. M., M. E. Moline and G. T. Williams. 1990. *Confronting Malpractice: Legal and Ethical Dilemmas in Psychotherapy.* Newbury Park, Calif.: Sage.

Beck, J. R., and R. K. Mathews. 1986. "A Code of Ethics for Christian Counselors." *Journal of Psychology and Christianity* 5(3): 78-84.

Bullis, R. K., and C. S. Mazur. 1993. *Legal Issues and Religious Counseling.* Louisville,

Ky.: Westminster/John Knox.

Carroll, M. A., H. B. Schneider and G. R. Wesley. 1985. *Ethics in the Practice of Psychology.* Englewood Cliffs, N.J.: Prentice-Hall.

Christian Association for Psychological Studies. 1993. *Ethical Guidelines for the Christian Association for Psychological Studies.* New Braunfels, Tex.: Author.

Corey, G., M. S. Corey and P. Callanan. 1993. *Issues and Ethics in the Helping Professions.* 4th ed. Monterey, Calif.: Brooks/Cole.

Keith-Spiegel, P., and G. P. Koocher. 1985. *Ethics in Psychology: Professional Standards and Cases.* Hillsdale, N.J.: Random House.

Kilbourg, R. R., P. E. Nathan and R. W. Thoreson, eds. 1986. *Professionals in Distress: Issues, Syndromes and Solutions in Psychology.* Washington, D.C.: American Psychological Association.

King, R. R. 1986. "Developing a Proposed Code of Ethics for the Christian Association for Psychological Studies." *Journal of Psychology and Christianity* 5(3): 85-90.

Levicoff, S. 1991. *Christian Counseling and the Law.* Chicago: Moody Press.

Malony, H. N. 1986. "Codes of Ethics: A Comparison." *Journal of Psychology and Christianity* 5(3): 94-101.

Ohlschlager, G., and P. Mosgofian. 1992. *Law for the Christian Counselor.* Dallas: Word.

Pope, K. S., B. G. Tabachnick and P. Keith-Spiegel. 1987. "Ethics of Practice: The Beliefs and Behaviors of Psychologists as Therapists." *American Psychologist* 42(1): 993-1006.

Pope, K. S., and M. J. T. Vasquez. 1991. *Ethics in Psychotherapy and Counseling: A Practical Guide for Psychologists.* San Francisco: Jossey-Bass.

Reeck, D. 1982. *Ethics for the Professions: A Christian Perspective.* Minneapolis: Augsburg.

Steere, J. 1984. *Ethics in Clinical Psychology.* Cape Town, South Africa: Oxford University Press.

Steininger, M., J. D. Newell and L. T. Garcia. 1984. *Ethical Issues in Psychology.* Homewood, N.J.: Dorsey Press.

Swenson, L. C. 1993. *Psychology and Law for the Helping Professions.* Pacific Grove, Calif.: Brooks/Cole.

Van Hoose, W. H., and L. V. Paradise. 1979. *Ethics in Counseling and Psychotherapy.* Cranston, R.I.: Carroll Press.

---

[1] The author has arranged these descriptors into three categories.

[2] If anything, the CAPS code may err in the direction of excess on this point. The author was a CAPS board member at the time these guidelines were drafted. The concern to develop a pastoral care network evolved in the context of a difficult membership issue that profoundly influenced the tone and direction of the eventual guide.

Appendix A

THE ETHICAL BEHAVIOR OF CHRISTIAN THERAPISTS
Mark S. Oordt

Much has been written on ethics in psychotherapy and counseling. Articles, chapters, books and formal codes of ethics have addressed these issues in an effort to regulate practice as well as provide guidance to practitioners. Until recently, however, little has been done to assess and report on the actual beliefs and behaviors of therapists and counselors.

The work of Pope and his colleagues has begun to address this gap in the literature by systematically gathering data on how clinicians are, in reality, approaching the issues of ethics in their work with hurting or mentally ill people. Pope, Tabachnick and Keith-Spiegel (1987) surveyed members of the APA's division on psychotherapy and asked them to respond to 83 ethically questionable behaviors with regard to how often they occurred in their own practice and the degree to which they regarded the behaviors as ethical. This work provided the first large-scale survey of ethical behavior of psychotherapists. Researchers have since studied the ethical beliefs of certified counselors (Gibson and Pope, 1993), social workers, psychiatrists, psychologists (Borys and Pope, 1989) and educators in psychology (Tabachnick, Keith-Spiegel and Pope, 1991) in the general arena of ethics as well as with regard to specific ethical issues (e.g., dual relationships, sexuality, etc.).

A few Christian psychotherapists have addressed the issue of therapeutic ethics from a Christian standpoint. Malony (1986) has suggested that the duty of Christian mental health professionals is to transcend the concept of justice as being the center of our ethical standards and form our ethics on a basis of love. He cites Jesus' Sermon on the Mount (Mt 5) as a call to this standard. Beck and Matthews (1986) have suggested that the Christian's code of ethics in psychotherapy can be a "higher, more definitive code than

is possible in a pluralistic framework" (p. 79) and that the foundation on which to base professional conduct exists for Christians in the Scriptures.

In contrast to discussions of what Christian psychotherapeutic ethics should be, little has been done to assess the actual beliefs and practices of the Christian practitioner. Data on the ethical beliefs and behaviors of clinicians "in the field" have the potential, however, to be quite useful. The ethical standards and guidelines of the various professions (psychologists, social workers, psychiatrists, counselors) are not completely objective or absolute. They are rooted in the values, beliefs and experiences of those who devise and interpret them (Van Hoose and Paradise, 1979). Therefore ethics may be affected more by the beliefs and values of practicing psychotherapists than by ethical theory or codes. To varying degrees the values that underlie therapy ethics may be similar or dissimilar to the set of values that would be considered by most to be Christian values.

Oordt (1990) conducted a survey of Christian clinicians in order to better understand their ethical beliefs and practices. Two hundred Ph.D.-level psychologists working in clinical settings were randomly selected from the 1988 membership directory of CAPS. CAPS is a professional association "committed to vigorous international Christian witness in psychology, theology, sociology and related theoretical and applied disciplines in the helping professions" (CAPS, 1988, p. 4). The assumption was made that members of CAPS would be people who defined themselves as Christians and who would serve as a diverse sample of practitioners, since CAPS has no denominational affiliation. The sample was restricted to psychologists (and not all types of psychotherapists), as one goal of the survey was to compare the results for this Christian sample with the general sample of psychologists surveyed by Pope et al. (1987).

Participants were mailed a questionnaire devised by Pope et al. (1987). The questionnaire asked participants to indicate the extent ("never," "rarely," "sometimes," "fairly often" and "very often") to which they had engaged in 83 behaviors in their practice of psychotherapy, as well as the degree to which they believed each of these behaviors to be ethical ("unquestionably not," "under rare circumstances," "don't know/not sure," "under many circumstances" and "unquestionably yes"). Questionnaires were returned by 69 of those surveyed.

The following discussion of the ethics of Christian psychotherapists is based on the results of this pilot study. The focus is specifically on the *behavior* of Christian therapists; however, their beliefs, as both reported and inferred from their behavior, are also included. A more focused discussion of these data on beliefs can be found elsewhere (Oordt, 1990).

The Practices of Christian Psychotherapists
Ethical codes, such as those established by the APA (1990), the American Association for Counseling and Development (1988) and the American Personal Guidance Association (1974), serve to guide practitioners in ethical behaviors as well as set a standard for ethical professional practice. It is clear, however, that the norms, values, experiences and prejudices of those who devise and interpret these codes affect how psychotherapy is practiced (Van Hoose and Paradise, 1979). It is reasonable to assume that a therapist's religious beliefs and attitudes are likely to play a role in his or her application of ethical guidelines and principles. The incidence of various behaviors in the practice of this sample of Christian psychotherapists may shed light on how this occurs.

Boundary Issues
Psychotherapy is a uniquely relational endeavor. Depending on one's theoretical approach, the therapeutic relationship can be seen as the context in which the necessary conditions are provided for change to occur (Rogers, 1961) or as the agent of change itself (as with more psychodynamic approaches). The psychotherapeutic relationship is at once personal, even intimate, and professional. The imbalance of power in the relationship and the focus on the life and experiences of the client make it different from the typical social relationship and create a potential for much harm to be done if the relationship is misused. Therefore it has been traditionally thought that the well-being of the client calls for certain limits, or boundaries, to be set on the client-therapist relationship (APA, 1990).

Just as psychotherapy is rooted in relationship, so is Christianity. The Christian church is a community of individuals called into relationship with each other as a unified body (Acts 4:32-35; 1 Cor 1:10). The Christian ethic is rooted in how we relate to one another (Mt 5:42-43; 19:18-19), and the Christian view of relationship has boundaries outlined in Scripture, ranging from how we treat those in need (Mt 25:34-40) to the use of discretion in sexual intimacies (1 Cor 6).

These issues raise the question of how the Christian view of relationship might integrate or conflict with the boundaries placed on the psychotherapy relationship. Christians responding to the survey revealed little variation from each other in their self-reports of boundary-related behavior in psychotherapy.

Physical contact. Physical contact with clients, and sexual behavior in particular, is a sensitive area. One hundred percent of respondents stated that they never engaged in sex or erotic activity with a current client or clinical supervisee and never had disrobed in the presence of a client. Three percent admitted to becoming sexually involved with former clients (it is notable that 29 percent of those responding found this to be ethical at least "under rare circumstances," with 4 percent being unsure). Two percent reported having allowed a client to disrobe either rarely or sometimes. While 88 percent of the respondents admitted to being sexually attracted to clients at least rarely, none of these reported ever telling the client of their attraction. Ninety-one percent reported never or only rarely engaging in sexual fantasy about a client, with the other 9 percent reporting such fantasy occurring sometimes. Less erotic contact was reported with a slightly greater frequency, with 55 percent of the therapists reporting that they hugged their clients either sometimes, fairly often or very often, and 9 percent stating they kissed a client rarely.

What many might consider to be nonintimate touching, such as offering or accepting a handshake, was engaged in by 99 percent of the sample at least sometimes, and the other 1 percent reported its occurrence only rarely.

These data are encouraging as they suggest the absence of explicitly sexual contact between Christian therapists and clients. Other studies surveying general samples of therapists have found the incidence of erotic or sexual contact with psychotherapists to range from 1.9 percent to 7.7 percent (Holroyd and Brodsky, 1977; Pope et al., 1987). It is possible that the difference with the Christian sample may be attributed to a traditional Christian value system or traditional Christian teaching. It is also possible that the small sample size in the survey of Christian therapists or the likely reluctance of Christians to admit to sexual contact with patients (given the combined pressure of prohibition from both their profession and their religion) revealed an artificially low incidence rate.

Dual relationships. The ethical code of the APA (1990) prohibits any form of "dual relationships," meaning that the relationship between therapist and client must remain only a professional one and not extend into social or business contexts. Since the ethical behavior questionnaire surveyed psychologists, it would be expected that the incidence of social contact or business interactions with clients would be low, as it would be reasonable to assume that these therapists adhere to their profession's code of ethics.

A large majority of the respondents reported that they maintain fairly firm boundaries around their therapist-client relationships. Ninety percent or more stated that they never or only rarely have invited a client to a party or social event or accepted an invitation to a client's social event. Only 68 percent, however, reported never or only rarely attending a client's special event, such as a wedding. Inviting clients to an open house was also more common than inviting them to parties or social events (15 percent reported doing so at least sometimes), perhaps because of the professional setting in which the socializing would occur. Ninety-two percent and 96 percent of the sample stated they had never gone into business with a client or former client, respectively (the other 8 percent and 4 percent reported doing so rarely). Seventy-

five percent reported never or rarely being social friends with former clients.

Likewise, Christian therapists report being fairly cautious in allowing people with whom they have nontherapy relationships to become therapy clients. A majority stated that they rarely or never provided therapy to friends (84 percent), students, supervisees or employees (91 percent).

Clearly these data support the idea that Christian psychotherapists tend to exercise caution in loosening the boundaries of their professional relationships. Adding to this evidence is the fact that 90 percent or more of the respondents reported rarely or never engaging in the following: accepting or giving gifts over $50 in value, selling goods to clients, lending money to clients, borrowing money from clients or asking favors of clients (such as a ride home).

Still, some of the responses suggest that these clinicians, on the whole, tended not to relate to clients with extreme professional coldness or aloofness. A majority reported that at least sometimes they addressed clients by their first name (99 percent) and allowed clients to address them by first name (92 percent), used self-disclosure as a therapy technique (90 percent) and, as mentioned above, offered or accepted handshakes (99 percent). Forty-nine percent had accepted gifts worth less than $5.

Sexual Issues

In addition to the issues of sexual activity between a psychotherapist and a client addressed above, ethical issues can come into play when psychotherapy utilizes sexual behavior, role plays, nudity, etc., as part of treatment. This may be an area of special sensitivity for some Christians. Biblical passages specifically discouraging sexual immorality (Rom 13:13; 1 Cor 6:13), lust (Col 3:5), homosexuality (1 Cor 6:9) and adultery (Ex 20:14; Heb 13:4) would make it reasonable to assume that practicing Christians would avoid explicitly sexual behavior in psychotherapy. On the other hand, it may be that Christian psychotherapists, in a genuine effort to help people fully experience their God-given sexuality, may turn to the variety of techniques used by some secular therapists.

The responses of the Christian therapists surveyed indicates that they rarely if ever utilize sexual behavior in treatment. None reported ever having used sexual surrogates with clients or disrobing in the presence of a client. The use of nude therapy or "growth" groups was denied by over 97 percent of the respondents, as was the toleration of clients' disrobing in therapy.

The issue of homosexuality revealed more divergence. The contemporary Christian church certainly is not unified by a single view of homosexuality. Some preach it as sin while others openly ordain homosexual clergy. Likewise, mental health professionals have vacillated in their views. Until the *DSM-III* (APA, 1980) was published, homosexuality was considered a form of psychopathology by accepted psychiatric nomenclature. This is no longer the case. So the question arises as to how Christian mental health professionals, who have allegiances to both their profession and their religion, resolve this apparent conflict.

The wide distribution of responses to the question of whether the Christian therapists had treated homosexuality per se as pathological suggests that this issue poses a difficult judgment. In terms of reported behavior, 47 percent stated they never or rarely treated it as pathological, 22 percent did so sometimes, and 31 percent did so fairly often or very often. Clearly there is a variety of beliefs and opinions about the issue, as well as much ambiguity. It is notable that almost one-quarter of the respondents stated they were "unsure" whether treating homosexuality as pathological is right or wrong. Homosexuality is an issue warranting more discussion among Christian psychotherapists, especially those who feel caught between competing value systems.

Financial Issues

It is interesting that many of the items on the survey that revealed a great deal of ambiguity regarding ethical beliefs had to do with financial issues. It is not surprising, therefore, that respondents varied a great deal in their reported behavior with regard to financial issues. Approximately one-third reported charging a client nothing for therapy at least sometimes, and it was rare that a client would be terminated for not being able to pay. Most reported never or rarely accepting goods or services in lieu of payment. Issues related to various means of collecting unpaid fees or to

charging for missed appointments were reported to be difficult judgments for many. Their behavior, however, was less ambiguous. Most showed reluctance in using collection agencies (only 22 percent reported doing so at least sometimes) or lawsuits (only 8 percent had done so sometimes). Furthermore, 87 percent had allowed clients to run up a large unpaid bill. It seems that this sample was not willing to push the issue of payment to the extreme or let it interfere with ongoing therapy.

Confidentiality

Confidentiality is an essential aspect of psychotherapy. A client's confidence that what he or she says will not leave the therapist's office significantly contributes to an environment of trust and openness that may otherwise be impossible. Clinicians in the survey reported strong commitment to protecting the intimate and private world of clients from others who have no legitimate need to know. One hundred percent reported rarely or never discussing clients by name with friends, and 91 percent reported never or rarely disclosing confidential data unintentionally.

Yet when a therapist judges the breaking of confidentiality to be in the best interest of the client, a dilemma is created. When these two "goods" (maintaining the sanctity of confidentiality and protecting the welfare of the client) come into conflict, a decision must be made as to which is the greater benefit. Only two-thirds of the respondents indicated that they violated confidentiality, at least sometimes, when a patient was suicidal or when child abuse was revealed. Only one-third reported breaking confidentiality, at least sometimes, if a client was homicidal.

This is surprising given the prevalence of laws mandating the reporting of risk for harm to oneself or another. It is possible that these responses reflect confusion about what the questionnaire was asking. The question was intended to elicit data on how often, when presented with patients at risk for harm, do respondents break confidentiality. Instead, respondents may have read the question as asking about the frequency of these types of cases in their practices. The latter could certainly produce a lower incidence rate as the nature of some therapy practices could preclude confronting a suicidal, homicidal or child-abusing patient with any frequency. This is the most likely explanation for these responses given the fact that three-quarters of the respondents reported a belief that breaking confidentiality for these reasons is "unquestionably" ethical. On the other hand, it is certainly also possible that people do not break confidentiality in these circumstances despite their strong beliefs that it is ethical to do so.

Accountability and Protecting the Profession

Christians are called to be accountable for themselves and for others (Mt 18:15-17). It is therefore not surprising that a large majority of the respondents (87 percent) stated it was "unquestionably" ethical or ethical "under many circumstances" to file an ethics complaint against a colleague. It is notable, however, that a majority (76 percent) also reported never having done so. Could this mean that Christian psychologists are unwilling to practice what they believe to be appropriate? Does it mean that many Christian therapists have never been faced with a situation to report? Or is it conceivable that these therapists follow the Christian teaching in Matthew 18:15-17 and confront colleagues personally before resorting to a formal complaint? It is worth noting that the general sample of psychologists (e.g., not exclusively Christian) surveyed by Pope et al. (1987) showed a noticeably lower percentage who had never filed an ethical report (although such a comparison between numbers in different studies must be seen as tentative).

Helping a client file a complaint regarding a colleague was seen as "unquestionably" ethical or ethical "under many circumstances" by a fewer proportion of respondents (56 percent) than filing a complaint oneself. The reason for this can only be guessed—perhaps something to do with the therapist's presumption of having better knowledge of what constitutes an ethical violation or a concern for the welfare of the client who filed the complaint. Again, a majority (70 percent) reported never having engaged in this behavior.

While accepting the responsibility for "policing" the profession of psychotherapy is important for maintaining high standards of care, it is equally important that individuals hold themselves accountable. The ultimate responsibility falls on each psychotherapy provider for acting ethically and for monitoring one's own capability to do so.

Three behaviors on the survey addressed this issue, and the responses suggest that Christian psychotherapists are not as cautious as they might be in monitoring themselves. Sixty-six percent admitted to having worked when too distressed to be effective. Furthermore, 32 percent reported they had provided services outside their area of competence. No one reported that they had provided service while working under the influence of alcohol.

Miscellaneous Behaviors

Psychotherapy is a helping endeavor. It is probably reasonable to assume that many Christian psychotherapists, in one way or another, see their work as corresponding to the Christian mission of loving others and caring for those in need. Integrating this ideal vision of psychotherapy with the practical realities of providing mental health care in contemporary society, however, can be a dilemma. This is evident in the fact that only 13 percent of the respondents stated it is unethical to avoid certain clients for fear of being sued. Forty-three percent reported engaging in this behavior at least rarely. Apparently these therapists find it unrealistic to accept all who come needing service, because of the fear of possible consequences.

The issue of suicide is another area that can raise serious ethical and moral questions. How do therapists with a Christian worldview approach clients who have decided they no longer wish to live? Is it ever ethical to accept a client's decision to commit suicide? Within the Christian community there are differences of opinion. In the survey sample 17 percent stated it was ethical under rare conditions and 6 percent stated it was ethical under many conditions or always. Eight percent reported having accepted a client's decision to end his or her life.

Conclusion

The ethical beliefs and behaviors of this sample of Christian psychotherapists appear to be generally consistent with the ethical guidelines of the APA (1990). Christian psychotherapists appear to be cautious in maintaining professional boundaries with clients while still being open to relating in a human, open and warm manner (e.g., handshakes, self-disclosure, use of first names). Confidentiality is valued, as is the need to hold colleagues accountable, although reporting of ethical violations is not common. Those issues found to be most difficult for Christian therapists dealt largely with finances. This concurs with the results of Pope et al. (1987) that finances are a particularly difficult issue with psychotherapists in general. Additionally, homosexuality is a topic needing more guidance and discussion.

While I have used the term *psychotherapist* throughout this chapter, it is important to recall that the sample consisted of specifically Ph.D.-level psychologists. The degree to which these data generalize to Christian psychiatrists, social workers, master's-level psychologists, pastoral counselors, lay counselors or any other provider of psychotherapy services is unknown. Ph.D. psychologists are diligently trained according to a specific ethical code (APA, 1990) and are likely to be influenced by the values inherent in that code, perhaps more so than those in other professions who are trained according to the standards of their disciplines. Some descriptive data exist on the ethical beliefs and behaviors of social workers, psychiatrists (Borys and Pope, 1989) and counselors (Gibson and Pope, 1993); however, none use a specifically Christian sample.

It is also essential to address limitations of research, such as those on which our discussion was based. The small sample size and the possibility for bias and distortion on a self-report measure should be considered in deciding to what degree the results reflect the true incidents of these behaviors.

Nevertheless, the data do provide a general overview from which hypotheses and further questions for examination can be generated. Additional research aimed at understanding the ethical beliefs and practices of Christian mental health providers would add to what has begun here.

References

American Association for Counseling and Development. 1988. *Ethical Standards*. Alexandria, Va.: Author.

American Personnel and Guidance Association. 1974. *Code of Ethics*. Washington, D.C.: Author.

American Psychiatric Association. 1980. *Diagnostic and Statistical Manual of Mental Disorders*. 3rd ed. Washington, D.C.: Author.

American Psychological Association. 1990. "Ethical Principles of Psychologists." *American Psychologist* 43: 390-95.

Beck, J. R., and R. K. Matthews. 1986. "A Code of Ethics for Christian Counselors." *Journal of Psychology and Christianity* 5(3): 78-84.

Borys, D. S., and K. S. Pope. 1989. "Dual Relationships Between Therapist and Client: A National Study of Psychologists, Psychiatrists and Social Workers." *Professional Psychology: Research and Practice* 20(5): 283-293.

Christian Association for Psychological Studies. 1988. *The International Directory of the Christian Association for Psychological Studies*. Farmington Hills, Mich.: Author.

Gibson, W. T., and Pope, K. S. 1983. "The Ethics of Counseling: A National Survey of Certified Counselors." *Journal of Counseling and Development* 71: 330-36.

Holroyd, J. C., and A. M. Brodsky. 1977. "Psychologists' Attitudes and Practices Regarding Erotic and Nonerotic Physical Contact with Patients." *American Psychologist* 32: 843-49.

Malony, H. N. 1986. "Codes of Ethics: A Comparison." *Journal of Psychology and Christianity* 5(3): 94-101.

Oordt, M. S. 1990. "Ethics of Practice Among Christian Psychologists: A Pilot Study." *Journal of Psychology and Theology* 18(3): 255-60.

Pope, K. S., B. G. Tabachnick and P. Keith-Spiegel. 1987. "Ethics of Practice: The Beliefs and Behaviors of Psychologists as Therapists." *American Psychologist* 42: 993-1006.

Rogers, C. R. 1961. *On Becoming a Person*. Boston: Houghton Mifflin.

Tabachnick, B. G., P. Keith-Spiegel and K. S. Pope. 1991. "Ethics of Teaching: Beliefs and Behaviors of Psychologists as Educators." *American Psychologist* 46: 506-15.

Van Hoose, W. H., and L. V. Paradise. 1979. *Ethics in Counseling and Psychotherapy: Perspectives in Issues and Decision Making*. Cranston, R.I.: Carroll.

Appendix B

ETHICAL CODES AND GUIDELINES

Ethical Principles of Psychologists and Code of Conduct (APA)

Introduction

The American Psychological Association's (APA's) Ethical Principles of Psychologists and Code of Conduct (hereinafter referred to as the Ethics Code) consists of an Introduction, a Preamble, six General Principles (A-F), and specific Ethical Standards. The Introduction discusses the intent, organization, procedural considerations, and scope of application of the Ethics Code. The Preamble and General Principles are *aspirational* goals to guide psychologists toward the highest ideals of psychology. Although the Preamble and General Principles are not themselves enforceable rules, they should be considered by psychologists in arriving at an ethical course of action and may be considered by ethics bodies in interpreting the Ethical Standards. The Ethical Standards set forth *enforceable* rules for conduct as psychologists. Most of the Ethical Standards are written broadly, in order to apply to psychologists in varied roles, although the application of an Ethical Standard may vary depending on the context. The Ethical Standards are not exhaustive. The fact that a given conduct is not specifically addressed by the Ethics Code does not mean that it is necessarily either ethical or unethical.

Membership in the APA commits members to adhere to the APA Ethics Code and to the rules and procedures used to implement it. Psychologists and students, whether or not they are APA members, should be aware that the Ethics Code may be applied to them by state psychology boards, courts, or other public bodies.

This Ethics Code applies only to psychologists' work-related activities, that is, activities that are part of the psychologists' scientific and professional functions or that are psychological in nature. It includes the clinical or counseling practice of psychology, research, teaching, supervision of trainees, development of assessment instruments, conducting assessments, educational counseling, organizational consulting, social intervention, administration, and other activities as well. These work-related activities can be distinguished from the purely private conduct of a psychologist, which ordinarily is not within the purview of the Ethics Code.

The Ethics Code is intended to provide standards of professional conduct that can be applied by the APA and by other bodies that choose to adopt them. Whether or not a psychologist has violated the Ethics Code does not by itself determine whether he or she is legally liable in a court action, whether a contract is enforceable, or whether other legal consequences occur. These results are based on legal rather than ethical rules. However, compliance with or violation of the Ethics Code may be admissible as evidence in some legal proceedings, depending on the circumstances.

In the process of making decisions regarding their professional behavior, psychologists must consider this Ethics Code, in addition to applicable laws and psychology board regulations. If the Ethics Code establishes a higher standard of conduct than is required by law, psychologists must meet the higher ethical standard. If the Ethics Code standard appears to conflict with the requirements of law, then psychologists make known their commitment to the Ethics Code and take steps to resolve the conflict in a responsible manner. If neither law nor the Ethics Code resolves an issue, psychologists should consider other professional materials[1] and the dictates of their own conscience, as well as seek consultation with others within the field when this is practical.

The procedures for filing, investigating, and resolving complaints of unethical conduct are described in the current Rules and Procedures of the APA Ethics Committee. The actions that APA may take for violations of the Ethics Code include actions such as reprimand, censure, termination of APA membership, and referral of the matter to other bodies. Complainants who seek remedies such as monetary damages in alleging ethical violations by a psychologist must resort to private negotiation, administrative bodies, or the courts. Actions that violate the Ethics Code may lead to the imposition of sanctions on a psychologist by bodies other than APA, including state psychological associations, other professional groups, psychology boards, other state or federal agencies, and payors for health services. In addition to actions for violation of the Ethics Code, the APA Bylaws provide that APA may take action against a member after his or her conviction of a felony, expulsion or suspension from an affiliated state psychological association, or suspension or loss of licensure.

---

[1]Professional materials that are most helpful in this regard are guidelines and standards that have been adopted or endorsed by professional psychological organizations. Such guidelines and standards, whether adopted by the American Psychological Association (APA) or its Divisions, are not enforceable as such by this Ethics Code, but are of educative value to psychologists, courts, and professional bodies. Such materials include, but are not limited to, the APA's *General Guidelines for Providers of Psychological Services* (1987), *Specialty Guidelines for the Delivery of Services by Clinical Psychologists, Counseling Psychologists, Industrial/Organizational Psychologists, and School Psychologists* (1981), *Guidelines for Computer Based Tests and Interpretations* (1987), *Standards for Educational and Psychological Testing* (1985), *Ethical Principles in the Conduct of Research With Human Participants* (1982), *Guidelines for Ethical Conduct in the Care and Use of Animals* (1986), *Guidelines for Providers of Psychological Services to Ethnic, Linguistic, and Culturally Diverse Populations* (1990), and *Publication Manual of the American Psychological Association* (3rd ed., 1983). Materials not adopted by APA as a whole include the APA Division 41 (Forensic Psychology)/American Psychology—Law Society's *Specialty Guidelines for Forensic Psychologists* (1991).

Preamble

Psychologists work to develop a valid and reliable body of scientific knowledge based on research. They may apply that knowledge to human behavior in a variety of contexts. In doing so, they perform many roles, such as researcher, educator, diagnostician, therapist, supervisor, consultant, administrator, social interventionist, and expert witness. Their goal is to broaden knowledge of behavior and, where appropriate, to apply it pragmatically to improve the condition of both the individual and society. Psychologists respect the central importance of freedom of inquiry and expression in research, teaching, and publication. They also strive to help the public in developing informed judgments and choices concerning human behavior. This Ethics Code provides a common set of values upon which psychologists build their professional and scientific work.

This Code is intended to provide both the general principles and the decision rules to cover most situations encountered by psychologists. It has as its primary goal the welfare and protection of the individuals and groups with whom psychologists work. It is the individual responsibility of each psychologist to aspire to the highest possible standards of conduct. Psychologists respect and protect human and civil rights, and do not knowingly participate in or condone unfair discriminatory practices.

The development of a dynamic set of ethical standards for a psychologist's work-related conduct requires a personal commitment to a lifelong effort to act ethically; to encourage ethical behavior by students, supervisees, employees, and colleagues, as appropriate; and to consult with others, as needed, concerning ethical problems. Each psychologist supplements, but does not violate, the Ethics Code's values and rules on the basis of guidance drawn from personal values, culture, and experience.

General Principles
Principle A: Competence

Psychologists strive to maintain high standards of competence in their work. They recognize the boundaries of their particular competencies and the limitations of their expertise. They provide only those services and use only those techniques for which they are qualified by education, training, or experience. Psychologists are cognizant of the fact that the competencies required in serving, teaching, and/or studying groups of people vary with the distinctive characteristics of those groups. In those areas in which recognized professional standards do not yet exist, psychologists exercise careful judgment and take appropriate precautions to protect the welfare of those with whom they work. They maintain knowledge of relevant scientific and professional information related to the services they render, and they recognize the need for ongoing education. Psychologists make appropriate use of scientific, professional, technical, and administrative resources.

Principle B: Integrity

Psychologists seek to promote integrity in the science, teaching, and practice of psychology. In these activities psychologists are honest, fair, and respectful of others. In describing or reporting their qualifications, services, products, fees, research, or teaching, they do not make statements that are false, misleading, or deceptive. Psychologists strive to be aware of their own belief systems, values, needs, and limitations and the effect of these on their work. To the extent feasible, they attempt to clarify for relevant parties the roles they are performing and to function appropriately in accordance with those roles. Psychologists avoid improper and potentially harmful dual relationships.

Principle C: Professional and Scientific Responsibility

Psychologists uphold professional standards of conduct, clarify their professional roles and obligations, accept appropriate responsibility for their behavior, and adapt their methods to the needs of different populations. Psychologists consult with, refer to, or cooperate with other professionals and institutions to the extent needed to serve the best interests of their patients, clients, or other recipients of their services. Psychologists' moral standards and conduct are personal matters to the same degree as is true for any other person, except as psychologists' conduct may compromise their professional responsibilities or reduce the public's trust in psychology and psychologists. Psychologists are concerned about the ethical compliance of their colleagues' scien-tific and professional conduct. When appropriate, they consult with colleagues in order to prevent or avoid unethical conduct.

Principle D: Respect for People's Rights and Dignity

Psychologists accord appropriate respect to the fundamental rights, dignity, and worth of all people. They respect the rights of individuals to privacy, confidentiality, self-determination, and autonomy, mindful that legal and other obligations may lead to inconsistency and conflict with the exercise of these rights. Psychologists are aware of cultural, individual, and role differences, including those due to age, gender, race, ethnicity, national origin, religion, sexual orientation, disability, language, and socioeconomic status. Psychologists try to eliminate the effect on their work of biases based on those factors, and they do not knowingly participate in or condone unfair discriminatory practices.

Principle E: Concern for Others' Welfare

Psychologists seek to contribute to the welfare of those with whom they interact professionally. In their professional actions, psychologists weigh the welfare and rights of their patients or clients, students, supervisees, human research participants, and other affected persons, and the welfare of animal subjects of research. When conflicts occur among psychologists' obligations or concerns, they attempt to resolve these conflicts and to perform their roles in a responsible fashion that avoids or minimizes harm. Psychologists are sensitive to real and ascribed differences in power between themselves and others, and they do not exploit or mislead other people during or after professional relationships.

Principle F: Social Responsibility

Psychologists are aware of their professional and scientific responsibilities to the community and the society in which they work and live. They apply and make public their knowledge of psychology in order to contribute to human welfare. Psychologists are concerned about and work to mitigate the causes of human suffering. When undertaking research, they strive to advance human welfare and the science of psychology. Psychologists try to avoid misuse of their work. Psychologists comply with the law and encourage the development of law and social policy that serve the interests of their patients and clients and the public. They are encouraged to contribute a portion of their professional time for little or no personal advantage.

Ethical Standards
1. General Standards

These General Standards are potentially applicable to the professional and scientific activities of all psychologists.

1.01 *Applicability of the Ethics Code.* The activity of a psychologist subject to the Ethics Code may be reviewed under these Ethical Standards only if the activity is part of his or her work-related functions or the activity is psychological in nature. Personal activities having no connection to or effect on psychological roles are not subject to the Ethics Code.

1.02 *Relationship of Ethics and Law.* If psychologists' ethical responsibilities conflict with law, psychologists make known their commitment to the Ethics Code and take steps to resolve the conflict in a responsible manner.

1.03 *Professional and Scientific Relationship.* Psychologists provide diagnostic, therapeutic, teaching, research, supervisory, consultative, or other psychological services only in the context of a defined professional or scientific relationship or role. (See also Standards 2.01, Evaluation, Diagnosis, and Interventions in Professional Context, and 7.02, Forensic Assessments.)

1.04 *Boundaries of Competence.* (a) Psychologists provide services, teach, and conduct research only within the boundaries of their competence, based on their education, training, supervised experience, or appropriate professional experience.

(b) Psychologists provide services, teach, or conduct research in new areas or involving new techniques only after first undertaking appropriate study, training, supervision, and/or consultation from persons who are competent in those areas or techniques.

(c) In those emerging areas in which generally recognized standards for preparatory training do not yet exist, psychologists nevertheless take reasonable steps to ensure the competence of their work and to protect patients, clients, students, research participants, and others from harm.

1.05 *Maintaining Expertise.* Psychologists who engage in assessment, therapy, teaching, research, organizational consulting, or other professional activities maintain a reasonable level of awareness of current scientific and professional information in their fields of activity, and undertake ongoing efforts to maintain competence in the skills they use.

1.06 *Basis for Scientific and Professional Judgments.* Psychologists rely on scientifically and professionally derived knowledge when making scientific or professional judgments or when engaging in scholarly or professional endeavors.

1.07 *Describing the Nature and Results of Psychological Services.* (a) When psychologists provide assessment, evaluation, treatment, counseling, supervision, teaching, consultation, research, or other psychological services to an individual, a group, or an organization, they provide, using language that is reasonably understandable to the recipient of those services, appropriate information beforehand about the nature of such services and appropriate information later about results and conclusions. (See also Standard 2.09, Explaining Assessment Results.)

(b) If psychologists will be precluded by law or by organizational roles from providing such information to particular individuals or groups, they so inform those individuals or groups at the outset of the service.

1.08 *Human Differences.* Where differences of age, gender, race, ethnicity, national origin, religion, sexual orientation, disability, language, or socioeconomic status significantly affect psychologists' work concerning particular individuals or groups, psychologists obtain the training, experience, consultation, or supervision necessary to ensure the competence of their services, or they make appropriate referrals.

1.09 *Respecting Others.* In their work-related activities, psychologists respect the rights of others to hold values, attitudes, and opinions that differ from their own.

1.10 *Nondiscrimination.* In their work-related activities, psychologists do not engage in unfair discrimination based on age, gender, race, ethnicity, national origin, religion, sexual orientation, disability, socioeconomic status, or any basis proscribed by law.

1.11 *Sexual Harassment.* (a) Psychologists

do not engage in sexual harassment. Sexual harassment is sexual solicitation, physical advances, or verbal or nonverbal conduct that is sexual in nature, that occurs in connection with the psychologist's activities or roles as a psychologist, and that either: (1) is unwelcome, is offensive, or creates a hostile workplace environment, and the psychologist knows or is told this; or (2) is sufficiently severe or intense to be abusive to a reasonable person in the context. Sexual harassment can consist of a single intense or severe act or of multiple persistent or pervasive acts.

(b) Psychologists accord sexual-harassment complainants and respondents dignity and respect. Psychologists do not participate in denying a person academic admittance or advancement, employment, tenure, or promotion, based solely upon their having made, or their being the subject of, sexual-harassment charges. This does not preclude taking action based upon the outcome of such proceedings or consideration of other appropriate information.

1.12 *Other Harassment.* Psychologists do not knowingly engage in behavior that is harassing or demeaning to persons with whom they interact in their work based on factors such as those persons' age, gender, race, ethnicity, national origin, religion, sexual orientation, disability, language or socioeconomic status.

1.13 *Personal Problems and Conflicts.* (a) Psychologists recognize that their personal problems and conflicts may interfere with their effectiveness. Accordingly, they refrain from undertaking an activity when they know or should know that their personal problems are likely to lead to harm to a patient, client, colleague, student, research participant, or other person to whom they may owe a professional or scientific obligation.

(b) In addition, psychologists have an obligation to be alert to signs of, and to obtain assistance for, their personal problems at an early stage, in order to prevent significantly impaired performance.

(c) When psychologists become aware of personal problems that may interfere with their performing work-related duties adequately, they take appropriate measures, such as obtaining professional consultation or assistance, and determine whether they should limit, suspend, or terminate their work-related duties.

1.14 *Avoiding Harm.* Psychologists take reasonable steps to avoid harming their patients or clients, research participants, students, and others with whom they work, and to minimize harm where it is foreseeable and unavoidable.

1.15 *Misuse of Psychologists' Influence.* Because psychologists' scientific and professional judgments and actions may affect the lives of others, they are alert to and guard against personal, financial, social, organizational, or political factors that might lead to misuse of their influence.

1.16 *Misuse of Psychologists' Work.* (a) Psychologists do not participate in activities in which it appears likely that their skills or data will be misused by others, unless corrective mechanisms are available. (See also Standard 7.04, Truthfulness and Candor.)

(b) If psychologists learn of misuse or misrepresentation of their work, they take reasonable steps to correct or minimize the misuse or misrepresentation.

1.17 *Multiple Relationships.* (a) In many communities and situations, it may not be feasible or reasonable for psychologists to avoid social or other nonprofessional contacts with persons such as patients, clients, students, supervisees, or research participants. Psychologists must always be sensitive to the potential harmful effects of other contacts on their work and on those persons with whom they deal. A psychologist refrains from entering into or promising another personal, scientific, professional, financial, or other relationship with such persons if it appears likely that such a relationship reasonably might impair the psychologist's objectivity or otherwise interfere with the psychologist's effectively performing his or her functions as a psychologist, or might harm or exploit the other party.

(b) Likewise, whenever feasible, a psychologist refrains from taking on professional or scientific obligations when preexisting relationships would create a risk of such harm.

(c) If a psychologist finds that, due to unforeseen factors, a potentially harmful multiple relationship has arisen, the psychologist attempts to resolve it with due regard for the best interests of the affected person and maximal compliance with the Ethics Code.

1.18 *Barter (With Patients or Clients).* Psychologists ordinarily refrain from accepting goods, services, or other nonmonetary remuneration from patients or clients in return for psychological services because such arrangements create inherent potential for conflicts, exploitation, and distortion of the professional relationship. A psychologist may participate in bartering *only* if (1) it is not clinically contraindicated, *and* (2) the relationship is not exploitative. (See also Standards 1.17, Multiple Relationships, and 1.25, Fees and Financial Arrangements.)

1.19 *Exploitative Relationships.* (a) Psychologists do not exploit persons over whom they have supervisory, evaluative, or other authority such as students, supervisees, employees, research participants, and clients or patients. (See also Standards 4.05—4.07 regarding sexual involvement with clients or patients.)

(b) Psychologists do not engage in sexual relationships with students or supervisees in training over whom the psychologist has evaluative or direct authority, because such relationships are so likely to impair judgment or be exploitative.

1.20 *Consultations and Referrals.* (a) Psychologists arrange for appropriate consultations and referrals based principally on the best interests of their patients or clients, with appropriate consent, and subject to other relevant considerations, including applicable law and contractual obligations. (See also Standards 5.01, Discussing the Limits of Confidentiality, and 5.06, Consultations.)

(b) When indicated and professionally appropriate, psychologists cooperate with other professionals in order to serve their patients or clients effectively and appropriately.

(c) Psychologists' referral practices are consistent with law.

1.21 *Third-Party Requests for Services.* (a) When a psychologist agrees to provide services to a person or entity at the request of a third party, the psychologist clarifies to the extent feasible, at the outset of the service, the nature of the relationship with each party. This clarification includes the role of the psychologist (such as therapist, organizational consultant, diagnostician, or expert witness), the probable uses of the services provided or the information obtained, and the fact that there may be limits to confidentiality.

(b) If there is a foreseeable risk of the psychologist's being called upon to perform conflicting roles because of the involvement of a third party, the psychologist clarifies the nature and direction of his or her responsibilities, keeps all parties appropriately informed as matters develop, and resolves the situation in accordance with this Ethics Code.

1.22 *Delegation to and Supervision of Subordinates.* (a) Psychologists delegate to their employees, supervisees, and research assistants only those responsibilities that such persons can reasonably be expected to perform competently, on the basis of their education, training, or experience, either independently or with the level of supervision being provided.

(b) Psychologists provide proper training and supervision to their employees or supervisees and take reasonable steps to see that such persons perform services responsibly, competently, and ethically.

(c) If institutional policies, procedures, or practices prevent fulfillment of this obligation, psychologists attempt to modify their role or to correct the situation to the extent feasible.

1.23 *Documentation of Professional and Scientific Work.* (a) Psychologists appropriately document their professional and scientific work in order to facilitate provision of services later by them or by other professionals, to ensure accountability, and to meet other requirements of institutions or the law.

(b) When psychologists have reason to believe that records of their professional services will be used in legal proceedings involving recipients of or participants in their work, they have a responsibility to create and maintain documentation in the kind of detail and quality that would be consistent with reasonable scrutiny in an adjudicative forum. (See also Standard 7.01, Professionalism, under Forensic Activities.)

1.24 *Records and Data.* Psychologists create, maintain, disseminate, store, retain, and dispose of records and data relating to their research, practice, and other work in accordance with law and in a manner that permits compliance with the requirements of this Ethics Code. (See also Standard 5.04, Maintenance of Records.)

1.25 *Fees and Financial Arrangements.* (a) As early as is feasible in a professional or scientific relationship, the psychologist and the patient, client, or other appropriate recipient of psychological services reach an agreement specifying the compensation and the billing arrangements.

(b) Psychologists do not exploit recipients of services or payors with respect to fees.

(c) Psychologists' fee practices are consistent with law.

(d) Psychologists do not misrepresent their fees.

(e) If limitations to services can be anticipated because of limitations in financing, this is discussed with the patient, client, or other appropriate recipient of services as early as is feasible. (See also Standard 4.08, Interruption of Services.)

(f) If the patient, client, or other recipient of services does not pay for services as agreed, and if the psychologist wishes to use collection agencies or legal measures to collect the fees, the psychologist first informs the person that such measures will be taken and provides that person an opportunity to make prompt payment. (See also Standard 5.11, Withholding Records for Nonpayment.)

1.26 *Accuracy in Reports to Payors and Funding Sources.* In their reports to payors for services or sources of research funding, psychologists accurately state the nature of the research or service provided, the fees or charges, and where applicable, the identity of the provider, the findings, and the diagnosis. (See also Standard 5.05, Disclosures.)

1.27 *Referrals and Fees.* When a psychologist pays, receives payment from, or divides fees with another professional other than in an employer-employee relationship, the payment to each is based on the services (clinical, consultative, administrative, or other) provided and is not based on the referral itself.

2. Evaluation, Assessment, or Intervention

2.01 *Evaluation, Diagnosis, and Interventions in Professional Context.* (a) Psychologists perform evaluations, diagnostic services, or interventions only within the context of a defined professional relationship. (See also Standard 1.03, Professional and Scientific Relationship.)

(b) Psychologists' assessments, recommendations, reports, and psychological diagnostic or evaluative statements are based on information and techniques (including personal interviews of the individual when appropriate) sufficient to provide appropriate substantiation for their findings. (See also Standard 7.02, Forensic Assessments.)

2.02 *Competence and Appropriate Use of Assessments and Interventions.* (a) Psychologists who develop, administer, score, interpret, or use psychological assessment techniques, interviews, tests, or instruments do so in a manner and for purposes that are appropriate in light of the research on or evidence of the usefulness and proper application of the techniques.

(b) Psychologists refrain from misuse of assessment techniques, interventions, results, and interpretations and take reasonable steps to prevent others from misusing the information these techniques provide. This includes refraining from releasing raw test results or raw data to persons, other than to patients or clients as appropriate, who are not qualified to use such information. (See also Standards 1.02, Relationship of Ethics and Law, and 1.04, Boundaries of Competence.)

2.03 *Test Construction.* Psychologists who develop and conduct research with tests and other assessment techniques use scientific procedures and current professional knowledge for test design, standardization, validation, reduction or elimination of bias, and recommendations for use.

2.04 *Use of Assessment in General and With Special Populations.* (a) Psychologists who perform interventions or administer, score, interpret, or use assessment techniques are familiar with the reliability, validation, and related standardization or outcome studies of, and proper applications and uses of, the techniques they use.

(b) Psychologists recognize limits to the certainty with which diagnoses, judgments, or predictions can be made about individuals.

(c) Psychologists attempt to identify situations in which particular interventions or assessment techniques or norms may not be applicable or may require adjustment in administration or interpretation because of factors such as individuals' gender, age, race, ethnicity, national origin, religion, sexual orientation, disability, language, or socioeconomic status.

2.05 *Interpreting Assessment Results.* When interpreting assessment results, including automated interpretations, psychologists take into account the various test factors and characteristics of the person being assessed that might affect psychologists' judgments or reduce the accuracy of their interpretations. They indicate any significant reservations they have about the accuracy or limitations of their interpretations.

2.06 *Unqualified Persons.* Psychologists do not promote the use of psychological assessment techniques by unqualified persons. (See also Standard 1.22, Delegation to and Supervision of Subordinates.)

2.07 *Obsolete Tests and Outdated Test Results.* (a) Psychologists do not base their assessment or intervention decisions or recommendations on data or test results that are outdated for the current purpose.

(b) Similarly, psychologists do not base such decisions or recommendations on tests and measures that are obsolete and not useful for the current purpose.

2.08 *Test Scoring and Interpretation Services.* (a) Psychologists who offer assessment or scoring procedures to other professionals accurately describe the purpose, norms, validity, reliability, and applications of the procedures and any special qualifications applicable to their use.

(b) Psychologists select scoring and interpretation services (including automated services) on the basis of evidence of the validity of the program and procedures as well as on other appropriate considerations.

(c) Psychologists retain appropriate responsibility for the appropriate application, interpretation, and use of assessment instruments, whether they score and interpret such tests themselves or use automated or other services.

2.09 *Explaining Assessment Results.* Unless the nature of the relationship is clearly explained to the person being assessed in advance and precludes provision of an explanation of results (such as in some organizational consulting, preemployment or security screenings, and forensic evaluations), psychologists ensure that an explanation of the results is provided using language that is reasonably understandable to the person assessed or to another legally authorized person on behalf of the client. Regardless of whether the scoring and interpretation are done by the psychologist, by assistants, or by automated or other outside services, psychologists take reasonable steps to ensure that appropriate explanations of results are given.

2.10 *Maintaining Test Security.* Psychologists make reasonable efforts to maintain the integrity and security of tests and other assessment techniques consistent with law, contractual obligations, and in a manner that permits compliance with the requirements of this Ethics Code. (See also Standard 1.02, Relationship of Ethics and Law.)

3. Advertising and Other Public Statements

3.01 *Definition of Public Statements.* Psychologists comply with this Ethics Code in public statements relating to their professional services, products, or publications or to the field of psychology. Public statements include but are not limited to paid or unpaid advertising, brochures, printed matter, directory listings, personal resumes or curricula vitae, interviews or comments for use in media, statements in legal proceedings, lectures and public oral presentations, and published materials.

3.02 *Statements by Others.* (a) Psychologists who engage others to create or place public statements that promote their professional practice, products, or activities retain professional responsibility for such statements.

(b) In addition, psychologists make reasonable efforts to prevent others whom they do not control (such as employers, publishers, sponsors, organizational clients, and representatives of the print or broadcast media) from making deceptive statements concerning psychologists' practice or professional or scientific activities.

(c) If psychologists learn of deceptive statements about their work made by others, psychologists make reasonable efforts to correct such statements.

(d) Psychologists do not compensate employees of press, radio, television, or other communication media in return for publicity in a news item.

(e) A paid advertisement relating to the psychologist's activities must be identified as such, unless it is already apparent from the context.

3.03 *Avoidance of False or Deceptive Statements.* (a) Psychologists do not make public statements that are false, deceptive, misleading, or fraudulent, either because of what they state, convey, or suggest or because of what they omit, concerning their research, practice, or other work activities or those of persons or organizations with which they are affiliated. As examples (and not in limitation) of this standard, psychologists do not make false or deceptive statements concerning (1) their training, experience, or competence; (2) their academic degrees; (3) their credentials; (4) their institutional or association affiliations; (5) their services; (6) the scientific or clinical basis for, or results or degree of success of, their services; (7) their fees; or (8) their publications or research findings. (See also Standards 6.15, Deception in Research, and 6.18, Providing Participants With Information About the Study.)

(b) Psychologists claim as credentials for their psychological work, only degrees that (1) were earned from a regionally accredited educational institution or (2) were the basis for psychology licensure by the state in which they practice.

3.04 *Media Presentations.* When psychologists provide advice or comment by means of public lectures, demonstrations, radio or television programs, prerecorded tapes, printed articles, mailed material, or other media, they take reasonable precautions to ensure that (1) the statements are based on appropriate psychological literature and practice, (2) the statements are otherwise consistent with this Ethics Code, and (3) the recipients of the information are not encouraged to infer that a relationship has been established with them personally.

3.05 *Testimonials.* Psychologists do not solicit testimonials from current psychotherapy clients or patients or other persons who because of their particular circumstances are vulnerable to undue influence.

3.06 *In-Person Solicitation.* Psychologists do not engage, directly or through agents, in uninvited in-person solicitation of business from actual or potential psychotherapy patients or clients or other persons who because of their particular circumstances are vulnerable to undue influence. However, this does not preclude attempting to implement appropriate collateral contacts with significant others for the purpose of benefiting an already engaged therapy patient.

4. Therapy

4.01 *Structuring the Relationship.* (a) Psychologists discuss with clients or patients as early as is feasible in the therapeutic relationship appropriate issues, such as the nature and anticipated course of therapy, fees, and confidentiality. (See also Standards 1.25, Fees and Financial Arrangements, and 5.01, Discussing the Limits of Confidentiality.)

(b) When the psychologist's work with clients or patients will be supervised, the above discussion includes that fact, and the name of the supervisor, when the supervisor has legal responsibility for the case.

(c) When the therapist is a student intern, the client or patient is informed of that fact.

(d) Psychologists make reasonable efforts to answer patients' questions and to avoid apparent misunderstandings about therapy. Whenever possible, psychologists provide oral and/or written information, using language that is reasonably understandable to the patient or client.

4.02 *Informed Consent to Therapy.* (a) Psychologists obtain appropriate informed consent to therapy or related procedures, using language that is reasonably understandable to participants. The content of informed consent will vary depending on many circumstances; however, informed consent generally implies that the person (1) has the capacity to consent, (2) has been informed of significant information concerning the procedure, (3) has freely and without undue influence expressed consent, and (4) consent has been appropriately documented.

(b) When persons are legally incapable of giving informed consent, psychologists obtain informed permission from a legally authorized person, if such substitute consent is permitted by law.

(c) In addition, psychologists (1) inform those persons who are legally incapable of giving informed consent about the proposed interventions in a manner commensurate with the persons' psychological capacities, (2) seek their assent to those interventions, and (3) consider such persons' preferences and best interests.

4.03 *Couple and Family Relationships.* (a) When a psychologist agrees to provide services to several persons who have a relationship (such as husband and wife or parents and children), the psychologist attempts to clarify at the outset (1) which of the individuals are patients or clients and (2) the relationship the psychologist will have with each person. This clarification includes the role of the psychologist and the probable uses of the services provided or the information obtained. (See also Standard 5.01, Discussing the Limits of Confidentiality.)

(b) As soon as it becomes apparent that the psychologist may be called on to perform potentially conflicting roles (such as marital counselor to husband and wife, and then witness for one party in a divorce proceeding), the psychologist attempts to clarify and adjust, or withdraw from, roles appropriately. (See also Standard 7.03, Clarification of Role, under Forensic Activities.)

4.04 *Providing Mental Health Services to Those Served by Others.* In deciding whether to offer or provide services to those already receiving mental health services elsewhere, psychologists carefully consider the treatment issues and the potential patient's or client's welfare. The psychologist discusses these issues with the patient or client, or another legally authorized person on behalf of the client, in order to minimize the risk of confusion and conflict, consults with the other service providers when appropriate, and proceeds with caution and sensitivity to the therapeutic issues.

4.05 *Sexual Intimacies With Current Patients or Clients.* Psychologists do not engage in sexual intimacies with current patients or clients.

4.06 *Therapy With Former Sexual Partners.* Psychologists do not accept as therapy patients or clients persons with whom they have engaged in sexual intimacies.

4.07 *Sexual Intimacies With Former Therapy Patients.* (a) Psychologists do not engage in sexual intimacies with a former therapy patient or client for at least two years after cessation or termination of professional services.

(b) Because sexual intimacies with a former therapy patient or client are so frequently harmful to the patient or client, and because such intimacies undermine public confidence in the psychology profession and thereby deter the public's use of needed services, psychologists do not engage in sexual intimacies with former therapy patients and clients even after a two-year interval except in the most unusual circumstances. The psychologist who engages in such activity after the two years following cessation or termination of treatment bears the burden of demonstrating that there has been no exploitation, in light

of all relevant factors, including (1) the amount of time that has passed since therapy terminated, (2) the nature and duration of the therapy, (3) the circumstances of termination, (4) the patient's or client's personal history, (5) the patient's or client's current mental status, (6) the likelihood of adverse impact on the patient or client and others, and (7) any statements or actions made by the therapist during the course of therapy suggesting or inviting the possibility of a posttermination sexual or romantic relationship with the patient or client. (See also Standard 1.17, Multiple Relationships.)

4.08 *Interruption of Services.* (a) Psychologists make reasonable efforts to plan for facilitating care in the event that psychological services are interrupted by factors such as the psychologist's illness, death, unavailability, or relocation or by the client's relocation or financial limitations. (See also Standard 5.09, Preserving Records and Data.)

(b) When entering into employment or contractual relationships, psychologists provide for orderly and appropriate resolution of responsibility for patient or client care in the event that the employment or contractual relationship ends, with paramount consideration given to the welfare of the patient or client.

4.09 *Terminating the Professional Relationship.* (a) Psychologists do not abandon patients or clients. (See also Standard 1.25e, under Fees and Financial Arrangements.)

(b) Psychologists terminate a professional relationship when it becomes reasonably clear that the patient or client no longer needs the service, is not benefiting, or is being harmed by continued service.

(c) Prior to termination for whatever reason, except where precluded by the patient's or client's conduct, the psychologist discusses the patient's or client's views and needs, provides appropriate pretermination counseling, suggests alternative service providers as appropriate, and takes other reasonable steps to facilitate transfer of responsibility to another provider if the patient or client needs one immediately.

5. Privacy and Confidentiality

These standards are potentially applicable to the professional and scientific activities of all psychologists.

5.01 *Discussing the Limits of Confidentiality.*

(a) Psychologists discuss with persons and organizations with whom they establish a scientific or professional relationship (including, to the extent feasible, minors and their legal representatives) (1) the relevant limitations on confidentiality, including limitations where applicable in group, marital, and family therapy or in organizational consulting, and (2) the foreseeable uses of the information generated through their services.

(b) Unless it is not feasible or is contraindicated, the discussion of confidentiality occurs at the outset of the relationship and thereafter as new circumstances may warrant.

(c) Permission for electronic recording of interviews is secured from clients and patients.

5.02 *Maintaining Confidentiality.* Psychologists have a primary obligation and take reasonable precautions to respect the confidentiality rights of those with whom they work or consult, recognizing that confidentiality may be established by law, institutional rules, or professional or scientific relationships. (See also Standard 6.26, Professional Reviewers.)

5.03 *Minimizing Intrusions on Privacy.* (a) In order to minimize intrusions on privacy, psychologists include in written and oral reports, consultations, and the like, only information germane to the purpose for which the communication is made.

(b) Psychologists discuss confidential information obtained in clinical or consulting relationships, or evaluative data concerning patients, individual or organizational clients, students, research participants, supervisees, and employees, only for appropriate scientific or professional purposes and only with persons clearly concerned with such matters.

5.04 *Maintenance of Records.* Psychologists maintain appropriate confidentiality in creating, storing, accessing, transferring, and disposing of records under their control, whether these are written, automated, or in any other medium. Psychologists maintain and dispose of records in accordance with law and in a manner that permits compliance with the requirements of this Ethics Code.

5.05 *Disclosures.* (a) Psychologists disclose confidential information without the consent of the individual only as mandated by law, or where permitted by law for a valid purpose, such as (1) to provide needed professional services to the patient or the individual or organizational client, (2) to obtain appropriate professional consultations, (3) to protect the patient or client or others from harm, or (4) to obtain payment for services, in which instance disclosure is limited to the minimum that is necessary to achieve the purpose.

(b) Psychologists also may disclose confidential information with the appropriate consent of the patient or the individual or organizational client (or of another legally authorized person on behalf of the patient or client), unless prohibited by law.

5.06 *Consultations.* When consulting with colleagues, (1) psychologists do not share confidential information that reasonably could lead to the identification of a patient, client, research participant, or other person or organization with whom they have a confidential relationship unless they have obtained the prior consent of the person or organization or the disclosure cannot be avoided, and (2) they share information only to the extent necessary to achieve the purposes of the consultation. (See also Standard 5.02, Maintaining Confidentiality.)

5.07 *Confidential Information in Databases.* (a) If confidential information concerning recipients of psychological services is to be entered into databases or systems of records available to persons whose access has not been consented to by the recipient, then psychologists use coding or other techniques to avoid the inclusion of personal identifiers.

(b) If a research protocol approved by an institutional review board or similar body requires the inclusion of personal identifiers, such identifiers are deleted before the information is made accessible to persons other than those of whom the subject was advised.

(c) If such deletion is not feasible, then before psychologists transfer such data to others or review such data collected by others, they take reasonable steps to determine that appropriate consent of personally identifiable individuals has been obtained.

5.08 *Use of Confidential Information for Didactic or Other Purposes.* (a) Psychologists do not disclose in their writings, lectures, or other public media, confidential, personally identifiable information concerning their patients, individual or organizational clients, students, research participants, or other recipients of their services that they obtained during the course of their work, unless the person or organization has consented in writing or unless there is other ethical or legal authorization for doing so.

(b) Ordinarily, in such scientific and professional presentations, psychologists disguise confidential information concerning such persons or organizations so that they are not individually identifiable to others and so that discussions do not cause harm to subjects who might identify themselves.

5.09 *Preserving Records and Data.* A psychologist makes plans in advance so that confidentiality of records and data is protected in the event of the psychologist's death, incapacity, or withdrawal from the position or practice.

5.10 *Ownership of Records and Data.* Recognizing that ownership of records and data is governed by legal principles, psychologists take reasonable and lawful steps so that records and data remain available to the extent needed to serve the best interests of patients, individual or organizational clients, research participants, or appropriate others.

5.11 *Withholding Records for Nonpayment.* Psychologists may not withhold records under their control that are requested and imminently needed for a patient's or client's treatment solely because payment has not been received, except as otherwise provided by law.

6. Teaching, Training Supervision, Research, and Publishing

6.01 *Design of Education and Training Programs.* Psychologists who are responsible for education and training programs seek to ensure that the programs are competently designed, provide the proper experiences, and meet the requirements for licensure, certification, or other goals for which claims are made by the program.

6.02 *Descriptions of Education and Training Programs.* (a) Psychologists responsible for education and training programs seek to ensure that there is a current and accurate description of the program content, training goals and objectives, and requirements that must be met for satisfactory completion of the program. This information must be made readily available to all interested parties.

(b) Psychologists seek to ensure that statements concerning their course outlines are accurate and not misleading, particularly regarding the subject matter to be covered, bases for evaluating progress, and the nature of course experiences. (See also Standard 3.03, Avoidance of False or Deceptive Statements.)

(c) To the degree to which they exercise control, psychologists responsible for announcements, catalogs, brochures, or advertisements describing workshops, seminars, or other non-degree-granting educational programs ensure that they accurately describe the audience for which the program is intended, the educational objectives, the presenters, and the fees involved.

6.03 *Accuracy and Objectivity in Teaching.* (a) When engaged in teaching or training, psychologists present psychological information accurately and with a reasonable degree of objectivity.

(b) When engaged in teaching or training, psychologists recognize the power they hold over students or supervisees and therefore make reasonable efforts to avoid engaging in conduct that is personally demeaning to students or supervisees. (See also Standards 1.09, Respecting Others, and 1.12, Other Harassment.)

6.04 *Limitation on Teaching.* Psychologists do not teach the use of techniques or procedures that require specialized training, licensure, or expertise, including but not limited to hypnosis, biofeedback, and projective techniques, to individuals who lack the prerequisite training, legal scope of practice, or expertise.

6.05 *Assessing Student and Supervisee Performance.* (a) In academic and supervisory relationships, psychologists establish an appropriate process for providing feedback to students and supervisees.

(b) Psychologists evaluate students and supervisees on the basis of their actual performance on relevant and established program requirements.

6.06 *Planning Research.* (a) Psychologists design, conduct, and report research in accordance with recognized standards of scientific competence and ethical research.

(b) Psychologists plan their research so as to minimize the possibility that results will be misleading.

(c) In planning research, psychologists consider its ethical acceptability under the Ethics Code. If an ethical issue is unclear, psychologists seek to resolve the issue through consultation with institutional review boards, animal care and use committees, peer consultations, or other proper mechanisms.

(d) Psychologists take reasonable steps to implement appropriate protections for the rights and welfare of human participants, other persons affected by the research, and the welfare of animal subjects.

6.07 *Responsibility.* (a) Psychologists conduct research competently and with due concern for the dignity and welfare of the participants.

(b) Psychologists are responsible for the ethical conduct of research conducted by them or by others under their supervision or control.

(c) Researchers and assistants are permitted to perform only those tasks for which they are appropriately trained and prepared.

(d) As part of the process of development and implementation of research projects, psychologists consult those with expertise concerning any special population under investigation or most likely to be affected.

6.08 *Compliance With Law and Standards.* Psychologists plan and conduct research in a manner consistent with federal and state law and regulations, as well as professional standards governing the conduct of research, and particularly those standards governing research with human participants and animal subjects.

6.09 *Institutional Approval.* Psychologists obtain from host institutions or organizations appropriate approval prior to conducting research, and they provide accurate information about their research proposals. They conduct the research in accordance with the approved research protocol.

6.10 *Research Responsibilities.* Prior to conducting research (except research involving only anonymous surveys, naturalistic observations, or similar research), psychologists enter into an agreement with participants that clarifies the nature of the research and the responsibilities of each party.

6.11 *Informed Consent to Research.* (a) Psychologists use language that is reasonably understandable to research participants in obtaining their appropriate informed consent (except as provided in Standard 6.12, Dispensing With Informed Consent). Such informed consent is appropriately documented.

(b) Using language that is reasonably understandable to participants, psychologists inform participants of the nature of the research; they inform participants that they are free to participate or to decline to participate or to withdraw from the research; they explain the foreseeable consequences of declining or withdrawing; they inform participants of significant factors that may be expected to influence their willingness to participate (such as risks, discomfort, adverse effects, or limitations on confidentiality, except as provided in Standard 6.15, Deception in Research); and they explain other aspects about which the prospective participants inquire.

(c) When psychologists conduct research with individuals such as students or subordinates, psychologists take special care to protect the prospective participants from adverse consequences of declining or withdrawing from participation.

(d) When research participation is a course requirement or opportunity for extra credit, the prospective participant is given the choice of equitable alternative activities.

(e) For persons who are legally incapable of giving informed consent, psychologists nevertheless (1) provide an appropriate explanation, (2) obtain the participant's assent, and (3) obtain appropriate permission from a legally authorized person, if such substitute consent is permitted by law.

6.12 *Dispensing With Informed Consent.* Before determining that planned research (such as research involving only anonymous questionnaires, naturalistic observations, or certain kinds of archival research) does not require the informed consent of research participants, psychologists consider applicable regulations and institutional review board requirements, and they consult with colleagues as appropriate.

6.13 *Informed Consent in Research Filming or Recording.* Psychologists obtain informed consent from research participants prior to filming or recording them in any form, unless the research involves simply naturalistic observations in public places and it is not anticipated that the recording will be used in a manner that could cause personal identification or harm.

6.14 *Offering Inducements for Research Participants.* (a) In offering professional services as an inducement to obtain research participants, psychologists make clear the nature of the services, as well as the risks, obligations, and limitations. (See also Standard 1.18, Barter [With Patients or Clients].)

(b) Psychologists do not offer excessive or inappropriate financial or other inducements to obtain research participants, particularly when it might tend to coerce participation.

6.15 *Deception in Research.* (a) Psychologists do not conduct a study involving deception unless they have determined that the use of deceptive techniques is justified by the study's prospective scientific, educational, or applied value and that equally effective alternative procedures that do not use deception are not feasible.

(b) Psychologists never deceive research participants about significant aspects that would affect their willingness to participate, such as physical risks, discomfort, or unpleasant emotional experiences.

(c) Any other deception that is an integral feature of the design and conduct of an experiment must be explained to participants as early as is feasible, preferably at the conclusion of their participation, but no later than at the conclusion of the research. (See also Standard 6.18, Providing Participants With Information About the Study.)

6.16 *Sharing and Utilizing Data.* Psychologists inform research participants of their anticipated sharing or further use of personally identifiable research data and of the possibility of unanticipated future uses.

6.17 *Minimizing Invasiveness.* In conducting research, psychologists interfere with the participants or milieu from which data are collected only in a manner that is warranted by an appropriate research design and that is consistent with psychologists' roles as scientific investigators.

6.18 *Providing Participants With Information About the Study.* (a) Psychologists provide a prompt opportunity for participants to obtain appropriate information about the nature, results, and conclusions of the research, and psychologists attempt to correct any misconceptions that participants may have.

(b) If scientific or humane values justify delaying or withholding this information, psychologists take reasonable measures to reduce the risk of harm.

6.19 *Honoring Commitments.* Psychologists take reasonable measures to honor all commitments they have made to research participants.

6.20 *Care and Use of Animals in Research.* (a) Psychologists who conduct research involving animals treat them humanely.

(b) Psychologists acquire, care for, use, and dispose of animals in compliance with current federal, state, and local laws and regulations, and with professional standards.

(c) Psychologists trained in research methods and experienced in the care of laboratory animals supervise all procedures involving animals and are responsible for ensuring appropriate consideration of their comfort, health, and humane treatment.

(d) Psychologists ensure that all individuals using animals under their supervision have received instruction in research methods and in the care, maintenance, and handling of the species being used, to the extent appropriate to their role.

(e) Responsibilities and activities of individuals assisting in a research project are consistent with their respective competencies.

(f) Psychologists make reasonable efforts to minimize the discomfort, infection, illness, and pain of animal subjects.

(g) A procedure subjecting animals to pain, stress, or privation is used only when an alternative procedure is unavailable and the goal is justified by its prospective scientific, educational, or applied value.

(h) Surgical procedures are performed under appropriate anesthesia; techniques to avoid infection and minimize pain are followed during and after surgery.

(i) When it is appropriate that the animal's life be terminated, it is done rapidly, with an effort to minimize pain, and in accordance with accepted procedures.

6.21 *Reporting of Results.* (a) Psychologists do not fabricate data or falsify results in their publications.

(b) If psychologists discover significant errors in their published data, they take reasonable steps to correct such errors in a correction, retraction, erratum, or other appropriate publication means.

6.22 *Plagiarism.* Psychologists do not present substantial portions or elements of another's work or data as their own, even if the other work or data source is cited occasionally.

6.23 *Publication Credit.* (a) Psychologists

take responsibility and credit, including authorship credit, only for work they have actually performed or to which they have contributed.

(b) Principal authorship and other publication credits accurately reflect the relative scientific or professional contributions of the individuals involved, regardless of their relative status. Mere possession of an institutional position, such as Department Chair, does not justify authorship credit. Minor contributions to the research or to the writing for publications are appropriately acknowledged, such as in footnotes or in an introductory statement.

(c) A student is usually listed as principal author on any multiple-authored article that is substantially based on the student's dissertation or thesis.

6.24 *Duplicate Publication of Data.* Psychologists do not publish, as original data, data that have been previously published. This does not preclude republishing data when they are accompanied by proper acknowledgment.

6.25 *Sharing Data.* After research results are published, psychologists do not withhold the data on which their conclusions are based from other competent professionals who seek to verify the substantive claims through reanalysis and who intend to use such data only for that purpose, provided that the confidentiality of the participants can be protected and unless legal rights concerning proprietary data preclude their release.

6.26 *Professional Reviewers.* Psychologists who review material submitted for publication, grant, or other research proposal review respect the confidentiality of and the proprietary rights in such information of those who submitted it.

7. Forensic Activities

7.01 *Professionalism.* Psychologists who perform forensic functions, such as assessments, interviews, consultations, reports, or expert testimony, must comply with all other provisions of this Ethics Code to the extent that they apply to such activities. In addition, psychologists base their forensic work on appropriate knowledge of and competence in the areas underlying such work, including specialized knowledge concerning special populations. (See also Standards 1.06, Basis for Scientific and Professional Judgments;

1.08, Human Differences; 1.15, Misuse of Psychologists' Influence; and 1.23, Documentation of Professional and Scientific Work.)

7.02 *Forensic Assessments.* (a) Psychologists' forensic assessments, recommendations, and reports are based on information and techniques (including personal interviews of the individual, when appropriate) sufficient to provide appropriate substantiation for their findings. (See also Standards 1.03, Professional and Scientific Relationship; 1.23, Documentation of Professional and Scientific Work; 2.01, Evaluation, Diagnosis, and Interventions in Professional Context; and 2.05, Interpreting Assessment Results.)

(b) Except as noted in (c), below, psychologists provide written or oral forensic reports or testimony of the psychological characteristics of an individual only after they have conducted an examination of the individual adequate to support their statements or conclusions.

(c) When, despite reasonable efforts, such an examination is not feasible, psychologists clarify the impact of their limited information on the reliability and validity of their reports and testimony, and they appropriately limit the nature and extent of their conclusions or recommendations.

7.03 *Clarification of Role.* In most circumstances, psychologists avoid performing multiple and potentially conflicting roles in forensic matters. When psychologists may be called on to serve in more than one role in a legal proceeding—for example, as consultant or expert for one party or for the court and as a fact witness—they clarify role expectations and the extent of confidentiality in advance to the extent feasible, and thereafter as changes occur, in order to avoid compromising their professional judgment and objectivity and in order to avoid misleading others regarding their role.

7.04 *Truthfulness and Candor.* (a) In forensic testimony and reports, psychologists testify truthfully, honestly, and candidly and, consistent with applicable legal procedures, describe fairly the bases for their testimony and conclusions.

(b) Whenever necessary to avoid misleading, psychologists acknowledge the limits of their data or conclusions.

7.05 *Prior Relationships.* A prior professional relationship with a party does not preclude psychologists from testifying as fact witnesses or from testifying to their services to the extent permitted by applicable law. Psychologists appropriately take into account ways in which the prior relationship might affect their professional objectivity or opinions and disclose the potential conflict to the relevant parties.

7.06 *Compliance With Law and Rules.* In performing forensic roles, psychologists are reasonably familiar with the rules governing their roles. Psychologists are aware of the occasionally competing demands placed upon them by these principles and the requirements of the court system, and attempt to resolve these conflicts by making known their commitment to this Ethics Code and taking steps to resolve the conflict in a responsible manner. (See also Standard 1.02, Relationship of Ethics and Law.)

8. Resolving Ethical Issues

8.01 *Familiarity With Ethics Code.* Psychologists have an obligation to be familiar with this Ethics Code, other applicable ethics codes, and their application to psychologists' work. Lack of awareness or misunderstanding of an ethical standard is not itself a defense to a charge of unethical conduct.

8.02 *Confronting Ethical Issues.* When a psychologist is uncertain whether a particular situation or course of action would violate this Ethics Code, the psychologist ordinarily consults with other psychologists knowledgeable about ethical issues, with state or national psychology ethics committees, or with other appropriate authorities in order to choose a proper response.

8.03 *Conflicts Between Ethics and Organizational Demands.* If the demands of an organization with which psychologists are affiliated conflict with this Ethics Code, psychologists clarify the nature of the conflict, make known their commitment to the Ethics Code, and to the extent feasible, seek to resolve the conflict in a way that permits the fullest adherence to the Ethics Code.

8.04 *Informal Resolution of Ethical Violations.* When psychologists believe that there may have been an ethical violation by another psychologist, they attempt to resolve the issue by bringing it to the attention of that individual if an informal resolution appears appropriate and the intervention does not violate any confidentiality rights that may be involved.

8.05 *Reporting Ethical Violations.* If an apparent ethical violation is not appropriate for informal resolution under Standard 8.04 or is not resolved properly in that fashion, psychologists take further action appropriate to the situation, unless such action conflicts with confidentiality rights in ways that cannot be resolved. Such action might include referral to state or national committees on professional ethics or to state licensing boards.

8.06 *Cooperating With Ethics Committees.* Psychologists cooperate in ethics investigations, proceedings, and resulting requirements of the APA or any affiliated state psychological association to which they belong. In doing so, they make reasonable efforts to resolve any issues as to confidentiality. Failure to cooperate is itself an ethics violation.

8.07 *Improper Complaints.* Psychologists do not file or encourage the filing of ethics complaints that are frivolous and are intended to harm the respondent rather than to protect the public.

This version of the APA Ethics Code was adopted by the American Psychological Association's Council of Representatives during its meeting, August 13 and 16, 1992, and is effective beginning December 1, 1992. Inquiries concerning the substance or interpretation of the APA Ethics Code should be addressed to the Director, Office of Ethics, American Psychological Association, 750 First Street, NE, Washington, DC 20002-4242.

This Code will be used to adjudicate complaints brought concerning alleged conduct occurring on or after the effective date. Complaints regarding conduct occurring prior to the effective date will be adjudicated on the basis of the version of the Code that was in effect at the time the conduct occurred, except that no provisions repealed in June 1989, will be enforced even if an earlier version contains the provision. The Ethics Code will undergo continuing review and study for future revisions; comments on the Code may be sent to the above address.

The APA has previously published its Ethical Standards as follows:

American Psychological Association. (1953). *Ethical standards of psychologists.* Washington, DC: Author.

American Psychological Association. (1958). Standards of ethical behavior for psychologists. *American Psychologist, 13,* 268-271.

American Psychological Association. (1963). Ethical standards of psychologists. *American Psychologist, 18,* 56-60.

American Psychological Association. (1968). Ethical standards of psychologists. *American Psychologist, 23,* 357-361.

American Psychological Association. (1977, March). Ethical standards of psychologists. *APA Monitor,* pp. 22-23.

American Psychological Association. (1979). *Ethical standards of psychologists.* Washington, DC: Author.

American Psychological Association. (1981). Ethical principles of psychologists. *American Psychologist, 36,* 633-638.

American Psychological Association. (1990). Ethical principles of psychologists (Amended June 2, 1989). *American Psychologist, 45,* 390-395.

Request copies of the APA's Ethical Principles of Psychologists and Code of Conduct from the APA Order Department, 750 First Street, NE, Washington, DC 20002-4242, or phone (202) 336-5510.

Ethical Guidelines for the Christian Association for Psychological Studies

Introduction

The Statement of Ethical Guidelines that follows was adopted by the voting membership of the Christian Association for Psychological Studies (CAPS) on June 15, 1992 by the completion of an election about the guidelines and several other propositions. The proposition about ethical guidelines stated "That agreement with the CAPS Statement of Ethical Guidelines be a requirement of membership." It passed by 84.1% of the ballots cast.

Thus, an overwhelming majority of the CAPS membership agreed strongly that guidance on ethical behaviors of members would be helpful. Many CAPS members do not belong to another professional association and therefore would not otherwise have written ethical guidelines to assist them in applying their Christian faith in their professional activities. The ethical guidelines that follow were eight years in the making, starting before the first draft of a code of ethics was presented at a CAPS Western Region convention in Buena Park, California on June 23, 1984. Since that time the "code" became "guidelines," they were reviewed by CAPS members during several convention forums, they were also presented—with pro and con discussions—in the Fall, 1986 issue (Vol. 5, No. 3) of the *Journal of Psychology and Christianity,* and they were edited during committee meetings and regular meetings of

the CAPS Board of Directors.

The CAPS Board hopes that the Statement of Ethical Guidelines will be helpful to our members and, thus, to the people whom they serve. The guidelines are distinctively Christian in nature and emphasize restoration and reconciliation rather than punishment, if they are breached.

Preamble

The Christian Association for Psychological Studies (CAPS) presents the following Statement of Ethical Guidelines as a set of ideals for conduct of its individual members. The Guidelines derive from CAPS' Statement of Faith, found in Article II of the CAPS Constitution and By-Laws:

The basis of this organization is belief in: God, the Father, who creates and sustains us; Jesus Christ, the Son, who redeems and rules us; and the Holy Spirit, who guides us personally and professionally, through God's inspired Word, the Bible, our infallible guide of faith and conduct, and through the communion of Christians.

These Guidelines are aimed at helping each member apply the message of the Gospel to his or her professional or pastoral service. The statements herein could not hope to explore all the richness of the Bible as it relates to ethical conduct. Rather, each believer in Christ has the capacity—even the privilege and duty—to explore the depths of God's Word and discover personal guidance for daily living. The following scripturally based principles exemplify the foundation upon which the more specifically applied Guidelines are based. The cited biblical passages are meant as representative sources, not "proof texts" for the concepts expressed.

Biblical Principles

We are, as human beings as well as Christians, prone to hurts, conflicts and sin (Romans 3:23). Difficulties, power struggles, trials and tribulations are normal and to be expected (Psalms 37:7; John 16:33; Romans 2:9). We are to grow and mature through the conflicts, problems, trials, tribulations and discipline that we experience (2 Corinthians 7:8-13a; 1 Thessalonians 5:18; James 1:2-4). We are to support and encourage each other (John 13:35; 15:17; Ephesians 4:32). We are to admonish and confront each other, especially those Christians in positions of leadership and trust. However, such confrontation is to be constructive rather than judgmental, done in love and with caution about our own short-comings (Proverbs 27:5; Matthew 18:15-17; Galatians 6:1). We are to demonstrate the lordship of Christ in our lives by servant-like leadership, a sense of community and a life-style that reflects the will of God (Matthew 20:25-28; John 12:26; Colossians 3:12-17; 1 Peter 4:8-11). We are to reach out to others in love and concern (Matthew 25:31-40; 2 Corinthians 1:3-7; Hebrews 13:16).

These Guidelines are meant in part as an encouragement for all CAPS members to reach out to other members who are in distress. They do not constitute a quasi-legal document designed for disciplinary purposes by the organization. The Guidelines are written with recognition of the priesthood of all believers.

Applicability of the Guidelines

This Statement of Ethical Guidelines is applicable to all current, dues-paid Regular Members and Associate Members of CAPS. While CAPS is not a licensing or accrediting agency, it does desire that members who provide mental health, pastoral, teaching or other personal services do so with the highest possible level of Christian ethics, whether the member is a professional, layperson or student. The Guidelines are therefore intended to benefit members, their colleagues and the persons whom they serve.

Articles of the Ethical Guidelines

Note: In an effort to avoid awkward and lengthy descriptions of persons whom members serve or with whom they work, the somewhat neutral word "client" is used. According to the perspective of members, words such as "peer," "parishioner," "communicant," "patient," "helpee," "counselee," "student," "subject" or even "prisoner" may be used. Also, the word "service" or "serving" is used frequently in the guidelines to describe what members do. Again, according to the perspective of members, words such as "helping ministries," "psychological professions," "counseling," "ministering," "pastoring," "teaching" or "researching" may be substituted. Admittedly, no word is neutral, since language shapes and reflects reality. Thus, the word "service" or its derivatives is meant to reflect Christ's statement that He came to serve, rather than to be served.

1. Personal Commitment as a Christian

1.1 I agree with the basis of CAPS, as stated in the Constitution and By-Laws.

1.2 I commit my service, whether as professional or layperson, to God as a special calling.

1.3 I pledge to integrate all that I do in service with Christian values, principles and guidelines.

1.4 I commit myself to Christ as Lord as well as Savior. Thus, direction and wisdom from God will be sought, while accepting responsibility for my own actions and statements.

1.5 I view my body as the temple of the Holy Spirit and will treat it lovingly and respectfully. Balance in my priorities and activities will be prayerfully sought.

2. Loving Concern for Clients

2.1 Clients will be accepted regardless of race, religion, gender, sexual orientation, income, education, ethnic background, value system, etc., unless such a factor would interfere appreciably with my ability to be of service.

2.2 I value human life, the sanctity of personhood, personal freedom and responsibility and the privilege of informed free choice by adults in matters of belief and action.

2.3 I will avoid exploiting or manipulating any client to satisfy my own needs.

2.4 I will abstain from unnecessary or prurient invasion of privacy.

2.5 I will take appropriate actions to help, even protect, those persons within my area of responsibility who are being endangered and are relatively dependent on other persons for their survival and well being.

2.6 Sexual contact or sexual exploitation—both covert and overt—with any client will be scrupulously avoided.

2.7 Members who provide professional services should make advance financial arrangements that protect the best interests of and are clearly understood by their clients. A portion of their services should be contributed towards work for which they receive little or no financial return.

3. Confidentiality

3.1 I will demonstrate utmost respect for the

confidentiality of the client and other persons in a professional or pastoral relationship.

3.2 I will carefully protect the identity of clients and their situations. Thus, I will avoid divulging information about clients, whether privately or publicly, unless I have received freely given, informed consent of the adult client or legal holder of confidentiality privilege for minor clients, in the form of expressed, written permission and the release of such information would be appropriate to the situation.

3.3 All records of counseling, teaching and research will be handled in a way that protects the clients and the nature of their situations from disclosure.

3.4 The limits of confidentiality, such as those based on civil laws, regulations and judicial precedent, will be explained to the client. Examples of limits or exceptions to confidentiality include such situations as (1) legal mandate, e.g., if child abuse is suspected or apparent; (2) when divulging information would prevent a clear and immediate danger to a person or persons; (3) legal proceedings in which the member does not have privilege.

4. Competency in Services Provided

4.1 I pledge to be well-trained and competent in providing services.

4.2 I will refrain from implying that I have qualifications, experiences and capabilities which are in fact lacking.

4.3 I will comply with applicable state and local laws and regulations regarding competency in the psychological and pastoral professions.

4.4 I will avoid using any legal exemptions from professional competency afforded in certain states to churches and other nonprofit organizations as a means of providing services that are beyond my training and expertise.

4.5 I will diligently pursue additional education, experience, professional consultation and spiritual growth in order to improve my effectiveness in serving persons in need.

5. My Human Limitations

5.1 I will do my best to be aware of my human limitations and biases. I admit that I do not have complete objectivity or spiritual maturity. Thus, I also will endeavor to establish and maintain a relationship of mutual accountability with another Christian colleague or mentor.

5.2 I will avoid fostering any misconception a client could have that I am omnipotent, or that I have all the answers.

5.3 I will refer clients whom I am not capable of helping, whether by lack of available time or expertise, or because of subjective, personal reasons. The referral will be done compassionately, clearly and completely, insofar as feasible.

5.4 I will resist efforts of any clients or colleagues to place demands for services on me that exceed my qualifications and/or the time available to minister, or that would impose unduly on my relationships with my own family, other persons or God.

6. Advertising and Promotional Activities

6.1 I will advertise or promote my services by Christian and professional standards, rather than only commercial standards.

6.2 Personal aggrandizement will be omitted from advertising and promotional activities.

6.3 Since CAPS is not a licensing or accrediting agency, I will avoid using membership in CAPS as an advertising promotional.

7. Research

7.1 Any research conducted will be done openly and will not jeopardize the welfare of any persons who are research subjects. The confidentiality of such subjects will be protected. They will provide informed, written consent for their participation in the research.

8. Professional Liability

8.1 The value of professional liability ("malpractice") insurance will be carefully considered, especially if a lawsuit, whether justified or not, would possibly drain financial resources of the organization with which I am associated.

9. Pastoral Care Network

9.1 CAPS will establish a network of representatives who will be available to respond to members in a pastoral manner. These representatives will endeavor to respond personally to members who seek their help or refer such persons to appropriate sources of help. Ideally, as part of the Body of Christ, the entire CAPS membership is intended to function in this pastoral way. The Pastoral Care Network provides deliberate structure to enhance this functioning.

10. Membership Revocation and Restoration

10.1 Although CAPS will not enforce these Ethical Guidelines with any investigative or disciplinary measure, I understand that if my professional license or certification has been revoked by any other professional organization or state board, then I may lose my membership status with CAPS. Such a decision will be made by a majority vote of the CAPS Board of Directors.

10.2 In the event of such a loss of membership, a process of reconciliation and restoration will be promptly instituted under the auspices of the CAPS Pastoral Care Network.

11. General Prudential Rule

11.1 Recognizing that no ethical guidelines are complete, I make my day-to-day decisions based on the criteria and principles stated in the Preamble. I will do my best to serve and to live in a way that is congruent with the stated basic principles of these guidelines and with my faith as a Christian.

Further Discussion: Paragraph 9 of the guidelines states that a pastoral care network will be established. The plan for implementing the CAPS Pastoral Care Network follows for your information.

The CAPS Pastoral Care Network Protocol for Giving Service to Troubled Members

Prologue: Our ultimate goal is to help our members practice professionally in an increasingly Christlike fashion. Our ultimate method is to love the member such that the person experiences God's grace and in that context re-examines his or her conduct or works through a professional hardship.

The steps of care we take must be understandable to the public, whether Christian or secular, whether professional or lay people.

Protocol:

1. We encourage all CAPS members to reach out in love to any member who may be in personal or professional difficulty. If the problem is a health crisis, loss of job, or similar distress, prayerful comfort and networking assistance are to be offered as appropriate. An individual's need for prayer support and other forms of personal encouragement may be made known to CAPS membership. This may *only* be done with the explicit permission of said member.

2. If the problem is that a CAPS member is found to be functioning in a manner which violates the CAPS Statement of Ethical Guidelines, another CAPS member may begin gentle confrontation of the member. If there is no improvement in the situation, the member may then enlist the help of a Pastoral Care Network representative. One or both of these individuals will call the member and invite him or her to lunch or breakfast or ask to come by the member's office, to talk prayerfully about a problem which may exist.

3. In face to face dialogues with members who may be behaving unprofessionally, our Pastoral Care Network representatives may use the CAPS Statement of Ethical Guidelines for discussion; they will use biblical bases for these ethical ideals to gently invite self-reexamination by the member. They will not take the stance of, "If you have violated the CAPS ethical standards, your membership may be terminated." Rather, they may want to ask, "How have you thought through for yourself this behavior which seems contrary to our understanding of biblical ethics?"

4. If the CAPS member or the Pastoral Care Network representative comes to believe even more strongly that an ethical principle is being violated, and if the member being confronted denies the charge, the CAPS member may decide to wait and pray and return for further discussion. If the ethical issue violates the standards of the member's professional license, the CAPS Pastoral Care Network representative would report that individual to the appropriate regulatory agency of the member's state.

5. *Under no circumstances* is any CAPS member or Pastoral Care Network representative authorized to make public statements about possible or actual ethical misbehavior by a member. Nor is a CAPS member *ever* to threaten another member with loss of CAPS membership, media publicity or revelations to that individual's employer or clients. There

are only two authorized responses in the case of a violation of ethical standards: (1) if the violation is of CAPS ideals but not of state licensure standards, the member is to be prayed for and talked with but *not* reported to anyone; (2) if the violation is of state legal or professional association ethical standards, the individual is to be reported, with full confidentiality otherwise, to the appropriate state agency and/or to the appropriate professional association.

6. If an individual has been removed from CAPS membership by vote of the Board of Directors according to the Ethical Guidelines (section 10), that person may be restored to full CAPS membership when the individual reapplies and is found to no longer be in violation of the CAPS ethical ideals or Statement of Faith.

7. A CAPS member who has been removed from membership by vote of the Board of Directors may appeal that decision by making a written statement to the CAPS Regional Director in which the member lives. The Regional Director and the President of the Board of Directors will decide how to provide a forum to hear the member's appeal and arrive at another vote.

8. CAPS members will receive training in giving pastoral care to members. Such training will involve knowledge of the Statement of Ethical Guidelines and of the protocol here presented. Where such can be done without violating confidentiality, experiences of other Pastoral Care persons may be passed along to all caregivers who may benefit from the work of these persons. Training for pastoral caregivers will be made available by each of the Regional Directors and/or representatives of the Pastoral Care Network as he or she sees fit.

American Association of Pastoral Counselors Code of Ethics

(Amended April 28, 1994)
(Procedures separated out April 17, 1993[1])

Principle 1: Prologue

As members[2] of the American Association of Pastoral Counselors, we are committed to the various theologies, traditions, and values of our faith communities and to the dignity and worth of each individual. We are dedicated to advancing the welfare of those who seek our assistance and to the maintenance of high standards of professional conduct and competence. We are accountable for our ministry whatever its setting. This accountability is expressed in relationships to clients, colleagues, students, our faith communities, and through the acceptance and practice of the principles and procedures of this Code of Ethics.

In order to uphold our standards, as members of AAPC we covenant to accept the following foundational premises:

A. To maintain responsible association with the faith group in which we have ecclesiastical standing.

B. To avoid discriminating against or refusing employment, educational opportunity or professional assistance to anyone on the basis of race, gender, sexual orientation, religion, or national origin.

C. To remain abreast of new developments in the field through both educational activities and clinical experience. We agree at all levels of membership to continue postgraduate education and professional growth including supervision, consultation, and active participation in the meetings and affairs of the Association.

D. To seek out and engage in collegial relationships, recognizing that isolation can lead to a loss of perspective and judgement.

E. To manage our personal lives in a healthful fashion and to seek appropriate assistance for our own personal problems or conflicts.

F. To diagnose or provide treatment only for those problems or issues that are within the reasonable boundaries of our competence.

G. To establish and maintain appropriate professional relationship boundaries.

Principle 2: Professional Practices

In all professional matters members of AAPC maintain practices that protect the public and advance the profession.

A. We use our knowledge and professional associations for the benefit of the people we serve and not to secure unfair personal advantage.

B. We clearly represent our level of membership and limit our practice to that level.

C. Fees and financial arrangements, as with all contractual matters, are always discussed without hesitation or equivocation at the onset and are established in a straightforward, professional manner.

D. We are prepared to render service to individuals and communities in crisis without regard to financial remuneration when necessary.

E. We neither receive nor pay a commission for referral of a client.

F. We conduct our practice, agency, regional and Association fiscal affairs with due regard to recognized business and accounting procedures.

G. Upon the transfer of a pastoral counseling practice or the sale of real, personal, tangible or intangible property or assets used in such practice, the privacy and well being of the client shall be of primary concern.

1. Client names and records shall be excluded from the transfer or sale.
2. Any fees paid shall be for services rendered, consultation, equipment, real estate, and the name and logo of the counseling agency.

H. We are careful to represent facts truthfully to clients, referral sources, and third party payors regarding credentials and services rendered. We shall correct any misrepresentation of our professional qualifications or affiliations.

1. We do not malign colleagues or other professionals.

Principle 3: Client Relationships

It is the responsibility of members of AAPC to maintain relationships with clients on a professional basis.

A. We do not abandon or neglect clients. If we are unable, or unwilling for appropriate reasons, to provide professional help or continue a professional relationship, every reasonable effort is made to arrange for continuation of treatment with another professional.

B. We make only realistic statements regarding the pastoral counseling process and its outcome.

C. We show sensitive regard for the moral, social, and religious standards of clients and communities. We avoid imposing our beliefs on others, although we may express them when appropriate in the pastoral counseling process.

D. Counseling relationships are continued only so long as it is reasonably clear that the clients are benefiting from the relationship.

E. We recognize the trust placed in and unique power of the therapeutic relationship. While acknowledging the complexity of some pastoral relationships, we avoid exploiting the trust and dependency of clients. We avoid those dual relationships with clients (e.g., business or close personal relationships) which could impair our professional judgement, compromise the integrity of the treatment, and/or use the relationship for our own gain.

F. We do not engage in harassment, abusive words or actions, or exploitative coercion of clients or former clients.

G. All forms of sexual behavior or harassment with clients are unethical, even when a client invites or consents to such behavior or involvement. Sexual behavior is defined as, but not limited to, all forms of overt and covert seductive speech, gestures, and behavior as well as physical contact of a sexual nature; harassment is defined as, but not limited to, repeated comments, gestures or physical contacts of a sexual nature.

H. We recognize that the therapist/client relationship involves a power imbalance, the residual effects of which are operative following the termination of the therapy relationship. Therefore, all sexual behavior or harassment as defined in Principle 3.G with former clients is unethical.

Principle 4: Confidentiality

As members of AAPC we respect the integrity and protect the welfare of all persons with whom we are working and have an obligation to safeguard information about them that has been obtained in the course of the counseling process.

A. All records kept on a client are stored or disposed of in a manner that assures security and confidentiality.

B. We treat all communications from clients with professional confidence.

C. Except in those situations where the identity of the client is necessary to the understanding of the case, we use only the first names of our clients when engaged in supervision or consultation. It is our responsibility to convey the importance of confidentiality to the supervisor/consultant; this is particularly important when the supervision is shared by other professionals, as in a supervisory group.

D. We do not disclose client confidences to anyone, except: as mandated by law; to prevent a clear and immediate danger to someone; in the course of a civil, criminal or disciplinary action arising from the counseling where the pastoral counselor is a defendant; for purposes of supervision or consultation; or by previously obtained written permission. In cases involving more than one person (as client) written permission must be obtained from all legally accountable persons who have been present during the counseling before any disclosure can be made.

E. We obtain informed written consent of clients before audio and/or video tape recording or permitting third party observation of their sessions.

F. We do not use these standards of confidentiality to avoid intervention when it is necessary, e.g., when there is evidence of abuse of minors, the elderly, the disabled, the physically or mentally incompetent.

G. When current or former clients are referred to in a publication, while teaching or in a public presentation, their identity is thoroughly disguised.

H. We as members of AAPC agree that as an express condition of our membership in the Association, Association ethics communications, files, investigative reports, and related records are strictly confidential and waive their right to use same in a court of law to advance any claim against another member. Any member seeking such records for such purpose shall be subject to disciplinary action for attempting to violate the confidentiality requirements of the organization. This policy is intended to promote pastoral and confessional communications without legal consequences and to protect potential privacy and confidentiality interests of third parties.

Principle 5: Supervisee, Student & Employee Relationships

As members of AAPC we have an ethical concern for the integrity and welfare of our supervisees, students and employees. These relationships are maintained on a professional and confidential basis. We recognize our influential position with regard to both current and former supervisees, students and employees, and avoid exploiting their trust and dependency. We make every effort to avoid dual relationships with such persons that could impair our judgement or increase the risk of personal and/or financial exploitation.

A. We do not engage in ongoing counseling relationships with current supervisees, students and employees.

B. We do not engage in sexual or other harassment of supervisees, students, employees, research subjects or colleagues.

C. All forms of sexual behavior, as defined in Principle 3.G, with our supervisees, students, research subjects and employees (except in employee situations involving domestic partners) are unethical.

D. We advise our students, supervisees, and employees against offering or engaging in, or holding themselves out as competent to engage in, professional services beyond their training, level of experience and competence.

E. We do not harass or dismiss an employee who has acted in a reasonable, responsible and ethical manner to protect, or intervene on behalf of, a client or other member of the public or another employee.

Principle 6: Interprofessional Relationships

As members of AAPC we relate to and cooperate with other professional persons in our community and beyond. We are part of a network of health care professionals and are expected to develop and maintain interdisciplinary and interprofessional relationships.

A. We do not offer ongoing clinical services to persons currently receiving treatment from another professional without prior knowledge of and in consultation with the other professional, with the clients' informed consent. Soliciting such clients is unethical.

B. We exercise care and interprofessional courtesy when approached for services by persons who claim or appear to have inappropriately terminated treatment with another professional.

Principle 7: Advertising
Any advertising by or for a member of AAPC, including announcements, public statements and promotional activities, is undertaken with the purpose of helping the public make informed judgements and choices.

A. We do not misrepresent our professional qualifications, affiliations and functions, or falsely imply sponsorship or certification by any organization.

B. We may use the following information to describe ourselves and the services we provide: name; highest relevant academic degree earned from an accredited institution; date, type and level of certification or licensure; AAPC membership level, clearly stated; address and telephone number; office hours; a brief review of services offered, e.g., individual, couple and group counseling; fee information; languages spoken; and policy regarding third party payments. Additional relevant information may be provided if it is legitimate, reasonable, free of deception and not otherwise prohibited by these principles. We may not use the initials "AAPC" after our names in the manner of an academic degree.

C. Announcements and brochures promoting our services describe them with accuracy and dignity, devoid of all claims or evaluation. We may send them to professional persons, religious institutions and other agencies, but to prospective individual clients only in response to inquires.

D. We do not make public statements which contain any of the following:

1. A false, fraudulent, misleading, deceptive or unfair statement.
2. A misrepresentation of fact or a statement likely to mislead or deceive because in context it makes only a partial disclosure of relevant facts.
3. A testimonial from a client regarding the quality of services or products.
4. A statement intended or likely to create false or unjustified expectations of favorable results.
5. A statement implying unusual, unique, or one-of-a-kind abilities, including misrepresentation through sensationalism, exaggeration or superficiality.
6. A statement intended or likely to exploit a client's fears, anxieties or emotions.
7. A statement concerning the comparative desirability of offered services.
8. A statement of direct solicitation of individual clients.

E. We do not compensate in any way a representative of the press, radio, television or other communication medium for the purpose of professional publicity and news items. A paid advertisement must be identified as such, unless it is contextually apparent that it is a paid advertisement. We are responsible for the content of such advertisement. Any advertisement to the public by radio or television is to be pre-recorded, approved by us and a recording of the actual transmission retained in our possession.

F. Advertisements or announcements by us of workshops, clinics, seminars, growth groups or similar services or endeavors, are to give a clear statement of purpose and a clear description of the experiences to be provided. The education, training and experience of the provider(s) involved are to be appropriately specified.

G. Advertisements or announcements soliciting research participants, in which clinical or other professional services are offered as an inducement, make clear the nature of the services as well as the cost and other obligations or risks to be accepted by participants in the research.

Code of Ethics Procedures
(Amended April 28, 1994)
As members of the American Association of Pastoral Counselors we are committed to accept the judgment of other members as to standards of professional ethics, subject to the procedures that follow. Refusal or failure to cooperate with an ethics investigation at any point may be considered grounds for Dismissal.

As members of AAPC we are bound by ethical standards to take action, according to the procedures outlined herein, when it appears that another member has violated the Code of Ethics. Whenever ethical questions arise and the answers do not appear to be clear, we consult with the Regional Ethics Committee for information and clarification.

A. General Procedures (For "Sexual Misconduct Cases" see "E")

1. While all ethical violations are recognized as serious, if an alleged violation is not threatening to the well-being of the member or others, we are encouraged first to approach the member in question to see if the matter can be resolved through clarification or remonstrance.

2. If this fails, or if an alleged violation appears to be a serious threat to the well-being of the member or others, the matter is immediately referred to the Regional Ethics Committee. This constitutes a formal complaint and shall be made in writing to the Regional Ethics Committee, which begins an investigation as soon as possible and in a deliberate and careful manner.

3. If members receive complaints of unethical conduct against them, they shall promptly report the complaints to the Regional Ethics Committee.

4. Regional Ethics Committees shall consult with the Association Chair or Committee immediately upon receipt of a complaint. The Executive Director of AAPC shall be notified by phone of the complaint.

5. A Regional Ethics Committee begins an investigation as soon as a complaint from a primary party has been received. A copy of the complaint (or a summary or a portion of it which indicates the nature of the complaint) is sent to the member against whom it is directed.

6. A Regional Ethics Committee may also begin an investigation based upon information obtained from other sources, including but not limited to:
   a. Notification of Suspension or Dismissal from another professional organization or from the member's endorsing faith group.
   b. The media.
   c. Knowledge that a member has been convicted of, or is engaged in conduct which could lead to the conviction of, a felony or of a misdemeanor related to the member's qualifications or functioning as a pastoral counselor.
   d. Knowledge that a member has had a professional license or certificate suspended or revoked.
   e. Knowledge that a member has shown a lack of competency to practice pastoral counseling due to impairment through physical or mental causes or the abuse of alcohol or other substances.

7. When a Regional Ethics Committee proceeds on its own initiative (in lieu of the receipt of a written complaint), it shall prepare a statement concerning the factual allegations against the member; a copy of this shall be sent to the member.

8. Complaints may be brought by anyone. Complaints by members shall be brought promptly, with due regard for client confidentiality.

9. Investigations usually include separate personal interviews by the Regional Ethics Committee with the person(s) who has made the complaint, with the member against whom the complaint has been made and with anyone else deemed necessary to obtain needed information. All parties involved are to be supported while at the same time not given unnecessary information or promises.

10. Notes are to be kept which include dates and brief summaries of all phone calls and meetings. These notes are to be kept confidential, including the use of initials instead of names whenever feasible. These notes should be clear enough to enable a reasonable person to conclude that the Regional Committee's investigation was adequate and its findings sufficient to sustain its determination(s).

11. At the discretion of the Regional Ethics Chair, legal counsel may be obtained to ensure that these procedures are followed accurately. The member against whom a complaint has been made may also seek legal counsel, at his/her own expense, but under no circumstances shall legal counsel be present at any Ethics Committee meet-

ing or investigative interview.

12. Any member of a Regional Ethics Committee who has or has had a close personal or collegial relationship with the member under investigation shall be excused from the investigation and deliberations of that case. If this includes the chairperson, a chair pro-temp shall be named. Regional Ethics Committees may recruit any member(s) of AAPC, from any region, for a specific investigation.

13. Confidentiality is crucial. However, when it is deemed to be in the best interest of protecting the public and the Association and its members, if a Regional or Association Ethics Committee is approached by a member of AAPC or of the public and is asked about allegations against a particular member, the committee member or chairperson may reveal to that person that (a) an investigation of the alleged violation(s) is in process, or (b) that the member is under discipline or either is or has been recommended for Dismissal. No other details are to be revealed.

14. Any member under investigation who moves to another region during the course of any disciplinary action shall notify in writing the Chairs of the Ethics Committees of both the former and new regions. A copy of each notification shall be sent to the other chairperson.
    a. Investigations shall be conducted and completed by the Ethics Committee of the region in which the alleged violation occurred.
    b. A copy of the complete file shall be sent to the Ethics Chair of the region into which the member relocates. That Chair shall be responsible for the management of the ongoing process until it is resolved in consultation with the original Ethics Chair.
    c. Responsibility for the management of the case shall be transferred to the Ethics Committee in the new region at a time that is deemed appropriate by both Regional Ethics Chairs.

15. Investigations can be held and disciplinary actions can be taken only against those who were members at the time the alleged violation of the Code took place. Conversely, if a member resigns during or after such violation, or during the course of an investigation, ethics procedures shall proceed to completion.

B. Actions

When an investigation is complete, there are four courses of action that an Ethics Committee may take:

1. Advice that the complaint is unfounded.

2. Admonishment. This action is meant to be educational when a member has been unaware of having violated the Code of Ethics.

3. Reprimand. This action is a serious reproof or rebuke of the member. It is based upon an assessment that the member has accepted responsibility for the violation and that the reprimand is adequate to ensure that it will not reoccur.

Actions 2 and 3 may be taken only in those cases in which the violation is deemed not to be threatening to the well-being of the member or others. They are taken by the Regional Ethics Committees. The following is recommended by the Regional Ethics Committees for action by the Association Ethics Committee.

4. Dismissal. This action is taken when a violation of the Code is serious and demonstrates an essential lack of professional knowledge, procedures, and conduct, which are consistent with membership in AAPC.

   When deemed appropriate, the Association Ethics Committee, or a Board of Review on behalf of the Ethics Committee, may offer the member a voluntary reduction of membership level to a membership category which is more in keeping with the member's demonstrated level of pastoral functioning and need for supervision. The member is subsequently allowed to advance in membership categories through normal Membership Committee procedures; i.e., reattain required number of hours of supervision for advancement, reappear before Membership Committee, etc.

   When dismissed, and at the conclusion of possible appeals, the member shall submit membership certificate to the Executive Director. When a voluntary reduction of membership category has been accepted, the member shall submit existing membership certificate and may request a certificate for the new membership category at own expense.

The action of dismissal may be taken in any case but is mandated when a member has been found guilty in a court of law of a felony, or of a misdemeanor which is related to the member's functioning as a pastoral counselor.

C. Appeals Process and Records

With each of the four actions above, the action is communicated to the complainant and to the member by certified mail, return receipt requested, with notification that the decision may be appealed.

1. Actions 2 and 3 may be appealed to the Association Ethics Committee, at which point the Regional Ethics Chair forwards the complete file along with a summary of the case to the Association Ethics Chair.

   a. The Association Ethics Chair decides upon and organizes any additional investigation that may be necessary.

   b. When this is accomplished, the Association Ethics Committee reviews the case and meets either in person or by conference call to discuss the appeal and to reach a decision.

   c. If no appeal is received within 30 days of this receipt, a chronological summary (without names) of the case is sealed in an envelope with only the member's name on the outside. It is then sent to the Executive Director of AAPC for safekeeping.

   d. The summary is to be kept by the Executive Director of AAPC for a period of twenty years, or longer if another investigation is begun. In the event another investigation of that member begins, the summary may be sent upon request to a Regional or Association Ethics Committee.

2. Action 4 may be appealed to an Appeal Board through notification of the As-

sociation Chair. The Appeal Board shall be made up of the Chair of the Association Ethics Committee, the Vice President of AAPC, and a member-at-large in AAPC, chosen by the Association Ethics Chair. The Religious Endorsing Body (REB) representative shall be invited to participate as an observing (non-voting) member of the Appeal Board. The REB representative shall be informed of the details of a case only should they choose to participate on the Board. The Appeal Board may also include a representative of the AAPC Executive Director as a non-voting, observing member.

   a. The Association Ethics Chair, in consultation with legal counsel, decides upon and organizes any additional investigation that may be necessary.

   b. When this is accomplished, the Appeal Board shall review the case and meet either in person or by conference call to discuss the appeal. It then reaches a final decision about the appeal.

   c. If no appeal is received within 30 days of the above mentioned receipt, the procedure is the same as in 1.c.

   d. The file, with summary, shall be kept by the Executive Director of AAPC indefinitely and shall be destroyed one year after the Association learns of the member's death. A Regional or Association Ethics Committee may request this file if another complaint is received or investigation is begun regarding the member. In addition, in the case of Dismissal, the file shall also be sent upon request to a Regional or Association Membership Committee if the person reapplies for membership.

   e. If a member appeals a decision for Dismissal, the member shall cease all functioning as a pastoral counselor during the appeal.

3. Decisions by the Appeal Board regarding appeals are final.

D. Notifications

1. When issued a Reprimand the member

shall report this status in writing to a present or prospective employer, including supervisors and consultants, and copies shall be sent to the Regional Ethics Chair. Notifications of a Reprimand shall be sent by the Association Ethics Chair to the member's endorsing faith group, relevant state regulatory agencies and any and all other professional organizations to which the member belongs.

2. Determinations of Reprimand or Dismissal, once the appeal time or procedures are over, are publicized to the membership in the next AAPC Newsletter. The announcement is limited to the member's full name and highest earned degree, geographical location, the fact and date of Reprimand or Dismissal and the specific Principle(s) of the Code violated. If a member is dismissed for violation of Principle 8, first paragraph (refusal or failure to cooperate with an ethics investigation at any point), all other Principles alleged to have been violated shall also be listed.

3. In the case of Dismissal, the Association Ethics Chair, once the appeal time or procedures are over, shall notify the member's endorsing faith group, relevant state regulatory agencies, and any and all other professional organizations to which the member belongs. The specific information communicated is the same as above.

E. Sexual Misconduct Cases

When a complaint is received alleging sexual misconduct or violative harassment of Principle 3.G and H, the following procedures shall pertain:

1. Upon receipt of a complaint, or information of a potential complaint, the Regional Ethics Chair shall immediately contact the AAPC Executive Director and the Association Ethics Chair to advise them of all initial information received, forwarding to the Executive Director a completed Regional Ethics Committee special report form on the matter. An investigatory process shall commence under the direct guidance of the Association's legal counsel, util-

izing Regional Ethics committee members and resources as needed.

2. The Association Ethics Chair shall appoint a three member subcommittee of Association Committee members to receive the results of the investigation and act as a Board of Review for the case. The Regional Ethics Chair of the region from which the complaint arose shall be a member of the subcommittee, barring conflicts, and will not act as chair. Only members of the Association Ethics Committee may serve on the Board of Review. However, as a matter of discretion, the Association Ethics Chair may appoint to review boards a qualified fourth member in order to attain gender, racial, cultural, faith group, or sexual orientation balance and fairness. This person may be from the membership of AAPC, or, as deemed necessary, from the general public.

3. When acting as a Board of Review, the subcommittee shall act on behalf of the Association Ethics Committee, review results of the investigations, make provision as necessary for further fact finding and reach a decision on a disposition of the matter in accordance with Procedures B.1-4. The deliberations of the Board of Review are held in executive session and upon invitation open to the member, the complainant, and their respective counsel. Investigations, deliberation of facts, conclusions, and any disciplinary actions are not intended to replicate a court of law or legal process. Reasonableness and fairness shall be the standard for the Ethics Committee process rather than strict adherence to legal rules of evidence used in court.

4. The decision of the Board of Review may be appealed by the member only when the decision involves Reprimand or Dismissal. Appeals are made to an Appeal Board, as outlined in Section C.2. (above), which has final jurisdiction. Appeals must be made within 30 days of notification of the Board of Review's findings. If litigation is pending, the Board of Review may defer its decision to the outcome of such litiga-

tion, and on an interim basis impose nonappealable terms or conditions of discipline. If new and material facts are discovered within 30 days of the decision of the Board of Review, the member or complainant may ask the Board of Review for a re-hearing, provided that no appeal has been previously taken. A re-hearing is at the sole discretion of the Board of Review.

F. Board of Emergency Review

1. To protect the public welfare, the rights of AAPC members, and the interests of the Association, a Board of Emergency Review is established. This board consists of the President, the Vice President, the Executive Director, the Deputy Executive Director, and at least one AAPC Committee Chair of a relevant committee or his/her designee. The Board of Emergency Review shall have legal counsel present whenever action is to be taken.

2. Upon notification that a member's conduct and actions appear to be so egregious that waiting for action and decision through the normal committee process presents an unacceptable level of risk to the public, the member, or the Association, the Board of Emergency Review has the authority to meet, to consider the facts, and to temporarily withdraw membership credentials pending full investigation of the case.

3. Notification shall be made to the member in writing. Further, made to the committee investigating the case. The committee shall be notified that the Board of Emergency Review's decision to temporarily withdraw the member's credentials does not constitute a finding of guilt on the charges under investigation and does not absolve the committee of its responsibility to fully investigate the charges, render a decision, and make ultimate disposition of the case.

4. Notification shall be made to outside authorities, i.e., endorsing bodies, licensing boards, and other professional organizations to which the member belongs. These bodies will be notified in writing and told that the decision of the Board of Emergency Review does not constitute a finding of guilt on any charges but was taken only to protect the interests of the public, the member and/or the AAPC.

---

[1]The AAPC Code of Ethics and the Ethics Committee Procedures were separated by action of the AAPC membership on April 17, 1993. The Board of Governors is now authorized to modify ethics committee procedures without further action by the membership. Members should note that the substantive rule from the Code of ethics to be applied to an alleged violation will continue to be determined by the date of the alleged violation and not the date the complaint is received. However, as a result of the action taken, the current procedures in effect will be followed for all complaints brought after April 17, 1993, regardless of the date of alleged violation.

[2]The use of "member", "we," "us," and "our" refers to and is binding upon all levels of individual and institutional membership and affiliation of AAPC.

AAMFT Code of Ethics

The Board of Directors of the American Association for Marriage and Family Therapy (AAMFT) hereby promulgates, pursuant to Article 2, Section 2.013 of the Association's Bylaws, the Revised AAMFT Code of Ethics, effective August 1, 1991.

The AAMFT Code of Ethics is binding on Members of AAMFT in all membership categories, AAMFT Approved Supervisors, and applicants for membership and the Approved Supervisor designation (hereafter, AAMFT Member).

If an AAMFT Member resigns in anticipation of, or during the course of an ethics investigation, the Ethics Committee will complete its investigation. Any publication of action taken by the Association will include the fact that the Member attempted to resign during the investigation.

Marriage and family therapists are strongly encouraged to report alleged unethical behavior of colleagues to appropriate professional associations and state regulatory bodies.

1. Responsibility to Clients

Marriage and family therapists advance the welfare of families and individuals. They respect the rights of those persons seeking their assistance, and make reasonable efforts to ensure that their services are used appropriately.

1.1 Marriage and family therapists do not discriminate against or refuse professional service to anyone on the basis of race, gender, religion, national origin, or sexual orientation.

1.2 Marriage and family therapists are aware of their influential position with respect to clients, and they avoid exploiting the trust and dependency of such persons. Therapists, therefore, make every effort to avoid dual relationships with clients that could impair professional judgment or increase the risk of exploitation. When a dual relationship cannot be avoided, therapists take appropriate professional precautions to ensure judgment is not impaired and no exploitation occurs. Examples of such dual relationships include, but are not limited to, business or close personal relationships with clients. Sexual intimacy with clients is prohibited. Sexual intimacy with former clients for two years following the termination of therapy is prohibited.

1.3 Marriage and family therapists do not use

their professional relationships with clients to further their own interests.

1.4 Marriage and family therapists respect the right of clients to make decisions and help them to understand the consequences of these decisions. Therapists clearly advise a client that a decision on marital status is the responsibility of the client.

1.5 Marriage and family therapists continue therapeutic relationships only so long as it is reasonably clear that clients are benefiting from the relationship.

1.6 Marriage and family therapists assist persons in obtaining other therapeutic services if the therapist is unable or unwilling, for appropriate reasons, to provide professional help.

1.7 Marriage and family therapists do not abandon or neglect clients in treatment without making reasonable arrangements for the continuation of such treatment.

1.8 Marriage and family therapists obtain written informed consent from clients before videotaping, audiorecording, or permitting third party observation.

2. Confidentiality

Marriage and family therapists have unique confidentiality concerns because the client in a therapeutic relationship may be more than one person. Therapists respect and guard confidences of each individual client.

2.1 Marriage and family therapists may not disclose client confidences except: (a) as mandated by law; (b) to prevent a clear and immediate danger to a person or persons; (c) where the therapist is a defendant in a civil, criminal, or disciplinary action arising from the therapy (in which case client confidences may be disclosed only in the course of that action); or (d) if there is a waiver previously obtained in writing, and such information may be revealed only in accordance with the terms of the waiver. In circumstances where more than one person in a family receives therapy, each such family member who is legally competent to execute a waiver must agree to the waiver required by subparagraph (d). Without such a waiver from each family member legally competent to execute a waiver, a therapist cannot disclose information received from any family member.

2.2 Marriage and family therapists use client and/or clinical materials in teaching, writing, and public presentations only if a written waiver has been obtained in accordance with Subprinciple 2.1(d), or when appropriate steps have been taken to protect client identity and confidentiality.

2.3 Marriage and family therapists store or dispose of client records in ways that maintain confidentiality,

3. Professional Competence and Integrity

Marriage and family therapists maintain high standards of professional competence and integrity.

3.1 Marriage and family therapists are in violation of this Code and subject to termination of membership or other appropriate action if they: (a) are convicted of any felony; (b) are convicted of a misdemeanor related to their qualifications or functions; (c) engage in conduct which could lead to conviction of a felony, or a misdemeanor related to their qualifications or functions; (d) are expelled from or disciplined by other professional organizations; (e) have their licenses or certificates suspended or revoked or are otherwise disciplined by regulatory bodies; (f) are no longer competent to practice marriage and family therapy because they are impaired due to physical or mental causes or the abuse of alcohol or other substances; or (g) fail to cooperate with the Association at any point from the inception of an ethical complaint through the completion of all proceedings regarding that complaint.

3.2 Marriage and family therapists seek appropriate professional assistance for their personal problems or conflicts that may impair work performance or clinical judgment.

3.3 Marriage and family therapists, as teachers, supervisors, and researchers, are dedicated to high standards of scholarship and present accurate information.

3.4 Marriage and family therapists remain abreast of new developments in family therapy knowledge and practice through educational activities.

3.5 Marriage and family therapists do not engage in sexual or other harassment or exploitation of clients, students, trainees, supervisees, employees, colleagues, research subjects, or actual or potential witnesses or complainants in investigations and ethical proceedings.

3.6 Marriage and family therapists do not diagnose, treat, or advise on problems outside the recognized boundaries of their competence.

3.7 Marriage and family therapists make efforts to prevent the distortion or misuse of their clinical and research findings.

3.8 Marriage and family therapists, because of their ability to influence and alter the lives of others, exercise special care when making public their professional recommendations and opinions through testimony or other public statements.

4. Responsibility to Students, Employees, and Supervisees

Marriage and family therapists do not exploit the trust and dependency of students, employees, and supervisees.

4.1 Marriage and family therapists are aware of their influential position with respect to students, employees, and supervisees, and they avoid exploiting the trust and dependency of such persons. Therapists, therefore, make every effort to avoid dual relationships that could impair professional judgment or increase the risk of exploitation. When a dual relationship cannot be avoided, therapists take appropriate professional precautions to ensure judgment is not impaired and no exploitation occurs. Examples of such dual relationships include, but are not limited to, business or close personal relationships with students, employees, or supervisees. Provision of therapy to students, employees, or supervisees is prohibited. Sexual intimacy with students or supervisees is prohibited.

4.2 Marriage and family therapists do not permit students, employees, or supervisees to perform or to hold themselves out as competent to perform professional services beyond their training, level of experience, and competence.

4.3 Marriage and family therapists do not disclose supervisee confidences except: (a) as mandated by law; (b) to prevent a clear and immediate danger to a person or persons; (c) where the therapist is a defendant in a civil, criminal, or disciplinary action arising from the supervision (in which case supervisee confidences may be disclosed only in the course of that action); (d) in educational or training settings where there are multiple supervisors, and then only to other professional colleagues who share responsibility for the training of the supervisee; or (e) if there is a waiver previously obtained in writing, and then such information may be revealed only in accordance with the terms of the waiver.

5. Responsibility to Research Participants

Investigators respect the dignity and protect the welfare of participants in research and are aware of federal and state laws and regulations and professional standards governing the conduct of research.

5.1 Investigators are responsible for making careful examinations of ethical acceptability in planning studies. To the extent that services to research participants may be compromised by participation in research, investigators seek the ethical advice of qualified professionals not directly involved in the investigation and observe safeguards to protect the rights of research participants.

5.2 Investigators requesting participants' involvement in research inform them of all aspects of the research that might reasonably be expected to influence willingness to participate. Investigators are especially sensitive to the possibility of diminished consent when participants are also receiving clinical services, have impairments which limit understanding and/or communication, or when participants are children.

5.3 Investigators respect participants' freedom to decline participation in or to withdraw from a research study at any time. This obligation requires special thought and consideration when investigators or other members of the research team are in positions of authority or influence over participants. Marriage and family therapists, therefore, make every effort to avoid dual relationships with research participants that could impair professional judgment or increase the risk of exploitation.

5.4 Information obtained about a research participant during the course of an investigation is confidential unless there is a waiver previously obtained in writing. When the possibility exists that others, including family members, may obtain access to such information, this possibility, together with the plan for protecting confidentiality, is explained as part of the procedure for obtaining informed consent.

6. Responsibility to the Profession

Marriage and family therapists respect the rights and responsibilities of professional colleagues and participate in activities which advance the goals of the profession.

6.1 Marriage and family therapists remain accountable to the standards of the profession when acting as members or employees of organizations.

6.2 Marriage and family therapists assign publication credit to those who have contributed to a publication in proportion to their contributions and in accordance with customary professional publication practices.

6.3 Marriage and family therapists who are the authors of books or other materials that are published or distributed cite persons to whom credit for original ideas is due.

6.4 Marriage and family therapists who are the authors of books or other materials published or distributed by an organization take reasonable precautions to ensure that the organization promotes and advertises the materials accurately and factually.

6.5 Marriage and family therapists participate in activities that contribute to a better community and society, including devoting a portion of their professional activity to services for which there is little or no financial return.

6.6 Marriage and family therapists are concerned with developing laws and regulations pertaining to marriage and family therapy that serve the public interest, and with altering such laws and regulations that are not in the public interest.

6.7 Marriage and family therapists encourage public participation in the design and delivery of professional services and in the regulation of practitioners.

7. Financial Arrangements

Marriage and family therapists make financial arrangements with clients, third party payors, and supervisees that are reasonably understandable and conform to accepted professional practices.

7.1 Marriage and family therapists do not offer or accept payment for referrals.

7.2 Marriage and family therapists do not charge excessive fees for services.

7.3 Marriage and family therapists disclose their fees to clients and supervisees at the beginning of services.

7.4 Marriage and family therapists represent

facts truthfully to clients, third party payors, and supervisees regarding services rendered.

8. Advertising

Marriage and family therapists engage in appropriate informational activities, including those that enable laypersons to choose professional services on an informed basis.

General Advertising

8.1 Marriage and family therapists accurately represent their competence, education, training, and experience relevant to their practice of marriage and family therapy.

8.2 Marriage and family therapists assure that advertisements and publications in any media (such as directories, announcements, business cards, newspapers, radio, television, and facsimiles) convey information that is necessary for the public to make an appropriate selection of professional services. Information could include: (a) office information, such as name, address, telephone number, credit card acceptability, fees, languages spoken, and office hours; (b) appropriate degrees, state licensure and/or certification, and AAMFT Clinical Member status; and (c) description of practice. (For requirements for advertising under the AAMFT name, logo, and/or the abbreviated initials AAMFT, see Subprinciple 8.15, below).

8.3 Marriage and family therapists do not use a name which could mislead the public concerning the identity, responsibility, source, and status of those practicing under that name and do not hold themselves out as being partners or associates of a firm if they are not.

8.4 Marriage and family therapists do not use any professional identification (such as a business card, office sign, letterhead, or telephone or association directory listing) if it includes a statement or claim that is false, fraudulent, misleading, or deceptive. A statement is false, fraudulent, misleading, or deceptive if it (a) contains a material misrepresentation of fact; (b) fails to state any material fact necessary to make the statement, in light of all circumstances, not misleading; or (c) is intended to or is likely to create an unjustified expectation.

8.5 Marriage and family therapists correct, wherever possible, false, misleading, or inaccurate information and representations made by others concerning the therapist's qualifications, services, or products.

8.6 Marriage and family therapists make certain that the qualifications of persons in their employ are represented in a manner that is not false, misleading, or deceptive.

8.7 Marriage and family therapists may represent themselves as specializing within a limited area of marriage and family therapy, but only if they have the education and supervised experience in settings which meet recognized professional standards to practice in that specialty area.

Advertising Using AAMFT Designations

8.8 The AAMFT designations of Clinical Member, Approved Supervisor, and Fellow may be used in public information or advertising materials only by persons holding such designations. Persons holding such designations may, for example, advertise in the following manner:

☐ *Jane Doe, Ph.D., a Clinical Member of the American Association for Marriage and Family Therapy.*
Alternately, the advertisement could read: *Jane Doe, Ph.D., AAMFT Clinical Member.*
☐ *John Doe, Ph.D., an Approved Supervisor of the American Association for marriage and Family Therapy.*
Alternately, the advertisement could read: *John Doe, Ph.D., AAMFT Approved Supervisor.*
☐ *Jane Doe, Ph.D., A Fellow of the American Association for Marriage and Family Therapy.*
Alternately, the advertisement could read: *Jane Doe, Ph.D., AAMFT Fellow.*

More than one designation may be used if held by the AAMFT Member.

8.9 Marriage and family therapists who hold the AAMFT Approved Supervisor or the Fellow designation may not represent the designation as an advanced clinical status.

8.10 Student, Associate, and Affiliate Members may not use their AAMFT membership status in public information or advertising materials. Such listings on professional resumes are not considered advertisements.

8.11 Persons applying for AAMFT membership may not list their application status on any resume or advertisement.

8.12 In conjunction with their AAMFT membership, marriage and family therapists claim as evidence of educational qualifications only those degrees (a) from regionally accredited institutions or (b) from institutions recognized by states which license or certify marriage and family therapists, but only if such state regulation is recognized by AAMFT.

8.13 Marriage and family therapists may not use the initials AAMFT following their name in the manner of an academic degree.

8.14 Marriage and family therapists may not use the AAMFT name, logo, and/or the abbreviated initials AAMFT or make any other such representation which would imply that they speak for or represent the Association. The Association is the sole owner of its name, logo, and the abbreviated initials AAMFT. Its committees and divisions, operating as such, may use the name, logo, and/or the abbreviated initials, AAMFT, in accordance with AAMFT policies.

8.15 Authorized advertisements of Clinical Members under the AAMFT name, logo, and/or the abbreviated initials AAMFT may include the following: the Clinical Member's name, degree, license or certificate held when required by state law, name of business, address, and telephone number. If a business is listed, it must follow, not precede the Clinical Member's name. Such listings may not include AAMFT offices held by the Clinical Member, nor any specializations, since such a listing under the AAMFT name, logo, and/or the abbreviated initials, AAMFT, would imply that this specialization has been credentialed by AAMFT.

8.16 Marriage and family therapists use their membership in AAMFT only in connection with their clinical and professional activities.

8.17 Only AAMFT divisions and programs accredited by the AAMFT Commission on Accreditation for Marriage and Family Therapy Education, not businesses nor organizations, may use any AAMFT-related designation or affiliation in public information or advertising materials, and then only in accordance with AAMFT policies.

8.18 Programs accredited by the AAMFT Commission on Accreditation for Marriage and Family Therapy Education may not use the AAMFT name, logo, and/or the abbreviated initials, AAMFT. They may not state in printed program materials, program advertisements, and student advisement that their courses and training opportunities are accepted by AAMFT to meet AAMFT membership requirements.

This Code is published by:

American Association for Marriage and Family Therapy
1133 15th Street, NW, Suite 300
Washington, DC 200205-2710
(202) 452-0109

Violations of this Code should be brought in writing to the attention of the AAMFT Ethics Committee, 1133 15th Street, NW, Suite 300, Washington, DC 20005-2710 (telephone 202/452-0109).

Effective August 1, 1991

Code of Ethics and Standards of Practice of the American Counseling Association

As approved by Governing Council, April 1995. Effective July 1, 1995

Preamble

The American Counseling Association is an educational, scientific and professional organization whose members are dedicated to the enhancement of human development throughout the life span. Association members recognize diversity in our society and embrace a cross-cultural approach in support of the worth, dignity, potential, and uniqueness of each individual.

The specification of a code of ethics enables the association to clarify to current and future members, and to those served by members, the nature of the ethical responsibilities held in common by its members. As the code of ethics of the association, this document establishes principles that define the ethical behavior of association members. All members of the American Counseling Association are required to adhere to the Code of Ethics and the Standards of Practice. The Code of Ethics will serve as the basis for processing ethical complaints initiated against members of the association.

Section A: The Counseling Relationship
A.1. Client Welfare

a. Primary Responsibility. The primary responsibility of counselors is to respect the dignity and to promote the welfare of clients.

b. *Positive Growth and Development.* Counselors encourage client growth and development in ways that foster the clients' interest and welfare; counselors avoid fostering dependent counseling relationships.

c. *Counseling Plans.* Counselors and their clients work jointly in devising integrated, individual counseling plans that offer reasonable promise of success and are consistent with abilities and circumstances of clients. Counselors and clients regularly review counseling plans to ensure their continued viability and effectiveness, respecting clients' freedom of choice. (See A.3.b.)

d. *Family Involvement.* Counselors recognize that families are usually important in clients' lives and strive to enlist family understanding and involvement as a positive resource, when appropriate.

e. *Career and Employment Needs.* Counselors work with their clients in considering employment in jobs and circumstances that are consistent with the clients' overall abilities, vocational limitations, physical restrictions, general temperament, interest and aptitude patterns, social skills, education, general qualifications, and other relevant characteristics and needs. Counselors neither place nor participate in placing clients in positions that will result in damaging the interest and the welfare of clients, employers, or the public.

A.2. Respecting Diversity

a. *Nondiscrimination.* Counselors do not condone or engage in discrimination based on age, color, culture, disability, ethnic group, gender, race, religion, sexual orientation, marital status, or socioeconomic status. (See C.5.a., C.5.b., and D.1.i.)

b. *Respecting Differences.* Counselors will actively attempt to understand the diverse cultural backgrounds of the clients with whom they work. This includes, but is not limited to, learning how the counselor's own cultural/ethnic/racial identity impacts her/his values and beliefs about the counseling process. (See E.8. and F.2.i.)

A.3. Client Rights

a. *Disclosure to Clients.* When counseling is initiated, and throughout the counseling process as necessary, counselors inform clients of the purposes, goals, techniques,

procedures, limitations, potential risks and benefits of services to be performed and other pertinent information. Counselors take steps to ensure that clients understand the implications of diagnosis, the intended use of tests and reports, fees, and billing arrangements. Clients have the right to expect confidentiality and to be provided with an explanation of its limitations, including supervision and/or treatment team professionals; to obtain clear information about their case records; to participate in the ongoing counseling plans; and to refuse any recommended services and be advised of the consequences of such refusal. (See E.5.a. and G.2.)

b. *Freedom of Choice.* Counselors offer clients the freedom to choose whether to enter into a counseling relationship and to determine which professional(s) will provide counseling. Restrictions that limit choices of clients are fully explained. (See A.1.c.)

c. *Inability to Give Consent.* When counseling minors or persons unable to give voluntary informed consent, counselors act in these clients' best interests. (See B.3.)

A.4. Clients Served by Others

If a client is receiving services from another mental health professional, counselors, with client consent, inform the professional persons already involved and develop clear agreements to avoid confusion and conflict for the client. (See C.6.c.)

A.5. Personal Needs and Values

a. *Personal Needs.* In the counseling relationship, counselors are aware of the intimacy and responsibilities inherent in the counseling relationship, maintain respect for clients, and avoid actions that seek to meet their personal needs at the expense of clients.

b. *Personal Values.* Counselors are aware of their own values, attitudes, beliefs, and behaviors and how these apply in a diverse society, and avoid imposing their values on clients. (See C.5.a.)

A.6. Dual Relationships

a. *Avoid When Possible.* Counselors are aware of their influential positions with respect to clients, and they avoid exploiting the trust and dependency of clients. Counselors make every effort to avoid dual relationships with clients that could impair professional judgment or increase the risk of harm to clients. (Examples of such relationships include, but are not limited to, familial, social, financial, business, or close personal relationships with clients.) When a dual relationship cannot be avoided, counselors take appropriate professional precautions such as informed consent, consultation, supervision, and documentation to ensure that judgment is not impaired and no exploitation occurs. (See F.1.b.)

b. *Superior/Subordinate Relationships.* Counselors do not accept as clients superiors or subordinates with whom they have administrative, supervisory, or evaluative relationships.

A.7. Sexual Intimacies with Clients

a. *Current Clients.* Counselors do not have any type of sexual intimacies with clients and do not counsel persons with whom they have had a sexual relationship.

b. *Former Clients.* Counselors do not engage in sexual intimacies with former clients within a minimum of two years after terminating the counseling relationship. Counselors who engage in such relationship after two years following termination have the responsibility to thoroughly examine and document that such relations did not have an exploitative nature, based on factors such as duration of counseling, amount of time since counseling, termination circumstances, client's personal history and mental status, adverse impact on the client, and actions by the counselor suggesting a plan to initiate a sexual relationship with the client after termination.

A.8. Multiple Clients

When counselors agree to provide counseling services to two or more persons who have a relationship (such as husband and wife, or parents and children), counselors clarify at the outset which person or persons are clients and the nature of the relationships they will have with each involved person. If it becomes apparent that counselors may be called upon to perform potentially conflicting roles, they clarify, adjust, or withdraw from roles appropriately. (See B.2. and B.4.d.)

A.9. Group Work

a. *Screening.* Counselors screen prospective group counseling/therapy participants. To the extent possible, counselors select members whose needs and goals are compatible with goals of the group, who will not impede the group process, and whose well-being will not be jeopardized by the group experience.

b. *Protecting Clients.* In a group setting, counselors take reasonable precautions to protect clients from physical or psychological trauma.

A.10. Fees and Bartering (See D.3.a. and D.3.b.)

a. *Advance Understanding.* Counselors clearly explain to clients, prior to entering the counseling relationship, all financial arrangements related to professional services including the use of collection agencies or legal measures for nonpayment. (A.11.c.)

b. *Establishing Fees.* In establishing fees for professional counseling services, counselors consider the financial status of clients and locality. In the event that the established fee structure is inappropriate for a client, assistance is provided in attempting to find comparable services of acceptable cost. (See A.10.d., D.3.a., and D.3.b.)

c. *Bartering Discouraged.* Counselors ordinarily refrain from accepting goods or services from clients in return for counseling services because such arrangements create inherent potential for conflicts, exploitation, and distortion of the professional relationship. Counselors may participate in bartering only if the relationship is not exploitive, if the client requests it, if a clear written contract is established, and if such arrangements are an accepted practice among professionals in the community. (See A.6.a.)

d. *Pro Bono Service.* Counselors contribute to society by devoting a portion of their professional activity to services for which there is little or no financial return (pro bono).

A.11. Termination and Referral

a. *Abandonment Prohibited.* Counselors do not abandon or neglect clients in counseling. Counselors assist in making appropriate arrangements for the continuation of treatment, when necessary, during interruptions such as vacations, and following termination.

b. *Inability to Assist Clients.* If counselors

determine an inability to be of professional assistance to clients, they avoid entering or immediately terminate a counseling relationship. Counselors are knowledgeable about referral resources and suggest appropriate alternatives. If clients decline the suggested referral, counselors should discontinue the relationship.

c. *Appropriate Termination.* Counselors terminate a counseling relationship, securing client agreement when possible, when it is reasonably clear that the client is no longer benefiting, when services are no longer required, when counseling no longer serves the client's needs or interests, when clients do not pay fees charged, or when agency or institution limits do not allow provision of further counseling services. (See A.10.b. and C.2.g.)

A.11. Computer Technology

a. *Use of Computers.* When computer applications are used in counseling services, counselors ensure that: (1) the client is intellectually, emotionally, and physically capable of using the computer application; (2) the computer application is appropriate for the needs of the client; (3) the client understands the purpose and operation of the computer applications; and (4) a follow-up of client use of a computer application is provided to correct possible misconceptions, discover inappropriate use, and assess subsequent needs.

b. *Explanation of Limitations.* Counselors ensure that clients are provided information as a part of the counseling relationship that adequately explains the limitations of computer technology.

c. *Access to Computer Applications.* Counselors provide for equal access to computer applications in counseling services. (See A.2.a.)

Section B: Confidentiality
B.1. Right to Privacy

a. *Respect for Privacy.* Counselors respect their clients' right to privacy and avoid illegal and unwarranted disclosures of confidential information. (See A.3.a. and B.6.a.)

b. *Client Waiver.* The right to privacy may be waived by the client or their legally recognized representative.

c. *Exceptions.* The general requirement that counselors keep information confidential does not apply when disclosure is required to prevent clear and imminent danger to the client or others or when legal requirements demand that confidential information be revealed. Counselors consult with other professionals when in doubt as to the validity of an exception.

d. *Contagious, Fatal Diseases.* A counselor who receives information confirming that a client has a disease commonly known to be both communicable and fatal is justified in disclosing information to an identifiable third party, who by his or her relationship with the client is at a high risk of contracting the disease. Prior to making a disclosure the counselor should ascertain that the client has not already informed the third party about his or her disease and that the client is not intending to inform the third party in the immediate future. (See B.1.c and B.1.f.)

e. *Court Ordered Disclosure.* When court ordered to release confidential information without a client's permission, counselors request to the court that the disclosure not be required due to potential harm to the client or counseling relationship. (See B.1.c.)

f. *Minimal Disclosure.* When circumstances require the disclosure of confidential information, only essential information is revealed. To the extent possible, clients are informed before confidential information is disclosed.

g. *Explanation of Limitations.* When counseling is initiated and throughout the counseling process as necessary, counselors inform clients of the limitations of confidentiality and identify foreseeable situations in which confidentiality must be breached. (See G.2.a.)

h. *Subordinates.* Counselors make every effort to ensure that privacy and confidentiality of clients are maintained by subordinates including employees, supervisees, clerical assistants, and volunteers. (See B.1.a.)

i. *Treatment Teams.* If client treatment will involve a continued review by a treatment team, the client will be informed of the team's existence and composition.

B.2. Groups and Families

a. *Group Work.* In group work, counselors clearly define confidentiality and the parameters for the specific group being entered, explain its importance, and discuss the difficulties related to confidentiality involved in group work. The fact that confidentiality cannot be guaranteed is clearly communicated to group members.

b. *Family Counseling.* In family counseling, information about one family member cannot be disclosed to another member without permission. Counselors protect the privacy rights of each family member. (See A.8., B.3., and B.4.d.)

B.3 Minor or Incompetent Clients

When counseling clients who are minors or individuals who are unable to give voluntary, informed consent, parents or guardians may be included in the counseling process as appropriate. Counselors act in the best interests of clients and take measures to safeguard confidentiality. (See A.3.c.)

B.4. Records

a. *Requirement of Records.* Counselors maintain records necessary for rendering professional services to their clients and as required by laws, regulations, or agency or institution procedures.

b. *Confidentiality of Records.* Counselors are responsible for securing the safety and confidentiality of any counseling records they create, maintain, transfer, or destroy whether the records are written, taped, computerized, or stored in any other medium. (See B.1.a.)

c. *Permission to Record or Observe.* Counselors obtain permission from clients prior to electronically recording or observing sessions. (See A.3.a.)

d. *Client Access.* Counselors recognize that counseling records are kept for the benefit of clients, and therefore provide access to records and copies of records when requested by competent clients, unless the records contain information that may be misleading and detrimental to the client. In situations involving multiple clients, access to records is limited to those parts of records that do not include confidential information related to another client. (See A.8., B.1.a., and B.2.b.)

e. *Disclosure or Transfer.* Counselors obtain written permission from clients to disclose or transfer records to legitimate third parties unless exceptions to confidentiality exist as listed in Section B.1. Steps are taken to ensure that receivers of counseling records are sensitive to their confidential nature.

B.5. Research and Training

a. *Data Disguise Required.* Use of data derived from counseling relationships for purposes of training, research, or publication is confined to content that is disguised to ensure the anonymity of the individuals involved. (See B.1.g. and G.3.d.)

b. *Agreement for Identification.* Identification of a client in a presentation or publication is permissible only when the client has reviewed the material and has agreed to its presentation or publication. (See G.3.d.)

B.6. Consultation

a. *Respect for Privacy.* Information obtained in a consulting relationship is discussed for professional purposes only with persons clearly concerned with the case. Written and oral reports present data germane to the purposes of the consultation, and every effort is made to protect client identity and avoid undue invasion of privacy.

b. *Cooperating Agencies.* Before sharing information, counselors make efforts to ensure that there are defined policies in other agencies serving the counselor's clients that effectively protect the confidentiality of information.

Section C: Professional Responsibility
C.1. Standards Knowledge

Counselors have a responsibility to read, understand, and follow the Code of Ethics and the Standards of Practice.

C.2. Professional Competence

a. *Boundaries of Competence.* Counselors practice only within the boundaries of their competence, based on their education, training, supervised experience, state and national professional credentials, and appropriate professional experience. Counselors will demonstrate a commitment to gain knowledge, personal awareness, sensitivity, and skills pertinent to working with a diverse client population.

b. *New Specialty Areas of Practice.* Counselors practice in specialty areas new to them only after appropriate education, training, and supervised experience. While developing skills in new specialty areas, counselors take steps to ensure the competence of their work and to protect others from possible harm.

c. *Qualified for Employment.* Counselors accept employment only for positions for which they are qualified by education, training, supervised experience, state and national professional credentials, and appropriate professional experience. Counselors hire for professional counseling positions only individuals who are qualified and competent.

d. *Monitor Effectiveness.* Counselors continually monitor their effectiveness as professionals and take steps to improve when necessary. Counselors in private practice take reasonable steps to seek out peer supervision to evaluate their efficacy as counselors.

e. *Ethical Issues Consultation.* Counselors take reasonable steps to consult with other counselors or related professionals when they have questions regarding their ethical obligations or professional practice. (See H.1.)

f. *Continuing Education.* Counselors recognize the need for continuing education to maintain a reasonable level of awareness of current scientific and professional information in their fields of activity. They take steps to maintain competence in the skills they use, are open to new procedures, and keep current with the diverse and/or special populations with whom they work.

g. *Impairment.* Counselors refrain from offering or accepting professional services when their physical, mental or emotional problems are likely to harm a client or others. They are alert to the signs of impairment, seek assistance for problems, and, if necessary, limit, suspend, or terminate their professional responsibilities. (See A.11.c.)

C.3. Advertising and Soliciting Clients

a. *Accurate Advertising.* There are no restrictions on advertising by counselors except those that can be specifically justified to protect the public from deceptive practices. Counselors advertise or represent their services to the public by identifying their credentials in an accurate manner that is not false, misleading, deceptive, or fraudulent. Counselors may only advertise the highest degree earned which is in counseling or a closely related field from a college or university that was accredited when the degree was awarded by one of the regional accrediting bodies recognized by the Council on Postsecondary Accreditation.

b. *Testimonials.* Counselors who use testimonials do not solicit them from clients or other persons who, because of their particular circumstances, may be vulnerable to undue influence.

c. *Statements by Others.* Counselors make reasonable efforts to ensure that statements made by others about them or the profession of counseling are accurate.

d. *Recruiting Through Employment.* Counselors do not use their places of employment or institutional affiliation to recruit or gain clients, supervisees, or consultees for their private practices. (See C.5.e.)

e. *Products and Training Advertisements.* Counselors who develop products related to their profession or conduct workshops or training events ensure that the advertisements concerning these products or events are accurate and disclose adequate information for consumers to make informed choices.

f. *Promoting to Those Served.* Counselors do not use counseling, teaching, training, or supervisory relationships to promote their products or training events in a manner that is deceptive or would exert undue influence on individuals who may be vulnerable. Counselors may adopt textbooks they have authored for instruction purposes.

g. *Professional Association Involvement.* Counselors actively participate in local, state, and national associations that foster the development and improvement of counseling.

C.4. Credentials

a. *Credentials Claimed.* Counselors claim or imply only professional credentials possessed and are responsible for correcting any known misrepresentations of their credentials by others. Professional credentials include graduate degrees in counseling or closely related mental health fields, accreditation of graduate programs, national voluntary certifications, government-issued certifications or licenses, ACA professional membership, or any other credential that might indicate to the public specialized knowledge or expertise in counseling.

b. *ACA Professional Membership.* ACA professional members may announce to the public their membership status. Regular members may not announce their ACA membership in a manner that might imply they are credentialed counselors.

c. *Credential Guidelines.* Counselors follow the guidelines for use of credentials that have been established by the entities that issue the credentials.

d. *Misrepresentation of Credentials.* Counselors do not attribute more to their credentials than the credentials represent, and do not imply that other counselors are not qualified because they do not possess certain credentials.

e. *Doctoral Degrees From Other Fields.* Counselors who hold a master's degree in counseling or a closely related mental health field, but hold a doctoral degree from other than counseling or a closely related field do not use the title "Dr." in their practices and do not announce to the public in relation to their practice or status as a counselor that they hold a doctorate.

C.5. Public Responsibility

a. *Nondiscrimination.* Counselors do not discriminate against clients, students, or supervisees in a manner that has a negative impact based on their age, color, culture, disability, ethnic group, gender, race, religion, sexual orientation, or socioeconomic status, or for any other reason. (See A.2.a.)

b. *Sexual Harassment.* Counselors do not engage in sexual harassment. Sexual harassment is defined as sexual solicitation, physical advances, or verbal or nonverbal conduct that is sexual in nature, that occurs in connection with professional activities or roles, and that either: (1) is unwelcome, is offensive, or creates a hostile workplace environment, and counselors know or are told this; or (2) is sufficiently severe or intense to be perceived as harassment to a reasonable person in the context. Sexual harassment can consist of a single intense or severe act or multiple persistent or pervasive acts.

c. *Reports to Third Parties.* Counselors are accurate, honest, and unbiased in reporting their professional activities and judgments to appropriate third parties including courts, health insurance companies, those who are the recipients of evaluation reports, and others. (See B.1.g.)

d. *Media Presentations.* When counselors provide advice or comment by means of public lectures, demonstrations, radio or television programs, pre-recorded tapes, printed articles, mailed material, or other media, they take reasonable precautions to ensure that (1) the statements are based on appropriate professional counseling literature and practice; (2) the statements are otherwise consistent with the Code of Ethics and the Standards of Practice; and (3) the recipients of the information are not encouraged to infer that a professional counseling relationship has been established. (See C.6.b.)

e. *Unjustified Gains.* Counselors do not use their professional positions to seek or receive unjustified personal gains, sexual favors, unfair advantage, or unearned goods or services. (See C.3.d.)

C.6. Responsibility to Other Professionals

a. *Different Approaches.* Counselors are respectful of approaches to professional counseling that differ from their own. Counselors know and take into account the traditions and practices of other professional groups with which they work.

b. *Personal Public Statements.* When making personal statements in a public context, counselors clarify that they are speaking from their personal perspectives and that they are not speaking on behalf of all counselors or the profession. (See C.5.d.)

c. *Clients Served by Others.* When counselors learn that their clients are in a professional relationship with another mental health professional, they request release from clients to inform the other professionals and strive to establish positive and collaborative professional relationships. (See A.4.)

Section D: Relationships with Other Professionals

D.1. Relationships with Employers and Employees

a. *Role Definition.* Counselors define and describe for their employers and employees the parameters and levels of their professional roles.

b. *Agreements.* Counselors establish working agreements with supervisors, colleagues, and subordinates regarding counseling or clinical relationships, confidentiality, adherence to professional standards, distinction between public and private material, maintenance and dissemination of recorded information, workload, and accountability. Working agreements in each instance are specified and made known to those concerned.

c. *Negative Conditions.* Counselors alert their employers to conditions that may be potentially disruptive or damaging to the counselor's professional responsibilities or that may limit their effectiveness.

d. *Evaluation.* Counselors submit regularly to professional review and evaluation by their supervisor or the appropriate representative of the employer.

e. *In-Service.* Counselors are responsible for in-service development of self and staff.

f. *Goals.* Counselors inform their staff of goals and programs.

g. *Practices.* Counselors provide personnel and agency practices that respect and enhance the rights and welfare of each employee and recipient of agency services. Counselors strive to maintain the highest levels of professional services.

h. *Personnel Selection and Assignment.* Counselors select competent staff and assign responsibilities compatible with their skills and experiences.

i. *Discrimination.* Counselors, as either employers or employees, do not engage in or condone practices that are inhumane, illegal, or unjustifiable (such as considerations based on age, color, culture, disability, ethnic group, gender, race, religion, sexual orientation, or socioeconomic status) in hiring, promotion, or training. (See A.2.a. and C.5.b.)

j. *Professional Conduct.* Counselors have a responsibility both to clients and to the agency or institution within which services are performed to maintain high standards of professional conduct.

k. *Exploitive Relationships.* Counselors do not engage in exploitive relationships with individuals over whom they have supervisory, evaluative, or instructional control or authority.

l. *Employer Policies.* The acceptance of employment in an agency or institution implies that counselors are in agreement with its general policies and principles. Counselors strive to reach agreement with employers as to acceptable standards of conduct that allow for changes in institutional policy conducive to the growth and development of clients.

D.2. Consultation (See B.6.)

a. *Consultation as an Option.* Counselors may choose to consult with any other professionally competent persons about their clients. In choosing consultants, counselors avoid placing the consultant in a conflict of interest situation that would preclude the consultant being a proper party to the counselor's efforts to help the client. Should counselors be engaged in a work setting that compromises this consultation standard, they consult with other professionals whenever possible to consider justifiable alternatives.

b. *Consultant Competency.* Counselors are reasonably certain that they have or the organization represented has the necessary competencies and resources for giving the kind of consulting services needed and that appropriate referral resources are available.

c. *Understanding with Clients.* When providing consultation, counselors attempt to develop with their clients a clear understanding of problem definition, goals for change, and predicted consequences of interventions selected.

d. *Consultant Goals.* The consulting relationship is one in which client adaptability and growth toward self-direction are consistently encouraged and cultivated. (See A.1.b.)

D.3. Fees for Referral

a. *Accepting Fees from Agency Clients.* Counselors refuse a private fee or other remuneration for rendering services to persons who are entitled to such services through the counselor's employing agency or institution. The policies of a particular agency may make explicit provisions for agency clients to receive counseling services from members of its staff in private practice. In such instances, the clients must be informed of other options open to them should they seek private counseling services. (See A.10.a., A.11.b., and C.3.d.)

b. *Referral Fees.* Counselors do not accept a referral fee from other professionals.

D.4. Subcontractor Arrangements

When counselors work as subcontractors for counseling services for a third party, they have a duty to inform clients of the limitations of confidentiality that the organization may place on counselors in providing counseling services to clients. The limits of such confidentiality ordinarily are discussed as part of the intake session. (See B.1.e. and B.1.f.)

Section E: Evaluation, Assessment, and Interpretation
E.1. General

a. *Appraisal Techniques.* The primary purpose of educational and psychological assessment is to provide measures that are objective and interpretable in either comparative or absolute terms. Counselors recognize the need to interpret the statements in this section as applying to the whole range of appraisal techniques, including test and nontest data.

b. *Client Welfare.* Counselors promote the welfare and best interests of the client in the development, publication, and utilization of educational and psychological assessment techniques. They do not misuse assessment results and interpretations and take reasonable steps to prevent others from misusing the information these techniques provide. They respect the client's right to know the results, the interpretations made, and the bases for their conclusions and recommendations.

E.2. Competence to Use and Interpret Tests

a. *Limits of Competence.* Counselors recognize the limits of their competence and perform only those testing and assessment services for which they have been trained. They are familiar with reliability, validity, related standardization, error of measurement, and proper application of any technique utilized. Counselors using computer-based test interpretations are trained in the construct being measured and the specific instrument being used prior to using this type of computer application. Counselors take reasonable measures to ensure the proper use of psychological assessment techniques by persons under their supervision.

b. *Appropriate Use.* Counselors are responsible for the appropriate application, scoring, interpretation, and use of assessment instruments, whether they score and interpret such tests themselves or use computerized or other services.

c. *Decisions Based on Results.* Counselors responsible for decisions involving individuals or policies that are based on assessment results have a thorough understanding of educational and psychological measurement, including validation criteria, test research, and guidelines for test development and use.

d. *Accurate Information.* Counselors provide accurate information and avoid false claims or misconceptions when making statements about assessment instruments or techniques. Special efforts are made to avoid

unwarranted connotations of such terms as IQ and grade equivalent scores. (See C.5.c.)

E.3. Informed Consent

a. *Explanation to Clients.* Prior to assessment, counselors explain the nature and purposes of assessment and the specific use of results in language the client (or other legally authorized person on behalf of the client) can understand unless an explicit exception to this right has been agreed upon in advance. Regardless of whether scoring and interpretation are completed by counselors, by assistants, or by computer or other outside services, counselors take reasonable steps to ensure that appropriate explanations are given to the client.

b. *Recipients of Results.* The examinee's welfare, explicit understanding, and prior agreement determine the recipients of test results. Counselors include accurate and appropriate interpretations with any release of individual or group test results. (See B.1.a. and C.5.c.)

E.4. Release of Information to Competent Professionals

a. *Misuse of Results.* Counselors do not misuse assessment results, including test results, and interpretations, and take reasonable steps to prevent the misuse of such by others. (See C.5.c.)

b. *Release of Raw Data.* Counselors ordinarily release data (e.g., protocols, counseling or interview notes, or questionnaires) in which the client is identified only with the consent of the client or the client's legal representative. Such data are usually released only to persons recognized by counselors as competent to interpret the data. (See B.1.a.)

E.5. Proper Diagnosis of Mental Disorders

a. *Proper Diagnosis.* Counselors take special care to provide proper diagnosis of mental disorders. Assessment techniques (including personal interview) used to determine client care (e.g., locus of treatment, type of treatment, or recommended follow-up) are carefully selected and appropriately used. (See A.3.a. and C.5.c.)

b. *Cultural Sensitivity.* Counselors recognize that culture affects the manner in which clients' problems are defined. Clients' socioeconomic and cultural experience is considered when diagnosing mental disorders.

E.6. Test Selection

a. *Appropriateness of Instruments.* Counselors carefully consider the validity, reliability, psychometric limitations, and appropriateness of instruments when selecting tests for use in a given situation or with a particular client.

b. *Culturally Diverse Populations.* Counselors are cautious when selecting tests for culturally diverse populations to avoid inappropriateness of testing that may be outside of socialized behavioral or cognitive patterns.

E.7. Conditions of Test Administration

a. *Administration Conditions.* Counselors administer tests under the same conditions that were established in their standardization. When tests are not administered under standard conditions or when unusual behavior or irregularities occur during the testing session, those conditions are noted in interpretation, and the results may be designated as invalid or of questionable validity.

b. *Computer Administration.* Counselors are responsible for ensuring that administration programs function properly to provide clients with accurate results when a computer or other electronic methods are used for test administration. (See A.12.b.)

c. *Unsupervised Test-Taking.* Counselors do not permit unsupervised or inadequately supervised use of tests or assessments unless the tests or assessments are designed, intended, and validated for self-administration and/or scoring.

d. *Disclosure of Favorable Conditions.* Prior to test administration, conditions that produce most favorable test results are made known to the examinee.

E.8. Diversity in Testing

Counselors are cautious in using assessment techniques, making evaluations, and interpreting the performance of populations not represented in the norm group on which an instrument was standardized. They recognize the effects of age, color, culture, disability, ethnic group, gender, race, religion, sexual orientation, and socioeconomic status on test administration and interpretation and place test results in proper perspective with

other relevant factors. (See A.2.a.)

E.9. Test Scoring and Interpretation

a. *Reporting Reservations.* In reporting assessment results, counselors indicate any reservations that exist regarding validity or reliability because of the circumstances of the assessment or the inappropriateness of the norms for the person tested.

b. *Research Instruments.* Counselors exercise caution when interpreting the results of research instruments possessing insufficient technical data to support respondent results. The specific purposes for the use of such instruments are stated explicitly to the examinee.

c. *Testing Services.* Counselors who provide test scoring and test interpretation services to support the assessment process confirm the validity of such interpretations. They accurately describe the purpose, norms, validity, reliability, and applications of the procedures and any special qualifications applicable to their use. The public offering of an automated test interpretations service is considered a professional-to-professional consultation. The formal responsibility of the consultant is to the consultee, but the ultimate and overriding responsibility is to the client.

E.10. Test Security

Counselors maintain the integrity and security of tests and other assessment techniques consistent with legal and contractual obligations. Counselors do not appropriate, reproduce, or modify published tests or parts thereof without acknowledgment and permission from the publisher.

E.11. Obsolete Tests and Outdated Test Results

Counselors do not use data or test results that are obsolete or outdated for the current purpose. Counselors make every effort to prevent the misuse of obsolete measures and test data by others.

E.12. Test Construction

Counselors use established scientific procedures, relevant standards, and current professional knowledge for test design in the development, publication, and utilization of educational and psychological assessment techniques.

Section F: Teaching, Training, and Supervision

F.1. Counselor Educators and Trainers

a. *Educators as Teachers and Practitioners.* Counselors who are responsible for developing, implementing, and supervising educational programs are skilled as teachers and practitioners. They are knowledgeable regarding the ethical, legal, and regulatory aspects of the profession, are skilled in applying that knowledge, and make students and supervisees aware of their responsibilities. Counselors conduct counselor education and training programs in an ethical manner and serve as role models for professional behavior. Counselor educators should make an effort to infuse material related to human diversity into all courses and/or workshops that are designed to promote the development of professional counselors.

b. *Relationship Boundaries with Students and Supervisees.* Counselors clearly define and maintain ethical, professional, and social relationship boundaries with their students and supervisees. They are aware of the differential in power that exists and the student's or supervisee's possible incomprehension of that power differential. Counselors explain to students and supervisees the potential for the relationship to become exploitive.

c. *Sexual Relationships.* Counselors do not engage in sexual relationships with students or supervisees and do not subject them to sexual harassment. (See A.6. and C.5.b.)

d. *Contributions to Research.* Counselors give credit to students or supervisees for their contributions to research and scholarly projects. Credit is given through coauthorship, acknowledgment, footnote statement, or other appropriate means, in accordance with such contributions. (See G.4.b. and G.4.c.)

e. *Close Relatives.* Counselors do not accept close relatives as students or supervisees.

f. *Supervision Preparation.* Counselors who offer clinical supervision services are adequately prepared in supervision methods and techniques. Counselors who are doctoral students serving as practicum or internship supervisors to master's level students are adequately prepared and supervised by the training program.

g. *Responsibility for Services to Clients.* Counselors who supervise the counseling services of others take reasonable measures to ensure that counseling services provided to clients are professional.

h. *Endorsement.* Counselors do not endorse students or supervisees for certification, licensure, employment, or completion of an academic or training program if they believe students or supervisees are not qualified for the endorsement. Counselors take reasonable steps to assist students or supervisees who are not qualified for endorsement to become qualified.

F.2. Counselor Education and Training Programs

a. *Orientation.* Prior to admission, counselors orient prospective students to the counselor education or training program's expectations, including but not limited to the following: (1) the type and level of skill acquisition required for successful completion of the training, (2) subject matter to be covered, (3) basis for evaluation, (4) training components that encourage self-growth or self-disclosure as part of the training process, (5) the type of supervision settings and requirements of the sites for required clinical field experiences, (6) student and supervisee evaluation and dismissal policies and procedures, and (7) up-to-date employment prospects for graduates.

b. *Integration of Study and Practice.* Counselors establish counselor education and training programs that integrate academic study and supervised practice.

c. *Evaluation.* Counselors clearly state to students and supervisees, in advance of training, the levels of competency expected, appraisal methods, and timing of evaluations for both didactic and experiential components. Counselors provide students and supervisees with periodic performance appraisal and evaluation feedback throughout the training program.

d. *Teaching Ethics.* Counselors make students and supervisees aware of the ethical responsibilities and standards of the profession and the students' and supervisees' ethical responsibilities to the profession. (See C.1. and F.3.e.)

e. *Peer Relationships.* When students or supervisees are assigned to lead counseling groups or provide clinical supervision for their peers, counselors take steps to ensure that students and supervisees placed in these roles do not have personal or adverse relationships with peers and that they understand they have the same ethical obligations as counselor educators, trainers, and supervisors. Counselors make every effort to ensure that the rights of peers are not compromised when students or supervisees are assigned to lead counseling groups or provide clinical supervision.

f. *Varied Theoretical Positions.* Counselors present varied theoretical positions so that students and supervisees may make comparisons and have opportunities to develop their own positions. Counselors provide information concerning the scientific bases of professional practice. (See C.6.a.)

g. *Field Placements.* Counselors develop clear policies within their training program regarding field placement and other clinical experiences. Counselors provide clearly stated roles and responsibilities for the student or supervisee, the site supervisor, and the program supervisor. They confirm that site supervisors are qualified to provide supervision and are informed of their professional and ethical responsibilities in this role.

h. *Dual Relationships as Supervisors.* Counselors avoid dual relationships such as performing the role of site supervisor and training program supervisor in the student's or supervisee's training program. Counselors do not accept any form of professional services, fees, commissions, reimbursement, or remuneration from a site for student or supervisee placement.

i. *Diversity in Programs.* Counselors are responsive to their institution's and program's recruitment and retention needs for training program administrators, faculty, and students with diverse backgrounds and special needs. (See A.2.a.)

F.3. Students and Supervisees

a. *Limitations.* Counselors, through ongoing evaluation and appraisal, are aware of the academic and personal limitations of students and supervisees that might impede performance. Counselors assist students and supervisees in securing remedial assistance when needed, and dismiss from the training program supervisees who are unable to provide competent service due to academic or personal limitations. Counselors seek professional consultation and document their decision to dismiss or refer students or supervisees for assistance. Counselors assure that students and supervisees have recourse to address decisions made, to require them to seek assistance, or to dismiss them.

b. *Self-Growth Experiences.* Counselors use professional judgment when designing training experiences conducted by the counselors themselves that require student and supervisee self-growth or self-disclosure. Safeguards are provided so that students and supervisees are aware of the ramifications their self-disclosure may have, on counselors whose primary role as teacher, trainer, or supervisor requires acting on ethical obligations to the profession. Evaluative components of experiential training experiences explicitly delineate predetermined academic standards that are separate and not dependent on the student's level of self-disclosure. (See A.6.)

c. *Counseling for Students and Supervisees.* If students or supervisees request counseling, supervisors or counselor educators provide them with acceptable referrals. Supervisors or counselor educators do not serve as counselor to students or supervisees over whom they hold administrative, teaching, or evaluative roles unless this is a brief role associated with a training experience. (See A.6.b.)

d. *Clients of Students and Supervisees.* Counselors make every effort to ensure that the clients at field placements are aware of the services rendered and the qualifications of the students and supervisees rendering those services. Clients receive professional disclosure information and are informed of the limits of confidentiality. Client permission is obtained in order for the students and supervisees to use any information concerning the counseling relationship in the training process. (See B.1.e.)

e. *Standards for Students and Supervisees.* Students and supervisees preparing to become counselors adhere to the Code of Ethics and the Standards of Practice. Students and supervisees have the same obligations to clients as those required of counselors. (See H.1.)

Section G: Research and Publication
G.1. Research Responsibilities

a. *Use of Human Subjects.* Counselors plan, design, conduct, and report research in a manner consistent with pertinent ethical principles, federal and state laws, host institutional regulations, and scientific standards governing research with human subjects. Counselors design and conduct research that reflects cultural sensitivity appropriateness.

b. *Deviation from Standard Practices.* Counselors seek consultation and observe stringent safeguards to protect the rights of research participants when a research problem suggests a deviation from standard acceptable practices. (See B.6.)

c. *Precautions to Avoid Injury.* Counselors who conduct research with human subjects are responsible for the subjects' welfare throughout the experiment and take reasonable precautions to avoid causing injurious psychological, physical, or social effects to their subjects.

d. *Principal Researcher Responsibility.* The ultimate responsibility for ethical research practice lies with the principal researcher. All others involved in the research activities share ethical obligations and full responsibility for their own actions.

e. *Minimal Interference.* Counselors take reasonable precautions to avoid causing disruptions in subjects' lives due to participation in research.

f. *Diversity.* Counselors are sensitive to diversity and research issues with special populations. They seek consultation when appropriate. (See A.2.a. and B.6.)

G.2. Informed Consent

a. *Topics Disclosed.* In obtaining informed consent for research, counselors use language that is understandable to research participants and that: (1) accurately explains the purpose and procedures to be followed; (2) identifies any procedures that are experimental or relatively untried; (3) describes the attendant discomforts and risks; (4) describes the benefits or changes in individuals or organizations that might be reasonably expected; (5) discloses appropriate alternative procedures that would be advantageous for subjects; (6) offers to answer any inquiries concerning the procedures; (7) describes any limitations on confidentiality; and (8) instructs that subjects are free to withdraw their consent and to discontinue participation in the project at any time. (See B.1.f.)

b. *Deception.* Counselors do not conduct research involving deception unless alternative procedures are not feasible and the prospective value of the research justifies the deception. When the methodological requirements of a study necessitate concealment or deception, the investigator is required to explain clearly the reasons for this action as soon as possible.

c. *Voluntary Participation.* Participation in research is typically voluntary and without any penalty for refusal to participate. Involuntary participation is appropriate only when it can be demonstrated that participation will have no harmful effects on subjects and is essential to the investigation.

d. *Confidentiality of Information.* Information obtained about research participants during the course of an investigation is confidential. When the possibility exists that others may obtain access to such information, ethical research practice requires that the possibility, together with the plans for protecting confidentiality, be explained to participants as a part of the procedure for obtaining informed consent. (See B.1.e.)

e. *Persons Incapable of Giving Informed Consent.* When a person is incapable of giving informed consent, counselors provide an appropriate explanation, obtain agreement for participation and obtain appropriate consent from a legally authorized person.

f. *Commitments to Participants.* Counselors take reasonable measures to honor all commitments to research participants.

g. *Explanations After Data Collection.* After data are collected, counselors provide participants with full clarification of the nature of the study to remove any misconceptions. Where scientific or human values justify delaying or withholding information, counselors take reasonable measures to avoid causing harm.

h. *Agreements to Cooperate.* Counselors who agree to cooperate with another individual in research or publication incur an obligation to cooperate as promised in terms of punctuality of performance and with regard to the completeness and accuracy of the information required.

i. *Informed Consent for Sponsors.* In the pursuit of research, counselors give sponsors, institutions, and publication channels the same respect and opportunity for giving informed consent that they accord to individual research participants. Counselors are aware of their obligation to future research workers and ensure that host institutions are given feedback information and proper acknowledgment.

G.3. Reporting Results

a. *Information Affecting Outcome.* When reporting research results, counselors explicitly mention all variables and conditions known to the investigator that may have affected the outcome of a study or the interpretation of data.

b. *Accurate Results.* Counselors plan, conduct, and report research accurately and in a manner that minimizes the possibility that results will be misleading. They provide thorough discussions of the limitations of their data and alternative hypotheses. Counselors do not engage in fraudulent research, distort data, misrepresent data, or deliberately bias their results.

c. *Obligation to Report Unfavorable Results.* Counselors communicate to other counselors the results of any research judged to be of professional value. Results that reflect unfavorably on institutions, programs, services, prevailing opinions, or vested interests are not withheld.

d. *Identity of Subjects.* Counselors who supply data, aid in the research of another person, report research results, or make original data available take due care to disguise the identity of respective subjects in the absence of specific authorization from the subjects to do otherwise. (See B.1.g. and B.5.a.)

e. *Replication Studies.* Counselors are obligated to make available sufficient original research data to qualified professionals who may wish to replicate the study.

G.4. Publication

a. *Recognition of Others.* When conducting and reporting research, counselors are familiar with and give recognition to previous work on the topic, observe copyright laws, and give full credit to those to whom credit is due. (See F.1.d. and G.4.c.)

b. *Contributors.* Counselors give credit through joint authorship, acknowledgment, footnote statements, or other appropriate means to those who have contributed significantly to research or concept development in accordance with such contributions. The principal contributor is listed first and minor technical or professional contributions are acknowledged in notes or introductory statements.

c. *Student Research.* For an article that is substantially based on a student's dissertation or thesis, the student is listed as the principal author. (See F.1.d. and G.4.a.)

d. *Duplicate Submission.* Counselors submit manuscripts for consideration to only one journal at a time. Manuscripts that are published in whole or in substantial part in another journal or published work are not submitted for publication without acknowledgment and permission from the previous publication.

e. *Professional Review.* Counselors who review material submitted for publication, research, or other scholarly purposes respect the confidentiality and proprietary rights of those who submitted it.

Section H: Resolving Ethical Issues
H.1. Knowledge of Standards

Counselors are familiar with the Code of Ethics and the Standards of Practice and other applicable ethics codes from other professional organizations of which they are member, or from certification and licensure bodies. Lack of knowledge or misunderstanding of an ethical responsibility is not a defense against a charge of unethical conduct. (See F.3.e.)

H.2. Suspected Violations

a. *Ethical Behavior Expected.* Counselors expect professional associates to adhere to Code of Ethics. When counselors possess reasonable cause that raises doubts as to whether a counselor is acting in an ethical manner, they take appropriate action. (See H.2.d. and H.2.e.)

b. *Consultation.* When uncertain as to whether a particular situation or course of action may be in violation of Code of Ethics, counselors consult with other counselors who are knowledgeable about ethics, with colleagues, or with appropriate authorities.

c. *Organization Conflicts.* If the demands of an organization with which counselors are affiliated pose a conflict with Code of Ethics, counselors specify the nature of such conflicts and express to their supervisors or other responsible officials their commitment to Code of Ethics. When possible, counselors work toward change within the organization to allow full adherence to Code of Ethics.

d. *Informal Resolution.* When counselors have reasonable cause to believe that another counselor is violating an ethical standard, they attempt to first resolve the issue informally with the other counselor if feasible, providing that such action does not violate confidentiality rights that may be involved.

e. *Reporting Suspected Violations.* When an informal resolution is not appropriate or feasible, counselors, upon reasonable cause, take action such as reporting the suspected ethical violation to state or national ethics committees, unless this action conflicts with confidentiality rights that cannot be resolved.

f. *Unwarranted Complaints.* Counselors do not initiate, participate in, or encourage the filing of ethics complaints that are unwarranted or intend to harm a counselor rather than to protect clients or the public.

H.3. Cooperation with Ethics Committees

Counselors assist in the process of enforcing Code of Ethics. Counselors cooperate with investigations, proceedings, and requirements of the ACA Ethics Committee or ethics committees of other duly constituted associations or boards having jurisdiction over those charged with a violation. Counselors are familiar with the ACA Policies and Procedures and use it as a reference in assisting the enforcement of the Code of Ethics.

Standards of Practice

All members of the American Counseling Association (ACA) are required to adhere to the Standards of Practice and the Code of Ethics. The Standards of Practice represent minimal behavioral statements of the Code of Ethics. Members should refer to the applicable section of the Code of Ethics for further interpretation and amplification of the applicable Standard of Practice.

Section A: The Counseling Relationship

Standard of Practice One (SP-1): Nondiscrimination. Counselors respect diversity and must not discriminate against clients because of age, color, culture, disability, ethnic group, gender, race, religion, sexual orientation, marital status, or socioeconomic status. (See A.2.a.)

Standard of Practice Two (SP-2): Disclosure to Clients. Counselors must adequately inform clients, preferably in writing, regarding the counseling process and counseling relationship at or before the time it begins and throughout the relationship. (See A.3.a.)

Standard of Practice Three (SP-3): Dual Relationships. Counselors must make every effort to avoid dual relationships with clients that could impair their professional judgment or increase the risk of harm to clients. When a dual relationship cannot be avoided, counselors must take appropriate steps to ensure that judgment is not impaired and that no exploitation occurs. (See A.6.a. and A.6.b.)

Standard of Practice Four (SP-4): Sexual Intimacies with Clients. Counselors must not engage in any type of sexual intimacies with current clients and must not engage in sexual intimacies with former clients within a minimum of two years after terminating the counseling relationship. Counselors who engage in such relationship after two years following termination have the responsibility to thoroughly examine and document that such relations did not have an exploitative nature.

Standard of Practice Five (SP-5): Protecting Clients During Group Work. Counselors must take steps to protect clients from physical or psychological trauma resulting from interactions during group work. (See A.9.b.)

Standard of Practice Six (SP-6): Advance Understanding of Fees. Counselors must explain to clients, prior to their entering the counseling relationship, financial arrangements related to professional services. (See A.10.a-d. and A.11.c.)

Standard of Practice Seven (SP-7): Termination. Counselors must assist in making appropriate arrangements for the continuation of treatment of clients, when necessary, following termination of counseling relationships. (See A.11.a.)

Standard of Practice Eight (SP-8): Inability to Assist Clients. Counselors must avoid entering or immediately terminate a counseling relationship if it is determined that they are unable to be of professional assistance to a client. The counselor may assist in making an appropriate referral for the client. (See A.11.b.)

Section B: Confidentiality

Standard of Practice Nine (SP-9): Confidentiality Requirement. Counselors must keep information related to counseling services confidential unless disclosure is in the best interest of clients, is required for the welfare of others, or is required by law. When disclosure is required, only information that is essential is revealed and the client is informed of such disclosure. (See B.1.a.-f.)

Standard of Practice Ten (SP-10): Confidentiality Requirements for Subordinates. Counselors must take measures to ensure that privacy and confidentiality of clients are maintained by subordinates. (See B.1.h.)

Standard of Practice Eleven (SP-11): Confidentiality in Group Work. Counselors must clearly communicate to group members that confidentiality cannot be guaranteed in group work. (See B.2.a.)

Standard of Practice Twelve (SP-12): Confidentiality in Family Counseling. Counselors must not disclose information about one family member in counseling to another family member without prior consent. (See B.2.b.)

Standard of Practice Thirteen (SP-13): Confidentiality of Records. Counselors must maintain appropriate confidentiality in creating, storing, accessing, transferring, and disposing of counseling records. (See B.4.b.)

Standard of Practice Fourteen (SP-14): Permission to Record or Observe. Counselors must obtain prior consent from clients in order to electronically record or observe sessions. (See B.4.c.)

Standard of Practice Fifteen (SP-15): Disclosure or Transfer of Records. Counselors must obtain client consent to disclose or transfer records to third parties, unless exceptions listed in SP-9 exist. (See B.4.e.)

Standard of Practice Sixteen (SP-16): Data Disguise Required. Counselors must disguise the identity of the client when using data for training, research, or publication. (See B.5.a.)

Section C: Professional Responsibility
Standard of Practice Seventeen (SP-17): Boundaries of Competence. Counselors must practice only within the boundaries of their competence. (See C.2.a.)

Standard of Practice Eighteen (SP-18): Continuing Education. Counselors must engage in continuing education to maintain their professional competence. (See C.2.f.)

Standard of Practice Nineteen (SP-19): Impairment of Professionals. Counselors must refrain from offering professional services when their personal problems or conflicts may cause harm to a client or others. (See C.2.g.)

Standard of Practice Twenty (SP-20): Accurate Advertising. Counselors must accurately represent their credentials and services when advertising. (See C.3.a.)

Standard of Practice Twenty-one (SP-21): Recruiting Through Employment. Counselors must not use their place of employment or institutional affiliation to recruit clients for their private practices. (See C.3.d.)

Standard of Practice Twenty-two (SP-22): Credentials Claimed. Counselors must claim or imply only professional credentials possessed and must correct any known misrepresentations of their credentials by others. (See C.4.a.)

Standard of Practice Twenty-three (SP-23): Sexual Harassment. Counselors must not engage in sexual harassment. (See C.5.b.)

Standard of Practice Twenty-four (SP-24): Unjustified Gains. Counselors must not use their professional positions to seek or receive unjustified personal gains, sexual favors, unfair advantage, or unearned goods or services. (See C.5.e.)

Standard of Practice Twenty-five (SP-25): Clients Served by Others. With the consent of the client, counselors must inform other mental health professionals serving the same client that a counseling relationship between the counselor and client exists. (See C.6.c.)

Standard of Practice Twenty-six (SP-26): Negative Employment Conditions. Counselors must alert their employers to institutional policy or conditions that may be potentially disruptive or damaging to the counselor's professional responsibilities, or that may limit their effectiveness or deny clients' rights. (See D.1.c.)

Standard of Practice Twenty-seven (SP-27): Personnel Selection and Assignment. Counselors must select competent staff and must assign responsibilities compatible with staff skills and experiences. (See D.1.h.)

Standard of Practice Twenty-eight (SP-28): Exploitive Relationships with Subordinates. Counselors must not engage in exploitive relationships with individuals over whom they have supervisory, evaluative, or instructional control or authority. (See D.1.k.)

Section D: Relationship with Other Professionals
Standard of Practice Twenty-nine (SP-29): Accepting Fees from Agency Clients. Counselors must not accept fees or other

remuneration for consultation with persons entitled to such services through the counselor's employing agency or institution. (See D.3.a.)

Standard of Practice Thirty (SP-30): Referral Fees. Counselors must not accept referral fees. (See D.3.b.)

Section E: Evaluation, Assessment, and Interpretation

Standard of Practice Thirty-one (SP-31): Limits of Competence. Counselors must perform only testing and assessment services for which they are competent. Counselors must not allow the use of psychological assessment techniques by unqualified persons under their supervision. (See E.2.a.)

Standard of Practice Thirty-two (SP-32): Appropriate Use of Assessment Instruments. Counselors must use assessment instruments in the manner for which they were intended. (See E.2.b.)

Standard of Practice Thirty-three (SP-33): Assessment Explanations to Clients. Counselors must provide explanations to clients prior to assessment about the nature and purposes of assessment and the specific uses of results. (See E.3.a.)

Standard of Practice Thirty-four (SP-34): Recipients of Test Results. Counselors must ensure that accurate and appropriate interpretations accompany any release of testing and assessment information. (See E.3.b.)

Standard of Practice Thirty-five (SP-35): Obsolete Tests and Outdated Test Results. Counselors must not base their assessment or intervention decisions or recommendations on data or test results that are obsolete or outdated for the current purpose. (See E.11.)

Section F: Teaching, Training, and Supervision

Standard of Practice Thirty-six (SP-36): Sexual Relationships with Students or Supervisees. Counselors must not engage in sexual relationships with their students and supervisees. (See F.1.c.)

Standard of Practice Thirty-seven (SP-37): Credit for Contributions to Research. Counselors must give credit to students or supervisees for their contributions to research and scholarly projects. (See F.1.d.)

Standard of Practice Thirty-eight (SP-38): Supervision Preparation. Counselors who offer clinical supervision services must be trained and prepared in supervision methods and techniques. (See F.1.f.)

Standard of Practice Thirty-nine (SP-39): Evaluation Information. Counselors must clearly state to students and supervisees in advance of training, the levels of competency expected, appraisal methods, and timing of evaluations. Counselors must provide students and supervisees with periodic performance appraisal and evaluation feedback throughout the training program. (See F.2.c.)

Standard of Practice Forty (SP-40): Peer Relationships in Training. Counselors must make every effort to ensure that the rights of peers are not violated when students and supervisees are assigned to lead counseling groups or provide clinical supervision. (See F.2.e.)

Standard of Practice Forty-one (SP-41): Limitations of Students and Supervisees. Counselors must assist students and supervisees in securing remedial assistance, when needed, and must dismiss from the training program students and supervisees who are unable to provide competent service due to academic or personal limitations. (See F.3.a.)

Standard of Practice Forty-two (SP-42): Self-Growth Experiences. Counselors who conduct experiences for students or supervisees that include self growth or self disclosure must inform participants of counselors' ethical obligations to the profession and must not grade participants based on their nonacademic performance. (See F.3.b.)

Standard of Practice Forty-three (SP-43): Standards for Students and Supervisees. Students and supervisees preparing to become counselors must adhere to the Code of Ethics and the Standards of Practice of counselors. (See F.3.e.)

Section G: Research and Publication

Standard of Practice Forty-four (SP-44): Precautions to Avoid Injury in Research. Counselors must avoid causing physical, social, or psychological harm or injury to subjects in research. (See G.1.c.)

Standard of Practice Forty-five (SP-45): Confidentiality of Research Information. Counselors must keep confidential information obtained about research participants. (See G.2.d.)

Standard of Practice Forty-six (SP-46):

Information Affecting Research Outcome. Counselors must report all variables and conditions known to the investigator that may have affected research data or outcomes. (See G.3.a.)

Standard of Practice Forty-seven (SP-47): Accurate Research Results. Counselors must not distort or misrepresent research data, nor fabricate or intentionally bias research results. (See G.3.b.)

Standard of Practice Forty-eight (SP-48): Publication Contributors. Counselors must give appropriate credit to those who have contributed to research. (See G.4.a. and G.4.b.)

Section H: Resolving Ethical Issues

Standard of Practice Forty-nine (SP-49): Ethical Behavior Expected. Counselors must take appropriate action when they possess reasonable cause that raises doubts as to whether counselors or other mental health professionals are acting in an ethical manner. (See H.2.a.)

Standard of Practice Fifty (SP-50): Unwarranted Complaints. Counselors must not initiate, participate in, or encourage the filing of ethics complaints that are unwarranted or intended to harm a mental health professional rather than to protect clients or the public. (See H.2.f.)

Standard of Practice Fifty-one (SP-51): Cooperation with Ethics Committees. Counselors must cooperate with investigations, proceedings, and requirements of the ACA Ethics Committee or ethics committees of other duly constituted associations or boards having jurisdiction over those charged with a violation. (See H.3.)

References

The following documents are available to counselors as resources to guide them in their practices. These resources are not a part of the Code of Ethics and the Standards of Practice.

American Association for Counseling and Development/Association for Measurement and Evaluation in Counseling and Development. (1989). The responsibilities of users of standardized tests (revised). Washington, DC: Author.

American Counseling Association. (1988). American Counseling Association Ethical Standards. Alexandria, VA: Author.

American Psychological Association. (1985). Standards for educational and psychological testing (revised). Washington, DC: Author.

American Rehabilitation Counseling Association, Commission on Rehabilitation Counselor Certification, and National Rehabilitation Counseling Association. (1995). Code of professional ethics for rehabilitation counselors. Chicago, IL: Author.

American School Counselor Association. (1992). Ethical standards for school counselors. Alexandria, VA: Author.

Joint Committee on Testing Practices. (1988). Code of fair testing practices in education. Washington, DC: Author.

National Board for Certified Counselors. (1989). National Board for Certified Counselors Code of Ethics. Alexandria, VA: Author.

Prediger, D.J. (Ed.). (1993, March). Multicultural assessment standards. Alexandria, VA: Association for Assessment in Counseling.

Policies and Procedures for Responding to Members' Requests for Interpretations of the Ethical Standards

Revised by Governing Council April 1994. Effective July 1, 1994.

Section A: Appropriate Requests

1. ACA members may request that the Committee issue formal interpretations of the ACA Code of Ethics for the purpose of guiding the member's own professional behavior.

2. Requests for interpretations will not be considered in the following situations:

a. The individual requesting the interpretation is not an ACA member, or

b. The request is intended to determine whether the behavior of another mental health professional is unethical. In the event an ACA member believes the behavior of another mental health professional is unethical, the ACA member should resolve the issue directly with the professional, if possible, and should file an ethical complaint if appropriate.

Section B: Procedures

1. Members must send written requests for interpretations to the Committee at ACA Headquarters.

2. Questions should be submitted in the following format: "Does (counselor behavior) violate Sections _____ or any other sections of the ACA Ethical Standards?" Questions should avoid unique details, be general in nature to the extent possible, and be brief.

3. The Committee staff liaison will revise the question, if necessary, and submit it to the Committee Co-Chair for approval.

4. The question will be sent to Committee members who will be asked to respond individually.

5. The Committee Co-Chair will develop a consensus interpretation on behalf of the Committee.

6. The consensus interpretation will be sent to members of the Committee for final approval.

7. The formal interpretation will be sent to the member who submitted the inquiry.

8. The question and the formal interpretation will be published in the ACA newsletter, but the identity of the member requesting the interpretation will not be disclosed.

Policies and Procedures for Processing Complaints of Ethical Violations
Section A: General

1. The American Counseling Association, hereafter referred to as the "Association" or "ACA," is dedicated to enhancing human development throughout the life span and promoting the counseling profession.

2. The Association, in furthering its objectives, administers the Code of Ethics that have been developed and approved by the ACA Governing Council.

3. The purpose of this document is to facilitate the work of the ACA Ethics Committee ("Committee") by specifying the procedures for processing cases of alleged violations of the ACA Code of Ethics, codifying options for sanctioning members, and stating appeals procedures. The intent of the Association is to monitor the professional conduct of its members to promote sound ethical practices. ACA does not, however, warrant the performance of any individual.

Section B: Ethics Committee Members

1. The Ethics Committee is a standing committee of the Association. The Committee consists of six (6) appointed members, including two (2) Co-Chairs whose terms

overlap. Two members are appointed annually for three (3) year terms by the President-Elect; appointments are subject to confirmation by the ACA Governing Council. Any vacancy occurring on the Committee will be filled by the President in the same manner, and the person appointed shall serve the unexpired term of the member whose place he or she took. Committee members may be reappointed to not more than one (1) additional consecutive term.

2. One (1) of the Committee co-chairs is appointed annually by the President Elect from among the Committee members who have two (2) years of service remaining and serves as co-chair for two (2) years, subject to confirmation by the ACA Governing Council.

Section C: Role and Function

1. The Ethics Committee is responsible for:

a. Educating the membership as to the Association's Code of Ethics;

b. Periodically reviewing and recommending changes in the Code of Ethics of the Association as well as the Policies and Procedures for Processing Complaints of Ethical Violations;

c. Receiving and processing complaints of alleged violations of the Code of Ethics of the Association; and,

d. Receiving and processing questions.

2. The Committee shall meet in person or by telephone conference a minimum of three (3) times per year for processing complaints.

3. In processing complaints about alleged ethical misconduct, the Committee will compile an objective, factual account of the dispute in question and make the best possible recommendation for the resolution of the case. The Committee, in taking any action, shall do so only for cause, shall only take the degree of disciplinary action that is reasonable, shall utilize these procedures with objectivity and fairness, and in general shall act only to further the interests and objectives of the Association and its membership.

4. Of the six (6) voting members of the Committee, a vote of four (4) is necessary to conduct business. In the event a Co-Chair or any other member of the Committee has a personal interest in the case, he or she shall withdraw from reviewing the case.

5. In the event Committee members re-

cuse themselves from a complaint and insufficient voting members are available to conduct business, the President shall appoint former ACA Committee members to decide the complaint.

Section D: Responsibilities of the Committee

1. The Committee members have an obligation to act in an unbiased manner, to work expeditiously, to safeguard the confidentiality of the Committee's activities, and to follow procedures established to protect the rights of all individuals involved.

Section E: Responsibilities of the Co-Chairs Administering the Complaint

1. In the event that one of the Co-Chairs administering the complaint [has a] conflict of interest in a particular case, the other Co-Chair shall administer the complaint. The Co-Chair administering the complaint shall not have a vote in the decision.

2. In addition to the above guidelines for members of the Committee, the Co-Chairs, in conjunction with the Headquarters staff liaison, have the responsibilities of:

a. Receiving, via ACA Headquarters, complaints that have been certified for membership status of the accused;

b. Determining whether the alleged behavior(s), if true, would violate ACA's Code of Ethics and whether the Committee should review the complaint under these rules;

c. Notifying the complainant and the accused member of receipt of the case by certified mail return receipt requested;

d. Notifying the members of the Committee of the case;

e. Requesting additional information from complainants, accused members and others;

f. Presiding over the meetings of the Committee;

g. Preparing and sending, by certified mail, communications to the complainant and accused member on the recommendations and decisions of the Committee; and

h. Arranging for legal advice with assistance and financial approval of the ACA Executive Director.

Section F: Jurisdiction

1. The Committee will consider whether individuals have violated the ACA Code of Ethics if those individuals:

a. Are current members of the American Counseling Association; or

b. Were ACA members when the alleged violations occurred.

2. Ethics committees of divisions, branches, corporate affiliates, or other ACA entities must refer all ethical complaints involving ACA members to the Committee.

Section G: Eligibility to File Complaints

1. The Committee will receive complaints that ACA members have violated one or more sections of the ACA Code of Ethics from the following individuals:

a. Members of the general public who have reason to believe that ACA members have violated the ACA Code of Ethics.

b. ACA members, or members of other helping professions, who have reason to believe that other ACA members have violated the ACA Code of Ethics.

c. The Co-Chair of the Committee on behalf of the ACA membership when the Co-Chair has reason to believe through information received by the Committee that ACA members have violated the ACA Code of Ethics.

2. If possible, individuals should attempt to resolve complaints directly with accused members before filing ethical complaints.

Section H: Time Lines

1. The time lines set forth in these standards are guidelines only and have been established to provide a reasonable time framework for processing complaints.

2. Complainants or accused members may request extensions of deadlines when appropriate. Extensions of deadlines will be granted by the Committee only when justified by unusual circumstance.

Section I: Nature of Communication

1. Only written communications regarding ethical complaints against members will be acceptable. If telephone inquiries from individuals are received regarding the filing of complaints, responding to complaints, or providing information regarding complaints, the individuals calling will be informed of the written communication requirement and asked to comply.

2. All correspondence related to an ethical complaint must be addressed to the Ethics

Committee, ACA Headquarters, 5999 Stevenson Avenue, Alexandria, VA 22304, and must be marked "confidential." This process is necessary to protect the confidentiality of the complainant and the accused member.

Section J: Filing Complaints

1. Only written complaints, signed by complainants, will be considered.

2. Individuals eligible to file complaints will send a letter outlining the nature of the complaint to the Committee at the ACA Headquarters.

3. The ACA staff liaison to the Committee will communicate in writing with complainants. Receipt of complaints and confirmation of membership status of accused members as defined in Section F.1., above, will be acknowledged to the complainant. Proposed formal complaints will be sent to complainants after receipt of complaints have been acknowledged.

4. If the complaint does not involve a member as defined in Section F.1., above, the staff liaison shall inform the complainant.

5. The Committee Co-Chair administering a complaint will determine whether the complaint, if true, would violate one or more sections of the ethical standards or if the complaint could be properly decided if accepted. If not, the complaint will not be accepted and the complainant shall be notified.

6. If the Committee Co-Chair administering the complaint determines that there is insufficient information to make a fair determination of whether the behavior alleged in the complaint would be cause for action by the Committee, the ACA staff liaison to the Committee may request further information from the complainant or others.

7. When complaints are accepted, complainants will be informed that copies of the formal complaints plus evidence and documents submitted in support of the complaint will be provided to the accused member and that the complainant must authorize release of such information to the accused member before the complaint process may proceed.

8. The ACA staff liaison, after receiving approval of the Committee Co-Chair administering a complaint, will formulate a formal complaint which will be presented to the complainants for their signature.

a. The correspondence from complainants will be received and the staff liaison and Committee Co-Chair administering the complaint will identify all ACA Code of Ethics that might have been violated if the accusations are true.

b. The formal complaint will be sent to complainants with a copy of these Policies and Procedures, a copy of the ACA Code of Ethics, a verification affidavit form and an authorization and release of information form. Complainants will be asked to sign and return the completed complaint, verification affidavit and authorization and release of information forms. It will be explained to complainants that sections of the codes that might have been violated may be added or deleted by the complainant before signing the formal statement.

c. If complainants elect to add or delete sections of the ethical standards in the formal complaint, the unsigned formal complaint shall be returned to ACA Headquarters with changes noted and a revised formal complaint will be sent to the complainants for their signature.

9. When the completed formal complaint, verification affidavit form and authorization and release of information form are presented to complainants for their signature, they will be asked to submit all evidence and documents they wish to be considered by the Committee in reviewing the complaint.

Section K: Notification of Accused Members

1. Once signed formal complaints have been received, accused members will be sent a copy of the formal complaint and copies of all evidence and documents submitted in support of the complaint.

2. Accused members will be asked to respond to the complaint against them. They will be asked to address each section of the ACA Code of Ethics they have been accused of having violated. They will be informed that if they wish to respond they must do so in writing within sixty (60) working days.

3. Accused members will be informed that they must submit all evidence and documents they wish to be considered by the Committee in reviewing the complaint within sixty (60) working days.

4. After accused members have received notification that a complaint has been

brought against them, they will be given sixty (60) working days to notify the Committee Co-Chair (via ACA Headquarters) in writing, by certified mail, if they wish to request a formal face-to-face hearing before the Committee. Accused members may waive their right to a formal hearing before the Committee. (See Section P: Hearings).

5. If the Committee Co-Chair determines that there is insufficient information to make a fair determination of whether the behavior alleged in the complaint would be cause for action by the Committee, the ACA staff liaison to the Committee may request further information from the accused member or others. The accused member shall be given thirty (30) working days from receipt of the request to respond.

6. All requests for additional information from others will be accompanied by a verification affidavit form which the information provider will be asked to complete and return.

7. The Committee may, in its discretion, delay or postpone its review of the case with good cause, including if the Committee wishes to obtain additional information. The accused member may request that the Committee delay or postpone its review of the case for good cause if done so in writing.

Section L: Disposition of Complaints

1. After receiving the responses of accused members, Committee members will be provided copies of: (a) the complaint, (b) supporting evidence and documents sent to accused members, (c) the response, and (d) supporting evidence and documents provided by accused members and others.

2. Decisions will be rendered based on the evidence and documents provided by the complainant and accused member or others.

3. The Committee Co-Chair administering a complaint will not participate in deliberations or decisions regarding that particular complaint.

4. At the next meeting of the Committee held no sooner than fifteen (15) working days after members received copies of documents related to a complaint, the Committee will discuss the complaint, response, and supporting documentation, if any, and determine the outcome of the complaint.

5. The Committee will determine whether each Code of Ethics the member has been accused of having violated was violated based on the information provided.

6. After deliberations, the Committee may decide to dismiss the complaint or to dismiss charges within the complaint.

7. In the event it is determined that any of the ACA Code of Ethics have been violated, the Committee will impose for the entire complaint one or a combination of the possible sanctions allowed.

Section M: Withdrawal of Complaints

1. If the Complainant and accused member both agree to discontinue the complaint process, the Committee may, at its discretion, complete the adjudication process if available evidence indicates that this is warranted. The Co-Chair of the Committee, on behalf of the ACA membership, shall act as complainant.

Section N: Possible Sanctions

1. Reprinted Remedial requirements may be stipulated by the Committee.

2. Probation for a specified period of time subject to Committee review of compliance. Remedial requirements may be imposed to be completed within a specified period of time.

3. Suspension from ACA membership for a specified period of time subject to Committee review of compliance. Remedial requirements may be imposed to be completed within a specified period of time.

4. Permanent expulsion from ACA membership. This sanction requires a unanimous vote of those voting.

5. The penalty for failing to fulfill in a satisfactory manner a remedial requirement imposed by the Committee as a result of a probation sanction will be automatic suspension until the requirement is met, unless the Committee determines that the remedial requirement should be modified based on good cause shown prior to the end of the probationary period.

6. The penalty for failing to fulfill in a satisfactory manner a remedial requirement imposed by the Committee as a result of a suspension sanction will be automatic permanent expulsion unless the Committee determines that the remedial requirement should be modified based on good cause shown prior to the end of the suspension period.

7. Other corrective action.

Section O: Notification of Results

1. Accused members shall be notified of Committee decisions regarding complaints against them.

2. Complainants will be notified of Committee decisions after the deadline for accused members to file appeals or, in the event an appeal is filed, after a filed appeal decision has been rendered.

3. After complainants are notified of the results of their complaints as provided in Section O., Paragraph 2 above, if a violation has been found and accused members have been suspended or expelled, counselor licensure, certification, or registry boards, other mental health licensure, certification, or registry boards, voluntary national certification boards, and appropriate professional associations will also be notified of the results. In addition, ACA divisions, state branches, the ACA Insurance Trust, and other ACA-related entities will also be notified of the results.

4. After complainants have been notified of the results of their complaint as provided in Section O., Paragraph 2 above, if a violation has been found and accused members have been suspended or expelled, a notice of the Committee action that includes the sections of the ACA ethical standards that were found to have been violated and the sanctions imposed will be published in the ACA newsletter.

Section P: Hearings

1. At the discretion of the Committee, a hearing may be conducted when the results of the Committee's preliminary determination indicate that additional information is needed.

2. When accused members, within sixty (60) working days of notification of the complaint, request a formal face-to-face or telephone conference hearing before the Committee a hearing shall be conducted. (See Section K.6.)

3. The accused shall bear all their expenses associated with attendance at hearings requested by the accused.

4. The Committee Co-Chair shall schedule a formal hearing on the case at the next scheduled Committee meeting and notify both the complainant and the accused member of their right to attend the hearing in person or by telephone conference call.

5. The hearing will be held before a panel made up of the Committee and if the accused member chooses, a representative of the accused member's primary Division. This representative will be identified by the Division President and will have voting privileges.

Section Q: Hearing Procedures

1. Purpose

a. A hearing will be conducted to determine whether a breach of the ethical standards has occurred and, if so, to determine appropriate disciplinary action.

b. The Committee will be guided in its deliberations by principles of basic fairness and professionalism, and will keep its deliberations as confidential as possible, except as provided herein.

2. Notice

a. The accused members shall be advised in writing by the Co-Chair administering the complaint of the time and place of the hearing and the charges involved at least forty-five (45) working days before the hearing. Notice shall include a formal statement of the complaints lodged against the accused member and supporting evidence.

b. The accused member is under no duty to respond to the notice, but the Committee will not be obligated to delay or postpone its hearing unless the accused so requests in writing, with good cause reviewed at least fifteen (15) working days in advance. In the absence of such 15 day advance notice and postponement by the Committee, if the accused fails to appear at the hearing, the Committee shall decide the complaint on record. Failure of the accused member to appear at the hearing shall not be viewed by the Committee as sufficient grounds alone for taking disciplinary action.

3. Conduct of the Hearing

a. Accommodations. The location of the hearing shall be determined at the discretion of the Committee. The Committee shall provide a private room to conduct the hearing and no observers or recording devices other than a recording device used by the Committee shall be permitted.

b. Presiding Officer. The Co-Chair in charge of the case shall preside over the hearing and deliberations of the Committee. At the conclusion of the hearing and deliberations of the Committee, the Co-Chair shall promptly notify the accused member and complainant of the Committee's decision in writing as provided in Section O., Paragraphs 1 and 2, above.

c. Record. A record of the hearing shall be made and preserved, together with any documents presented in evidence, at ACA Headquarters for a period of three (3) years. The record shall consist of a summary of testimony received or a verbatim transcript, at the discretion of the Committee.

d. Right to Counsel. The accused member shall be entitled to have legal counsel present to advise and represent them throughout the hearing. Legal counsel for ACA shall also be present at the hearing to advise the Committee and shall have the privilege of the floor.

e. Witnesses. Either party shall have the right to call witnesses to substantiate his or her version of the case.

f. The Committee shall have the right to call witnesses it believes may provide further insight into the matter. ACA shall, in its sole discretion, determine the number and identity of witnesses to be heard.

g. Witnesses shall not be present during the hearing except when they are called upon to testify and shall be excused upon completion of their testimony and any cross-examination.

h. The Co-Chair administering the complaint shall allow questions to be asked of any witness by the opposition or members of the Committee if such questions and testimony are relevant to the issues in the case.

i. The Co-Chair administering the complaint will determine what questions and testimony are relevant to the case. Should the hearing be disturbed by irrelevant testimony, the Co-Chair administering the complaint may call a brief recess until order can be restored.

j. All expenses associated with counsel on behalf of the parties shall be borne by the respective parties. All expenses associated with witnesses on behalf of the accused shall be borne by the accused when the accused requests a hearing. If the Committee requests the hearing, all expenses associated with witnesses shall be borne by ACA.

4. Presentation of Evidence

a. The staff liaison, or the Co-Chair administering the complaint shall be called upon

first to present the charge(s) made against the accused and to briefly describe the evidence supporting the charge. The person presenting the charges shall also be responsible for examining and cross-examining witnesses on behalf of the complainant and for otherwise presenting the matter during the hearing.

b. The complainant or a member of the Committee shall then be called upon to present the case against the accused. Witnesses who can substantiate the case may be called upon to testify and answer questions of the accused and the Committee.

c. If the accused has exercised the right to be present at the hearing, he or she shall be called upon last to present any evidence which refutes the charges against him or her. This includes witnesses as in Subsection (3) above.

d. The accused will not be found guilty simply for refusing to testify. Once the accused member chooses to testify, however, he or she may be cross-examined by the complainant and members of the Committee.

e. The Committee will endeavor to conclude the hearing within a period of approximately three (3) hours. The parties will be requested to be considerate of this time frame in planning their testimony.

f. Testimony that is merely cumulative or repetitious may, at the discretion of the Co-Chair administering the complaint, be excluded.

5. Relevancy of Evidence

a. The Hearing Committee is not a court of law and is not required to observe formal rules of evidence. Evidence that would be inadmissible in a court of law may be admissible in the hearing before the Committee, if it is relevant to the case. That is, if the evidence offered tends to explain, clarify, or refute any of the important facts of the case, it should generally be considered.

b. The Committee will not consider evidence or testimony for the purpose of supporting any charge that was not set forth in the notice of the hearing or that is not relevant to the issues of the case.

6. Burden of Proof

a. The burden of proving a violation of the ethical standards is on the complainant and/or the Committee. It is not up to the accused to prove his or her innocence of any wrong-doing.

b. Although the charge(s) need not be proved "beyond a reasonable doubt," the Committee will not find the accused guilty in the absence of substantial, objective, and believable evidence to sustain the charge(s).

7. Deliberation of the Committee

a. After the hearing is completed, the Committee shall meet in a closed session to review the evidence presented and reach a conclusion. ACA legal counsel may attend the closed session to advise the Committee if the Committee so desires.

b. The Committee shall be the sole trier of the facts and shall weigh the evidence presented and assess the credibility of the witnesses. The act of a majority of the members of the Committee present shall be the decision of the Committee. A unanimous vote of those voting is required for permanent expulsion from ACA membership.

c. Only members of the Committee who were present throughout the entire hearing shall be eligible to vote.

8. Decision of the Committee

a. The Committee will first resolve the issue of the guilt or innocence of the accused on each charge. Applying the burden of proof in subsection (5), above, the Committee will vote by secret ballot, unless the members of the Committee consent to an oral vote.

b. In the event a majority of the members of the Committee do not find the accused guilty, the charges shall be dismissed. If the Committee finds the accused member has violated the Code of Ethics, it must then determine what sanctions, in accordance with Section N: Possible Sanctions, shall be imposed.

c. As provided in Section O., above, the Co-Chair administering the complaint shall notify the accused member and complainant of the Committee's decision in writing.

Section R: Appeals

1. Decisions of the ACA Ethics Committee that members have violated the ACA Code of Ethics may be appealed by the member found to have been in violation based on one or both of the following grounds:

a. The Committee violated its policies and procedures for processing complaints of ethical violations; and/or

b. The decision of the Committee was arbitrary and capricious and was not supported by the materials provided by the complainant and accused member.

2. After members have received notification that they have been found in violation of one or more ACA Code of Ethics, they will be given thirty (30) working days to notify the Committee in writing by certified mail that they are appealing the decision.

3. An appeal may consist only of a letter stating one or both of the grounds of appeal listed in subsection 1 above and the reasons for the appeal.

4. Appealing members will be asked to identify the primary ACA division to which he or she belongs. The ACA President will appoint a three (3) person appeals panel consisting of two (2) former ACA Ethics Committee Chairs and the President of the identified division. The ACA attorney shall serve as legal advisor and have the privilege of the floor.

5. The three (3) member appeals panel will be given copies of the materials available to the Committee when it made its decision, a copy of the hearing transcript if a hearing was held, plus a copy of the letter filed by the appealing member.

6. The appeals panel generally will render its decision regarding an appeal which must receive a majority vote within sixty (60) working days of their receipt of the above materials.

7. The decision of the appeals panel may include one of the following:

a. The decision of the Committee is upheld.

b. The decision of the Committee is reversed and remanded with guidance to the Committee for a new decision. The reason for this decision will be given to the Committee in detail in writing.

8. When a Committee decision is reversed and remanded, the complainant and accused member will be informed in writing and additional information may be requested first from the complainant and then from the accused member. The Committee will then render another decision without a hearing.

9. Decisions of the appeals panel to uphold the Committee decision are final.

Section S: Substantial New Evidence

1. In the event that substantial new evidence is presented in a case in which an appeal was not filed, or in a case which a final decision has been rendered, the case may be reopened by the Committee.

2. The Committee will consider substantial new evidence and if it is found to be substantiated and capable of exonerating a member who was expelled, the Committee will reopen the case and go through the entire complaint process again.

Section T: Records

1. The records of the Committee regarding complaints are confidential except as provided herein.

2. Original copies of complaint records will be maintained in locked files at ACA Headquarters or at an off-site location chosen by ACA.

3. Members of the Committee will keep copies of complaint records confidential and will destroy copies of records after a case has been closed or when they are no longer a member of the Committee.

Section U: Legal Actions Related to Complaints

1. Complaints and accused members are required to notify the Committee if they learn of any type of legal action (civil or criminal) being filed related to the complaint.

2. In the event any type of legal action is filed regarding an accepted complaint, all actions related to the complaint will be stayed until the legal action has been concluded. The Committee will consult with legal counsel concerning whether the processing of the complaint will be stayed if the legal action does not involve the same complainant and the same facts complained of.

3. If actions on a complaint are stayed, the complainant and accused member will be notified.

4. When actions on a complaint are continued after a legal action has been concluded, the complainant and accused member will be notified.

For information on ordering the *ACA Code of Ethics and Standards of Practice* write to:

ACA Distribution Center
P.O. Box 531
Annapolis Junction, MD 20701-0531
or call 301-470-4ACA (301-470-4222); toll free
1-800-422-2648; fax 301-604-0158.

Other Sources for Codes of Ethics

American Association of Christian Counselors, P.O. Box 739, Fairfax, VA 24551. This association is currently devising a code of ethics which is likely to be adopted in the year 2000. Copies of a provisional statement may be obtained from the address above.

American Psychiatric Association, 1400 K Street NW, Washington, DC 20005. The American Psychiatric Association publishes *The Principles of Medical Ethics with Annotations Especially Applicable to Psychiatry*.

American Psychological Association, 1200 17th Street NW, Washington, DC 20036. In addition to its ethical code, which is printed elsewhere in this appendix, this association has published its *Rules and Procedures*, which contains the association's procedures for handling ethics complaints and cases. A copy of these rules may be found in the *American Psychologist* 47 (1992): 1612-28. The organization has also published a number of other specialty guidelines which are listed as a footnote to the introduction to the ethical code.

National Association of Social Workers, 7981 Eastern Avenue, Silver Spring, MD 20910.

National Board for Certified Counselors, P.O. Box 5406, Greensboro, NC 27435.

Appendix C

SAMPLE CONSENT FORMS

The forms included on the pages that follow are samples of the types of forms that are used for release of information and informed consent. It should be understood that laws regarding what must be incorporated in such forms vary from state to state. In addition, information included in the forms will vary according to the type of counseling done (e.g., counseling centers that serve only certain treatment populations or conditions) or the counseling setting (church-based center, private practice, etc.). Readers may wish to consult with other professionals in their locale or seek legal consultation before constructing their own forms.

Mail_____ File_____

Consent for Release of Confidential Information

I authorize _____ to release to _____ to obtain from _____
Person(s)_____
Organization_____
Address _____
City _____ State _____ Zip _____ Phone _____
the following information:

___ Progress Notes/Report
___ Treatment Plan
___ Discharge Summary

___ Psychosocial History
___ Psychiatric Evaluation
___ Contents of entire file

___ Psychological Report/Testing
___ Medications/Medical History
___ Other (specify) _____

This information is for the purpose of continued treatment or (specify)
_____

This information is disclosed from records whose confidentiality is protected by Federal law. Federal regulations (42CFR Part 2) prohibit any further disclosure of this information without specific written consent of the person to whom it pertains, or as otherwise permitted by such regulations. A general authorization for the release of medical or other information is not sufficient for this purpose. The Federal rules restrict any use of this information to criminally investigate or prosecute any alcohol or drug abuse patient. This information is to be destroyed upon fulfillment of stated purpose.

Such release may include information regarding a communicable or venereal disease which may include, but is not limited to, diseases such as hepatitis, syphilis, gonorrhea and the human immunodeficiency virus, also know as acquired immune deficiency syndrome (AIDS).

Oklahoma state law (76 O.S. Supp. 1986 Section 19) provides that psychiatric records may not be provided to a patient, their guardians or agents, without consent of the treating physician or an order from a court of competent jurisdiction.

I understand that my records are protected under the federal and state confidentiality regulations and cannot be released without my written consent unless otherwise provided for in said regulations. I also understand that I may revoke this consent at any time in writing unless action has already been taken based upon it and that in any event, this consent expires automatically in twelve months.

By signing below, I hereby release the above parties from any and all liability resulting from the release of this information.

Patient _____ Date of Birth _____

Signature of Patient _____ Date _____

Parent or Guardian _____ Date _____
(if patient is a minor)

Witness _____ Date _____ Rev 9/96

Insurance/Payment Information

Responsible Party

Last Name _____ First Name _____ M.I. _____

Address _____

City _____ State ____ Zip _____ Home Phone (___) _____

Date of Birth _____ SSN _____ Relationship to Patient _____

Employer _____ Address_____

Occupation _____ Business Phone (___)_____

Spouse Name _____ SSN _____

Primary Insurance Co _____ Effective Date_____
Insured's Name _____ DOB _____ SSN _____

Address (if different) _____

Policy No _____ Group No _____ Relationship to Patient_____

Secondary Insurance Co _____ Effective Date_____
Insured's Name _____ DOB _____ SSN _____

Address (if different) _____

Policy No _____ Group No _____ Relationship to Patient_____

I (we) authorize payment of medical benefits to the provider herein for all medical/psychological services rendered. I (we) authorize the provider to release any information required to process my insurance claims. I (we) authorize my insurance benefits to be paid directly to _____. I (we) understand that I (we) am (are) financially responsible for payment of any insurance deductible, copayments, and non-covered charges or services. A photocopy of this signature is valid as the original.

Signature of Responsible Party _____ Date _____

Signature of Spouse _____ Date _____
(required if marital treatment)
Please provide us with your insurance card in order to have a copy on file. Please notify us of any changes to your insurance.
Rev 9/96

Consent for Psychological Services to Child(ren)

In order for minor children to receive psychological services, it is necessary for the parent or legal guardian to grant permission for such services to occur.

Names and dates of birth of child(ren) to receive psychological services:

Name _____ Date of Birth _____

Name _____ Date of Birth _____

Name _____ Date of Birth _____

Name _____ Date of Birth _____

Name of person requesting services _____
Your relationship to child(ren): Parent Stepparent Grandparent Guardian Other __
Are you the legal parent or custodian of the above-named children?
    Yes _____ No _____
I hereby swear that I have a legal right to obtain treatment for the above named child(ren).
        Yes _____ No _____

In instances of divorce, it is essential that the legal custodian of the child(ren) grant permission for the services.
    If you are a divorced parent, a stepparent, a grandparent, a guardian, or other, you may be asked to provide a copy of the court order which names you the legal custodian of the above children. Are you willing to do so? Yes _____ No _____
    If the answer to any of the above questions is "No," psychological services cannot be provided to the above-named child(ren) until a copy of the court order which names you the legal custodian is provided to this office.
I acknowledge that both natural parents, even though divorced, may have a right to obtain from the provider named below information regarding the nature and course of treatment of the child(ren).

    I, _____, consent to _____ of

_____ providing psychological services to the child(ren)
named above. These services may include:
    _____ clinical interviews of the child(ren)
    _____ psychological testing of the child(ren)
    _____ counseling/psychotherapy
    _____ other services: _____

_____   _____
Signature of person giving consent   Date   Rev 9/96

Important Information for New Clients

Welcome to _____. We ask that you read the following information and bring any questions you might have to our office staff.

Appointments. The counseling service recognizes that scheduling an appointment for mental health services must accommodate other commitments such as family and work. Our professional staff is available during the weekdays, as well as some evening and Saturday appointments. When necessary, same-day appointments are usually available.

Individual appointments are generally forty-five to fifty (45-50) minutes in length and are held exclusively for you. If for *any* reason you are unable to keep your appointment, it is essential for you to *notify our office by noon on the day preceding your scheduled appointment.* Otherwise you will be charged for the time reserved for you. Insurance companies reimburse for services rendered; therefore, charges for a missed appointment will not be billed to the insurance company. It is the patient's responsibility to pay for the missed appointment.

Continuity of treatment is an important part of benefiting from treatment. We encourage you to plan ahead to avoid any last-minute disruption to your appointment time. If you do need to reschedule an appointment, we will cooperate in accommodating your preferences.

Fees. The fees for a 45-50 minute session are $90 for a Ph.D. level therapist and $80 for a Master's level therapist. Please see the attached **Fee Schedule** for specific services and fees.

Payments. Payment in full is expected at the time services are rendered unless prior payment arrangements have been made in writing.

Please understand that you, the patient, are fully responsible for the payment of all the fees for services provided *regardless* of the extent of any insurance coverage you may have. It is not our policy to accept the amount an insurance company may pay as payment in full if the amount is less than the regular fee. If you are unable to pay for psychological services, we will be happy to refer you to an appropriate local agency.

It is the policy of this office to turn seriously delinquent accounts over to a collection agency. Only information which is nonclinical in nature will be given to the collection agency for this purpose.

Insurance Coverage and Reimbursement. Services in this office may be covered by health insurance plans. As a courtesy to you, we will verify benefits and file your insurance upon receipt of your insurance card and information. Until the benefits have been verified, you will be expected to pay in full at the time of the services.

If you belong to an HMO, a PPO, or another managed care plan, it is your responsibility to be aware of your benefits, as well as the procedures and limitations which they require. It is your responsibility to discuss the psychological services offered under your plan with your case manager and obtain authorization to be treated or to seek an initial consultation *prior* to your first appointment here. Please be aware that many managed care plans require preauthorization of services and/or periodic review of treatment and reauthorization of additional visits.

In those instances where you are a member of an HMO or a PPO or where our office has a preferred provider relationship, you will be expected to make the copayment at the time the service is rendered.

Emergency Calls. The counseling service office is staffed Monday-Friday 8:00 a.m.-5:00 p.m. After hours emergencies are handled through the answering service. Should you require immediate attention, please go to the emergency room of a local hospital.

Consultations. In order to maximize the benefit you receive from services, it is important to coordinate care. We may ask that you give us permission to contact your primary care physician as needed in order to review your treatment plan and to provide coordinated care to you. If you do not have a primary care physician, your therapist may recommend that you obtain one if needed.

Certain patients may be referred to other professionals for specialized services. Examples would include referral to a physician for medical problems or hospitalization. Though a consultant may be recommended, patients are encouraged to state their own preferences for consultants if the need should arise.

Psychological Testing. In order to better understand a patient's problems and to facilitate treatment, psychological tests are sometimes utilized. In such cases the purpose of taking the tests will be explained and the results will be reviewed with you. Fees for testing are separate from fees for regular visits and vary according to the tests used. Estimates of the cost of testing will be furnished upon request and in advance of test administration.

Confidentiality. All information which you reveal to your therapist, including test results, notes, and records, is confidential and will not be released to any outside person or agency without your written authorization. When more than one family member is seen during a session, each of these legally competent individuals must sign such an authorization. There are several circumstances which require release of information without patient consent: (1) if, in the therapist's opinion, revealing the information would be necessary to prevent a person's death or serous injury, (2) if a patient is being evaluated or is in treatment by order of a court of law, the results of the evaluation and/or treatment must be revealed to the court, (3) in instances where there is evidence or suspicion of child neglect or abuse. In addition, most insurance companies require information regarding diagnosis and a description of services rendered in order to process the claims. Each client agrees that he/she shall not assert a waiver of the confidential and privileged nature of any Counselor/Client communication, including but not limited to an assertion of waiver based upon the presence of a third party, including Client's spouse.

Responding to a Subpoena. In the event that a subpoena for records or testimony is received, it is the policy of the counseling service to (1) notify the client in writing and provide the client with a copy of the subpoena; (2) either have the client provide the counseling service with a written waiver of objection to the subpoena (an authorization form for honoring the subpoena will be provided) or have the client indicate that an objection will be filed (with a copy sent to the counseling service). Unless otherwise previously agreed in writing, all services and expenses incurred by the provider for court related issues will be charged to the client and subject to regular payment policies. Any time required for contact with attorneys, depositions or courtroom proceedings will be subject to the established professional fees and regular payment policies.

I, the undersigned, acknowledge that I have read, understand, and accept the provisions of the above material entitled **Important Information for New Clients** and **Fee Schedule**. I understand that I am free at any time to ask questions or discuss these provisions with my therapist.

A Final Note. Once again, if you have any questions about any of these policies or any aspect of your treatment in this office, please feel free to ask.

_____   _____

Patient, Parent, or Guardian Signature   Date

I have received a copy of this document_____

_____

Therapist Signature/Date

Consent for Evaluation and/or Treatment

The decision to begin psychotherapy is one which may have important consequences for the rest of your life. Research has shown that when individuals enter this type of treatment with a good understanding of what they are about to undertake, they are likely to achieve more favorable results.

What Is Psychotherapy or Counseling? In Psychotherapy you will work with a trained mental health professional to work out strategies for handling problems of daily living. In addition, therapy can lead to personal growth through clarification of your thoughts and feelings about yourself, others, and events in your life. The majority of the time you spend in therapy will consist of talking about the issues you have presented. However, in addition other methods may be employed such as relaxation and assertiveness training. Treatment can involve an individual, family, couple, or group depending on the nature of the problem. The specific form of therapy will also depend on the theoretical orientation of your therapist. You may wish to ask your therapist about his or her approach at the start of therapy so that you will know what to expect during treatment. The length of treatment varies depending on the therapist, the patient, and the nature of the problems but typically will last 8-12 sessions for relatively specific problems. For more severe problems or those that might affect many areas of your life or those that have persisted for a long time, therapy may be significantly longer. Usually after several sessions the therapist can give you an estimated length of treatment.

Therapist Responsibilities. Your therapist will usually devote the first several sessions to assessing the nature and extent of your concerns and problems. After identifying the specific problem areas, the two of you will agree on a therapy plan that includes goals, methods to accomplish these goals, and the approximate length of time needed. Periodically, you may jointly review your progress and reformulate goals.

Patient Responsibilities. You will also have certain responsibilities in therapy. It is important for you to attend all of your scheduled appointments on time. Equally important is your responsibility to be as active, open, and honest as possible with your therapist. Your most important responsibility, however, is to work toward the goals you and the therapist have agreed upon. Having weekly sessions will be of little benefit to you without additional effort outside of the therapy office. This can include thinking about the material covered in your sessions, making yourself aware of your behavior, or working on specific assignments made by your therapist.

Effectiveness and Risks of Treatment. Psychotherapy is as much an art as it is a science. While many people have been shown to benefit from it, the results cannot be guaranteed. Whether or not a particular individual will benefit from psychotherapy depends on many factors, including how serious the problems are, how long the individual has had these problems, how well the person functioned before the problems began, how much support is available from family members and/or friends, and how motivated the individual is. On average, two thirds of all clients show improvement during therapy.

It is important to be aware of the possible risks of being involved in psychotherapy. Although psychotherapy is unlikely to be harmful, it may stir up uncomfortable or painful thoughts or feelings. However, these periods will be temporary. There may also be times when a person feels discouraged because he or she is not making noticeable progress. Progress in therapy is typically not steady; however, the overall gains should outweigh these potential risks.

Questions or concerns about your treatment should first be raised with your therapist. If, after discussing your concerns with your therapist, you are still not satisfied, you might consider seeking a second opinion or changing to a different therapist. Competent therapists recognize that they will be able to serve the needs of some clients better than others. If you believe your therapist's behavior is either unethical or does not adhere to professional standards, you again have several alternatives. You may bring the matter to the attention of the counseling service director. You may also choose to contact the appropriate state or national professional association or the state licensing or certification board.

Alternative Sources of Help. You should be aware that other helping systems exist that may be used in conjunction with or in place of therapy. Before engaging in one of these activities you should discuss the decision with your therapist to assure that it will be a useful option for you at this time. You may want to consider: individual self help such as educational books, recreational activities, or changes in your job or living situation; peer support groups such as Parents Without Partners, Alcoholics Anonymous, or Weight Watchers; crisis intervention services including crisis hotlines, rape crisis centers, and shelters for battered women; assistance from other kinds of agencies such as legal, vocational, or pastoral counseling.

Other Questions For Your Therapist. What are the therapist's qualifications to help you (credentials, training, experience)? What is the therapist's treatment orientation or philosophy? What are the therapist's values in areas that may have special pertinence to you (such as divorce, religion, alternative lifestyles)? Are you permitted to phone the therapist between sessions or after hours? What arrangements does the therapist have for emergencies or for when he or she is out of the office?

I acknowledge that I have received, read, and understand the documents, IMPORTANT INFORMATION FOR NEW CLIENTS and FEE SCHEDULE. I do hereby seek and consent to participate in evaluation and/or treatment at this counseling service.

I am aware that the practice of psychotherapy is not an exact science and so predictions of the effects are not precise or guaranteed. I acknowledge that no guarantees have been made to me regarding the results of treatment or procedures provided at this counseling service.

I am aware that I may terminate my treatment at any time without consequence, but that I will still be responsible for payment for the services which I have received.

I am aware that any cancellations of appointments must be made **by noon on the day prior to my appointment** and if I do not cancel or do not keep the appointment I will be charged for the appointment.

I am aware that an authorized agent of my insurance carrier or other third-party payor may request and be provided with information about the type, cost, and dates of any services or treatments I receive so that payment may be provided to the counseling service.

I am aware that if I have not paid for services received, my treatment may be discontinued by my therapist.

I am aware that this office is not responsible for any personal property or valuables I bring into its facilities. I acknowledge that, if I or anyone else whom I am legally responsible for deliberately causes damage or steals any property of this office, I will be held financially responsible for its replacement.

I certify, with my signature below, that I have read, had explained to me when necessary, fully understand, and agree with the contents of this CONSENT FOR EVALUATION and/or TREATMENT.

_____   _____

Patient Signature   Date

I have received a copy of this document_____

_____   _____

Witness   Date

Rev 9/96

Confidential Client Information

Today's Date _____ Case No. _____

Client's Name _____ M ____ F ____ Date of Birth _____ Age _____

Address _____ City _____ State _____ Zip _____

Social Security No. _____ Occupation _____ Employer _____

Telephone: Home _____ Work _____ Pager _____ Education_____

Marital Status: Single_____ Married_____ Separated_____ Divorced_____ Widow_____

Previous Marriages: Yes____ No____ Dates: 1:_____ 2:_____ 3: _____
Spouse's Name _____ Date of Birth _____ Age_____

Spouse's SSN _____ Spouse's Employer _____ Tel _____

Children_____ Age_____ Date of Birth_____ Grade_____ Living With _____
_____ Age _____ Date of Birth_____Grade _____Living With ___
_____ Age _____ Date of Birth_____Grade _____Living With ___
_____ Age _____ Date of Birth_____Grade _____Living With ___

Emergency Contact Person (other than household member):

Name _____ Address_____

Relationship _____ Telephone (H)_____ (W) _____

Please describe any current/recent medical problems _____

_____

Please list all current medications you are taking _____

_____

Family Physician _____ Phone_____

Referred by _____

Have you or any family member received previous counseling or psychotherapy?

Outpatient? Yes No Providers and dates: _____

Inpatient? Yes No Facility and dates: _____

In what way would you like the therapist to assist you? _____

_____

_____

Please rate each of the following concerns as they apply to you *at the present time* on a scale of 1-5 (1 = not a problem, no concern; 5 = a very strong or severe concern or problem)

Feelings of sadness, crying, being "down"	1	2	3	4	5
My mind feels like it's racing	1	2	3	4	5
Unwanted thoughts in my mind	1	2	3	4	5
Sometimes I can't control what I do	1	2	3	4	5
Sleep problems	1	2	3	4	5
Feeling worthless	1	2	3	4	5
Problems with anger/temper	1	2	3	4	5
Feeling like things aren't real	1	2	3	4	5
Problems with my eating	1	2	3	4	5
There are things too painful to talk about	1	2	3	4	5
Concerns about my sexuality	1	2	3	4	5
Use of alcohol and/or drugs	1	2	3	4	5
Doing things over and over	1	2	3	4	5
Seeing or hearing things that others don't	1	2	3	4	5
Feeling anxious/nervous	1	2	3	4	5
Being close to people	1	2	3	4	5
Spiritual concerns	1	2	3	4	5
Pain and/or health concerns	1	2	3	4	5

Are there current or past relationships that are a particular concern for you? Please describe briefly: _____

_____

What are the most significant stresses that you are currently dealing with? _____

_____

_____

_____

What do you consider to be your most important strengths? _____

_____

_____

_____

Is your spiritual life meaningful to you? Yes___ No___

Would you like this area to be part of your counseling? Yes___ No___

Are there other areas of concern that you would like to let us know about that have not been covered? _____

_____

_____

We appreciate your taking the time to give us this important information. We hope that this visit and all of your future visits to our clinic will meet your expectations.

Contributors

Stephen H. Allison (Ph.D., Graduate School of Psychology, Fuller Theological Seminary) is director of health services and assistant professor of psychology at Abilene Christian University. He is also a clinical psychologist with Clinical Associates of Abilene and has served as president of CAPS.

James M. Alsdurf (Ph.D., Graduate School of Psychology, Fuller Theological Seminary) is a clinical psychologist and a consultant to the State of Minnesota Department of Disability Determination. He serves as contributing editor for the *Journal of Psychology and Theology* and has coauthored *Battered into Submission* and *Eating Disorders* (IVP).

James R. Beck (Ph.D., Rosemead School of Psychology, Biola University) is a licensed psychologist and professor of counseling at Denver Seminary. He serves as associate editor of the *Journal of Psychology and Christianity* and as contributing editor for the *Journal of Pastoral Counseling*. He has authored numerous books and articles.

Colleen Benson (R.N., Ph.D., Rosemead School of Psychology, Biola University) is a clinical psychologist at Covina Psychological Services in Covina, California. She is also a past president of CAPS and chairs the CAPS Pastoral Care and Ethics Committee.

Jeffrey S. Berryhill (Ph.D., Graduate School of Psychology, Fuller Theological Seminary) is a clinical psychologist and cofounder of Cornerstone Family Counseling, P.C., in Fairfax, Virginia. He provides consultation to churches, Christian schools and families in matters of child abuse and child custody and was previously the associate editor of *Clinician's Research Digest*.

Bill Blackburn (Ph.D., Southern Seminary) has been pastor of Trinity Baptist Church in Kerrville, Texas, since 1984. He is the author of five books, including *What You Should Know About Suicide*. He has done postdoctoral work at Oxford University in biblical studies and medical ethics.

Richard E. Butman (Ph.D., Graduate School of Psychology, Fuller Theological Seminary) is professor of psychology at Wheaton College and a licensed clinical psychologist. He is coauthor (with Stanton L. Jones) of *Modern Psychotherapies: A Comprehensive Christian Appraisal* (IVP).

Ioma L. Hawkins (Ph.D., California School of Professional Psychology—Los Angeles) is a clinical psychologist in private practice in Torrance, California, and a member of the Ethics Committee of the California State Psychological Association. She was formerly associate professor and director of clinical training at the Rosemead School of Psychology, Biola University.

James H. Jennison (Ph.D., Graduate School of Psychology, Fuller Theological Seminary) is a clinical psychologist in private practice and an associate clinical professor in physical medicine and rehabilitation at the University of California, Irvine.

Stanton L. Jones (Ph.D., Arizona State University) was previously chair of the department of psychology at Wheaton College and the Dr. Arthur P. Rech and Mrs. Jean May Rech Professor of Psychology. After a year as visiting scholar and fellow at Cambridge University, he recently assumed the post of provost of Wheaton College.

Horace C. Lukens Jr. (Ph.D., University of Maine) is a clinical psychologist at Family Medical Care and is on the teaching faculty at In His Image Family Practice Residency Training Program of Tulsa, Oklahoma. He also serves on the CAPS Southwest region board of directors.

H. Newton Malony (Ph.D., George Peabody College of Vanderbilt University, ABPP) is senior professor in the Graduate School of Psychology at Fuller Theological Seminary. He is the author of numerous books and articles and was a previous president of CAPS as well as of Division 36 of the APA.

Mark R. McMinn, (h.D., Vanderbilt University, ABPP) is the Dr. Arthur P. Rech and Mrs. Jean May Rech Professor of Psychology at Wheaton College, where he directs the doctoral program in clinical psychology. He is the author of numerous books and articles, and his most recent book is *Psychology, Theology and Spirituality in Christian Counseling* (Tyndale).

Katheryn Rhoads Meek, M.A., is a student in the doctoral program of clinical psychology at Wheaton College. She has authored or coauthored numerous journal articles and chapters pertaining to professional ethics in psychology.

Mark Oordt (Ph.D., Graduate School of Psychology, Fuller Theological Seminary) is a clinical psychologist in Lakenheath, England.

Richard L. Price (Ph.D., Graduate School of Psychology, Fuller Theological Seminary) has nineteen years of experience as a military psychologist.

Angela M. Sabates (Ph.D., Northwestern University) is assistant professor of psychology at Palm Beach Atlantic College in West Palm Beach, Florida. She formerly led the child and adolescent treatment team at the Minirth-Meier-Byrd Clinic in Virginia as well as maintained a private practice.

Steven J. Sandage (M.S., Virginia Commonwealth University, M.Div., Trinity Evangelical Divinity School) is completing a psychology internship at a Virginia prison and is a doctoral student in counseling psychology at Virginia Commonwealth University. He is coauthor of *To Forgive Is Human* (IVP) and author of other books and articles.

Randolph K. Sanders (Ph.D., Graduate School of Psychology, Fuller Theological Seminary) is executive director of CAPS and is a clinical psychologist in private practice in New Braunfels, Texas, as well as an award-winning author. He serves on the board of his denomination's state ethics and social concerns agency.

John F. Shackelford (Psy.D., Rosemead School of Psychology, Biola University) is a clinical psychologist in private practice in Richardson, Texas. He is a former CAPS Southwest regional director.

Siang-Yang Tan (Ph.D., McGill University) is associate professor of psychology at Fuller Theological Seminary and senior pastor of First Evangelical Church in Glendale, California. He also serves as associate editor for the *Journal of Psychology and Christianity* and a consulting editor for *Professional Psychology: Research and Practice.* His books include *Lay Counseling* (Zondervan).

Alan Tjeltveit (Ph.D., Graduate School of Psychology, Fuller Theological Seminary) is associate professor of psychology at Muhlenberg College in Allentown, Pennsylvania, and the author of several articles on psychotherapy ethics.

Everett L. Worthington Jr. (Ph.D., University of Missouri) is professor of psychology at Virginia Commonwealth University. He has published numerous books and articles, including *Marriage Counseling: A Christian Approach to Counseling Couples* (InterVarsity). He is also editor of *Marriage & Family: A Christian Journal.*

Mark A. Yarhouse, M.A., is a doctoral student in clinical psychology at Wheaton College and is staff therapist at the Outreach Community Center in Carol Stream, Illinois.

Index